Intellectics and Computational Logic

APPLIED LOGIC SERIES

VOLUME 19

Managing Editor

Dov M. Gabbay, *Department of Computer Science, King's College, London, U.K.*

Co-Editor

John Barwise, *Department of Philosophy, Indiana University, Bloomington, IN, U.S.A.*

Editorial Assistant

Jane Spurr, *Department of Computer Science, King's College, London, U.K.*

SCOPE OF THE SERIES
Logic is applied in an increasingly wide variety of disciplines, from the traditional subjects of philosophy and mathematics to the more recent disciplines of cognitive science, computer science, artificial intelligence, and linguistics, leading to new vigor in this ancient subject. Kluwer, through its Applied Logic Series, seeks to provide a home for outstanding books and research monographs in applied logic, and in doing so demonstrates the underlying unity and applicability of logic.

The titles published in this series are listed at the end of this volume.

Intellectics and Computational Logic

Papers in Honor of Wolfgang Bibel

edited by

STEFFEN HÖLLDOBLER

Dresden University of Technology, Germany

KLUWER ACADEMIC PUBLISHERS

DORDRECHT / BOSTON / LONDON

A C.I.P. Catalogue record for this book is available from the Library of Congress.

ISBN 978-90-481-5438-8

Published by Kluwer Academic Publishers,
P.O. Box 17, 3300 AA Dordrecht, The Netherlands.

Sold and distributed in North, Central and South America
by Kluwer Academic Publishers,
101 Philip Drive, Norwell, MA 02061, U.S.A.

In all other countries, sold and distributed
by Kluwer Academic Publishers,
P.O. Box 322, 3300 AH Dordrecht, The Netherlands.

Printed on acid-free paper

WOLFGANG BIBEL

TABLE OF CONTENTS

STEFFEN HÖLLDOBLER

PREFACE

Intellectics is the field of science, where, on the one hand, an understanding of the functions, structure and operations of the human intellect is attempted and, on the other hand, artificial systems are tested to see to what extent they can substitute or complement such functions. The name "intellectics" was introduced in the early 1980s by Wolfgang Bibel as a linguistically correct name for the united fields of artificial intelligence and cognitive science.

The field of intellectics can be divided into the subareas cognitive modeling, natural communication, robotics, machines and, at the very heart of it, knowledge based systems. The core of any intellectics system itself consists of a knowledge base together with an inference component. It is – and always was – this core which is the focus point of the research carried out by Wolfgang Bibel. Moreover, he is – and always was – a strong advocate for a formal basis of this core within a computational logic.

Based on a solid education in physics, mathematics and, in particular, in mathematical logic, Wolfgang Bibel was among the few scientist who recognized the chances and potentials of artificial intelligence and cognitive science in the late 1960s. From this time on he devoted his energy to establish this field of science in Germany and Europe. Although he sometimes faced considerable difficulties, his efforts were extremely successful. Looking at the most influential events in the history of intellectics in Germany and Europe one almost always discovers the name of Wolfgang Bibel. The German Workshops on Artificial Intelligence, the German Spring Schools on Artificial Intelligence, the European Coordination Committee for Artificial Intelligence and the integration of our colleagues working in Eastern Europe are just a few of the activities that were co–founded and strongly supported by Wolfgang Bibel. Just a few months ago the German research focus programme on deduction, which was running since 1992 and was headed by Wolfgang Bibel, came to a very successful end. Today Germany is among the leading nations in this area.

Wolfgang Bibel's own research was always focussed on deduction and computational logic. He is convinced that the knowledge needed to solve problems should be represented in a logic language and that calculi equipped with intelligent strategies are adequate mechanisms for solving these problems. In more than one hundred and fifty publications and more than one hundred scientific talks Wolfgang Bibel has argued for his ideas. Under his guidance several automated theorems provers were developed, which demonstrated the strength and power of "his" connection method in international competitions. At the same time he was always interested in the applications of deduction and, in particular, he made considerable contributions to the areas of automated programming, program synthesis, logic programming, deductive planning and knowledge based systems.

Wolfgang Bibel has received numerous awards, among which the following ones are the most prestigious: In 1990 he has been awarded the title of an "AAAI Fellow" by the American Association for Artificial Intelligence (AAAI) "in Recognition of Significant Contributions to the Field of Artificial Intelligence". In 1996 he has received the German Research Excellence Award for Artificial Intelligence from the Association of German AI Institutions. In 1999 he has received the Donald E. Walker Distinguished Service Award for his outstanding contributions and service to the international AI community.

This book is a collection of papers by distinguished researchers, colleagues and former students of Wolfgang Bibel, who at one time have worked together with him. The papers were collected on the occasion of Wolfgang Bibel's sixtieth birthday. They were all reviewed by second readers. In the papers technical problems related to intellectics and computational logic are discussed. The range of subjects presented includes automated deduction, logic programming, the logic based approach to intellectics, reasoning about actions and causality, knowledge representation and reasoning as well as applications thereof. Each contribution contains new, unpublished and reviewed results. The collection provides a state of the art account of the current capabilities and limitations of a computational logic approach to intellectics.

In addition, Christoph Kreitz has added a prolog and an epilog. Both were written while Christoph Kreitz was working in Wolfgang Bibel's group in Darmstadt on the occasion of a christmas party. This shall demonstrate that working with Wolfgang Bibel was not just challenging and inspiring but also fun.

ACKNOWLEDGMENTS

I am grateful to the second readers who carefully read the manuscripts and provided valuable additional information:

Susanne Biundo	Gerhard Brewka	Hans-Jürgen Bürckert
Ricardo Caferra	Christian Eckes	Norbert Eisinger
Uwe Egly	Bertram Fronhöfer	Ulrich Furbach
Christoph Kreitz	Reinhold Letz	David McAllester
Hans Jürgen Ohlbach	Horst Reichel	Enno Sandner
Torsten Schaub	Josef Schneeberger	Hans-Peter Störr
	Michael Thielscher	

In fact, Norbert Eisinger contributed that much to the paper that the authors decided to make him a co-author.

Maria Tiedemann helped a lot to come up with a complete list of researchers who had worked together with Wolfgang Bibel. Hans–Peter Störr produced the Latex style as well as the final layout. Maja von Wedelstedt was involved in many administrative tasks related to this book project. I would like to express many thanks to all of them.

Steffen Hölldobler

Prologue

In the beginning The Scientist created the Intellectics and the connection method. And the connection method was without form and unexplored. Darkness was upon the field of automated deduction and the spirit of the scientist was hovering over the logical inferences.

And The Scientist said, „Let there be derivability," and there was derivability. And The Scientist saw that derivability was good and he divided the derivable from the unprovable. The Scientist called the derivable „valid" and the unprovable „invalid". And there was winter semester and summer semester — the first academic year.

And The Scientist said, „Let there be a syntactical construct between the formulae, to separate formula from formula." So The Scientist made the syntactical construct and separated the valid formulae from the invalid. And it was so. The Scientist called the syntactical construct „complementary matrix". And there was winter semester and summer semester — the second academic year.

And The Scientist said, „Let the complex formulae be gathered together to one place and let simple formulae appear." And it was so. The Scientist called the simple formulae „propositional logic" and the complex formulae he called „predicate logic". And The Scientist saw that it was good.

Then The Scientist said, „Let the propositional logic bring forth normal forms, atoms, literals, and clauses which contain literals, connections between two literals, and paths through matrices, each

according to its kind." And it was so. The propositional logic brought forth normal forms, atoms, literals, and clauses which contain literals, connections between two literals, and paths through matrices, each according to its kind. And The Scientist saw that it was good. And there was winter semester and summer semester — the third academic year.

And The Scientist said, „Let there be representations of matrices, to separate valid formulae from the invalid, and to characterize inference methods. And let them be representations of matrices to give light upon the proofs." And it was so. The Scientist created two important representations — the positive one to rule direct proofs, and the negative representation to rule indirect proofs. He also made representations for non-normal forms. And The Scientist set them in the world of matrices, to give light upon the proofs and to separate valid formulae from the invalid. And The Scientist saw that it was good. And there was winter semester and summer semester — the fourth academic year.

And The Scientist said, „Let the predicate logic bring forth abundantly the terms that have free variables, and substitutions that may unify atomic formulae to span connections among the matrices." So The Scientist created the great terms of predicate logic and every variable and function symbol that occurs within the language of predicate logic according to its kind, and every substitution of variables according to the unification algorithm. And The Scientist saw that it was good. And The Scientist implemented them and said, „Be fruitful, and multiply. Simplify the predicate logic, and fill the matrices with span-

S. Hölldobler (ed.), Intellectics and Computational Logic, 1–2.

ning connections" And there was winter semester and summer semester — the fifth academic year.

And The Scientist said, „Let the propositional logic bring forth proof strategies according to the connection method; extension steps which follow connections, backtracking steps to undo unsolvable paths, and reductions to simplify the matrices, each according to its kind." And it was so. The Scientist created reductions to simplify the matrices, extension steps which follow connections according to their kinds, and backtracking steps to undo unsolvable paths according to their kinds. And The Scientist saw that it was good.

Then The Scientist said, „Let us train young researchers in our image, after our likeness; and let them have dominion over the clause instances, unification algorithms, proof strategies, reductions, and over all the automated deduction, and over every inference technique that shows up in the literature." So The Scientist trained young researchers in his own image, in the image of The Scientist he trained them; as master and PhD students he supervised them.

And The Scientist employed them as research associates and said unto them, „Be fruitful, and multiply; replenish the scientific literature, and subdue the field of automated deduction. And have dominion over the clause instances, unification, reductions, and every proof strategy that uses spanning connections." And The Scientist said, „Behold, I have given you every atom which occurs in the language of predicate logic, literals, clauses, connections between literals, and paths through matrices. To you it shall be a foundation. And to all the proof methods, reductions, unifications, and spanning connections — everything that can test validity — I give every formula as benchmark." And it was so.

The Scientist took the young researchers and put them into the field of deduction, to work in it and fill it with publications. And The Scientist commanded them, „Every area of the field you may freely investigate; but resolution you shall not investigate. For when you do so, you shall surely perish."

And The Scientist saw every thing that he had made, and, behold, it was very good. And there was winter semester and summer semester — the sixth academic year.

Thus the Intellectics and the connection method were finished in all their complexity. And in the seventh academic year The Scientist ended his work which he had made; and in the seventh academic year he took a sabbatical. And The Scientist welcomed the seventh academic year and called it valuable, because there were no academic duties and he had completed everything that he had created.

Christoph Kreitz, Department of Computer Science
Cornell University, Ithaca, NY, 14850, U.S.A.

P. BAUMGARTNER, N. EISINGER AND U. FURBACH

A CONFLUENT CONNECTION CALCULUS

1. INTRODUCTION

This work is concerned with basic issues of the design of calculi and proof procedures for first-order connection methods and tableaux calculi. Calculi we have in mind include connection calculi (Bibel, 1987; Eder, 1992), first-order clausal tableaux with rigid variables (Fitting, 1990), more recent developments like A-ordered tableaux (Klingenbeck and Hähnle, 1994; Hähnle and Klingenbeck, 1996), and tableaux with selection function (Hähnle and Pape, 1997). Let us refer to all these calculi by the term "rigid variable methods". Recently complexity issues for those kinds of calculi have been considered in (Voronkov, 1998; Voronkov, 1997).

We emphasise that in this paper we do *not* consider model elimination (ME) (Loveland, 1968). Although ME can be presented as a tableau calculus (Letz et al., 1994; Baumgartner and Furbach, 1993), it is *not* proof confluent. The same holds for Restart ME (Baumgartner et al., 1997) and related methods. These calculi are not even proof-confluent at the propositional level and cannot be treated by the methods presented here. Nevertheless they are the basis of some high performance theorem provers like SETHEO (Letz et al., 1992) or Protein (Baumgartner and Furbach, 1994).

In this paper we propose a new technique for the design of proof procedures for rigid variable methods. The new technique is motivated by the desire to get more efficient proof procedures and implementations thereof than those which have been developed so far.

The proposed technique should also be applicable to calculi which *avoid* rigid variables in the first place, like SATCHMO (Manthey and Bry, 1988), MGTP (Fujita and Hasegawa, 1991), hyper tableaux (Baumgartner et al., 1996) and ordered semantic hyper linking (Plaisted and Zhu, 1997). Usually the price for getting around rigid variables in these approaches is that they involve some uninformed ground instantiation in special cases. These special cases may be irrelevant for most typical applications, but nevertheless these calculi are likely to profit from techniques enabling them to handle rigid variables as well.

A more recent development is the disconnection method (Billon, 1996). Unlike the calculi mentioned above, and like our calculus below, it avoids blind instantiation

3

S. Hölldobler (ed.), Intellectics and Computational Logic, 3–26.

by the use of unification. Unlike our method and unlike the free variable methods mentioned above, the disconnection method does not deal with "free variables"[1]. In free variable methods, a branch or a path is considered as "solved" if it contains a pair (K, L) of literals that are complementary; in the disconnection method, the respective "\$-closed" condition on (K, L) is that K and L are equal after instantiating all variables with the same (new) constant \$. For instance, $(P(X, Y), \neg P(Z, Z))$ is considered as complementary. The disconnection method has inference rules to further instantiate clauses derived so far, but the parent clauses of an inference step have to be kept. This instantiation is driven by connections that are not \$-closed. Since substitutions are applied locally to clauses, a previously \$-closed connection may become open again. If the clause containing $\neg P(Z, Z)$ is further instantiated to, say, $\neg P(a, a)$ this implies that the connection $(P(X, Y), \neg P(a, a))$ is no longer \$-closed. In free variable methods this effect is avoided because, clearly, complementary literals *remain* complementary after instantiation; there is no need to check previously closed paths after instantiation whether they are still closed. On the other hand, for the disconnection method only one variant per clause needs to be kept; this is not possible in free variable methods.

In sum, we feel that theses approaches are rather different. A more rigid and systematic comparison would be interesting future work.

Our approach is based on the observation that current proof procedures for rigid variable methods rely on the following weak completeness theorem:

> *Weak completeness:* a clause set S is unsatisfiable if and only if *there is* a derivation from S which is also a refutation.

The search space thus is the space of *derivations*; it requires a tentative control regime such as backtracking, which explores *all* possible derivations.

Proof confluent calculi like the ones mentioned at the beginning of the introduction, however, should admit a *strong* completeness theorem of the form:

> *Strong completeness:* a clause set S is unsatisfiable if and only if *every* (fair) derivation from S is a refutation.

Consequently, proof procedures following this theorem can do with an irrevocable control regime that needs to develop only *one single* derivation and may safely ignore alternatives as it proceeds. They can thus *reuse* information which would be lost in a backtracking intensive approach. Typically they enumerate *models* but not *derivations* (the hyper tableaux calculus (Baumgartner et al., 1996) is an example that enumerates models, model elimination (Loveland, 1968) is an example for the enumeration of derivations).

Put abstractly, the source to gain efficiency is that there are usually many derivations for the *same* model, and all but one derivation can be avoided. Table 1 summarises the issues addressed so far.

In this paper, we will develop a strong completeness result for a modified connection calculus (the CCC calculus, Section 3) together with first steps towards a respective proof procedure.

This result closes a strange gap in Table 1: the connection calculus in (Bibel, 1987) is proof confluent on the propositional level, but its first-order version is not.

Calculus	Completeness	Proof procedure	Enumeration of
CCC Bibel's prop. CC Tableaux	Strong	No Backtracking	models
Bibel's first-order CC ME	Weak	Backtracking	derivations

Table 1 Properties of calculi. CCC is the new *confluent connection calculus* of Section 3. For Bibel's connection calculi (CC) we refer to (Bibel, 1987).

This is the only calculus we are aware of having this property. Although other free-variable methods, such as the first-order tableaux calculus in Fitting's book (Fitting, 1990) *are* proof-confluent, they are *implemented* as if they were non-confluent. This yields unnecessary inefficiencies, and the main motivation for the work presented in this paper is to find a cure for them.

The rest of this paper is structured as follows: in the next section we will briefly summarise the idea behind connection and tableaux calculi. The problems with them will be illustrated using an example. Then, after having introduced some preliminaries, we define our new calculus CCC (confluent connection calculus), suggest a rather general search strategy and prove its fairness. The subsequent section contains the completeness proof. Finally we conclude the paper by indicating some future work.

2. CURRENT APPROACHES

Let us first briefly recall the basic idea of current proof procedures for rigid variable methods and identify the tackled source of inefficiency.

2.1. Prawitz Procedures

"Usual" proof procedures like the one used in the 3TAP prover (Hähnle et al., 1994), the LeanTAP prover (Beckert and Posegga, 1995)), the connection procedure proposed in (Bibel, 1987), and the one in Fitting's Book (Fitting, 1990) follow an idea suggested by Prawitz (Prawitz, 1960) and can be seen as more or less direct translation of the following formulation of the Herbrand-Skolem-Gödel theorem (we can restrict our attention to clause logic here):

> A clause set S is unsatisfiable if and only if there is a finite set S' of variants of clauses of S and there is a substitution δ such that $S'\delta$ is unsatisfiable, where $S'\delta$ is viewed as a propositional clause set.

Now, in accordance with the theorem, proof procedures for rigid variable methods typically realise the following scheme to prove that given clause set $S = \{C_1, \ldots, C_n\}$

is unsatisfiable. Following Voronkov (Voronkov, 1998; Voronkov, 1997), we call it *The Procedure*:

Procedure 1. (The Procedure)

(i) Let $\mu = 1$ called *multiplicity*.

(ii) Let $S^\mu = \{C_1^1, \ldots, C_1^\mu$
$$\vdots$$
$$C_n^1, \ldots, C_n^\mu\}$$

be a set of pairwise variable-disjoint clauses, such that C_i^j is a variant of C_i for $1 \leq i \leq n, 1 \leq j \leq \mu$. It is usual to call S^μ an *amplification* of S.

(iii) Check if there is a substitution δ such that $S^\mu\delta$ is propositionally unsatisfiable.

(iv) If such a δ exists, then stop and return "unsatisfiable"; otherwise let $\mu = \mu + 1$ and go to step (ii). □

Completeness of *The Procedure* is achieved by, first, a fairness condition in the generation of the amplifications S^μ in step (ii), namely by uniformly taking $1, 2, 3, \ldots$ variants of every clause in S in round $1, 2, 3, \ldots$, and, second, by exhaustively searching for substitutions in step (iii).

2.2. Connection Methods

How is step (iii) in *The Procedure* realised? Our primary interest is in connection methods (also called matrix methods), hence we will briefly recall the idea: define a matrix to be any set of quantifier free formulae. For our purposes it suffices to consider clause sets only. Notice that S^μ is a matrix. A *path* through a matrix is obtained by taking exactly one literal from every clause. A connection is a pair of literals, which can be made complementary by application of a substitution; with each connection we associate a most general unifier σ achieving this. In order to realise step (iii), proof procedures for connection calculi search for a substitution δ such that every path through $S^\mu\delta$ contains a pair of complementary literals (we say that δ *closes* S^μ). If such a δ exists S must be unsatisfiable: take some arbitrary ground instance of $S^\mu\delta$ and observe that this set is propositionally unsatisfiable, because any possible way to satisfy a conjunction of disjunctions is excluded by virtue of the complementary literals.

For δ, it is sufficient to search through the *finite* space of most general unifiers making literals along paths (or branches) complementary (this guarantees the termination of step (iii). See e.g. (Bibel, 1987) for a concrete procedure to decide if a δ exists which renders all paths complementary. For our purposes it suffices to rephrase the underlying idea: let $p_1, p_2, \ldots, p_n$ be any enumeration of all paths through the current amplification. It can be shown by usual lifting techniques that there is δ which simultaneously renders all paths as complementary if and only if there is a sequence $p_1\delta_1, p_2\delta_1\delta_2,\ldots,p_n\delta_1\cdots\delta_n$, where δ_i is a most general unifier associated with a connection in $p_i\delta_1\cdots\delta_{i-1}$. In other words, by defining $\delta := \delta_1\cdots\delta_n$ one recognises that δ can be computed incrementally. Notice, however, that the "there is" quantification is to be translated in a backtracking-oriented procedure.

Example 2. (Connection method) Consider the following unsatisfiable clause set:

$$S = \{P(X)\vee Q(X),\ \neg P(c),\ \neg P(a)\vee\neg P(b),\ \neg Q(a),\ \neg Q(b)\}$$

We write a matrix as a vertical sequence of clauses. Hence S^1 and S^2 look like this[2]:

	S^2:	$P(X^1)\vee Q(X^1)$
S^1:	$P(X^1)\vee Q(X^1)$	$P(X^2)\vee Q(X^2)$
	$\neg P(c)$	$\neg P(c)$
	$\neg P(a)\vee\neg P(b)$	$\neg P(a)\vee\neg P(b)$
	$\neg Q(a)$	$\neg Q(a)$
	$\neg Q(b)$	$\neg Q(b)$

A path is obtained by traversing the matrix from top to bottom, picking up one literal from every clause.

The Procedure starts with $\mu = 1$, i.e. with S^1. By looking at the path through S^1 which passes through $P(X^1)$ one recognises that there are three candidate MGUs $\delta_1^1 = \{X^1/a\}$, $\delta_2^1 = \{X^1/b\}$ and $\delta_3^1 = \{X^1/c\}$. Since none of $S^1\delta_1^1$, $S^1\delta_2^1$ and $S^1\delta_3^1$ is propositionally unsatisfiable, *The Procedure* has to consider S^2. An incremental computation of a substitution δ which closes S^2 might proceed as follows: it starts by considering the connection $(P(X^1),\neg P(c))$ which results in $\delta_1^2 = \{X^1/c\}$. The next connection would be $(Q(X^2),\neg Q(a))$ with MGU $\delta_2^2 = \{X^2/a\}$. The combined substitution $\delta_1^2\delta_2^2 = \{X^1/c, X^2/a\}$ does not close the matrix, neither will $\delta_1^2\delta_3^2$, where $\delta_3^2 = \{X^2/b\}$. Hence, backtracking occurs until eventually the "right" substitution $\delta = \{X^1/a,\ X^2/b\}$ is computed, which closes S^2.   □

2.3. *Proof Search with Tableaux*

Typically, the search for δ in step (iii) is organised as the construction of a free-variable tableau where a branch in a tableau stands for a path through the current amplification. According to Bibel (Bibel, 1987), any method which explores paths through a matrix in a systematical way qualifies as a connection calculi. Undoubtedly, this holds for tableaux calculi. Hence, tableaux calculi are connection calculi.

For space efficiency reasons it is prohibitive to explicitly represent in step (iii) all paths through S^μ in memory. For example, only 15 clauses consisting of 3 literals result in more than 14 million paths. A respective tableau thus has in the worst case the same number of branches. Hence, one possibility for step (iii) is to only keep in memory one path p (or branch in a tableau) at a time. A closing substitution δ_p is guessed, and if δ_p cannot be extended to a substitution δ which simultaneously closes all paths, then backtracking occurs and a different candidate δ_p is guessed. If all that fails, then a completely new tableau construction is started when entering step (iii) in the next round.

We emphasise that this is a common idea in all proof procedures for free-variable tableaux and connection calculi we are aware of. Let us refer to any such instance of *The Procedure* as a "tableau procedure". We are aware that there are numerous improvements; which, however will not be considered in the present paper, since we are interested in a basic weakness which is intrinsic to the tableau procedure.

2.4. Drawback of Current Approaches

The tableau procedure from the previous section suffers from an unnecessarily large search space. For illustration, and in order to contrast it to our approach below, take the following example:

Example 3. (Incestuous Graph) Consider the graph in Figure 1. All edges shall be directed from top to bottom. The graph illustrates in an obvious way the clause set S to the right of it, which is written in the usual notation for Horn clauses. The R-clauses[3] denote the edges between successive layers, and the RT-clauses define the transitive closure of the R relation.

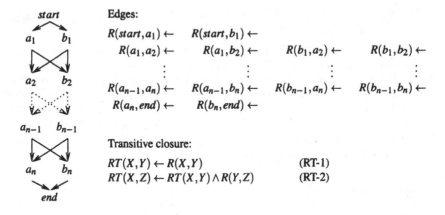

Figure 1   Incestuous graphs.

Since the *end* node is reachable from the *start* node, the clause $RT(start, end)$ is a logical consequence of S, in other words, $S \cup \{\neg RT(start, end)\}$ is unsatisfiable. Notice that the length of any path through the graph from *start* to *end* is $n + 1$, but that there are 2^n, i.e. exponentially many, different paths from *start* to *end*. However, even a naive procedure which successively marks reachable nodes (in a greedy way) beginning with *start* would terminate after $O(n)$ steps with every node (and hence also *end*) as marked. Notably, bottom-up evaluation with hyper resolution (Robinson, 1965) or related calculi like hyper tableau (Baumgartner et al., 1996) or PUHR tableaux (Bry and Yahya, 1996) would exactly achieve this when applied to the clause set[4]. □

The tableau procedure performs very poorly on this example. We will discuss why. In brief, the tableau procedure enumerates *proofs*, and there are exponentially many proofs that $RT(start, end)$ is a logical consequence of S, whereas a better approach here is to enumerate *models*, and there is only one model of S (which also contains $RT(start, end)$).

In order to derive $RT(start, end)$, the procedure needs at least $\mu_n \in O(n)$ variants of RT-clauses. This is because with k variants of RT-clauses not more than k nodes reachable in the graph from *start* are contained in that subset of the RT-relation which is a logical consequence of $S^k\delta$ (for any δ). In other words, $O(n)$ variants of RT-clauses are needed to derive $RT(start, end)$.

More explicitly, consider the following set (RT-2)^g of ground instances of (RT-2):

$$\left[\begin{array}{l} RT(start, end) \leftarrow RT(start, a_n) \wedge R(a_n, end) \\ RT(start, end) \leftarrow RT(start, b_n) \wedge R(b_n, end) \end{array} \right]$$

$$\left[\begin{array}{l} RT(start, a_n) \leftarrow RT(start, a_{n-1}) \wedge R(a_{n-1}, a_n) \\ RT(start, a_n) \leftarrow RT(start, b_{n-1}) \wedge R(b_{n-1}, a_n) \end{array} \right] \quad \left[\begin{array}{l} RT(start, b_n) \leftarrow RT(start, a_{n-1}) \wedge R(a_{n-1}, b_n) \\ RT(start, b_n) \leftarrow RT(start, b_{n-1}) \wedge R(b_{n-1}, b_n) \end{array} \right]$$

$$\vdots \qquad\qquad\qquad \vdots$$

$$\left[\begin{array}{l} RT(start, a_2) \leftarrow RT(start, a_1) \wedge R(a_1, a_2) \\ RT(start, a_2) \leftarrow RT(start, b_1) \wedge R(b_1, a_2) \end{array} \right] \quad \left[\begin{array}{l} RT(start, b_2) \leftarrow RT(start, a_1) \wedge R(a_1, b_2) \\ RT(start, b_2) \leftarrow RT(start, b_1) \wedge R(b_1, b_2) \end{array} \right]$$

We want to identify a *minimal* subset X of (RT-2)^g such that X together with (sufficiently many) ground instances of (RT-1) plus the other facts is unsatisfiable. To do so, proceed as follows: choose one of the two clauses in the topmost group (a "group" is denoted by enclosing its clauses in brackets). Depending on the RT-literal in the body, walk down to the respective left or right group below it. Choose any of the two clauses in that group. Proceed as in the first step, and go on until a bottommost group is reached.

This selection determines a minimal set X as claimed: obviously, we have to make all n selections, because otherwise some RT-literal in the body of some clause would remain unprovable. But these n selections suffice, because the RT-literal in the body of the clause in the bottommost group can be reduced by an instance of the (RT-1) clause to an R-literal. This leaves us only with R-literals, which all are given as facts.

Of course, (RT-2)^g is not the full set of ground instances of (RT-2). All other ground instances of (RT-2) are similar to (RT-2)^g and they represent the relations $RT(a_1, end)$, $RT(b_1, end)$, $RT(a_2, end)$, ... instead of $RT(start, end)$. It is easy to figure out that this full set of ground instances of (RT-2) comprises $O(n^3)$ clauses.

The just sketched procedure allows to identify $O(2^n)$ different sets X because in each group 2 selections are possible. Hence, for *every* path from *start* to *end* there is a corresponding amplification S^μ of S and there is a ground substitution γ such that the path from *start* to *end* is represented in $S^\mu\gamma$ by respective instances of the RT-clauses.

That is, there are exponentially many ways to instantiate S^μ so that $RT(start, end)$ is a logical consequence of the instantiated set.

This indicates the weakness with the tableau procedure; the general problem with the tableau procedure is that too much information is lost during computation and so is computed over and over again. There are two phenomena:

Loss in inner loop: Suppose S^μ as given, for some μ, and we are in step (iii) of *The Procedure*. Recall from above that the tableau procedure searches through the space of candidate substitutions δ such that $S^\mu\delta$ is propositionally unsatisfiable. As concluded above, there are $O(2^n)$ different paths from *start* to *end* and each of these is represented by $S^n\gamma$ for some γ. If e.g. $\mu = n - 1$ there still are $O(2^n)$ different paths, and, again, each of these is represented by a ground instance of S^μ. Further, each of these ground instances is obtainable as some instance of $S^\mu\delta$ which is generated in step (iii) as a solution candidate. None of these, however, will lead to a proof, because μ is not sufficiently large.

Now consider the situation where the first candidate substitutions correspond to choosing the edges from *start* to a_1 to a_2. The procedure will explore the search space of paths originating from a_2, which will not lead to a proof. After some backtracking the candidate substitutions will correspond to chosing the edges from *start* to b_1 to a_2, and the procedure will reexplore the very same search space of paths originating from a_2, and it will fail again.

This repetition of work occurs at all backtracking choice-points, causing exponential redundancy within step (iii).

Loss in outer loop: When returning from step (iv) to step (ii), the set of paths through S^μ in round μ is a strict subset of the set of paths through $S^{\mu+1}$. Since all substitutions δ searched for S^μ are lost on backtracking, each of these will be computed again for $S^{\mu+1}$.

We note that keeping all the substitutions δ for S^μ when exploring $S^{\mu+1}$ would be no solution, as there are exponentially many.

For further illustration of this drawback think of a respective control regime within a level-saturation resolution proof procedure: after unsuccessful termination of level n and on entering level $n + 1$ one would *delete* all clauses derived in level n and start with the plain input set again! Probably no-one would seriously consider this.

On the other hand, the outer loop on μ in *The Procedure* is a form of iterative deepening, and it is well-known that, in the limit, iterative deepening has the same search space as a procedure which would instantly guess the "right" μ. Consequently, the true problem lies in the loss of information in the inner loop.

To sum up, there are possibly exponentially many ways to compute the same information. In our example, there are $O(2^k)$ ways to prove that $RT(start, a_k)$ holds, and all of these will be computed. In other words, there is a large potential for *reuse* which is not exploited.

We thus now turn to our confluent connection calculus which avoids the problem. Like the mentioned bottom-up evaluation with hyper resolution, it will solve the incestuous graph problem in polynomially many inference steps (see the remarks in the conclulsions).

3. A CONFLUENT CONNECTION CALCULUS

In this section we indroduce the confluent version of a connection calculus. For this we briefly have to set up the usual prerequisites. After indroducing the calculus together with an abstract notion of fairness, we show how this fairness can be realised and finally we prove strong completeness.

3.1. Preliminaries

For a literal L we denote by $|L|$ the atom of L, i.e. $|A| = A$ and $|\neg A| = A$ for any atom A. Literals K and L are *complementary* iff K and L have different sign and $|L| = |K|$.

By var(*object*) we denote the set of variables occurring in *object*, where *object* is a term, a literal, a clause or a set of these. Our notion of a *substitution* is the usual one (Baader and Schulz, 1998), and, as usual, we confuse a substitution with its homomorphic extension to terms, literals, clauses and clause sets. For a substitution σ, we denote by dom(σ) the (finite) set $\{X \mid X\sigma \neq X\}$, by cod($\sigma$) the set $\{X\sigma \mid X \in \text{dom}(\sigma)\}$ and by vcod(σ) the set var(cod(σ)). Substitution γ is a *ground* substitution iff vcod(γ) = $\emptyset$; it is a *ground substitution for object* iff additionally var(*object*) $\subseteq$ dom(γ). A substitution σ is idempotent, if $X\sigma\sigma = X\sigma$ for each variable X. This is the case iff dom(σ) $\cap$ vcod(σ) = $\emptyset$.

A clause is a finite disjunction of literals. In the following, S is the given finite input clause set, and M is a matrix for S, i.e. a set of clauses, each of which is an instance of a clause from S. It is worth emphasizing that in a matrix we consider clauses *not* to be individually universally quantified. That is, all variables are free, and thus applying a substitution, say, $\{Y/a\}$ to the matrix $\{\neg P(Y), P(Y) \vee Q(Y)\}$ would affect all occurrences of Y.

A *connection with substitution* σ is a pair of literals (L, K) such that $L\sigma$ and $K\sigma$ are complementary. A *connection* is a pair of literals that is a connection with some substitution. In these definitions, we replace "substitution σ" by "MGU σ" only if additionally $\sigma = \text{unify}(\{|K|, |L|\})$, where unify returns any most general unifier of its argument. Below we make use of the following assumption:

Assumption 4. *If a set Q of atoms is unifiable, then* unify(Q) *returns an idempotent most general unifier σ with (i)* dom(σ) $\subseteq$ var(Q) *and (ii)* vcod(σ) $\subseteq$ var(Q).

Notice that this is a very mild assumption: (i) says that σ operates on the variables of Q only, and (ii) says that σ must not introduce new variables. Clearly, this is satisfied by any "standard" unification procedure.

A *path* through a matrix M is a set of literals, obtained by taking exactly one literal from each clause of M. A path is *closed* iff it contains a pair of complementary literals, otherwise it is *open*. A matrix is *open* iff there is a (at least one) path through it that is open, otherwise it is *closed*.

Notice that there is exactly one path through the "empty" matrix $\{\}$, which is the empty set $\{\}$ of literals; notice further that this path is open. On the other hand, if a matrix M contains the empty clause, then there is no path through M, in particular no open path, and the matrix is closed.

3.2. The Calculus

We are going to define the calculus *CCC* (Confluent Connection Calculus). The constituents are the inference rules, the notion of a derivation, and a fairness condition for derivations.

Definition 5. (CCC inference rules and derivation) *The inference rule* variant step *on M is defined as follows:*

$$\frac{M}{M \cup \text{new}(S)} \quad \text{if} \begin{cases} 1. & \text{new}(S) \text{ contains exactly one variant of each clause of } S, \text{ and} \\ 2. & \text{the members of new}(S) \text{ are pairwise variable disjoint and each} \\ & \text{of them is variable disjoint with each clause in } M. \end{cases}$$

The inference rule connection step *on (K, L) in M is defined as follows:*

$$\frac{M}{M \cup M\sigma} \quad \text{if} \begin{cases} 1. & \text{there are clauses } C \in M \text{ and } D \in M \text{ such that } C = K \vee R_K \text{ and} \\ & D = L \vee R_L \text{ for some clauses } R_K \text{ and } R_L, \text{ and} \\ 2. & \{K, L\} \subseteq p \text{ for some open path } p \text{ through } M, \text{ and} \\ 3. & (K, L) \text{ is a connection with MGU } \sigma. \end{cases}$$

The set $(M \cup M\sigma) \setminus M$ is called the set of new *clauses (of this inference step). If conditions 1 to 3 above hold for M and (K, L), we say that a connection step is* applicable *to (K, L) in M or that (K, L) is a* candidate *for a connection step in M.*

We say that a connection step on (K, L) in M is progressive *if $M \cup M\sigma \neq M$ (i.e. at least one clause in the conclusion is new). If $M \cup M\sigma = M$ we say that it is* non-progressive. *Note that a connection step on a connection (K, L) with $|K| = |L|$ is impossible and therefore neither progressive nor non-progressive – any path containing $\{K, L\}$ would be closed, contradicting condition 2. above.*

Any sequence

$$D = (\{\} = M_0), M_1, \ldots, M_n, \ldots$$

is called a derivation *from S, provided that M_{i+1} is obtained from M_i, which is open, by a single application of one of the inference rules (for $i \geq 0$). A* refutation *is a derivation that contains (i.e. ends in) a closed matrix.*

Notice that we do not have inference rules that delete clauses. Thus, every derivation has the following *chain property*:

$$(\{\} = M_0) \subseteq M_1 \subseteq \cdots \subseteq M_n \subseteq \cdots$$

The inclusions are not strict, because non-progressive steps are allowed as well (though they are not needed at all).

3.3. Example

Suppose the given input clause set is $S = \{\neg P(X), \; P(Y) \vee Q(Y), \; \neg Q(Z)\}$. Clearly, S is unsatisfiable. We develop a refutation.

We have to start with the empty matrix M_0. Only a variant step can be applied to M_0, hence M_1 is just a copy of S. For each matrix M_i we discuss the possibilities for one open path through M_i, which is indicated by underlining.

M_1:

$$\underline{\neg P(X)} \qquad (C_1)$$
$$\underline{P(Y)} \vee Q(Y) \qquad (C_2)$$
$$\underline{\neg Q(Z)} \qquad (C_3)$$

The underlined path is open, and we carry out a connection step on $(\neg P(X), P(Y))$. Suppose that unify returns $\sigma_1 = \{Y/X\}$. This step is progressive and results in the following matrix[5]:

M_2:

$$\neg P(X) \qquad (C_1)$$
$$P(X) \vee \underline{Q(X)} \qquad (C_2\sigma_1)$$
$$\underline{\neg Q(Z)} \qquad (C_3)$$
$$P(Y) \vee \underline{Q(Y)} \qquad (C_2)$$

Now there are two connections in the underlined open path to which a connection step is applicable: $(Q(X), \neg Q(Z))$ and $(\neg Q(Z), Q(Y))$. By applying a connection step to the former we would obtain a closed matrix, thus ending the refutation. In order to make the example more illustrative, let us instead apply a connection step to $(\neg Q(Z), Q(Y))$ with MGU $\sigma_2 = \{Y/Z\}$. This gives us:

M_3:

$$\underline{\neg P(X)} \qquad (C_1)$$
$$P(X) \vee \underline{Q(X)} \qquad (C_2\sigma_1)$$
$$\underline{\neg Q(Z)} \qquad (C_3)$$
$$\underline{P(Z)} \vee Q(Z) \qquad (C_2\sigma_2)$$
$$P(Y) \vee \underline{Q(Y)} \qquad (C_2)$$

Here the underlined path offers three possibilities. First, the connection $(Q(X), \neg Q(Z))$ is still a candidate for a connection step, but we disregard it for the same reason as in the previous matrix. Second, the connection step on $(\neg Q(Z), Q(Y))$ with MGU $\{Y/Z\}$ would not be progressive and therefore not interesting (if unify would return $\{Z/Y\}$ instead, the step would be progressive, though). Third, a connection step on $(\neg P(X), P(Z))$ is progressive no matter which of the two MGUs unify returns.

Suppose that this step is applied with $\sigma_3 = \{Z/X\}$:

M_4:		
	$\neg P(X)$	(C_1)
	$P(X) \vee Q(X)$	$(C_2\sigma_1)$
	$\neg Q(X)$	$(C_3\sigma_3)$
	$P(X) \vee Q(X)$	$(C_2\sigma_2\sigma_3)$
	$P(Y) \vee Q(Y)$	(C_2)
	$\neg Q(Z)$	(C_3)
	$P(Z) \vee Q(Z)$	$(C_2\sigma_2)$

Note that $P(X) \vee Q(X)$ occurs twice in this listing. Since matrices are sets, deleting one of these occurrences would represent the same set.

M_4 is closed because either path through the first three clauses alone is closed. Hence we have found a refutation.

3.4. Fairness

Control strategies for any kind of rule-based system usually depend on some notion of fairness, when several rules or rule instances are applicable and one of them has to be selected for the next step. In matrix M_2 above, two connections were candidates for progressive connection steps, and one of them was selected to derive M_3, while the other was disregarded. In M_3 the disregarded connection was again a candidate for a progressive connection step and was again disregarded. Fairness is a condition on the choices made by the strategy to prevent that an applicable step is disregarded forever.

In many cases, especially with control strategies for logical calculi, fairness can be defined very simply as *exhaustiveness*: every step that is applicable to any state will ultimately be performed. There are standard text book procedures to implement exhaustive strategies effectively; in particular, resolution calculi can be treated this way.

This simple approach is sufficient if the underlying rules are commutative in the following sense: whenever two steps are applicable in some state, each of them remains applicable in the successor state produced by the other. If, on the other hand, the rules are not commutative, then the application of one step might destroy the applicability of the other. Such a phenomenon makes exhaustiveness an inherent impossibility and turns fairness into a more difficult question.

Unfortunately, our system is of the non-commutative variety. As an example let

$$M_i = \{\underline{\neg P(a)} \vee R, \quad \underline{P(X)}, \quad \underline{\neg Q(a)}, \quad \underline{Q(Y)} \vee P(Y), \quad \ldots\}$$

where the underlined path through M_i is open. Both $(\neg P(a), P(X))$ and $(\neg Q(a), Q(Y))$ are candidates for progressive connection steps in M_i. Disregarding the former and applying the latter yields

$$M_{i+1} = \{\neg P(a) \vee R, \quad P(X), \quad \neg Q(a), \quad Q(a) \vee P(a), \quad Q(Y) \vee P(Y), \quad \ldots\} .$$

Now any path through M_{i+1} containing the disregarded connection $(\neg P(a), P(X))$ is closed. This is a consequence of the presence of the clauses $\neg Q(a)$ and $Q(a) \vee P(a)$ in M_{i+1}. Therefore a connection step on the first connection, which would introduce the new clause $P(a)$, is no longer applicable – the second condition in the definition of a connection step can no longer be satisfied for this connection. Note that other paths through M_{i+1} are still open, though.

By the way, had we selected the other applicable step in M_i, the next matrix would have been

$$M'_{i+1} = \{\neg P(a) \vee \underline{R}, \quad \underline{P(a)}, \quad \underline{P(X)}, \quad \underline{\neg Q(a)}, \quad \underline{Q(Y)} \vee P(Y), \quad ...\}$$

in which the disregarded connection $(\neg Q(a), Q(Y))$ is still a candidate for a progressive connection step as shown by the underlined open path through M'_{i+1}. Selecting this connection next we can achieve that the new clauses of both steps are present.

Should the presence of all of these clauses happen to be indispensable for closing the matrix, it might be that the sequence $M_0, \ldots, M_i, M_{i+1}$ cannot be extended to a refutation whereas the sequence $M_0, \ldots, M_i, M'_{i+1}$ can – this would be a typical case of non-confluence. Fortunately, it turns out that our calculus *is* confluent: in all such situations, either none or both sequences can be continued to a refutation. The example illustrates why this is not a trivial property.

Coming back to fairness, the simple exhaustiveness definition is not possible, and we need a more complex definition. With this definition we will prove below our main result, that any fair derivation from an unsatisfiable clause set is a refutation (strong completeness).

Definition 6. (Fairness) *A derivation $D = M_0, M_1, \ldots, M_i, \ldots$ is fair iff it is a refutation or else the following two conditions are satisfied:*

1. *For every $i \geq 0$ there is a $j \geq i$ such that M_{j+1} results from M_j by a variant step.*

2. *For every $i \geq 0$ and every connection (K, L) with MGU σ that is a candidate for a progressive connection step in M_i there is a $j \geq i$ such that one of the following is true:*

   (a) $M_i \sigma \subseteq M_j$.

   (b) Every path p through M_j with $\{K, L\} \subseteq p$ is closed.

Condition 1 simply requires variant steps to be performed "every now and then".

Condition 2.(a) formalises that any progressive connection step that remains applicable sufficiently long must ultimately be performed. More precisely, the condition does not enforce that this very step be performed, but only that its effect be achieved at some point – regardless whether by this step or by some other.

In a nice case, if Condition 2.(a) holds, the connection (K, L) is irrelevant from M_j onward, because any connection step on (K, L) in some later matrix would result in clauses that have been introduced up to M_j anyway.

However, perhaps contrary to the intuition, this is not always so. The reason is that the MGU σ of the connection, say $\{X/Y\}$, may be applicable to clauses containing the variable X *that are derived only later in the derivation.* Hence, applying σ at a later time may well be progressive. Condition 2.(a) covers this possibility: let the later time be i', then there must again be a time j' at which the clauses that are new for $M_{j'}$ have been introduced.

Condition 2.(b) captures the case that a connection step loses its applicability because of other steps.

3.5. Achieving Fairness

Our notion of fairness – Definition 6 – is defined as an abstract mathematical property derivations may or may not enjoy. In order to implement a proof procedure, however, we need not only the property, but an effective strategy for the construction of a derivation that is guaranteed to have this property.

Fortunately, the existence of such a strategy can be demonstrated with a fairly simple approach: use an iteratively increasing bound T that serves both as a limit for the term nesting depth and as a trigger for the application of variant steps.

More precisely, we call a progressive connection step T-*progressive*, if at least one (but not necessarily all) of its new clauses has a term nesting depth not exceeding T. Building on this, we define an effective strategy as follows (in contrast to *The Procedure* in Section 2):

Procedure 7. (The CCC Procedure)

(i) Initialise M with the empty matrix and T with the maximum term nesting depth of the clauses in S.

(ii) While M is open repeat:

  (a) Modify M by applying one variant step.

  (b) Increment T.

  (c) Modify M by applying a T-progressive connection step.
  Repeat until saturation, i.e., until no such step is applicable any more. □

The sequence of values of M over time corresponds to the constructed derivation. Let us denote these values by $M_0, M_1, \ldots, M_i, \ldots$

Note that this strategy is indeed irrevocable in the sense described in the introduction. It never backtracks to previous values of M or makes any other provision for reconsidering alternatives at a later point in time. A subtle difference to *The Procedure* given in Section 2 concerns the generated amplifications. One might think that each iteration through (a) creates the next amplification S^μ of S. However, during the application of T-progressive connection steps in phase (c), the current M_i is extended by new clauses yielding M_{i+1}, whereas S^μ in *The Procedure* would only be instantiated, but not extended. In a sense our connection steps combine instantiation with (partial) amplification.

Theorem 8. *Any derivation (from any finite input clause set) constructed by Procedure 7 is fair.*

Proof: We first make sure that the saturation phase (c) always terminates. Each connection step has to be T-progressive, which means that it introduces at least one instance $C\sigma$ of some clause with $C \in M$ and $C\sigma \notin M$. The clause $C\sigma$ is either a variant or a proper instance of C. The total number of different variants that may be introduced in this way is finite, because Assumption 4 implies that $\text{var}(C\sigma) \subseteq \text{var}(M)$, which is finite (only variant steps introduce new variables, and $|\text{var}(\text{new}(S))|$ is finite). The total number of proper instances that may be introduced is also finite, because their term nesting depth is limited by T, which remains fixed during (c). Thus, after finitely many applications of connection steps all applications producing a clause within the term nesting limit will be used up, and (c) terminates.

Next, if the constructed derivation is a refutation, it is fair by definition. So suppose it is not a refutation. This means that the procedure above does not terminate.

Each of (a), (b), (c) terminates, therefore nontermination implies that (a) is performed periodically with finite intervals in between. Hence the derivation satisfies Condition 1 in the fairness definition.

For Condition 2 consider any point in time i where a progressive connection step is applicable to some connection (K, L) in M_i, and let $D_1, \ldots, D_n$ be the new clauses of this step (progressive means that there is at least one such clause).

Case 1: M_i is the value of M at the beginning or during the saturation phase (c) for some value of T. Let m be the maximum term nesting depth of the clauses $D_1, \ldots, D_n$. If $m \leq T$, let $i' = i$. Otherwise let i' be the smallest point in time where $M_{i'}$ is the value of M at the beginning of phase (c) and where T has been incremented sufficiently often so that its value is greater or equal to m. (This may require several iterations of the body of the *while* loop, but only finitely many changes to M.)

By construction we have in either case that $M_{i'}$ is the value of M during the saturation phase (c) when each of $D_1, \ldots, D_n$ has a term nesting depth not exceeding the current value of T. Now let j be the point in time right after termination of this saturation phase, when phase (a) would be next. We show that for this j Condition 2.(a) or Condition 2.(b) holds.

Assume to the contrary that neither holds, i.e., $D_k \notin M_j$ for one of the clauses $D_1, \ldots, D_n$ and some path p through M_j with $\{K, L\} \subseteq p$ is open. This means that a connection step is applicable to (K, L) in M_j and that it is T-progressive, because by construction the term nesting depth of D_k does not exceed T. Hence the saturation phase (c) is not yet completed, contradicting the definition of the time point j. Therefore the assumption is wrong and Condition 2.(a) or Condition 2.(b) holds.

Case 2: M_i is the value of M at the beginning of phase (a). Then M_{i+1} is obtained from M_i by a variant step. It is straightforward to see that in this case any progressive connection step on (K, L) in M_i is also a progressive connection step on (K, L) in M_{i+1}. Moreover, M_{i+1} is the value of M at the beginning of the saturation phase (c), thus we can construct $j \geq i + 1$ as in the previous case, again satisfying Condition 2.

Altogether this proves all requirements of the fairness definition. $\square$

Of course there are certainly much better strategies. The procedure above is only meant as a proof that fair derivations can be effectively constructed.

What remains, now, is to show that the fairness of derivations, no matter how achieved, ensures confluence. This result is established in the next section.

4. COMPLETENESS

Definition 9. (Bounded downward closed clause set) *Let S be a finite clause set, and γ be a ground substitution for S. Define a set of sets $S \downarrow \gamma$ as follows:*

$$S \downarrow \gamma = \{ S\delta \mid S\delta\gamma = S\gamma \text{ for some substitution } \delta \}$$

That is, $S \downarrow \gamma$ is the set of instances of S, (including S, variants of S and $S\gamma$ itself) that can further be instantiated to $S\gamma$ by γ itself. Notice that if $S\delta' \in S \downarrow \gamma$ and $S\delta'\delta''\gamma = S\gamma$ for some δ'', then also $S\delta'\delta'' \in S \downarrow \gamma$ by simply taking $\delta = \delta'\delta''$. In this sense $S \downarrow \gamma$ is "downward closed".

Lemma 10. $S \downarrow \gamma$ *is a finite set of finite sets.*

Proof: We are given that S is finite. We show that $\bigcup(S \downarrow \gamma)$ is finite. Clearly, this suffices to show that $S \downarrow \gamma$ is a finite set of finite sets. In order for $\bigcup(S \downarrow \gamma)$ to be infinite, the clauses $C\delta$ in $\bigcup(S \downarrow \gamma)$ would have to grow (i) without bound wrt. term depth, or (ii) for some (at least one) clause $C\delta$ in $\bigcup(S \downarrow \gamma)$ there would have to be infinitely many variants of $C\delta$ in $\bigcup(S \downarrow \gamma)$. Now, (i) is impossible because the condition $C\delta\gamma = C\gamma$ can not be maintained if the term depth of $C\delta$ is higher than that of $C\gamma$. Hence, the term depth of $C\delta$ is limited. Similarly, (ii) cannot be the case, because having infinitely many variants $M = \{C\delta_1, \ldots, C\delta_n, \ldots\} \subseteq \bigcup(S \downarrow \gamma)$ of some $C\delta \in \bigcup(S \downarrow \gamma)$ implies that var(M) is infinite as well. However, γ is a substitution and hence, by definition of substitution, dom(γ) is finite. Thus, γ instantiates only a finite subset of var(M), and there must be some $C\delta_j \in M$ for which $C\delta_j\gamma$ is not ground. However, by construction $C\delta_j \in S\delta_j$ for some $S\delta_j \in S \downarrow \gamma$, which contradicts with $S\delta_j\gamma = S\gamma$ the given fact that $S\gamma$ is ground. Hence, in sum, $\bigcup(S \downarrow \gamma)$ must be a finite set, and so $S \downarrow \gamma$ is a finite set of finite sets. $\square$

Lemma 11. *Let γ be a ground substitution, let $V \subseteq$ dom(γ) be a set of variables, and let σ be an idempotent substitution (i.e. $X\sigma = X\sigma\sigma$ for all variables X) with dom(σ) $\subseteq V$ and vcod(σ) $\subseteq V$. If there is a substitution δ such that $X\sigma\delta = X\gamma$ for every $X \in V$ then $X\sigma\gamma = X\gamma$ for every $X \in$ dom(γ).*

Proof: If $X \notin \mathrm{dom}(\sigma)$ the lemma holds trivially. Hence suppose now that $X \in \mathrm{dom}(\sigma)$. Let δ be the given substitution such that

$$X\sigma\delta = X\gamma. \tag{1}$$

Now consider $\mathrm{var}(X\sigma)$. If this set is empty, $X\sigma$ is ground and $X\sigma\delta = X\sigma\gamma$ holds trivially, and with (1) the lemma follows immediately. Hence we consider the case that $\mathrm{var}(X\sigma)$ is nonempty. It suffices to show that

$$Y\delta = Y\gamma, \text{ for every } Y \in \mathrm{var}(X\sigma), \tag{2}$$

because this implies $X\sigma\delta = X\sigma\gamma$, and with (1) the lemma follows immediately.

Now, to prove (2), recall that $Y \in \mathrm{vcod}(\sigma) \subseteq V$ and $X\sigma\delta = X\gamma$ for every $X \in V$ (as given). Thus, it holds in particular that

$$Y\sigma\delta = Y\gamma \tag{3}$$

We are given that σ is idempotent. Hence $\mathrm{dom}(\sigma) \cap \mathrm{vcod}(\sigma) = \emptyset$. Thus $Y \notin \mathrm{dom}(\sigma)$. Hence $Y = Y\sigma$. But then with (3), (2) follows immediately, which remained to be shown. □

The relevance of this lemma is to prove the following proposition, which serves a purpose analogous to that of the "lifting lemma" in resolution theory.

Proposition 12. *Let M be a matrix, p be a path through M, and γ be a ground substitution for M. Suppose that $\{K, L\} \subseteq p$ (for some literals K and L), that (K, L) is a connection with substitution γ, and that (K, L) is a connection with idempotent MGU σ. Then $M\gamma = M\sigma\gamma$.*

Proof: Let $V = \mathrm{var}(\{K, L\})$. By Assumption 4, σ is an idempotent substitution such that $\mathrm{dom}(\sigma) \subseteq V$ and $\mathrm{vcod}(\sigma) \subseteq V$. By the defining property of MGUs, there is a substitution δ such that $X\sigma\delta = X\gamma$ for every $X \in V$. But then Lemma 11 is applicable, and the result follows immediately. □

Definition 13. (Ordering on Clause Sets) *Let M and N be finite clause sets. Define $M \succ N$ iff $\mathrm{var}(M) \supset \mathrm{var}(N)$.*

It is easy to see that $\succ$ is an irreflexive and transitive relation, hence a strict (partial) ordering. Obviously, since $\mathrm{var}(M)$ is always finite, it is well-founded as well.

Lemma 14. (Path Extension) *Let $D = M_0, M_1, \ldots, M_n, \ldots$ be an infinite derivation from clause set S. Let M be a finite clause set, and suppose that $M \subseteq M_k$ for some k. Then there is a path p through M such that for every $i \geq k$ there is an open path p_i through M_i with $p \subseteq p_i$.*

That is, we can find a path p through M such that p will be part of some open path as the derivation proceeds.

Proof: Suppose, to the contrary, that for every path p through M there is a $i \geq k$ such that every path p_i through M_i with $p \subseteq p_i$ is closed. Let $\{i_1, \ldots, i_m\}$ be these time points, corresponding to the m paths p through M (matrices are finite).

Now consider $s = \max\{i_1, \ldots, i_m\}$ and let $j \in \{i_1, \ldots, i_m\}$ arbitrary.

Since $j \leq s$ the chain property gives us $M_j \subseteq M_s$. From $j \geq k$ and the chain property conclude that $M_k \subseteq M_j$. We are given that $M \subseteq M_k$. Altogether

$$M \subseteq M_k \subseteq M_j \subseteq M_s \text{ , for every } j \in \{i_1, \ldots, i_m\}. \tag{4}$$

Since the derivation is infinite, it contains no closed matrix, and through every open matrix there is, by definition, an open path. Hence let p_s be any open path through M_s. From 4 we conclude that there is an (open) path $p \subseteq p_s$ through M as well.

By the assumption made at the beginning of the proof, and using the subsequently defined naming of time points as $\{i_1, \ldots, i_m\}$, there is in particular for the just defined path p a time point $j \in \{i_1, \ldots, i_m\}$ such that every path p_j through M_j with $p \subseteq p_j$ is closed.

From the fact that p (resp. p_s) is a path through M (resp. M_s) and $p \subseteq p_s$ it follows with 4 that there is a path p' through M_j such that $p \subseteq p' \subseteq p_s$. Since p_s is an open path, p' is an open path as well (by $p' \subseteq p_s$). This, however, yields together with $p \subseteq p'$ a plain contradiction to the conclusion above, which stated that every path p_j through M_j with $p \subseteq p_j$ is closed. Hence, the assumption must have been wrong, and the lemma holds as claimed.   □

The main result of this paper is the following completeness theorem. Note that it assures completeness, whenever fairness is guaranteed; hence we have strong completeness and thus proof confluence.

Theorem 15. (Completeness) *Let S be the given input clause set. If S is unsatisfiable, then every fair derivation from S is a refutation.*

Proof: By Herbrand's theorem there is a finite set S^g of ground instances of clauses from S which is unsatisfiable. It can be presented as a finite set M of pairwise variable disjoint variants of clauses from S and a ground substitution γ such that $M\gamma = S^g$.

Now, let D be a fair derivation from S and assume contrary to the theorem that D is not a refutation.

Since D is fair, the variant rule must be applied infinitely often. Recall that we never delete clauses from matrices. Hence, at some time point, say l, it will thus be that $M \subseteq M_l$ (and hence also $M \subseteq \bigcup_{i \geq 0} M_i$). W.l.o.g. we can assume that each clause in M is syntactically identical to one of the variants introduced up to M_l; otherwise rename M (and γ) appropriately.

Now let $N \in M \downarrow \gamma$ be a minimal set wrt. $\succ$ such that $N \subseteq \bigcup_{i \geq 0} M_i$. We have to check that such a set N exists: since $M \subseteq \bigcup_{i \geq 0} M_i$ and it trivially holds that $M \in M \downarrow \gamma$ it is clear that M itself might be a candidate to be taken as N. Now, since $\succ$ is a well-founded ordering on finite clause sets, and the elements of $M \downarrow \gamma$ are finite (cf. Lemma 10), any chain $(N_0 := M) \succ N_1 \succ \cdots \succ N_{n-1} \succ N_n$ with $N_i \in M \downarrow \gamma$ and

$N_i \subseteq \bigcup_{i \geq 0} M_i$ must be finite, and we set $N := N_n$, provided that this chain cannot be extended to the right. Thus, N is minimal wrt. $\succ$ restricted to the elements in $\bigcup_{i \geq 0} M_i$.

The proof technique now is to construct an N' with $N' \in M \downarrow \gamma$ and $N' \subseteq \bigcup_{i \geq 0} M_i$ and $N \succ N'$, contradicting the minimality of N.

Since derivations have the chain property, the property $N \subseteq \bigcup_{i \geq 0} M_i$ implies by the fact that N is a finite set that

$$N \subseteq M_k \text{ , for some } k. \tag{5}$$

Therefore we can apply Lemma 14 and conclude that there is a path p through N such that for every $i \geq k$ there is an open path p_i through M_i with $p \subseteq p_i$. This result will be used further below – the immediate consequence that this p is open will be needed in a moment.

Clearly, $N\gamma$ is an unsatisfiable ground clause set, because $N \in M \downarrow \gamma$ means by definition that $N = M\delta$ for some δ such that $M\delta\gamma = M\gamma$, hence $N\gamma = M\gamma$, and $M\gamma$ was assumed to be ground and unsatisfiable above. Consequently, any path through $N\gamma$ contains a pair of complementary literals. In particular, $p\gamma$ contains a pair of complementary literals, say $K\gamma$ and $L\gamma$, where

$$\{K, L\} \subseteq p \text{ .} \tag{6}$$

In other words, (K, L) is a connection with substitution γ. But then (K, L) is a connection with MGU σ, where σ is computed by unify. Then Proposition 12 is applicable and we conclude that $N\sigma\gamma = N\gamma$. The element $N\sigma$ has the form $N\sigma = M(\delta\sigma)$ because $N = M\delta$. For this element we obtain by the previous equation and by $N\gamma = M\gamma$ the properties $M(\delta\sigma)\gamma = N\gamma = M\gamma$, which is just the definition for

$$N\sigma \in M \downarrow \gamma \text{ .} \tag{7}$$

The next subgoal is to show that $N\sigma$ is strictly smaller than N.

Since p is open and $\{K, L\} \subseteq p$ it trivially holds that $|K| \neq |L|$. On the other hand, σ is a most general unifier of $|K|$ and $|L|$. Hence there is at least one variable, say X, in $\{K, L\} \subseteq p$, for which $X\sigma \neq X$, that is, $X \in \text{dom}(\sigma)$. Now p is a path through N, therefore $X \in \text{var}(N)$.

Obviously, $\text{var}(N\sigma) \subseteq \text{var}(N) \cup \text{vcod}(\sigma)$. By Assumption 4 $\text{vcod}(\sigma) \subseteq \text{var}(\{K, L\}) \subseteq \text{var}(N)$, hence $\text{var}(N\sigma) \subseteq \text{var}(N)$.

The idempotence of σ implies $\text{dom}(\sigma) \cap \text{vcod}(\sigma) = \emptyset$, thus $X \notin \text{vcod}(\sigma)$ and $X \notin \text{var}(N\sigma)$. So we have $\text{var}(N\sigma) \subset \text{var}(N)$, which means nothing but

$$N \succ N\sigma \text{ .} \tag{8}$$

There remains to be shown that

$$N\sigma \subseteq \bigcup_{i \geq 0} M_i \text{ .} \tag{9}$$

We distinguish two cases, each leading to the conclusion 9.

Case 1:   For every $i \geq k$, it is not the case that (K, L) is a candidate for a progressive connection step in M_i.

As concluded above by the application of Lemma 14, for every $i \geq k$ there is an open path p_i through M_i with $p \subseteq p_i$. With the fact that $\{K, L\} \subseteq p$ (obtained in 6 above) it follows that $\{K, L\}$ is a candidate for a connection step in M_i, for every $i \geq k$.

Together with the assumption of this Case 1 we obtain that for every $i \geq k$ a connection step on (K, L) in M_i exists, but this connection step is non-progressive. Hence, for every $i \geq k$, $M_i \cup M_i \sigma = M_i$. But then with $N \subseteq M_k$ as obtained in 5 we get the following chain:

$$N\sigma \subseteq M_k \sigma \subseteq \bigcup_{i \geq k}(M_i \cup M_i \sigma) = \bigcup_{i \geq k} M_i \subseteq \bigcup_{i \geq 0} M_i .$$

Case 2:   This is the complement of Case 1. Hence suppose that for some $i \geq k$ the connection (K, L) is a candidate for a progressive connection step in M_i. We are given that the given derivation D is fair (cf. Def. 6). In particular, Condition 2 in the definition of fairness holds wrt. the connection (K, L) and M_i. Let $j \geq i$ be the point in time claimed there.

Assume that Condition 2.(b) is satisfied (this will yield a contradiction). This means that every path p' through M_j with $\{K, L\} \subseteq p'$ is closed. But at the same time, however, observing that $j \geq k$ (since $j \geq i$ and $i \geq k$) we concluded further above by application of Lemma 14 that there is an open path p_j through M_j with $p \subseteq p_j$. Since $\{K, L\} \subseteq p$ (as by 6) and thus $\{K, L\} \subseteq p_j$, we arrive at a contradiction to the just assumed by setting $p' = p_j$.

Hence Condition 2.(b) cannot be satisfied, and consequently Condition 2.(a) must be satisfied. This means that $M_i \sigma \subseteq M_j$. Recall that derivations have the chain property. From $i \geq k$ we thus get $M_k \subseteq M_i$. Together with $N \subseteq M_k$ then $N\sigma \subseteq M_i \sigma$, and so $N\sigma \subseteq M_j$ follows immediately. Clearly, $N\sigma \subseteq \bigcup_{i \geq 0} M_i$ as well. This completes Case 2.

Notice that in both cases we concluded with 9. Altogether, 7, 8, and 9 contradict the minimality of N.

Hence, the assumption that D is not a refutation must be wrong, and the theorem holds.   □

5. CONCLUSIONS

In this paper we have defined CCC, a confluent connection calculus on the first-order level. We gave a proof of its strong completeness and hence, of its proof confluence.

We demonstrated the drawback of a naive connection method by means of an example and we briefly discussed tableaux oriented proof procedures. More precisely, in Section 2.4 we identified an incestuous graph (IG) problem and argued that a prototypical proof procedure – *The Procedure* – exhibits an exponential search space. We did not rigorously argue that the proposed new proof procedure – *The CCC Procedure* – performs any better. However, it is indeed possible to solve the IG problem with *The CCC Procedure* in linear time (and space). To see this, observe first that the IG problem contains no function symbols. Further, it is possible to derive all required instances of the non-ground clauses (RT-1) and (RT-2) as descendant of *one single* variant of the (RT-1) and (RT-2) clauses, respectively. In other words, *The CCC procedure* will find the refutation during the *first* instance of the saturation phase (ii.c).

The CCC Procedure treats matrices, which are sets of clauses. Consequently, the order of clauses does not play any role for fairness or completeness. Hence, more refined proof procedures are free to represent sets as (duplicate-free) lists. A good strategy then would be to append new instances of clauses derived during the saturation phase or during variant steps at the end of the list, because then it is cheap to identify and represent those new closed paths that simply extend previously closed paths[6].

As a further ingredient, actual implementations of *The CCC Procedure* should include a "relevance test"[7]: consider, for example, a matrix $M \cup \{A \vee B\} \cup M'$, and suppose that p is some path through M, and that for every path p' through M' the path $p \cup \{A\} \cup p'$ is closed. Now, if $p \cup p'$ alone is closed (for every p'), then also $p \cup \{B\} \cup p'$ is closed (for every p'). In other words, if A is not relevant to obtain closed paths through M' in the context $p \cup \{A\}$, then no *search* for closed paths in M' in the context $p \cup \{B\}$ is needed.

Now, using the proposed list representation of matrices, and taking advantage of the relevance test, it can indeed be shown that *The CCC Procedure* solves the IG problem after $O(n)$ steps.

Our calculus achieves confluence by taking into account only derivations which obey a fairness condition. This condition is formulated as an abstract formal property of derivations. It allows to formulate a strong completeness theorem, stating that *any fair* derivation leads to a proof, provided that a proof exists at all.

The difficulty was to define the calculus in such a way that an *effective* fairness condition can be stated. Defining an effective fair strategy is much less straightforward than in resolution calculi (CCC is not commutative, unlike resolution).

That it is not trivial was observed already in (Bry and Eisinger, 1996). There, a rigid-variable calculus is defined and a strong completeness result is proven. However, the question how to define an *effective* fair strategy had to be left open. Thus, our new approach can be seen to address open issues there.

We came up with a strategy, which is based on a term-depth bound and we proved that this strategy indeed results in fair derivations.

We are aware of the fact, that this effective strategy is only a first step towards the design of an efficient proof procedure based on the CCC-calculus. We expect improvements over "usual" tableaux based implementations of connection calculi, which do not exploit confluence.

This article is a first step, a lot of work remains to be done. In particular the saturation step within our strategy for achieving fairness needs to be turned into a more algorithmic version. Another important topic is to avoid the generation of redundant clauses. To this end regularity, as it is implemented in clausal tableaux would be a first attempt. A further point would be to investigate under which conditions the variant inference rule can be dispensed with, or how to modify the calculus so that new variants of input clauses are introduced more sparsely.

ACKNOWLEDGMENTS

We are grateful to Donald Loveland for comments on an earlier version.

Peter Baumgartner, Ulrich Furbach
Universität Koblenz
Koblenz, Germany

Norbert Eisinger
Universität München
München, Germany

NOTES

1. This is not meant to disqualify the disconnection method; merely, we want to point out differences.

2. In the literature, matrices are also written horizontally.

3. By an X-clause we mean any clause whose predicate symbol of the head literal is X.

4. It is well-known that in general the time complexity to compute reachability in graphs is $O(n^3)$ (Warshall-algorithm).

5. In writing down the matrices, we use the strategy to apply the substitution "in place" to the old matrix, and append the uninstantiated versions of the clauses affected by the substitution at the bottom. This suggests that a tableau procedure can be defined as a specific variant of CCC. We plan to investigate this in the future.

6. This strategy resembles much a tableau procedure – one that takes advantage of *confluence*, however.

7. Similar to *condensing* in (Oppacher and Suen, 1988) or *level cut* in (Baumgartner et al., 1996). Although so simple, this technique is very helpful in practice.

REFERENCES

Baader, F. and Schulz, K. U. (1998). Unification Theory. In Bibel, W. and Schmitt, P. H., editors, *Automated Deduction. A Basis for Applications*. Kluwer Academic Publishers.

Baumgartner, P. and Furbach, U. (1993). Consolution as a Framework for Comparing Calculi. *Journal of Symbolic Computation*, 16(5):445–477.

Baumgartner, P. and Furbach, U. (1994). PROTEIN: A *PRO*ver with a *Theory* Extension *I*nterface. In Bundy, A., editor, *Automated Deduction – CADE-12*, volume 814 of *Lecture Notes in Artificial Intelligence*, pages 769–773. Springer. Available in the WWW, URL:
http://www.uni-koblenz.de/ag-ki/Systems/PROTEIN/.

Baumgartner, P., Furbach, U., and Niemelä, I. (1996). Hyper Tableaux. In *Proc. JELIA 96*, number 1126 in Lecture Notes in Artificial Intelligence. European Workshop on Logic in AI, Springer.

Baumgartner, P., Furbach, U., and Stolzenburg, F. (1997). Computing Answers with Model Elimination. *Artificial Intelligence*, 90(1–2):135–176.

Beckert, B. and Posegga, J. (1995). leanT^{A}P: Lean tableau-based deduction. *Journal of Automated Reasoning*, 15(3):339–358.

Bibel, W. (1987). *Automated Theorem Proving*. Vieweg, 2nd edition.

Billon, J.-P. (1996). The Disconnection Method. In (Miglioli et al., 1996).

Bry, F. and Eisinger, N. (1996). Unit resolution tableaux. Research Report PMS-FB-1996-2, Institut für Informatik, LMU München.

Bry, F. and Yahya, A. (1996). Minimal Model Generation with Positive Unit Hyper-Resolution Tableaux. In (Miglioli et al., 1996), pages 143–159.

Eder, E. (1992). *Relative Complexities of First Order Languages*. Vieweg.

Fitting, M. (1990). *First Order Logic and Automated Theorem Proving*. Texts and Monographs in Computer Science. Springer.

Fujita, H. and Hasegawa, R. (1991). A Model Generation Theorem Prover in KL1 using a Ramified-Stack Algorithm. In *Proc. of the Eigth International Conference on Logic Programming*, pages 535–548, Paris, France.

Hähnle, R., Beckert, B., and Gerberding, S. (1994). The Many-Valued Theorem Prover 3TAP. Interner Bericht 30/94, Universität Karlsruhe.

Hähnle, R. and Klingenbeck, S. (1996). A-Ordered Tableaux. *Journal of Logic and Computation*, 6(6):819–833.

Hähnle, R. and Pape, C. (1997). Ordered tableaux: Extensions and applications. In Galmiche, D., editor, *Automated Reasoning with Analytic Tableaux and Related Methods*, number 1227 in Lecture Notes in Artificial Intelligence, pages 173–187. Springer.

Klingenbeck, S. and Hähnle, R. (1994). Semantic tableaux with ordering restrictions. In Bundy, A., editor, *Automated Deduction — CADE 12*, LNAI 814, pages 708–722, Nancy, France. Springer-Verlag.

Letz, R., Mayr, K., and Goller, C. (1994). Controlled Integrations of the Cut Rule into Connection Tableau Calculi. *Journal of Automated Reasoning*, 13.

Letz, R., Schumann, J., Bayerl, S., and Bibel, W. (1992). SETHEO: A High-Performance Theorem Prover. *Journal of Automated Reasoning*, 8(2).

Loveland, D. (1968). Mechanical Theorem Proving by Model Elimination. *JACM*, 15(2).

Manthey, R. and Bry, F. (1988). SATCHMO: a theorem prover implemented in Prolog. In Lusk, E. and Overbeek, R., editors, *Proceedings of the 9th Conference on Automated Deduction, Argonne, Illinois, May 1988*, volume 310 of *Lecture Notes in Computer Science*, pages 415–434. Springer.

Miglioli, P., Moscato, U., Mundici, D., and Ornaghi, M., editors (1996). *Theorem Proving with Analytic Tableaux and Related Methods*, number 1071 in Lecture Notes in Artificial Intelligence. Springer.

Oppacher, F. and Suen, E. (1988). HARP: A Tableau-Based Theorem Prover. *Journal of Automated Reasoning*, 4:69–100.

Plaisted, D. A. and Zhu, Y. (1997). Ordered Semantic Hyper Linking. In *Proceedings of Fourteenth National Conference on Artificial Intelligence (AAAI-97)*.

Prawitz, D. (1960). An improved proof procedure. *Theoria*, 26:102–139.

Robinson, J. A. (1965). Automated deduction with hyper-resolution. *Internat. J. Comput. Math.*, 1:227–234.

Voronkov, A. (1997). Strategies in rigid-variable methods. In *15th International Joint Conference on Artificial Intelligence (IJCAI 97)*, Nagoya. International Joint Conference on Artificial Intelligence.

Voronkov, A. (1998). Herbrand's theorem, automated reasoning and semantic tableaux. In *IEEE Symposium on Logic in Computer Science*.

GERHARD BREWKA AND THOMAS EITER

PRIORITIZING DEFAULT LOGIC

1. INTRODUCTION

In nonmonotonic reasoning conflicts among defaults are ubiquitous. For instance, more specific rules may be in conflict with more general ones, a problem which has been studied intensively in the context of inheritance networks (Poole, 1985; Touretzky, 1986; Touretzky et al., 1991). When defaults are used for representing design goals in configuration tasks conflicts naturally arise. The same is true in model based diagnosis where defaults are used to represent the assumption that components typically are ok. In legal reasoning conflicts among rules are very common (Prakken, 1993) and keep many lawyers busy (and rich).

The standard nonmontonic formalisms handle such conflicts by generating multiple belief sets. In default logic (Reiter, 1980) and autoepistemic logic (Moore, 1985) these sets are called extensions or expansions, respectively. In circumscription (McCarthy, 1980) the belief sets correspond to different classes of preferred models.

Usually, not all of the belief sets are plausible. We often tend to prefer some of the conflicting rules and are interested in the belief sets generated by the preferred rules only. One way to achieve this is to re-represent the defaults in such a way that the unwanted belief sets are not generated, for instance by adding new consistency conditions to a default. This approach has the advantage that the logical machinery of the underlying nonmonotonic logic does not have to be changed. On the other hand, re-representing the defaults in this way is a very clumsy business. The resulting new defaults tend to be rather complex. Moreover, the addition of new information to the knowledge base may lead to further re-representations. In other words, elaboration tolerance is violated.

For this reason we prefer an approach where preferences among defaults can be represented via an explicit preference relation and where the logical machinery is extended accordingly. Indeed, for all major nonmonotonic formalisms, such prioritized versions have been proposed in the past. Among them are prioritized circumscription (Gelfond et al., 1989), hierarchic autoepistemic logic (Konolige, 1988), prioritized theory revision (Benferhat et al., 1993; Nebel, 1998), prioritized logic programming

27

S. Hölldobler (ed.), Intellectics and Computational Logic, 27–46.
© 2000 *Kluwer Academic Publishers.*

(Sakama and Inoue, 1996; Zhang and Foo, 1997), or prioritized abduction (Eiter and Gottlob, 1995).

Also several prioritized versions of Reiter's default logic, the logic we are dealing with in this paper, have been described in the literature (Marek and Truszczyński, 1993; Brewka, 1994a; Baader and Hollunder, 1995; Delgrande and Schaub, 1997), as well as of defeasible logics beyond default logic (Nute, 1994; Gelfond and Son, 1998). However, as we will show in Section 3, these approaches are not fully satisfactory. It turns out that some of them implicitly recast Reiter's default logic to a logic of graded beliefs, while others do overly enforce the application of rules with high priority, which leads to counterintuitive behavior.

Our approach takes a different perspective, which is dominated by the following two main ideas. The first is that the application of a default rule means to jump to a conclusion, and this conclusion is yet another assumption which has to be used globally in the program for the issue of deciding whether a rule is applicable or not. The second is that the rules must be applied in an order compatible with the priority information. We take this to mean that a rule is applied *unless it is defeated via its assumptions by rules of higher priorities.* This view is new and avoids the unpleasant behavior which is present with the other approaches. Our formalization of these ideas involves a dual of the standard Gelfond-Lifschitz reduction and a certain operator used to check satisfaction of priorities. In order to base our approach on firmer grounds, we set forth some abstract principles that, as we believe, any formalization of prioritized default logic should satisfy. We demonstrate that our approach satisfies these principles, while other approaches violate them.

The remainder of this paper is organized as follows. The next section recalls the basic definitions of default logic and introduces the notion of a prioritized default theory. Section 3 introduces two basic principles for preference handling, reviews some approaches to prioritized default logic and demonstrates that they fail to satisfy the principles. In Section 4, we then present our approach, by introducing the concept of preferred extensions. We will introduce this notion in a stepwise manner, starting with the simplest case, namely prerequisite-free normal defaults, which are also called supernormal defaults. We then extend our definition to prerequisite-free default theories, showing that an additional fixed point condition is needed to get the definition of preferred extensions right. Finally, we handle arbitrary default theories by reducing them to the prerequisite-free case. The reduction can be viewed as dual to the famous Gelfond/Lifschitz reduction for extended logic programs. In Section 5 we show how preference information can be expressed in the logical language. This makes it possible to reason not only with, but also about preferences among rules. Section 6 discusses related work, and concludes the paper by considering possible extensions and outlining further work.

The work reported here generalizes the approach presented in (Brewka and Eiter, 1998), which covers the fragment of default logic equivalent to extended logic programs, and extends the results.

2. PRIORITIZED DEFAULT THEORIES

We first recall the basic definitions underlying Reiter's default logic. A *default theory* is a pair $\Delta = (D, W)$ of a theory W containing first-order sentences and a set of defaults D. Each default is of the form $a : b_1, \ldots, b_n/c, n \geq 1$, where a, b_i, and c are first-order formulas. The intuitive meaning of the default is: if a is derived and the b_i are separately consistent with what is derived, then infer c. Formula a is called the *prerequisite*, each b_i a *justification*, and c the *consequent* of the default. For a default d we use $pre(d)$, $just(d)$, and $cons(d)$ to denote the prerequisite, the set of justifications, and the consequent of d, respectively; $\neg just(d)$ denotes $\{\neg a \mid a \in just(d)\}$. As usual, we assume that W and D are in skolemized form and that open defaults, i.e., defaults with free variables, represent the sets of their ground instances over the Herbrand universe (Reiter, 1980); a default theory with open defaults is closed by replacing open defaults with their ground instances. In what follows, we implicitly assume that default theories are closed before extensions etc are considered.

A (closed) default theory generates extensions which represent acceptable sets of beliefs which a reasoner might adopt based on the given default theory (D, W). Extensions are defined in (Reiter, 1980) as fixed points of an operator Γ_Δ. This operator Γ_Δ maps an arbitrary set of formulas S to the smallest deductively closed set S' that contains W and satisfies the condition: if $a : b_1, \ldots, b_n/c \in D$, $a \in S'$ and $\neg b_i \notin S$ then $c \in S'$. Intuitively, an extension is a set of beliefs containing W such that

1. as many defaults as consistently possible have been applied, and

2. only formulas possessing a non-circular derivation from W using defaults in D are contained.

Extensions can be characterized as follows (Marek and Truszczyński, 1993): Let $D^E = \{a/c \mid a : b_1, \ldots, b_n/c \in D, \neg b_i \notin E, i = 1, \ldots, n\}$ denote the *reduct* of D by E. Then E is an extension of T, if and only if $E = Th_{D^E}(W \cup D^E)$, where $Th_A(S)$ is the deductive closure of S in the monotonic rule system $FOL + A$, i.e., first-order logic augmented with the rules in A.

A default theory Δ may have zero, one or multiple extensions. The (skeptical) conclusions of Δ is the set of formulas contained in all extensions of Δ. Default theories possessing at least one extension will be called coherent. We say a default $a : b_1, \ldots, b_n/c$ is *defeated* by a set of formulas S, iff $\neg b_i \in S$ for some $i \in \{1, \ldots, n\}$.

A default $d = a : b/c$ is called *normal*, if b is logically equivalent to c; it is called *prerequisite-free*, if a is a logical truth, which is denoted by $\top$. Defaults which are both prerequisite-free and normal are called *supernormal*. A default theory is called *normal* (*prerequisite-free, supernormal*), if all of its defaults are normal (prerequisite-free, supernormal), respectively.

A default d is called *generating* in a set of formulas S, if $pre(d) \in S$ and $\neg just(d) \cap S = \emptyset$; denote by $GD(E, D)$ the set of all defaults from D which are generating in E. It is well-known (Reiter, 1980) that every extension of a default theory $\Delta = (D, W)$

is characterized through $GD(D, E)$, i.e.,

$$E = Th(W \cup cons(GD(D, E))) \qquad (1)$$

where $cons(D') = \{cons(d) \mid d \in D'\}$ for any set D'. Moreover, if Δ is prerequisite-free, then every E which satisfies (1) is an extension, cf. (Marek and Truszczyński, 1993).

We now introduce the notion of a prioritized default theory. Basically, we extend default theories with a strict partial order $<$ (i.e., $d \not< d$ and $d < d'$, $d' < d''$ implies $d < d''$) on the default rules. A default d will be considered preferred over default d', whenever $d < d'$ holds.

Definition 1. *A prioritized default theory is a triple $\Delta = (D, W, <)$ where (D, W) is a default theory and $<$ is a strict partial order on D.*

Partially ordered default theories have the advantage that the preference ordering among certain defaults can be left unspecified. This is important because in many cases there is no natural way of assigning preferences. However, the case of arbitrary partial orders can be reduced to particular refinements, namely well-orderings, in a canonical way. Recall that a partial order is a well-ordering, iff every subset of the elements has the least element; observe that any well-ordering is a total ordering.

Definition 2. *A fully prioritized default theory is a prioritized default theory $\Delta = (D, W, <)$ where $<$ is a well-ordering.*

Conclusions of prioritized default theories are defined in terms of preferred extensions, which are a subset of the classical extensions of Δ, i.e., the extensions of (D, W) according to (Reiter, 1980). The definition of preferred extension for fully prioritized default theories will be given in the next section. The general case of arbitrary prioritized default theories can then be reduced to this case as follows.

Definition 3. *Let $\Delta = (D, W, <)$ be a closed prioritized default theory. E is a prioritized extension of Δ iff E is a prioritized extension of a fully prioritized default theory $\Delta' = (D, W, <')$ such that $d < d'$ implies $d <' d'$.*

The preferred extensions of an open prioritized default theory Δ are the preferred extensions of Δ^* obtained by closing Δ. The partial order $<$ is inherited from D to the ground set of instances D^* in the obvious way. We assume here that no conflict arises, i.e., $d < d$ does not result for any $d \in D^*$; otherwise, no preferred extensions are defined.

In the remainder of this paper, we will restrict our discussion to fully prioritized default theories. Unless stated otherwise, all default theories are tacitly assumed to be closed.

3. PROBLEMS WITH EXISTING APPROACHES

Different prioritized versions of default logic have been proposed in the literature, e.g. (Marek and Truszczyński, 1993; Brewka, 1994a; Baader and Hollunder, 1995; Rintanen, 1995; Delgrande and Schaub, 1997). They do not behave as desired in certain situations, and we show that some of them fail to satisfy natural principles for preference handling in default logic.

3.1. Principles for priorities

The first principle can be viewed as a meaning postulate for the term "preference" and states what we consider a minimal requirement for preference handling in rule based systems:

Principle I. Let B_1 and B_2 be two extensions of a prioritized default theory Δ generated by the defaults $R \cup \{d_1\}$ and $R \cup \{d_2\}$, where $d_1, d_2 \notin R$, respectively. If d_1 is preferred over d_2, then B_2 is not a preferred extension of T.

We find it hard to see how the use of the term "preference among rules" could be justified in cases where Principle I is violated.

The second principle is related to relevance. It tries to capture the idea that the decision whether to believe a formula p or not should depend on the priorities of defaults contributing to the derivation of p only, not on the priorities of defaults which become applicable when p is believed:

Principle II. Let E be a preferred extension of a prioritized default theory $\Delta = (D, W, <)$, and let d be a (closed) default such that the prerequisite of d is not in E. Then E is a preferred extension of $\Delta' = (D \cup \{d\}, W, <')$ whenever $<'$ agrees with $<$ on priorities among defaults in D.

Thus, adding a rule which is not applicable in a preferred belief set can never render this belief set non-preferred unless new preference information changes preferences among some of the old rules (e.g. via transitivity). In other words, a belief set is not blamed for not applying rules which are not applicable.

We will see that each of the existing treatments of preferences for default logic, described in (Marek and Truszczyński, 1993; Brewka, 1994a; Baader and Hollunder, 1995; Rintanen, 1995), violates one of these principles.

3.2. Control of Reiter's quasi-inductive definition

The first group of proposals (Marek and Truszczyński, 1993; Brewka, 1994a; Baader and Hollunder, 1995) uses preferences to control the quasi-inductive definition of extensions (Reiter, 1980): in each step of the generation of extensions the defaults with highest priority whose prerequisites have already been derived are applied. Now what is wrong with this idea? The answer is: the preferred extensions do not take seriously what they believe. It may be the case that a less preferred default is applied although the prerequisite of a conflicting, more preferred default is believed in a preferred extension. As we will see, this can lead to situations where Principle I is violated.

The mentioned approaches differ in technical detail. We do not want to present the exact definitions here. Instead, we will illustrate the difficulties using an example for which all these approaches obtain the same result.

Example 4. Assume we are given the following default theory:

$$(1)\ a : b/b$$
$$(2)\ \top : \neg b/\neg b$$
$$(3)\ \top : a/a$$

Assume further that (1) is preferred over (2) and (2) over (3). This default theory has two classical extensions, namely $E_1 = Th(\{a, b\})$, which is generated by rules (1) and (3), and $E_2 = Th(\{a, \neg b\})$, which is generated by rules (2) and (3). The single preferred extension in the approaches mentioned above is E_2. The reason is that the prerequisite of (2) is derived before the prerequisite of (1) in the construction of the extension. The approaches thus violate Principle I.   □

The selection of E_2 in the previous example was already observed in (Brewka, 1994a). In that paper, the first author tried to defend his approach arguing that there is only weak evidence for the literal a in our example. We revise our view, however, and do not support this argument any longer. After all, default logic is not a logic of graded belief where degrees of evidence should play a role. Default logic models acceptance of belief based on defeasible arguments. Since a is an accepted belief, we believe rule (1) should be applied and E_1 should be the preferred extension in the example.

3.3. Rintanen's approach

An entirely different approach was proposed in (Rintanen, 1995). Rintanen uses a total order on (normal) defaults to induce a lexicographic order on extensions.

Call a normal default rule $r = a{:}b/b$ *applied* in a set of formulas E (denoted $r \in appl(E)$), if a and b are in E. An extension E is then preferred over extension E', if and only if there is a default $r \in appl(E) \setminus appl(E')$ satisfying the following condition: if r' is preferred over r and $r' \in appl(E')$, then $r' \in appl(E)$.

Unfortunately, also this approach leads to counterintuitive results and to a violation of our principles.

Example 5. Consider the following default theory:

$$(1)\ a : b/b$$
$$(2)\ \top : \neg a/\neg a$$
$$(3)\ \top : a/a$$

Again (1) is preferred over (2), and (2) over (3). The default theory has two classical extensions, namely $E_1 = Th(\{\neg a\})$ and $E_2 = Th(\{a, b\})$. Intuitively, since the decision whether to believe a or not depends on (2) and (3) only, and since (2) is preferred over (3), we would expect to conclude $\neg a$, in other words, to prefer E_1.

However, the approach of Rintanen prefers E_2. The reason is that in E_2 default (1) is applied. Belief in a is thus accepted on the grounds that this allows us to apply a default of high priority. This is far from being plausible and amounts to wishful thinking. It is also easy to see that Principle II is violated: E_1 clearly is the single preferred extension of rules (2) and (3) in Rintanen's approach. Adding rule (1) which is not applicable in E_1 makes E_1 a non-preferred extension.   □

The approach in (Rintanen, 1995) has been extended from normal to full default logic in (Rintanen, 1998). Moreover, variants of this approach are described in (Rintanen, 1998), which do not behave intuitively in certain situations either.

Since all the approaches discussed above suffer from drawbacks, we develop our new approach in the following section.

4. PREFERRED EXTENSIONS

In this section, we introduce our new notion of preferred extensions for fully prioritized default theories. As mentioned before, arbitrary prioritized default theories can be reduced to that case in a canonical manner.

We will consider the simplest case first, namely supernormal default theories. We then proceed to prerequisite-free default theories and, finally, to arbitrary default theories.

4.1. Supernormal default theories

Preference handling in prioritized supernormal default theories is rather easy. The obvious idea is to check the applicability of defaults in the order of preference. We first introduce an operator C which, given a fully prioritized prerequisite-free default theory Δ (which is not necessarily supernormal), produces tentative conclusions of Δ.

Call a default d active in a set of formulas S, if $pre(d) \in S$, $\neg just(d) \cap S = \emptyset$ and $cons(d) \notin S$ all hold. Intuitively, a default is active in S if it is applicable with respect to S and has not yet been applied.

Definition 6. *Let $\Delta = (D, W, <)$ be a fully prioritized prerequisite-free default theory. The operator C is defined as follows: $C(\Delta) = \bigcup_{\alpha \geq 0} E_\alpha$, where $E_0 = Th(W)$, and for every ordinal $\alpha > 0$,*

$$E_\alpha = \begin{cases} \underline{E_\alpha}, & \textit{if no default from } D \textit{ is active in } \underline{E_\alpha}; \\ Th(\underline{E_\alpha} \cup \{cons(d)\}) & \textit{otherwise, where} \\ & \quad d = \min_{<}\{d' \in D \mid d' \textit{ is active in } \underline{E_\alpha}\}, \end{cases}$$

where $\underline{E}_\alpha = \bigcup_{\beta < \alpha} E_\beta$. *(Note that for each successor ordinal* $\alpha = \beta + 1$, $\underline{E}_\alpha = E_\beta$.)

In the case of supernormal default theories, the operator C always produces an extension in the sense of Reiter and thus can directly be used to define preferred extensions:

Definition 7. *Let* $\Delta = (D, W, <)$ *be a fully prioritized supernormal default theory. E is the preferred extension of Δ if and only if $E = C(\Delta)$.*

It is obvious that there is always exactly one preferred extension. Note that the definition of this extension is fully constructive. It extends the notion of preferred subtheories as developed in (Brewka, 1989) to the infinite case.

4.2. *Prerequisite-free default theories*

Can we simply extend the definition for supernormal defaults to this case? The answer is obviously no. It may be the case that defaults are applied during the construction which are defeated later through the application of defaults of lower priority.

So, can we simply say: if the construction gives us an extension, then that extension is preferred? Unfortunately, the answer is again no.

Example 8. Consider the following default theory:

$$(1)\ \top : \neg b/a \qquad\qquad (3)\quad \top : a/a$$
$$(2)\ \top : \neg a/\neg a \qquad\qquad (4)\quad \top : b/b$$

Assume $(1) < (2) < (3) < (4)$. Applying operator C to this default theory yields $E = Th(\{a, b\})$. As easily seen, this is a classical extension. Nonetheless, one would certainly not say that this extension preserves priorities. What went wrong? Default (2) is defeated in E by applying a default which is less preferred than (2), namely default (3). In the construction of $C(\Delta)$ this remains unnoticed, since rule (1), although defeated in E, blocks the applicability of (2). In other words, without a special treatment of such cases, a rule (e.g. (3)) may inherit a high preference from a rule with the same consequent (namely (1)), even if that latter rule is not applicable in the extension. □

To avoid this, we have to impose an additional condition on an extension: in the construction of the tentative conclusions, we have to discard each rule whose consequent is in E, but which is defeated in E. Since we have to take E as the result of the construction into account, this amounts to adding a fixed point condition. What we will do is check whether we arrive at the same set of formulas after eliminating rules which are defeated in E and whose head is in E.

Definition 9. *Let* $\Delta = (D, W, <)$ *be a fully prioritized prerequisite-free default theory. Then, a set E of formulas is a prioritized extension of Δ, if and only if*

$$E = C(\Delta^{\star E}),$$

where $\Delta^{\star E}$ is obtained from Δ by deleting all defaults whose consequents are in E
and which are defeated in E.

This definition is coherent with the intuition that preferred extensions are distinguished classical extensions. Moreover, as in the case of supernormal theories, the preferred extension (if it exists) is unique.

Proposition 10. *Let $\Delta = (D, W, <)$ be a fully prioritized prerequisite-free default theory. Then, every preferred extension E of Δ is a classical extension, and Δ has at most one preferred extension.*

Proof: To show the first part, assume that E is a preferred extension of Δ. We show that

$$E = Th(W \cup cons(GD(D, E))) \qquad (2)$$

holds; since all defaults are prerequisite-free, this implies that E is a classical extension of Δ, cf. paragraph after Equation (1).

Since $E = C(\Delta^{\star E})$, no default from $D \setminus GD(D, E)$ is applied in the construction of E; hence, $E \subseteq Th(W \cup cons(GD(D, E)))$ follows. On the other hand, since each E_α is included in E and E does not defeat d, for every $d \in GD(D, E)$, it follows $cons(d) \in C(\Delta^{\star E})$; hence, $Th(W \cup cons(GD(D, E))) \subseteq E$ follows. This implies Equation (2), and proves that E is a classical extension of Δ.

For the second part, assume that different preferred extensions $E \neq E'$ exist. We derive a contradiction. Let d be the least default in D such that either (i) $d \in GD(D, E)$ and $cons(d) \notin E'$, or (ii) $d \in GD(D, E')$ and $cons(d) \notin E$. Since $E \neq E'$, d must exist. Consider first the case (i). It follows that $d \in D^{\star E'}$; for, otherwise $cons(d) \in E'$ holds, which is a contradiction. The default d must be defeated by E'; from the definition of $C(\Delta^{\star E})$, it follows that d is defeated by $Th(W \cup cons(K))$ for $K = \{d' \in GD(D, E') \mid d' < d\}$. From the minimality of d, it follows that for every $d' \in K$ it holds that $cons(d') \in E$. Hence, $Th(W \cup cons(K)) \subseteq E$, which means E defeats d. This is a contradiction to $d \in GD(D, E)$, however. The case (ii), i.e., $d \in GD(D, E')$ and $cons(d) \notin E$ is analogous. This proves the result. $\square$

4.3. General default theories

We will now reduce the general case to the prerequisite-free case. The basic idea is the following: in order to check whether an extension E of a fully prioritized default theory Δ is preferred, we evaluate the prerequisites of the default rules according to the extension E. Evaluating prerequisites means (1) eliminating prerequisites which are contained in the extension E from the corresponding rules, and (2) eliminating rules whose *prerequisites are not contained in* E. Observe that this operation can be viewed as a dual of the standard Gelfond/Lifschitz reduction from logic programming (Gelfond and Lifschitz, 1988), in which the justifications rather than the prerequisites are used to eliminate and simplify rules.

Finally, we check whether the resulting prerequisite-free theory Δ_E has E as its preferred extension.

Definition 11. *Let $\Delta = (D, W, <)$ be a fully prioritized default theory and E a set of formulas. The default theory $\Delta_E = (D_E, W, <_E)$ is obtained from Δ as follows: D_E results from D by*

1. *eliminating every default $d \in D$ such that $pre(d) \notin E$, and*

2. *replacing $pre(d)$ by $\top$ in all remaining defaults;*

$<_E$ is inherited from $<$ as follows: for any rules d and d' in D_E, $d <_E d'$ holds if and only if $d1 < d1'$ holds for the $<$-least rules $d1$ and $d1'$ in D which give rise to d and d' (i.e., $d1_E = d$ and $d1'_E = d'$), respectively.

The resulting default theory is clearly prerequisite-free. We thus can define preferred extensions for general default theories as follows:

Definition 12. *Let $\Delta = (D, W, <)$ be a fully prioritized default theory. Then, E is a prioritized extension of Δ, if (i) E is a classical extension of Δ, and (ii) E is a prioritized extension of Δ_E.*

Let us show that the problematic examples discussed in Section 3 are handled correctly in our approach:

Example 13. Consider the default theory Δ:

(1) $a : b/b$
(2) $\top : \neg b/\neg b$
(3) $\top : a/a$

Again we assume that (1) is preferred over (2) and (2) over (3). This default theory has two classical extensions, namely $E_1 = Th(\{a, b\})$ and $E_2 = Th(\{a, \neg b\})$. Δ_{E_1} consists of the rules

(1) $\top : b/b$
(2) $\top : \neg b/\neg b$
(3) $\top : a/a$

It is not difficult to see that $C(\Delta_{E_1}) = E_1$. Since there are no rules whose head is in E_1 but which are defeated in E_1, E_1 is a preferred extension. On the contrary, E_2 is not preferred. Note that the dual E_2-reduct of Δ is the same as the dual E_1-reduct, and that $C(\cdot)$ applied to the reduct does not reproduce E_2.   □

Example 14. Consider the following default theory Δ':

(1) $a : b/b$
(2) $\top : \neg a/\neg a$
(3) $\top : a/a$

Again (1) is preferred over (2), and (2) over (3). The default theory has two classical extensions, namely $E_1 = Th(\{\neg a\})$ and $E_2 = Th(\{a, b\})$. We argued in Section 3 that E_1 should be preferred. Consider Δ'_{E_1}:

(2) $\top : \neg a / \neg a$
(3) $\top : a / a$

Clearly, $C(\Delta'_{E_1}) = E_1$, and since again there are no rules defeated in E_1 whose head is in E_1, we have that E_1 is preferred.

E_2 is not preferred since $C(\Delta'_{E_2}) = Th(\{b, \neg a\})$ which differs from E_2. □

The following proposition tells us that all rules which are not generating in a preferred extension must be defeated by some appropriate generating rules, which must have higher priority.

Proposition 15. *Let $\Delta = (W, D, <)$ be a fully prioritized ground default theory, and let E be a classical extension of Δ. Then, E is a preferred extension of Δ, if and only if for each default $d \in D$ such that $pre(d) \in E$ and $cons(d) \notin E$, there exists a set of defaults $K_d \subseteq \{d' \in GD(D, E) \mid d' < d\}$ such that d is defeated in $Th(W \cup cons(K_d))$.*

Proof: ($\Leftarrow$) Suppose that for every default d such that $pre(d) \in E$ and $cons(d) \notin E$ a set $K_d \subseteq \{d' \in GD(D, E) \mid d' < d\}$ exists such that $Th(W \cup cons(K_d))$ defeats d. By (transfinite) induction on the sets E_α, $\alpha \geq 1$, we show that the least active default d_E from $D_E^{\star E}$ in $\underline{E}_\alpha$, provided one exists, stems from some $d \in GD(D, E)$ and $cons(d) \in E_\alpha$ holds.

For $\alpha = 1$, the statement holds. Indeed, the least rule d_E of $D_E^{\star E}$ is active. Let d be the least parent of d_E in D, i.e., $d = \min_{<}\{d' \mid d'_E = d_E\}$. Assuming that $d \in D \setminus GD(D, E)$, we obtain $K_d = \emptyset$, and hence d is defeated by $E_0 = Th(W)$. This contradicts that d_E is active in $\underline{E}_1 = E_0$, however. Thus, $d \in GD(D, E)$ holds, and $cons(d) \in E_\alpha$ follows.

Let then $\alpha > 1$ and assume the statement holds for all $1 \leq \beta < \alpha$. Suppose the least default d_E from $D_E^{\star E}$ active in $\underline{E}_\alpha$ exists, and that its least parent in D is not in $GD(D, E)$. The induction hypothesis implies that for each $d' \in GD(D, E)$ such that $d' < d$ it holds that $cons(d') \in \underline{E}_\alpha$. Hence, $Th(W \cup cons(K_d)) \subseteq \underline{E}_\alpha$, which implies that d is defeated by $\underline{E}_\alpha$. This contradicts that d_E is active. Thus, if d_E exists, then $d \in GD(D, E)$ holds; clearly, $cons(d) \in E_\alpha$. This concludes the induction, from which $C(\Delta_E^{\star E}) = Th(W \cup cons(GD(D, E)))$ follows. By Equation (1), it follows $E = C(\Delta_E^{\star E})$, which means that E is a preferred extension.

($\Rightarrow$) Suppose E is a preferred extension, but some $d \in D$ such that $pre(d) \in E$ and $cons(d) \notin E$ is not defeated by any $Th(W \cup cons(K))$, where $K \subseteq \{d' \in GD(D, E) \mid d' < d\}$. Let d be the least such rule in D. Since E is a preferred extension, for every $d' \in GD(D, E)$ we have $cons(d') \in C(\Delta_E^{\star E})$. By the minimality of d, it follows that d_E becomes the least active rule in $D_E^{\star E}$ at some step α, and up to this point, only consequents of active reducts d'_E of $d' \in K$ have been added, i.e.,

$\underline{E}_\alpha = Th(W \cup cons(K))$ holds. Since $\underline{E}_\alpha$ does not defeat d_E, the rule is applied, which implies $C(\Delta_E^{*E}) \neq E$. Consequently, E is not a preferred extension, which is a contradiction. $\qquad\square$

Exploiting this proposition, we can establish that the principles for a prioritization approach from above are both satisfied by our approach.

Proposition 16. *The approach to preferred extensions satisfies both Principles I and II as described in Section 3.*

Proof: *Principle I.* Let $\Delta = (W, D, <)$ be a prioritized default theory, and let E, E' be classical extensions of Δ such that $GD(D, E) = R \cup \{d\}$ and $GD(D, E') = R \cup \{d'\}$, where $d_1, d_2 \notin R$ and $d < d'$. We have to show that E' is not a preferred extension of Δ.

Towards a contradiction, suppose E' is a preferred extension. Let $\Delta' = (W, D, <')$ be a full prioritization of Δ. Since $d \in GD(D, E)$, it holds that $pre(d) \in Th(W \cup cons(R))$; hence, d survives the dual GL-reduction with rspect E', and d, d' give rise to defaults $d_{E'}, d'_{E'} \in D_{E'}$, respectively.

Since $d \notin GD(D, E')$, it follows that $pre(d) \in E'$ but $cons(d) \notin E'$. Hence, by Proposition 15, it follows that d is defeated by $Th(W \cup cons(K))$ for some $K \subseteq \{d'' \in GD(D, E') \mid d'' < d\}$. It follows that $K \subseteq R$ holds. Since d is defeated by $Th(W \cup cons(K))$ and $Th(W \cup cons(K)) \subseteq E$, it follows that d is defeated by E. This contradicts $d \in GD(D, E)$; satisfaction of Principle I follows.

Principle II. Let E be a preferred extension of $\Delta = (W, D, <)$, and let d be a (closed) default such that $pre(d) \notin E$. We have to show that E is a preferred extension of $\Delta' = (D \cup \{d\}, W, <')$ where $<'$ is compatible with $<$.

Consider the dual reduct of Δ' with respect E, i.e., $\Delta'_E = ((D \cup \{d\})_E, W, <'_E)$. Then, the default d is eliminated in the dual reduct, and we have $\Delta'_E = \Delta_E$. Since E is a preferred extension of Δ_E, it follows immediately that E is a preferred extension of Δ'. Thus, Principle II is satisfied. (Remark: the proof can be easily adapted for an open default d, if closing d does not lead to inconsistency of $<'$.) $\qquad\square$

Thus, our approach satisfies these general benchmarks for a prioritization logic.

On the other hand, a less desirable property of the approach is that in some cases no preferred extension may exist. This is what happens in Example 8; it is easily checked that neither of the two classical extensions $E = Th(\{a, b\})$ and $E' = Th(\{\neg a, b\})$ is a preferred extension.

Another example shows that in general, normal prioritized default theories may have no preferred extension. Thus, the property that supernormal default theories always have extensions is lost if prerequisites are allowed in the defaults.

Example 17. Consider the following defaults:

    (1) $a : \neg b / \neg b$
    (2) $\top : b / b$
    (3) $b : a / a$

This default theory has the unique classical extension $E = Th(\{a, b\})$. However, assuming $(1) < (2) < (3)$, E is not preferred, since preference of (1) requires to conclude $\neg b$. □

Intuitively, if no preferred extension exists, then the priorities as specified by the user are incompatible with the way in which defaults must be executed to generate an extension. In the preceding example, this is clearly the case.

There are different possibilities to react to such an inconsistency, and some of them have been discussed in (Brewka and Eiter, 1998). There are two main directions for handling such inconsistencies. One direction is to stop on occurrence of such an inconsistency and notify the user that there is an inconsistency in the priorities. The other would be trying to overcome this inconsistency, by reconciling the priority information and the logical entrenchment of default application by relaxing or modifying the priority information in a way such that preferred extensions become possible.

We believe that in general, the first direction is preferable to the second one since the user becomes explicitly aware that there is something wrong with his preferences, which cannot be satisfied. However, we could require that an approach to priorities should be consistent in the sense that if classical extensions exist, then some of them should always be selected by the prioritization method. In this case, a relaxation of our preferred extension approach would be desirable, which selects the preferred extensions if some exist and some classical extensions, according to some rationale, if no preferred extensions exist.

There are different possibilities for generalizing the preferred extensions to such "weakly" preferred extensions. One such possibility is to allow a minimal reordering of the defaults in D, i.e., E becomes a preferred extension after switching as few neighbored defaults in $<$ as possible, cf. (Brewka and Eiter, 1998). Another approach would be to remove preferences between defaults, e.g., to relax the ordering $<$ as little as possible such that preferred extensions exist. We do not pursue these possibilities any further here. However, we observe some limitations of such weakly preferred extensions.

We call a function χ which selects a subset $\chi(\Delta)$ from the classical extensions of a prioritized default theory D a *consistent preference relaxation* (CPR) of preferred extensions, if $\chi(\Delta)$ selects all and only preferred extensions if preferred extensions exist, and selects some (arbitrary) classical extensions provided some classical extension exists. Then, the following holds.

Proposition 18. *Every consistent preference relaxation χ of preferred extensions must violate both Principle I and Principle II.*

Proof: (Sketch) To show that no CPR χ can satisfy Principle I in general, we consider a prioritized default theory $\Delta = (W, D, <)$ such that Δ has classical extensions but no preferred extensions, and such that χ can not select any of the classical extensions without violating Principle I. Define

$$W = \{b_i \rightarrow (b_{i+1} \wedge c), \ a_i \leftrightarrow \neg b_i \mid i \geq 0\},$$
$$D = \{\top : a_i/a_i, \ \top : b_i/b_i \mid i \geq 0\} \cup \{\top : \neg c/\bot\},$$

where all a_i, b_i and c are propositional atoms, and let $<$ be the well-ordering such that

$$\left.\begin{array}{l} \top : a_i/a_i \;<\; \top : b_i/b_i \;<\; \top : a_{i+1}/a_{i+1}, \\ \top : a_i/a_i \;<\; \top : \neg c/\bot, \; \top : b_i/b_i \;<\; \top : \neg c/\bot \end{array}\right\} i \geq 0,$$

where $\bot$ denotes falsity. It can be seen that the classical extensions of Δ are of the form

$$E^i = Th(W \cup cons(\{\top : a_k/a_k, \; \top : b_j/b_j \mid 0 \leq k < i, j \geq i\})), \quad i \geq 0.$$

Moreover, for each $i \geq 0$, it holds that $GD^i = GD(D, E^i)$ and $GD^{i+1} = GD(D, E^{i+1})$ are of the form $GD^i = R \cup \{d'\}$ and $GD^{i+1} = R \cup \{d\}$ such that $d < d'$, where $R = GD^i \cap GD^{i+1}$, $d = \top : a_i/a_i$, and $d' = \top : b_i/b_i$.

Hence, if χ satisfies Principle I, then it must not select E^i. Since this holds for all $i \geq 0$, χ cannot select any classical extension. Observe that no preferred extensions exist (cf. Proposition 16). This proves unsatisfiability of Principle I.

That also Principle II is unsatisfiable for any CPR χ is exemplified by the following prioritized default theory $\Delta = (\emptyset, D, \{1 < 2\})$, which is rephrased from (Brewka and Eiter, 1998):

(1) $\top : \neg b/c$
(2) $\top : a/b$

The unique classical extension of Δ is $E = Th(\{b\})$, which must be selected by χ. Augment Δ by a default (0) $c : \top/\neg a$, such that $0 < 1$ and $0 < 2$; let Δ' be the resulting default theory. Clearly, $pre(0) \notin E$. However, E cannot be selected by χ, since Δ' has the unique preferred extension $E' = Th(\{\neg a, c\})$. Hence, χ violates Principle II. $\square$

This result tells us that we have to sacrifice the principles if we want to have a "weakly" preferred extension for each coherent default theory. We take this as additional support for our view that the preferences should be reconsidered in situations where no preferred extension exists.

Observe that the prioritized default theory Δ showing the failure of Principle I is infinite. It turns out that this is essential. In fact, over a finite (closed) Δ, the following CPR χ satisfying Principle I is possible. In the case in which Δ has a preferred extension, χ just returns hat collection. In the case in which no preferred extension exists, fix a well-ordering $<'$ compatible with $<$ in $\Delta = (D, W, <)$, and define a relation $\prec$ on the classical extensions of Δ by $E \prec E'$ iff $GD(D, E) = R \cup \{d\}$, $GD(D, E') = R \cup \{d'\}$ where $d, d' \notin R$ and $d <' d'$. Let then χ select the minimal elements of $\prec$, i.e., the classical extensions E such that $E' \not\prec E$ for all other classical extensions E'. It can be shown that $\prec$ is irreflexive, and moreover that $\prec$ has some minimal element. Hence, $\chi(\Delta, <')$ selects some classical extension(s), if some exist. Moreover, by construction of $\prec$ it is easily seen that χ satisfies Principle I.

5. EXPRESSING PREFERENCES IN THE LANGUAGE

For several applications like legal reasoning it is important to reason not only with, but also about the preferences among default rules. Such preferences often depend on the particular context at hand, and it is not possible to assign preferences independently of a particular context.

To make reasoning about default priorities possible, we must be able to refer to defaults explicitly, and we must introduce a special predicate symbol representing default preferences. We thus extend our logical language in two respects.

1. We introduce a distinct set of rule names N. A naming function assigns a unique name to default rules. Formally, default names are simply ground terms in the underlying language.

2. We use the reserved two-place infix predicate symbol $\prec$ to represent default priority. For instance, if d_1 and d_2 are default names, then $d_1 \prec d_2$ is a formula with the intended meaning: d_1 has priority over d_2.

Definition 19. *A preferential default theory is a triple $\Delta = (D, W, name)$ where*

1. (D, W) *is a default theory,*

2. $name : D \to N$ *is an injective function, and*

3. W *contains axioms guaranteeing that $\prec$ is a strict partial order.*

Note that we do not restrict the appearance of $\prec$ to W. It is possible (and useful) to have defaults which derive priority relations among other defaults.

An extension of a preferential default theory $\Delta = (D, W, name)$ is just a classical extension of (D, W). The question now is how to define preferred extensions for preferential default theories.

All the derived preference information now is contained in the extensions of Δ. What we need is a way to eliminate an extension if it contains priority information which is in conflict with the way the extension was generated.

Given the techniques developed for prioritized default theories, it is not difficult to see how this can be done. Basically, an extension E of a preferential default theory is preferred iff E is a preferred extension of a fully prioritized default theory $(D, W, <)$ such that $<$ is compatible with the preference information in E. Compatibility is tested by generating a syntactic description of $<$ in terms of $\prec$ and checking whether this description is consistent with E.

Definition 20. *Let $\Delta = (D, W, name)$ be a preferential default theory, and let E be a classical extension of Δ. We say $<$ is compatible with E if and only if*

$$E \cup \{d_i \prec d_k \mid r_i < r_k, name(r_i) = d_i, name(r_k) = d_k\}$$

is consistent.

Definition 21. *Let* $\Delta = (D, W, name)$ *be a preferential default theory. Then, a set of formulas E is a preferred extension of Δ if and only if E is a preferred extension of some fully prioritized default theory $(D, W, <)$ such that $<$ is compatible with E.*

Example 22. Let's consider the following scenario. Your mother expects you to visit her on Sundays. Your wife likes the opera and expects you to join her whenever Mozart is played. Unfortunately, visiting your mother and simultaneously going to the opera is impossible. Normally, the rules representing your mother's wishes must have preference over those representing your wife's wishes. However, on your wife's birthday, you definitely should give preference to her.

This scenario can be modeled as the following preferential default theory.[1] The set of defaults D contains the following three rules:

$$(d_1) \qquad sunday : visit(mother)/visit(mother)$$

$$(d_2) \qquad play(mozart) : go(opera)/go(opera)$$

$$(d_3[d, d']) \quad mother\_rule(d) \wedge wife\_rule(d') : d \prec d'/d \prec d'$$

The following formulas are in the background theory W:

$$birthday(wife) \wedge wife\_rule(d) \wedge mother\_rule(d') \rightarrow d \prec d',$$
$$mother\_rule(d_1),$$
$$wife\_rule(d_2),$$
$$\neg(visit(mother) \wedge go(opera)).$$

Now assume the following facts hold in addition (i.e., are in W):

$$sunday, \qquad play(mozart).$$

We obtain two classical extensions. Note that both extensions contain the preference information $d_1 \prec d_2$. It is easy to see that there is no total preference relation $<$ compatible with this information such that E_2 is a preferred extension of $(D, W, <)$. Only the first extension is preferred and you should visit your mother.

Now consider what happens if we add $birthday(wife)$. Again we obtain two extensions, E_1' containing $visit(mother)$, and E_2' containing $go(opera)$. In this case the preference information in both extensions is $d_2 \prec d_1$. Note that the applicability of default $d_3[d_1, d_2]$ is blocked. Now E_1' cannot be reconstructed as preferred extension of a fully prioritized theory $(D, W, <)$ such that $<$ is compatible with E_1'. The extension E_2', on the other hand, can be reconstructed in such a way: just use an ordering with $r_2 < r_1$ where $name(r_1) = d_1$ and $name(r_2) = d_2$. That is, you should join your wife and go to the opera.   □

6. RELATED WORK AND CONCLUSION

In this paper, we have presented an approach, based on the ideas of (Brewka and Eiter, 1998), to incorporating priority information into default logic. This approach overcomes problems of previous approaches with respect to general principles which, as we argue, any prioritized variant of default logic should satisfy. For space reasons, a detailed comparison of our approach to the many other variants of prioritized default logic is necessarily superficial.

Rintanen's approach and the approaches in (Marek and Truszczyński, 1993; Brewka, 1994b; Baader and Hollunder, 1995; Brewka, 1996) have already been briefly mentioned. The latter handle priorities such that in the (re)construction of an extension, only some of the applicable defaults can be fired in each step.

In (Delgrande and Schaub, 1997) priorities are handled by encoding them into the object-level rather than constraining the construction of extensions at the meta-level. It turns out that in this approach some reasonable default theories do not possess any preferred extensions at all. For instance, no preferred extension exists for Example 4.

Other approaches, somewhat less related to our work, are concerned with handling specificity by respecting logical entrenchment of rules. In (Delgrande and Schaub, 1994), an approach to handling specificity is developed which rewrites the defaults, based on their logical entrenchment, such that more specific rules are preferred. This is in the spirit of early versions of Nute's defeasible logic, cf. (Nute, 1994). Nute distinguishes defeasible and certain rules and presents a semantics with strong proof theoretic flavor for answering queries to the system.

Further related work is present in the context of logic programming, where different proposals to enhance extended logic programs with priorities have been made, cf. (Sakama and Inoue, 1996; Zhang and Foo, 1997; Gelfond and Son, 1998). Possible extensions of these approaches to full default logic remain to be explored; however, on the common fragment of extended logic programs, these approaches differ from ours. For an extended discussion of these approaches and the ones mentioned above, see (Brewka and Eiter, 1999). For a discussion of further approaches to priorities and specificity in default logic, see (Delgrande and Schaub, 1994; Baader and Hollunder, 1995; Brewka, 1996).

Several issues remain for future work. First of all, procedures for reasoning from prioritized default theories need to be investigated. In the finite propositional case, brave and cautious reasoning in prioritized and classical default logic are polynomial time equivalent, and thus, by the results in (Gottlob, 1992), Σ_2^p and Π_2^p-complete, respectively. In fact, a suitable full prioritization of $\Delta = (W, D, <)$ such that E is a preferred extension of $\Delta' = (W, D, <')$ can be guessed, and the condition $E = C(\Delta_E^{*E})$ can be checked in polynomial time with an NP oracle. As a consequence, theorem provers for Reiter's default logic can be used after a polynomial transformation for solving reasoning tasks in prioritized default logic. The design of genuine algorithms for prioritized default logic remains to be explored.

Another issue are approximations of preferred extensions. As we have shown, consistent preference relaxations (CPRs) of preferred extensions are subject to certain limitations. It would be interesting to see to what extent relaxations satisfying Principle I and II are possible, as well as for which weakenings of the principles CPRs do exist.

ACKNOWLEDGMENTS

This work was partially supported by the Austrian Science Fund in the context of the Ludwig Wittgenstein Labor für Informationssysteme (Project N Z29-INF) and by Deutsche Forschungsgemeinschaft (Forschergruppe Kommunikatives Verstehen).

Gerhard Brewka
University of Leipzig
Leipzig, Germany

Thomas Eiter
Technische Universität Wien
Vienna, Austria

NOTES

1. We define *name* implicitly by putting the name of a default in front of the default.

REFERENCES

Baader, F. and Hollunder, B. (1995). Priorities on Defaults with Prerequisite and their Application in Treating Specificity in Terminological Default Logic. *Journal of Automated Reasoning*, 15:41–68.

Benferhat, S., Cayrol, C., Dubois, D., Lang, J., and Prade, H. (1993). Inconsistency Management and Prioritized Syntax-Based Entailment. In Bajcsy, R., editor, *Proceedings of the Thirteenth International Joint Conference on Artificial Intelligence (IJCAI-93)*, pages 640–645. Morgan Kaufman.

Brewka, G. (1989). Preferred Subtheories: An Extended Logical Framework for Default Reasoning. In *Proceedings IJCAI '89*, pages 1043–1048.

Brewka, G. (1994a). Adding Priorities and Specificity to Default Logic. In *Proceedings JELIA '94*, LNAI 838, pages 247–260. Springer.

Brewka, G. (1994b). Reasoning About Priorities in Default Logic. In *Proceedings AAAI '94*, pages 940–945.

Brewka, G. (1996). Well-Founded Semantics for Extended Logic Programs with Dynamic Preferences. *Journal of Artificial Intelligence Research*, 4:19–36.

Brewka, G. and Eiter, T. (1998). Preferred Answer Sets for Extended Logic Programs. In Cohn, A., Schubert, L., and Shapiro, S., editors, *Proceedings Sixth International Conference on Principles of Knowledge Representation and Reasoning (KR-98)*, pages 86–97.

Brewka, G. and Eiter, T. (1999). Preferred Answer Sets for Extended Logic Programs. *Artificial Intelligence*, to appear.

Delgrande, J. and Schaub, T. (1994). A General Approach to Specificity in Default Reasoning. In *Proceedings Fourth International Conference on Principles of Knowledge Representation and Reasoning (KR-94)*, pages 146–157.

Delgrande, J. and Schaub, T. (1997). Compiling Reasoning With and About Preferences into Default Logic. In *Proceedings IJCAI '97*, pages 168–174.

Eiter, T. and Gottlob, G. (1995). The Complexity of Logic-Based Abduction. *Journal of the ACM*, 42(1):3–42.

Gelfond, M. and Lifschitz, V. (1988). The Stable Model Semantics for Logic Programming. In *Logic Programming: Proceedings Fifth Intl Conference and Symposium*, pages 1070–1080, Cambridge, Mass. MIT Press.

Gelfond, M., Przymusinska, H., and Przymusinski, T. (1989). On the Relationship Between Circumscription and Negation as Failure. *Artificial Intelligence*, 38:75–94.

Gelfond, M. and Son, T. (1998). Reasoning with Prioritized Defaults. In *Selected Papers presented at the Workshop on Logic Programming and Knowledge Representation (LPKR '97), Port Jefferson*, volume 1471 of *LNAI*, pages 164–223. Springer.

Gottlob, G. (1992). Complexity Results for Nonmonotonic Logics. *Journal of Logic and Computation*, 2(3):397–425.

Konolige, K. (1988). Hierarchic Autoepistemic Theories for Nonmonotonic Reasoning. In *Proceedings AAAI '88*, pages 439–443.

Marek, W. and Truszczyński, M. (1993). *Nonmonotonic Logics – Context-Dependent Reasoning*. Springer.

McCarthy, J. (1980). Circumscription – A Form of Non-Monotonic Reasoning. *Artificial Intelligence*, 13:27–39.

Moore, R. (1985). Semantical Considerations on Nonmonotonic Logics. *Artificial Intelligence*, 25:75–94.

Nebel, B. (1998). How Hard is it to Revise a Belief Base ? In Dubois, D. and Prade, H., editors, *Handbook on Defeasible Reasoning and Uncertainty Management Systems*, volume III: Belief Change, pages 77–145. Kluwer Academic.

Nute, D. (1994). Defeasible Logic. In Gabbay, D., Hogger, C., and Robinson, J., editors, *Handbook of Logic in Artificial Intelligence and Logic Programming*, volume III, pages 353–395. Clarendon Press, Oxford.

Poole, D. (1985). On the Comparison of Theories: Preferring the Most Specific Explanation. In *Proceedings IJCAI '85*, pages 144–147.

Prakken, H. (1993). *Logical Tools for Modelling Legal Argument*. Dissertation, Vrije Universiteit Amsterdam.

Reiter, R. (1980). A Logic for Default Reasoning. *Artificial Intelligence*, 13:81–132.

Rintanen, J. (1995). On Specificity in Default Logic. In Mellish, C., editor, *Proceedings IJCAI '95*, pages 1474–1479. AAAI Press.

Rintanen, J. (1998). Lexicographic Priorities in Default Logic. *Artificial Intelligence*, 106:221–265.

Sakama, C. and Inoue, K. (1996). Representing Priorities in Logic Programs. In *Proceedings IJCSLP-96*, pages 82–96, Bonn, Germany. MIT-Press.

Touretzky, D. (1986). *The Mathematics of Inheritance*. Pitman Research Notes in Artificial Intelligence, London.

Touretzky, D., Thomason, R., and Horty, J. (1991). A Skeptic's Menagerie: Conflictors, Preemptors, Reinstaters, and Zombies in Nonmonotonic Inheritance. In *Proceedings IJCAI '91*, pages 478–485.

Zhang, Y. and Foo, N. (1997). Answer Sets for Prioritized Logic Programs. In *Proceedings ILPS 97*, pages 69–83.

STEFAN BRÜNING AND TORSTEN SCHAUB

A CONNECTION CALCULUS FOR HANDLING
INCOMPLETE INFORMATION

1. INTRODUCTION

In many AI applications default reasoning plays an important role since many subtasks
involve reasoning from incomplete information. This is why there is a great need for
systematic methods that allow us to integrate default reasoning capabilities. In fact,
the two last decades have provided us with a profound understanding of the underlying
problems and have resulted in well-understood formal approaches to default reasoning.
Therefore, we are now ready to build advanced default reasoning systems. For this
undertaking, we have chosen Reiter's default logic (Reiter, 1980) as our point of
departure.

Default logic augments classical logic by *default rules* that differ from standard
inference rules in sanctioning inferences that rely upon given as well as absent information. Knowledge is represented in default logics by *default theories* (D, W) consisting
of a consistent set of formulas W, also called facts, and a set of default rules D. A
default rule $\frac{\alpha : \beta}{\gamma}$ has two types of antecedents: A *prerequisite* α which is established
if α is derivable and a *justification* β which is established if β is consistent. If both
conditions hold, the *consequent* γ is concluded by default. A set of such conclusions
(sanctioned by default rules and classical logic) is called an *extension* of an initial set
of facts: Given a set of formulas W and a set of default rules D, any such extension
E is a deductively closed set of formulas containing W such that, for any $\frac{\alpha : \beta}{\gamma} \in D$,
if $\alpha \in E$ and $\neg\beta \notin E$ then $\gamma \in E$. (A formal introduction to default logic is given in
Section 2.)

In what follows, we are interested in implementing the basic approach to query-
answering in default logic that allows for determining whether a formula is in *some*
extension of a given default theory. Unlike other approaches that address this problem
by encapsulating the underlying theorem prover as a separate module, we are proposing
a rather different approach that integrates default reasoning into existing automated
theorem provers. In order to comply with the methodology underlying query-oriented
classical theorem provers, it is more or less indispensable to center the overall approach
around *local* proof procedures (ie. proof procedures that allow for deciding whether

47

S. Hölldobler (ed.), *Intellectics and Computational Logic*, 47–66.
© 2000 *Kluwer Academic Publishers*.

a set of default rules forms a default proof by looking at the constituent rules only). This is because such procedures permit validating a default inference step during the goal-directed proof search in a locally determinable way (see Section 2 for details).

The methodology presented in this paper has its origins in an approach to default query-answering proposed in (Schaub, 1995). This approach furnishes a mating-based characterization of default proofs inside the framework provided by the connection method (Bibel, 1987). This characterization forms the basis for adapting existing efficient connection calculi for query-answering in so-called *semi-monotonic* default logics. (The advantage of these default systems is that they allow for the afore-mentioned local proof procedures, as we detail in Section 2.) In fact, there already exist very successful implementations of connection calculi for classical logic, eg. SETHEO (Letz et al., 1992) or KoMeT (Bibel et al., 1994). In this paper we show how the basic inference steps underlying these connection calculi, namely the *extension step* and the *reduction step*, can be adapted to be used for default reasoning.

Our overall contribution can thus be looked at from different perspectives: First, we show how the notion of a proof provided by a connection calculus can be refined to capture (semi-monotonic) default proofs and how standard techniques for implementing and improving connection calculi based proof systems (regularity, lemmas) can be adapted and extended to default reasoning. And finally, one can view our contribution as a step towards a logic programming system integrating disjunction, classical as well as default negation.

To give a more precise overview of our approach, we start by noting that default logic is among the *consistency-based* approaches to default reasoning. In these formalisms, a logical formalization of a consistency-driven procedure is added to a standard logic. As explained above, this is done in default logic by means of the justification of a default rule. In this way, default reasoning is mapped onto a *deductive* task and a *consistency checking* task. Of course, this carries over to the resulting proof procedures for query-answering, too.

As anticipated above, we address the deductive task of default query-answering by a top-down backward-chaining calculus which has its roots in connection calculi for classical logic (eg. see (Bibel, 1987; Bibel, 1993)). This integrated approach allows us to push the concepts needed for handling defaults from the underlying calculus, over the corresponding proof procedure, into elaborated implementation techniques available for connection calculi, such as compilation techniques (eg. see (Stickel, 1984)).

The paper is organized as follows. We provide in Section 2 an introduction to default logic along with its basic proof theory (for normal default theories). Section 3 introduces then a corresponding connection calculus that is proven to be sound and complete for query-answering in (normal) default logic. Finally, Section 3.1 discusses some important calculi refinements which are indispensable in view of an implementation. While our integral approach addresses full-fledged (semi-monotonic) default logics, which support local proof procedures, we restrict our exposition to so-called *normal* default theories over a propositional language. This restriction is justified by the fact that except for consistency checking all techniques developed for normal default theories carry over to the general case without any modifications.

We draw the reader's attention right from the start to the fact that this paper focuses on proof theoretical issues. A more detailed description of a corresponding implementation along with experimental analysis can be found in (Nicolas and Schaub, 1998). Note, however, that the implementation described in (Nicolas and Schaub, 1998) is *not* based on the calculus proposed in this paper but on a closely related calculus called *Default Model Elimination* (or DME for short) presented in (Schaub and Brüning, 1996). DME relies on so-called connection tableaux as basic proof objects whereas the calculus presented in Section 3 uses matrices for this purpose. Due to the close relatioship of both calculi, the implementation results in (Nicolas and Schaub, 1998) are transferable to the calculus proposed in the present paper.

2. DEFAULT LOGIC

This section introduces Reiter's classical default logic along with some important formal concepts needed for providing a proof theory adequate for our purposes.

As already sketched in the introductory section, default logic augments classical logic by *default rules* of the form $\frac{\alpha : \beta}{\gamma}$. Such a rule is called *normal* if β is equivalent to γ; it is called *semi-normal* if β implies γ. We sometimes denote the *prerequisite* α of a default rule δ by $Prereq(\delta)$, its *justification* β by $Justif(\delta)$ and its *consequent* γ by $Conseq(\delta)$. Accordingly, $Prereq(D)$ is the set of prerequisites of all default rules in D; $Justif(D)$ and $Conseq(D)$ are defined analogously. A set of default rules D and a set of consistent formulas W form a *default theory* (D, W) that may induce a single or multiple *extensions* in the following way (Reiter, 1980).

Definition 1. *Let* (D, W) *be a default theory. For any set of formulas* S, *let* $\Gamma(S)$ *be the smallest set of formulas* S' *such that*

1. $W \subseteq S'$,

2. $Th(S') = S'$,

3. For any $\frac{\alpha : \beta}{\gamma} \in D$, *if* $\alpha \in S'$ *and* $S \cup \{\beta\}$ *is consistent then* $\gamma \in S'$.

A set of formulas E *is a classical extension of* (D, W) *iff* $\Gamma(E) = E$.

Observe that E must be a fixed point of Γ. Any such set represents a possible set of beliefs about the world at hand.

As already put forward in (Reiter, 1980), query-answering in default logics is most feasible in the presence of the property of *semi-monotonicity*: If $D' \subseteq D$ for two sets of default rules, then if E' is an extension of (D', W), there is an extension E of (D, W) such that $E' \subseteq E$. Given this property, it is sufficient to consider a relevant subset of default rules while answering a query, since applying other default rules would only enlarge and thus preserve a partial extension at hand. In Reiter's default logic, semi-monotonicity is enjoyed by normal default theories. Moreover, all major variants of default logic such as classical default logic (Reiter, 1980), justified default logic (Łukaszewicz, 1988), cumulative default logic (Brewka, 1991), constrained default logic (Delgrande et al., 1994), and rational default logic (Mikitiuk and Truszczyński, 1993) coincide on this particular fragment. This is why we have chosen normal default theories as an initial exemplar for our approach. We show in (Schaub and Nicolas, 1997) how general default theories are treated in the aforementioned variants, provided they enjoy semi-monotonicity.

In the presence of semi-monotonicity, extensions are constructible in a truly iterative way by applying one applicable default rule after another by appeal to a rather local notion of consistency:

Theorem 2. *Let* (D, W) *be a normal default theory and let* E *be a set of formulas. Then,* E *is an extension of* (D, W) *iff there is some maximal* $D' \subseteq D$ *that has an enumeration* $\langle \delta_i \rangle_{i \in I}$ *such that for* $i \in I$, *we have:*

$$E = \mathit{Th}(W \cup \mathit{Conseq}(D')) \qquad (1)$$

$$W \cup \mathit{Conseq}(\{\delta_0, \ldots, \delta_{i-1}\}) \vdash \mathit{Prereq}(\delta_i) \qquad (2)$$

$$W \cup \mathit{Conseq}(\{\delta_0, \ldots, \delta_{i-1}\}) \not\vdash \neg \mathit{Conseq}(\delta_i) \qquad (3)$$

This type of characterization was first given in (Schwind, 1990) (except for Condition (3) reflecting an *incremental* approach, as opposed to a rather *global* approach requiring $W \cup \mathit{Conseq}(D') \not\vdash \bot$).

Condition (2) spells out that D' has to be grounded in W. In general, a set of default rules D is *grounded* in a set of facts W iff there exists an enumeration $\langle \delta_i \rangle_{i \in I}$ of D that satisfies Condition (2). Condition (3) expresses the notion of *incremental consistency*. Here, the "consistent" application of a default rule is checked at each step, whereas this must be done wrt the *final* extension in a non-semi-monotonic default logic.

These notions lead us to the following notion of a *default proof* from normal default theories, on which we build our initial formal characterization of query-answering:

Definition 3. *Let* (D, W) *be a normal default theory and* φ *a formula. A normal default proof for* φ *from* (D, W) *is a finite sequence of default rules* $\langle \delta_i \rangle_{i \in I}$ *with* $\delta_i \in D$ *for all* $i \in I$ *such that* $W \cup \{\mathit{Conseq}(\delta_i) \mid i \in I\} \vdash \varphi$ *and Condition* (2) *and* (3) *are satisfied for all* $i \in I$.

The following immediate consequence of Theorem 2 assures that a query is in some extension of the (normal) default theory at hand iff it has a (normal) default proof:

Theorem 4. *Let* (D, W) *be a normal default theory and* φ *a formula. Then,* $\varphi \in E$ *for some extension* E *of* (D, W) *iff there is a normal default proof for* φ *from* (D, W).

That is, for verifying whether φ is in some extension of a default theory (D, W), it is enough to determine a grounded and consistent set of default rules $D_\varphi \subseteq D$ that allows for proving φ from the facts in W and the consequents of all default rules in D_φ.

Now, given the concept of a default proof, let us elucidate the computational advantage of *local* proof procedures provided by semi-monotonicity: For deciding whether a set of default rules forms a default proof, it is sufficient to investigate the constituent rules only. A local proof procedure must thus never consider a rule in $(D \setminus D_\varphi)$ for deciding whether D_φ is a default proof for some query φ. Note that in the absence of a property like semi-monotonicity a proof procedure must necessarily consider all default rules in the given default theory. This is, for instance, the case for general default theories under Reiter's interpretation. Finally, we emphasize that we are not interested in semi-monotonicity as such, it is rather the resulting localness of proof procedures that we draw upon, since this is an essential feature of the connection calculi based theorem provers that we are aiming at.

As an example, consider the following set of statements about a child predisposed to an allergy against milk products:"children normally eat ice-cream", "ice-cream usually contains milk", "ice-cream usually contains sugar", and "milk is an allergen in case of a predisposition". The corresponding default theory along with facts child ∧ predispo (expressing that the considered child has the aforementioned predisposition) is the following one:

$$\left(\left\{ \frac{child : icecream}{icecream}, \frac{icecream : milk}{milk}, \frac{icecream : sugar}{sugar} \right\}, \right.$$
$$\left. \{child, predispo, milk \wedge predispo \rightarrow allergen\} \right) \tag{4}$$

For instance, we can explain the presence of an allergen in the above situation by proving allergen from child ∧ predispo by means of default proof:

$$\left\langle \frac{child : icecream}{icecream}, \frac{icecream : milk}{milk} \right\rangle. \tag{5}$$

Importantly, this proof can be found by a top-down backward-chaining procedure that starts from the query by ignoring irrelevant default rule $\frac{icecream : sugar}{sugar}$. This illustrates the great advantage of local proof procedures.

For the most part of the paper, we follow (Schaub, 1995) in dealing with default theories in atomic format in the following sense: For a default theory (D, W) in language $\mathcal{L}_\Sigma$ over some alphabet Σ, let $\mathcal{L}_{\Sigma'}$ be the language over the alphabet Σ', obtained by adding three new propositions, named $\alpha_\delta, \beta_\delta, \gamma_\delta$ for each $\delta \in D$. Then, (D, W) is mapped into default theory (D', W') in $\mathcal{L}_{\Sigma'}$ where

$$D' = \left\{ \frac{\alpha_\delta : \beta_\delta}{\gamma_\delta} \;\middle|\; \delta \in D \right\}$$
$$W' = W \cup \{ Prereq(\delta) \rightarrow \alpha_\delta, \beta_\delta \rightarrow Justif(\delta), \gamma_\delta \rightarrow Conseq(\delta) \mid \delta \in D \}$$

The resulting default theory (D', W') is called the *atomic format* of the original default theory, (D, W). As shown in (Rothschild, 1993), this transformation does not affect the computation of queries to the original default theory. That is in terms of default proofs, given a query φ in $\mathcal{L}_\Sigma$, then φ has a default proof from (D, W) iff φ has a default proof from (D', W'). We can therefore restrict our attention to atomic default rules without loosing generality. The advantages of atomic default rules over arbitrary ones are, first, that their constituents are not spread over several clauses while transforming them into clausal format (see Section 3) and, second, that these constituents are uniquely referable to. The motivations for this format are somehow similar to the ones for definitional clausal form in automated theorem proving (Eder, 1992). For default reasoning, the naming of defaults was first done by Poole in (Poole, 1988).

For clarity, we refrain from turning default rules into their atomic counterparts whenever they are composed of atomic components. This is for instance the case with Default theory (4).

3. QUERY ANSWERING IN DEFAULT LOGICS

As mentioned in the introductory section, our approach is rooted in the mating-based characterization of default proofs developed in (Schaub, 1995). Such matings are used in connection calculi as a structure-oriented means for characterizing the unsatisfiability of formulas (cf. (Bibel, 1987)).[1] We confine ourselves in what follows to an introduction to its underlying ideas, needed for a better understanding of the connection calculus, presented in the major part of this section.

First of all, we introduce the following conventions: We let L^c denote the literal complementary to L. We mainly deal with formulas in *conjunctive normal form* (CNF), which are given by a conjunction of disjunctions of literals. To ease notation, we denote such formulas in clausal form, that is, a formula in CNF is given as a set of clauses, where a *clause* is a set of literals $\{L_1, \ldots, L_n\}$ representing a disjunction $L_1 \vee \ldots \vee L_n$. A clause is called *negative* iff it contains only negative literals.

The mating-based characterization of default proofs relies on the idea that an atomic default rule $\frac{\alpha : \beta}{\gamma}$ can be decomposed into a *classical implication* $\alpha \rightarrow \gamma$ along with two proof-theoretic conditions on the usage of the resulting clause $\{\neg\alpha, \gamma\}$; these conditions are referred to as *admissibility* and *compatibility*. Intuitively, both of them rely on a sequence of clauses, stemming from default rules only, which is induced by the underlying mating (see (Schaub, 1995)). Such a sequence amounts to an enumeration of default rules $\langle \delta_i \rangle_{i \in I}$, as given in Theorem 2 and Definition 3. In fact, while admissibility provides the proof-theoretic counterpart of Condition (2), that is groundedness, compatibility enforces the notion of consistency described in Condition (3).

Now, in order to find out whether a formula φ is in some extension of a default theory (D, W), we proceed as follows: First, we transform the default rules in D into a set of indexed implications W_D. In our example, this encoding yields the set

$$W_D = \left\{ \text{child}_{\delta_1} \rightarrow \text{icecream}_{\delta_1}, \ \text{icecream}_{\delta_2} \rightarrow \text{milk}_{\delta_2}, \ \text{icecream}_{\delta_3} \rightarrow \text{sugar}_{\delta_3} \right\}. \tag{6}$$

The indexes denote the respective default rules in (4) from left to right. [2]

Second, we transform both W and W_D into their clausal forms, C_W and C_D. The clauses in C_D are called *δ-clauses*; they are of the form $\{\neg\alpha_\delta, \gamma_\delta\}$; all other clauses are referred to as *ω-clauses*. In our example, we obtain the following clause set for

$C_W \cup C_D$:

$$\{\{\text{predispo}\}, \{\text{child}\}, \{\neg\text{predispo}, \neg\text{milk}, \text{allergen}\}\} \tag{7}$$
$$\cup \quad \{\{\neg\text{child}_{\delta_1}, \text{icecream}_{\delta_1}\}, \{\neg\text{icecream}_{\delta_2}, \text{milk}_{\delta_2}\}, \{\neg\text{icecream}_{\delta_3}, \text{sugar}_{\delta_3}\}\}$$

Finally, a query φ is derivable from (D, W) iff the set of clauses $C_W \cup C_D \cup \{\{\neg\varphi\}\}$ is unsatisfiable and if it agrees with the (mating-based) concepts of admissibility and compatibility.

A default connection calculus

We develop in the sequel a proof procedure which finds a (default) refutation for $\neg\varphi$ from clause set $C_W \cup C_D$ iff there exists a default proof for φ from (D, W).

We address this problem by means of a calculus based on the connection method (Bibel, 1987; Bibel, 1993). The main focus of this calculus is to provide an adequate basis for the implementation of a default proof system. The mating-based approach in (Schaub, 1995) provides a purely declarative characterization of default proofs, which is much too abstract for this purpose. In particular, it does not provide means for representing derivations and it cannot reflect the relation between goals and their subgoals.

The basic inference steps of connection calculi are called *extension* and *reduction step*. Intuitively, an extension step amounts to Prolog's use of input resolution: A (sub)goal L is resolved with an input clause $\{L^c, K_1, \ldots, K_n\}$ resulting in the new subgoals $K_1, \ldots, K_n$. For illustration, let us consider the clauses in (7) along with query allergen: We can resolve initial goal $\neg$allergen with clause $\{\neg\text{predispo}, \neg\text{milk}, \text{allergen}\}$. The resulting subgoal $\neg$milk can then be resolved with clause $\{\text{milk}_{\delta_2}, \neg\text{icecream}_{\delta_2}\}$ and so on. The reduction step renders the inference system complete for (full) propositional clause logic: A subgoal is solved if it is complementary to one of its ancestor (sub)goals. In our example, we thus obtain the set $\{\neg\text{allergen}, \neg\text{milk}\}$ of ancestor goals after the two aforementioned extension steps; this allows for applying subsequently reduction steps to putative subgoals allergen and milk.

For incorporating default reasoning into such a calculus, both inference steps have to be adapted appropriately: First, one has to take care of groundedness (cf. Condition (2)). To this end, we have to guarantee that whenever a δ-clause $\{\neg\alpha_\delta, \gamma_\delta\}$ is used as input clause, (i) only γ_δ is resolved upon, and (ii) after such an "extension step" the ancestors of the resulting subgoal $\neg\alpha_\delta$ must not be used for subsequent reduction steps. Moreover, (iii) each such "extension step" must guarantee the consistency with the previous proof segment (cf. Condition (3)).

The calculus presented in this section relies on matrices as basic proof objects. A *matrix* consists of a multiset of clauses.[3] Matrices are usually displayed in a two-dimensional way: The elements of a matrix, i.e. the clauses are listed horizontally whereas the elements of clauses are listed vertically (see Figure 1 for some matrices). Literals in a matrix are either marked as *open* or *closed*. Only literals marked as open are subject to the application of inference steps. A *connection* is an unordered pair of literals with the same predicate symbol but different signs. A connection is called *complementary* iff the literals are identical except for the sign. Connections in a matrix are indicated as arcs linking the respective literals. In what follows, we restrict the definitions to the propositional case.

The first inference step to be introduced is the so-called *initialization step*; it allows to build initial matrices consisting of one clause. Throughout the following definitions, let $CS = C_W \cup C_D$ be a set of input clauses, comprising a set C_W of ω-clauses and a set C_D of δ-clauses, and let M be an arbitrary yet fixed matrix such that for every $c \in M, c \in CS$.

Definition 5. (Initialization step) *Matrix M' is obtained by an initialization step in the following way.*

- *Let c be the copy of a negative ω-clause in CS.*

- *Set $M' = \{c\}$.*

- *Every literal in c is marked as open.*

c is called start clause.

For extending matrices, we define two different variants of extension steps. The first variant is restricted to use input clauses from C_W (ie. ω-clauses) for tableau expansion; this is identical to the extension step in classical connection calculi.

Definition 6. (ω-Extension step) *Matrix M' is obtained from M by an ω-extension step in the following way.*

- *Select in M a literal L which is marked as open.*

  Let $c = \{L_1, \ldots, L_n\}$ be the copy of a ω-clause in CS such that $L^c = L_i$ for some $i \in \{1, \ldots, n\}$.

- *$M' = M \cup \{c\}$.*

- *Finally, mark L_i and L as closed and every literal in $c \setminus \{L_i\}$ as open.*

For extending matrices by δ-clauses from C_D, we introduce δ-extension steps. To begin with, their definition must reflect the fact that defaults are *inference rules* rather than formulas: A clause $\{\neg\alpha_\delta, \gamma_\delta\}$ from C_D can only be applied to an open literal $\neg\gamma_\delta$. Taking into account that the calculus presented in this section is a top-down backward-chaining calculus, this amounts to the application of the underlying default rule. Note that taking $\{\neg\alpha_\delta, \gamma_\delta\}$ as an ordinary ω-clause allows for applying a ω-extension step to an open literal α_δ; this corresponds to reasoning by contraposition, which denies the inference rule character of default rules. Such inferences are disallowed by δ-extension steps:

Definition 7. (δ-**Extension step**) *Matrix $\mathcal{M}'$ is obtained from $\mathcal{M}$ by a δ-extension step in the following way.*

- *Select in $\mathcal{M}$ a an open literal L.*

  Let $c = \{\neg\alpha_\delta, \gamma_\delta\}$ be the copy of a δ-clause in $\mathcal{CS}$ such that $L^c = \gamma_\delta$.

- $\mathcal{M}' = \mathcal{M} \cup \{c\}$.

- *Finally, mark L and γ_δ as closed and mark $\neg\alpha_\delta$ as open.*

In what follows, we need the following vocabulary: Considering Definition 6 (Definition 7, respectively), we call L_i (γ_δ) an ω-*extension literal* (δ-*extension literal*), and each element of $\{L_1, \ldots, L_n\} \setminus \{L_i\}$ ($\{\neg\alpha_\delta\}$), ω-*extension-resulting literal* (δ-*extension-resulting literal*). We sometimes omit the prefixes ω- and δ- whenever it is clear from the context.

If an extension step (δ- or ω-extension step) is applied to an open literal L, the literals added by this extension step to the respective matrix are called the *descendants* of L. Further, if L_1 is a descendant of L_2 and L_2 is a descendant of L_3 then L_1 is also called a descendant of L_3. If L_1 is a descendant of L_2 then L_2 is also called an *ancestor* of L_1. The descendants of L which are extension-resulting literals are called the *subgoals* of L. A sequence $\langle L_1, \ldots, L_n \rangle$ of literals where (i) L_1 is an element of the start clause and (ii) L_{i+1} is the subgoal of L_i for $1 \le i < n$ is called *goal path*.[4] If L_n is marked as open then p is called *open goal path*.

As argued above, the use of δ-clauses for matrix extension must reflect the properties of default rules. Apart from being an inference rule, default rules must be applied in a consistency-preserving way. Transposed to δ-clauses, we must guarantee that a δ-extension step with δ-clause $\{\neg\alpha_\delta, \gamma_\delta\}$ does not violate Consistency criterion (3) in Theorem 2. To this end, it is sufficient to check whether γ_δ is consistent with all other δ-extension literals in the current derivation. (Note that δ-extension literals correspond (as long as normal default rules are considered) to the justifications of the respective default rules.)

Definition 8. (**Compatible δ-extension step**) *Let $\mathcal{M}$ be a matrix and let $\{\gamma_{\delta_1}, \ldots, \gamma_{\delta_j}\}$ be the set of δ-extension literals occurring in $\mathcal{M}$.*

A δ-extension step with δ-clause $\{\neg\alpha_\delta, \gamma_\delta\}$ applied to $\mathcal{M}$ is called compatible if $C_W \cup \{\{\gamma_{\delta_1}\}, \ldots, \{\gamma_{\delta_j}\}\} \cup \{\{\gamma_\delta\}\}$ is consistent.

Observe that although this definition is in accord with consistency condition (2) regarding their common *incremental* flavor, it involves a different set of underlying default rules. This is because the latter condition is conceived in a bottom-up fashion, while Definition 8 relies on a top-down approach. For a default rule δ_k in an entire default proof $\langle \delta_i \rangle_{i \in I}$, the former criterion involves default rules in $\langle \delta_i \rangle_{i < k}$, while the latter considers default rules in $\langle \delta_i \rangle_{i > k}$.

Even though all these conceptions involve multiple default rules or δ-clauses, respectively, it is always sufficient to restrict our attention to those used in the actual

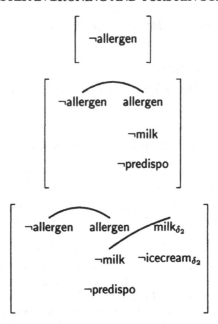

Figure 1 The matrices generated by three derivation steps from Clause set (7) and start clause {¬allergen}.

derivation only. This is due to the notion of localness backed up by semi-monotonicity. Nonetheless compatibility has a special status because it necessitates a more global treatment as opposed to ω- and δ-extension steps. We come back to this issue at the end of this section.

Actually, Definition 7 furnishes only one-half of the machinery needed for ensuring the inference rule character of default rules. Intuitively, this is because we must also eliminate reasoning by cases for δ-clauses. This is done by restricting the well-known reduction step in classical connection calculi. The sole difference is that subgoals of a δ-extension-resulting literal $\neg\alpha_\delta$ must not be solved by reduction steps using ancestors of $\neg\alpha_\delta$. There must thus exist an independent default proof of $\neg\alpha_\delta$, which ignores all ancestors of $\neg\alpha_\delta$.

Definition 9. (Reduction step) *Matrix $\mathcal{M}'$ is obtained from $\mathcal{M}$ in the following way.*

- *Select in $\mathcal{M}$ an open goal path $p = \langle L_1, \ldots, L_k, L \rangle$.*

- *If for some $i \in \{1, \ldots, k\}$, $L_i = L^c$, and every descendant of L_i on p is a ω-extension-resulting literal, then mark L as closed.*

Consider the three matrices depicted in Figure 1. The first matrix $\mathcal{M}_1$ is generated by an initialization step with start clause {¬allergen}. The second matrix $\mathcal{M}_2$ is generated from $\mathcal{M}_1$ by applying an ω-extension step with ω-clause {allergen, ¬milk, ¬predispo} to the sole open literal ¬allergen. The third tableau emerges from $\mathcal{M}_2$ by the application of a δ-extension step with δ-clause {¬icecream$_{\delta_2}$, milk$_{\delta_1}$} to open literal ¬milk.

. The above inference steps provide us with a sound and complete calculus, as given in the next definition:

Definition 10. (Default Extension Calculus) *A sequence* $\langle \mathcal{M}_1, \ldots, \mathcal{M}_n \rangle$ *of matrices is called a <u>DEC-derivation</u> for a clause set* CS *(called the set of input clauses) if*

- $\mathcal{M}_1$ *is obtained by an initialization step and*

- *for* $1 < i \leq n$, $\mathcal{M}_i$ *is obtained from* $\mathcal{M}_{i-1}$ *by applying to* $\mathcal{M}_{i-1}$ *either*

  - *a reduction step,*

  - *a ω-extension step, or*

  - *a compatible δ-extension step.*

  A DEC-derivation is called a <u>DEC-refutation</u> if it generates a matrix containig no open literals.

For convenience, we sometimes identify the elements of a derivation (namely the matrices) with their generating inference steps: We thus write $\langle d_1, \ldots, d_n \rangle$ instead of $\langle \mathcal{M}_1, \ldots, \mathcal{M}_n \rangle$, where each d_i denotes the instance of the respective inference rule used for obtaining $\mathcal{M}_i$.

Let L be an open literal in a matrix $\mathcal{M}$. A *DEC-subderivation* $\mathcal{D}$ for L is a sequence of derivation steps where the first element of $\mathcal{D}$ selects L and each further element selects a descendant of L. $\mathcal{D}$ is called a *DEC-subrefutation* if after applying $\mathcal{D}$ to $\mathcal{M}$, L has no descendant which is marked as open. We sometimes omit the prefix DEC whenever it is clear from the context.

We continue the example developed in Figure 1. A DEC-refutation for query allergen from Clause set (7) can be constructed as follows: First, a ω-extension step with ω-clause {predispo} is applied to open literal ¬predispo of the third matrix in Figure 1. Second, a δ-extension step with δ-clause {¬child$_{\delta_1}$, icecream$_{\delta_1}$} is applied to open literal ¬icecream$_{\delta_2}$. As a result, we get a matrix (the first matrix in Figure 2) containing a single open literal. This open literal is solved via an application of a ω-extension step with unit clause {child}. Hence, every literal in the resulting matrix (the second one in Figure 2) is marked as closed and so we have found a DEC-refutation of allergen from Clause set (7).

The following theorem tells us that a mechanism generating DEC-derivations in an exhaustive manner constitutes a sound and complete proof mechanism for query answering in default logic (here, restricted to normal default theories).

Theorem 11. *Let* (D, W) *be a normal default theory and* φ *be an atomic formula. Let* CS *be the clausal representation of the atomic format of* (D, W).

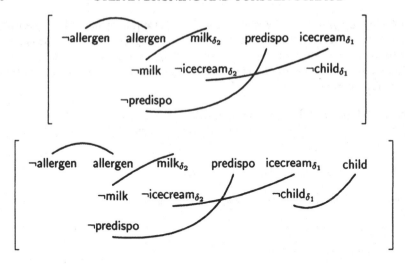

Figure 2   Generating a DEC-refutation from Clause set (7) and start clause $\{\neg \text{allergen}\}$.

Then, there is a default proof for φ from (D, W) iff there is a DEC-refutation for CS with start clause $\{\varphi^c\}$.

Proof: (Sketch)

(Only-if-part) The proof of the only-if-part is an induction on the number n of defaults used in the default proof for φ.

If $n = 0$ we have $W \vdash \varphi$. Hence we must show that DEC is a complete calculus for propositional logic. This is an quite easy task because DEC behaves exactly like ordinary connection calculi (as defined for example in (Bibel, 1987)) in case no δ-extension steps are involved in the course of a deduction. This is because

- the definition of initialization steps and ω-extension steps is exactly the same as for classical propositional connection calculi,

- δ-extension steps do not enter the derivation, and

- if no δ-clauses are used during a derivation, DEC-reduction steps correspond exactly to classical reduction steps.

For $n > 0$, let $\delta_1, \ldots, \delta_n$ be in accord with Theorem 2. Then there exists a default proof D_1 for $Prereq(\delta_1)$ from $(\emptyset, W)$ and a default proof D_2 for φ from $(\{\delta_2, \ldots, \delta_n\}, W \cup \{\{Conseq(\delta_1)\}\})$. For D_1 and D_2 there must exist (due to the induction hypothesis) corresponding DEC-refutations R_1 and R_2. The proof of the only-if case is completed by showing that R_1 and R_2 can be combined in such a way that the resulting refutation is a DEC-refutation for CS with start clause $\{\varphi^c\}$.

The if-case can be proved in a similar way.   □

The restriction to atomic queries is no limitation of the approach, since an arbitrary query formula ϕ can always be replaced by an atomic one, say φ, and an additional formula $\phi \to \varphi$ in W.

The resulting DEC-calculus provides us with a homogeneous and systematic characterization of default proofs that leaves room for diverse design decisions as regards the ultimate implementation. In fact, a salient feature of our approach is that it relies on a local proof procedure employing an incremental consistency check. As a result, all inference steps of our DEC-calculus are executable in a more or less local fashion. This comprises the reduction step, searching among ancestor literals, as well as the verification of compatibility for δ-extension steps which involves inspecting all δ-extension literals occurring in the matrix at hand. But even though the latter allows for ignoring all default clauses outside the current derivation, it has nonetheless a special status due to the involved consistency check. Of course, such a consistency check can be mapped, roughly speaking, onto "unsuccessful" derivations that yield matrices comprising at least one open literal. This would amount to a generalization of Prolog's "negation-as-failure" mechanism to full clause logic. We argue however that such an approach is infeasible due to the combinatoric explosion of (repeated) saturations; this gets even worse in the presence of disjunctions.

Moreover, it is not even necessary to continuously perform exhaustive consistency checks, once we can actually *represent* and then eventually *reuse* the result of a successful consistency check. In (Brüning and Schaub, 1996) we propose the following approach to incremental consistency checking: We start with a model of the initial set of facts. Each time, we apply a δ-extension step, we check whether the actual model satisfies the underlying default assumptions, that is – in terms of Definition 8 – we check whether the actual model bears witness for the satisfiability of $C_W \cup \{\{\gamma_{\delta_1}\}, \ldots, \{\gamma_{\delta_j}\}\} \cup \{\{\gamma_{\delta}\}\}$. If this is the case, we continue proving. If not, we try to generate a new model of the initial set of facts satisfying the current as well as all default assumptions underlying the DEC-derivation at hand. If we succeed, we simply continue proving under the new model. Otherwise, we know that the δ-extension step cannot be applied in a compatible way (since there is no model for the continuation of our current derivation with the δ-clause at hand). In this way, we restrict the generation of new models to the ultimately necessary ones.

3.1. Extensions and refinements

3.1.1. Lemma handling

Lemma handling is an important means for eliminating redundancy in automated theorem proving (cf. (Astrachan and Stickel, 1992)). This task is however more difficult in our context, since proofs may depend on default rules and their induced consistency requirements.

In fact, in classical connection calculi, a lemma l is simply a set of literals that allows for marking an open literal as closed if the corresponding open goal path contains all elements of l. It is well known that, given two clause sets CS and CS'

with $CS' \subseteq CS$, and a lemma l (generated during a derivation for CS'), then l can be applied safely during derivations for CS. That is, given a goal path p with open literal L generated during a derivation for CS, L can be marked as closed if p contains every element of l.

Unlike this classical approach, it is impossible to simply use such lemmas, like l, during a derivation in default theorem proving. This is because the subrefutation from which l was generated might depend on a set of δ-clauses C_{DS}. The use of l during a derivation employing defaults not consistent with C_{DS} would lead to incorrect results. In the context of default theorem proving, we therefore have to extend the concept of lemmas:

Definition 12. (DEC-Lemma) *Let C_W be a set of ω-clauses, C_D be a set of δ-clauses, and let $\mathcal{M}$ be a matrix generated from some DEC-derivation for $C_W \cup C_D$. Let L be some literal in $\mathcal{M}$ whith a non-empty set of descendants such that every descendant of L is marked as closed, ie. there exists a subrefutation $\mathcal{D}$ for L. Further, let $L_1, \ldots, L_n$ be the ancestors of L used for reduction steps in $\mathcal{D}$ and let $S \subseteq C_W \cup C_D$ be the set of input clauses used in $\mathcal{D}$.*

Then, $l = \{L, L_1, \ldots, L_n\}$ is called a __DEC-lemma__ wrt S and the set of default rules $\{\delta \mid \{\neg\alpha_\delta, \gamma_\delta\} \in (C_D \cap S)\}$.

Formal underpinnings for this notion can be given by appeal to so-called *lemma default rules* (Schaub, 1992). Restricted to normal default theories, a lemma default rule δ_l for a formula l from (D, W), is constructed from a default proof $\langle \delta_i \rangle_{i \in I}$ for l in the following way:

$$\delta_l = \frac{: \bigwedge_{\delta_i \in I} Conseq(\delta)}{l}$$

Since this results in a non-normal default rule, the precise meaning has to be fixed wrt a full-fledged default logic. For full-fledged Reiter's default logic, it is shown in (Schaub, 1992) that E is an extension of (D, W) iff E is an extension of $(D \cup \{\delta_l\}, W)$.

Our approach is justified by the following result.

Theorem 13. *Let C_W be a set of ω-clauses and C_D be a set of δ-clauses such that $W \cup Conseq(D)$ is consistent. Let l be a DEC-lemma wrt some subset of $C_W \cup C_D$ and some set of default rules $D' \subseteq D$. Further, let $\mathcal{M}$ be a matrix generated by a DEC-derivation from $C_W \cup C_D$, and let $\langle K_1, \ldots, K_v, \ldots, K_m \rangle$ be an open goal path in $\mathcal{M}$.*

If $K_{v+1}, \ldots, K_m$ are ω-extension-resulting literals and $l \subseteq \{K_v, \ldots, K_m\}$, then K_m can be marked as closed (without loosing soundness).

Proof: (Sketch)
Let $l = \{L_1, \ldots, L_n, L\}$ be in accord with Definition 12 and let $C_{D'}$ be the set of default rules used in the subrefutation of L. First, it is quite easy to recognize that for every element $K \in l$, there exists a DEC-refutation for $C_{D'} \cup C_W \cup \{\{L_1\}, \ldots, \{L_n\}, \{L\}\}$ with start clause $\{K\}$. Now, let l and $\langle K_1, \ldots, K_m \rangle$ be in accord with Theorem 13. For simplicity we assume that $K_m \in l$, otherwise lemma l could have been applied

earlier in course of the derivation. Then, we know that there exists a DEC-refutation for $C_{D'} \cup C_W \cup \{\{L_1\}, \ldots, \{L_n\}, \{L\}\}$ with start clause $\{\{K_m\}\}$. This DEC-refutation can be applied to K_m without violating consistency (note that $D' \subseteq D$). Further, since $l \subseteq \{K_v, \ldots, K_m\}$, each extension step using one of the unit clauses from $\{\{L_1\}, \ldots, \{L_n\}, \{L\}\}$ can be replaced by a reduction step. The resulting subrefutation for K_m is a proper DEC-subrefutation for K_m from $C_{D'} \cup C_W$. $\square$

As a corollary to this result, we obtain that soundness is preserved when extending DEC-derivations with an appropriate *Lemma step*, which can be given shape as follows. For this, let $\mathcal{M}$ and $l = \{L_1, \ldots, L_n\}$ be in accord with Theorem 13:

Definition 14. (Lemma step) *Matrix $\mathcal{M}'$ is obtained from $\mathcal{M}$ in the following way.*

- *Select in $\mathcal{M}$ an open goal path $\langle K_1, \ldots, K_v, \ldots, K_m \rangle$.*

- *If $K_{v+1}, \ldots, K_m$ are ω-extension-resulting literals*

  and $\{L_1, \ldots, L_n\} \subseteq \{K_v, \ldots, K_m\}$, then mark K_m as closed.

In view of an implementation, one has to take care of the fact that using lemma mechanisms in an unrestricted fashion leads to the generation of a flood of useless lemmas swamping the storage. One approach to overcome this problem is the distinction between *static* and *dynamic lemmas* (see (Linke and Schaub, 1995)). Another (complementary) possibility is to restrict the use of lemmata to *unit lemmas*, which consist of one literal only. Experimental results have shown that the use of such refined variants of DEC-Lemmata can significantly reduce the time required for finding DEC-refutations.

Besides reducing redundancy during the search for DEC-refutations, DEC-lemmas can be further used for communicating information from DEC-derivations to an attached consistency checker. This allows a potentially synergistic treatment of theorem proving and model handling. For details we refer to (Brüning and Schaub, 1996).

3.1.2. Loop checking by blockwise regularity

Regularity provides a highly efficient means for restricting the search space in proof procedures based on top-down backward-chaining calculi. Applied to a classical connection calculus, it forbids that in the course of a subderivation for some literal L another occurrence of L is generated as open literal. Using this refinement, the number of possible derivations decreases considerably in many cases (eg. see (Letz et al., 1992; Letz et al., 1994)).

Unfortunately, this important refinement for classical connection calculi cannot be applied to DEC without loosing completeness. However, as we will show in the sequel, it is possible to adapt regularity to the needs of default reasoning. This leads us to what we call *blockwise regularity*, which requires (i) that no open literal L_1 is equal to one of its ancestors L_2 unless there is a δ-extension-resulting literal between

L_1 and L_2, and (ii) that the use of δ-clauses as input clauses reflects the ordering given by the groundedness-property of default-proofs.

In fact, on the pure classical parts of a default proof, blockwise regularity behaves exactly like ordinary regularity, whereas in the parts of a derivation involving δ-clauses, it avoids the application of δ-extension steps which, otherwise, would lead to the generation of redundant subderivations. Besides pruning large parts of the search space, blockwise regularity also guarantees completeness since it is necessarily violated by infinite goal paths.

The following definition introduces the concept of blocks which is required for a formal definition of blockwise regularity. Roughly spoken, a block can be considered as a sequence of literals in a matrix to which the full (classical) regularity restriction can be applied without loosing completeness.

Definition 15. (Block) *Let $\mathcal{M}$ be a matrix generated by a DEC-derivation for a clause set $\mathcal{CS}$ and let $s = \langle L_1, \ldots, L_n \rangle$ be a literal sequence in $\mathcal{M}$ where L_i is the immediate ancestor of L_{i+1} for $1 \leq i < n$. s is called a <u>block</u> iff*

1. L_1 is a δ-extension resulting literal or is an element of the start clause, and

2. each L_i with $1 < i \leq n$ is a ω-extension literal or a ω-extension resulting literal.

Condition 2. asserts simply that literal L_i stems from a ω-clause in $\mathcal{CS}$.

As mentioned above, blockwise regularity demands that the use of δ-clauses as input clauses during a DEC-derivation must reflect the ordering of defaults which is given by the groundedness property of default proofs. Taking Theorem 2 into account, this implies that in the course of a DEC-derivation a δ-clause corresponding to default δ_i must not be used during a subrefutation of $Prereq(\delta_j)$ if $i \geq j$.[5] Naturally, a complete enumeration $\langle \delta_i \rangle_{i \in I}$ which is in accord with Theorem 2 is unknown in the course of a DEC-derivation.[6] A matrix generated by a DEC-derivation, however, induces a partial ordering of the involved δ-clauses (see the following definition). Hence, blockwise regularity forbids those derivations generating matrices whose induced partial ordering is not in accord with an enumeration as given in Theorem 2.

Definition 16. (Ordering of δ-clauses) *Let $\mathcal{M}$ be a matrix generated by a DEC-derivation for a clause set $\mathcal{CS}$. If for some pair of literals in $\mathcal{M}$, say L_1 and L_2,*

- *L_2 is a descendant of L_1,*

- *a δ-extension step with δ-clause d_1 has been applied to L_1, and*

- *a δ-extension step with δ-clause d_2 has been applied to L_2*

we set $d_2 <_\delta d_1$. For any δ-clauses d_1, d_2, and d_3, if $d_1 <_\delta d_2$ and $d_2 <_\delta d_3$ we set $d_1 <_\delta d_3$.

Then, blockwise regularity is defined as follows.[7]

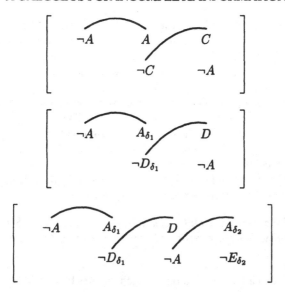

Figure 3   Some matrices illustrating blockwise regularity.

Definition 17. (Blockwise regularity) *Let $\mathcal{M}$ be a matrix generated by a DEC-derivation D for a clause set CS. $\mathcal{M}$ is called <u>blockwisely regular</u> iff the following two conditions hold.*

1. For each block $\langle L_1, \ldots, L_n \rangle$ in $\mathcal{M}$, $L_i \neq L_j$ for all $1 \leq i < j \leq n$.

2. For each pair (d_1, d_2) of δ-clauses used in the course of D with $d_1 = \{\neg\alpha_1, \gamma_1\}$ and $d_2 = \{\neg\alpha_2, \gamma_2\}$, if $d_1 <_\delta d_2$, then $\gamma_1 \neq \gamma_2$.

We call a DEC-derivation D blockwisely regular iff the matrix generated by D is blockwisely regular.

Note that Condition 2. not only demands that the use of δ-clauses reflects the ordering of defaults in a grounded default proof (as discussed above). It further reflects the fact that for a default proof it is not necessary to use two defaults with the same consequent. For instance, Condition 2. guarantees that there are no two literals on one goal path which are proved by using δ-clauses stemming from defaults having the same consequence.

The effect of blockwise regularity can be illustrated by the matrices shown in Figure 3, which are generated by different derivations for a clause set comprising ω-clauses

$$c_1 = \{\neg A\}, \; c_2 = \{A, \neg C\}, \; c_3 = \{C, \neg A\}, \; c_4 = \{D, \neg A\}$$

and δ-clauses

$$d_1 = \{A_{\delta_1}, \neg D_{\delta_1}\}, \; d_2 = \{A_{\delta_2}, \neg E_{\delta_2}\}.$$

The first matrix is build by an initialization step with clause c_1 and two ω-extension steps with clauses c_2 and c_3, respectively. This matrix obviously violates blockwise regularity since it contains a block with two occurrences of literal $\neg A$. The derivation generating the second matrix also starts with an initialization step using clause c_1 but applies a δ-extension step with clause d_1 and a ω-extension step with clause c_4. This matrix is blockwisely regular although it contains a goal path with open literal $\neg A$ which has an identical ancestor (in the start clause). The third matrix is obtained by extending the second matrix via a δ-extension step with clause d_2. Now, since $\{A_{\delta_1}, \neg D_{\delta_1}\} <_\delta \{A_{\delta_2}, \neg E_{\delta_2}\}$, Condition 2. of Definition 17 is violated and therefore the matrix is not blockwisely regular.

The following theorem guarantees that every derivation which is not blockwise regular can be pruned away without loosing completeness.

Theorem 18. *If there exists a DEC-refutation for a clause set CS which violates blockwise regularity, then there exists a blockwise regular DEC-refutation for CS.*

Proof: (Sketch)
One has to prove that a DEC-refutation R which violates blockwise regularity can be transformed into a DEC-refutation R' that is blockwisely regular. This is done in two steps: First, each violation of Condition 2. is eliminated by reordering R. For instance, if we have two literals in $\mathcal{M}$, say L_1 and L_2, where L_2 is a descendant of L_1, and the δ-clauses used by the δ-extension steps applied to L_1 and L_2 are not in accord with Condition 2., the subrefutation for L_2 can be directly applied to L_1.

Second, each block violating condition 1. is eliminated by replacing the involved sequence s of ω-extension and reduction steps by, roughly speaking, another sequence s' of ω-extension and reduction steps where s' uses the same input clauses than s. This is possible since (classical) regularity does not affect completeness for (classical) connection calculi.   □

4. CONCLUSION

We proposed a top-down proof procedure for handling incomplete information based on default logic and a connection calculus: The Default Extension Calculus. This proof procedure has its roots in the connection method based approach to default query-answering in (Schaub, 1995). This consequent integration of classical automated theorem proving techniques and novel default logic technology is a salient feature of the approach. Moreover, we put forward appropriate enhancements of well-known concepts in automated theorem proving, like blockwise regularity and lemma handling, for further improving the performance of our inference engine.

Stefan Brüning
TLC GmbH,
Frankfurt, Germany

Torsten Schaub
Universität Potsdam,
Potsdam, Germany.

NOTES

1. The connection method is usually presented as an affirmative method for characterizing the *validity* of formulas. For our purposes it is however more convenient to present the connection method as a framework to prove the unsatisfiability of the negation of formulas. Since this is just the dual task, it makes no difference concerning the employed notations and mechanisms.

2. Of course, these indexes do not influence two literals' complementarity.

3. Hence, a matrix may contain several copies of the same clause. This is not necessary for a purely declarative approach; the definition of our calculus however is simplified by considering multisets instead of sets. In what follows we do not distinguish between set and multiset notation.

4. Note that a goal path is not necessarily a path as defined, for instance, in (Bibel, 1987; Bibel, 1993). There, a path through a matrix is a sequence of literals with one literal from each clause in the matrix.

5. This does not imply that a DEC-refutation which violates this criterion is incorrect. It only implies that such a DEC-refutation includes redundancies which should be avoided.

6. Otherwise, there is no need to search for a refutation.

7. In (Schaub and Brüning, 1996) a related Definition of blockwise regularity is given. There, however, the ordering of defaults given by the groundedness property is not taken into account.

REFERENCES

Astrachan, O. and Stickel, M. (1992). Caching and lemmaizing in model elimination theorem provers. In Kapur, D., editor, *Proceedings of the Conference on Automated Deduction*, volume 607 of *Lecture Notes in Artificial Intelligence*, pages 224–238. Springer Verlag.

Bibel, W. (1987). *Automated Theorem Proving*. Vieweg Verlag, Braunschweig, second edition.

Bibel, W. (1993). *Deduction: Automated Logic*. Academic Press, London.

Bibel, W., Brüning, S., Egly, U., and Rath, T. (1994). KoMeT. In Bundy, A., editor, *Proceedings of the Conference on Automated Deduction*, number 814 in Lecture Notes in Artificial Intelligence, pages 783–787. Springer Verlag. System description.

Brewka, G. (1991). Cumulative default logic: In defense of nonmonotonic inference rules. *Artificial Intelligence*, 50(2):183–205.

Brüning, S. and Schaub, T. (1996). A model-based approach to consistency-checking. In Ras, Z. and Michalewicz, M., editors, *Proceedings of the Ninth International Symposium on Methodologies for Intelligent Systems*, volume 1079 of *Lecture Notes in Artificial Intelligence*, pages 315–324. Springer Verlag.

Delgrande, J., Schaub, T., and Jackson, W. (1994). Alternative approaches to default logic. *Artificial Intelligence*, 70(1-2):167–237.

Eder, E. (1992). *Relative Complexities of First Order Calculi*. Vieweg Verlag, Braunschweig.

Letz, R., Bayerl, S., Schumann, J., and Bibel, W. (1992). SETHEO: A high-performance theorem prover. *Journal of Automated Reasoning*, 8(2):183–212.

Letz, R., Mayr, K., and Goller, C. (1994). Controlled integrations of the cut rule into connection tableau calculi. *Journal of Automated Reasoning*, 13(3):297–338.

Linke, T. and Schaub, T. (1995). Lemma handling in default logic theorem provers. In Froidevaux, C. and Kohlas, J., editors, *Proceedings of European Conference on Symbolic and Quantitative Approaches to Reasoning and Uncertainty*, volume 946 of *Lecture Notes in Artificial Intelligence*, pages 285–292. Springer Verlag.

Łukaszewicz, W. (1988). Considerations on default logic — an alternative approach. *Computational Intelligence*, 4:1–16.

Mikitiuk, A. and Truszczyński, M. (1993). Rational default logic and disjunctive logic programming. In Nerode, A. and Pereira, L., editors, *Proceedings of the Second International Workshop on logic Programming and Non-monotonic Reasoning.*, pages 283–299. MIT Press.

Nicolas, P. and Schaub, T. (1998). The XRay system: An implementation platform for local query-answering in default logics. In Hunter, A. and Parsons, S., editors, *Applications of Uncertainty Formalisms in Information Systems*, volume 1455 of *Lecture Notes in Artificial Intelligence*, pages 354–378. Springer Verlag.

Poole, D. (1988). A logical framework for default reasoning. *Artificial Intelligence*, 36:27–47.

Reiter, R. (1980). A logic for default reasoning. *Artificial Intelligence*, 13(1-2):81–132.

Rothschild, A. (1993). Algorithmische Untersuchungen zu Defaultlogiken. Diplomarbeit, FG Intellektik, FB Informatik, TH Darmstadt, Alexanderstraße 10, D-64283 Darmstadt, Germany.

Schaub, T. (1992). On constrained default theories. In Neumann, B., editor, *Proceedings of the European Conference on Artificial Intelligence*, pages 304–308. John Wiley & sons.

Schaub, T. (1995). A new methodology for query-answering in default logics via structure-oriented theorem proving. *Journal of Automated Reasoning*, 15(1):95–165.

Schaub, T. and Brüning, S. (1996). Prolog technology for default reasoning. In Wahlster, W., editor, *Proceedings of the European Conference on Artificial Intelligence*, pages 105–109. John Wiley & sons.

Schaub, T. and Nicolas, P. (1997). An implementation platform for query-answering in default logics: Theoretical underpinnings. In Ras, Z. and Skowron, A., editors, *Proceedings of the Tenth International Symposium on Methodologies for Intelligent Systems*, Lecture Notes in Artificial Intelligence. Springer Verlag.

Schwind, C. (1990). A tableaux-based theorem prover for a decidable subset of default logic. In Stickel, M., editor, *Proceedings of the Conference on Automated Deduction*. Springer Verlag.

Stickel, M. (1984). A Prolog technology theorem prover. *New Generation Computing*, 2:371–383.

RICARDO CAFERRA AND NICOLAS PELTIER

THE CONNECTION METHOD, CONSTRAINTS AND
MODEL BUILDING

1. INTRODUCTION

1.1. Simultaneous Search for Refutations and Models

Since 1990, we investigate an approach, and develop corresponding methods, specially devoted to simultaneous search for refutations and models. Its aim is to capture the standard attitude of a human being faced to a conjecture : trying *simultaneously* to *prove* or to *disprove* it. It is indeed very likely that search for a counter-example of a given formula often helps to find a proof, and conversely: informations deduced during proof search often guide the search for a counter-example.

The methods we have proposed are extensions of proof procedures, based on the use of *constraints*. Instead of standard clauses and formulae, they consider *constrained clauses*, and *constrained formulae* (or c-clauses and c-formulae for short), i.e. pairs $[F : \mathcal{X}]$, where F is a clause (resp. formula) and $\mathcal{X}$ a constraint formula. The constraint formula $\mathcal{X}$ specifies conditions on variables of the formula F. Usual clauses and first-order formulae are particular cases of c-clauses and c-formulae. Standard refutation rules can be straightforwardly extended to constrained clauses: it suffices to add in the constraint conditions allowing the applications of these rules. For example, instead of performing unification between two terms t and s, we simply *delay* this unification by adding the constraint $t = s$ to the considered clause. Similarly, it is possible to add conditions *preventing* applications of the refutations and simplification rules (such as subsumption, elimination of tautologies etc.). This second possibility leads to a new kind of rules, called *disinference rules*, allowing to discard *instances* of the clauses or formulae that are not necessary to obtain a proof. Some of these rules make possible to derive new unit clauses that are *not* logical consequences of the original formula, thus implementing what we have called "non-consequence relations" (Caferra and Peltier, 1997a). The unit clauses so produced can be considered as partial models of the clause they belong to. The standard properties of the method (soundness, refutational completeness etc.) are preserved. The use of disinference rules allows to prune the search space in a stronger way than usual simplification rules do. The price

S. Hölldobler (ed.), Intellectics and Computational Logic, 67–84.

to pay is that we have to handle constraints that may be much more complicated than standard unification problems. Moreover, for some clauses, our methods are also able to transform the formula at hand into a satisfiable set of unit c-clauses, which can be considered as a representation of an Herbrand model of the original formula.

This idea has been applied to the resolution calculus (Caferra and Zabel, 1992; Bourely et al., 1994; Peltier, 1997b) and to the tableaux method (Caferra and Zabel, 1993; Peltier, 1997c). In this work, we show how to use it to extend the connection method presented in (Eder, 1990). Besides, a *systematic* way of model building, this extension also allows to solve the tautological circuit problem (Bibel, 1981) in a very natural and elegant way. Moreover, we also show how to include in it the use of term schematization techniques.

1.2. The Connection method

The connection method (CM for short) was originally introduced by W. Bibel (see for example (Bibel, 1981; Bibel, 1982) and references there). Andrews (Andrews, 1981) proposed a similar one, called "matings".

It provides a framework for theorem proving and a clever way to test the validity of a formula (not necessarily in clausal form) by checking all its *paths*. Roughly speaking, a *path through* a matrix is a set of occurrences of the literals that corresponds, in the case of a matrix in normal form, to literals in one disjunct of the disjunctive normal form. It can be shown that a formula is unsatisfiable iff all paths through its matrix contain two complementary literals. As Lee and Plaisted remark in (Lee and Plaisted, 1994) "a path corresponds roughly to a model". One of the contributions of the present work is a method to *avoid* that a path contains two complementary literals, thus yielding a model.

2. PRELIMINARIES

2.1. Basic notions

We assume the reader is familiar with the usual terminology of automated deduction and first-order logic. We briefly review in this section some of the basic notions used throughout this work.

Let Σ be a set of function symbols, Ω be a set of predicate symbols and $\mathcal{X}$ be a (countable) infinite set of variables. Let $arity$ be a function mapping each symbol in $\Sigma \cup \Omega$ to a natural number (the *arity* of the symbol). Function symbols of arity 0 are called *constants* and will be denoted by $a, b, c, \ldots$ $\overline{x}, \overline{y}, \overline{z}, \ldots$ will denote tuples of variables. The set of *terms* $\tau(\Sigma, \mathcal{V})$ is defined as usual over the alphabet $\Sigma, \mathcal{V}$ (where $\mathcal{V} \subseteq \mathcal{X}$). $\overline{t}$ will denote tuples of terms. If $\mathcal{V}$ is empty, $\tau(\Sigma, \mathcal{X})$ is denoted by $\tau(\Sigma)$.

An *atom* is of the form $P(t_1, \ldots, t_n)$, where $P \in \Omega$, $arity(P) = n$ and $\forall i \in [1..n].t_i \in \tau(\Sigma, \mathcal{X})$. A *literal* is either an atom or the negation of an atom. If P is a literal, $\neg P$ denotes the literal with the same predicate symbol and the same arguments than P but with different sign. A *clause* is a finite set (or a disjunction) of literals. First-order formulae are built as usual over atoms by using the logical symbols $\vee, \wedge, \neg, \exists, \forall \ldots$. By $Var(E)$ we denote the set of (free) variables occurring in the expression (term, clause, atom, literal...) E. If $Var(E) = \emptyset$ (i.e. E does not contain free variables) then E is called *ground*. The notion of *substitution* is defined as usual. The result of applying a substitution σ to an expression (term, atom, clause etc.) E is denoted by $E\sigma$. The domain of a substitution σ is the set of variables x such that $x\sigma \not\equiv x$ (noted $Dom(\sigma)$). If for all variables $x \in Dom(\sigma)$, $x\sigma$ is ground then σ is called *ground*. Substitutions will be represented by sets : $\{x_1 \rightarrow t_1, \ldots, x_n \rightarrow t_n\}$.

A *position* is a finite sequence of integers. We denote by Λ the empty sequence and by "." the concatenation operator between sequences. The set of positions in a term (or in an atomic formula) t is denoted by $Pos(t)$ and inductively defined as follows: $Pos(t) = \{\Lambda\}$, iff t is a variable; $Pos(f(t_1, \ldots, t_n)) = \{\Lambda\} \cup \{i.p/p \in Pos(t_i)\}$. If $p \in Pos(t)$, we denote by $t_{|p}$ the term at position p in t. This is formally defined as follows. $t_{|\Lambda} = t$ and $f(t_1, \ldots, t_n)_{|i.p} = t_{i|p}$.

2.2. Equational problems

As explained in the Introduction, the constraints used in the initial version of our method for simultaneous search for refutations and models are *equational constraints*. These constraints are equational formulae interpreted in the Herbrand universe. Definitions and rules below are from (Comon and Lescanne, 1989).

Let Σ be a set of function symbols. We note $\tau(\Sigma)$ the sets of ground terms built on the signature Σ (i.e. the Herbrand universe).

Definition 1. *An equational formula $\mathcal{P}$ is either an equation $s = t$, where s and t are two terms, $\perp$ (false) $\top$ (true) or of the form: $P \vee Q$, $P \wedge Q$, $\neg P$, $\exists x.P$, $\forall x.P$ where P and Q are two equational formula. The free variables $\overline{x}$ of $\mathcal{P}$ are called the unknowns.*

We say that a substitution σ of variables $\overline{x}$ *validates* an equational formula $\mathcal{P}$ iff the formula $\mathcal{P}\sigma$ is true in the Herbrand universe. More precisely:

Definition 2. *A ground substitution σ validates an equational formula $\mathcal{P}$ iff one of the following statements holds:*

$\mathcal{P}$ is an equation $t = u$ and $t\sigma$ and $u\sigma$ are syntactically identical.

$\mathcal{P}$ is a disequation $t \neq u$ and $t\sigma$ and $u\sigma$ are syntactically different.

$\mathcal{P}$ is $\top$.

$\mathcal{P}$ is a conjunction of formulae which are all validated by σ.

$\mathcal{P}$ is a disjunction of formulae and at least one disjunct is validated by σ.

$\mathcal{P}$ is of the form: $\exists x.\mathcal{P}'$, and there exists a term $t \in \tau(\Sigma)$ such that σ validates $\mathcal{P}'\{x \rightarrow t\}$

$\mathcal{P}$ *is of the form:* $\forall x.\mathcal{P}'$, *and for all term* $t \in \tau(\Sigma)$, σ *validates* $\mathcal{P}'\{x \to t\}$

The set of substitutions σ that validate $\mathcal{P}$ is called the set of *solutions of* $\mathcal{P}$ and is noted $Sol(\mathcal{P})$.

Example 3. *The formula*

$$\mathcal{P} : x \neq y \land \forall z.x \neq f(z)$$

is an equational formula. The unknowns of $\mathcal{P}$ *are* x *and* y. *The substitution* σ *defined by:* $\sigma(x) = a$ *and* $\sigma(y) = f(a)$ *is a solution of* $\mathcal{P}$. *Indeed the formula* $\mathcal{P}\sigma : a \neq f(a) \land \forall z.a \neq f(z)$ *is true in the Herbrand universe, on the signature on* $\mathcal{P}$.

The decidability of equational formulae has been proven in (Comon and Lescanne, 1989) where an algorithm is given in order to transform any equational formula into a union of formulae in a so-called "definition with constraints" solved form, from which the solutions of the formula can easily be extracted. This algorithm is given as a set of transformation rules (that are proven sound and terminating) allowing to reach the solved form of any equational formula.

It is not possible nor useful to recall here all these transformation rules (the interested reader can see (Comon and Lescanne, 1989) or (Caferra and Zabel, 1992)). The rules below are some of the key rules of the system. They will be frequently used in this paper.

clash (C), decomposition (D) and occur check (O)

$$(C_1) \quad f(t_1, \ldots, t_m) = g(u_1, \ldots, u_n) \quad \mapsto \quad \bot \qquad \text{if } f \neq g$$

$$(C_2) \quad f(t_1, \ldots, t_m) \neq g(u_1, \ldots, u_n) \quad \mapsto \quad \top \qquad \text{if } f \neq g$$
$$(D_1) \quad f(t_1, \ldots, t_m) = f(u_1, \ldots, u_m) \quad \mapsto \quad \bigwedge_{i=1}^{m} t_i = u_i$$
$$(D_2) \quad f(t_1, \ldots, t_m) \neq f(u_1, \ldots, u_m) \quad \mapsto \quad \bigvee_{i=1}^{m} t_i \neq u_i$$
$$(O_1) \quad z = t \quad \mapsto \quad \bot \qquad \text{if } z \text{ occurs in } t, z \not\equiv t$$
$$(O_2) \quad z \neq t \quad \mapsto \quad \top \qquad \text{if } z \text{ occurs in } t, z \not\equiv t$$

replacement (R)

$$(R_1) \quad z = t \land P \quad \mapsto \quad z = t \land P(z \leftarrow t)$$
$$(R_2) \quad z \neq t \lor P \quad \mapsto \quad z \neq t \lor P(z \leftarrow t)$$

The whole set of rules given in (Comon and Lescanne, 1989) will be noted R. If $\mathcal{P}$ is reduced to $\mathcal{P}'$ by R, we note: $\mathcal{P} \to_R \mathcal{P}'$. An improved version of the constraint-solving algorithm has been implemented. The system is called ECS_{ATINF} (Peltier, 1998) and can be freely downloaded on the WEB (http://www-leibniz.imag.fr/ATINF/Welcome.html).

2.3. Constrained clauses

We introduce the notion of constrained clause (or c-clause).

Definition 4. *A constrained clause (or a c-clause for short) is a pair* $[C : \mathcal{X}]$ *where:*

- C *is a set of literals (in the standard sense).*

- $\mathcal{X}$ *is an equational formula.*

If C *is unit then* $[C : \mathcal{X}]$ *is called a* c-literal.

Roughly speaking, a constrained clause denotes the set of its ground instances. For any c-clause $[C : \mathcal{X}]$ we denote by ground_instances($[C : \mathcal{X}]$) the set $\{C\sigma/\sigma \in Sol(\mathcal{X})\}$. A total Herbrand interpretation (i.e. whose domain is the Herbrand universe) $\mathcal{I}$ *validates* a c-clause $[C : \mathcal{X}]$ iff it validates all ground clauses in ground_instances($[C : \mathcal{X}]$). Clearly, if $\mathcal{X} \equiv \top$, $[C : \mathcal{X}]$ is equivalent to the clause C. Hence *standard clauses are particular cases of c-clauses.*

Example 5. *Let* $\Sigma = \{0, succ\}$. *Let* C_1 *and* C_2 *be the two following clauses:*
  $C_1 : [P(x) \lor R(x) : \forall z.x \neq succ(z)]$ *and* $C_2 : [P(x,y) \lor R(y) : x \neq y]$.
  C_1 *denotes the set of ground clauses:* $\{P(t) \lor R(t)/\forall s.t \neq succ(s)\}$ *i.e.* $\{P(0) \lor R(0)\}$ *(since for all term t not equal to 0, $t = succ(s)$ for some s).*
  C_2 *denotes the set of ground clauses:* $\{P(t,s) \lor R(s)/t \neq s\}$. *In contrast to the previous case, this set of ground clauses cannot be denoted by a finite set of standard clauses.*

2.4. Representing Herbrand models as sets of unit c-clauses

It is intuitively clear (thinking for example to the Herbrand base) that sets of unit c-clauses can be used to represent Herbrand interpretations. This is done as follows.

Definition 6. *A Herbrand interpretation* $\mathcal{I}$ *is said to be an* eq-interpretation *iff there exists a finite set of unit c-clauses S such that for any ground literal P:* $\mathcal{I} \models P$ *iff* $P \in$ ground_instances(S). *In this case* $\mathcal{I}$ *is said to* correspond *to S. Obviously when an eq-interpretation satisfies a formula* $\mathcal{F}$, *we say that it is a eq-model of* $\mathcal{F}$.

Theorem 7. *Let* $\mathcal{F}$ *be a first-order formula and S be a finite set of unit c-clauses. The problem of checking whether the eq-interpretation corresponding to S is a (counter) model of* $\mathcal{F}$ *is decidable.*

Proof: See (Caferra and Peltier, 1997b). The idea of the proof is to transform the problem $\mathcal{I} \models \mathcal{F}$? into an equational problem and then to solve this problem using the algorithm in (Comon and Lescanne, 1989).   □

Remark 8. *The set of satisfiable formulae having an eq-model is denoted by Eqmodel. Many classes of satisfiable formulae belong to the Eqmodelclass: the (function-free) monadic class, the Bernays-Schönfinkel class, the PVD and OCC1N (Fermüller et al., 1993) classes etc.*

3. FROM CM TO CRAMC

We can now describe the proposed extension of the CM. This method will be called CRAMC (Connection method for **R**efutation **a**nd **M**odel **C**onstruction). As already mentioned, the ideas and techniques underlying our method have been applied to semantic tableaux (Caferra and Zabel, 1993) and to the resolution calculus (Caferra and Zabel, 1992; Caferra and Zabel, 1993). It is therefore a natural idea to apply the same approach to extend the CMs (Bibel, 1981) and the matings (Andrews, 1981). The solution of the tautological circuit problem in the CM using the distautology generation rule (Caferra and Zabel, 1992) shows that our approach fits particularly well some key features of the CM.

Unlike the resolution calculus and like tableaux, the CM can handle arbitrary formulae of first-order logic (in skolemized normal form). We will restrict ourselves in this paper to formulae in clausal form. As stated in (Eder, 1990), this restriction does not affect the search space if structural transformation (see for example (Plaisted and Greenbaum, 1986; Boy de la Tour, 1992; Egly, 1996)) is used to transform formulae into clausal form. Moreover, following (Eder, 1990), we describe the extended CM in terms of unsatisfiability and models instead of validity and counter-example (this is dual to the original presentation of the CM).

A *deduction* using the CM can be completely described by a finite sequence of *structured matrices*, i.e. tuples (M, p, D, σ), where M is a matrix (a conjunction of clauses), p is the active path (i.e. the path currently tested), D is a sequence of clauses and σ a unifier (Eder, 1990). A *circuit* corresponds to a tautological resolvent in the resolution method and are therefore undesirable in a deduction. In (Bibel, 1981), a method to avoid these circuits in the ground case is given. In this paper, we show that the use of equational problems provides a much more powerful language which allows to design a method which effectively avoids tautological circuits in the *non-ground* case. A systematic and more powerful way of building models is also presented. More precisely, we propose an extension of the CM, where the unifier σ is replaced by an *equational formula* (see Definition 1). By using equational formulae more conditions can be specified on the free variables occurring in the current path. *Negative* constraints as well as positive ones can be expressed.

3.1. Structured matrices with constraints

We give in this section a new definition of structured matrix (Eder, 1990). The original definition is extended in two ways. First, unifiers are replaced by equational formulae, allowing to specify *negative* conditions on the variables as well as positive ones. Second, the literals occurring in the path may be universally quantified. This allows to express finitely *infinite* paths through the matrices, as we will see in the next sections.

Definition 9. *A* connection *in a matrix or in a formula is a pair* $(\forall \overline{x}[P : \mathcal{X}], \forall \overline{y}[\neg P' : \mathcal{Y}])$ *such that* $\mathcal{X} \wedge \mathcal{Y} \wedge P = P'$ *is satisfiable.*

If $c = (\forall \bar{x}[P : \mathcal{X}], \forall \bar{y}[\neg P' : \mathcal{Y}])$ is a connection, we denote by c^+ the formula $\mathcal{X} \wedge \mathcal{Y} \wedge P = P'$, and by c^- the formula $\mathcal{X} \wedge \forall \bar{x}, \bar{y}. \neg \mathcal{X} \vee \neg \mathcal{Y} \vee P \neq P'$.

Definition 10. *A path is a (finite) sequence of formulae of the form $\forall x_1, \ldots, x_n.[P : \mathcal{X}]$, where P is a unit literal. A path is said to be* complementary *iff it contains a connection.*

Remark 11. *A path may contain "rigid" (i.e. free) variables, as well as universally quantified ones. For example, the sequence $P(a), \forall x.[R(x,y) : x \neq a]$ is a path. It represents the infinite path $(P(a), R(t_1, y), R(t_2, y), R(t_3, y), \ldots)$ where $(t_1, t_2, t_3, \ldots)$ are the ground terms different from a.*

Definition 12. *A* c-structured *matrix (i.e. a structured matrix with constraints) is a tuple $(M, p, D, \mathcal{X})$, where:*

- *M is a matrix (a conjunction of clauses).*

- *p is a path (the* active *path).*

- *D is a sequence of clauses.*

- *$\mathcal{X}$ is an equational problem.*

3.2. The new rules

Now we give the definition of rules that are extensions of those of the CM defined in (Eder, 1990).

Definition 13. *A c-structured matrix $(M, q, E, \mathcal{Y})$ is obtained from a c-structured matrix $(M, p, D, \mathcal{X})$ by an* **extension step,** *noted*

$$(M, p, D, \mathcal{X}) \vdash_{ext} (M, q, E, \mathcal{Y})$$

iff there are $k, L_1, \ldots, L_{k+1}, d_1, \ldots, d_{k+1}, e, c, C, C', C''$ such that the following conditions hold.

- *$p = (L_1, \ldots, L_k)$ and $D = (d_1, \ldots, d_{k+1})$ and $L_{k+1} \in d_{k+1}$.*

- *$q = (L_1, \ldots, L_{k+1})$ and $E = (d_1, \ldots, d_{k+1} \setminus \{L_{k+1}\}, e)$.*

- *c is a variant of a clause in M.*

- *C is the set of connection between elements of q and elements of $c \setminus e$.*

- *$C_1 \subseteq C$.*

- *$C_2 = C \setminus C_1$.*

- $C' = \{(L(\bar{s}), \neg L(\bar{t}))/L(\bar{s}) \in e \wedge \neg L(\bar{t}) \in \bigcup_{i=1}^{k+1} d_i\}$.

- $C'' = \{(L(\bar{s}), \forall \bar{x}.[L(\bar{t}) : \mathcal{X}])/L(\bar{s}) \in e \wedge \forall \bar{x}.[L(\bar{t}) : \mathcal{X}] \in q\}$.

$$\mathcal{Y} = \bigwedge_{c \in \mathcal{C}_1} c^+ \wedge \bigwedge_{c \in \mathcal{C}_2} c^- \wedge \bigwedge_{(L(\bar{s}), \neg L(\bar{t})) \in C'} \bar{s} \neq \bar{t} \wedge \bigwedge_{(L(\bar{s}), \forall \bar{x}.[\neg L(\bar{t}) : \mathcal{X}]) \in C''} \forall \bar{x}.\bar{s} \neq \bar{t} \vee \neg \mathcal{X}$$

$\mathcal{Y}$ is satisfiable.

The original feature of the c-extension step in CRAMC is the introduction of equational problems ($\mathcal{X}$ or $\mathcal{Y}$) instead of the unifiers used in extension step of the CM. The equational problems allow to express relevant information on problems covering more details than those the CM can handle. The first condition corresponds to the unification between complementary literals in the chosen set of connections $\mathcal{C}_1$. The second condition corresponds to the addition of conditions *preventing unification* between the remaining connections (i.e. between the pairs of potentially complementary literals that have *not* been chosen).

The third and fourth conditions prevent the derivation of *tautological circuits*: the idea of the third condition is to prevent unification between a literal in the current path and the complementary of literals occurring in the remaining subgoals (i.e. in the clauses in D). The fourth condition prevents unification between a literal occurring in the current path and the clause chosen in the extension step.

The truncation defined below aims at removing the last literals of the active path if there are no unsolved subgoals in the last corresponding clauses. This rule is identical to the *truncation rule* defined in (Eder, 1990).

Definition 14. *We say that a c-structured matrix* $(M, q, E, \mathcal{Y})$ *is obtained from a c-structured matrix* $(M, p, D, \mathcal{X})$ *by a* **truncation step**, *noted*

$$(M, p, D, \mathcal{X}) \vdash_{tru} (M, q, E, \mathcal{Y})$$

iff

- $p = (L_1, \ldots, L_k)$,

- $D = (d_1, \ldots, d_{j+1}, \emptyset, \ldots, \emptyset)$ *with* $k - j$ *occurrences of* $\emptyset$,

- $q = (L_1, \ldots, L_j)$,

- *and* $E = (d_1, \ldots, d_{j+1})$, *where* $0 \leq j < k$.

Finally, we introduce the *factorization step*, which is an easy adaptation of the factorization step in (Eder, 1990), adapted to constraint. Its goal is to avoid to solve more than once a literal occurring several times in the matrix. As for the extension step unification between the two literals is replaced by the adding of the constraints making these two literals equal.

Definition 15. *We say that a c-structured matrix* $(M, q, E, \mathcal{Y})$ *is obtained from a c-structured matrix* $(M, p, D, \mathcal{X})$ *by a* **factorization step**, *noted*

$$(M, p, D, \mathcal{X}) \vdash_{fac} (M, q, E, \mathcal{Y})$$

if there are $L_1, \ldots, L_k, d_1, \ldots, d_{k+1}, L, K$ *such that*

1. $p = q = (L_1, \ldots, L_k)$,

2. $D = (d_1, \ldots, d_{k+1})$,

3. $L \in d_{k+1}$,

4. $E = (d_1, \ldots, d_{k+1} \setminus \{L\})$,

5. $K \in d_1 \cup \ldots \cup d_k$ *and* K *has the same sign as* L,

6. $\mathcal{Y} = \mathcal{X} \wedge K = L$ *is satisfiable.*

We also define a *disfactorization step* with no counterpart in the standard CM. It adds conditions preventing application of the factorization step. This constraint on the free variables occurring in the path may result in a search space pruning.

Definition 16. *We say that a c-structured matrix* $(M, q, D, \mathcal{Y})$ *is obtained from a c-structured matrix* $(M, p, D, \mathcal{X})$ *by a* **disfactorization step**, *noted*

$$(M, p, D, \mathcal{X}) \vdash_{disfac} (M, p, D, \mathcal{Y})$$

iff

1. $\mathcal{Y} = \mathcal{X} \wedge K \neq L$ *is satisfiable.*

Remark 17. *The factorization and dis-factorization rules are not necessary for completeness. They only aim at reducing search space. There is no equivalent (or similar) rule to the disfactorization step in the CM in its present state.*

We define a simplification rule allowing to instantiate variables whose value is known.

Definition 18. *We say that a c-structured matrix* $(M, q, E, \mathcal{Y})$ *is obtained from a c-structured matrix* $(M, p, D, \mathcal{X})$ *by a* **simplification step**, *noted,*

$$(M, p, D, \mathcal{X}) \vdash_{simp} (M, q, D, \mathcal{Y})$$

iff

1. $\mathcal{Y} = \mathcal{X} \wedge x = t$.

2. $q = d\{x \to t\}$.

3. $E = D\{x \to t\}$.

3.3. Connection derivation

Obviously, there is nothing new in the following

Definition 19. *A connection derivation of a matrix M is a finite sequence $(S_0, \ldots, S_k)$ of c-structured matrices such that $S_0 = (M, (), (c), \top)$, for some clause $c \in M$, $S_k = (M, (), (\emptyset), \mathcal{X})$, where $\mathcal{X}$ is satisfiable, and S_i is obtained from S_{i-1} $(1 \le i \le k)$ by an* extension, truncation, factorization, disfactorization *or* simplification *step. M is said to be* derivable in the CM *iff there exists a connection derivation of M.*

4. THE PROPERTIES OF THE CRAMC PROCEDURE

The soundness and completeness of the CRAMC procedure are direct consequences of the following lifting lemma.

Lemma 20. *(lifting lemma) Let $\mathcal{S} = (M_i, p_i, D_i, \mathcal{X}_i)$ $(1 \le i \le n)$ be a sequence of c-structured matrices. $\mathcal{S}$ is a CRAMC derivation iff there exists a ground solution σ of $\bigwedge_{i=1}^{n} \mathcal{X}_i$ such that $(ground\_instances(M_i), p'_i, D_i\sigma, \mathcal{X}_i\sigma)$ is a ground CRAMC derivation.*

Proof: (sketch) By induction on the length of the derivation (it suffices to consider each rule separately).   □

Theorem 21. *CRAMC is sound and refutationally complete.*

Proof: (sketch) In the ground case, the soundness and completeness of the CRAMC procedure can be proven using the same techniques as in (Bibel, 1981). Then this result can be lifted to the non ground case, using Lemma 20.   □

5. EXPRESSING INFINITE PATHS

In this section, we present some techniques for preventing the generation of infinite paths. The idea is to use the more powerful language of disequations and universal quantifiers in order to express these paths finitely. Firstly, we integrate in our calculus some advanced features of tableaux, namely a modified truncation rule and an introduction of universal quantifiers rule. These features are essential for the model building presented in this paper, particularly combined with the specific rules for extracting models that will be presented later.

5.1. Marked literals

We need to extend the definition of c-structured matrix, as follows.

Definition 22. *A* marked c-structured matrix *is a pair $(\mathcal{M}, S)$ where $\mathcal{M}$ is a c-structured matrix and S a subsequence of the active path of $\mathcal{M}$ (the* marked literals*).*

Intuitively, marked literals are simply the literals that are *responsible* for the failure in detecting contradiction of the previously tested paths (i.e literals occurring in a connection of one of these paths).

We modify CRAMC's rule as follows.

- **Extension step.** The set of literals L such that there exists a connection $(L, R) \in C_1$ is added to S.

- **Factorization and disfactorization steps.** S is not modified.

- **Truncation step.** See below.

In order to take advantage of the information introduced by the use of marked literals, the truncation step can be modified as follows.

Definition 23. *We say that a c-structured matrix* $(M, q, E, \mathcal{Y})$ *is obtained from a c-structured matrix* $(M, p, D, \mathcal{X})$ *by a* **truncation step,**

$$(M, p, D, \mathcal{X}) \vdash_{tru} (M, q, E, \mathcal{Y})$$

iff

- $p = (L_1, \ldots, L_k)$,

- $D = (d_1, \ldots, d_{j+1}, d_{j+2}, \ldots, d_{k+1})$ *where* $d_{k+1} = \emptyset$, $\forall n \in [j+2, k]$ *either* L_n *is not marked or* d_n *is empty.*

- $q = (L_1, \ldots, L_j)$,

- *and* $E = (d_1, \ldots, d_{j+1})$, *where* $0 \leq j < k$.

The soundness of the new truncation step follows directly from the following lemma.

Lemma 24. *Let* (M_i, p_i, D_i, X_i) $(1 \leq i \leq n)$ *be a CRAMC derivation and let* $\mathcal{M}$ *be the set of marked literals at step* n. *Let* $p_n = (L_1, \ldots, L_k)$ *and* $D_n = (d_1, \ldots, d_{k+1})$. *Then, for any path through* $\mathcal{M}_n$ *containing* $\mathcal{M}$, *either* $\mathcal{M}_n$ *contains a literal in* d_{k+1} *or* $\mathcal{M}$ *is complementary.*

Proof: By induction on the length of the derivation.   □

Example 25. *Let* $S = \{Q(a), P(x) \vee R(x), \neg P(x), \neg Q(x) \vee Q(f(x))\}$

Let us apply the CRAMC method on S. *We start from* $(S, \emptyset, P(x_1) \vee R(x_1), \top)$. *We obtain:*

$(S, \emptyset, P(x_1) \vee R(x_1), \top)$
$\vdash_{ext}$ $(S, P(x_1), (R(x_1), \neg Q(x_2) \vee Q(f(x_2))), \top)$
$\vdash_{ext}$ $(S, (P(x_1), \neg Q(x_2)), (R(x_1), Q(f(x_2)), \emptyset)), x_3 = x_1)$
          (because of the connection $\neg P(x_3), P(x_1)$)

Here only $P(x_1)$ is marked. The literal $\neg Q(x_2)$ is not marked. Hence the truncation step gives:

$$(S, \emptyset, R(x_1), \top)$$

instead of

$$(S, P(x_1), (R(x_1), Q(f(x_2))), \top).$$

Applying the standard truncation step instead of the new rule defined in this section would have lead to consider the path $P(x_1), Q(f(x_2))$, which is clearly redundant.

5.2. The introduction of quantifiers rule

We add to the CRAMC method a rule that is essentially new, i.e. it is not an extension of a rule of standard CM. This new rule allows to introduce universal quantifiers into the current path. It aims at preventing further infinitely many applications of the *extension* rule.

Definition 26. *We say that a c-structured matrix $(M, q, D, \mathcal{Y})$ is obtained from a c-structured matrix $(M, p, D, \mathcal{X})$ by an **introduction of quantifier** step,*

$$(M, p, D, \mathcal{X}) \vdash_{\forall\text{-}int} (M, q, D, \mathcal{Y})$$

iff

1. $p = (L_1, \ldots, \forall \overline{x}.[L_i : \mathcal{U}], \ldots, L_k)$

2. $q = (L_1, \ldots, \forall y, \overline{x}.[L_i : \mathcal{U} \wedge \mathcal{X}], L_{i+1}, \ldots, L_k).$

3. $\mathcal{Y} = \exists y.\mathcal{X}.$

   where y occurs only in $\forall \overline{x}.[L_i : \mathcal{U}]$.

Example 27. *Let S be a set of clauses of the form: $S = S' \cup \{P(x) \vee R(x), \neg R(y)\}$.*
   Let us apply the CRAMC method on S. We start from $(S, \emptyset, P(x_1) \vee R(x_1), \top)$. We choose the literal $R(x_1)$ and the clause $\neg R(y)$ for the first extension step. We obtain: $(S, R(x_1), (P(x_1), \emptyset), x_1 = y_1)$ (because of the connection $R(x_1), \neg R(y_1)$). i.e. (after constraint solving and simplification): $(S, R(x_1), (P(x_1), \emptyset), \top)$ Then, applying the truncation step, we get: $(S, \emptyset, P(x_1), \top)$. After application of the extension step, we get: $(S, P(y_1), \emptyset, \top)$. Here we can apply the introduction of quantifier rule. We get:

$$(S, \forall y_1.[P(y_1) : \top], \emptyset, \top)$$

This express the fact that any non-complementary path through the matrix must contain $P(t)$ for any term t.

5.3. *Using term schematizations*

Term schematization is another more powerful way of denoting infinite paths. Roughly speaking, using term schematizations it is possible to express infinite sets of structurally similar terms. For example, they allow to denote the set of terms $\{f^n(x)\}$, which cannot be expressed by first-order terms.

Recently (and independently of model building needs), many different term schematization formalisms have been proposed: recurrence terms (Chen et al., 1990), ω-terms (Chen and Hsiang, 1991), I-terms (Comon, 1992), R-terms (Salzer, 1992), and primal grammars (Hermann, 1992; Hermann, 1994). These formalisms have been mainly used in order to study infinite loops and divergence, for example in theorem proving (Salzer, 1994) or in term rewriting. In (Peltier, 1997a), it is shown how to use term schematization for representing and building Herbrand models of first-order formulae.

For some of these languages, unification is known to be decidable, and algorithms have been proposed in order to solve *unification* problems. An exhaustive bibliography can be found in (Hermann, 1994; Salzer, 1994). Particularly interesting for the present work is the notion of *integer terms* (*I-terms* for short), i.e. *terms with integer exponents* introduced by Comon (Comon, 1992) who proposed a unification algorithm for his language. In (Peltier, 1997a), it is proven that the first-order theory of terms with integer exponents (i.e. the theory involving conjunctions, disjunctions, negations, universal and existential quantifiers instead of simple unification problems) is decidable.

Here we show how to incorporate I-terms into CRAMC in order to extend the capabilities of the CM. The idea is to use the powerful language of I-terms in order to denote infinite paths: for example, the path $P(a), P(f(a)), P(f(f(a))), \ldots$ can be denoted by $(\forall n.P(f^n(a)))$.

First we recall the definition of I-terms (Comon, 1992; Peltier, 1997a).

5.3.1. *Syntax of I-terms*

Definition 28. *Let V_M be a set of variables, called* integer variables. *The set T of* terms with integer exponents (*I-terms*) *and the set $T_\diamond$ of* terms with multiple holes *are the least sets that satisfy the following properties:*

$$f(\bar{s}) \in T \qquad \Leftarrow \quad \bar{s} \in T^{arity(f)}$$
$$\mathcal{X} \subset T$$
$$f(s_1, \ldots, s_n) \in T_\diamond \quad \Leftarrow \quad \forall i \leq n.s_i \in T_\diamond \cup T \wedge \exists i \leq n.s_i \in T_\diamond \wedge n = arity(f)$$
$$s^n.t \in T \qquad \Leftarrow \quad s \in T_\diamond \wedge t \in T \wedge n \in V_N \wedge s \neq \diamond$$
$$\diamond \in T_\diamond$$

$\mathcal{X}$ represents the set of all variables, V_N the set of integer variables and $\Rightarrow$ is self-explaining.

The notions of formulae, clauses, constrained clauses, equational formulae etc. can be straightforwardly extended to I-terms.

Example 29. $t_n = f(g(\diamond)^n.a, h(\diamond)^n.b)$, $s_n = f(\diamond, \diamond)^n.a$ *are examples of I-terms.*

5.3.2. Semantic of I-terms

Assignment of terms, formulae E etc. containing I-terms are pairs $(\mathcal{I}, \sigma)$ where $\mathcal{I}$ is an interpretation (in the standard sense) and σ a function mapping each non integer variables from E into an element of the domain of $\mathcal{I}$ and each integer variable of E into a positive integer. In order to give a semantics to I-terms, it is enough to specify the value of an assignment $(\mathcal{I}, \sigma)$ on a term $t^n.u$. Roughly speaking, a term $t^n.u$, where $\diamond$ occurs at a set of positions P in t is either equivalent to u (if the value of n in the assignation is 0) or equivalent to $t[t^m.u]_P$ where m is a new integer variable of value $n - 1$.

Definition 30. Let $\mathcal{A} = (\mathcal{I}, \sigma)$ be an assignation and let $t^n.u$ be a I-term. Then $\mathcal{A}(t^n.u) = \mathcal{A}(u)$ if $\mathcal{A}(n) = 0$, else $\mathcal{A}(t^n.u) = (\mathcal{I}, \sigma \cup \{y \to v\})(t\{\diamond \leftarrow y\})$, where $v = (\mathcal{I}, \sigma \cup \{m \to \mathcal{A}(n) - 1\})(t^m.u)$, m is a new variable.

5.3.3. The I-term introduction rule

In (Salzer, 1992; Peltier, 1997a) rules are defined in order to automatically generate I-terms into sets of clauses. However, these methods are defined in the context of the resolution calculus: they use self-resolving clauses belonging to the set of clauses in order to automatically generate I-terms, obtained by repeated applications of the resolution on these clauses. For example, the clause $\neg P(x) \vee P(f(x))$ can be replaced by the clause $\neg P(x) \vee P(f^n(x))$ where n is a new integer variable. Indeed, this last clause can be obtained from the initial one $\neg P(x) \vee P(f(x))$ by n application of the resolution rule. However, this method is neither feasible in the context of the CM nor in tableaux since self-resolving clauses will *not* be explicitly generated.

Indeed, the CM lacks the lemma building property of the resolution method. Consider for example the set of clauses $S = \{\neg P(x) \vee R(x), \neg R(x) \vee P(f(x))\}$. Here the clause $\neg P(x) \vee P(f(x))$ is a logical consequence of S. It can be generated by applying the resolution rule. However, if we apply the CM, the clause $\neg P(x) \vee P(f(x))$ will not be explicitly generated. Instead, we generate the infinite path: $(R(x_1), P(f(x_1)), R(f(x_1)), P(f(f(x_1)))$, etc.

In (Klingenbeck, 1996), a variant of the inductive rule presented in (Salzer, 1992) is used in the context of tableaux. However, this method is too weak since it is only applied as a pre-processing step on clauses belonging to the initial set of formulae.

Here we propose a new method, allowing to detect and finitely express such infinite paths.

Definition 31. We say that a c-structured matrix $(M, q, D, \mathcal{Y})$ is obtained from a c-structured matrix $(M, p, D, \mathcal{X})$ by an **introduction of I-terms** step, noted

$$(M, p, D, \mathcal{X}) \vdash_{I\text{-}int} M, p, D, \mathcal{Y})$$

iff

1. $p = (L_1, \ldots, L_k)$.

2. $D = (L_1, \ldots, L_k)$.

3. *there exists a subsequence (L_i, L_j) of p $(i < j)$ such that $L_i \equiv P[x]_p$ and $L_j \equiv P[t]_p$ (where x is a variable occurring in t).*

4. *x does not occur in d_n, for $i < n \le j$.*

5. *x does not occur in $\mathcal{X}$.*

6. $t' = t\{x \to \diamond\}$.

7. $q = (L_1, \ldots, L_k, P[t'^n.x])$.

Example 32. *Let $S = \{P(x) \vee P(f(x)), \neg P(x) \vee \neg P(f(x))\}$. CRAMC gives:*

$$\begin{aligned}
& (S, \emptyset, P(x_1) \vee P(f(x_1)), \top) \\
\vdash_{ext} \quad & (S, P(x_1), (P(f(x_1)), \neg P(f(x_3))), x_1 = x_3) \\
\vdash_{simp} \quad & (S, P(x_1), (P(f(x_1)), \neg P(f(x_1))), \top) \\
\vdash_{ext} \quad & (S, (P(x_1), \neg P(f(x_1))), (\neg P(f(x_1)), \emptyset, P(f(x_4))), x_4 = f(x_1)) \\
\vdash_{ext} \quad & (S, (P(x_1), \neg P(f(x_1)), P(f(f(x_1)))), (\neg P(f(x_1)), \emptyset, \emptyset, \neg P(x_5) \vee \neg P(f(x_5))), \top)
\end{aligned}$$

Here, we can apply the introduction of I-terms, instead of indefinitely applying the extension rule. We obtain:

$$(S, (P(x_1), \neg P(f(x_1)), P(f(f(\diamond)))^n.x_1), (\neg P(f(x_1)), \emptyset, \emptyset, \neg P(x_5) \vee \neg P(f(x_5))), \top).$$

Then by applying the introduction of quantifier rule, we get:

$$(S, (P(x_1), \neg P(f(x_1)), \forall n.P(f(f(\diamond)))^n.x_1), (\neg P(f(x_1)), \emptyset, \emptyset, \neg P(x_5) \vee \neg P(f(x_5))), \top).$$

We obtain a finite description of an infinite path. This path can be straightforwardly transformed into a model of the initial formula, simply by instantiating the variable $x_1 \to a$.

6. THE MODEL GENERATION RULE

We now present a method for extracting models for (possible infinite) satisfiable paths through the matrix. This method is almost identical to the one presented in (Caferra and Zabel, 1993) in the context of tableaux. This is natural considering the close relationship between tableaux and the CM. The idea is the following. Paths through a matrix can be seen as potential models of the set of clauses (see also Plaisted's quotation in Section 1.2). Generating paths corresponds therefore to generating models of the set of clauses. However, these paths are in general infinite, which prevents to exhibit a model, excepted in some very particular cases.

If a path p does not contain a contradiction, it can be seen as a *partial* model of the set of clauses. The idea of our method is to transform it into a *total* one. For doing that, we will use a very simple approach. Models are simply generated by considering the *universal closure* of the unit literal in the clause (i.e. we replace a literal $p(t)$

by $\forall x_1, \ldots, x_n.p(t)$, where $\{x_1, \ldots, x_n\} = Var(p(t))$. Obviously, this is not sound in general, since we can get an unsatisfiable set of c-clauses from a satisfiable one. Therefore, we add a rule in order to remove contradictions in the set of c-clauses. The idea is simply to discard the instances of a given unit c-clause, that are negations of instances of another unit c-clause in the set.

More formally, consider the following rule:

The Removing Contradictory Instances (RCI) rule.

$$\frac{[L(\bar{t}) : \mathcal{X}] \qquad [\neg L(\bar{s}) : \mathcal{Y}]}{[L(\bar{t}) : \mathcal{X}] \qquad [\neg L(\bar{s}) : \mathcal{Y} \wedge \forall \bar{y}.\bar{t} \neq \bar{s} \vee \neg \mathcal{X})]}$$

where $\bar{y} = Var([L(\bar{t}) : \mathcal{X}])$.

Clearly, the nondeterministic application of the **RCI rule** on a given set of c-clauses terminates (the number of clash, i.e. the number of pair of complementary literals strictly decreases). Hence we denote by $\text{RCI}^*(S)$ a normal form of S w.r.t. the **RCI rule**.

Let p be a path, i.e. a sequence of literal $p_1, \ldots, p_k$ and $\mathcal{X}$ be an equational formulae. We denote by $\text{model}(p, \mathcal{X})$ the set $\text{RCI}^*(\{[p_i : \mathcal{X}]/1 \leq i \leq n\})$.

$$\frac{(M, p, D, \mathcal{X})}{\mathcal{I}}$$

If $\mathcal{I} = \text{model}(p, \mathcal{X})$, $\mathcal{I} \models M$ (This test is decidable by Theorem 7).

7. CONCLUSION

We have proposed an extension of the CM based on equational constraints. This extension consists essentially in using the language of equational constraints for expressing negative conditions on the free variables and for expressing finitely *infinite* paths through the matrix. In particular we show how to detect tautological circuits through the matrix and how to incorporate the use of term schematization into the method.

Hopefully, this work will contribute to a deeper understanding of the CM, particularly on its model building abilities. It should also show the generality and modularity of implementing non-consequence relations by using constraints. Another interesting feature is that the approach is easy to combine with powerful formalisms (see Section 5.3). The proposed extension, essentially based on constraint handling should not be very difficult to incorporate to existing (possibly parallel) implementations of the CM. The tool described in (Peltier, 1998) could be used for this purpose.

Laboratory LEIBNIZ-IMAG
Grenoble, FRANCE

REFERENCES

Andrews, P. (1981). Theorem-proving via general matrices. *Journal of the Association of Computing Machinery*, 28(2):193–214.

Bibel, W. (1981). On matrices with connections. *Journal of the Association of Computing Machinery*, 28:633–645.

Bibel, W. (1982). A comparative study of several proof procedures. *Artificial Intelligence*, 18:269–293.

Bourely, C., Caferra, R., and Peltier, N. (1994). A method for building models automatically. Experiments with an extension of Otter. In *Proceedings of CADE-12*, pages 72–86. Springer. LNAI 814.

Boy de la Tour, T. (1992). An optimality result for clause form translation. *Journal of Symbolic Computation*, 14:283–301.

Caferra, R. and Peltier, N. (1997a). Model building in the cross-roads of consequence and non-consequence relations. FTP'97 (International Workshop First-Order Theorem Proving). Technical Report RISC-Linz Report Series No. 97-50, page 40-44.

Caferra, R. and Peltier, N. (1997b). A new technique for verifying and correcting logic programs. *Journal of Automated Reasoning*, 19(3):277–318.

Caferra, R. and Zabel, N. (1992). A method for simultaneous search for refutations and models by equational constraint solving. *Journal of Symbolic Computation*, 13:613–641.

Caferra, R. and Zabel, N. (1993). Building models by using tableaux extended by equational problems. *Journal of Logic and Computation*, 3:3–25.

Chen, H. and Hsiang, J. (1991). Logic programming with recurrence domains. In *Automata, Languages and Programming (ICALP'91)*, pages 20–34. Springer, LNCS 510.

Chen, H., Hsiang, J., and Kong, H. (1990). On finite representations of infinite sequences of terms. In *Conditional and Typed Rewriting Systems, 2nd International Workshop*, pages 100–114. Springer, LNCS 516.

Comon, H. (1992). On unification of terms with integer exponents. Technical report, LRI, Orsay, France.

Comon, H. and Lescanne, P. (1989). Equational problems and disunification. *Journal of Symbolic Computation*, 7:371–475.

Eder, E. (1990). *Relative Complexities of First-Order Logic Calculi*. Vieweg.

Egly, U. (1996). On different structure-preserving translations to normal form. *Journal of Symbolic Computation*, 21:1–22.

Fermüller, C., Leitsch, A., Tammet, T., and Zamov, N. (1993). *Resolution Methods for the Decision Problem*. LNAI 679. Springer.

Hermann, M. (1992). On the relation between primitive recursion, schematization, and divergence. In *Proceeding 3rd Conference on Algebraic and Logic Programming*, pages 115–127. Springer, LNCS 632.

Hermann, M. (1994). Divergence des systèmes de réécriture et schématisation des ensembles infinis de termes. Habilitation, Université de Nancy I, and CRIN-CNRS Inria-Lorraine, Nancy, France.

Klingenbeck, S. (1996). *Counter Examples in Semantic Tableaux*. PhD thesis, University of Karlsruhe.

Lee, S. and Plaisted, D. (1994). Problem solving by searching for models with a theorem prover. *Artificial Intelligence*, 69:205–233.

Peltier, N. (1997a). Increasing the capabilities of model building by constraint solving with terms with integer exponents. *Journal of Symbolic Computation*, 24:59–101.

Peltier, N. (1997b). *Nouvelles Techniques pour la Construction de Modèles finis ou infinis en Déduction Automatique*. PhD thesis, Institut National Polytechnique de Grenoble.

Peltier, N. (1997c). Simplifying formulae in tableaux. Pruning the search space and building models. In *Proceeding of Tableaux'97*, pages 313–327. Springer. LNAI 1227.

Peltier, N. (1998). System description: an equational constraints solver. In *Proceedings of CADE-15*. Springer.

Plaisted, D. and Greenbaum, S. (1986). A structure-preserving clause form translation. *Journal of Symbolic Computation*, 2:293–304.

Salzer, G. (1992). The unification of infinite sets of terms and its applications. In *Logic Programming and Automated Reasoning (LPAR'92)*, pages 409–429. Springer, LNAI 624.

Salzer, G. (1994). Primal grammar and unification modulo a binary clause. In *Proc. of CADE-12*, pages 72–86. Springer. LNAI 814.

ROBERT DEMOLOMBE AND LUIS FARIÑAS DEL CERRO

TOWARDS A LOGICAL CHARACTERISATION OF SENTENCES OF THE KIND "SENTENCE *P* IS ABOUT OBJECT *C*"

1. INTRODUCTION

There are many dynamic applications where the set of represented objects may change. Some new objects are introduced in the representations, others are ruled out. For instance, an aircraft may be traced by a radar, and at a given time, for some technical reasons, the aircraft is no more in the scope of the radar. Another example may be found in a database which is used for personnel management in a company. When an employee leaves the company we may want to "erase" the overall information about this employee, because this information is no longer of interest. A similar situation may happen in the case of a patient who leaves a hospital. For privacy reasons, we may desire that the patient no longer "exists" in the database. In all these examples, we want to characterise a situation where there is an object that disappears, in the sense that in our representation of the world we have no more pieces of information about this object. Then, an important problem is to find a formal definition of the property that in a set of sentences that represents our knowledge about the world there is no sentence about a given object. Another important related problem, which **is not** investigated in this paper, is to determine how to change this set of sentences when an object disappears.

The same problem arises in the field of information retrieval. When we have structured data stored in a database, the standard technique to retrieve information is to ask a query which may formally be represented by an open sentence in a first order predicate language. The corresponding answer is a set of tuples of objects for which the formula is true. Another kind of query, that cannot be asked in current database systems, and that may be very useful when people have no idea about the kind of predicates that are used to represent information, is to request all the information regarding a given object. For example, queries of the kind, "tell me everything you know about John". Here again we need a formal characterisation of sentences that are "about John", or, in general, about an oject.

85

S. Hölldobler (ed.), Intellectics and Computational Logic, 85–99.

This problem has also been investigated by a few philosophers, like R. Carnap (Carnap, 1937) and H. Putnam (Putnam, 1958) , and, later, by N. Goodman in (Goodman, 1961) . In his paper Goodman provides a syntactic characterisation of the property that a sentence is about an object or is "absolutely" about an object. He analyses several possible definitions and shows that this characterisation is far to be trivial. In particular, he shows that we cannot directly relate the fact that a sentence mentions an object name, and the fact that this sentence is about this object.

For example, the sentence *in everywhere in the province of Languedoc there are vineyards*, represented by: $\forall x(Languedoc(x) \rightarrow vineyards(x))$, does not mention the city of Carcassonne. However, since the city of Carcassonne is in the province of Languedoc, this sentence is about Carcassonne, in the sense that it informs us about Carcassonne. Indeed, from the fact *Languedoc(Carcassonne)*, and the former sentence, we can infer *vineyard(Carcassonne)*. In general, a sentence of the form $\forall x F(x)$ is about objects named by c because we can infer from it $F(c)$.

Conversely, there are sentences that mention an object and that are not about this object. A trivial example is the tautology *there are vineyards in Oslo or there are not vineyards in Oslo*, formally represented by $vineyards(Oslo) \vee \neg vineyards(Oslo)$, which is not about Oslo because it gives no information about the city of Oslo. A less trivial example is the sentence $vineyards(Carcassonne) \wedge (vineyards(Carcassonne) \vee vineyards(Oslo))$ which is not about Oslo since it is logically equivalent to the sentence $vineyards(Carcassonne)$.

An important feature of the formal analysis presented in this paper is that it directly refers to properties of propositions which are represented in the language in some syntactical form. In fact, it is based on the idea that a definition of the concept of aboutness in the semantics is more appropriate than in the syntax to give an intrinsic characteristion of this concept. From this point of view, our approach is different from Goodman, whose analysis, at least at the begining of his paper, is based on syntactical considerations.

The idea that motivates the formal definitions presented in next section is that a sentence which is not about a given object is a sentence that does not allow us to distinguish states of the world whose descriptions only differ by the truth-value assignment to atomic sentences that mention this object. Conversely, a sentence which is about an object may be true in some of these states, and false in others.

In the next section we introduce the logical framework in which a definition of the property that a sentence is not about an object is given. We start from the definition of "sentences not being about an object", because it is easier to have an intuitive understanding of this formal definition than of "being about", whose definition directly follows from the first one. Then, we analyse formal properties of this concept with regard to logical connectives and quantifiers, and also with regard to logical consequence. In section 3, we give a definition of the fact that a theory is about a given object. It is shown that the fact that a theory is about an object is not directly related to the fact it contains some sentences that are about this object. Section 4 presents suggestions to extend the definitions to languages with equality predicates. In the conclusion we present a list of open problems concerning the application and automatisation of the treatment of aboutness.

2. SENTENCES ABOUT AN OBJECT

Definition 1. (Syntactical definition of language L_c) *We define a first order predicate calculus language L_c, where c is some given constant symbol. Neither function symbols nor the equality predicate are allowed in the language. Terms are either variable symbols or constant symbols.*
   L_c is defined by the following rules.

   1. If p is an n-ary predicate and t is a n-tuple of terms, then $p(t) \in L_c$.

   2. If $F \in L_c$ and $G \in L_c$, then $(\neg F) \in L_c$ and $(F \vee G) \in L_c$.

   3. if $F \in L_c$, then $(\exists x F) \in L_c$ and $(\exists x \neq c \, F) \in L_c$ [1].

   4. All the sentences in L_c are defined by rules 1, 2 and 3.

As usual we adopt the following notations: $p \wedge q \stackrel{\text{def}}{=} \neg((\neg p) \vee (\neg q))$, $p \rightarrow q \stackrel{\text{def}}{=} (\neg p) \vee q$, $p \leftrightarrow q \stackrel{\text{def}}{=} (p \rightarrow q) \wedge (q \rightarrow p)$ and $\forall x \neq c \, F \stackrel{\text{def}}{=} \neg(\exists x \neq c \, \neg F)$. Paranthesis will be omittted when there will be no risk of misinterpretation.
   Quantifiers of the form $\forall x \neq c$ and $\exists x \neq c$ are called "restricted quantifiers".

Definition 2. (Interpretation) *Let's consider a language L_c as defined in Definition 1. An interpretation M of L_c is a tuple $M = < D, i >$ such that*

- *D is a non empty set of individuals,*

- *i is a function that assigns*

   - *to each predicate symbol of arity n a subset of D^n,*
   - *to each variable symbol an element of D,*
   - *to each constant symbol an element of D,*

In the following D will be called the domain of the interpretation, and i will be called the interpretation function, or, for short, the interpretation.
   Notation: the domain of M will be denoted by D_M and the interpretation function of M will be denoted by i_M.

Definition 3. (Satisfiability conditions) *Let M be an interpretation of the language L_c. The fact that a formula F of L_c is true in M is denoted by $M \models F$, and is inductively defined as follows.*

- *If F is an atomic sentence of the form p(t), where t is a tuple of constant symbols or variable symbols, we have $M \models F$ iff $i_M(t) \in i_M(p)$.*

- *$M \models \neg F$ and $M \models F \vee G$ are defined from $M \models F$ and $M \models G$ as usual.*

- *$M \models \exists x F$ iff there exists an interpretation $M_{x/d}$ that only differs from M by the interpretation of variable symbol x, such that $i_{M_{x/d}}(x)$ is the element d of $D_{M_{x/d}}$ and $M_{x/d} \models F$.*

- *$M \models \exists x \neq c\, F$ iff there exists an interpretation $M_{x/d}$ that only differs from M by the interpretation of variable symbol x, such that $i_{M_{x/d}}(x)$ is the element d of $D_{M_{x/d}}$ and $i_{M_{x/d}}(c)$ is not d and $M_{x/d} \models F$.*

A formula F is a valid formula iff for every interpretation M we have $M \models F$. This is denoted by $\models F$.

The most important part of the paper concerns the notion of variants, which provides a foundation for our definition of aboutness.

Definition 4. (Variants of an interpretation with regard to an object) *Let L_c be a language as defined in Definition 1. We call variants of M with regard to c the set M^c of interpretations M' defined from M in the following way.*

- $D_{M'} = D_M$

- *$i_{M'} = i_M$ for every variable symbol and constant symbol,*

- *$i_{M'}$ is defined from i_M for each predicate symbol as follows: if p is a predicate symbol of arity n*

    - *if t is a n-tuple of terms of language L_c that contain no occurence of the constant symbol c, then $i_{M'}(t) \in i_{M'}(p)$ iff $i_M(t) \in i_M(p)$,*

    - *if an element $< d_1, \ldots, d_n >$ of D^n is such that, for every j in [1,n], $d_j \neq i_M(c)$, then $< d_1, \ldots, d_n > \in i_{M'}(p)$ iff $< d_1, \ldots, d_n > \in i_M(p)$.*

The set of variants M' of interpretation M with regard to an object named with the constant symbol c is denoted by M^c. Notice that M belongs to M^c, and that, if M' belongs to M^c, M belongs to M'^c too.

Roughly speaking, the set M^c is the set of interpretation that only differs from M by the truth assignement of atomic sentences where c appears as an argument. The M^c definition is a bit complicated, its justification is that, in informal terms, a sentence is not about an object named by c iff its truth value does not change in all the variants of a given interpretation. Examples below can help to understand Definition 4.

Example 1. Let L_c be a language with the unique unary predicate symbol p, and the constant symbols a, b and c. Let M be an interpretation of L_c defined by: $D = \{d_1, d_2, d_3, d_4\}$, $i_M(a) = d_1$, $i_M(b) = d_2$, $i_M(c) = d_3$, and $i_M(p) = \{d_1, d_3, d_4\}$ (see Figure 1).

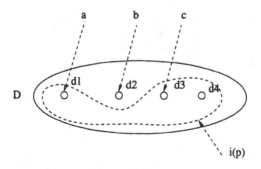

Figure 1 Example 1.

According to Definition 4, for every variant M' in M^c, $i_{M'}(p)$ contains d_1, because d_1 is the interpretation of the constant symbol a, which is different from constant symbol c. Therefore, the sentence $p(a)$ is true in every variant M'. At the opposite extreme, there are variants M' of M such that d_3 is not in $i_{M'}(p)$, because d_3 is the interpretation of c. In these variants $p(c)$ is false, although it is true in M.

Example 2. Let us consider another interpretation which is the same as in example 1, except that the constant symbols a and c are interpreted by d_3, and $i_M(p) = \{d_3, d_4\}$ (see Figure 2).

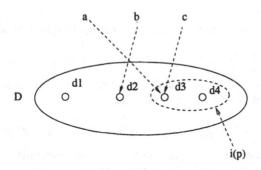

Figure 2 Example 2.

In this example, for every variant M' in M^c, d_3 is in $i_{M'}(p)$ because d_3 is the interpretation of the constant symbol a. Since d_3 is also the interpretation of c, and the interpretation of constant symbols remains unchanged in all the variants of M, the sentence $p(c)$ is true in every variant of M.

Notice that $\exists x \neq c\ p(x)$ is true in M, and it is also true in every variant of M because d_4 belongs to $i_{M'}(p)$ for every variant M' in M^c.

Example 3. Let us now consider an interpretation which is the same as in example 1, except that the interpretation of the predicate symbol p is $i_M(p) = \{d_3\}$ (see Figure 3). Then, there is a variant of M where $i_M(p) = \emptyset$. Therefore the sentence $\exists x p(x)$ is true in M, but it is false in some variant in M^c.

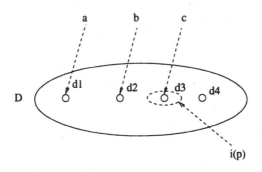

Figure 3   Example 3.

Definition 5. (Sentences that are not about an object) *Let F be a sentence of language L_c. We say that F is not about an object named by the constant symbol c iff for every interpretation M, we have $M \models F$ iff for every interpretation M' in M^c we have $M' \models F$.*

The fact that F is not about object c is denoted by $NA(F,c)$. In short we have:

$$NA(F,c) \ holds \ iff \ \forall M(M \models F \ iff \ \forall M' \in M^c \ M' \models F)$$

We say that a formula F is about the object c, if it is not the case that $NA(F,c)$. This fact is denoted by $A(F,c)$. In short we have:

$$A(F,c) \ holds \ iff \ \exists M(\exists M' \in M^c(M \models F \ and \ M' \not\models F))$$

It can be checked that, according to Definition 5, sentence $p(a)$ is not about object c, and that sentences $p(c)$ and $\exists x p(x)$ are about object c.

Theorem 6. *If sentences F and G are logically equivalent, then $NA(F,c)$ iff $NA(G,c)$.*
   In short: $\models F \leftrightarrow G \Rightarrow (NA(F,c) \leftrightarrow NA(G,c))$.

Theorem 7. *Sentence F is not about object c iff sentence $\neg F$ is not about object c.*
   In short: $NA(F,c) \leftrightarrow NA(\neg F,c)$.

Proof: We first prove that $NA(F,c) \Rightarrow NA(\neg F,c)$.

Let M be an interpretation such that $M \models \neg F$. If there exists an interpretation M' in M^c such that $M' \not\models \neg F$, we have $M' \models F$. Since we have $NA(F, c)$, from Definition 5, for every M'' in M'^c we have $M'' \models F$. From Definition 4 we have $M \in M'^c$, therefore $M \models F$.

To prove that $NA(\neg F, c) \Rightarrow NA(F, c)$, from the former result we have $NA(\neg F, c) \Rightarrow NA(\neg\neg F, c)$, and from Theorem 6 we have $NA(\neg\neg F, c) \leftrightarrow NA(F, c)$. □

Theorem 8. *If both sentences F and G are not about object c, then sentence $F \vee G$ is not about object c.*

In short: $NA(F, c)$ *and* $NA(G, c) \Rightarrow NA(F \vee G, c)$.

Proof: If $M \models F \vee G$, then we have either $M \models F$ or $M \models G$. Assume we have $M \models F$. Since we have $NA(F, c)$, for every M' in M^c we have $M' \models F$ and therefore $M' \models F \vee G$. In the case where we have $M \models G$ the same conclusion follows. Then we have $NA(F \vee G, c)$. □

Theorem 9. *If both sentences F and G are not about object c, then sentence $F \wedge G$ is not about object c.*

In short: $NA(F, c)$ *and* $NA(G, c) \Rightarrow NA(F \wedge G, c)$.

Proof: From $NA(F, c)$ and $NA(G, c)$, by Theorem 7 we have $NA(\neg F, c)$ and $NA(\neg G, c)$, and by Theorem 8 we have $NA(\neg F \vee \neg G, c)$. By Theorem 7 again we have $NA(\neg(\neg F \vee \neg G), c)$, and by Theorem 6 we have $NA(F \wedge G, c)$. □

Theorem 10. *If the sentence $F(c)$ is not about the object c, then $F(c)$ is logically equivalent to $\forall x F(x)$.*

In short: $NA(F(c), c) \Rightarrow \models F(c) \leftrightarrow \forall x F(x)$.

Proof: Assume $NA(F(c), c)$. Let M be an interpretation such that $M \models F(c)$. Let $M_{c/d}$ be an interpretation whose only difference from M is that the constant symbol c is interpreted by some indiviual d in D_M. That is $i_{M_{c/d}}(c) = d$. There exists M' in M^c, such that for every atomic sentence of the form $p(t)$, where t is a tuple that contains at least one occurence of c, we have $i_{M'}(t) \in i_{M'}(p)$ iff $i_{M_{c/d}}(t) \in i_{M_{c/d}}(p)$. That is because M^c contains all the variants of M with regard to c.

Since we have $NA(F(c), c)$, from definition 4, $M \models F(c)$ implies $M' \models F(c)$. Then, we have $M_{c/d} \models F(c)$. The same conclusion can be drawn for any element in D_M. That is, for every d in D_M we have $M_{c/d} \models F(c)$, which from the definition of satisfiability means $M \models \forall x F(x)$.

We have shown that $\forall M(M \models F(c) \Rightarrow M \models \forall x F(x))$. Then we have $\models F(c) \rightarrow \forall x F(x)$. From properties of first order logic we also have $\models \forall x F(x) \rightarrow F(c)$. Then, finally, we have $\models F(c) \leftrightarrow \forall x F(x)$. □

One might intuitively explain Theorem 10 by the fact that sentences that contain no restricted quantifiers and are not about c are sentences where sub-formulas in the scope of quantifiers are tautologies or contradictions. However, this explanation would be wrong. Take, for example, the sentence $p(a) \wedge \exists x(p(x) \vee q(x))$, which is logically equivalent to $p(a)$.

We now present several "negative" properties, that is properties that one may expect to hold, but in fact do not hold.

Theorem 11. *The fact that sentences F and G are both about object c does not imply that sentence $F \vee G$ is about object c.*
   In short: $A(F,c)$ and $A(G,c) \not\Rightarrow A(F \vee G, c)$.

Proof: Take $F = p(c)$ and $G = \neg p(c)$. It is easy to check that both F and G are about c, while $p(c) \vee \neg p(c)$ is not about c.   □

Theorem 12. *The fact that sentences F and G are both about object c does not imply that sentence $F \wedge G$ is about object c.*
   In short: $A(F,c)$ and $A(G,c) \not\Rightarrow A(F \wedge G, c)$.

Proof: Take the same instance of F and G as in the proof of Theorem 11.   □

Using contraposition, Theorems 11 and 12 could respectively be presented in the form:
   $NA(F \vee G, c) \not\Rightarrow NA(F,c)$ or $NA(G,c)$
   $NA(F \wedge G, c) \not\Rightarrow NA(F,c)$ or $NA(G,c)$

Theorem 13. *If sentence F logically implies G it is not necessarily the case that $A(F,c)$ implies $A(G,c)$.*
   In short: $\models F \rightarrow G \not\Rightarrow (A(F,c) \Rightarrow A(G,c))$.

Proof: Take $F = p(a) \wedge p(c)$ and $G = p(a)$. We have $\models F \rightarrow G$. We can also check that we have $A(p(a) \wedge p(c), c)$ but we do not have $A(p(a), c)$.   □

Theorem 14. *If sentence F logically implies G it is not necessarily the case that $A(G,c)$ implies $A(F,c)$.*
   In short: $\models F \rightarrow G \not\Rightarrow (A(G,c) \Rightarrow A(F,c))$.

Proof: Take $F = p(a)$ and $G = p(a) \vee p(c)$. We have $A(p(a) \vee p(c), c)$ because there is an intepretation M where $p(a) \vee p(c)$ is true, because $p(a)$ is false and $p(c)$ is true, and M has a variant where $p(a)$ is false and $p(c)$ is false, that is, where $p(a) \vee p(c)$ is false. Moreover we do not have $A(p(a), c)$.   □

Using contraposition, Theorems 13 and 14 could respectively be presented in the form:
   $\models F \rightarrow G \not\Rightarrow (NA(G,c) \Rightarrow NA(F,c))$
   $\models F \rightarrow G \not\Rightarrow (NA(F,c) \Rightarrow NA(G,c))$
The most important properties are listed below.

$\models F \leftrightarrow G \Rightarrow (NA(F, c) \Leftrightarrow NA(G, c))$

$NA(F, c) \Leftrightarrow NA(\neg F, c)$

$NA(F, c)$ and $NA(G, c) \Rightarrow NA(F \vee G, c)$

$NA(F, c)$ and $NA(G, c) \Rightarrow NA(F \wedge G, c)$

$\models F \leftrightarrow G \Rightarrow (A(F, c) \Leftrightarrow A(G, c))$

$A(F \vee G, c) \Rightarrow A(F, c)$ or $A(G, c)$

$A(F \wedge G, c) \Rightarrow A(F, c)$ or $A(G, c)$

$\models F \rightarrow G \not\Rightarrow (NA(F, c) \Rightarrow NA(G, c))$

$\models F \rightarrow G \not\Rightarrow (NA(G, c) \Rightarrow NA(F, c))$

$\models F \rightarrow G \not\Rightarrow (A(F, c) \Rightarrow A(G, c))$

$\models F \rightarrow G \not\Rightarrow (A(G, c) \Rightarrow A(F, c))$

So far, in this paper, the property of aboutness has only been defined in the semantics. An important issue is to find a corresponding definition in the syntax. That is to find a syntactical characterisation of the set of sentences that are, or are not, about an object c. Unfortunately, at the present time we do not have such a complete characterisation. However, we shall present in the following a syntactical characterisation and we conjecture that its extension by logical equivalence is complete,

Definition 15. (Syntactical definition of language L'_c) *We define a sub set L'_c of the first order language L_c as follows:*

1. *If p is an n-ary predicate and t is a n-tuple of terms with no occurence of the constant symbol c, then $p(t) \in L'_c$.*

2. *If $F \in L'_c$ and $G \in L'_c$, then $(\neg F) \in L'_c$ and $(F \vee G) \in L'_c$.*

3. *if $F \in L'_c$, then $(\exists x \neq c \, F) \in L'_c$.*

4. *All the sentences in L'_c are defined by rules 1, 2 and 3.*

Theorem 16. *If F is a sentence in L'_c then F is not about the object c.*
   In short: $F \in L_c \Rightarrow NA(F, c)$.

Proof: The proof is by induction on the number n of logical connectives or quantifiers in sentence F.

For $n = 0$ we have F of the form $p(t)$. If F is in L'_c there is no occurence of constant c in t. Then, if $p(t)$ is true in an interpretation M, from Definition 4 of variants of M, $p(t)$ is true in all the variants in M^c, which means, from Definition 5, that $p(t)$ is not about object c.

For $n > 0$.

If F is of the form $F = \neg G$, from the definition of L'_c, G is in L'_c. Then, by the induction hypothesis, we have $NA(G, c)$, and, from Theorem 7, we have $NA(\neg G, c)$.

If F is of the form $F = G \vee H$, from the definition of L'_c, G and H are in L'_c. Then, by the induction hypothesis, we have $NA(G, c)$ and $NA(H, c)$, and by Theorem 8, we have $NA(G \vee H, c)$.

If F is of the form $F = \exists x \neq c\, G$, if M is an interpretation such that $M \models \exists x \neq c\, G$, from the definition of satisfiability conditions there exists an interpretation $M_{x/d}$ such that (1) $i_{M_{x/d}}(x) \neq i_{M_{x/d}}(c)$ and (2) $M_{x/d} \models G$.

From the definition of L'_c, G is in L'_c, and by the induction hypothesis we have $NA(G, c)$. Then, from (2), in every variant M' in $M^c_{x/d}$ we have $M' \models G$.

Since the interpretation of variable symbols and constant symbols is not changed in the variants of an interpretation, for every M' in $M^c_{x/d}$ we have $i_{M'}(x) \neq i_{M'}(c)$.

Therefore we have (3) $\forall M' \in M^c_{x/d}\, (M' \models G$ and $i_{M'}(x) \neq i_{M'}(c))$.

Let M'' be a variant of M, that is $M'' \in M^c$. The interpretation $M''_{x/d}$ which only differs from M'' by the interpretation of the variable symbol x (that is $i_{M''_{x/d}}(x) = d$) is a variant of $M_{x/d}$. That is $M''_{x/d} \in M^c_{x/d}$. Then, from (3), we have $M''_{x/d} \models G$ and $i_{M''_{x/d}}(x) \neq i_{M''_{x/d}}(c)$, and, by the definition of satisfiability, we have $M'' \models \exists x \neq c\, G$.

Since $\exists x \neq c\, G$ is true in all the variants M'' in M^c, $\exists x \neq c\, G$ is not about object c. $\qquad \square$

A trivial consequence of Theorems 6 and 16 is that any sentence in L_c logically equivalent to some sentence in L'_c is not about object c. In short:

$(\models F \leftrightarrow G$ and $G \in L'_c) \Rightarrow NA(F, c)$

We have not found any counter example showing that the implication in the other direction does not hold.

As pointed out by Goodman in (Goodman, 1961) the fact that a sentence mentions object c is not necessarily related to the fact that this sentence is about object c.

First, the fact that c does not occur in a sentence F does not imply that F is not about c. For instance, we have $A(\exists x p(x), c)$ and $A(\forall x p(x), c)$. This can be intuitively understood if we think of $\exists x p(x)$ (resp. $\forall x p(x)$) as an infinite disjunction (resp. conjunction) whose one disjunct (resp. conjunct) is $p(c)$. Notice that for restricted quantifiers we have $NA(\exists x \neq c\, p(x), c)$ and $NA(\forall x \neq c\, p(x), c)$.

Second, the fact that c occurs in a sentence F does not imply that F is about object c. Examples that come in mind are tautologies of the form $G(c) \vee \neg G(c)$ where c occurs in G. But these are not the only examples. Since $\models F \rightarrow G$ implies $\models F \leftrightarrow F \wedge G$, if we have $NA(F, c)$ and c occurs in G, then, by Theorem 6, we have $NA(F \wedge G, c)$ and c occurs in $F \wedge G$. Take, for example, $F = p(a)$ and $G = p(a) \vee p(c)$; we have $NA(p(a) \wedge (p(a) \vee p(c)), c)$.

3. THEORIES ABOUT AN OBJECT

In the previous section we have defined the notion of aboutness for a sentence alone. Theorems 12 and 13 have shown that aboutness is not stable with regard to conjunction with other sentences, or with regard to logical consequence. That means that we also have to consider aboutness of a sentence in a particular "context". That is, if we understand the fact that sentence F is about object c in the sense that, if we know that F is true then we know something about the object named c, then it may be that when we learn that F is true we learn or we do not learn something about c, depending on the context of the overall set of knowledge in which the information that F is true has been acquired.

For instance, if we acquire the fact that $p(a) \lor p(c)$ is true in an empty context, that is, in a context where we **only know** that $p(a) \lor p(c)$ is true, then we learn something about object c. Indeed, if in addition we learn that $p(a)$ is false then we know that $p(c)$ is true. However, if we are in a context where we know that $p(a)$ is true, then the fact that $p(a) \lor p(c)$ is true tell us nothing about the object c, because there is no situation compatible with this context where $p(a) \lor p(c)$ may be false.

The intuitive idea is that when we know that a set of sentences is true, to determine whether this set of sentences informs us about c, we cannot consider each sentence independently.

For instance, if we know that $murder(John) \lor murder(Peter)$ is true, to determine whether this sentence tells us something about $Peter$, we have to distinguish, on the one hand, situations where we also know that $murder(John)$ is true, since in that situations $murder(John) \lor murder(Peter)$ gives no information about $Peter$, and, on the other hand, situations where we only know that $murder(John) \lor murder(Peter)$ is true, since in those situations we do know something about $Peter$.

These comments suggest that it is useful to define the notion of aboutness for a set of sentences which is closed under logical consequence, that is, for what we call a "theory". The idea is to define a theory T that is about object c as a theory that informs us about c, in the sense that there are models of T who have variants with regard to c which are not models of T.

Let $\mathcal{F}$ be a set of sentences in L_c. We say that $\mathcal{F}$ is a base for a theory T iff T is the closure of $\mathcal{F}$ under logical consequence. This is denoted by $Base(T) = \mathcal{F}$.

Let us consider, for instance, a theory T_1 such that $Base(T_1) = \{p(a)\}$, and T_2 such that $Base(T_2) = \{p(a) \lor p(c)\}$. It is assumed that both theories are defined on the same language. The theory T_2 is about object c, or informs about c, because we can find a model M of T_2, and a variant of M with regard to c, which is not a model of T_2. In the other case, though sentence $p(a) \lor p(c)$ belongs to theory T_1, every variant of every model of T_1, is a model of T_1, and sentence $p(a) \lor p(c)$ is true in every variant, because $p(a)$ is true in all these variants. That means that theory T_1 is not about object c though it contains a sentence which, if it is considered alone, is about object c.

Theory T_1 is more informative than theory T_2, in the sense that it has less models than T_2, but it is less informative than T_2 about c. Intuitively, when we know that T_1 is true, to know whether $p(c)$ is true we have to know that $p(c)$ iteslf is true, while when we know that T_2 is true, to know whether $p(c)$ is true we only have to know that $p(a)$ is false.

Now, we give a formal definition of aboutness for a theory.

Definition 17. (Theories that are not about an object) *Let T be a theory formed with sentences of language L_c. We say that T is not about an object named with the constant symbol c iff for every interpretation M, M is a model of T iff every interpretation M' in M^c is a model of T.*

The fact theory T is not about object c is denoted by $NA'(T,c)$ and the fact M is a model of T is denoted by $M(T)$. In short:

$$NA'(T,c) \text{ holds iff } \forall M(M(T) \text{ iff } \forall M' \in M^c \ M'(T))$$

We say that T is about the object c, if it is not the case that we have $NA'(T,c)$. This fact is denoted by $A'(T,c)$. In short terms we have:

$$A'(F,c) \text{ holds iff } \exists M(\exists M' \in M^c(M(T) \text{ and not } M'(T))$$

The set of models of a theory T is denoted by $\mathcal{M}(T)$, and the set of variants of models of T, that is, the set of interpretations M' such that there exists M in $\mathcal{M}(T)$ such that $M' \in M^c$, is denoted by $\mathcal{M}^c(T)$.

Definition 18. (Restriction of a theory with regard to an object) *Let T be a theory, we say that the theory T^c is the restriction of theory T with regard to object c iff T^c is the theory whose set of models is the set of variants with regard to c of the models of T.*

In short T^c is the theory such that $\mathcal{M}(T^c) = \mathcal{M}^c(T)$.

Theorem 19. *For any theory T, the theory T^c defined in Definition 18 is not about object c.*
In short we have $NA'(T^c,c)$.

Proof: Let M be a model of T^c. By definition of $\mathcal{M}(T^c)$, M is a variant of a model of T. The variants of M are also variants of some model of T. Then, they are in $\mathcal{M}(T^c)$, and therefore they are models of T^c. □

Notice that since $\mathcal{M}(T)$ is included in $\mathcal{M}(T^c)$, T^c is included in T. T^c is the largest theory included in T which is not about object c, because T^c contains all the sentences which are true in every model in $\mathcal{M}^c(T)$.

4. RESEARCH DIRECTIONS FOR EXTENSION TO EQUALITY

An interesting possible extension of the work presented in this paper is to consider a first order language with an equality predicate.

In the definition of $NA(F,c)$ we have considered variants M' of a given interpretation M, where the interpretation of variable symbols and constant symbols are the same in M' and in M, and where the only changes are about the predicate interpretations with regard to the domain element d which interprets the constant symbol c, that is such that $d = i_M(c)$.

However, in cases where d is also the interpretation of another constant symbol, for instance when $i_M(a) = i_M(c)$, predicate interpretations are not changed with regard to d. The reason is that we wanted to know whether modifications of the truth value of properties about c, like $p(..., c, ...)$, can change the truth value of a given sentence F, but we did not want to modify the truth values of properties about a like $p(..., a, ...)$.

Now, if we extend the language with an equality predicate, the first question that comes in mind is: *"do we have to change, in the variants of M, the interpretation of the equality predicate, as we did for other predicates?"*. A possible answer is *"no"*.

An argument in this sense is that, if we change the interpretation of equality, we also have to change the interpretation of constant symbols. For example, if in M we have $i_M(a) = i_M(c)$ and $i_M(c) = d$, $a = c$ is true in M, and, if there is a variant M' where $a = c$ is false, in M' we have $i_{M'}(a) \neq i_{M'}(c)$, that is $i_{M'}(a) \neq d$ or $i_{M'}(c) \neq d$. That would lead to a change in the meaning of the constant symbols in the variants of M. If we change the meaning of constant symbols, we change the objects named by the constant symbols in the variants of M, and it does not make sense any more to say that a sentence informs about an object named by the constant symbol c if the meaning of c changes from variants to variants.

Then, another question is : *"do we have to change the definition of variants?"*. We think that a natural answer is *"yes"*. In particular in the situations where **we know** that $a = c$. Inded, if we know, for instance, that $p(a) \wedge a = c$ is true, we know that $p(c)$ is true. So, it is quite obvious that sentence $p(a) \wedge a = c$ is about c. If we do not change the definitions presented in section 2, and if equality is treated like any other predicate, we face the conclusion that $p(a) \wedge a = c$ is not about c.

Therefore, we propose to change the definition of variants in Definition 4 in such a way that, **in a context where we know** that, for instance, $a = c$, the interpretation of predicates is also changed for the domain element which is is the interpretation of c, even if this element is also the interpretation of a constant symbol different of c. According to this new definition, though we have rigid interpretation of constant symbols, if $p(a)$ is true in M and we know that $a = c$, the truth value of $p(a)$ will change in the variants of M.

In other contexts where we have no information about $a = c$ Definition 4 should not be changed. In more formal terms, when $M \models p(a) \wedge a = c$, the new definition should make a distinction between the case where we consider sentence $F = p(a) \wedge a = c$, and the case where we consider the sentence $G = p(a)$.

This definition would lead to the conclusion that $a = c$ is not about c. That seems to be counterintuitive, but it is not so odd if the **only** information we know is $a = c$. The reason why we may intuitively believe that $a = c$ informs about c is that, if we know some fact about a, we know the same fact about c, but if we know nothing about a, from $a = c$ we can infer nothing about c.

However, the problem requires a more detailed analysis for sentences which are not of the form $F(a) \wedge a = c$. For instance, we intuitively understand that $p(a) \wedge$

$(a = b \lor a = c)$ should be about c, as it is the case for $p(a) \land (p(b) \lor p(c))$. But $p(a) \land (a = c \lor \neg a = c)$ should not be about c. And what about sentences of the kind $p(a) \rightarrow a = c$ or $(p(a) \land a = c) \lor (q(b) \land b = c)$?

5. CONCLUSION

A formal definition of the concept of aboutness has been given semantically for sentences and for theories. We have also proved properties that show that the notion of not being about an object is compositional for logical connectives, but not for quantifiers. The notion of being about is compositional only for negation. Moreover, these notions are closed neither under logical consequence nor under logical antecedents. Many of these results are not intuitive, but they are consistent with properties of the notion of being absolutely about demonstrated by Goodman in (Goodman, 1961).

The language L'_c gives a syntactical characterisation of a sub set of sentences that are not about the object named by c. It is a basic open question to know whether the class of sentences that are about c is decidable.

We have also given the definition of a theory being, or not being, about an object. In the case where a theory is about an object we have defined the largest sub-theory that is not about this object. This may be used as a foundation for the definition of the operation of "retracting" an object from a theory.

There are many open problems related to the formal definition of aboutness. One is to investigate to what extent the concept of aboutness for topics, for instance as is introduced by Demolombe and Jones in (Demolombe and Jones, pear) (see also (Epstein, 1990; L. Fariñas del Cerro and V. Lugardon, 1994; Lewis, 1988)), is related to the concept of aboutness for objects. We guess they are orthogonal, because the fact that a sentence is about a given topic mainly depends on the meaning of the sentence, it is independent of its extension. In particular two logically equivalent sentences are not necessarily about the same topics, while they are about the same object.

In the area of belief revision many people have attempted to characterise parts of a theory that are invariant with respect to contraction of the theory by a sentence (C. Alchourron and Makinson, 1985). It is rather tempting to use the notion of aboutness for that purpose.

The definition of T^c (Definition 18) is not constructive. An interesting open problem is to find a constructive method to determine the base of a theory T^c as a function of the base of T.

To answer queries of the form "tell me every thing you know about John" we need to define inference rules to derive consequences of the basis $\mathcal{F}$ of a theory T that are about a given object c, in the context of T. That is, sentences that are true in some model M of T, and are false in some variant M' in M^c. If we regard $\mathcal{F}$ as the conjunction sentences that are in $\mathcal{F}$, from Theorem 14 we know that if $\mathcal{F}$ is about object c, it is not necessarily the case that any consequence G of $\mathcal{F}$ is about c. Then, a practical problem is to find additional conditions on $\mathcal{F}$ and G that allow us to restrict the generation of consequences to those that are about c.

Finally, an interesting field for future investigation is to try to extend the automated deduction method, based on the connection method, defined by Wolfang Bible (Bibel, 1981; Bibel, 1983), to sentences that are about the same objects. The intuitive idea is to connect two sentences that are about at least one common object, in order to make more efficient the derivation of sentences that are about a given object.

ACKNOWLEDGMENTS

We are very grateful to Hans-Jurgen Ohlbach who has made many valuable comments about the paper, and who suggested interesting changes or extensions. We also want to thank David Pearce for his great help in the preparation of this paper.

Robert Demolombe
ONERA
Toulouse, France

Luis Fariñas del Cerro
IRIT
Toulouse, France

NOTES

1. Here $x \neq c$ is used as a notation to denote restricted quantifiers, it is not taken as a sentence with an occurence of equality predicate.

REFERENCES

Bibel, W. (1981). Matrices with Connections. *Journal of the ACM*, 28:633–645.

Bibel, W. (1983). Mating in Matrices. *Cmmunications of the ACM*, 26:844–852.

C. Alchourron, P. G. and Makinson, D. (1985). On the logic of theory change : Partial meet contraction and revision functions. *The journal of symbolic logic*, 50(2).

Carnap, R. (1937). The logical syntax of language.

Demolombe, R. and Jones, A. (1999). On sentences of the kind "sentence "p" is about topic "t": some steps toward a formal-logical analysis. In H-J. Ohlbach and U. Reyle, editor, *Logic, Language and Reasoning. Essays in Honor of Dov Gabbay*. Kluwer Academic Press.

Epstein, R. (1990). *The Semantic Foundations of Logic, Volume1: Propositional Logic*. Kluwer Academic.

Goodman, N. (1961). About. *Mind*, LXX(277).

L. Fariñas del Cerro and V. Lugardon (1994). Sequents for dependence logic. *Logique et Analyse*, 133-134.

Lewis, D. K. (1988). Relevant implication. *Theoria*, LIV(3).

Putnam, H. (1958). Formalization of the concept "About". *Philosophy of Science*, XXV:125–130.

ELMAR EDER

THE CUT RULE IN THEOREM PROVING

1. INTRODUCTION

It was one of the most influential merits of Wolfgang Bibel in automated theorem proving to develop and to realize — in the form of the connection method (Bibel, 1987) — the idea of taking a cut-free affirmative proof calculus and of applying its rules in a backward direction, with redundancies and irrelevant information removed in order to allow efficient automation. In the case of an input sentence in disjunctive normal form, this implies that a *complementary compound instance* of the input sentence is generated, i.e., a finite set of ground instances of its clauses through which all paths are complementary.

In the history of first order logic, the first calculi developed had as a central rule the cut rule. However, the cut rule makes a calculus hard to handle for proof theory as well as for backward automated reasoning where it gives rise to an infinite branching factor at each node of the search tree. Therefore a number of sound and complete calculi without cut have been developed for first order logic, starting with Gerhard Gentzen's famous cut elimination theorem for his sequent calculus (Gentzen, 1935). On the other hand, it has been shown (Orevkov, 1979) that, for some classes of formulas, cut elimination in the sequent calculus necessarily leads to extraordinarily longer proofs. A similar result was proved in (Statman, 1979) from which it follows that the number of instances of clauses needed for a complementary compound instance may be extremely (non-elementarily) large compared to the length of a shortest proof in a calculus with cut rule.

The question arises whether a calculus such as resolution which is based on a forward application of the cut rule can overcome this disadvantage. It turned out that resolution has the same shortcoming. In fact, a refined connection calculus — consolution (Eder, 1992) — can even simulate resolution step by step.

It is the goal of this paper to investigate the pros and cons of the cut rule in different types of calculi — affirmative/refutational, forward/backward. In Sect. 2 some basic notations used throughout the paper are defined. Section 3 contains a definition of the sequent calculus with and without cut and states a few of its properties. In Sect. 4 the connection method and its relation to the cut-free sequent calculus as well as Orevkov's

S. Hölldobler (ed.), Intellectics and Computational Logic, 101–123.
© 2000 *Kluwer Academic Publishers.*

and Statman's result on the complexity of cut elimination and its implications for other calculi are discussed. It is argued that it may be necessary to use a backward cut calculus in some areas of automated deduction, and it is outlined how this could be done. Resolution and the sequent calculus with and without cut and the connection method are compared to each other. It is discussed how the cut relates to definitions and to introductions of tautologies of the form $D \rightarrow D$. In Sect. 5 definitions are given of what is a affirmative/refutation, forward/backward, and cut-free/cut calculus. This gives a classification of most calculi used for theorem proving. It is proved that Statman's and Orevkov's result holds for a wide class of cut-free calculi. In Sect. 6 measures for the time needed to read a proof and for the time needed to find a proof of a valid sentence in a calculus are given. A few results are shown concerning these measures for calculi in general and for the sequent calculus with and without cut. In Sect. 7, some of the better known calculi are classified according to the classification criteria.

2. PRELIMINARIES

In this paper the set $\{0, 1, 2, \dots\}$ of natural numbers is denoted $\mathbb{N}$. It is assumed that, in addition to the constants of the basic language of first order predicate logic, there are countably infinitely many *parameters* which will be used only in proof calculi as auxiliary constants. We shall use a, b, c as syntactic variables to denote parameters and x, y, z to denote variables. As propositional connectives we take $\neg$, $\wedge$, $\vee$, and $\rightarrow$. *Terms* and *Formulas* are defined the usual way where constants of the basic language as well as parameters are allowed to occur in formulas. The language $\mathfrak{L}^{par}$ is the set of formulas. The language $\mathfrak{L}$ is the set of parameter-free formulas. A formula is *closed* or a *sentence* if no variable occurs free in it. The set of sentences of $\mathfrak{L}$ is denoted $\mathfrak{S}$ and the set of sentences of $\mathfrak{L}^{par}$ by $\mathfrak{S}^{par}$. Formulas are denoted by capital Latin letters from the beginning of the alphabet: $A, \dots, H$, also with indices. $A \leftrightarrow B$ is a shorthand for $(A \rightarrow B) \wedge (B \rightarrow A)$. The *degree* $\deg F$ of a formula F is defined by $\deg F := 1$ if F is atomic, $\deg \neg F := \deg F + 1$, $\deg F \circ G := \deg F + \deg G + 1$ for a binary connective $\circ$, and $\deg QxF := \deg F + 1$ for a quantifier Q. A *substitution* is a function from the set of variables to the set of terms which has finite support. The substitution with support $\{x_1, \dots, x_n\}$ which maps x_1 to $t_1, \dots, x_n$ to t_n, is denoted $\{x_1 \backslash t_1, \dots, x_n \backslash t_n\}$. The substitution is *ground* if the terms $t_1, \dots, t_n$ are ground. Now let F be a formula and σ a ground substitution. Then the formula obtained from the formula F by replacing each free occurrence of a variable x in F with the term $x\sigma$, is denoted $F\sigma$. It is called the result of *applying* the substitution σ to F. If $F\sigma$ is closed then we shall say that $F\sigma$ is a *substitution instance* of the formula F. Semantic equivalence of two formulas F and G is denoted $F \sim G$. A tuple or sequence of objects $z_1, \dots, z_n$ is denoted $\langle z_1, \dots, z_n \rangle$. Its *length* $|\langle z_1, \dots, z_n \rangle|$ is n. If Z is any set then the set of finite sequences $\{\langle z_1, \dots, z_n \rangle \mid n \in \mathbb{N} \text{ and } z_1, \dots, z_n \in Z\}$ of elements of Z is denoted Z^*. In particular, if Z is an alphabet then Z^* is the set of strings over Z. If Y and Z are sets then a *binary relation* between (elements of) Y

and (elements of) Z is a subset of $Y \times Z$. For a binary relation $\rho \subseteq Y \times Z$ and for $y \in Y$ and $z \in Z$, the shorthand $y\rho z$ is used for $\langle y, z \rangle \in \rho$.

In order to investigate the role of the cut rule, a calculus has first to be chosen. The first calculus to be developed for predicate logic was Gottlob Frege's Begriffsschrift (Frege, 1879). Similar calculi were developed by David Hilbert and other authors. These calculi were primarily designed as affirmative calculi which allow to prove any valid parameter-free sentence F, i.e. to prove that F is indeed valid. However, these calculi can also be used to prove semantic entailments $S \models F$ where S is a set of sentences from $\mathfrak{S}$, and F is a sentence from $\mathfrak{S}$. This is done the following way.

The calculus has a number of *rules* stating that under certain conditions a new sentence F (the *conclusion*) can be deduced in one step from zero or more already derived sentences $F_1, \ldots, F_k$ (the *premises*). In this case we shall write $\langle F_1, \ldots, F_k \rangle \triangleright F$. A Rule is written as a figure $\frac{\Phi_1 \ldots \Phi_k}{\Phi}$ where $\Phi_1, \ldots, \Phi_k$ are strings from the language of the calculus which denote the premises $F_1, \ldots, F_k$, and Φ is a string denoting the conclusion F. The figure $\frac{F_1 \ldots F_k}{F}$ is said to be an *instance* of the rule $\frac{\Phi_1 \ldots \Phi_k}{\Phi}$. For example, for every sentence A and every sentence B, the figure $\frac{A \quad A \to B}{B}$ is an instance of the modus ponens rule "$\frac{A \quad A \to B}{B}$". In the first figure the characters "A" and "B" stand for formulas while in the second figure the quotation marks indicate that "A" and "B" stand for themselves as symbols of the calculus. A restriction may be added to a rule to indicate that it is applicable only under a certain condition. A rule with zero premises is called an *axiom scheme*. An axiom scheme $\frac{}{\Phi}$ is more shortly written as Φ. When referring to a rule, the quotation marks will be omitted if this does not lead to ambiguities.

3. THE SEQUENT CALCULUS

In this section Gerhard Gentzen's sequent calculus is described which was introduced in (Gentzen, 1935). It has been adapted slightly from Gentzen's original paper to incorporate function symbols.

The sequent calculus does not work directly with sentences but with so-called sequents. A *sequent* is a string of characters of the form

$$A_1, \ldots, A_\mu \Longrightarrow B_1, \ldots, B_\nu$$

where $\mu, \nu \geq 0$ and $A_1, \ldots, A_\mu, B_1, \ldots, B_\nu$ are sentences from $\mathfrak{S}^{\text{par}}$. The sentences $A_1, \ldots, A_\mu$ form the *antecedent* and the sentences $B_1, \ldots, B_\nu$, the *succedent* of the sequent. The sequent has the same informal meaning as the sentence

$$A_1 \wedge \cdots \wedge A_\mu \to B_1 \vee \cdots \vee B_\nu.$$

We use capital Greek letters as syntactic variables to denote finite sequences $A_1, \ldots, A_\mu$ of sentences separated by commas. So, every sequent has the form $\Gamma \Longrightarrow \Theta$. The axioms are the sequents consisting of one sentence in the antecedent and the same sentence in the succedent. In addition there are two kinds of inference rules, structural and operational inference rules. For each propositional connective and each quantifier, there is at least one operational rule for its introduction in the antecedent and one operational rule for its introduction in the succedent:

3.1. The Rules

Axiom scheme:

$$D \Longrightarrow D$$

Structural inferences (thinning, contraction, interchange, cut):

$$\frac{\Gamma \Longrightarrow \Theta}{D, \Gamma \Longrightarrow \Theta} \qquad\qquad \frac{\Gamma \Longrightarrow \Theta}{\Gamma \Longrightarrow \Theta, D} \qquad \text{(Th)}$$

$$\frac{D, D, \Gamma \Longrightarrow \Theta}{D, \Gamma \Longrightarrow \Theta} \qquad\qquad \frac{\Gamma \Longrightarrow \Theta, D, D}{\Gamma \Longrightarrow \Theta, D} \qquad \text{(Con)}$$

$$\frac{\Delta, D, E, \Gamma \Longrightarrow \Theta}{\Delta, E, D, \Gamma \Longrightarrow \Theta} \qquad\qquad \frac{\Gamma \Longrightarrow \Theta, E, D, \Lambda}{\Gamma \Longrightarrow \Theta, D, E, \Lambda} \qquad \text{(Int)}$$

$$\frac{\Gamma \Longrightarrow \Theta, D \qquad D, \Delta \Longrightarrow \Lambda}{\Gamma, \Delta \Longrightarrow \Theta, \Lambda} \qquad \text{(Cut)}$$

Operational inferences (introduction rules for $\neg, \wedge, \vee, \rightarrow, \forall, \exists$ in the antecedent and in the succedent):

$$\frac{\Gamma \Longrightarrow \Theta, A}{\neg A, \Gamma \Longrightarrow \Theta} \quad (\neg A) \qquad\qquad \frac{A, \Gamma \Longrightarrow \Theta}{\Gamma \Longrightarrow \Theta, \neg A} \quad (\neg S)$$

$$\frac{A, \Gamma \Longrightarrow \Theta}{A \wedge B, \Gamma \Longrightarrow \Theta} \qquad\qquad \frac{B, \Gamma \Longrightarrow \Theta}{A \wedge B, \Gamma \Longrightarrow \Theta} \qquad (\wedge A)$$

$$\frac{\Gamma \Longrightarrow \Theta, A \qquad \Gamma \Longrightarrow \Theta, B}{\Gamma \Longrightarrow \Theta, A \wedge B} \qquad (\wedge S)$$

$$\frac{A, \Gamma \Longrightarrow \Theta \qquad B, \Gamma \Longrightarrow \Theta}{A \vee B, \Gamma \Longrightarrow \Theta} \qquad (\vee A)$$

$$\frac{\Gamma \Longrightarrow \Theta, A}{\Gamma \Longrightarrow \Theta, A \vee B} \qquad\qquad \frac{\Gamma \Longrightarrow \Theta, B}{\Gamma \Longrightarrow \Theta, A \vee B} \qquad (\vee S)$$

$$\frac{\Gamma \Longrightarrow \Theta, A \quad B, \Delta \Longrightarrow \Lambda}{A \to B, \Gamma, \Delta \Longrightarrow \Theta, \Lambda} \quad (\to A) \qquad \frac{A, \Gamma \Longrightarrow \Theta, B}{\Gamma \Longrightarrow \Theta, A \to B} \quad (\to S)$$

$$\frac{F\{x\backslash t\}, \Gamma \Longrightarrow \Theta}{\forall x F, \Gamma \Longrightarrow \Theta} \quad (\forall A) \qquad \frac{\Gamma \Longrightarrow \Theta, F\{x\backslash a\}}{\Gamma \Longrightarrow \Theta, \forall x F}[\text{epc}] \quad (\forall S)$$

$$\frac{F\{x\backslash a\}, \Gamma \Longrightarrow \Theta}{\exists x F, \Gamma \Longrightarrow \Theta}[\text{epc}] \quad (\exists A) \qquad \frac{\Gamma \Longrightarrow \Theta, F\{x\backslash t\}}{\Gamma \Longrightarrow \Theta, \exists x F} \quad (\exists S)$$

It is required that all sentences which are members of any of the premise sequents or of the conclusion sequent are sentences from $\mathfrak{S}^{\text{par}}$. The rules ($\forall$S) and ($\exists$A) are subject to the *eigen parameter condition* [epc] which requires that the *eigen parameter a* must not occur in the conclusion. The sentence D in the cut rule is called the *cut sentence*.

3.2. The Calculus

Definition 1. *A* derivation *or* proof *in the sequent calculus is a finite sequence of sequents each of which is obtained from previous sequents of the sequence by application of a rule. The last sequent of a derivation is called its* end sequent. *A derivation of a parameter-free sentence F is a derivation with end sequent $\Longrightarrow F$.*

Gerhard Gentzen proved in (Gentzen, 1935)

Proposition 2. (soundness and completeness of the sequent calculus) *There is a derivation for a parameter-free sentence F in the sequent calculus if and only if F is valid.*

Definition 3. *The* cut-free sequent calculus *is the calculus obtained from the (full) sequent calculus by removing the cut rule.*

The main result of (Gentzen, 1935) is the following:[1]

Proposition 4. (Gentzen's Hauptsatz, cut elimination theorem) *Every derivation of a parameter-free sentence F in the full sequent calculus can be transformed to a proof of F in the cut-free sequent calculus.*

Thus, every valid sentence of $\mathfrak{S}$ has also a derivation in the cut-free sequent calculus.

3.3. The Subformula Property

The cut-free sequent calculus has a very pleasant property, the *subformula property*. It says that every sentence which is a member of a premise of a rule instance is a substitution instance of a subformula of a sentence which is a member of the conclusion.

Every rule of the cut-free sequent calculus has the subformula property as is easily verified. The cut rule does not have the subformula property since the cut sentence D does in general not occur in the conclusion.

The cut elimination theorem is of great importance in proof theory because it allows to prove the consistency of calculi. But it is also of great importance in automated theorem proving because, due to the subformula property, the cut-free sequent calculus lends itself to automatic backward reasoning. The idea is to start from the sentence which is to be proved and to construct a derivation in the cut-free sequent calculus by applying the rules backward starting from the conclusion and constructing the premises. Due to the subformula property, there is only a finite number of ways to apply to a given sentence a rule of the calculus in the backward direction. Namely, the wanted premises can only be made up essentially of subformulas of sentences occurring in the conclusion. Thus the branching factor of the search tree is finite. The only problem occurs with the substitutions in the rules ($\forall$A) and ($\exists$S) where infinitely many substitutions are possible. This problem is solved in automated theorem proving through the use of unification. This means that the term t is not determined at the time when the rule is applied backward. Rather, for example in ($\forall$A), the "sequent" $F, \Gamma \implies \Theta$ is taken instead of the premise, and the substitution $\{x \backslash t\}$ which is to be applied to it is only determined later through unification when an axiom is constructed.

4. CALCULI FOR AUTOMATED THEOREM PROVING
WITH AND WITHOUT CUT

4.1. Analytic Calculi

Analytic calculi are proof calculi based on a backward application of the rules of a calculus which has the subformula property. Usually this calculus is a cut-free sequent calculus.[2] The name comes from the fact that these calculi work by decomposing (or analyzing) a sentence. This is a very efficient method because it involves comparatively little search. Examples of analytic calculi for automated theorem proving are the *tableau calculus* (Beth, 1955; Beth, 1959; Smullyan, 1971), and the *connection method* developed by Wolfgang Bibel (Bibel, 1987); see also (Bibel, 1992). In fact, W. Bibel's starting point in the development of the connection method was a version of the cut-free sequent calculus.

The connection method can be viewed as a refinement of the cut-free sequent calculus with the rules applied in backward direction. Essentially, the sequent corresponding to any stage of a connection proof process is a sequent whose antecedent is empty and whose succedent consists of substitution instances of those subformulas of the input sentence through which the active path passes.[3] Choosing a connection in the connection method corresponds to a backward application of the rule ($\neg$S) followed by a backward application of the axiom scheme (i.e., an elimination of an axiom) in the cut-free sequent calculus. Choosing a clause for extension of the active path in the connection method corresponds to backward applications of operational inference rules. In the case of a formula in disjunctive normal form, this is a backward application of the rule ($\exists$S) followed by a backward application of the rule ($\wedge$S). In all cases, the rules of thinning, contraction, and interchange may have to be applied as well in order to rearrange the formulas within a sequent. Also, the factorization of the connection method has its counterpart in the cut-free sequent calculus, namely a backward application of the thinning rule to produce a sequent that has already previously been produced by a backward application of a rule. Note that, due to the way we have defined a derivation in the cut-free sequent calculus, a sequent which is used twice as a premise need only be derived once. Thus the natural graphical representation of a derivation is not a tree but a directed acyclic graph (dag). Factorization in the connection method can be seen as a merging of two nodes of a derivation tree of the cut-free sequent calculus into one node. A connection proof without factorization corresponds to a derivation tree in the cut-free sequent calculus while a connection proof with factorization corresponds to a derivation dag.

On the other hand, every derivation of a sentence in negation normal form in the cut-free sequent calculus can be transformed to a connection proof, essentially by

1. reading the derivation in a backward direction

2. removing redundant information contained in the sequent derivation through using the structure sharing techniques provided by the connection method

3. replacing the (ground) substitution instances of subformulas of the input sentence which occur in the sequent derivation with the same subformulas instantiated only partially through unification.

Again, when a sequent is used twice as a premise in the sequent derivation then there will in general be a factorization involved in the corresponding connection proof (or otherwise the size of the connection proof might blow up exponentially in terms of the size of the sequent proof). If no sequent is used twice as a premise then no factorization is necessary in the connection proof.

For sentences which are not in negation normal form, a sequent derivation may contain axioms of the form $D \Longrightarrow D$ where D is not atomic. This cannot happen for an input formula in negation normal form. Therefore, in the standard connection method connections are allowed only between literals. In the sequent counterpart this means that only axioms $D \Longrightarrow D$ with atomic D are allowed. Let us call this the atomic cut-free sequent calculus. However, it is easily verified that the following holds. Let A be a sentence $\neg A_1$ or $A_1 \circ A_2$ with a binary connective $\circ$ or QxF with a quantifier Q. In the latter case let $A_1 := F\{x\backslash a\}$ where a is a parameter not occurring in F. Then the sequent $A \Longrightarrow A$ is derivable in at most three steps from the sequent(s) $A_i \Longrightarrow A_i$ in the atomic cut-free sequent calculus. By induction, it follows that each sequent $D \Longrightarrow D$ has a derivation in the atomic cut-free sequent calculus in at most $3 \cdot \deg D$ steps. Also, a derivation of a sentence in the sequent calculus can easily be transformed to a derivation of its negation normal form.[4] For the connection method this means that every backward derivation of a formula F in the cut-free sequent calculus can be simulated efficiently as a proof of the negation normal form of F in the connection method. An alternative would be to extend the definition of the connection method to sentences which are not in negation normal form and to allow connections between identical subformulas of opposite polarity. This would essentially allow a step by step simulation. On the other hand, it is doubtful whether this improves efficiency since — from what has been said above — a connection proof "proving" such a nonatomic connection by using only atomic connections, can be done in linear time, just like the time needed to check that two subformulas are identical.

The connection method exploits the subformula property to the maximal extent for automated theorem proving, since it actually represents the sentences of sequents of the sequent calculus as structures defined on top of the input sentence (or its matrix). So, it combines the efficiency of search and the optimal structure sharing guaranteed by the subformula property.

Automated theorem proving based on backward reasoning in the full sequent calculus is a much harder task since the cut rule does not satisfy the subformula property. In a backward application of the cut rule, there is an infinite number of possible cut sentences. So the search tree has an infinite branching factor at each node. Here the cut elimination theorem shows that these problems can be overcome by using the cut-free sequent calculus if soundness and completeness are the only issues of interest. In fact, for a great class of sentences this approach is a very efficient one as the success of theorem provers based on this approach and of Prolog has shown. However, this does not hold of all sentences as the following result of R. Statman shows which implies that also non-analytic calculi based on a backward full sequent calculus should be considered for automated theorem proving.

4.2. The Cost of Cut Elimination versus the Cost of the Cut

R. Statman (Statman, 1979) and V. Orevkov (Orevkov, 1979) proved independently of each other that there is a class of sentences for which cut elimination necessarily makes a derivation extremely (non-elementarily) much longer. More precisely, for a valid sentence F in disjunctive normal form, the *Herbrand complexity* is defined to be the number of clauses of the smallest complementary compound instance of F.

Proposition 5. (Statman) *Let the function* $s \colon \mathbb{N} \to \mathbb{N}$ *be defined by* $s(0) := 1$ *and* $s(n+1) := 2^{s(n)}$. *Then there is an infinite sequence* $\langle F_1, F_2, \ldots \rangle$ *of valid sentences from* $\mathfrak{S}$ *in disjunctive normal form such that the length of* F_n *and the length of the shortest derivation of* F_n *in the full sequent calculus grow exactly exponentially with* $n \to \infty$, *but the Herbrand complexity of* F_n *grows like* $s(n)$ *with* $n \to \infty$.

This implies that the size of the shortest connection proof as well as the size of the shortest proof in the cut-free sequent calculus of F_n grows at least like $s(n)$ and the size of the shortest resolution proof of F_n grows at least like $s(n-1)$ for $n \to \infty$. If first order logic is augmented by the concept of definitions then the sentence F_n can be stated so that it has even length $O(n)$ and that its shortest derivation in the full sequent calculus has also length $O(n)$.

From Statman's result it follows that if we define $f(0, n) := n$ and $f(k + 1, n) := 2^{f(k,n)}$ for all $n, k \in \mathbb{N}$ and if we choose a fixed $k \in \mathbb{N}$, then the length of the shortest derivation of F_n in the cut-free sequent calculus (or in the connection calculus, or by resolution) grows faster than $f(k, N)$ in terms of the length N of the shortest derivation of F_n in the full sequent calculus. This is called a *non-elementary* growth. Orevkov gave another class of valid sentences for which he also proved that the shortest proofs in the cut-free sequent calculus are non-elementarily much longer than the shortest proofs in the full sequent calculus.

This implies even that the following holds.

Observation 6. *There are classes of sentences for which a stupid search process which enumerates all strings and tests them whether they are derivations of the input sentence in the full sequent calculus, is more efficient than the most sophisticated strategy for the cut-free sequent calculus.*

Moreover, in informal logical reasoning in mathematics, the cut rule is used very frequently. This indicates that maybe we have to somehow learn to use the cut rule without producing a search tree with an infinite branching factor.

One way to do this is to remember that we had the same problem with the substitution occurring in the rules ($\forall$A) and ($\exists$S) and solved it through unification. We could use metavariables for formulas. Then, in a backward application of the cut rule, we can introduce instead of the cut sentence a metavariable for it which gets its value only later through some kind of unification on the level of formulas. In fact, it has been shown in (Eder, 1996) for a Frege-Hilbert calculus that it is possible to build a calculus on this idea. This calculus has a finite branching factor of its search tree for any sentence. The same method can be used for the full sequent calculus. This gives the advantage that the manageable search space of the analytic method can be combined with the power of the cut rule if the cut rule is applied only by need. However, still the cut rule can be applied at every step of a proof, and it is very difficult to decide when there is a need (for the sake of efficiency) to apply the cut rule and at which place to apply it. A mathematician makes essential use of the cut rule in his informal proofs only at well chosen places, and at the moment there seems to be no way to mimic in the computer the process of choosing the right places. So it seems that a finitely branching search tree is only the first small step, and the major work will be to develop efficient strategies for the decision when to apply the cut rule.

4.3. Resolution and the Cut Rule

In propositional logic, a clause $\{\neg A_1, \ldots, \neg A_\mu, B_1, \ldots, B_\nu\}$ of the resolution calculus (with $A_1, \ldots, A_\mu, B_1, \ldots, B_\nu$ being atomic formulas) can be viewed as a sequent $A_1, \ldots, A_\mu \Longrightarrow B_1, \ldots, B_\nu$. Then the resolution rule on clauses corresponds to the cut rule on sequents. Resolution can be viewed as a fragment of the sequent calculus consisting only of the cut rule, the contraction rule (which corresponds to factorization), and the interchange rule. We want to see how resolution relates to the full sequent calculus in first order logic. In first order logic, the semantics of a clause c is the universal closure, say F_c, of the disjunction of its literals. But we are not allowed to take the universal closure of a sequent. Therefore we have to take the sequent $\Longrightarrow F_c$ in the sequent calculus.

Proposition 7. (resolution $\mapsto$ forward sequent refutation with cut) *Let S be a set of clauses and let there be a resolution derivation of a clause e from S. Then, in the full sequent calculus, there is a derivation of the sequent $\Longrightarrow F_e$ from the sequents $\Longrightarrow F_c$ with $c \in S$. Its size grows at most quadratically in terms of the size of the resolution derivation.*

Proof: We show that if a clause e is a resolvent of two clauses c and d then there is a derivation of $\Longrightarrow F_e$ from $\Longrightarrow F_c$ and $\Longrightarrow F_d$. We have $F_c = \forall C$, $F_d = \forall D$, and $F_e = \forall E$ with disjunctions C, D, and E of literals, where $\forall$ denotes universal closure. Let σ be the mgu of the resolution step, composed with a substitution which renames variables to parameters. From the axiom $C\sigma \Longrightarrow C\sigma$ we derive $\forall C \Longrightarrow C\sigma$ with $(\forall A)$ and, using $\Longrightarrow \forall C$ and the cut rule, $\Longrightarrow C\sigma$. Similarly we get $\Longrightarrow D\sigma$. Let A and $\neg A$ be the literals resolved upon in the resolution step, instantiated with σ. From the axiom $A \Longrightarrow A$ obtains $\neg A, A \Longrightarrow$ with $(\neg A)$. Applying interchange, contraction, and cut to it and to $\Longrightarrow C\sigma$ and $\Longrightarrow D\sigma$ yields $\Longrightarrow E\sigma$. With $(\forall S)$ obtains $\Longrightarrow \forall E$. □

Note that to a forward resolution refutation corresponds a forward refutation in the full sequent calculus.

Proposition 8. (tree resolution $\mapsto$ backward sequent affirmation without cut)
Let S be a set of clauses with a resolution refutation tree T. Let F be a formula in disjunctive normal form whose positive matrix representation is S. Then there is a derivation of S in the cut-free sequent calculus. Its size grows at most polynomially in terms of the size of T.

Proof: We show by induction on the deduction that if a clause c is derivable by resolution from S, and $\{L_1, \ldots, L_n\}$ is a ground instance of c, then the sequent $\Longrightarrow F$ is derivable in the cut-free sequent calculus from the sequents $\Longrightarrow F, L_j$ $(j = 1, \ldots, n)$. If $c \in S$ then the rules $(\wedge S)$, $(\vee S)$, and $(\exists S)$ yield the sequent $\Longrightarrow F, F$. Then apply contraction. Now assume that two clauses d and e are are derivable by resolution from S, that c is a resolvent of d and e, and that c' is a ground instance of c. Then there are ground instances $d' = \{K_1, \ldots, K_m\}$ of d and $e' = \{L_1, \ldots, L_n\}$ of e such that c' is a resolvent of d' and e'. By induction hypothesis, there are derivations D_1 of $\Longrightarrow F$ from $\Longrightarrow F, K_i$ $(i = 1, \ldots, m)$, and D_2 of $\Longrightarrow F$ from $\Longrightarrow F, L_j$ $(j = 1, \ldots, n)$. Let K and L be the literals of d' and e', resp., resolved upon. Now, by adding to the succedent of each sequent of D_2 the literal K, a derivation of $\Longrightarrow F, K$ from $\Longrightarrow F, K, L_j$ $(j = 1, \ldots, n)$ is obtained (except, perhaps a few more interchange steps are needed). But the latter sequents are either obtained by thinning from sequents $\Longrightarrow F, L_j$ with $L_j \neq L$ or are the sequent $\Longrightarrow F, K, L$ which obtains from an axiom by ($\neg$S), thinning, and interchange. So we have a derivation D_2° of $\Longrightarrow F, K$ from the sequents $\Longrightarrow F, L_j$ with $L_j \neq L$. Let D be D_2° followed by D_1. Then D is the wanted derivation. Application of the result just shown to the empty clause yields the assertion. $\square$

Note that to a forward resolution refutation corresponds a backward affirmation in the cut-free sequent calculus. Note also that to a resolution refutation tree corresponds a sequent derivation dag. This dag is a tree only if no factorization is involved in the resolution refutation. It also implies that a resolution refutation tree can be transformed efficiently to a derivation in the connection calculus with factorization. Since for every resolution refutation there is a resolution refutation tree which is at most exponentially longer, it follows that the cut-free sequent calculus as well as the connection calculus with factorization can simulate resolution at exponential cost. And, in fact, the number of proof steps is exponential in terms of the number of resolution steps in the worst case, as is shown in (Eder, 1992) where it is proved that the number of Herbrand instances needed and hence the size of the matrix may blow up exponentially. It is interesting to note, however, that — although the number of paths blows up double exponentially — still the number of paths that have actually to be checked is exponential in the size of the resolution refutation.

4.4. The Cut Rule, Definitions, Introduction of Tautologies, Skolemization

The *tautology rule* (Taut) for the sequent calculus reads $\dfrac{D \to D, \Gamma \Longrightarrow \Theta}{\Gamma \Longrightarrow \Theta}$. The cut can be simulated in the cut-free sequent calculus augmented by (Taut), namely by (Th), ($\to$A), and (Taut) with D being the cut formula. Note that (Taut) does not fulfill the subformula property. Also, adding the rule $\dfrac{}{D|\overline{D}}$ to the tableau calculus yields a calculus which can efficiently simulate the full sequent calculus.

Definition 9. *A definition w.r.t. a set of sentences $S \subseteq \mathfrak{S}^{par}$ is the universal closure of a formula $L \leftrightarrow D$ where $L = P(x_1, \ldots, x_n)$ for some predicate symbol P which neither occurs in D nor in a sentence of S, and where $x_1, \ldots, x_n$ are the free variables of D.*

The *definition rule* (Def) reads $\dfrac{A, \Gamma \Longrightarrow \Theta}{\Gamma \Longrightarrow \Theta}$ where A is a definition w.r.t. Γ and Θ. The cut can be simulated in the cut-free sequent calculus augmented by (Def), namely by (Th), ($\to$A), (Int), (Con), ($\wedge$A), and (Def) with A being a definition $P \leftrightarrow D$ where D is the cut formula and P is a new nullary[5] predicate symbol.

Definitions can be eliminated at exponential cost in the full sequent calculus by simple expansion. This is not possible in the cut-free sequent calculus. There the cost is non-elementary, by Statman's theorem. Introduction of tautologies $D \to D$ as axioms makes no sense since they can be obtained from axioms by ($\to$S). Introduction of definitions as axioms into the cut-free sequent calculus cannot simulate the cut rule efficiently. Such axioms cannot contribute to the proof since they contain a new predicate symbol and therefore, by the subformula property, cannot occur in a derivation. For the connection method this means that considering the pair $\langle L, D \rangle$ as a connection does not help whereas it seems that introducing a definition as a new clause (of the non-normal form connection calculus) can simulate the cut. Note that the short proofs of Statman's formulas in the full sequent calculus make essential use of non-normal form and that also any definition containing a quantifier is non-normal form. Similarly, it seems that allowing to add tautological clauses $\{D, \neg D\}$ in the connection method allows simulation of the full sequent calculus.

M. Baaz and A. Leitsch have shown in (Baaz and Leitsch, 1992) that the cut rule can be simulated in clausal logic through extension using re-Skolemization. Introduction of Skolem function symbols allows a similar speed-up of proofs as the cut rule. However, through transformation to prenex normal form the speed-up through Skolemization is destroyed as shown in (Baaz and Leitsch, 1994). Independently it has been shown in (Eder, 1992) that the cut-free sequent calculus can be simulated by resolution via the structure-preserving normal form transformation. The cut rule as well as introduction of definitions can be simulated by the extension rule.

5. CLASSIFICATION OF PROOF CALCULI

In the last section it has been argued that analytic calculi allow a comparatively efficient proof search with a search tree whose branching factor is finite, whereas the cut rule gives rise to an infinite branching factor unless a complex device is used to delay decisions taken in the search to a later stage of the search process. However, clauses in resolution can be viewed as a kind of sequents of atomic formulas lifted to the first order level.[6] Then the resolution rule is the cut rule of the sequent calculus lifted to the first order level through unification. So resolution is actually a calculus based entirely on the cut rule. Still, search in resolution does do not have an infinite branching factor. In fact, resolution is the most frequently used calculus in automated theorem proving, and very efficient theorem provers have been built with it. On the other hand, despite the fact that resolution uses the cut rule and despite Statman's result, shortest proofs in the cut-free sequent calculus are only exponentially longer than in resolution in the worst case. So, how can these discrepancies be explained?

The answer is that we have to distinguish between affirmative and refutation calculi and between forward and backward reasoning. Resolution is a refutation calculus whose rules are applied forward. The sequent calculus is a calculus usable for affirmation or for refutation. If the cut rule is removed, it remains complete for affirmation, but not for refutation. In the last section we considered it for forward and for backward reasoning.

In the case of resolution, the only rule is essentially the cut rule applied in a forward direction and used for refutation. Thus only analytic atomic cuts occur, in the sense that the cut formulas are atomic subformulas of the input sentence. This explains why the branching factor of the search tree is finite and why the lengths of shortest proofs of Statman's formulas are non-elementary.

In order to get a better feeling of the properties of rules such as the cut rule, we have to ask what is a calculus.

Definition 10. *A* deduction relation *on a set $\mathfrak{X}$ is a pair $\langle \mathfrak{X}, \rhd \rangle$ where $\rhd$ is a relation between $\mathfrak{X}^*$ and $\mathfrak{X}$, i.e., $\rhd \subseteq \mathfrak{X}^* \times \mathfrak{X}$.*

Definition 11. *Let $\mathcal{D}$ be a deduction relation $\langle \mathfrak{X}, \rhd \rangle$ and let $U \subseteq \mathfrak{X}$. Then*

1. *A derivation from U in $\mathcal{D}$ is a finite sequence $\langle X_1, \ldots, X_n \rangle$ of elements of $\mathfrak{X}$ such that for each $j = 1, \ldots, n$ one of the following two propositions holds.*

   (a) $X_j \in U$.

   (b) There are $j_1, \ldots, j_k < j$ such that $\langle X_{j_1}, \ldots, X_{j_k} \rangle \rhd X_j$.

2. *Let $X \in \mathfrak{X}$. A derivation of X from U in $\mathcal{D}$ is a derivation $\langle X_1, \ldots, X_n \rangle$ from U in $\mathcal{D}$ such that $X_n = X$.*

3. *An element $X \in \mathfrak{X}$ is derivable from U in $\mathcal{D}$, in symbols $U \vdash_{\mathcal{D}} X$, if there is a derivation of X from U in $\mathcal{D}$. Instead of $\emptyset \vdash_{\mathcal{D}} X$ we write $\vdash_{\mathcal{D}} X$.*

Definition 12. *A locally sound deduction relation is a deduction relation $\langle \mathfrak{S}^{\mathrm{par}}, \rhd \rangle$ on the set $\mathfrak{S}^{\mathrm{par}}$ of sentences such that, for all $S \subseteq \mathfrak{S}$ and for all $F_1, \ldots, F_k, F \in \mathfrak{S}^{\mathrm{par}}$ with $\langle F_1, \ldots, F_k \rangle \rhd F$, the following implication holds. If $S \models F_1, \ldots, S \models F_k$ then $S \models F$.*

Note that this is equivalent to $\forall^{\mathrm{par}} F_1, \ldots, \forall^{\mathrm{par}} F_k \models \forall^{\mathrm{par}} F$ where $\forall^{\mathrm{par}} F$ denotes the universal closure of the result of renaming in F the parameters to new variables. A simple induction argument yields

Proposition 13. (soundness of locally sound deduction relations) *Let $\mathcal{D}$ be a locally sound deduction relation. Let $S \subseteq \mathfrak{S}$ and $F \in \mathfrak{S}$ with $S \vdash_{\mathcal{D}} F$. Then $S \models F$.*

All proof calculi are based on some deduction relation. For a Frege-Hilbert calculus, this is a locally sound deduction relation $\mathcal{D}$ on the set $\mathfrak{S}^{\mathrm{par}}$ of sentences. In some calculi, however, the objects occurring in a derivation (elements of $\mathfrak{X}$) are not sentences but sentences augmented by some additional structure (e.g. sequents in the sequent calculus) or ripped of some of their structure (e.g. clauses in the resolution calculus). In these calculi, each parameter-free sentence F allowed as input to the calculus must first be translated to an element $\psi(F)$ of $\mathfrak{X}$. The concept of a deduction relation defined above has to be augmented for such a calculus with the function ψ.

Definition 14. *By a* standard calculus *we mean a quadruple $\langle \mathfrak{E}, \mathfrak{X}, \psi, \rhd \rangle$ such that*

1. *$\mathfrak{E} \subseteq \mathfrak{S}$.*

2. *$\langle \mathfrak{X}, \rhd \rangle$ is a deduction relation.*

3. $\psi: \mathfrak{E} \to \mathfrak{X}$.

Example 15. *Every Frege-Hilbert calculus can be viewed as a standard calculus* $\langle \mathfrak{E}, \mathfrak{X}, \psi, \rhd \rangle$ *where* $\mathfrak{E}$ *is the set* $\mathfrak{S}$ *of parameter-free sentences,* $\mathfrak{X}$ *is the set* $\mathfrak{S}^{\text{par}}$ *of sentences,* $\psi: \mathfrak{S} \to \mathfrak{S}^{\text{par}}$ *is given by* $\psi(F) := F$, *and* $\rhd$ *is the relation on* $\mathfrak{S}^{\text{par}*} \times \mathfrak{S}^{\text{par}}$ *given by the rules of the calculus.*

Example 16. *Resolution is a standard calculus* $\langle \mathfrak{E}, \mathfrak{X}, \psi, \rhd \rangle$ *where* $\mathfrak{E}$ *is the set of universal closures of disjunctions of literals of* $\mathfrak{L}$, $\mathfrak{X}$ *is the set of clauses built from literals of* $\mathfrak{L}$, $\psi(F)$ *is the clause representing the sentence* $F \in \mathfrak{E}$, *and* $\langle X_1, X_2 \rangle \rhd X$ *if and only if the clause* X *is a resolvent of the clauses* X_1 *and* X_2.

Definition 17. *The* sequent calculus *(SC) is the standard calculus* $\langle \mathfrak{E}, \mathfrak{X}, \psi, \rhd \rangle$ *where*

1. $\mathfrak{E}$ *is the set* $\mathfrak{S}$ *of parameter-free sentences.*

2. $\mathfrak{X}$ *is the set of sequents.*

3. $\psi(F)$ *is the sequent* $\implies F$, *for every parameter-free sentence* F.

4. $\rhd$ *is the relation between* $\mathfrak{X}^*$ *and* $\mathfrak{X}$ *defined by the axiom scheme and rules given above.*

The cut-free sequent calculus *(cfSC) is defined the same way except that the cut rule is not considered as a rule of the calculus.*

Definition 18. *Let* C *be a standard calculus* $\langle \mathfrak{E}, \mathfrak{X}, \psi, \rhd \rangle$ *and let* $S \subseteq \mathfrak{E}$. *Then* $\psi(S) := \{\psi(F) \mid F \in S\}$. *Now, let* $F \in \mathfrak{E}$.

1. *A derivation from* S *in* C *is a derivation from* $\psi(S)$ *in* $\langle \mathfrak{X}, \rhd \rangle$.

2. *A derivation of* F *from* S *in* C *is a derivation of* $\psi(F)$ *from* $\psi(S)$ *in* $\langle \mathfrak{X}, \rhd \rangle$.

3. F *is derivable from* S *in* C, *in symbols* $S \vdash_C F$, *if* $\psi(S) \vdash_{\langle \mathfrak{X}, \rhd \rangle} \psi(F)$. *Instead of* $\emptyset \vdash_C F$ *we write* $\vdash_C F$.

Now we can make a first classification of proof calculi.

Definition 19. *An* affirmative calculus *is a standard calculus used for proving* $\vdash_C F$ *for some* $F \in \mathfrak{S}$. *A* refutation calculus *is a standard calculus used for proving* $S \vdash_C \bot$ *for some* $S \subseteq \mathfrak{S}$. *A* forward calculus *is a standard calculus used in such a way that premises are generated before conclusions.* *A* backward calculus *is a standard calculus used in such a way that conclusions are generated before premises.*

For the sequent calculus and for a parameter-free sentence F, the sequent $\psi(F)$ is $\implies F$. On the other hand, not every sequent occurring in a derivation has the form $\implies F$. But in order to define a property of local soundness for standard calculi in a similar way as for deduction relations, it is necessary to associate a formula F with each sequent S. We shall denote this by $S\phi F$ where $\phi \subseteq \mathfrak{X} \times \mathfrak{S}^{\text{par}}$.

Definition 20. *Let $\mathfrak{X}$ be a set, let $\phi \subseteq \mathfrak{X} \times \mathfrak{S}^{\text{par}}$, let $S \subseteq \mathfrak{S}$ be a set of parameter-free sentences, and let $X \in \mathfrak{X}$. Then $S \models_\phi X$ means that for every sentence $F \in \mathfrak{S}^{\text{par}}$ with $X\phi F$, the proposition $S \models F$ holds.*

Definition 21. *A locally sound calculus is a standard calculus $\langle \mathfrak{E}, \mathfrak{X}, \psi, \triangleright \rangle$ such that there exists a ϕ such that the following propositions hold.*

1. *$\phi \subseteq \mathfrak{X} \times \mathfrak{S}^{\text{par}}$.*

2. *For all $X \in \mathfrak{X}$ and $F, G \in \mathfrak{S}^{\text{par}}$, the following implication holds. If $X\phi F$ and $X\phi G$ then $F \sim G$.*

3. *$\psi(F)\phi F$ for all $F \in \mathfrak{E}$.*

4. *For all $S \subseteq \mathfrak{E}$ and for all $X_1, \ldots, X_k, X \in \mathfrak{X}$ with $\langle X_1, \ldots, X_k \rangle \triangleright X$, the following implication holds. If $S \models_\phi X_1, \ldots, S \models_\phi X_k$ then $S \models_\phi X$.*

We call ϕ a correspondence relation *of the calculus.*

Every Frege-Hilbert calculus is a locally sound calculus with ϕ being the equality relation $\{\langle F, F \rangle \mid F \in \mathfrak{S}^{\text{par}}\}$ on the set $\mathfrak{S}^{\text{par}}$ of sentences. If $S \subseteq \mathfrak{S}$ and $F \in \mathfrak{S}^{\text{par}}$ then $S \models_\phi F$ holds if and only if $S \models F$ holds.

Resolution is also a locally sound calculus where $X\phi F$ holds if and only if F is a universal closure of a disjunction of parameter-free literals and X is the clause representing F. If $S \subseteq \mathfrak{S}$ and $X\phi F$ then $S \models_\phi X$ holds if and only if $S \models F$ holds.

The sequent calculus is locally sound with the relation ϕ being given by:
$$(A_1, \ldots, A_\mu \implies B_1, \ldots, B_\nu)\phi F \quad \text{iff} \quad F = (\neg A_1 \vee \cdots \vee \neg A_\mu \vee B_1 \vee \cdots \vee B_\nu).$$

Proposition 22. (soundness of locally sound calculi) *Let $C = \langle \mathfrak{E}, \mathfrak{X}, \psi, \triangleright \rangle$ be a locally sound calculus. Let $S \subseteq \mathfrak{E}$ and $F \in \mathfrak{E}$ such that $S \vdash_C F$. Then $S \models F$.*

Proof: We use the notations of the above definitions. Let $\langle X_1, \ldots, X_n \rangle$ be a derivation of F from S in C. For all $G \in S$ it holds $\psi(G)\phi G$. Therefore, for all sentences H, if $\psi(G)\phi H$ then $S \models H$. Hence $S \models_\phi \psi(G)$. By induction on j it follows that $S \models_\phi X_j$ for $j = 1, \ldots, n$. In particular $S \models_\phi X_n$. But $\psi(F)\phi F$, i.e. $X_n\phi F$. Hence $S \models F$. $\qquad\qquad \square$

The full sequent calculus is complete in the sense that $S \models F$ implies $S \vdash_{\text{SC}} F$. By the cut elimination theorem, every valid sentence of $\mathfrak{L}$ is derivable in the cut-free sequent calculus. If $\models F$ then $\vdash_{\text{cfSC}} F$. However, it does not hold that if $S \models F$ then $S \vdash_{\text{cfSC}} F$. In particular, cfSC is not complete for refutation.

Now, what is a cut-free calculus? Requiring a locally sound calculus guarantees that each proof step in the calculus has its counterpart in first order logic.[7] However, this does not suffice to prove any useful results on the complexity of proving. Namely, every calculus $\mathcal{C}$ can be coded into a cut-free calculus $\mathcal{C}'$ as follows. Let F be a non-trivial valid input sentence. Then F has at least two possibly negated instances of subformulas, F_0 and F_1 with $F_0 \models F$ and $F_1 \models F$. Now, any derivation D of F in $\mathcal{C}$ can be coded as a sequence of 0's and 1's: $\langle b_1, \ldots, b_n \rangle$. Let F_D be the sentence $F \vee F_{b_1} \vee \cdots \vee F_{b_n}$. Let $\mathcal{C}'$ have the axioms F_D where D is a derivation of F in $\mathcal{C}$, and the rule $\frac{F_D}{F}$. If $\mathcal{C}$ is a locally sound calculus then $\mathcal{C}'$ is a locally sound calculus which is cut-free in the sense that the subformula property holds. If the deduction relation of $\mathcal{C}$ is decidable then so is the deduction relation of $\mathcal{C}'$. In $\mathcal{C}'$ each valid sentence has a derivation in two steps. But each derivation of a sentence F in $\mathcal{C}'$ is a derivation of F in $\mathcal{C}$ slightly recoded, and vice versa. So any adequate (sound and complete) calculus (even the full sequent calculus) can hide behind a cut-free calculus. So we have to be more careful about a definition of 'cut-free'.

The completeness of most proof calculi is based on the fundamental theorem by Herbrand, Gödel, Gentzen, Henkin, Hasenjäger, Beth, and Smullyan. It can be found in (Stegmüller and Varga von Kibéd, 1984).

Definition 23. *A regular sequence is a finite sequence* $\langle A_1, \ldots, A_n \rangle$ *of sentences of* $\mathfrak{S}^{\text{par}}$ *such that each* A_j *has one of the following forms*

1. $\forall x F \to F\{x \backslash t\}$

2. $F\{x \backslash t\} \to \exists x F$

3. $\exists x F \to F\{x \backslash a\}$ *where a occurs neither in F nor in any A_i with $i < j$*

4. $F\{x \backslash a\} \to \forall x F$ *where a occurs neither in F nor in any A_i with $i < j$.*

Then the set $R = \{A_1, \ldots, A_n\}$ *is a regular set. The parameters a in 3. and 4. are the eigen parameters of R. The formulas $\forall x F$ in 1. and in 4. and $\exists x F$ in 2. and in 3. are the principal sentences.*

Note that if R is a regular set then every interpretation for $\mathfrak{L}$ can be extended to an interpretation on $\mathfrak{L}^{\text{par}}$ which is a model of R. Therefore $F \in \mathfrak{S}$ and $R \models F$ implies $\models F$. On the other hand, every proof of a sentence $F \in \mathfrak{S}$ in the sequent calculus can be transformed to a derivation of F from a regular set using only propositional rules (in particular the cut).

Proposition 24. (Fundamental Theorem) *Let F be a valid sentence from $\mathfrak{S}$. Then F follows propositionally from a regular set whose principal sentences are substitution instances of subformulas of F.*

Definition 25. *Let $\mathcal{C}$ be a locally sound calculus* $\langle \mathfrak{E}, \mathfrak{X}, \psi, \triangleright \rangle$ *with correspondence relation* ϕ. *Let* $f, g, h \colon \mathbb{N} \to \mathbb{N}$. *Assume that, for all* $X_1, \ldots, X_k, X \in \mathfrak{X}$ *with* $\langle X_1, \ldots, X_k \rangle \triangleright X$ *the following conditions hold.*

1. $k \leq f(\deg F)$.

2. *For every sentence $F \in \mathfrak{S}^{\text{par}}$ with $X \phi F$, there are sentences $F_1, \ldots, F_k \in \mathfrak{S}^{\text{par}}$ with $X_1 \phi F_1, \ldots, X_k \phi F_k$, such that*

   (a) *Each F_i is propositionally equivalent to a disjunction of possibly negated substitution instances of subformulas of F.*

   (b) *There is a regular set R whose eigen parameters do not occur in F and whose cardinality is at most $g(\deg F)$ such that F follows propositionally from $\{F_1, \ldots, F_k\} \cup R$.*

   (c) $\deg F_i \leq h(\deg F)$ *for $i = 1, \ldots, k$.*

Then we say that $\mathcal{C}$ is an f, g, h-bounded cut-free calculus.

The cut-free sequent calculus is an f, g, h-bounded cut-free calculus with $f(n) = 2$, $g(n) = 1$, $h(n) = 2n + 1$.

Proposition 26. *Let f, g, h be polynomials on $\mathbb{N}$ and let $\mathcal{C}$ be an f, g, h-bounded cut-free calculus. Then the lengths of the shortest proofs of Statman's sentences in $\mathcal{C}$ have non-elementary growth.*

Proof: Assume there is a proof $\langle X_1, \ldots, X_r \rangle$ of the n-th Statman sentence F_n in $\mathcal{C}$ in r steps. Then $\psi(F_n) = X_r$. According to the definition of an f, g, h-bounded cut-free calculus, we obtain a sequence $G = \langle G_1, \ldots, G_r \rangle$ with $X_i \phi G_i$, and a regular set R. The construction starts from G_r and goes backward. Corresponding to each backward step in $\mathcal{C}$, new premises are introduced into G, and a new regular set is added to R by set union. There are no eigen parameters since F_n is in disjunctive normal form. By assumption there is a $c > 0$ such that $f(x), g(x), h(x) \leq x^c$ for all x. Hence all sentences in the derivation have at most degree $(\deg F_n)^{c^r}$. Let m be the cardinality of R. Then $m \leq r \cdot (\deg F_n)^{c^{r+1}} \leq e(r + \deg F_n)$ for some elementary function e. But, by Statman's theorem, the growth of m for in terms of n is non-elementary while the growth of $\deg F_n$ is elementary (exponential). Since the sum and the composition of two elementary functions is elementary, it follows that r has non-elementary growth in terms of n and therefore also in terms of the length of F_n. $\square$

6. COMPLEXITY MEASURES FOR SEARCH

6.1. Formal Systems

In the following we assume an alphabet Σ of cardinality $N \geq 2$.

Definition 27. *A formal system over the alphabet Σ is a recursive binary relation $\mathfrak{D} \subseteq \Sigma^* \times \Sigma^*$ on the set of strings. If $P \mathfrak{D} F$ holds then we say that the string P is a proof of the string F in $\mathfrak{D}$. We also say that F is provable in $\mathfrak{D}$.*

Assume a sufficiently powerful computation model $\mathcal{M}$ such as a multitape Turing machine or a programming language suited for efficient implementation of algorithms. Then we can speak of the number of time steps that an algorithm formulated in $\mathcal{M}$ takes to terminate. By an *algorithm on* Σ we mean an algorithm formulated in $\mathcal{M}$ which takes a string from Σ^* as its input and tries to produce a string of Σ^* as its output.

Definition 28. *A formal system* $\mathfrak{D}$ *is* verbose *if the following conditions hold.*

1. $P\mathfrak{D}F$ implies $|F| \leq |P|$.

2. $P\mathfrak{D}F$ can be decided in $\mathcal{M}$ in time $O(|P|)$.

If we have an arbitrary formal system $\mathfrak{D}$ then it can be checked whether a string P is a proof of a string F. Now add a complete transcript of the checking process to the string P yielding a string P'. Let the formal system $\mathfrak{D}'$ be defined as follows. $Q\mathfrak{D}'F$ if and only if there is a P such that $P\mathfrak{D}F$ and $Q = P'$. Then $\mathfrak{D}'$ is a verbose formal system with the same provable strings as $\mathfrak{D}$. So it is not a severe restriction to require of a formal system that it is verbose. In a sense this restriction means that proofs are required to be spelled out in detail.

6.2. Proof Complexity and Search Complexity

Now we want to give a measure of how complex it is to prove a string in a formal system. There are two issues of interest, namely the length of the shortest proof and the time needed by an efficient search algorithm to find a proof. Accordingly, we define two complexity measures: the *proof complexity* and the *search complexity*. Roughly, the proof complexity of a valid sentence F is the time needed to read a proof of F, and the search complexity is the time needed to write (find) a proof of F.

Definition 29. *Let $\mathfrak{D}$ be a formal system on Σ and let $F \in \Sigma^*$. Then the* proof complexity $p^{\mathfrak{D}}(F)$ *of F in $\mathfrak{D}$ is the length of a shortest proof of F in $\mathfrak{D}$ if F is provable, and ∞ otherwise.*

In order to define the search complexity, we have to consider algorithms which take as input a string F and try to produce as output a proof P of F. Since we have assumed a fixed computation model, there exists an enumeration of all algorithms on Σ. Search strategies for formal systems can be viewed as functions mapping each input string F to an infinite sequence $\langle P_1, P_2, \dots \rangle$ of output strings which are to be tested whether they are proofs of F in the formal system. Now we define a universal strategy which does not depend on the formal system but nevertheless will serve as a strategy which is best in terms of time complexity modulo a constant factor for all verbose formal systems.

Definition 30. *Let $F \in \Sigma^*$ and let n and k be two positive integers with $k \leq n$. Then the string $F_{nk} \in \Sigma^*$ is defined as follows. If the k-th algorithm of the enumeration* *terminates upon input F in at most 2^{n-k} time steps then F_{nk} is its output. Otherwise F_{nk} is the empty string.*

Definition 31. *The* universal strategy *is the function $\mathcal{U}$ mapping each $F \in \Sigma^*$ to the infinite sequence $\langle F_{11}, F_{21}, F_{22}, F_{31}, F_{32}, F_{33}, F_{41}, \ldots \rangle$.*

Definition 32. *Let $\mathfrak{D}$ be a verbose formal system on Σ and let $F \in \Sigma^*$. Then the* search complexity *$\mathfrak{s}^{\mathfrak{D}}(F)$ of F in $\mathfrak{D}$ is the number 2^n where n is the smallest positive integer such that there is a positive integer $k \leq n$ such that F_{nk} is a proof of F in $\mathfrak{D}$. If such an n does not exist then $\mathfrak{s}^{\mathfrak{D}}(F) := \infty$.*

Proposition 33. *Let $\mathfrak{D}$ be a verbose formal system on Σ. Then the following propositions hold.*

1. *There is a constant c and an algorithm on Σ which produces from every input $F \in \Sigma^*$ in at most $c \cdot \mathfrak{s}^{\mathfrak{D}}(F)$ time steps a proof P of F in $\mathfrak{D}$ if F is provable in $\mathfrak{D}$, and which does not terminate otherwise. Moreover, $|P| \leq \mathfrak{s}^{\mathfrak{D}}(F)$.*

2. *For every algorithm on Σ there is a positive constant c such that for every input $F \in \Sigma^*$ the algorithm either produces no proof of F in $\mathfrak{D}$ or takes at least $c \cdot \mathfrak{s}^{\mathfrak{D}}(F)$ time steps to produce a proof of F in $\mathfrak{D}$.*

Proof: To show 1., consider the following algorithm, suitably formulated in $\mathcal{M}$.

> Upon input F, generate successively the members of $\mathcal{U}(F)$ testing each whether it is a proof of F in $\mathfrak{D}$. If a proof of F is found then yield it as an output and terminate.

It is easily verified that the sequence $\mathcal{U}(F)$ can be generated and tested in $\mathcal{M}$ up to a member F_{nk} in time $O(2^n)$. If F is provable then a proof $P = F_{nk}$ is found when $2^n = \mathfrak{s}^{\mathfrak{D}}(F)$, hence in time $O(\mathfrak{s}^{\mathfrak{D}}(F))$. Then $|P| = |F_{nk}| \leq 2^{n-k} \leq \mathfrak{s}^{\mathfrak{D}}(F)$. Otherwise the algorithm does not terminate. To show 2., let an algorithm on Σ be given. It is the k-th algorithm of the enumeration for some positive integer k. The constant $c := 2^{-k-1}$ does the job. $\qquad\square$

It is obvious that for every verbose formal system $\mathfrak{D}$ there is a positive constant c such that $\mathfrak{p}^{\mathfrak{D}}(F) \leq \mathfrak{s}^{\mathfrak{D}}(F) \leq c \cdot N^{\mathfrak{p}^{\mathfrak{D}}(F)}$.

Note that the above results imply that there is a strategy which is best, in terms of time complexity modulo a constant factor, for all *adequate* (i.e., sound and complete) proof calculi for first order logic. But there is no best proof calculus. In fact, from Blum's speed-up theorem[8] (Blum, 1967) (see also (Enderton, 1977)) follows:

Proposition 34. *Let $f \colon \mathbb{N}^2 \to \mathbb{N}$ be recursive. Then there is an infinite sequence $\langle F_0, F_1, \ldots \rangle$ of valid sentences such that the following holds. For every adequate verbose formal system $\mathfrak{D}$ there is an adequate verbose formal system $\mathfrak{D}'$ and a nonnegative integer n_0 such that for all $n \geq n_0$ it holds $f(n, \mathfrak{p}^{\mathfrak{D}'}(F_n)) < \mathfrak{p}^{\mathfrak{D}}(F_n)$ and $f(n, \mathfrak{s}^{\mathfrak{D}'}(F_n)) < \mathfrak{s}^{\mathfrak{D}}(F_n)$.*

Kurt Gödel has remarked in (Gödel, 1936) that such a speed-up by an arbitrary recursive function is achieved when going from a system for i-th order logic to a system for $(i+1)$-th order logic. This is much more than is achieved through the cut rule, but of course causes the same and even more problems for automation than the cut rule. For example, in higher order logic unification is undecidable. But it indicates that locally sound deduction relations (which can be viewed as calculi reasoning entirely within first order logic) might not be able to achieve the potential efficiency of systems allowing a detour through higher order logic for proving first order sentences. A simple example are the sentences

$$\forall v\, P(0, v, s(v))$$
$$\wedge\quad \forall u \forall w \Big(P\big(u, s(0), w\big) \to P\big(s(u), 0, w\big) \Big)$$
$$\wedge\quad \forall u \forall v \forall w \forall x \Big(P\big(s(u), v, w\big) \wedge P\big(u, w, x\big) \to P\big(s(u), s(v), x\big) \Big)$$
$$\to\quad \exists x\, P\big(s^n(0), 0, x\big)$$

whose Herbrand complexities are $\geq p(n, 0)$ where p is the Peter-Ackermann function but which have short proofs in second order logic. Since the speed-up through the cut rule is only primitive recursive, the lengths of their shortest proofs even in the full sequent calculus grow faster than any primitive recursive function.

From what has been said so far follows

Proposition 35. *Let $\mathfrak{D}$ and $\mathfrak{D}'$ be two verbose formal systems with the same set $\mathfrak{A}$ of provable strings. If every proof P of any string F in $\mathfrak{D}$ can be transformed to a proof P' of F in $\mathfrak{D}'$ with $|P'| \leq f(|P|)$ then $\mathfrak{p}^{\mathfrak{D}'}(F) \leq f(\mathfrak{p}^{\mathfrak{D}}(F))$ for each $F \in \mathfrak{A}$. If, moreover, P' is computable from P in time $g(|P|)$ in $\mathcal{M}$ where g is monotonically increasing then there is a constant c such that $\mathfrak{s}^{\mathfrak{D}'}(F) \leq c \cdot g(\mathfrak{s}^{\mathfrak{D}}(F))$ for all $F \in \mathfrak{A}$. On the other hand there is a constant c such that, if $f : \mathbb{N} \to \mathbb{N}$ is monotonically increasing and if there is a proof P in $\mathfrak{D}$ of a string F such that each proof of F in $\mathfrak{D}'$ has length $\geq f(|P|)$ then $\mathfrak{p}^{\mathfrak{D}'}(F) \geq f(\mathfrak{p}^{\mathfrak{D}}(F))$ and $\mathfrak{s}^{\mathfrak{D}'}(F) \geq \mathfrak{p}^{\mathfrak{D}'}(F) \geq f(\log_N \mathfrak{s}^{\mathfrak{D}}(F) - c)$.*

This means that results stating that every proof of a formula in one calculus can/cannot be efficiently transformed to a proof in another calculus yield not only estimates comparing complexities of proof in the two calculi but also estimates comparing complexities of search.

For example, let $\mathfrak{D}$ and $\mathfrak{D}'$ be the formal system realizing the cut-free and the full sequent calculus, resp. Then $\mathfrak{p}^{\mathfrak{D}'}(F) \leq \mathfrak{p}^{\mathfrak{D}}(F)$ for all sentences F, and there is a positive constant c such that $\mathfrak{s}^{\mathfrak{D}'}(F) \leq c \cdot \mathfrak{s}^{\mathfrak{D}}(F)$. On the other hand, there is an infinite sequence $\langle F_1, F_2, \ldots \rangle$ of valid sentences with $|F_n| \to \infty$ and $\mathfrak{p}^{\mathfrak{D}'}(F_n) \to \infty$ ($n \to \infty$), and a non-elementary function $f : \mathbb{N} \to \mathbb{N}$ such that $\mathfrak{p}^{\mathfrak{D}}(F_n) \geq f(\mathfrak{p}^{\mathfrak{D}'}(F_n))$ and $\mathfrak{s}^{\mathfrak{D}}(F_n) \geq f(\mathfrak{s}^{\mathfrak{D}'}(F_n))$ for all $n \in \mathbb{N}$. This gives the somewhat paradoxical result that not only proof complexity but also search complexity is better modulo a constant factor in the full sequent calculus than in the cut-free sequent calculus.

7. CONCLUSION

Now, let us see how some of the known calculi can be classified as to affirmation/refutation, forward/backward, with cut/cut-free, search with finite/infinite branching factor.

	with cut	cut-free
affirmation forward	Frege-Hilbert calculi, sequent calculus, natural deduction; infinite branching	cut-free sequent calculus; infinite branching; non-elementary slow-down through cut elimination
affirmation backward	backward Frege-Hilbert calculi, backward sequent calculus; infinite branching, can be overcome only through a sort of unification on the level of formulas	analytic calculi (backward sequent calculus, tableau calculus, connection method); finite branching; non-elementary slow-down through cut elimination
refutation forward	Frege-Hilbert calculi, full sequent calculus, resolution, tableau calculus (branch closure is an application of the cut rule); finite or infinite branching	no complete calculus possible
refutation backward	no known calculus; infinite branching	no complete calculus possible

Note that a calculus can usually be viewed from different viewpoints. First, it can be applied forward or backward or some combination of both. Second, the objects occurring in a derivation may be interpreted in different ways. E.g., for a given input formula F in conjunctive normal form in the resolution calculus, a resolvent occurring in the refutation can either be interpreted as the formula G which it represents in the usual setting, or it can be interpreted as the formula $F \to G$. From the former viewpoint, resolution is a part of the forward sequent calculus with cut for refutation. From the latter viewpoint, resolution is a forward affirmative calculus with a semi-analytic cut in the sense that all formulas occurring in the derivation are composed of possibly negated substitution instances of subformulas (a liberalized version of the subformula property). The connection method is a backward cut-free sequent calculus for affirmation, but it can also be viewed as a forward calculus with semi-analytic cut, proving for an input sentence F that $P \to F$ holds where P is the conjunction of the paths still to be proved complementary. Thus, depending on the viewpoint, cut-freeness and infinite branching mean different things.

Usually, infinite branching cannot be proved for a class of calculi since a node with infinite branching factor can always be transformed to a binary tree with infinitely many nodes, and the resulting calculus is often in the same class.

University of Salzburg
Salzburg, Austria

NOTES

1. In the proof of his Hauptsatz, Gentzen shows how applications of the cut rule can be eliminated from a tree derivation in the full sequent calculus. Note however that an arbitrary derivation of a formula can be transformed to a tree derivation of the same formula (at exponential cost at most).

2. Note however that a sequent calculus with the cut rule restricted to analytic cuts also yields an analytic calculus.

3. The connection method has been formulated by W. Bibel for arbitrary sentences in negation normal form, and this is what we assume here. Of course, the connection method can easily be generalized to full first order logic. Then the active path would consist of signed subformulas of the input sentence. Subformulas with positive/negative sign would correspond to members of the succedent/antecedent in the sequent derivation. On the other hand, the connection method — as most calculi in automated theorem proving — is for simplicity usually only applied to sentences in clausal form, since an arbitrary first order sentence can be efficiently transformed to a clausal form, called definitional form, using definitions and Skolemization as shown in (Eder, 1992).

4. The transform of a sequent is obtained by negating the sentences of its antecedent and moving them to the succedent and then transforming each of the sentences to negation normal form. The number of operational inferences of the derivation does not increase. It may merely be necessary to insert a few applications of the interchange rule which are not counted as inference steps in the corresponding connection proof.

5. since D has no free variables

6. the negative literals of the clause corresponding to the atomic formulas in the antecedent of the sequent and the positive literals of the clause corresponding to the atomic formulas in the succedent of the sequent.

7. This excludes, for example, higher order calculi which can bring a tremendous speed-up also for first order sentences.

8. The speed-up theorem says that for every recursive $g: \mathbb{N}^2 \to \mathbb{N}$ there is a recursive $h: \mathbb{N} \to \{0, 1\}$ whose computation by Turing machines has speed-up g in the sense that for every Turing machine M computing $h(n)$ from n in $t(n)$ steps there is a Turing machine M' computing $h(n)$ from n in $s(n)$ steps where $g(n, s(n)) < t(n)$ for all sufficiently large $n \in \mathbb{N}$. The idea of the proof of Prop. 34 is the following. Choose g so that it grows sufficiently stronger than f, e.g., $g(n, N) := n \cdot f(n, n \cdot N)$ if f is monotonically increasing. Computation of $h(n)$ can be done by proving a sentence F_n which is either the sentence $T \to h(n) = 0$ or the sentence $T \to h(n) = 1$ for some suitable first order theory T. In an adequate verbose formal system $\mathfrak{D}$, a proof of F_n can be found in time $O(\mathfrak{s}^{\mathfrak{D}}(F_n))$. Therefore there is a Turing machine M computing $h(n)$ in time $c \cdot \mathfrak{s}^{\mathfrak{D}}(F_n)$. For $n \in \mathbb{N}$ let C_n be the computation of $h(n)$ from n by the Turing machine M' obtained from M by the speed-up theorem. Adding to $\mathfrak{D}$ the pairs $\langle C_n, F_n \rangle$ yields the required system $\mathfrak{D}'$.

REFERENCES

Baaz, M., Egly, U., and Leitsch, A. (1998). Extension Methods in Automated Deduction. In Bibel, W. and Schmitt, P., editors, *Automated Deduction — A Basis for Applications*, volume II, part 4, chapter 12, pages 331–360. Kluwer.

Baaz, M. and Leitsch, A. (1992). Complexity of resolution proofs and function introduction. *Annals of Pure and Applied Logic*, 57:181–215.

Baaz, M. and Leitsch, A. (1994). On Skolemization and Proof Complexity. *Fundamenta Informaticae*, 20:353–379.

Beth, E. W. (1955). Semantic entailment and formal derivability. *Mededlingen der Koninklijke Nederlandse Akademie van Wetenschappen*, 18(13):309–342.

Beth, E. W. (1959). *The Foundations of Mathematics*. North-Holland, Amsterdam.

Bibel, W. (1987). *Automated Theorem Proving*. Artificial Intelligence. Vieweg, Braunschweig/Wiesbaden, second edition.

Bibel, W. (1992). *Deduktion, Automatisierung der Logik*, volume 6.2 of *Handbuch der Informatik*. Oldenbourg Verlag.

Blum, M. (1967). A machine-independent theory of the complexity of recursive functions. *Journal of the ACM*, 14:322–366.

Eder, E. (1992). *Relative Complexities of First Order Calculi*. Artificial Intelligence. Vieweg, Wiesbaden. (Wolfgang Bibel and Walther von Hahn, editors).

Eder, E. (1996). Backward reasoning in systems with cut. In *Artificial Intelligence and Symbolic Computation, International Conference, AISMC-3*, Lecture Notes in Computer Science 1138, pages 339–353. Springer.

Egly, U. (1998). Cuts in Tableaux. In Bibel, W. and Schmitt, P., editors, *Automated Deduction — A Basis for Applications*, volume I, part 1, chapter 4, pages 103–132. Kluwer.

Enderton, H. B. (1977). Elements of recursion theory. In Barwise, J., editor, *Handbook of Mathematical Logic*, volume 90 of *Studies in Logic and the Foundations of Mathematics*, chapter C.1. North-Holland.

Feferman, S. et al. (1986). *Kurt Gödel. Collected Works*, volume I. Oxford University Press.

Frege, G. (1879). Begriffsschrift, eine der arithmetischen nachgebildete Formelsprache des reinen Denkens. Halle. Engl. Transl. in (Heijenoort, 1967), pp. 1–82.

Gentzen, G. (1935). Untersuchungen über das logische Schließen. *Mathematische Zeitschrift*, 39:176–210, 405–431. Engl. transl. in (Szabo, 1969), pp. 68–131.

Gödel, K. (1936). Über die Länge von Beweisen. Ergebnisse eines mathematischen Kolloquiums 7, 23–24. Printed in German and in Engl. transl. in (Feferman et al., 1986).

Heijenoort, J. v. (1967). *From Frege to Gödel. A Source Book in Mathematical Logic, 1879–1931*. Source Books in the History of the Sciences. Harvard University Press, Cambridge, Massachusetts.

Orevkov, V. P. (1979). Lower Bounds for Increasing Complexity of Derivations after Cut Elimination. *Zapiski Nauchnykh Seminarov Leningradskogo Otdeleniya Matematicheskogo Instituta im V. A. Steklova AN SSSR*, 88:137–161. English translation in *J. Soviet Mathematics*, 2337–2350, 1982.

Smullyan, R. M. (1971). *First-Order Logic*. Ergebnisse der Mathematik und ihrer Grenzgebiete. Springer-Verlag, Berlin, Heidelberg, New York.

Statman, R. (1979). Lower bounds on herbrand's theorem. *Proc. AMS*, 75.

Stegmüller, W. and Varga von Kibéd, M. (1984). *Strukturtypen der Logik*, volume 3 of *Probleme und Resultate der Wissenschaftstheorie und Analytischen Philosophie*. Springer-Verlag, Berlin, Heidelberg, New York, Tokyo.

Szabo, M. E. (1969). *The Collected Papers of Gerhard Gentzen*. Studies in Logic and the Foundations of Mathematics. North-Holland, Amsterdam.

UWE EGLY AND HANS TOMPITS

SOME STRENGTHS OF NONMONOTONIC REASONING

1. INTRODUCTION

A characteristic feature of human reasoning is its ability to draw *rational* conclusions in situations where not all relevant information is known. In fact, except for the most trivial cases, we always reason *with an incomplete body of knowledge* describing the current situation we are arguing about. We are constantly forced to make assumptions which may turn out to be wrong in the light of new, more accurate information. Consequently, statements inferred by this kind of reasoning are *defeasible*, i.e., capable of being defeated. Because of this feature, logics formalizing such reasoning patterns are called *nonmonotonic*.

Although our natural common sense constantly employs the adoption and retraction of assumptions based on incomplete information, formalizing nonmonotonic inferences turns out to be rather intricate. The most prominent approaches of nonmonotonic reasoning systems are *default logic* (Reiter, 1980), *circumscription* (McCarthy, 1980), and *autoepistemic logic* (Moore, 1983). Furthermore, principles employed in data bases and logic programming, like the *closed world assumption* (Reiter, 1978) and *negation as failure* (Clark, 1978), are closely related to nonmonotonic inference formalisms.

Since in daily life situations, defeasible assumptions are used to make the reasoning process simpler, one of the motivations in the development of nonmonotonic logics was the expectation that the inclusion of nonmonotonic rules should make automated reasoning systems likewise more efficient. For instance, in the context of reasoning about actions, instead of specifying a myriad of situations where a planned action might go wrong, the idea is to include a simple nonmonotonic rule stating that, if there is no evidence to the contrary, assume that the action will succeed.

Unfortunately, although nonmonotonic inference strategies work fine for humans, in formalizations they actually *increase* the inherent complexity. More exactly, it turned out that the relevant reasoning tasks in almost all nonmonotonic systems are computationally more involving than the corresponding reasoning tasks in classical logic (see, e.g., (Gottlob, 1992; Eiter and Gottlob, 1993); an overview can be found

S. Hölldobler (ed.), Intellectics and Computational Logic, 125–141.

in (Cadoli and Schaerf, 1993)). Evidently, it is hardly surprising that this predicament is generally regarded as a major setback with respect to the original motivations. On the other hand, these complexity results show only one side of the coin: they describe how nonmonotonic logics behave *in the worst case*, but they give no indication *how we might benefit from nonmonotonic rules*. Interestingly, this aspect of nonmonotonic reasoning has not received its due attention so far.

As indicated by the above example given for the domain of actions, an advantage of nonmonotonic rules is the capability to represent knowledge in a *compact form*. This mechanism has been investigated in (Cadoli et al., 1994) and (Cadoli et al., 1995). Roughly speaking, the results in these papers show that propositional nonmonotonic systems allow a "super-compact" representation of knowledge as compared to classical (monotonic) logic. We will briefly discuss this issue in Section 3.

Another benefit of nonmonotonic rules is their potential to decrease the proof length of formulae in quite a drastic way. This phenomenon is of relevance if nonmonotonic techniques are embedded in automated deduction systems, because then the relative efficiency of the chosen calculus becomes a crucial property. In this paper, we will survey some results taken from (Egly and Tompits, 1997a; Egly and Tompits, 1998; Tompits, 1998), which show to what extent the presence of nonmonotonic rules can simplify the search for proofs.

The idea of our approach is the following. We compare, in specific first-order cut-free sequent calculi for default logic and for circumscription, the minimal proof length of "purely classical" proofs—i.e., of proofs *without* applications of nonmonotonic rules—with proofs where nonmonotonic rules have been applied. The proof systems we use are slight extensions of cut-free sequent-type calculi developed in (Bonatti, 1996) and (Bonatti and Olivetti, 1997b) for propositional versions of default logic and circumscription, respectively. It turns out that, for certain infinite classes of formulae $(H_k)_{k \geq 1}$, the minimal proof length of any classical proof of H_k is *nonelementary in k*, i.e., the proof length is greater than $s(k)$, where $s(0) := 1$ and $s(n+1) := 2^{s(n)}$, for all $n \geq 0$, but a short (elementary) proof with *one* application of a nonmonotonic rule exists.

To see the huge difference between these two proof lengths, consider the case $k = 5$. The proof with the nonmonotonic rule consists of about 300 sequents, but the minimal "classical" proof length is greater than 10^{19200}. Now, assume that we have a computer with a clock frequency of 1GHz, performing one inference step per clock cycle. Furthermore, according to modern physics, the age of the universe is about 20 billion years, which is about 10^{17} seconds. Even if that computer has run since the big bang, only 10^{26} inference steps would be computed!

The reason for the extreme decrease of proof length lies in the fact that the nonmonotonic rules can simulate certain instances of the cut rule, and the formulae under consideration possess short proofs in a classical sequent system with cut (like Gentzen's LK_{cut}), but any such proof without cut is nonelementary. The formulae we respectively use are modifications of formulae introduced in (Orevkov, 1979).

A motivation for this comparison between classical and nonmonotonic proof length can be given as follows. Usually, nonmonotonic techniques are applied in case a classical proof cannot be found. Although this is a reasonable procedure in decidable systems, it is not appropriate for undecidable systems like first-order logic. Indeed, if we integrate nonmonotonic rules into first-order theorem provers, we have to invoke nonmonotonic mechanisms *after a certain amount of time*, whenever the goal formula has not been proven classically up to this point. Accordingly, it may happen that a formula is provable both classically *and* with the help of nonmonotonic rules. The results described in this paper show that, in certain cases, the theorem prover may easier find a proof because the presence of nonmonotonic rules yields a much smaller search space.

The paper is organized as follows. In Section 2, we review the basic facts about default logic and circumscription, and in Section 3, we briefly discuss how nonmonotonic systems can represent knowledge in a compact form. Section 4 deals with results on the proof complexity of nonmonotonic calculi, and we conclude with some general comments in Section 5.

2. PRELIMINARIES

Throughout this paper we use a first-order language consisting of *variables, function symbols, predicate symbols, logical connectives, quantifiers* and *punctuation symbols.* *Terms* and *formulae* are defined according to the usual formation rules. We will identify nullary predicate symbols with *propositional atoms*, and nullary function symbols with (*object*) *constants*. A formula is *closed* iff it contains no free variables; and a formula is *ground* iff it is both closed and quantifier-free.

As classical proof system we use the (cut-free) sequent calculus LK, whose formal objects are (*classical*) *sequents* $S := \Gamma \vdash \Sigma$, where Γ, Σ are finite sequences of first-order formulae. (Γ is the *antecedent* of S, and Σ is the *succedent* of S.) Recall that the informal meaning of a sequent $A_1, \ldots, A_n \vdash B_1, \ldots, B_m$ is the same as the informal meaning of the formula $(\bigwedge_{i=1}^{n} A_i) \rightarrow (\bigvee_{i=1}^{m} B_i)$. Moreover, LK_0 is the propositional version of LK, i.e., without quantifier rules and restricted to ground formulae, and LK_{cut} is the system LK extended by the *cut rule*:

$$\frac{\Gamma_1 \vdash \Sigma_1, A \qquad A, \Gamma_2 \vdash \Sigma_2}{\Gamma_1, \Gamma_2 \vdash \Sigma_1, \Sigma_2} \; cut$$

The *length* of a proof (in any of the systems used in this paper) is defined as the number of sequents occurring in it. We will use "$|\alpha|$" to denote the length of a proof α.

Let t be the function with $t(x, 0) := 2^x$ and $t(x, n+1) := 2^{t(x,n)}$, for all $n \in \mathbf{N}$. A function $f : \mathbf{N} \rightarrow \mathbf{N}$ is called *elementary* iff there is a Turing machine M and a constant $c \in \mathbf{N}$ such that M computes f and the computing time $T_M(x)$ of M with input x obeys the relation $T_M(x) \leq t(x, c)$, for all $x \in \mathbf{N}$.

Note that, for each fixed $n \in \mathbf{N}$, the function $t(\cdot, n)$ itself is elementary. On the other hand, the function s, defined by $s(n) := t(0, n)$, is *nonelementary*.

2.1. Default Logic

In default logic, nonmonotonic conclusions are sanctioned by special kinds of inference rules, called *defaults*. In contrast to classical inference rules, defaults contain additional consistency conditions which must be satisfied in order to apply the default.

Definition 1. *Let $A, B_1, \ldots, B_n, C$ be first-order formulae. A default d is an expression of the form*

$$\frac{A : B_1, \ldots, B_n}{C}.$$

A is the prerequisite, *$B_1, \ldots, B_n$ are the* justifications, *and C is the* consequent *of the default d. If $n = 0$, the default is* justification-free, *and if $A = \top$, the default is* prerequisite-free. *If $A, B_1, \ldots, B_n, C$ are closed (ground) formulae, the default is closed (ground). A set of defaults D is closed (ground) iff all defaults in it are closed (ground).*

A default theory is an ordered pair $T = \langle W, D \rangle$, where W is a set of closed formulae, called the premises *of T, and D is a set of defaults. We say that T is closed iff D is closed, and T is finite iff both W and D are finite.*

Informally, the default d has the following meaning: If A is believed, and $B_1, \ldots, B_n$ are *consistent with what is believed* (i.e., there is no evidence that $\neg B_1, \ldots, \neg B_n$ hold), then C is believed.

Furthermore, for a default theory $T = \langle W, D \rangle$, the set W represents absolute (though in general incomplete) knowledge about the world ("hard facts"), whilst D represents *defeasible* knowledge ("rules of thumb").

Fundamental objects in default logic are *extensions* of closed default theories. Intuitively, an extension characterizes a possible totality of beliefs that an agent may adopt on the basis of a given default theory $T = \langle W, D \rangle$. To be more precise, a set E of closed formulae serves as an extension of T iff a certain *fixed-point condition* is obeyed. We will not give a detailed definition of an extension though, because we are only interested in a proof-theoretical characterization of default logic (see (Reiter, 1980) for a comprehensive definition of an extension).

There are two basic reasoning tasks in the context of default logic, namely *brave reasoning* and *skeptical reasoning*. The former task is the problem of checking whether a closed formula A belongs to *at least one* extension of a given closed default theory T, whereas the latter task examines whether A belongs to *all* extensions of T. It is well-known that these problems are intrinsically "harder" than classical reasoning. More exactly, for the propositional case, both reasoning tasks are at the second level of the polynomial hierarchy (Gottlob, 1992), whilst for the general first-order case, already in the seminal paper (Reiter, 1980) it was shown that checking whether E is an extension of a given default theory T is not recursively enumerable.

2.2. Circumscription

Reasoning under circumscription is based on the idea that objects satisfying a certain predicate expression P are considered to be the *only* objects satisfying it. Roughly speaking, the positive information about P is treated as a *sufficient part* of a definition of P, and the circumscription of P "completes" this definition by *minimizing the extension of P*. In this process, one can determine which predicate symbols shall be minimized, which predicate symbols shall retain their meaning, and which ones can be varied. Contrary to classical reasoning, under circumscription, logical consequence is evaluated in terms of models which are *minimal* in a certain sense.

Definition 2. *Let M, N be two models of a finite set of closed formulae S, and let P, R be finite sets of predicate symbols such that P and R are disjoint. We call M a $(P; R)$-submodel of N, symbolically $M \preceq_{P;R} N$, iff the following conditions are satisfied:*

1. *M and N have the same domain;*

2. *M and N have the same interpretation for each predicate symbol in R;*

3. *the interpretation of each predicate symbol $F \in P$ in M is a subset of the interpretation of F in N.*

Note that in condition 3, if F is a propositional atom, then F must be true in N whenever it is true in M.

Clearly, the relation $\preceq_{P;R}$ is a pre-order. The minimal objects with respect to this ordering are called $(P; R)$-*minimal*. Observe that in the relation $\preceq_{P;R}$, all function symbols are allowed to vary.

Definition 3. *Under the circumstances of Definition 2, we say that a formula A is* entailed by S (with circumscribed predicate symbols P and fixed predicate symbols R), written $S \models_{P;R} A$, iff A is true in all $(P; R)$-minimal models of S.

Historically, circumscription was proposed in (McCarthy, 1980), where the minimization principle is encoded as a certain *second-order formula*. Subsequently, circumscription has been advanced by many AI researchers resulting in a whole family of different circumscription techniques. Our version of circumscription is a special form of the one given in (Lifschitz, 1985).

3. COMPACT REPRESENTATIONS

Extending a logic (or a calculus) by additional inference principles often simplifies the representational task. As an example, consider the small Prolog-like logic program in Figure 1. This program, which is assumed to run on some retailer's computer, consists of a data base of invalid credit cards and some further program clauses. Variables start

```
inval(4987_7765_9995_7348).
inval(8667_1438_7691_2299).
inval(4711_4712_4813_0700).

credit(std,A)        :-  A < 1000.
credit(gold,A)       :-  A < 5000.
credit(platinum,A)   :-  A < 100000.
pay(CC,K,A)          :-  ~inval(CC), credit(K,A).
```

Figure 1 The Prolog program clauses for the credit card example.

with an uppercase letter whereas constants are written in lowercase letters including "_" and digits. The predicate credit checks whether there is enough credit for the purchase, depending on the kind of the credit card (given by the first argument). The pay predicate checks whether the credit card (number) given in CC is not invalid and whether there is enough credit for the amount A of money for the transaction. Let us process the query G

```
:-  pay(1745_9821_4437_8476, gold, 898).
```

and explain where nonmonotonicity plays an important role.

In order to solve G, we unify it with the only program clause with predicate pay, resulting in the new goal H of the following form:

```
:-  ~inval(1745_9821_4437_8476), credit(gold,898).
```

The first subgoal of H is ~ inval(1745_9821_4437_8476) which checks that the given credit card is *not* invalid. Observe that ~ is not classical negation but *negation as failure*. The goal immediately behind the negation sign is processed in the standard way but the result (succeed or fail) is complemented. In our case here, the query

```
:-  inval(1745_9821_4437_8476).
```

fails because the given credit card number is not in the data base. As a result, the (sub)goal ~inval(1745_9821_4437_8476) succeeds. Therefore, the second subgoal of H is processed and eventually goal G succeeds. Hence, the credit card payment is possible.

What is the benefit of such a procedure with negation as failure with respect to the size of the problem representation? Observe that, in our credit card example above, only a small number of credit cards are declared invalid. Hence, the size of the data base consisting of all invalid credit cards is small as compared to the size of the data base containing all credit cards. If no negation as failure is available, the problem representation changes: all valid credit card numbers have to be stored because the "classical" validity check would then be formalized by a predicate `valid(CC)` occurring in the single clause which contains the predicate `pay`—with the undesirable consequence that the data base has to be changed to hold all *valid* credit cards. This new data base is much larger than the old one.

The above example shows that nonmonotonic inference principles are beneficial for the representation of problems. Although in this particular instance there is only a minor saving from a theoretical point of view (only a constant saving is possible), the practical benefit is obvious. There are slightly more complicated examples of propositional data bases where an exponential saving can be achieved.

The possibility for such "super-compact" representations with nonmonotonic inference principles has been analysed in (Cadoli et al., 1994) and (Cadoli et al., 1995). Basically, these investigations show that if nonmonotonic knowledge bases are "compiled" into classical logic (i.e., the compiled theory derives the same class of queries as the nonmonotonic knowledge base), then there are cases where the compiled knowledge base is exponentially larger than the original nonmonotonic knowledge base. Thus, the intractability of nonmonotonic reasoning can be regarded as the price one has to pay for having super-compact representations of knowledge.

In our example above, the program with negation as failure can be compiled into a "completed program" (together with an appropriate equality theory) (Clark, 1978). Again, the logic program is a more compact representation than the completed program.

Representation of knowledge is only one aspect—the *processing* of knowledge is another one. The intriguing question related with the second aspect is whether we can benefit from nonmonotonic rules (or from information provided by them) in the reasoning process as well. This question, however, does not have a unique answer, since a compact representation is, in some sense, contrary to fast reasoning. Assume we have a propositional Prolog program P and, instead of negation as failure, the *closed world assumption* (CWA). The basic idea underlying CWA is the extension of P by the set

$$ext(P) \quad = \quad \{\neg A \mid A \text{ is a positive propositional literal and } P \not\models A\}.$$

Instead of compiling the program (i.e., extending P by $ext(P)$), one can use P alone and add an inference rule of the form "if A is not derivable, then $\neg A$ is derivable". In this case, one has a more compact representation but reasoning takes longer if negative literals are required. Although the additional reasoning time seems to be neglectable because of the decidability of propositional Horn clauses in polynomial time, matters get more complicated in clause logic or in first-order logic.

In the next section, we consider the question whether the particular information provided by nonmonotonic inference rules—specified with respect to some given calculus—can yield a significant improvement regarding the search for proofs.

4. CLASSICAL VERSUS NONMONOTONIC PROOF LENGTHS

It is interesting to observe that it took more than a decade before two of the most widely used nonmonotonic systems are characterized in purely proof-theoretical terms (see, e.g., (Amati et al., 1996; Niemelae, 1996a; Niemelae, 1996b; Olivetti, 1992)). In the following, we use cut-free sequent-style systems based on the calculi introduced by Bonatti and Olivetti for brave propositional default reasoning, and for propositional circumscription, respectively (Bonatti, 1996; Bonatti and Olivetti, 1997b).[1] The advantage of using these calculi lies in the fact that they are conceptually simple, and, at the same time, well-suited for proof-theoretical investigations.

Both of the calculi proposed by Bonatti and Olivetti enjoy a common structure: they consist of a propositional sequent calculus for classical logic, a propositional *anti-sequent* calculus (the so-called *complementary* system, taking care of the consistency check), and certain nonmonotonic inference rules.

The ingenious part in their approach is the use of the complementary system *formalizing invalid statements*, i.e., an *anti-sequent* $\Gamma \not\vdash \Theta$ is provable in the complementary sequent calculus iff the corresponding classical sequent $\Gamma \vdash \Theta$ is invalid. In general, two logical systems are *complementary* iff objects derivable in one system are *not* derivable in the other system and vice versa.[2]

Since the subsequent results depend on the use of first-order formulae, the calculi of Bonatti and Olivetti have to be slightly generalized. However, due to the undecidability of first-order logic, there cannot be a both sound and complete formalization of *arbitrary* first-order non-theorems. If one wants to construct such a sound and complete axiomatization of invalid statements, only a *decidable* subclass of first-order formulae can be used. In fact, for the intended purpose, it suffices to generalize only the "classical parts" of the systems of Bonatti and Olivetti, but the "complementary parts" remain propositional. Basically, this means that general closed first-order formulae are allowed as possible queries instead of only propositional formulae. It can easily be shown that the soundness and completeness results given in (Bonatti, 1996; Bonatti and Olivetti, 1997b) hold for these versions of the calculi as well (for a thorough presentation of the topics discussed in this section, see (Tompits, 1998)).

4.1. Proof-Theoretical Framework

In this section, we present the calculus B for brave default reasoning and the calculus C for circumscription, respectively, which are slight generalizations of the systems proposed in (Bonatti, 1996; Bonatti and Olivetti, 1997b). In the next section, we discuss how the nonmonotonic inference rules, present in these calculi, can tremendously reduce proof length.

In the remainder of this paper, the expression $\hat{s}$ stands for the set of elements occurring in a sequence s. Furthermore, the empty sequence is denoted by ϵ.

Let us start with a description of the complementary sequent calculus LK_0^r.

Definition 4. *Let Γ and Θ be finite sequences of ground formulae. An* anti-sequent *is an ordered pair of the form $\Gamma \not\vdash \Theta$.*

The anti-sequent $\Gamma \not\vdash \Theta$ is said to be *true* iff the corresponding classical sequent $\Gamma \vdash \Theta$ is invalid.

LOGICAL RULES

$$\frac{\Gamma_1, A, \Gamma_2, B, \Gamma_3 \nvdash \Theta}{\Gamma_1, (A \wedge B), \Gamma_2, \Gamma_3 \nvdash \Theta} \wedge l^r$$

$$\frac{\Gamma \nvdash \Theta_1, A, \Theta_2}{\Gamma \nvdash \Theta_1, (A \wedge B), \Theta_2} \wedge r_1^r \qquad\qquad \frac{\Gamma \nvdash \Theta_1, B, \Theta_2}{\Gamma \nvdash \Theta_1, (A \wedge B), \Theta_2} \wedge r_2^r$$

$$\frac{\Gamma_1, A, \Gamma_2 \nvdash \Theta}{\Gamma_1, (A \vee B), \Gamma_2 \nvdash \Theta} \vee l_1^r \qquad\qquad \frac{\Gamma_1, B, \Gamma_2 \nvdash \Theta}{\Gamma_1, (A \vee B), \Gamma_2 \nvdash \Theta} \vee l_2^r$$

$$\frac{\Gamma \nvdash \Theta_1, A, \Theta_2, B, \Theta_3}{\Gamma \nvdash \Theta_1, (A \vee B), \Theta_2, \Theta_3} \vee r^r$$

$$\frac{\Gamma_1, \Gamma_2 \nvdash \Theta_1, A, \Theta_2}{\Gamma_1, (A \to B), \Gamma_2 \nvdash \Theta_1, \Theta_2} \to l_1^r \qquad\qquad \frac{\Gamma_1, B, \Gamma_2 \nvdash \Theta}{\Gamma_1, (A \to B), \Gamma_2 \nvdash \Theta} \to l_2^r$$

$$\frac{\Gamma_1, A, \Gamma_2 \nvdash \Theta_1, B, \Theta_2}{\Gamma_1, \Gamma_2 \nvdash \Theta_1, (A \to B), \Theta_2} \to r^r$$

$$\frac{\Gamma_1, \Gamma_2 \nvdash \Theta_1, A, \Theta_2}{\Gamma_1, \neg A, \Gamma_2 \nvdash \Theta_1, \Theta_2} \neg l^r \qquad\qquad \frac{\Gamma_1, A, \Gamma_2 \nvdash \Theta_1, \Theta_2}{\Gamma_1, \Gamma_2 \nvdash \Theta_1, \neg A, \Theta_2} \neg r^r$$

STRUCTURAL RULES: CONTRACTION

$$\frac{\Gamma_1, A, \Gamma_2, A, \Gamma_3 \nvdash \Theta}{\Gamma_1, A, \Gamma_2, \Gamma_3 \nvdash \Theta} cl^r \qquad\qquad \frac{\Gamma \nvdash \Theta_1, A, \Theta_2, A, \Theta_3}{\Gamma \nvdash \Theta_1, A, \Theta_2, \Theta_3} cr^r$$

Figure 2 Rules of the anti-sequent calculus LK$_0^r$.

The axioms of the complementary sequent calculus LK$_0^r$ are anti-sequents of the form $\Phi \nvdash \Psi$, where Φ and Ψ are finite sequences of closed atomic formulae such that $\hat{\Phi} \cap \hat{\Psi} = \emptyset$ and $(\{\bot\} \cap \hat{\Phi}) \cup (\{\top\} \cap \hat{\Psi}) = \emptyset$. The inference rules of LK$_0^r$ comprise of the logical rules and the structural rules, which are given in Figure 2.[3]

Theorem 5. *Let $S = \Gamma \nvdash \Theta$ be an anti-sequent, and let $d(S)$ be the logical complexity of S, i.e., the number of logical connectives occurring in S.*

(i) *If S is provable in* LK$_0^r$, *then it is true.*

(ii) *If S is true, then there is a proof α of S such that $|\alpha| \leq d(S) + 1$.*

AXIOMS

$$\Gamma; \varepsilon \vdash \varepsilon; \varepsilon$$

LOGICAL RULES

$$\frac{\Gamma \vdash A}{\Gamma; \varepsilon \vdash A; \varepsilon} \; l_1 \qquad\qquad \frac{\Gamma \not\vdash A}{\Gamma; \varepsilon \vdash \varepsilon; A} \; l_2$$

$$\frac{\Gamma; \varepsilon \vdash \Sigma_1; \Theta_1 \quad \Gamma; \varepsilon \vdash \Sigma_2; \Theta_2}{\Gamma; \varepsilon \vdash \Sigma_1, \Sigma_2; \Theta_1, \Theta_2} \; cu$$

$$\frac{\Gamma; \Delta_1, \Delta_2 \vdash \Sigma; \Theta_1, A, \Theta_2}{\Gamma; \Delta_1, (A:B_1,\ldots,B_n/C), \Delta_2 \vdash \Sigma; \Theta_1, \Theta_2} \; d_1$$

$$\frac{\Gamma; \Delta_1, \Delta_2 \vdash \Sigma_1, \neg B, \Sigma_2; \Theta}{\Gamma; \Delta_1, (A:\ldots,B,\ldots/C), \Delta_2 \vdash \Sigma_1, \Sigma_2; \Theta} \; d_2$$

$$\frac{\Gamma_1, C, \Gamma_2; \Delta_1, \Delta_2 \vdash \Sigma_1; \Theta_1, \neg B_1, \ldots, \neg B_n, \Theta_2 \qquad \Gamma_1, \Gamma_2; \varepsilon \vdash \Sigma_2, A; \varepsilon}{\Gamma_1, \Gamma_2; \Delta_1, (A:B_1,\ldots,B_n/C), \Delta_2 \vdash \Sigma_1, \Sigma_2; \Theta_1, \Theta_2} \; d_3$$

STRUCTURAL RULES: CONTRACTION

$$\frac{\Gamma_1, A, \Gamma_2, A, \Gamma_3; \Delta \vdash \Sigma; \Theta}{\Gamma_1, A, \Gamma_2, \Gamma_3; \Delta \vdash \Sigma; \Theta} \; cl_1^d$$

$$\frac{\Gamma; \Delta_1, (A:B_1,\ldots,B_n/C), \Delta_2, (A:B_1,\ldots,B_n/C), \Delta_3 \vdash \Sigma; \Theta}{\Gamma; \Delta_1, (A:B_1,\ldots,B_n/C), \Delta_2, \Delta_3 \vdash \Sigma; \Theta} \; cl_2^d$$

$$\frac{\Gamma; \Delta \vdash \Sigma_1, A, \Sigma_2, A, \Sigma_3; \Theta}{\Gamma; \Delta \vdash \Sigma_1, A, \Sigma_2, \Sigma_3; \Theta} \; cr_1^d \qquad \frac{\Gamma; \Delta \vdash \Sigma; \Theta_1, A, \Theta_2, A, \Theta_3}{\Gamma; \Delta \vdash \Sigma; \Theta_1, A, \Theta_2, \Theta_3} \; cr_2^d$$

Figure 3 Additional axioms and rules of the calculus B.

Corollary 6. *The anti-sequent* $\Gamma \not\vdash \Theta$ *is provable in* LK_0^r *iff the classical sequent* $\Gamma \vdash \Theta$ *is not provable in* LK_0.

Next, the sequent calculus B for brave default reasoning will be introduced.

Definition 7. *By a* (brave) *default sequent we understand an ordered quadrupel of the form* $\Gamma; \Delta \vdash \Sigma; \Theta$, *where* Γ *and* Θ *are finite sequences of ground first-order* *formulae, Δ is a finite sequence of ground defaults, and Σ is a finite sequence of closed first-order formulae.*

A default sequent $\Gamma; \Delta \mathrel{\vdash\!\!\!\sim} \Sigma; \Theta$ is *true* iff there is an extension E of the default theory $\langle \hat{\Gamma}, \hat{\Delta} \rangle$ such that $\hat{\Sigma} \subseteq E$ and $\hat{\Theta} \cap E = \emptyset$ (E is called a *witness* of $\Gamma; \Delta \mathrel{\vdash\!\!\!\sim} \Sigma; \Theta$).

The default sequent calculus B consists of classical sequents, anti-sequents and default sequents. It incorporates the systems LK for classical sequents and LK$_0^r$ for anti-sequents. The additional axioms and inference rules of B are given in Figure 3.

Rules l_1 and l_2 respectively combine classical sequents and anti-sequents with default sequents. Rule cu is the rule of "classical union"; it allows the joining of information in case that no default is present. Rules d_1, d_2, and d_3 are the default introduction rules. More specifically, d_1 and d_2 sanction the introduction of defaults which are not "active" in the given context (in d_1, the prerequisite of the default cannot be derived, and, in d_2, the negation of a justification of the default is derivable), whilst d_3 is the "proper" default introduction rule—here, both the prerequisite and no negation of a justification can be derived. The structural rules were not part of Bonatti's original formulation, because he defined default sequents via *sets* rather than sequences as we do.

Theorem 8. *A default sequent is provable in* B *iff it is true.*

Finally, we introduce the circumscription calculus C.

Definition 9. *By a circumscription sequent we understand an ordered 5-tuple of the form* $\Lambda; \Gamma \vdash_{P;R} \Sigma$, *where* Λ *is a finite sequence of propositional atoms,* Γ *is a finite sequence of propositional formulae,* Σ *is a finite sequence of closed first-order formulae, and P, R are finite sets of propositional atoms such that* $(P \cup \hat{\Lambda}) \cap R = \emptyset$.

A circumscription sequent $\Lambda; \Gamma \vdash_{P;R} \Sigma$ is *true* iff for any $(P \cup \hat{\Lambda}; R)$-minimal model M of $\hat{\Gamma}$ satisfying $\hat{\Lambda}$, at least one element of $\hat{\Sigma}$ is true in M. Obviously, the circumscription sequent $\epsilon; \Gamma \vdash_{P;R} A_1, \ldots, A_n$ is the syntactical counterpart of $\hat{\Gamma} \models_{P;R} A_1 \vee \ldots \vee A_n$.

The circumscription sequent calculus C consists of classical sequents, anti-sequents and circumscription sequents. Similar to the system B, it incorporates the systems LK for classical sequents and LK$_0^r$ for anti-sequents. The additional inference rules for circumscription sequents are depicted in Figure 4.

Let us briefly explain these rules. The first two rules, C_1 and C_2, represent two opposing situations how circumscription sequents can be introduced: for rule C_1, it holds that if its premise is true then its conclusion is *vacuously* true, whilst rule C_2 states that classical entailment implies minimal entailment. Rule C_3 distinguishes the case when a minimized atom q is respectively true or false in a minimal model; similar considerations apply for rule C_4 and a fixed atom r. Incidentally, the latter rule implements a variant of the atomic cut rule, restricted to propositional variables from the fixed atoms R as cut formulae.

Theorem 10. *A circumscription sequent is derivable in* C *iff it is true.*

LOGICAL RULES

$$\frac{\Gamma_1, \neg p_1, \ldots, \neg p_n, \Gamma_2 \nvdash q}{\Lambda_1, q, \Lambda_2; \Gamma_1, \Gamma_2 \vdash_{\{p_1, \ldots, p_n\}; \emptyset} \Sigma} \; C_1 \qquad\qquad \frac{\Lambda, \Gamma \vdash \Sigma}{\Lambda; \Gamma \vdash_{P;R} \Sigma} \; C_2$$

$$\frac{\Lambda_1, q, \Lambda_2; \Gamma_1, \Gamma_2 \vdash_{P;R} \Sigma_1 \qquad \Lambda_1, \Lambda_2; \Gamma_1, \neg q, \Gamma_2 \vdash_{P;R} \Sigma_2}{\Lambda_1, \Lambda_2; \Gamma_1, \Gamma_2 \vdash_{P \cup \{q\}; R} \Sigma_1, \Sigma_2} \; C_3$$

$$\frac{\Lambda; \Gamma_1, r, \Gamma_2 \vdash_{P;R} \Sigma_1 \qquad \Lambda; \Gamma_1, \neg r, \Gamma_2 \vdash_{P;R} \Sigma_2}{\Lambda; \Gamma_1, \Gamma_2 \vdash_{P; R \cup \{r\}} \Sigma_1, \Sigma_2} \; C_4$$

For the rule C_1, the propositional atom q must be present.

STRUCTURAL RULES: CONTRACTION

$$\frac{\Lambda_1, q, \Lambda_2, q, \Lambda_3; \Gamma \vdash_{P;R} \Sigma}{\Lambda_1, q, \Lambda_2, \Lambda_3; \Gamma \vdash_{P;R} \Sigma} \; cl_1^c \qquad\qquad \frac{\Lambda; \Gamma_1, A, \Gamma_2, A, \Gamma_3 \vdash_{P;R} \Sigma}{\Lambda; \Gamma_1, A, \Gamma_2, \Gamma_3 \vdash_{P;R} \Sigma} \; cl_2^c$$

$$\frac{\Lambda; \Gamma \vdash_{P;R} \Sigma_1, A, \Sigma_2, A, \Sigma_3}{\Lambda; \Gamma \vdash_{P;R} \Sigma_1, A, \Sigma_2, \Sigma_3} \; cr^c$$

Figure 4   Additional rules of the calculus C.

4.2. Shortening Proofs

How can the nonmonotonic rules, present in the calculi B and C, be used to make the reasoning process simpler? The basic idea is to compare, in these specific calculi, the minimal proof length of "purely classical" proofs with proofs (of the same goal formula!) where nonmontonic rules have been applied. It turns out that, for some classes of formulae, the proof without applications of nonmonotonic rules is nonelementarily longer than the proof where nonmonotonic rules have been applied. Since for first-order cut-free sequent calculi the size of the search space is elementarily related to the minimal proof length if, say, breadth-first search is assumed, a nonelementary decrease of the search space is also achieved. Note that, in the absence of the nonmonotonic rules, the nonelementarily larger search space cannot be compensated by clever search strategies!

Our discussion is based on a sequence of formulae introduced in (Orevkov, 1979) which possess short LK$_{cut}$-proofs, with one application of the cut rule, but only extremely long (cut-free) LK-proofs. The short proofs in B and C result from the possibility that the particular instance of the cut rule, necessary to obtain a short LK$_{cut}$-proof, can be simulated by applications of nonmonotonic rules.

We begin with the definition of the sequence $(F_k)_{k\geq 1}$ of formulae, introduced in (Orevkov, 1979).

Definition 11. *Let* $(F_k)_{k\geq 1}$ *be the sequence of formulae where*

$$F_k := \forall x \left((\forall w_0 \exists v_0 \, p(w_0, x, v_0) \wedge C(x)) \rightarrow B_k(x)\right)$$

and

$$C(x) := \forall uvw \, (\exists y \, (p(y, x, u) \wedge \exists z \, (p(v, y, z) \wedge p(z, y, w))) \rightarrow p(v, u, w))$$
$$B_k(x) := \exists v_k \, (p(x, x, v_k) \wedge \exists v_{k-1} \, (p(x, v_k, v_{k-1}) \wedge \ldots \wedge \exists v_0 \, p(x, v_1, v_0)) \ldots).$$

Intuitively, $p(x, y, z)$ represents the relation $x + 2^y = z$, and F_k "computes" certain numbers using a recursive definition of the function $\varphi(x, y) := x + 2^y$.

Let $\mathsf{SK}(F_k) = (\forall w_0 \, p(w_0, b, g(w_0)) \wedge C(b)) \rightarrow B_k(b))$ be the skolemized form of F_k. The basic properties of F_k and $\mathsf{SK}(F_k)$ are summarized in the next proposition.

Proposition 12. (Orevkov, 1979) *Let* $(F_k)_{k\in\mathbb{N}}$ *be the infinite sequence of formulae defined above.*

(a) *There is an* $\mathsf{LK}_{\mathrm{cut}}$-*proof* ψ_k *of* $\vdash F_k$ *such that* $|\psi_k| \leq c_1 \cdot k + c_2$, *for some constants* c_1, c_2.

(b) *For any (cut-free)* LK-*proof* α *of* $\vdash F_k$ *or* $\vdash \mathsf{SK}(F_k)$, *it holds that* $|\alpha| \geq 2\cdot\mathsf{s}(k) + 1$.

Thus, eliminating the cut yields a nonelementary increase of proof length.

On the other hand, it is well-known that each $\mathsf{LK}_{\mathrm{cut}}$-proof using only closed cut formulae can easily be converted into a cut-free LK-proof of another end sequent, by simply replacing applications of cut by introductions of the connective "$\rightarrow$" in the antecedent of (classical) sequents. Moreover, this new proof has the same length as the original proof with cut. Applying a similar method to the $\mathsf{LK}_{\mathrm{cut}}$-proof ψ_k of $\vdash F_k$ yields an LK-proof ϕ_k of $\forall x \, (A_k(x) \rightarrow A_k(x)) \vdash F_k$, where A_k is the cut formula occurring in the proof ψ_k. The universal quantifier $\forall x$ is necessary because A_k contains the free variable x.

This short LK-proof ϕ_k can be used to obtain a short (cut-free) B-proof as follows. Intuitively, the construction is based on the idea that the cut-encoding formula $\forall x \, (A_k(x) \rightarrow A_k(x))$ is derived by means of default inference rules. Now, since the consistency check in B requires quantifier-free formulae, the quantifiers in $\forall x \, (A_k(x) \rightarrow A_k(x))$ have to be eliminated. As shown in (Egly and Tompits, 1997a) (and, more detailed, also in (Tompits, 1998)), this can be done with an at most triple-exponential increase of proof length. There are two main steps to achieve this: the first one is to skolemize the proof ϕ_k (eliminating essentially universal quantifiers), and the second one is to eliminate the remaining quantifiers by a technique similar to the method of constructing a Herbrand disjunction out of a given closed first-order formula containing only essentially existential quantifiers.[4] The result of these manipulations is a short LK-proof ϑ_k of a sequent $D_k \vdash SK(F_k)$, where D_k is a ground formula. This LK-proof, in turn, yields a short B-proof of the default sequent $T_k := \varepsilon; (T : D_k/D_k) \mathrel{\vdash\!\!\!\sim} SK(F_k); \varepsilon$, which is given below:

$$
\cfrac{
  \cfrac{
    \cfrac{\cfrac{\vartheta_k}{D_k \vdash SK(F_k)}}{D_k; \varepsilon \mathrel{\vdash\!\!\!\sim} SK(F_k); \varepsilon} \; l_1
    \qquad
    \cfrac{\cfrac{\xi_k}{D_k \not\vdash \neg D_k}}{D_k; \varepsilon \mathrel{\vdash\!\!\!\sim} \varepsilon; \neg D_k} \; l_2
  }{D_k; \varepsilon \mathrel{\vdash\!\!\!\sim} SK(F_k); \neg D_k} \; cu
  \qquad
  \cfrac{\cfrac{\vdash T}{\varepsilon; \varepsilon \mathrel{\vdash\!\!\!\sim} T; \varepsilon} \; l_1}{\;}
}{\varepsilon; (T : D_k/D_k) \mathrel{\vdash\!\!\!\sim} SK(F_k); \varepsilon} \; d_3
$$

(ξ_k is a short LK_0^r-proof, which can be obtained from Theorem 5.)

On the other hand, deriving $SK(F_k)$ "classically" in B is tantamount to deriving the default sequent $C_k := \varepsilon; \varepsilon \mathrel{\vdash\!\!\!\sim} SK(F_k); \varepsilon$ in B. However, each such B-proof of C_k is nonelementary in k, because it must incorporate an LK-proof of $\vdash SK(F_k)$ (cf. Proposition 12(b)). This discussion can be summarized as follows:

Theorem 13. *There is an infinite sequence of first-order formulae $(F_k)_{k\geq 1}$ and an infinite sequence of quantifier-free closed formulae $(D_k)_{k\geq 1}$ such that the following holds:*

(a) *There is a B-proof of $T_k = \varepsilon; (T : D_k/D_k) \mathrel{\vdash\!\!\!\sim} SK(F_k); \varepsilon$ whose length is triple-exponential in k.*

(b) *The minimal proof length of $C_k = \varepsilon; \varepsilon \mathrel{\vdash\!\!\!\sim} SK(F_k); \varepsilon$ in B is greater than $\mathbf{s}(k)$.*

We like to point out that a similar result does *not* hold if one simply assumes a default of the form $d := (T : A/F_k)$, for some formula A. The reason is that, due to the syntactical constraints of the system B, the formulae in the default must be ground, but any ground instance of F_k has a logical complexity which is nonelementary, hence, any B-proof using d is nonelementary too.

Now we turn our attention to the system C. Observe that, in order to simulate an application of cut, it is necessary that the cut formula occurs in *both* polarities in the input formula. In our case, the formula A_k occurs both positively *and* negatively in the sequent $\forall x\, (A_k(x) \to A_k(x)) \vdash F_k$. If we replace one occurrence of A_k by a globally new propositional atom q, then the simulation of cut breaks down.

Lemma 14. *Let $H_k := (\forall x\, (A_k(x) \to q)) \to F_k$ $(k \geq 1)$, where q is a propositional atom which does not occur elsewhere in A_i or F_i $(0 \leq i \leq k)$. Then, the length of any LK-proof α of $\vdash H_k$ is greater than $c \cdot \mathbf{s}(k)$, for some constant c.*

Proof: See (Egly and Tompits, 1998) or (Tompits, 1998). $\square$

Consider the circumscription sequent $S_k := \epsilon; r \to q \vdash_{q;\emptyset} H_k$, where r is a propositional atom not occurring in H_k. In contrast to the nonelementary lower bound on proof length in LK for $\vdash H_k$, the sequent S_k possesses a short C-proof. The reason is that the circumscription of the atomic formula q results in a classical sequent of the form $r \to q, \neg q \vdash H_k$, in which q has both a positive and a negative occurrence. This additional positive occurrence of q (given by the formula $\neg q$ in the antecedent of the sequent) allows to use "one half" of the cut-free part of the short $\mathsf{LK_{cut}}$-proof ψ_k of $\vdash F_k$, yielding a short LK-proof ϱ_k of $r \to q, \neg q \vdash H_k$.

The short C-proof of S_k has the following form:

$$
\cfrac{\cfrac{\cfrac{\not\vdash r, q}{r \to q \not\vdash q} \to l^r}{q; r \to q \vdash_{\emptyset;\emptyset} H_k} C_1 \qquad \cfrac{\varrho_k}{\epsilon; r \to q, \neg q \vdash_{\emptyset;\emptyset} H_k} C_2}{\epsilon; r \to q \vdash_{q;\emptyset} H_k} C_3, cr^c
$$

In contrast to this short C-proof, the "classical counterpart" of S_k, namely the sequent $C'_k := \epsilon; r \to q \vdash_{\emptyset;\emptyset} H_k$, has only nonelementary long C-proofs, for the following reasons. The sequent C'_k can only be proven by an application of rule C_2, with the classical sequent $W_k := r \to q \vdash H_k$ as the premise of this rule application. But the additional information given by $r \to q$ does not reduce the proof length mainly because q occurs only in one polarity in W_k, and consequently H_k must be proven, which is nonelementary according to Lemma 14.

Theorem 15. *There is an infinite sequence $(H_k)_{k \geq 1}$ of first-order formulae for which the following holds.*

(a) *There exists a C-proof of $S_k = \epsilon; r \to q \vdash_{q;\emptyset} H_k$ whose length is linear in k.*

(b) *The minimal proof length of $C'_k = \epsilon; r \to q \vdash_{\emptyset;\emptyset} H_k$ in C is greater than $c \cdot \mathsf{s}(k)$, for some constant c.*

In (Egly and Tompits, 1997b) it is shown that a similar result holds for Herbrand complexity as well, if circumscription is used as a preprocessing activity.[5]

5. CONCLUSION

We have discussed two topics concerning nonmonotonic reasoning, namely the possibility to get compact representations of knowledge and the influence of information provided by nonmonotonic reasoning on cut-free proofs. Although nonmonotonic reasoning is, in the worst case, harder than classical reasoning, the results just described demonstrate that the other way around is also possible: in the *best* case, nonmonotonic reasoning is much simpler than classical (cut-free) reasoning. Moreover, since the search space which has to be inspected by a prover is elementarily related to the length of a (shortest) cut-free proof (provided that a fair search strategy like breadth-first search or depth-first search with iterative deepening is used), the size of the search space remains elementary for the considered reasoning problems. This coincides with the general idea that nonmonotonic reasoning is considered as a fast, but *unsound* approximation of classical reasoning in the sense that, if a statement is classically derivable, then it is also derivable by nonmonotonic means.

Albeit the classes of formulae used to establish these results are constructed in regard to show the best case for the speed-up, one should observe that even simpler and more natural examples may exist, which become easier to prove by considering additional (relevant) knowledge.

Technische Universität Wien
Wien, Austria

NOTES

1. The same authors introduced also a calculus for skeptical default reasoning (Bonatti and Olivetti, 1997a); but we do not consider this system in the following—similar results as those described in this paper hold for (an extension of) the skeptical calculus as well.

2. The term "complementary proof-system" is due to Varzi (Varzi, 1990).

3. Note that the contraction rules are included for convenience only; they are not necessary in order to obtain completeness of the calculus.

4. This method derives from a technique presented in (Baaz and Leitsch, 1994).

5. Herbrand complexity is a "calculus-independent" complexity measure which is based on Herbrand's Theorem.

REFERENCES

Amati, G., Aiello, L. C., Gabbay, D., and Pirri, F. (1996). A Proof Theoretical Approach to Default Reasoning I: Tableaux for Default Logic. *Journal of Logic and Computation*, 6(2):205–231.

Baaz, M., and Leitsch, A. (1994). On Skolemization and Proof Complexity. *Fundamenta Informaticae*, 20:353–379.

Bibel, W., Hölldobler, S., and Schaub, T. (1993). *Wissensrepräsentation und Inferenz*. Vieweg, Braunschweig.

Bonatti, P. A. (1996). Sequent Calculi for Default and Autoepistemic Logics. In Miglioli, P., Moscato, U., Mundici, D., and Ornaghi, M., editors, *Proceedings TABLEAUX'96*, Springer LNCS 1071, pages 127–142, 1996.

Bonatti, P. A., and Olivetti, N. (1997a). A Sequent Calculus for Skeptical Default Logic. In Galmiche, D., editor, *Proceedings TABLEAUX'97*, Springer LNAI 1227, pages 107–121.

Bonatti, P. A., and Olivetti, N. (1997b). A Sequent Calculus for Circumscription. In Nielsen, M., and Thomas, W., editors, *Proceedings CSL'97*, Springer LNCS 1414, pages 98–114.

Cadoli, M., Donini, F. M., and Schaerf, M. (1994). Is Intractability of Non-Monotonic Reasoning a Real Drawback? In *Proceedings of the AAAI National Conference on Artificial Intelligence*, pages 946–951, MIT Press.

Cadoli, M., Donini, F. M., and Schaerf, M. (1995). On Compact Representation of Propositional Circumscription. In *Proceedings STACS '95*, Springer LNCS 900, pages 205–216.

Cadoli, M., and Schaerf, M. (1993). A Survey of Complexity Results for Non-Monotonic Logics. *Journal of Logic Programming*, 17:127–160.

Clark, K. L. (1978). Negation as Failure. In *Logic and Databases*, Plenum, New York, pages 293–322.

Egly, U., and Tompits, H. (1997a). Non-Elementary Speed-Ups in Default Reasoning. In Gabbay, D. M., Kruse, R., Nonnengart, A., and Ohlbach, H. J., editors, *Proceedings ECSQARU-FAPR'97*, Springer LNAI 1244, pages 237–251.

Egly, U., and Tompits, H. (1997b). Is Nonmonotonic Reasoning Always Harder? In Dix, J., Furbach, U., and Nerode, A., editors, *Proceedings LPNMR'97*, Springer LNAI 1265, pages 60–75.

Egly, U., and Tompits, H. (1998). On Proof Complexity of Circumscription. In de Swart, H., editor, *Proceedings TABLEAUX'98*, Springer LNAI 1397, pages 141–155.

Eiter, T., and Gottlob, G. (1993). Propositional Circumscription and Extended Closed World Reasoning are Π_2^P-complete. *Journal of Theoretical Computer Science*, 114(2):231–245. Addendum in vol. 118, page 315, 1993.

Gottlob, G. (1992). Complexity Results for Nonmonotonic Logics. *Journal of Logic and Computation*, 2:397–425.

Lifschitz, V. (1985). Computing Circumscription. In *Proceedings of IJCAI'85*, Morgan Kaufmann, Los Altos, CA, pages 121–127.

McCarthy, J. (1980). Circumscription—A Form of Non-Monotonic Reasoning. *Artificial Intelligence*, 13:27–39.

Moore, R. (1985). Semantical Considerations on Non-Monotonic Logic. *Artificial Intelligence*, 25:75–94.

Niemelä, I. (1996a). A Tableau Calculus for Minimal Model Reasoning. In Miglioli, P., Moscato, U., Mundici, D., and Ornaghi, M., editors, *Proceedings TABLEAUX'96*, Springer LNAI 1071, pages 278–294.

Niemelä, I. (1996b). Implementing Circumscription Using a Tableau Method. In Wahlster, W., editor, *Proceedings ECAI'96*, John Wiley & Sons Ltd., Chichester, pages 80–84.

Olivetti, N. (1992). Tableaux and Sequent Calculus for Minimal Entailment. *Journal of Automated Reasoning*, 9:99–139.

Orevkov, V. P. (1979). Lower Bounds for Increasing Complexity of Derivations after Cut Elimination. *Zapiski Nauchnykh Seminarov Leningradskogo Otdeleniya Matematicheskogo Instituta im V. A. Steklova AN SSSR*, 88:137–161. English translation in *Journal of Soviet Mathematics*, 2337–2350, 1982.

Reiter, R. (1978). On Closed-World Data Bases. In *Logic and Databases*, pages 55–76, Plenum, New York.

Reiter, R. (1980). A Logic for Default Reasoning. *Artificial Intelligence*, 13:81–132.

Tompits, H. (1998). *On Proof Complexities of First-Order Nonmonotonic Logics*. Dissertation, Technische Universität Wien.

Varzi, A. (1990). Complementary Sentential Logics. *Bulletin of the Section of Logic*, 19:112–116.

JUTTA EUSTERBROCK

COMPOSING RE-USABLE SYNTHESIS METHODS THROUGH GRAPH-BASED VIEWPOINTS

1. THE NEED OF ABSTRACTION IN SYSTEM SYNTHESIS

The overall goal in the field of systems for automated synthesis, such as program synthesis, design, configuration or scheduling, is to construct plans or executable systems that conform with user-needs and adapt to changing environments. The Internet will be a foundation for a future generation of synthesis systems, providing for instance, tools for constructing graphical user-interfaces and comprehensive domain-specific information. Formal methods for synthesis should be like mathematical theorems in the sense that they state the assumptions which yield correctness, completeness or efficiency, and once methods have been deployed, they are re-usable, can be seamlessly combined with various tools and never have to be recoded manually.

Theoretical progress towards a formal theory of synthesis stems from several directions. Research has shown that it is necessary to use multiple knowledge representation and reasoning mechanisms, abstraction, meta-level (Bundy, 1988; Eusterbrock, 1996; Kreitz, 1993; Lowry and Van Baalen, 1997) and schema-guided or generic approaches (Heissel et al., 1995; Flener et al., 1998), rather than uniform general purpose deductive methods (Green, 1981). In his pioneering work, D. Smith derived formalisations of various general schemas for algorithm design, like the well-known "Divide-and-Conquer" (cf. (Smith, 1985)) or "Global Search" programs. (Kreitz, 1993) emphasises that it needs a formalisation of the meta-theory of programming and formally proven synthesis methods and that general purpose strategies such as the LOPS strategy (cf. (Bibel, 1980)) need to be formalised in order to yield an implementational framework for synthesis.

Research in knowledge-based systems has led to multi-level architectures and libraries of re-usable generic problem solving methods, most often on a pragmatic basis, aiming at efficient and effective reasoning for generic tasks and taking into account several kinds of strategic knowledge (cf. (van Harmelen and Balder, 1992)). Experimental studies have provided evidence that automated synthesis of complex efficient algorithms, based on formal methods is possible, if substantial domain-specific problem solving knowledge is provided (cf. (Eusterbrock, 1992a)).

S. Hölldobler (ed.), Intellectics and Computational Logic, 143–158.

The comprehensive SEAMLESS multi-layer architecture (Eusterbrock, 1996) is intended to provide a framework for (1) the partitioning of synthesis fragments such as types, synthesis knowledge, methods for construction and learning tasks into reusable units, and (2) the composition of units into effective domain-specific synthesis systems, combining approaches from knowledge-based systems and synthesis with formal methods. Three layers are distinguished: domain knowledge, generic abstractions, and distributed knowledge sources. Each layer can be divided uniformly into the three levels, data types, declarative and executable specifications. Generic theories are sorted declarative specifications. Sorts, variables, functions and predicates are intended to capture generic types, actions, goals and strategic synthesis knowledge. Correctness axioms constrain their semantics. Generic tasks can be specified through formulas on generic variables. Generic synthesis methods are executable specifications (meta-interpreters) for the construction of solutions to instantiated generic tasks, similar to proof plans (Bundy, 1988). They are derived as meta-level theorems with respect to associated generic theories. SEAMLESS *viewpoints* (VPs) are independent intermediate distributable components, introduced for the loose bridging of multi-paradigm knowledge sources on different abstraction layers. A VP specifies how various domain-specific knowledge sources correspond to a generic theory. Using these correspondences as application specific context, any associated generic method can then be specialised for the domain-specific knowledge.

Taking a theoretical basis for granted, having some experimental success, it has long been claimed that formal methods are bound to be increasingly applied for synthesising realistic application systems. There is still a considerable dichotomy between research in automated synthesis, and the wide-spread application of commercial and public environments for information storage, retrieval and system development, such as CASE tools (cf. (Fugetta, 1993)), databases or the popular World-Wide Web. User requirements and domain models tend to hard to capture as what can be expressed by a logical formalism does not match with common representation, for instance entity relationship diagrams or examples. Therefore, putting logic-based synthesis into practice requires the provision of comprehensive domain data, construction knowledge and synthesis objects using precise formal specifications. More importantly, in order to deal with intractable complexities, domain-specific knowledge, such as solved cases, has to be operationalised. Finally, deductive results have to be communicated back in a user-friendly way, for example by graphical support. Traditionally, synthesis systems are devised as stand-alone approaches. They rely on the user to pass information to the system as and when it needs it to perform certain deductions, however this is a tedious and difficult task and guidelines are missing. Developers of knowledge-based systems (Gray and et al, 1997; Maluf and Wiederhold, 1997) are now realising the potential of integrating reasoning and external resources, located across distributed networks.

Re-use oriented system design has been proposed by practical software engineers as a practical solution for achieving high-quality user-friendly systems. Current Internet technologies make re-use oriented synthesis a viable option as they allow the loose coupling of distributed systems in such a way that they keep their autonomy, eg. based on a Blackboard architecture (cf. (Schwartz, 1995)). In order to combine the results of synthesis research with the more pragmatic re-use paradigm, we need to access and integrate heterogeneous domain data, development tools and various kinds of synthesis knowledge, built upon different paradigms, in synthesis applications. There are several standardisation efforts on semantics-based information or knowledge sharing and inter-operable systems. Agent-based communication mandates a universal communication language and ontological commitments in which inconsistencies and notational variations are being eliminated. Establishing communication between multi-paradigm components which range from conventional databases to meta-level synthesis systems and user-provided domain-specific problem solving knowledge through knowledge sharing based on a syntactical variant of any plain formalism can be complicated and sometimes impossible. Communication between a synthesis system and a knowledge resource needs some higher abstraction mechanism rather than mere translation into a common format and a polishing up of notational variants.

This chapter will propose to adopt the viewpoint concept to make heterogeneous knowledge on different abstraction levels accessible for meta-level synthesis based on formal methods. Viewpoints address three main points: (1) A functional interface and physical access to distributed data and computational resources based on a Blackboard cooperation shall be provided; (2) Abstract data types are specialised by correspondences to concrete (partial) structures of object-level resources, eg. software architecture or the conceptual models of a presentation. As a major point, it is suggested to map a wide range of heterogeneous object-level structures into graphs; (3) Generic terms are specialised by lifting formulas which relate the truth of meta-level and domain-specific knowledge, so that correctness axioms are preserved. Lifting encapsulates domain-specific problem-solving knowledge, such as relationships between requirements and solutions. Using such a viewpoint as a dynamically added context for the application of a synthesis method, (truth) values for meta-level representations of selected domain-specific knowledge can be derived on demand.

2. SEAMLESS FOR RE-USE-BASED SYNTHESIS

It is often difficult to re-use synthesis and knowledge-based systems outside of their original context. The SEAMLESS framework addresses re-use in two ways:

- A synthesis process is seen as an evolutionary knowledge construction process, divided into the development steps "Specification, Experimentation, Abstraction, Maintenance, Learning and Extraction for System Synthesis". A knowledge-based synthesis system is conceived to provide generic methods and data types which assist automation of the above development steps.

- A multi-layer architecture provides a coherent concept for (1) partitioning various kinds of knowledge fragments on different layers of abstraction into an easy extensible collection of re-usable abstract and concrete components and (2) building a domain-specific synthesis system by the seamless composition of knowledge components into a network of resources.

The SEAMLESS architecture (cf. (Eusterbrock, 1996) and Figure 1) to model synthesis knowledge is based upon the definition of three hierarchically organised abstraction layers. The layers refer to the organisation of

- Domain Knowledge;

- Generic Domain Abstractions;

- Distributed Knowledge Sources.

The layers in Figure 1 are abstractions from lower layers and may be regarded as separated knowledge bases associated with distinguished formal specifications. Two views are possible: a layer may be seen as meta-layer, controlling the behaviour of the lower (object) layers, as well as an object layer which is available to manipulation by higher layers and provides services to them. The communication among layers is realized by *viewpoints*. Each layer is subdivided into the levels data types, axiomatic theories and derived executable specifications. *Tasks* to be solved on different levels and layers are submitted as *goals* in a Prolog-like style. Solutions are generated by interpretation.

Multi–Layer Knowledge Modeling and Interaction

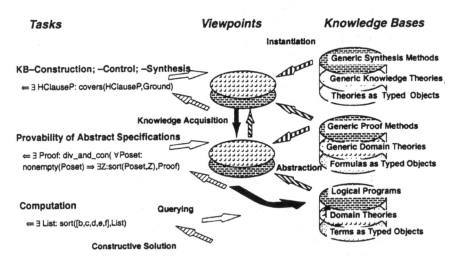

Figure 1   SEAMLESS Layers

Using SEAMLESS, at least three user-groups are involved: (1) method developers who want to evolve the collection of reasoning components to incorporate new capabilities; (2) design-experts who actually want to re-use synthesis methods and add their own context-specific design knowledge to get a domain-specific synthesis system; (3) end-users who want to use synthesised systems for their domain-specific purposes.

Different user groups will view the system from different perspectives. Therefore some users may need a more detailed insight into a specific layer than others. For instance, developers of logic-based methods and data types will need to have every of the three layers at their fingertips, while design-experts are only interested in augmenting high-level abstract applications with domain-specific knowledge.

3. THE OPEN GENERIC SYNTHESIS FRAMEWORK

When taking a logic-based approach, a synthesis process like configuration, design or program generation is generally considered to be a reasoning process, starting from a given domain theory $DomainTheory$. A solution in the form of a logic program LP is derived which fulfills the specified goal $Goal$, eg. functionality in the form of pre- and postconditions, and further constraints $Constraints$ on the program itself like efficiency conditions

$$DomainTheory \vdash LP$$
$$LP \vdash Goal$$
$$Constraints(LP)$$

A generic approach is favoured, rather than general-purpose proof procedures – which leads to serious theoretical and practical problems, because $Constraints$ are already meta-level properties. In principle, generic synthesis is realized as a meta-level constructive proof of a $Task$ having the form

$$Task \doteq \leftarrow \exists LP : (Goal \leftarrow LP) \wedge Constraints(LP)$$

whereby the meta-level variable LP is being substituted by a term which refers to an object-level program.

Abstract data types and data structures have to be introduced to enable automated constructive meta-level reasoning. This applies particularly to object-level expressions such as goals, constraint formulas, logic programs, architecture or database schemas which are subject to reasoning and modifying operations during the synthesis process. Abstract data types are collections of abstract objects which share common properties, and provide construction, selection, transformation and decision procedures. An ADT is specified by its signature and axioms which constitute the basis for correct applications. Data structures shall provide re-usable implementations. Data structures in logic programming are based on term representations and implementations of procedures through canonical term rewrite rules which preserve specifications.

Generic theories for domain clustering Generic theories are considered to be abstract open frameworks which are the starting point for method developers as well as domain experts. Generic theories are intended to axiomatise generic problem-solving knowledge over a range of similar problems in terms of recurrent concepts, problem-solving actions, knowledge categories and the relationships that exist between them, supposing that a broad range of domain-specific problem solving knowledge can be classified by few generic building blocks. Basic predicates characterise properties of domain theories which shall ensure that associated synthesis methods have some desirable properties such as termination. Having categories for additional (derived) strategic problem solving knowledge is the most important feature of this generic SEAMLESS approach – which distinguishes it significantly from schema-guided, transformational frameworks (cf. (Flener et al., 1998; Smith, 1993)).

Definition 1. *A generic theory is a declarative specification* $< S, F, P, \Delta >$ *where* S *is a set of sorts,* F *a set of operator symbols, and* P *a set of predicate symbols, divided into disjoint subsets* P_b, P_s, *called basic and strategic.* Δ *is a set of formulas, called correctness axioms, which constrain the interpretation and well-formed use of expressions.*

To exemplify the concept of a generic theory, a knowledge-based divide-and-conquer theory is defined (cf. (Eusterbrock, 1992b)).

Open Knowledge-based Divide-and-Conquer Framework

- *Sorts* goal, cost, req $\doteq$ [goal, cost], domain, truth, plan

- *Basic definitions*

    - truth_conjunction(T', T'', T) shall implement the table for the conjunction of truth-values, dependent on the chosen logic.

    - $<_{goal}$ denotes a well-founded ordering on goals; minimal verifies the minimality condition.

    - decompose(Req, Dom, Req', Req'') partitions a requirement Req into Req' and Req'', Req', Req'' $<_{goal}$ Req, applying a domain element Dom, which is selected querying split(Req, Dom), so that the solution Plan for Req can be assembled from its subsolutions Sub', Sub'' as it is described by a relation compose(Split, Sub', Sub'', Plan).

- *Strategic Knowledge*

    - known_case(Req, Plan, Truth) represents known relationships between request and constructive solutions. Using a 3-valued logic, Truth = maybe could state the knowledge that there is some evidence for the solvability of Req. In the cases Truth = false, Truth = true, it is already known whether any solution exists.

    - behav_equiv(Req, Plan, ReqEq, PlanEq) represents the behavioural equivalence of Request Req, ReqEq and relationships between the associated solutions Plan, PlanEq.

    - necessary(Req, Plan, ReqRed, PlanR) represents necessary conditions.

- sufficient(Req, Plan, ReqGen, PlanGen) represents a generalisation relation among requirements. Mathematical experience shows that in many cases a generalised problem is easier to solve than the original.
- upper_bound and lower_bound are intended to capture cost constraints.
- further generic predicates may be used to capture control knowledge.

Constructive generic synthesis methods   The question arises how to synthesise methods, which are executable and correct and how to re-use them across several contexts. The formal approach is to consider the definitions for a generic synthesis method as a computational theory, which is derived from the axioms stated by the associated generic theory so that the given generic task can be deduced.

$$GenericTheory \vdash GenericMethod$$
$$GenericMethod \vdash Task$$

Computational theory means that a logic programming system exists which can interpret the definitions, supposing that executable definitions for the open predicates and data types have been provided. The definitions in Figure 2 give an example for a knowledge-based generic synthesis method, formalising the "Divide-and-Conquer" paradigm, and aiming to incorporate various types of strategic knowledge in an explicit way.

Generic Synthesis Method		Knowledge_Based_Divide_and_Conquer
Based on		$Open - KBDQ - theory$
Defined predicates		kdq : req × plan × truth → bool
Definitions		
kdq(Req, Plan, Truth)	←	known_case(Req, Plan, Truth).
kdq(Req, Plan, Truth)	←	behav_equiv(Req, Plan, ReqEq, PlanEq)
		∧ known_case(ReqEq, Truth, PlanEq).
kdq(Req, Plan, false)	←	necessary(Req, Plan, ReqRed, PlanRed)
		∧ known_case(ReqRed, false, PlanRed).
kdq(Req, Plan, true)	←	sufficient(Req, Plan, ReqGen, PlanGen)
		∧ known_case(ReqGen, true, PlanGen).
kdq(Req, Plan, Truth)	←	minimal(Req, Plan, Truth).
kdq(Req, Plan, Truth)	←	split(Req, Split)
		∧ decompose(Req, Split, Req′, Req″)
		∧ kdq(Req′, P′, B′)
		∧ kdq(Req″, P″, B″)
		∧ truth_conjunction(B′, B″, Truth)
		∧ compose(Split, P′, P″, Plan).

Figure 2   Simplified Scheme of Knowledge-based Divide-and-Conquer

4. VIEWPOINTS FOR RE-USING DOMAIN INFORMATION

The result of the open generic synthesis framework is a task-structure- and class specific, abstract and domain-independent, highly generic synthesis approach. In order to serve as a practical development tool, the abstract generic theories should be instantiated with concrete domain-specific notations, techniques and strategies. The SEAMLESS approach aims to re-use pre-existing heterogeneous information sources in a loosely coupled way, based on *viewpoints* (VPs).

The term viewpoint has been borrowed from the Software Engineering Community, where it is widely acknowledged that different users and different applications have different views on object resources and that viewpoints assist effective development (cf. (Nuseibeh et al., 1994)): "A viewpoint is a loosely coupled, locally managed, distributable object, encapsulating partial representation knowledge, development process knowledge, application architectures and specification knowledge, eg. functionality or behaviour, about a (software) component and its domain relevant for re-use."

Generally, a viewpoint in the SEAMLESS architecture is a user-definable, intermediate and distributable component between knowledge resources on different abstraction layers. A VP instantiates a generic theory so that correctness axioms are preserved by describing how heterogeneous domain-specific knowledge fragments on different abstraction levels correspond to the sorts, functions and predicates. Using these correspondences as a context, any generic synthesis method associated with the given generic theory can then be specialised for the specific domain. Figure 3 illustrates the interplay between the multi-paradigm resources.

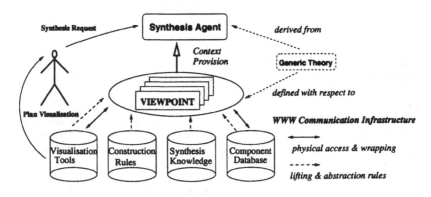

Figure 3 The Cooperation Architecture

Aiming at accessing distributed heterogeneous information and knowledge, the aspects concerned in specialising a generic synthesis method are as follows.

1. **Communication and access** A VP has to ensure physical access to pre-existing knowledge resources or application programs, such as databases or graphical user

interfaces through the logic-based target language. Having linked a database or a program to a VP, entries may be selected or function values may be computed by querying predicates. There are various ways to integrate reasoning systems with external multi-paradigm knowledge sources. Communication could be based on message exchanging, a common protocol and an intermediate interchange format. For example, the HTTP protocol enables network connectivity across heterogeneous networks and hardware platforms, URLs provide an universal transparent addressing scheme and blackboard systems allow to exchange information physically (cf. (de Bosschere and Tarau, 1996)) and provide the basis for sophisticated cooperation models when building complex distributed systems (cf. (Schwartz, 1995)). One of the proposed interchange formats is called KIF (Knowledge Interchange Format) which is a prefix version of first-order predicate calculus with various extensions. Integration could also be based on interface functions in the usual way. Generally, mediators are used for the integration of heterogeneous information sources. KOMET (cf. (Calmet et al., 1997)) is an example for a mediator-based system that uses annotated order-sorted logic to represent and integrate heterogeneous information sources. An external information source is considered to supply a set of functions and relations. SLG resolution is used to derive simple queries which correspond to source-specific requests. The following example shows how relational databases can be introduced using the KOMET language.

```
computer(string, string, bool) : [bool].
computer(Name, CPU, CDROM) : true ← DB1 :: laptop(Name, CPU, CDROM, Battery).
computer(Name, CPU, CDROM) : true ← DB2 :: workstation(Name, CPU, CDROM).
```

2. **Data types and views** Generic sorts and functions refer to abstract data types. Knowledge-based reasoning within a logic-based setting typically relies on explicit term representations of domain-specific object-level structure. Types have to represent semantical structure and organisation of the underlying systems, such as programs, software architecture, database schemas, declarative domain declarations or requirements, and to implement selection, construction or transformation procedures. (Novak, 1994) introduces the concept of a view which describes correspondences between semantical expressions and abstract data types in a correctness preserving way. This technology is being applied in the SEAMLESS framework to relate meta-level abstract types with domain variables, data structures and conceptual models. For instance, consider the atom relation(computer(name, cpu, cdrom)) which views the DB relation computer having relation attributes name, cpu, cdrom as term of type *relation* on the meta-level. Using view correspondences, the procedures of the abstract type, implemented as term rewrite rules, can then be specialised to operate on the concrete domain structures.

3. **Knowledge transformation through lifting** Development process knowledge is provided by lifting definitions (cf. (McCarthy and Buvac, 1998; Guha and Lenat, 1994; van Harmelen and Balder, 1992)). They relate the truth of domain-specific knowledge with meta-level knowledge representations. In other words, they

provide domain-specific substitutions of formulas for the variables of the generic predicate, asserting that it is true in the domain-specific context. Technically, lifting definitions consist of a finite set of designed clauses. They are of the form (i) *Head* or (ii) *Head* ← *Body*, where *Head* is an atom and *Body* is a conjunction of atoms or equations. An atom is an expression of $p(t_1, \ldots, t_n)$ where p is a predicate and each t_i is either a variable or a term. The head is required to be made of meta-level symbols; predicates which occur in the body are either generic predicates, interface predicates or auxiliary predicates which are defined elsewhere. A directed equation $X = p(t_1, \ldots, t_r)$ assigns a domain expression as the value for a meta-variable. All variables which appear in the head must be defined in the body. Correctness axioms must be preserved. For example, to describe a decomposition property with respect to a specific context, one may state

```
decompose(∃O, C : online_service(O)  ∧  computer(C)  ∧  connect(O, C),
                Split, Req1, Req2)  ←  Split = ∃O, C : connect(O, C)
∧ Req1 = ∃O : online_service(O)  ∧  Req2 = ∃C : computer(C).
```

In this case, correctness with respect to a "Divide-and-Conquer" theory means, that the correctness axioms for decomposition translate into corresponding axioms and that there exist a related composition statement.

```
compose(connect(f(O), f(C)), online_service(f(O)), computer(f(C)), Plan)
  ←  connect(f(O), f(C))  ∧  Plan = f(O) ⊕ f(C).
```

The most important feature of this viewpoint approach is that it allows to represent and store and relationships between and properties of object-level expressions, such as architecture or requirements, explicitly and in a flexible way. This distinguishes it significantly from related frameworks for synthesis (Flener et al., 1998; Smith, 1993) where generic predicates only provide an interface to declarative object-level descriptions. Especially derived knowledge, such as solved cases, or uncertain knowledge can be operationalised. This could result in more efficient synthesis processes. Complexity properties of programs can be expressed as meta-level properties and used to guide the synthesis of efficient or optimal programs.

Contextual proving   Having these annotations, a human designer as well as a generic synthesis method, can find a solution in a very effective way, even without having any domain-specific knowledge, by simply applying generic constructive reasoning. Once implemented,

■ Viewpoints provide the context in which generic, formally verified methods are used by identifying the assertions pertaining to the local environment:

■ Object-level values, expressions and synthesis knowledge may be queried - also in a Prolog-like style - by high-level applications using the vocabulary introduced by the associated generic theory.

This means a domain-specific solution LP is synthesised by constructively proving

$$(GenMethod >> VP) \vdash$$
$$(\leftarrow generic\_synthesis(\exists LP : (Goal \leftarrow LP) \wedge Constraints(LP)))$$

where $>>$ denotes the context (cf. (Cicekli, 1989)) which is dynamically added.

5. CAPTURING STRUCTURE THROUGH GRAPH-BASED ABSTRACTION

Representing the structure of object-level expressions and the computational operations on the meta-level by terms and term rewrite rules in a nearly one-to-one way is costly. It might result in well-known exponential complexities, if the meta-models form the assumptions for constructive reasoning. More importantly, a specific abstract data type has to be devised and implemented for any class of object-level expressions which is being coupled to the knowledge-based synthesis system. It needs abstraction mechanism in order to get effective synthesis procedures. Graphs are perhaps the most common natural means for capturing abstractions of semi-structured data, documents, processes, or complex programs, hardware- and software systems. Generally, nodes represent data or values and edges represent the relationships between them. The well-known configuration system XCON (McDermott, 1982) used directed graphs for the representation of connected hardware components. A software system may be modularised as a graph or configuration of "components" and "connectors" (cf. (Garlan, 1995)). Even commercial software transformation systems use graphs as a means to represent and manipulate abstract software structure. A complex site in the World-Wide Web has a natural abstraction as a graph where node parameters may be bound to page locations (URL's) and links describe structural and semantical relationships between parts of the hyper-document. Several query languages use graphs to model and use regular path-expressions to navigate through graphs. For example, UnQL (cf. (Fernandez and Suciu, 1998)) is a language for querying semi-structured data that can be modelled as labelled graphs. There is a natural mapping of declarative formulas into conceptual graphs through the ϕ operator (cf. (Sowa, 1984)).

As graphs have been proven very useful for solving various practical engineering tasks, they are employed in the SEAMLESS framework as a means to share structure between "real-world" semi-structured knowledge resources and constructive methods for knowledge-based synthesis. In the SEAMLESS framework, directed hypergraphs are used as basic means to represent the general structure of connected components on different levels of abstraction, whereas nodes refer to values or components and links refer to relationships. A representation graph (nested graph) maybe an elementary graph, where nodes are associated with names or concrete values, or an advanced graph, composed of graphs itself. In (Eusterbrock, 1997) term representatives and term rewriting rules for implementing directed graphs and their operations were devised. Moreover, some desirable properties could be proven. A well-founded ordering which yields a procedure for constructing canonical forms for equivalence classes of terms representing classes of isomorphic directed acyclic graphs was constructed. These results reduce *graph inclusion* to *term subsumption* and *graph intersection* to *term unification.* Operations, such as graph composition, are implemented through term rewriting. Terms provide a simple, but versatile, mechanism for representing arbitrary data. The particular way in which a directed graph is associated with a given declarative specification, program, algorithm, database schema, collection of WWW addresses or a system model, is not important so long as homomorphic mappings exist from domain structures into canonical graph terms so that graph theoretical decomposition, composition and inclusion properties translate into corresponding laws on the object level.

Then a synthesis process can be viewed as a graph decomposition and construction process. A functional or service-oriented existential quantified requirement specification is broken down into manageable pieces and a solution graph is constructed bottom-up, re-using graph-theoretical properties. Automated synthesis is based on domain-independent generic methods that use (1) context-specific lifted domain-specific knowledge as formulas over graph terms, and (2) graph-theoretical properties for retrieval and constructive reasoning through general purpose unification and subsumption procedures on graph terms. The existence of a well-founded ordering on graph terms ensures termination.

6. MULTIPLE VIEWS BY UNFOLDING CANONICAL TERMS

Canonical graph terms serve as indices on the abstractions of interest, such as declarative domain theories, software or document structures and provide the means for effective constructive reasoning. Using canonical forms to store the abstract structure of constructed systems avoids maintaining a combinatorial number of transformations into all the different formats required for multiple purposes. However, across a range of end-users and applications, there is typically no best way to view the derived terms:

- Term representations might be sufficient for processing by further logic-based applications;

- For easy understanding, visualisations could be most appropriate;

- For the application of synthesised results, it is necessary to have executable source code in the desired target language.

Within the SEAMLESS system, in general and as in (Marlin, 1996), multiple views are obtained by unfolding the canonical expressions. Generated views may be executable or serve as input for further applications. So far the following different views on constructed graph terms can be derived:

(1) More readable representations of complex terms, using simple pretty-print programs.

(2) Executable programs. Program extraction is based on composing software components by instantiating a given generic program schema with domain-specific

functions and data types, using the viewpoint rules downwards from the meta-level to the object-level, providing function values and parameters by traversing graph terms and using programming knowledge about the target environment.

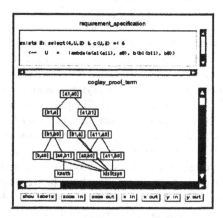

Figure 4   Visualisation of a synthesised decision graph

(3) Visual representations of nested graph terms are synthesised invoking the CoGLay graph layout tool kit through communication mechanism. CoGLay takes string representations of nested graphs, obtained through rewriting terms, and some layout constraints as input in order to compute a layout which satisfies aesthetic criteria and visualises derived results through a World-Wide Web interface as it is shown in Figure 4 (cf. (Eusterbrock and Nicolaides, 1996)).

7. CONCLUSIONS

A future generation of knowledge-based synthesis systems will be based on the Internet. In this paper, it is proposed to adopt the SEAMLESS framework aimed at re-use and based on *viewpoints* to achieve loose composition of logic-based meta-level synthesis methods and distributed knowledge resources built upon different paradigms in an additive way. A viewpoint provides the assumptions pertaining to the local environment represented in terms of an explicit generic theory, based on the principles of sharing abstract structure through graphs and modelling synthesis knowledge by formulas, containing graph terms and graph term variables. Abstracting structure through graphs provides a natural means to achieve cooperating problem solving systems which integrate heterogeneous components such as visualisation systems or database schemas even if they have been built upon different paradigms. Viewpoints allow for a significant amount of re-use by providing the dynamic context with a formally derived synthesis method. The major achievement of this paper is that it needs few new theoretical results to incorporate logic-based synthesis methods within a distributed multi-paradigm environment when adopting the SEAMLESS architecture. The buted multi-paradigm environment when adopting the SEAMLESS architecture. The challenging task that remains is to provide the associations which relate domain objects and composition operators with graph concepts and to instantiate generic problem solving concepts with concrete domain-specific problem solving knowledge.

So far, viewpoint concepts have not been discussed within Logic Programming. Using viewpoints seem to be in agreement with many other current developments on "middle layers" and "contexts" in computing for re-use, knowledge integration, distributed computing and software engineering. The usage of the concept viewpoint stems from software engineering (cf. (ACM, 1996; Nuseibeh et al., 1994)). The need for viewpoints when building open distributed systems is also recognised by the efforts on standardisation (ISO/IEC 10746-4, 1995). The proposed viewpoint concept comprises the wide use of schematic mapping functions and theory morphism, which translate expressions from one set of vocabulary to the vocabulary of an underlying theory so that natural language semantics or correctness axioms are preserved, as a basis for re-use in different areas (cf. (Novak, 1994; Srinivas and Jüllig, 1995; Smith, 1993)). The mediator which is an independent layer between applications and information resources was introduced as a very general concept by Wiederhold (cf. (Wiederhold, 1992)), resulting in various implementational realizations. Information sources, especially databases, are linked to the mediator using wrapper components which translate queries from the mediator format to the source and vice-versa. The most crucial operations are knowledge unification by translation into a common format and intersection in the sense that inconsistencies and notational variations are being resolved. The CYC system ((Guha and Lenat, 1994)) uses contexts or microtheories to tailor reasoning to a particular domain, using the modal predicate $ist(C\,p)$, meaning proposition p is true in context C. Lifting is employed for translating axioms from one context to another. Lifting formulas in the presented framework are used for describing abstract properties of domain knowledge and data rather than rewriting statements into a common format so that they can be queried in an uniform way. The SEAMLESS viewpoint approach stresses the need for multiple perspectives, user-defined abstractions on domain data and the incorporation of various kinds of synthesis knowledge in order to get a flexible representation which enables effective constructive meta-level reasoning.

Based on the SEAMLESS architecture, we implemented a knowledge-based program synthesis and learning system (Eusterbrock, 1992b) and applied it to the discovery of a non-trivial previously unknown mathematical algorithm (Eusterbrock, 1992a). The viewpoint architecture targeting at re-usable synthesis methods is currently being applied in the distributed KRAFT (Knowledge Re-Use and Transformation) environment (cf. (Gray and et al, 1997)) to provide synthesis tools for the constraint-based system design using distributed heterogeneous information sources.

ACKNOWLEDGMENTS

The SEAMLESS architecture is a reflection on the comprehensive research on synthesis methods and knowledge representation techniques, having started in the DFG project "Program Synthesis from Examples" at the Technical University of Darmstadt, taking into account experience from more practical work at the GMD on knowledge-based system configuration, the Internet and re-use in software engineering. Recent work in the KRAFT project at the University of Aberdeen has brought a database perspective into my mind. Especially, I want to thank Jon Atle Gulla for fruitful discussions on using viewpoints as a means to integrate CASE tools and logic-based synthesis methods and Michalis Nicolaides for intensive work on the integration of the visualisation component.

Computing Science Department, University of Aberdeen
Aberdeen AB24 3UE, Scotland, United Kingdom

REFERENCES

A. Brogi, S. C. and Turini, F. (1998). The use of renaming in composing general programs.

ACM (1996). Proc. International Workshop on Multiple Perspectives in Software Development (View-points'96), San Francisco, ACM Symposium on Foundations of Software Engineering.

Bibel, W. (1980). Syntax-directed, semantics supported program synthesis. *Artificial Intelligence*, 14:243–261.

Bundy, A. (1988). The use of explicit plans to guide inductive proofs. In Lusk, E. and Overbeek, R., editors, *Proc. 9th International Conference on Automated Deduction*, pages 111–120. Lecture Notes in Computer Science 310, Springer.

Calmet, J., Jekutsch, S., Kullmann, P., and Schü, J. . (1997). Komet - a system for the integration of heterogenous information sources. In *Proc. ISMIS'97*, pages 318–327. Springer Verlag.

Cicekli, I. (1989). Design and implementation of an abstract metaprolog engine for metaprolog. In Abramson, H. and Rogers, M., editors, *Meta-Programming in Logic Programming*, pages 417–434. MIT Press.

de Bosschere, K. and Tarau, P. (1996). Blackboard-based extensions in Prolog. *Software - Practice and Experience*, 26(1):49–69.

Eusterbrock, J. (1992a). Errata to "Selecting the top three elements" by M. Aigner: A Result of a computer assisted proof search. *Discrete Applied Mathematics*, 41:131–137.

Eusterbrock, J. (1992b). *Wissensbasierte Verfahren zur Synthese mathematischer Beweise: Eine kombina-torische Anwendung*, volume 10 of *DISKI*. INFIX.

Eusterbrock, J. (1996). A multi-layer architecture for knowledge-based system synthesis. In *Proc. ISMIS*, pages 582–592. Springer Verlag.

Eusterbrock, J. (1997). Canonical term representations of isomorphic transitive DAGs for efficient knowledge-based reasoning. In *Proceedings of the International KRUSE Symposium, Knowledge Retrieval, Use and Storage for Efficiency*, pages 235–249.

Eusterbrock, J. and Nicolaides, M. (1996). The visualization of constructive proofs by compositional graph layout: A world-wide web interface. *Proc. CADE Visual Reasoning Workshop, Rutgers University*.

Fernandez, M. and Suciu, D. (1998). Optimizing regular path expressions using graph schemas. In *Proc. Int'l Conference on Data Engineering 1998*, page to appear.

Flener, P., Lau, K., and Ornaghi, M. (1998). On correct program schemas. In Fuchs, N., editor, *Proc. LOPSTR'97*, pages 124–143. Lecture Notes in Computer Science.

Fugetta, A. (1993). A classification of case technology. *COMPUTER*, pages 25–38.

Garlan, D. (1995). Research directions in software architecture. *ACM Computing Surveys*, 27(2):257–260.

Goh, C. H., Madnick, S. E., and Siegel, M. D. (1995). Ontologies, contexts, and mediation: Representing and reasoning about semantic conflicts in heterogeneous and autonomous systems. Technical report, Sloan School of Management Working Paper 3848.

Gray, P. and et al (1997). KRAFT: Knowledge fusion from distributed databases and knowledge bases. In Wagner, R., editor, *Proc. Int'l Workshop on Databases and Expert Systems (DEXA'97)*, pages 682–691. IEEE Press.

Green, C. (1981). Application of theorem proving to problem solving. In Webber, B. L., editor, *Readings in Artificial Intelligence*, pages 202–222. Tioga Publishing Company.

Guha, R. and Lenat, D. (1994). Enabling agents to work together. *Communciations of the ACM*, 37(7):–.

Heissel, M., Santen, T., and Zimmermann, D. (1995). A generic system architecture for strategy-based software development. Technical report, Technische Universität Berlin.

ISO/IEC 10746-4 (1995). Information Technology - Open Distributed Processing - Reference Model - Open Distributed Processing. Part 4: Architectural Semantics.

Kreitz, C. (1993). Metasynthesis - deriving programs that develop programs. Habilitationsschrift, Technische Hochschule Darmstadt, 1992.

Lowry, M. and Van Baalen, J. (1997). Meta-Amphion: Synthesis of efficient domain-specific program synthesis systems. *Automated Software Engineering*, 4(2):199–242.

Maluf, D. and Wiederhold, G. (1997). Abstraction of representation of interoperation. In *Proc. ISMIS'97*, pages 441–455. Springer Verlag.

Marlin, C. (1996). Multiple views based on unparsing canonical representations - the multiview architecture. In *Proc. International Workshop on Multiple Perspectives in Software Development (Viewpoints'96)*, pages 217–221. Association for Computing Machinery.

McCarthy, J. and Buvac, S. (1998). Formalizing context (expanded notes). http://www-formal.standford.edu/jmc/mccarthy-buvac-98/index.html.

McDermott, J. (1982). R1: A rule based configurer of computer systems. *Artificial Intelligence*, 19:29–88.

Novak, G. (1994). Composing reusable software components through views. In *Knowledge-Based Software Engineering Conference*, pages 39–47.

Nuseibeh, B., Kramer, J., and Finkelstein, A. (1994). A framework for expressing the relationships between multiple views in requirements specification. *IEEE Transactions on Software Engineering*, 20(10):760–772.

Schwartz, D. (1995). *Cooperating Heterogenous Systems*. Kluwer Academic Publishers.

Smith, D. (1985). Top-down synthesis of divide-and-conquer algorithms. *Artificial Intelligence*, 27:43–96.

Smith, D. (1993). Constructing specification morphisms. *Journal Symbolic Computation*, 15:571–606.

Sowa, John, F. (1984). *Conceptual Structures, Information Processing in Mind and Machine*. Addison Wesley.

Srinivas, Y. and Jüllig, R. (1995). SPECWARE (TM): Formal support for composing software. In *Proceedings of the International Conference on the Mathematics of Program Construction*. Pitman Publ.

van Harmelen, F. and Balder, J. (1992). $(ML)^2$: A formal language for KADS models. In *Proc. of the 10th European Conference on Artificial Intelligence*, pages 582–586. John Wiley & Sons.

Wiederhold, G. (1992). Mediators in the architecture of future information systems. *IEEE Computer*, pages 38–49.

Wiederhold, G., Rathmann, P. Barsalou, T., Lee, B., and Quass, D. (1990). Partitioning and composing knowledge. *Information Systems*, 15(1):61–72.

BERTRAM FRONHÖFER

PROOF STRUCTURES AND MATRIX GRAPHS

1. INTRODUCTION

For a sequent of Linear Logic, different sequent derivations may exist which differ only in unimportant aspects, as e.g. the order in which certain 'independent' subderivations are performed.

Example 1. *Consider, for instance, the following two derivations of the same sequent:*

$$
\cfrac{
C \vdash C \quad
\cfrac{
\cfrac{A \vdash A \quad B \vdash B}{A, B \vdash A \otimes B} \mathbf{R_\otimes}
}{A \otimes B \vdash A \otimes B} \mathbf{L_\otimes}
}{C, A \otimes B \vdash C \otimes (A \otimes B)} \mathbf{R_\otimes}
$$

$$
\cfrac{
\cfrac{
C \vdash C \quad
\cfrac{A \vdash A \quad B \vdash B}{A, B \vdash A \otimes B} \mathbf{R_\otimes}
}{C, A, B \vdash C \otimes (A \otimes B)} \mathbf{R_\otimes}
}{C, A \otimes B \vdash C \otimes (A \otimes B)} \mathbf{L_\otimes}
$$

Since these two derivations only differ in inessential ways—interchanging the second and third derivation step brings about the same result—in (Girard, 1987) a uniform notation (for sequent derivations of Linear Logic) was proposed—so-colled proof nets (correct proof structures)—which 'subsumes' these two derivations. Sequent derivations presented by means of this uniform notation were called *proof structures*, and if they satisfy certain conditions which assure that they represent correct sequent derivations (of Linear Logic), then they were called *proof nets*. At several places in the literature on Linear Logic the question has been raised whether and how proof nets are related to matrices of the Connection Method—see, for instance, (Galmiche, 1993) and (Roorda, 1991).

S. Hölldobler (ed.), Intellectics and Computational Logic, 159–173.

The analysis of this relationship carried out in this paper will yield the following results:

1. We show how proof structures can be translated into matrices and vice versa. These translations show that matrices and proof structures differ basically in minor formal aspects, which are due to the philosophy inherent in the Connection Method (as presented in (Bibel, 1982)) to abstract from a formula tree everything which is redundant for determining theoremhood; a philosophy which is motivated by the interest in theorem proving.

2. We reformulate the Danos-Regnier-Criterion for the correctness of proof structures on the basis of matrices: Danos and Regnier derived so-called switch graphs from a proof structure and established the correctness of the proof structure through conditions on all the derived switch graphs. We present an analogous construction on matrices, which yields so-called completely unnested matrices.

3. We show a correspondence between switch graphs and completely unnested matrices, and prove—similar to Danos and Regnier—the 'correctness of a matrix' (i.e. that it represents a theorem of Linear Logic) on the basis of conditions which must be fulfilled by all derived completely unnested matrices. These conditions to be imposed on completely unnested matrices are also fairly similar to the ones for switch graphs.

4. We finally show a further correctness criterion for matrices based on a set of properties (LL-matrix), which are equivalently shared by a matrix (with a set of connections) and all its completely unnested matrices.

The paper is organised as follows:

In Section 2 we will review the Connection Method and cite a theorem (Theorem 5) about the characterisation of sequents derivable in Linear Logic by means of matrices (or better matrix graphs), which we proved in (Fronhöfer, 1996). In Section 3 we recapitulate the necessary concepts about proof structures, proof nets, switch graphs, etc.

Thereafter, in Section 4, we discuss a fairly straightforward translation of proof structures into matrix graphs and vice versa, and identify those matrix graphs which correspond to proof structures (see Lemma 8).

Analogously to the derivation of switch graphs from proof structures a similar procedure will be defined for matrix graphs—which generates so-called completely unnested matrix graphs—and it will be shown that both transformations produce equivalent derived structures—see Lemma 10—which, as we will show in Lemma 11, share basically the same properties. In this way the Danos-Regnier-Correctness-Criterion carries immediately over to a rather similar criterion on matrices, and we have thus obtained an alternative to the criterion of Theorem 5.

In Section 5 we show that the conditions stipulated in Theorem 5 for matrix graphs are equivalent to the same conditions on all their derived completely unnested matrix graphs. These results are summarized in Theorem 19.

For reasons of space the proofs of the lemmata and theorems had to be omitted, but can be found in (Fronhöfer, 1999).

2. THE CONNECTION METHOD

We will first shortly review the main concepts of the Connection Method. (For details we refer the reader to (Fronhöfer, 1996) where the Connection Method is developed in view of its application to the multiplicative fragments of substructural logics like Contraction Free, Linear or Relevance.)

If we consider the propositional language consisting (apart from the propositional variables) of the logical connectives conjunction, disjunction and negation (the latter only being allowed before propositional variables), in case of classical logic the Connection Method works as follows (see (Bibel, 1982) for details): We transform a formula into clausal normal form (where the Connection Method in contrast to Resolution traditionally does not negate the formula) which we denote as a set of sets of literals. (A literal is either a propositional variable or a negated propositional variable; the sets of literals are called clauses or columns). An undirected pair of two opposite literals, i.e. they have the same propositional variable, but one of them is negated while the other one is not, is called a *connection*. If we select from each clause/column a literal, then the obtained set of literals is called a *path*, and it is called a *complementary path* iff it contains a connection. A matrix is called *complementary* iff each path contains a connection, and in exactly this case the formula we started from is a theorem of classical propositional logic.

If we consider for Linear Logic the similar language fragment consisting of the connectives $\otimes$, $\sharp$ and $\perp$ ($\perp$ again just applied to propositional variables) we get less theorems than in classical logic—due to the absence of weakening and contraction—and consequently we have to impose additional conditions on the matrix apart from being complementary.

However, there are 3 issues which require modifications of our 'classical' matrices:

1. We cannot make use of clausal normal form matrices any longer, and we have to exploit the non-normal form version of the Connection Method, which has also already been worked out for classical logic (see (Bibel, 1982)), where the columns of a matrix may (recursively) contain further matrices (rows) as elements. (This is a consequence of the absence of contraction and weakening in Linear Logic, which are required to establish the distributivity of $\otimes$ and $\sharp$.)

Being compelled to deeper nesting of our matrices we may exploit this to preserve as much as possible of the tree structure of the given formula: Since every node in a formula tree has at most two sons, we may get matrices where each row or column has at most two elements, and we will call such matrices *binary*. Since sequents may consist of more than two formulae, we must allow more than two top-level columns in the matrix, in which case we speak of a *semi-binary* matrix.

Example 2. *For the sequent* $\vdash A^{\perp}, A \otimes (B^{\perp} \sharp C^{\perp}), B \otimes C$ *we get the following semi-binary matrix in set notation:* $\{\overline{A}, \{A, \{\overline{B}, \overline{C}\}\}, \{B, C\}\}$, *where we denote negation by overlining.*

It is common practice with the Connection Method to display matrices two-dimensionally as is shown here for the matrix above (together with the set of all possible connections).

In a matrix columns correspond to conjunctions while rows correspond to disjunctions. Note that due to the strict alternation of rows and columns in matrices we may get more nestings than connectives, e.g. in case of a formula like $A \otimes (B \otimes C)$ we would get the matrix $\{\{A, \{\{B, C\}\}\}\}$.

2. Due to the difference of $A \otimes A$ from A in Linear Logic we have to keep different occurrences of literals etc. in the matrices. We have to *distinguish different occurrences of (logical) literals*, which will be done by upper indices. We will sometimes omit them if no confusion may arise, e.g. if there are no different occurrences which must be distinguished. Literals are negated or unnegated propositional variables: $\overline{K}$ denotes the complementary one to K, where K may be a negated or unnegated propositional variable. $\overline{K}^1$ is an occurrence of $\overline{K}$ and not the negation of an occurrence K^1.

3. Finally, while for classical logic it was sufficient to consider the set of all connections of a matrix, this set may now be too large and we have to consider suitable subsets. The problem is that some interesting properties of sets of connections, which we will consider below, will not be inherited by their supersets. For this reason we have to state more explicitly which sets of connections we are considering, which leads to the concept of a *matrix graph* $(\mathcal{M}, \mathfrak{S})$, i.e. a pair consisting of a matrix $\mathcal{M}$ and a particular set of connections $\mathfrak{S}$.

More precisely we get the following:

A *normal form matrix* is a set of sets (columns) of literals. Absence of the necessary distributive laws disallows the transformation of a formula into a normal form matrix. We just achieve negation normal form, which corresponds to *(non-normal form) matrices* with deeper nestings: Set of sets of sets ..., respectively a row of columns of rows ... The symbol $\in$ denotes set membership, $\Subset$ its reflexive transitive closure. Absence of idempotence of conjunction and disjunction requires keeping different *occurrences* of (logical) literals in the matrix. More formally we get:

- Each occurrence L^1 of a logical literal is a matrix.
- If $\mathcal{M}_1, \ldots, \mathcal{M}_n$ $(n \geq 1)$ are matrices, then the set $\{\mathcal{M}_1, \ldots, \mathcal{M}_n\}$ is a matrix.
- The empty set is a matrix.

We denote by m_o the translation of sequents into matrices which satisfies the requirements **1** and **2** above, i.e. we don't apply distributive nor idempotent laws for the connectives $\otimes$ and $\sharp$.

We assume matrices $\mathcal{M}$ to be *fully flattened*, i.e. rows or columns $\{\{\mathcal{N}'_1, \ldots, \mathcal{N}'_n\}\} \neq \mathcal{M}$ will be replaced by $\mathcal{N}'_1, \ldots, \mathcal{N}'_n$, and rows or columns $\{L^1\}$ will be replaced by L^1.

A *path* $\mathfrak{p}$ *in a row* $\mathcal{N} = \{\mathcal{C}_1, \ldots, \mathcal{C}_n\} \Subset \mathcal{M}$ is the (necessarily disjoint) union of paths $\mathfrak{p}_1$ *in* $\mathcal{M}_1, \ldots, \mathfrak{p}_n$ *in* $\mathcal{M}_n$ with $\mathcal{M}_i \in \mathcal{C}_i$. If $\mathcal{C}_i$ or $\mathcal{M}_i$ is an occurrence L^1 of a literal, then the respective path is $\{L^1\}$. If there is a literal L in a path $\mathfrak{p}$ and also $L \Subset \mathcal{N}$ with $\mathcal{N} \Subset \mathcal{M}$, then we say that $\mathfrak{p}$ is a path *through* $\mathcal{N}$.

Two literals $L^1, K^1 \Subset \mathcal{M}$ are called *horizontally related* ($L^1 \overset{h}{\sim} K^1$), iff there is a path $\mathfrak{p}$ in $\mathcal{M}$ with $L^1, K^1 \in \mathfrak{p}$. Otherwise they are called *vertically related* ($L^1 \overset{v}{\sim} K^1$). (Note that $L^1 = K^1$ (same occurrence!) implies $L^1 \overset{h}{\sim} K^1$.)[1]

An undirected pair of two opposite literals, i.e. they have the same propositional variable, but one of them is negated while the other one is not, is called a *connection*.

A *complementary path* in a matrix graph $(\mathcal{M}, \mathfrak{S})$ is a path $\mathfrak{p}$ which *contains a connection* of $\mathfrak{S}$, i.e. there are literals $L^1 \Subset \mathcal{M}$ and $K^1 \Subset \mathcal{M}$ with $(K^1, L^1) \in \mathfrak{S}$ and $K^1, L^1 \in \mathfrak{p}$. A set of connections $\mathfrak{S}$ is called *spanning* for a matrix $\mathcal{M}$ iff every path in $\mathcal{M}$ contains at least one connection from $\mathfrak{S}$. A *complementary matrix graph* is a matrix graph $(\mathcal{M}, \mathfrak{S})$ such that $\mathfrak{S}$ is a spanning set of connections for $\mathcal{M}$.

When speaking about the multiplicative fragment of Contraction Free Logic we intend the set of all well-formed propositional formulae built with the multiplicative connectives $\otimes$ (conjunction), $\multimap$ (implication), $\sharp$ (disjunction) and $\perp$. Since we have less theorems than in case of respective connectives of classical logic, we have to impose additional conditions on our matrix graphs in order to characterize theorems of linear logic. These conditions will be explained in the following:

Linearity means that each literal may be involved in at most one connection and *total connectedness* means each literal must be involved in at least one connection. A matrix graph $(\mathcal{M}, \mathfrak{S})$ is called *uniquely connected* iff all literals in $\mathcal{M}$ are involved in exactly one connection of $\mathfrak{S}$. We call a connection $(K, L) \in \mathfrak{S}$ *essential* in a matrix graph $(\mathcal{M}, \mathfrak{S})$ iff there is a path $\mathfrak{p}$ in $\mathcal{M}$ with $K, L \in \mathfrak{p}$ and which contains no further connection from $\mathfrak{S}$. Otherwise a connection is called *superfluous*.

A matrix graph $(\mathcal{M}, \mathfrak{S})$ is called *minimal* iff none of the connections in $\mathfrak{S}$ is superfluous.

For defining the property of *acyclicity* we need some further concepts.

Given a matrix graph $(\mathcal{M}, \mathfrak{S})$. A list $\left[[L_1, K_1], \ldots, [L_n, K_n] \right]$ of ordered pairs of (occurrences of) literals from $\mathcal{M}$ such that $\{(L_1, K_1), \ldots, (L_n, K_n)\} \subset \mathfrak{S}$ is called a *connection chain* or simply a *chain* iff for $i = 1, \ldots, n-1$ holds: $K_i \overset{v}{\sim} L_{i+1}$ (thus $K_i \neq L_{i+1}$). If the literals K_n and L_1 are horizontally/vertically related, then the connection chain is called *open/closed*.

A connection chain $\left[[L_1, K_1], \ldots, [L_n, K_n] \right]$ is called *regular* iff

1. for $i, j = 1, \ldots, n$ the L_i and K_j are all mutually different, i.e. for $i \neq j$ we have $L_i \neq L_j$, $L_i \neq K_j$ and $K_i \neq K_j$ as occurrences of literals in the matrix

2. for $i = 1, \ldots, n$ holds: $L_i \overset{h}{\sim} L_{k \neq i}$ and $L_i \overset{h}{\sim} K_{l \neq i-1 \bmod n}$ (with $k, l = 1, \ldots, n$)

3. for $i = 1, \ldots, n$ holds: $K_i \overset{h}{\sim} K_{k \neq i}$ and $K_i \overset{h}{\sim} L_{l \neq i+1 \bmod n}$ (with $k, l = 1, \ldots, n$)

$$K_i \overset{h}{\sim} K_j$$
$$K_i \overset{h}{\sim} L_{j+1}$$
$$L_{i+1} \overset{h}{\sim} K_j$$
$$L_{i+1} \overset{h}{\sim} L_{j+1}$$

$$K_i \overset{v}{\sim} K_j$$
$$K_i \overset{h}{\sim} L_{j+1}$$
$$L_{i+1} \overset{h}{\sim} K_j$$
$$L_{i+1} \overset{v}{\sim} L_{j+1}$$

Figure 1   Regular Chains and Twist Knots

The relationships which are valid between two vertical pairs in a regular chain are shown in Figure 1 on top.

A closed regular chain is called a *cycle*. A matrix graph $(\mathcal{M}, \mathfrak{S})$ is called *cycle-free* or *acyclic* iff it contains no cycle.

For illustrating the concept of regular chains, we will introduce some terminology for speaking in more detail about 'irregularities' in connection chains. Roughly spoken, irregularities occur if the literals in a chain are not 'sufficiently' horizontally related to each other.

A *knot* in a chain $\left[[L_1, K_1], \ldots, [L_n, K_n]\right] \subset \mathfrak{S}$ consists of two pairs of literals $K_i \overset{v}{\sim} L_{i+1}$ and $K_j \overset{v}{\sim} L_{j+1}$, $i, j \leq n-1$ and $i \neq j$, such that *at least one* of the following vertical relationships holds: $K_i \overset{v}{\sim} K_j$, $K_i \overset{v}{\sim} L_{j+1}$, $L_{i+1} \overset{v}{\sim} K_j$ or $L_{i+1} \overset{v}{\sim} L_{j+1}$. A knot is called *degenerated* iff $L_{i+1} = K_j$ or $K_i = L_{j+1}$ (as occurrences of literals in the matrix). A knot is called a *twist knot* if *all* the relationships in Figure 1 (bottom) hold.

Twist knots are a phenomenon of matrices in non-normal form. In order to provide some intuition about connection chains in non-normal form matrices, let us look at the following examples which show the difference between closed chains and cycles.

Example 3. *Consider, for instance, the linear complementary matrix graph in Figure 2 on the left. (The matrix has 3 top-level columns! The central one has two rows, each of which has two columns.)*

This matrix graph contains a closed chain $\left[[A, \overline{A}], [\overline{C}, C], [\overline{D}, D], [B, \overline{B}]\right]$ *which has a twist knot between the vertical pairs* $\overline{A} \overset{v}{\sim} \overline{C}$ *and* $B \overset{v}{\sim} D$. *However, the matrix graph is still cycle-free, because this mentioned closed chain—which is the only one— does not satisfy all the horizontal relationships between literals which are required for cycles (as shown in Figure 1 on top).*

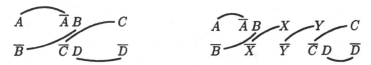

Figure 2 Chains, Twist Knots and Twist Chains

The example above can be made even more complicated: The twist knot can be 'stretched' along two coinciding subchains—however, of different direction of traversal—as is shown by the complementary matrix graph in Figure 2 on the right (with 5 top-level columns). It contains a closed chain

$$\left[[A,\overline{A}],[\overline{X},X],[\overline{Y},Y],[\overline{C},C],[\overline{D},D],[Y,\overline{Y}],[X,\overline{X}],[B,\overline{B}]\right] \text{ with a 'stretched'}$$

twist knot extending over the vertical pairs $\overline{A} \overset{v}{\sim} \overline{X}$ and $B \overset{v}{\sim} \overline{X}$, twice $X \overset{v}{\sim} \overline{Y}$ and finally $Y \overset{v}{\sim} \overline{C}$ and $Y \overset{v}{\sim} D$. We call the subchain $\left[[\overline{X},X],[\overline{Y},Y]\right]$ a twist chain.

All properties of matrix graphs which we will use in the following are invariant under flattening and unflattening steps. Therefore, we will not care about the exact nesting structure of the matrices we will have to deal with. It is usually most convenient to assume all matrices to be fully flattened.

As a kind of abbreviation we define: A matrix graph $(\mathcal{M}, \mathfrak{S})$ is called an *LL-matrix* iff it is semi-binary, acyclic, uniquely connected and minimal.

The following Lemma shows that LL-matrices are complementary.

Lemma 4. *A matrix graph $(\mathcal{M}, \mathfrak{S})$ which is uniquely connected and acyclic is complementary.*

We showed in (Fronhöfer, 1996):

Theorem 5. *For a sequent S of the propositional language described above there exists a Linear Logic sequent derivation iff there is an LL-matrix $(\mathrm{m}_o(S), \mathfrak{S})$.*

Note that the matrix graph of Example 2 fulfils all the properties requested by Theorem 5.

3. PROOF STRUCTURES

The other formalism which plays a role here are proof structures. The following definition is from (Gallier, 1991).

Proof Structures are certain finite unoriented connected node-labeled graphs with the following properties:

1. For every node labeled with a literal, there is a single arc from the entry point of that literal to the entry point of a literal with the same name and opposite sign,

2. For every node labeled with $A \otimes B$ or $A \sharp B$, there are two distinct nodes labeled with A and B respectively, such that the exit of A is connected to one of the two entry points of $A \otimes B$ (resp. $A \sharp B$) and the exit of B is connected to one of the two entry points of $A \otimes B$ (resp. $A \sharp B$), each by a single arc,

3. The exit point of every node is connected to at most one other node.

Example 6. *The following graph is a proof structure. (Actually it's even a proof net according to the definition given further below).*

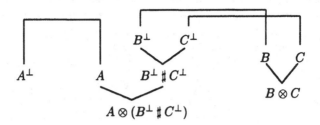

Let us also mention that this proof structure represents the sequent

$$\vdash A^{\perp}, A \otimes (B^{\perp} \sharp C^{\perp}), B \otimes C$$

Note that in the literature on proof structures/nets a pair of arcs which go to the entry points of a common node is generally depicted by a horizontal straight line. Our notation suggests more directly that proof structures are graphs and it is also more convenient for the notation of the derived switch graphs to be defined below.

For comparison, let us also display the matrix corresponding to the sequent above according to the mapping $\mathfrak{m}_o$ together with the set of all connections.

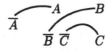

Note that this matrix graph fulfils all the properties for a derivable sequent of Linear Logic according to Theorem 5.

Originally, correctness of proof structures was defined by the so-called 'long-trip-condition' (see (Girard, 1987)) and proof structures which fulfil this condition were called *proof nets*.

There has also been proposed by Danos and Regnier in (Danos and Regnier, 1989) an alternative correctness criterion for proof structures, of which we will analyse in the sequel how it relates to matrices. We define in a proof structure N:

Arcs connecting the exit points of nodes labeled with formulae A or B to entry points of a node labeled with the formula $A \otimes B$ as well as arcs connecting entry points of nodes labeled with literals are called *solid*. Arcs connecting the exit points of nodes labeled with formulae A or B to entry points of a node labeled with the formula $A \,\natural\, B$ are called *soft*.

A *switch graph* N^s derived from the proof structure N is a (not unique) subgraph of N which is obtained by deleting at every node labeled with a disjunction exactly one of the two soft arcs at its entry points, while keeping the other soft arc.

A node where one of the two soft arcs has been deleted will be called *degenerated*.

Finally, a proof structure N is *correct*—and will be called a *proof net*—iff it satisfies the *Danos-Regnier-Criterion*, i.e. iff every switch graph N^s derived from N is a connected and acyclic graph.

Example 7. *From the proof structure presented in Example 6 we can derive two switch graphs depending on whether we cut the arc between $B^\perp$ and $B^\perp \,\natural\, C^\perp$ or the arc between $C^\perp$ and $B^\perp \,\natural\, C^\perp$. For instance, the second possibility yields the following switch graph:*

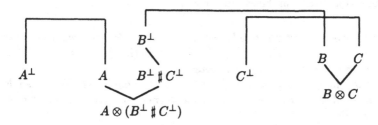

4. TRANSLATIONS

We will show next how proof structures can be translated into matrix graphs and vice versa. The details of these procedures are rather tedious and we refer to Appendix I of (Fronhöfer, 1999).

Intuitively, we can understand a proof structure as a graph composed of a set of formula trees, i.e. binary finite trees, whose nodes are each labeled with a formula which corresponds to the subtree/subformula at this node. We will call the arcs of these trees *m-arcs* and each (maximal) connected subgraph, which consists only of m-arcs, will be called a *(maximal) m-component*. (The proof structure of Example 6, for instance, has 3 maximal m-components whose root nodes are labeled with the formulae $A^\perp$, $A \otimes (B^\perp \,\natural\, C^\perp)$ and $B \otimes C$.) Furthermore, there are additional arcs (which we will call *c-arcs*) which connect the leaves of these formula trees and it is required for proof structures that each leaf must be connected to exactly one other leaf and the labels of two connected leaves must be opposite literals.

Comparing Examples 2 and 6 it becomes fairly obvious that the parts of the proof structure which consist of m-arcs correspond to a matrix, while the c-arcs correspond to connections. This allows to define a pair $(\tau_\mathcal{M}, \tau_\Theta)$ of mappings which translate a proof structure N into a matrix graph $(\tau_\mathcal{M}(\mathsf{N}), \tau_\Theta(\mathsf{N}))$ where $\tau_\mathcal{M}$ transforms the maximal m-components of N into the top-level columns of the matrix $\tau_\mathcal{M}(\mathsf{N})$ and

$\tau_{\mathfrak{S}}$ converts the c-arcs of N into a set $\tau_{\mathfrak{S}}(N)$ of connections. (The basic principle is that $\tau_{\mathcal{M}}$ transforms subtrees of maximal m-components, which are labeled by a conjunction (resp. disjunction) into a column (resp. row) of the matrix.)

We will not go into further details here, because due to the strict alternation of OR- and AND-nodes (i.e. rows and columns) in matrices, while proof structures allow OR-nodes (resp. AND-nodes) as sons of OR-nodes (resp. of AND-nodes), the exact definition of the translation $(\tau_{\mathcal{M}}, \tau_{\mathfrak{S}})$ is a little bit complex.

For a uniquely connected semi-binary matrix graph $(\mathcal{M}, \mathfrak{S})$ we can also define a reverse translation into a proof structure by a triple of mappings $(\tau_{\otimes}, \tau_{\sharp}, \tau_{C})$. Here again the details are a little bit tricky, but intuitively the mappings $\tau_{\otimes}$ and $\tau_{\sharp}$ generate from the rows and columns in $\mathcal{M}$ the nodes of a proof structure (together with the necessary m-arcs) which are labeled by conjunctions and disjunctions respectively. The mapping τ_{C} finally generates links between the leaves of maximal m-components from the connections in $\mathfrak{S}$.

With the translations just indicated we can prove that proof structures correspond to uniquely connected semi-binary matrix graphs:

Lemma 8. *Given a proof structure* N. *Then* $(\tau_{\mathcal{M}}(N), \tau_{\mathfrak{S}}(N))$ *is a uniquely connected semi-binary matrix graph and* $(\tau_{\otimes}, \tau_{\sharp}, \tau_{C})((\tau_{\mathcal{M}}(N), \tau_{\mathfrak{S}}(N)))$ *is again a proof structure which is isomorphic to* N *as unlabeled graph.*

Given a uniquely connected semi-binary matrix graph $(\mathcal{M}, \mathfrak{S})$. *Then* N $:= (\tau_{\otimes}, \tau_{\sharp}, \tau_{C})((\mathcal{M}, \mathfrak{S}))$ *is a proof structure and* $(\tau_{\mathcal{M}}(N), \tau_{\mathfrak{S}}(N))$ *yields the matrix graph* $(\mathcal{M}^{s}, \mathfrak{S})$.

Having now identified the semi-binary uniquely connected matrix graphs as those which correspond to proof structures, we will next look out for counterparts of switch graphs. Deletion of a soft link cuts off part of a maximal m-component and generates a new maximal one, i.e. a subformula tree becomes 'independent'. In matrices this means 'liberating' subcolumns from the 'surrounding nesting structure' and promoting them to top-level columns, a process which we will call unnesting.

Given a semi-binary matrix $\mathcal{M}$ with a row $\mathcal{R} \in \mathcal{M}$ and $\mathcal{R} \equiv \{C_1, C_2\}$. We call an *unnesting step* the transformation which moves up a column $C_i \in \mathcal{R}$ to the top-level, i.e. we obtain the matrix graph $\mathcal{M}[C_i] := \mathcal{M}' \cup \{C_i\}$ where $\mathcal{M}'$ is obtained from $\mathcal{M}$ by deleting C_i from $\mathcal{R}$. Just for the purpose of later translation into a switch graph we mark the row $\mathcal{R}$ as *degenerated*.

Iterative application of unnesting steps to a matrix $\mathcal{M}$ yields eventually a (not unique) normal-form matrix $\mathcal{M}^{u}$, which will be called a *completely unnested matrix of* $\mathcal{M}$. In case of a matrix graph $(\mathcal{M}, \mathfrak{S})$ we call $(\mathcal{M}^{u}, \mathfrak{S})$ a *completely unnested matrix graph of* $(\mathcal{M}, \mathfrak{S})$.

Example 9. *For the derived switch graph from Example 7 we get analogously the completely unnested matrix* $\{\overline{A}, \{A, \{\overline{B}\}\}, \overline{C}, \{B, C\}\}$ *(with 4 top-level columns) and together with the set of all connections we get the matrix graph*

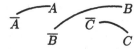

Let us mention that for a given semi-binary matrix $\mathcal{M}$ which contains r subrows $\mathcal{R}$ with $\mathcal{R} \neq \mathcal{M}$, which consist of two elements, the number of different completely unnested matrices is 2^r.

Note that a completely unnested matrix $\mathcal{M}^u$ is basically in clausal normal form, since none of its subrows has more than one element, although it is deeper nested. These additional nestings must also be taken into account when translating completely unnested matrix graphs into switch graphs—we have to create OR-nodes with only one son—and vice versa, OR-nodes where one soft arc has been cut must result in additional nestings when translating switch graphs into completely unnested matrix graphs. (We denote by $\tau_{\mathcal{M}}^s$ and $\tau_{\sharp}^u$ the respective necessary modifications of the mappings $\tau_{\mathcal{M}}$ and $\tau_{\sharp}$ when dealing with switch graphs resp. with completely unnested matrices.)

We get the following Lemma which shows that constructing switch graphs is tantamount to constructing completely unnested matrices.

Lemma 10. *Given a proof structure* N *and the matrix graph* $(\mathcal{M}, \mathfrak{S}) := (\tau_{\mathcal{M}}(N), \tau_{\mathfrak{S}}(N))$.

Then for every switch graph N^s *derived from* N *by a series* $\sigma = \{\sigma_1, \ldots, \sigma_m\}$ *of deletions of soft arcs, a series of unnesting steps* $\nu = \{\nu_1, \ldots, \nu_m\}$ *exists, which results in a completely unnested matrix graph* $(\mathcal{M}^u, \mathfrak{S})$ *such that the diagram*

$$
\begin{array}{ccc}
N & \xrightarrow{(\tau_{\mathcal{M}}, \tau_{\mathfrak{S}})} & (\mathcal{M}, \mathfrak{S}) \\
\downarrow{\sigma} & & \vdots\,\nu \\
N^s & \xrightarrow{(\tau_{\mathcal{M}}^s, \tau_{\mathfrak{S}})} & (\mathcal{M}^u, \mathfrak{S})
\end{array}
$$

is commutative.

Then for every completely unnested matrix graph $(\mathcal{M}^u, \mathfrak{S})$ *as the result of unnesting steps* $\nu = \{\nu_1, \ldots, \nu_m\}$, *a series* $\sigma = \{\sigma_1, \ldots, \sigma_m\}$ *of deletions of soft arcs exists, which derives a switch graph* N^s *from* N *such that the diagram*

$$
\begin{array}{ccc}
(\mathcal{M}, \mathfrak{S}) & \xrightarrow{(\tau_{\otimes}, \tau_{\sharp}, \tau_C)} & N \\
\downarrow{\nu} & & \vdots\,\sigma \\
(\mathcal{M}^u, \mathfrak{S}) & \xrightarrow{(\tau_{\otimes}, \tau_{\sharp}^u, \tau_C)} & N^s
\end{array}
$$

is commutative.

The Danos-Regnier-Criterion says that a proof structure is a proof net iff all derived switch graphs are acyclic connected graphs. We will show that the translation of proof structures into matrix graphs—if applied to switch graphs—carries over the conditions of connectedness and acyclicity of graphs to similar properties of matrices and vice versa. For this purpose we have to define first what connectedness traditionally means for matrix graphs:

A normal form matrix graph $(\mathcal{M}, \mathfrak{S})$ is called *not interconnected* iff there are two non-empty subsets of columns $\mathcal{M}_1, \mathcal{M}_2 \subset \mathcal{M}$ with $\mathcal{M} = \mathcal{M}_1 \dot{\cup} \mathcal{M}_2$ and $\mathfrak{S} = \mathfrak{S}|_{\mathcal{M}_1} \dot{\cup} \mathfrak{S}|_{\mathcal{M}_2}$. Otherwise the matrix graph $(\mathcal{M}, \mathfrak{S})$ is called *interconnected*.

Lemma 11. *Given a switch graph* S *and a uniquely connected matrix graph* $(\mathcal{M}, \mathfrak{S})$ $= (\tau_{\mathcal{M}}(S), \tau_{\mathfrak{S}}(S))$. *Then* S *is acyclic and connected iff* $(\mathcal{M}, \mathfrak{S})$ *is acyclic and interconnected.*

What we have found out so far is which matrix graphs correspond to proof structures and which matrix graphs correspond to (connected and acyclic) switch graphs. This allows to formulate the following theorem, which we inherit from the Regnier-Danos-Criterion for proof structures:

Theorem 12. *Given a sequent* S *with multiplicative formulae.*
If there is a uniquely connected matrix graph $(\mathfrak{m}_o(S), \mathfrak{S})$ *such that all its derived completely unnested matrix graphs are interconnected and acyclic, then* S *is derivable without contraction and weakening.*
If there is a derivation D *of* S *in Linear Logic, then this derivation can be translated into a matrix graph* $(\mathsf{DM}_M(D), \mathsf{DS}_M(D))$ *and all the completely unnested matrix graphs derived from it are interconnected and acyclic.*

5. LL-MATRICES

The rest of the paper will be devoted to a direct proof that this description of matrix graphs which characterize sequents (and theorems) of Multiplicative Linear Logic (as given in Theorem 12) is equivalent to the one presented in Theorem 5.

We showed in Lemma 11 that connected and acyclic switch graphs translate to uniquely connected, semi-binary, normal-form matrix graphs which are acyclic and interconnected. Theorem 19 below proves the important equivalence that these matrix graphs are LL-matrices and vice versa.

We have the following preparatory Lemmata:

Lemma 13. *A normal-form matrix graph* $(\mathcal{M}, \mathfrak{S})$ *which is uniquely connected, acyclic and interconnected, is minimal.*
On the other hand, if a matrix graph $(\mathcal{M}, \mathfrak{S})$ *is an LL-matrix, then it is semi-binary, interconnected and acyclic.*

Example 14. *Note that interconnectedness doesn't generally entail minimality in a uniquely connected, acyclic and complementary matrix graph. For instance in the matrix graph*

either the connection $(\overline{A}, A)$ *or* $(B, \overline{B})$ *is redundant. Note that in contrast to the proof of Lemma 13, where we dealt with normal-form matrices, here dropping one of these two connections doesn't lead to isolated middle columns in the resulting minimal spanning set of connections.*

What is now left to be shown is that for a matrix graph the LL-matrix property is equivalent to the LL-matrix property of all its derived completely unnested matrix graphs. We get:

Lemma 15. *Given a matrix graph* $(\mathcal{M}, \mathfrak{S})$ *which is an LL-matrix. Then all derived completely unnested matrix graphs* $(\mathcal{M}^u, \mathfrak{S})$ *are LL-matrices as well.*

Lemma 16. *Given a matrix graph* $(\mathcal{M}, \mathfrak{S})$. *If all completely unnested matrix graphs* $(\mathcal{M}^u, \mathfrak{S})$ *are acyclic, then* $(\mathcal{M}, \mathfrak{S})$ *is acyclic.*

Of course, it's clear that in general a cycle $\mathbb{C}$ in $(\mathcal{M}, \mathfrak{S})$ is no more present in an arbitrary derived completely unnested matrix graph, because arbitrary unnesting steps may convert a vertical pair of literals in $\mathbb{C}$ into a horizontal one, which breaks up the cycle into an open regular chain (or into several ones).

Lemma 17. *Given a matrix graph* $(\mathcal{M}, \mathfrak{S})$. *If there is a minimal completely unnested matrix graph* $(\mathcal{M}^u, \mathfrak{S})$, *then* $(\mathcal{M}, \mathfrak{S})$ *is minimal.*

Example 18. *The following matrix graph* $(\mathcal{M}, \mathfrak{S})$ *shows that being an LL-matrix does not follow if just one derived completely unnested matrix* $(\mathcal{M}^u, \mathfrak{S})$ *is an LL-matrix.*

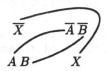

We get the following two completely unnested matrices (the further two are 'symmetric' cases, where instead of the column $\overline{A}$ *the column* $\overline{B}$ *is moved to the top-level).*

Only the first one is an LL-matrix, while the second one is cyclic and not interconnected. (Compare Lemma 16 where acyclicity is demanded for all derived completely unnested matrix graphs.)

We summarize the results proved so far in the next theorem which gives two alternative characterisations of LL-matrices:

Theorem 19. *For a semi-binary matrix graph* $(\mathcal{M}, \mathfrak{S})$ *the following statements are equivalent:*

(1) $(\mathcal{M}, \mathfrak{S})$ *is an LL-matrix.*
(2) *All completely unnested matrix graphs derived from* $(\mathcal{M}, \mathfrak{S})$ *are LL-matrices.*
(3) *All completely unnested matrix graphs derived from* $(\mathcal{M}, \mathfrak{S})$ *are uniquely connected, acyclic and interconnected.*

6. CONCLUSION

The far-reaching accordance between proof nets and matrices prompts the following question which can be paraphrased in two ways:

- "Are Girard's proof nets a reinvention of the wheel?"
- "Are Bibel's matrices an anticipation of proof nets?"

The best chance to arrive at a fair judgement might lie in shifting our focus to the differences between the two formalisms instead of emphasizing the similarities as we did up to now. Moreover, we think that for a historical assessment formal tools should not only be considered in their own right, but should be evaluated in the context in which they were created and with regard to the purpose for which they were/are meant to be used.

Here we must not forget that proof nets came not alone, but in the wake of a newly assembled logical system, for which proof nets represent quite faithfully the gist of sequent derivations. On the other hand, matrix graphs represent the essence of derivations in classical logic—their intended domain of application—only in an extremely condensed way: A derivation may be exponentially larger than the corresponding matrix. (This raises even the question whether a complementary matrix is entitled to be called a proof.)

Attempting to give fair treatment to the Connection Method, we must take into account its intended application for Automated Theorem Proving: This intention inspired profound transformations of formulae (e.g. normal-form matrices) and reductions of matrices (e.g. deletion of pure clauses, evaluation of isolated connections) as well as reductions applied to the set of all connections (e.g. deletion of tautological circuits; see (Bibel, 1982)). Even greater investments were made in the development of proof search techniques on matrices. For the latter purpose many distinguishing features of formulae which were irrelevant for their validity—e.g. associative nestings of connectives—were neglected and got lost in abstracting transformations. The way we shaped here the concept of the mapping m_o is indeed an effort in the opposite direction: We tried to keep as much as necessary of a formula's binary tree structure. The outcome are matrix representations of formulae which are a great deal more complex than traditionally with the Connection Method. Above all, let us point out that in the context of the Connection Method matrices were mainly viewed as representations of formulae and not as alternative notations for derivations. (It seems that issues like cut elimination on matrices have never been thought of before (Fronhöfer, 1996).)

Let us conclude with a historical analogy and compare the invention of matrices/proof nets with the discovery of America and relate Girard/Bibel to Christopher Columbus. We'd like to say that Girard didn't reinvent the wheel in the same sense as Columbus *did not* reinvent the wheel when he discovered America, despite the landing of Viking sailing vessels on the coast of North America some centuries before him. On the other hand, we'd like to say that Bibel didn't discover proof nets in the same sense as Columbus *did not* discover America, but just found some islands which he thought situated off the shores of China and Japan.

Technische Universität München
München, Germany

NOTES

1. Note that in general the relations $\overset{h}{\sim}$ and $\overset{v}{\sim}$ are not transitive. However, the relation $\overset{v}{\sim}$ is transitive in normal-form matrices, a circumstance which simplifies considerably the theory of connection chains.

REFERENCES

Bibel, W. (1982). *Automated Theorem Proving*. Vieweg.

Danos, V. and Regnier, L. (1989). The structure of multiplicatives. *Archive for Mathematical Logic*, 28:181–203.

Fronhöfer, B. (1996). *The Action-as-Implication Paradigm: Formal Systems and Application*, volume 1 of *Computer Science Monographs*. CSpress, München, Germany. (revised version of Habilitationsschrift, TU München 1994).

Fronhöfer, B. (1999). Proof Structures and Matrix Graphs. Technical report, Technische Universität München. available from ftp://ftp.informatik.tu-muenchen.de/local/lehrstuhl/jessen/Automated_Reasoning/Reports/.

Gallier, J. (1991). Constructive Logics. Part II: Linear Logic and Proof Nets. PRL Research Report 9, DEC.

Galmiche, D. (1993). Proof search methods in linear logic. In *Workshop on "Theorem Proving with Analytic Tableaux and Related Methods"*. Université d'Aix-Marseilles II, Faculté des Sciences de Luminy.

Girard, J.-Y. (1987). Linear Logic. *Theoretical Computer Science*, 50:1–102.

Roorda, D. (1991). *Resource Logics: Proof-theoretical Investigations*. PhD thesis, University of Amsterdam.

CHRISTOPH S. HERRMANN

AI AND COGNITIVE SCIENCE:
FEEDBACK LEADS TO A NEW NEURAL CONCEPT

1. AI IN FEEDBACK LOOPS

The major goal of Artificial Intelligence (AI) is to investigate natural and artificial intelligence.

- On the one hand, AI is intended to produce a better understanding of natural intelligence by evaluating the "behavior" of artificially intelligent mechanisms.

- On the other hand, artificially intelligent systems are meant to enhance human performance in the form of tools for automating cognitive taks.

Since it is not yet understood how intelligence is organized in the human brain, technical simulations of intelligent systems yield interesting results for psychologists that may serve as a basis for psychological theory and paradigm development (see e.g. (Anderson, 1995), p. 11). In this article, artificial neural networks (ANNs) will serve as illustrations of two feedback loops in which AI is involved. ANNs are derivatives of propositional networks that were developed in Psychology to represent semantic relations (Norman and Rumelhardt, 1975). Their development and computational investigation has been a topic of AI research and results of this research were subsequently used by cognitive psychologist to evaluate their hypotheses (Rumelhart and McClelland, 1986). This two-way interaction between AI and Biology/Psychology constitutes a feedback loop depicted in Figure 1a by the grey arrows.

Some cognitive models have worked out rather well. A process of model development divorced from the purpose of evaluating psychological models and has lead to AI applications being applied in various industrial fields which has proved their utilitarian value in automizing intelligent tasks (so-called *thinking tools*, as Bibel calls them (Bibel, 1992a)). A second feedback loop was thereby established where industrial needs were implemented into the tools of AI. This is indicated by the white arrows in Figure 1a.

175

S. Hölldobler (ed.), Intellectics and Computational Logic, 175–188.
© 2000 *Kluwer Academic Publishers.*

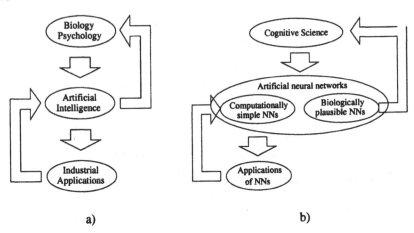

Figure 1 Two interdisciplinary feedback loops of Artificial Intelligence (a). The different demands of the two individual feedback loops lead to different specializations in the field of artificial neural networks.

1.1. Specialization by feedback

Both loops had advantages for all of the involved parties. Interestingly, the different demands from the two disciplines feeding into AI made the qualitative parameters of AI tools diverge into two directions. They can both be though of as evolutionary processes that were driven by different constraints. This is shown in Figure 1b for our case of artificial neural networks. Demands from industry drove the ANN development into fast and efficient architectures which resulted to be computationally simple. On the other hand, cognitive scientists were interested in having close-to-real models of the cortical processors—leading to biologically plausible ANNs.

In the following, we will demonstrate how the two families of neurons differ from each other. Then we are going to illustrate how the psychological demand for explaining binding leads to a new type of neuron. During the course of the paper we will keep coming back to the principle of feedback on different scales.

1.2. Feedback loops in AI

In order to achieve stable performance in technical as well as in biological systems, the concept of negative feedback has been applied. This principle is relatively simple: The positive value of the output is subtracted from the input, thus limiting the next output, thereby stabilizing the output value. However, negative feedback loops typically bear the problem of accidentally inducing oscillations (see e.g. (Gray and Meyer, 1984), p. 466) which may happen whenever there is a time delay in feeding back the output of a system to its input. For the model artificial neuron this oscillation bears a potential benefit and as such can explain the effect of spike bursts. In Section 3, we will introduce a model for an artificial neuron with a negative feedback loop.

1.3. ANNs in principle

The idea to simulate neural activity by a simplified integrate-and-fire neuron was introduced in 1943 by Mc Culloch and Pitts (McCulloch and Pitts, 1943). In 1949 Hebb formulated the Hebbian learning rule that adjusts the weights on the inputs of an artificial neural network. After a while Minsky and Papert showed that rather simple artificial neurons, so-called single layer perceptrons, can only be used to learn linearly seperable functions (Minsky and Papert, 1969). In order to solve more complex functions, as resembled e.g. by the logical operation XOR, so-called multi-layer-perceptrons are necessary. For these basic ANNs, no learning algorithm was known at that time, which lead to a pause in ANN research. The delta learning rule, that is based on the backpropagation[1] of the network output error was already found in 1969 (Bryson and Ho, 1969) but became only popular by the results of the Parallel Distributed Processing group in 1986 (Rumelhart and McClelland, 1986).

Since then, the development of ANNs has diverged into the two above-mentioned directions of *computationally simple* and *biologically plausible* architectures, which will be discussed in detail in the following two sections.

1.4. Computationally simple artificial neuron

The biological neuron receives inputs over afferent axons from other neurons via synapses into its dendritic tree as shown in Figure 2a. It sums up received input over time in its soma and generates output on its efferent axon if a certain threshold is surpassed. This axon connects to other neurons where the process is repeated. This procedure is modulated by elements that sum up their weighted inputs, in the fashion depicted in Figure 2b.

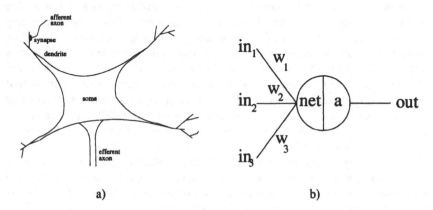

a)   b)

Figure 2   Biological and artificial neuron.

Figure 3 demonstartes that each of i inputs in_i is first mutiplied by its weight term w_i and subsequently all weighted inputs are summed, leading to the net input *net* (shown in the top left formula in Figure 3). The activation of the neuron then depends upon exceeding a threshold θ as given in the bottom left formula. This activation function is shown in the diagram in Figure 3.

$$net = \sum_i in_i \cdot w_i$$

$$a = \frac{1}{1+e^{-(net-\theta)}}$$

Figure 3 Summation of neuron inputs (top left), activation of neuron (bottom left) and sigmoidal activation function with thresholds $\theta = 0$ (—) and $\theta = 5$ ($\cdots$).

Nevertheless, the true electrical behaviour of a neuron is much more complicated.

1.5. The biologically plausible neuron

To better understand neural computation, one has to move from this simplified artificial neuron to a more biologically plausible neuron. Typically, the input to a neuron is by no means a constant digital value but an analog signal that varies over time. As in the case of the retina which inputs to other neurons, there will be frequent spikes during periods of light stimulation as depicted in Figure 4a (see e.g. (Churchland and Sejnowski, 1992), p. 54). Since amplitudes are being attenuated the further they travel in the cortex, coding neural information by frequency rather than amplitude bears the advantage of secure transmission over relatively long cortical distances. The neural mechanism of frequency-coding the input values works as follows. The dendrites of a neuron behave like RC-filters[2] and thus influence the shape of incoming potantials (Segev, 1995), an incoming excitatory postsynaptic current (EPSC) (see Figure 4b top) will generate an excitatory postsynaptic potential (EPSP) which is flattened and its peak delayed in time (see Figure 4b bottom). The soma of the neuron then accumulates the incoming EPSPs until a threshold is reached (see Figure 4c top) and it fires a single action potential onto its efferent axon (see Figure 4c bottom) reseting its soma potential. Since the soma then starts to re-accumulate EPSPs subsequently, the next spike comes sooner the higher the dendritic input—leading to a spike frequency proportional to the input value.

This type of behaviour has been modelled in so-called integrate-and-fire neurons (see e.g. (Hansel et al., 1998) or (Softky and Koch, 1995)). In these models the soma not only accumulates input, but more realistically also discharges itself over time, inputs have to come at a minimum frequency to charge the soma to a sufficient potential for it to fire. Models that take account of this phenomenon are called *leaky integrate-and-fire models* (Bugmann, 1997). With these models it is possible to establish syn-fire-chains if multiple neurons are interconnected (Eckhorn et al., 1990). Networks of spiking neurons have led to the so-called *third generation of neural network models* (Maass,

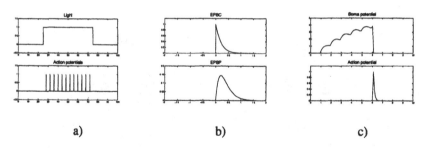

Figure 4 Retinal action potential in reaction to light (a), relation between EPSP and EPSP (b) and somatic integration of EPSPs until firing an action potential (c).

1997). However, the problem remains that the single neuron is not capable of some features observed in biological neurons.

2. THE BINDING PROBLEM

When multiple features of a single object have to be identified as belonging together in order to form a coherent representation this is believed to be done by the binding processes. A problem arises when multiple objects are perceived. The features from one object have to be disentangled from the features of another object by selective binding. Since this is not trivial, it is referred to in terms of *binding problem* (see e.g. (Rumelhart and McClelland, 1986)). In the human brain the binding process may be investigated by experiments with visual illusions. Usually, objects are bound together according to Gestalt criteria of object goodness (see e.g. (Sternberg, 1996), pp. 120). One of the Gestalt criteria is common fate, i.e. if two objects have something in common they will be bound together. Gray and Singer used stimuli exhibiting common fate for the investigation of the binding process in cats (Gray and Singer, 1989). They showed two vertical bars to the cats that were either moving into the same or in opposite directions. When the bars move into the same direction, they generate the illusion of one long moving bar and the two neurons that represent each bar fire synchronously. When the two bars move into opposite directions the neurons do not fire synchronously. This has lead to the assumtion that synchrony in neural discharges plays an important role in the binding process (Engel et al., 1992). In a neural model that uses synchrony for binding predicates to objects Shastri and Ajjanagadde have shown that this mechanism may very well be used in artificial systems for the task of binding (Shastri and Ajjanagadde, 1993).

Another type of visual illusion may occur due to the figure-ground separation (Grossberg, 1995). In Figure 5a one sees three black disks with missing pies (which are called pac-men :-). By simply rearranging these disks one perceives a white triangle on top of three black spheres in Figure 5b. These illusory figures are called Kanizsa-figures.

Figure 5   Three black pac-men on white ground a) and a Kanizsa triangle b).

Using Kanizsa figures, Tallon-Baudry et al. showed that there is a significant increase in gamma-oscillations in the human electroencephalogram (EEG) when illusory contous were perceived in contrast to perceiving pac-men (Tallon-Baudry et al., 1997). Herrmann et al. showed that these gamma-oscillation are synchronous to stimulus onset (Herrmann et al., 1998). Gamma-oscillations are waves with frequencies in the range of about 40 to 80 Hz (Başar-Eroglu et al., 1996). They are being generated by the above-mentioned EPSPs of pyramidal neurons in the visual cortex (see e.g. (Niedermeyer and Lopes da Silva, 1993), p. 20). It is known that pyramidal neurons fire in bursts, as shown by the spikes in Figure 6 (Bargas and Galarrage, 1995). The resulting EEG would be a sinusoidal wave forming an envelope on top of the spike bursts, as shown by the sine wave in Figure 6.

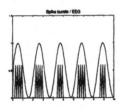

Figure 6   Generation of the EEG from spike bursts of EPSPs.

Since synchrony plays an important role in binding, Singer et al. argue that coincidence detection (a mechanism to detect synchrony) may be more important to the neural processing than the accumulation of inputs (König et al., 1996).

Summarizing the above phenomena that play key roles in the cortical processing of information, we think an artificial neuron should work as close to the biological neuron as possible and thus have the following properties:

- Code information in frequency

- Detect coincidence

- Fire in spike bursts

3. THE ARTIFICIAL AUTOSYNAPSE NEURON

Almost every neuron has a so-called *autosynapse* (also called autapse), that feeds back axonal action potentials to the own dendritic tree (Tamas et al., 1997).

This autosynapse offers a new functionality, since it is usually inhibitory rather than excitatory and further given that inhibitory synapses are typically located near to the soma (see e.g. (Greger and Windhorst, 1996), p. 1108), gives them longer time-constants than excitatory, soma-distant synapses. Inhibition leads to a decrease of membrane resistance in the dendrite, thus decreaseing the time-constant (see e.g. (Dudel et al., 1996), p. 120). We will model this relation in our *artificial autosynapse neuron* (AAN).

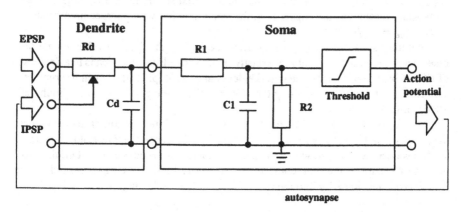

Figure 7   Artificial autosynapse neuron.

In our approach, pseudo action potential are being generated to serve as EPSCs by a spike generator with a constant frequency. By applying equation 1 the EPSCs look like those in Figure 4b (top).

$$\text{EPSC}_i(t) = A_{EPSC} \cdot e^{-(t-T_i)/\tau_{axon}} \tag{1}$$

The time constant, τ_{axon}, is 1ms and the amplitude, A_{EPSP} is 90μV for all incoming action potentials. T_i is the time at which one of i EPSCs arrives at the synapse. The dendritic tree is modeled by an RC-filter, as shown in Figure 7. This leads to

$$\text{EPSP}_i(t) = \text{EPSC}_i(t) \cdot (1 - e^{-(t-T_i)/\tau_{dendrite}}) \tag{2}$$

where $\tau_{dendrite} = R_d/C_d$ which is typically in the range of 10 to 30 ms for excitatory EPSPs. EPSPs on the dendritic tree are temporally and spatially integrated by the neuron (see e.g. (Schmidt and Thews, 1990), p. 52). In our approach the spatial integration is implemented by a superposition of all i incoming EPSPs, temporal integration is achieved by the accumulation of the superimposed EPSPs in the soma.

$$\text{EPSP}(t) = \sum_{j=1}^{i} \text{EPSP}_j(t) \tag{3}$$

The soma of our neuron is modeled by equation 4 which constitutes a leaky integrate-and-fire architecture.

$$\text{Soma}(t) = \text{EPSP}(t) \cdot (1 - e^{-t/\tau_{charge}}) \cdot e^{-t/\tau_{discharge}} \tag{4}$$

Here, the first exponential term represents the accumulation of EPSPs in the capacitor ($\tau_{discharge} = R_1/C1$) while the second exponential stands for the leakage that automatically discharges the capacitor at the same time but with a larger time constant ($\tau_{discharge} = R_2/C_1$).

Inhibitory synapses have quite a different effect on the dendrites than excitatory ones. They decrease the membrane resistivity of the dendrite which leads to a decrease of EPSPs by a factor of 10 (see e.g. (Dudel et al., 1996), p. 120) or even to complete cancellation of EPSPs by shunting them for a while (see e.g. (Greger and Windhorst, 1996), p. 1108).

We have modeled this behaviour by decreasing the time constant of the excitatory synapse by a factor of 10 as soon as the integrated IPSP exceeds a threshold. When the IPSP has decreased again, which happens with a much lower time-constant than for excitatory synapses, the time-constant for excitatory EPSP is being recovered. This introduces a non-linearity into the functional behavior of the model.

4. RESULTS

4.1. Frequency coding

In order to frequency-code its amplitude input, the neuron simply shunts the input voltage at the time of an action potential. Once shunted, it takes a time proportional to the amplitude of the input amplitude to again reach the threshold and fire again. Thus, the frequency of the action potentials is proportional to the input. This can be seen in Figure 8 for a low input which needs longer to load the soma to the threshold (top row) and for a higher input which loads the soma faster(bottom row).

4.2. Coincidence detection

The further away an EPSP arrives from the soma the more it will be attenuated by the resistance and capacitance along the dendritic tree. This makes coincidence detection more important for EPSPs of soma-distant synapses than for soma-near synapses.

If n action potential arrive at the exact same time on the dendrites of an axon, they add up to $n \cdot A_{EPSC}$. In contrast, if two spikes arrive with a time difference of Δt they only add up to $A_{EPSP} \cdot e^{-\Delta t/\tau_{dendrite}} + A_{EPSP}$. With a time-constant of $\tau_{dendrite} = 10$ ms the amplitude decreases to $n \cdot 0.9 \cdot A_{EPSP}$ if n EPSCs arrive with

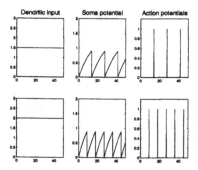

Figure 8   Higher amplitudes at the dendrites lead to higher firing rates (bottom row) than lower amplitudes (top row).

a mean time difference of 1 ms. If the time jitter of input is about 7 ms the EPSP amplitude decreases to half the size of synchronous EPSCs. This effect becomes more important, the further away from the soma an EPSC arrives, since the time-constant decreases with increasing distance from the soma. According to (Segev, 1995) the time-constant in the dendritic tips is about one tenth of that at the soma. This would mean that incoming EPSCs would be about halfed compared to synchronous ones if they arrive with a mean time difference of 0.7 ms.

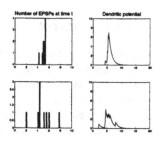

Figure 9   Coincidence detection yields much higher soma potentials for more synchronous inputs (top row) than for input arriving at random times (bottom row).

Figure 9 demonstrates how the phenomenon of integrating inputs with exponential decay automatically leads to a mechanism of coincidence detection. In the top row spikes arrive at the dendrites of the neuron at about 5 ms rather synchronously (time jitter $<\pm 1$ ms) resulting in a soma potential twice the size of the more randomly distributed spikes in the bottom row. There the spikes have a time jitter of about ± 3 ms.

It is interesting to see that the coincidence detection proposed by (König et al., 1996) happens automatically if realistic dendritic time-constants are taken into account.

4.3. Spike burst activity

The main result of our work is the finding that the *artificial autosynapse neuron* (AAN) is capable of generating spike bursts comparable to those obtained in the biological neural system. Figure 10 shows the constant frequency of spikes input to the dendritic tree of our AAN. In the first stage of the simulation, these pseudo action potentials are being superimposed and integrated by the soma. Whenever the some reaches a threshold of 0.4 an action potential is generated at the axon output and the soma potential is reset. This leads to a constant firing with a frequency that is proportional to the integrated input of the neuron. The action potentials at the axonal output are being again RC-filtered and accumulated to the feedback potential. When this feedback reaches a value of 0.3, the time-constant of the dendrite is reduced by a factor of 10. This starts the second phase of the simulation. The time constant is now so short, that EPSPs no longer superimpose, because they have completely decayed before the next spike occurs. This results in a soma potential which is below threshold which results in no further action potentials being generated along the axon with the additional result that the feedback slowly decays. When it has reached the value 0.1 the time-constant of the dendrite recovers, subsequently the simulation goes on as in the first phase and starts to oscillate between these two phases. This oscillation generates the spike bursts seen in the action potentials of Figure 10 (axon out) where all the neural potentials have been simulated.

5. CONCLUSIONS

We have described a biologically plausible artificial neuron which is able to generate spike bursts on its efferent axon. Since these spike bursts are the neural equivalent of binding object features together, this introduces a new possibility to evaluate psychological hypotheses by means of this model.

The architecture introduced above may be able to explain a mechanism of using two types of information for neural processing—receptive and contextual information—as proposed by Phillips and Singer (Phillips and Singer, 1997). The paradigm suggests that receptive input, e.g. from the retina, is in some way modified if additional contextual information gives evidence for known contextual perceptions in the data. Since pac-men do not induce gamma-oscillations unless they form a Kanizsa figure which are contextually more meaningful, one could assume that the proposed contextual information is coded in inhibitory potentials, leading to gamma oscillations.

The way in which we introduced inhibition in our approach is based on findings reported in literature. Other ways of implementing inhibition would also suffice the need for feedback. However, it is important to have negative feedback in form of inhibition to make the neuron generate spike bursts.

soft computing. Those computation which are better done by the computer than by humans, like calculations or database searches, will be done by crisp programs that are based on binary decisions. In contrast, more cognitive tasks will be solved by soft computing which simulates the vagueness of humans.

Acknowledgements I wish to thank Burkhard Maess and Thomas Knösche for valuable technical discussions on my model and Mark Elliott for psychological discussions and his polish on my English.

Max–Planck–Institute of Cognitive Neuroscience
Leipzig, Germany

NOTES

1. For this reason it is also called backpropagation algorithm.
2. An RC-filter is electronically composed of a resistor R and a capacitor C which leads to its name.

REFERENCES

Anderson, J. (1995). *Cognitive psychology and its implications.* Freeman.

Arbib, M. (1995). *Handbook of Brain Theory and Neural Networks.* MIT Press.

Başar-Eroglu, C., Strüber, D., Schürmann, M., Stadler, M., and Başar, E. (1996). Gamma-band responses in the brain: a short review of psychophysiological correlates and functional significance. *International Journal of Psychophysiology,* 24:101–112.

Bargas, J. and Galarrage, E. (1995). Ion channels: Keys to neuronal specialization. In *(Arbib, 1995),* pages 496–501.

Bibel, W. (1992a). *Deduktion: Automatisierung der Logik.* Vieweg.

Bibel, W. (1992b). Intellectics. In *(Shapiro, 1992),* pages 705–706.

Bryson, A. and Ho, Y.-C. (1969). *Applied Optimal Control.* Blaisdell.

Bugmann, G. (1997). Biologically plausible neural computation. *Biosystems,* 40(1–2):11–19.

Churchland, P. and Sejnowski, T. (1992). *The computational brain.* MIT Press.

Dudel, J., Menzel, R., and Schmidt, R. (1996). *Neurowissenschaft.* Springer.

Eckhorn, R., Dicke, P., Kruse, W., and Reitböck, H. (1990). Stimulus-related facilitation and synchronization among visual cortical areas: experiments and models. In Schuster, H. and Singer, W., editors, *Nonlinear Dynamics and Neural Networks,* pages 57–75. VCH.

Engel, A., König, P., Kreiter, A., Schillen, T., and Singer, W. (1992). Temporal coding in the visual cortex: new vistas on integration in the nervous system. *Trends in Neuroscience,* 15(6):218–226.

Gray, C. and Singer, W. (1989). Stimulus-specific neuronal oscillations in orientation columns of cat visual cortex. *Proceedings of the National Academy of Sciences USA,* 86:1698–1702.

Gray, P. and Meyer, R. (1984). *Analysis and Design of Analog Integrated Circuits.* John Wiley & Sons.

Greger, R. and Windhorst, U. (1996). *Comprehensive Human Physiology.* Springer.

Grossberg, S. (1995). Figure-ground separation. In *(Arbib, 1995),* pages 395–399.

Hansel, D., Mato, G., Meunier, C., and Neltner, L. (1998). On numerical simulations of integrate-and-fire neural networks. *Neural Computation*, 10(2):467–483.

Herrmann, C. S. (1995). A hybrid fuzzy-neural expert system for diagnosis. In Mellish, C. S., editor, *Proceedings of the 14th International Joint Conference on Artificial Intelligence (IJCAI)*, pages 494–500. Morgan Kaufman.

Herrmann, C. S. (1996). *Ein hybrides KI–System zur medizinischen Diagnose: am Beispiel der Elektroenzephalographie*. PhD thesis, TH Darmstadt, FG Intellektik. DISKI 145, Infix Verlag, St. Augustin.

Herrmann, C. S., Pfeifer, E., and Mecklinger, A. (1998). Gamma-oscillations during perception of illusory contours. *International Journal of Psychophysiology*, 30(1-2):133–134.

König, P., Engel, A., and Singer, W. (1996). Integrator or coincidence detector? the role of the cortical neuron revisited. *Trends in Neuroscience*, 19(4):130–137.

Maass, W. (1997). Networks of spiking neurons — the third generation of neural network models. *Neural Networks*, 10(9):1659–1671.

McCulloch, W. and Pitts, W. (1943). A logical calculus of the ideas immanent in nervous activity. *Bulletin of Mathematical Biophysics*.

Minsky, M. and Papert, S. (1969). *Perceptrons: An Introduction to Computational Geometry*. MIT Press.

Niedermeyer, E. and Lopes da Silva, F. (1993). *Electroencephalography, Basic Principles, Clinical Applications and Related Fields*. William & Wilkins.

Norman, D. and Rumelhardt, D. (1975). *Explorations in Cognition*. Freeman.

Phillips, W. and Singer, W. (1997). In search of common foundations for cortical computation. *Behavioral and brain Sciences*, 20:657–722.

Rumelhart, D. and McClelland, J. (1986). *Parallel Distributed Processing: Explorations in the Microstructure of Cognition*. MIT Press.

Schmidt, R. and Thews, G. (1990). *Physiologie des Menschen*. Springer.

Segev, I. (1995). Dendritic processing. In *(Arbib, 1995)*, pages 282–288.

Shapiro, S. C. (1992). *Encyclopedia of Artificial Intelligence*. John Wiley.

Shastri, L. and Ajjanagadde, V. (1993). From associations to systematic reasoning: A connectionist representation of rules, variables and dynamic bindings using temporal synchrony. *Behavioural and Brain Sciences*, 16(3):417–494.

Softky, W. and Koch, C. (1995). Single–cell models. In *(Arbib, 1995)*, pages 879–884.

Sternberg, R. (1996). *Cognitive Psychology*. Harcours Brace.

Tallon-Baudry, C., Bertrand, O., Wienbruch, C., Ross, B., and Pantev, C. (1997). Combined EEG and MEG recordings of visual 40 Hz responses to illusory triangles in human. *Neuroreport*, 8:1103–1107.

Tamas, G., Buhl, E., and Somogyi, P. (1997). Massive autaptic self-innervation of gabaergic neurons in cat visual cortex. *Journal of Neuroscience*, 17(16):6352–6364.

Zadeh, L. (1965). Fuzzy sets. *Information and Control*, 8:338–353.

C. KREITZ, J. OTTEN, S. SCHMITT, AND B. PIENTKA

MATRIX-BASED
CONSTRUCTIVE THEOREM PROVING

1. INTRODUCTION

Formal methods for program verification, optimization, and synthesis rely on complex mathematical proofs, which often involve reasoning about computations. Because of that there is no single automated proof procedure that can handle all the reasoning problems occurring during a program derivation or verification. Instead, one usually relies on proof assistants like NuPRL (Constable et al., 1986), Coq (Dowek and et. al, 1991), Alf (Altenkirch et al., 1994) etc., which are based on very expressive logical calculi and support interactive and tactic controlled proof and program development. Proof assistants, however, suffer from a very low degree of automation, since all their inferences must eventually be based on sequent or natural deduction rules. Even proof parts that rely entirely on predicate logic can seldomly be found automatically, as there are no complete proof search procedures embedded into these systems. It is therefore desirable to extend the reasoning power of proof assistants by integrating well-understood techniques from automated theorem proving.

Matrix-based proof search procedures (Bibel, 1981; Bibel, 1987) can be understood as compact representations of tableaux or sequent proof techniques. They avoid the usual redundancies contained in these calculi and are driven by *complementary connections*, i.e. pairs of atomic formulae that may become leaves in a sequent proof, instead of the logical connectives of a proof goal. Although originally developed for classical logic, the *connection method* has recently been extended to a variety of non-classical logics such as intuitionistic logic (Otten and Kreitz, 1995), modal logics (Kreitz and Otten, 1999), and fragments of linear logic (Kreitz et al., 1997; Mantel and Kreitz, 1998). Furthermore, algorithms for converting matrix proofs into sequent proofs have been developed (Schmitt and Kreitz, 1995; Schmitt and Kreitz, 1996), which makes it possible to view matrix proofs as plans for predicate logic proofs that can be executed within a proof assistant (Bibel et al., 1996; Kreitz et al., 1996).

Viewing matrix proofs as proof plans also suggests the integration of additional proof planning techniques into the connection method. Rewrite techniques such as rippling (Bundy et al., 1993), for instance, have successfully been used as proof planners

189

S. Hölldobler (ed.), Intellectics and Computational Logic, 189–205.

for inductive theorem proving but are relatively weak as far as predicate logic reasoning is concerned. A recent extension (Pientka and Kreitz, 1998) has demonstrated that rippling techniques and logical proof search can be combined and used successfully for constructive theorem proving and the synthesis of inductive programs.

In this paper we will present a coherent account of matrix methods for constructive theorem proving and show how to extend them by integrating rippling techniques into the unification process. We will first present a non-clausal extension of Bibel's original connection method in Section 2 and adapt it to constructive logic in Section 3. Section 4 describes the conversion of matrix proofs into sequent proofs. In Section 5 we discuss the integration of rippling techniques into matrix methods. We conclude with a discussion of possible applications of our work to program synthesis and verification.

2. THE CONNECTION METHOD FOR NON-CLAUSAL FORM

The connection method (Bibel, 1981; Bibel, 1987) was originally designed as proof search method for formulas in clause normal form. But as normalization of formulas is often costly and as many non-classical logics do not have normal forms, it is necessary to develop connection methods for formulas in non-clausal form. Bibel (Bibel, 1987) already describes a non-clausal version of his connection method. The version that we will present here is more general. It is based on Wallen's matrix characterizations of logical validity (Wallen, 1990) and can easily be adapted to a variety of logics.

Since matrix proofs can be viewed as compact representations of analytic tableaux, many notions from tableaux calculi carry over to matrix methods. The main difference is that tableaux proofs are based on rules that decompose a formula, generate subformulae, and eventually close off proof branches, while matrix methods operate directly on the formula tree and search for connections, i.e. pairs of identical literals with different polarities that could close a branch in a tableaux proof. In this section we will first introduce the basic concepts used in matrix methods, characterize logical validity in terms of these concepts, and then develop the proof procedure on the basis of the matrix characterization.

A *formula tree* is the representation of a formula F as a syntax tree. Each node corresponds to exactly one subformula F_s of F and is marked with a unique name $a_0, a_1, \ldots$, its *position*. The *label* of a position u denotes the major connective of F_s or the formula F_s, if it is atomic. In the latter case, u is called an *atomic position* (or *atom*) and can also be identified by its label. The *tree ordering* $<$ of F is the partial ordering on the positions in the formula tree where the *root* is the smallest position with respect to this tree ordering.

Each position in a formula tree is associated with a polarity and a principal type. The *polarity* (0 or 1) of a position is determined by the label and polarity of its parent. The root position has polarity 0. The *principal type* of a position is determined by its polarity and its label. Atomic positions have no principal type. Polarities and types of positions are defined in the table below. For example, a position labelled with $\Rightarrow$ and polarity 1 has principal type β and its successor positions have polarity 0 and 1, respectively. For a given formula we denote the sets of γ- and δ-positions by Γ and Δ.

principal type α successor polarity	$(A\wedge B)^1$ A^1, B^1	$(A\vee B)^0$ A^0, B^0	$(A\Rightarrow B)^0$ A^1, B^0	$(\neg A)^1$ A^0	$(\neg A)^0$ A^1
principal type β successor polarity	$(A\wedge B)^0$ A^0, B^0	$(A\vee B)^1$ A^1, B^1	$(A\Rightarrow B)^1$ A^0, B^1		
principal type γ successor polarity	$(\forall x A)^1$ A^1	$(\exists x A)^0$ A^0	principal type δ successor polarity	$(\forall x A)^0$ A^0	$(\exists x A)^1$ A^1

A *quantifier multiplicity* $\mu_Q:\Gamma\to\mathbb{N}$ (briefly μ) encodes the number of distinct instances of γ-subformulas that need to be considered during the proof search. By F^μ we denote an *indexed formula*, i.e. a formula and its multiplicity. We consider multiple instances of subformulas according to the multiplicity of its corresponding position in the formula tree and extend the tree ordering accordingly. For technical reasons we substitute variables in atomic formulas by the corresponding quantifier positions, i.e. γ- and δ-positions. Figure 1 shows the formula tree, marked with polarities, principal types, and a multiplicity, for the formula $F_1 \equiv$

$$\forall x Sx \wedge \forall y(\neg(Ty \Rightarrow Ry) \Rightarrow Py) \Rightarrow \neg\exists z((Pz \Rightarrow Qz)\wedge(Tz \Rightarrow Rz)) \Rightarrow \neg\neg Pa \wedge Sa \wedge Sb,$$

where the multiplicity of the subformula $\forall x Sx$ is 2.

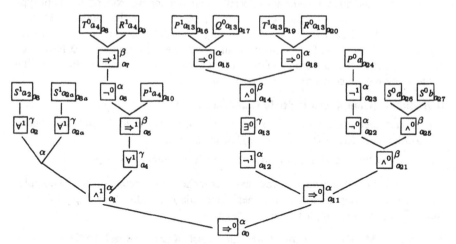

Figure 1 Formula tree for F_1^μ with $\mu(a_2)=2$

The *matrix(-representation)* of a formula F is a two-dimensional representation of its atomic formulas without connectives and quantifiers, which is better suited for illustration purposes. In a matrix representation α-related positions appear side by side and β-related positions appear on top of each other, where two positions u and v are α-*related* (or β-*related*), denoted $u\sim_\alpha v$ ($u\sim_\beta v$), iff $u\neq v$ and the greatest common ancestor of u and v w.r.t. the tree ordering $<$ is of principal type α (or β). u is α-*related* (β-*related*) to a set S of positions if $u\sim_\alpha v$ ($u\sim_\beta v$) for all $v \in S$. The matrix representation of F_1^μ is given in Figure 2.

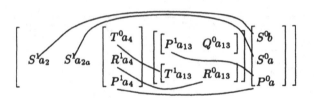

Figure 2   Matrix of the formula F_1

The matrix characterizations of logical validity (Bibel, 1981; Bibel, 1987; Wallen, 1990; Kreitz et al., 1997) depend on the concepts of paths, connections, and complementarity. A *path* through a formula F is a maximal set of mutually α-related atomic positions of its formula tree. It can be visualized as a maximal horizontal line through the matrix representation of F. A *connection* is a pair of atomic positions labelled with the same predicate symbol but with different polarities. A connection is *complementary* if its atomic formulas are unifiable by an admissible substitution.

The precise definition of complementarity depends on the logic under consideration. For classical logic, we only need to consider quantifier- or first-order substitutions. A *(first-order) substitution* σ_Q (briefly σ) is a mapping from positions of type γ to terms over $\Delta \cup \Gamma$. It induces a relation $\sqsubset_Q \subseteq \Delta \times \Gamma$ in the following way: if $\sigma_Q(u) = t$, then $v \sqsubset_Q u$ for all $v \in \Delta$ occurring in t. The relation $\sqsubset_Q$ expresses the *eigenvariable condition* of the sequent calculus, where eigenvariables $v \in \Delta$ have to be introduced before they are assigned to variables $u \in \Gamma$. Together with the tree ordering $<$ the relation $\sqsubset_Q$ determines a reduction ordering $\lhd$.

Definition 1. (Complementarity in Classical Logic)
- A first-oder substitution σ_Q is *admissible* with respect to F^μ iff the induced *reduction ordering* $\lhd := (< \cup \sqsubset_Q)^+$ is irreflexive.

- A connection $\{u, v\}$ is σ_Q-*complementary* iff $\sigma_Q(label(u)) = \sigma_Q(label(v))$.

As paths through matrices correspond to branches of tableaux proofs and complementary connections to closing branches, a formula F is valid if every path through some F^μ contains a complementary connection.

Theorem 2. (Matrix Characterization for Classical Logic (Bibel, 1987))
A formula F is (classically) valid iff there is a multiplicity μ, an admissible substitution σ and a set of σ-complementary connections such that every path through F^μ contains a connection from this set.

Example 3. *The matrix for F_1^μ in Figure 2 has 18 paths, each containing one of the connections $\{S^1 a_2, S^0 b\}$, $\{S^1 a_{2a}, S^0 a\}$, $\{T^0 a_4, T^1 a_{13}\}$, $\{R^1 a_4, R^0 a_{13}\}$, $\{P^1 a_4, P^0 a\}$, and $\{P^1 a_{13}, P^0 a\}$. The six connections are complementary under the first-order substitution $\sigma_Q = \{a_2 \backslash b, \ a_{2a} \backslash a, \ a_4 \backslash a, \ a_{13} \backslash a\}$. As no δ-positions occur in σ_Q, the induced reduction ordering $\lhd$ is the tree ordering $<$ and irreflexive. Thus σ_Q is admissible and F_1 is valid.*

According to the above characterization the validity of a formula F can be proven by showing that all paths through the matrix representation of F^μ contain a complementary connection. Obviously it is not very efficient to check all possible paths for complementary connections. Instead, a path checking algorithm should be driven by the connections: once a complementary connection has been identified all paths containing this connection can be eliminated from further consideration. This technique is similar to Bibel's connection method for classical logic (Bibel, 1987), but our algorithm is more general and useful for proof search in various non-classical logics.

The key notions of our path checking algorithm are active paths, active subgoals, and open goals. The *active path* $\mathcal{P}$ specifies those paths that are currently investigated for complementarity. All paths that contain $\mathcal{P}$ and an element u of the *active subgoal* $\mathcal{C}$ have already been proven to contain a complementary connection. All paths that contain $\mathcal{P}$ and an element v of the *open goal* $\mathcal{E}$ must still be tested for complementarity. If the latter can be proven complementary as well then all paths containing the active path are complementary. The algorithm will recursively check whether all paths containing the empty active path are complementary.

Let $\mathcal{A}$ denote the set of all atomic positions in the formula F. A *subpath* $\mathcal{P} \subseteq \mathcal{A}$ is a (not necessarily maximal) set of mutually α-related atomic positions. A subpath $\mathcal{P} \subseteq \mathcal{A}$ is a path iff there is no $u \in \mathcal{A}$ with $u{\sim}_\alpha \mathcal{P}$. A *subgoal* $\mathcal{C} \subseteq \mathcal{A}$ is a set of mutually β-related atomic positions. During proof search certain tuples $(\mathcal{P}, \mathcal{C})$ consisting of a non-complementary subpath $\mathcal{P}$ and a subgoal $\mathcal{C}$ with $u{\sim}_\alpha \mathcal{P}$ for all $u \in \mathcal{C}$ will be called *active goals*. $\mathcal{P}$ will be the *active path* and $\mathcal{C}$ the *active subgoal*. The *open goal* $\mathcal{E} \subseteq \mathcal{A}$ with respect to an active goal $(\mathcal{P}, \mathcal{C})$ is the set of atomic positions v with $v{\sim}_\alpha \mathcal{P}$ and $v{\sim}_\beta \mathcal{C}$.

Example 4. *In Figure 2 the sets* $\mathcal{P}_1{=}\{S^1a_2, S^1a_{2a}, T^1a_{13}, P^0a\}$, $\mathcal{P}_2{=}\{S^1a_2, S^1a_{2a}, R^1a_4, S^0b\}$, *and* $\mathcal{P}_3{=}\{T^0a_4, T^1a_{13}, R^0a_{13}\}$ *are subpaths for the formula* F_1. $\mathcal{C}_1{=}\{T^0a_4\}, \mathcal{C}_2{=}\{Q^0a_{13}, T^1a_{13}\}$, *and* $\mathcal{C}_3{=}\{S^1a_2\}$ *are subgoals.* $(\mathcal{P}_1, \mathcal{C}_1)$, $(\mathcal{P}_2, \mathcal{C}_2)$, *and* $(\mathcal{P}_3, \mathcal{C}_3)$ *are active goals. The set* $\{R^1a_4, P^1a_4\}$ *is the open goal w.r.t. the active goal* $(\mathcal{P}_1, \mathcal{C}_1)$; *the empty set* $\emptyset$ *is the open goal w.r.t.* $(\mathcal{P}_2, \mathcal{C}_2)$ *or* $(\mathcal{P}_3, \mathcal{C}_3)$.

We call an active goal $(\mathcal{P}, \mathcal{C})$ *provable* with respect to a formula F iff for the open goal $\mathcal{E}$ w.r.t. $(\mathcal{P}, \mathcal{C})$ and for all $v \in \mathcal{E}$ all paths $\mathcal{P}'$ through F with $P \cup \{v\} \subseteq \mathcal{P}'$ are complementary. This definition leads to a more algorithmic characterization of validity.

Theorem 5. *A formula F is valid iff there is a multiplicity μ and an admissible substitution σ such that the active goal $(\emptyset, \emptyset)$ w.r.t. F^μ is provable.*

The above characterization holds uniformly for a variety of logics and leads to a general path-checking algorithm that, coupled with an appropriate definition of complementarity, can be used as proof search procedure for all these logics. The path checking algorithm is implicitly described by the following theorem, which gives sufficient and necessary conditions for provability.

```
letrec prove(F,n) =
  let σ,μ = initialize(F,n)  in
   let CON = connections(Fμ)  in
    letrec provable(P,C,σ) =
      letrec check-connections(D,A,σ) =
        let Ā ∈ D  in                                        (* may fail *)
          (let σ₁ = unify-check(A,Ā,Fμ,σ)  in
            let σ₂ = provable(P,C∪{A},σ₁)  in
              if Ā ∈ P  then σ₂   else provable(P∪{A},{Ā},σ₂)
          ) ?   check-connections(D−{Ā},A,σ)              (* next Ā *)
      in
      letrec check-extension(E,σ) =
        let A ∈ E  in                                        (* may fail *)
          (let D = {Ā ∈ A|{A,Ā} ∈ CON ∧ (Ā ∈ P ∨ Ā∼α(P∪{A}))}  in
             check-connections(D,A,σ)
          ) ?   check-extension({u ∈ E|u∼αA},σ)            (* next A *)
      in
      let E = {A ∈ A| A∼αP ∧ A∼βC}  in
       if E = ∅  then σ   else check-extension(E,σ)
    in
       provable(∅,∅,σ)  ?       prove(F,n+1)
 in
   prove(F,1)
```

Figure 3   Uniform path checking algorithm

Theorem 6.

Let (P,C) be an active goal and $E := \{v \in A|v\sim_\alpha P \wedge v\sim_\beta C\}$ the open subgoal w.r.t. (P,C). The active goal (P,C) is provable iff

1. *the open goal E is empty, or*

2. *there is a complementary connection $\{A,\bar{A}\}$ with $A \in E$, such that the active goal $(P,C\cup\{A\})$ is provable and (1) $\bar{A} \in P$ or (2) $\bar{A}\sim_\alpha(P\cup\{A\})$ and the active goal $(P \cup \{A\}, \{\bar{A}\})$ is provable.*

Figure 3 describes a simple uniform path-checking algorithm based on the above theorems. The function provable checks the provability of an active goal (P,C) under an already computed substitution σ. It returns a new substitution, if it succeeds, and fails otherwise (? denotes failure catching). The variable E describes the positions A which may be used to extend the active path. If E is empty, then provable succeeds because of Theorem 6.1. Otherwise provable recursively checks all possible values for A (in E) and $\bar{A}$ (in D) according to Theorem 6.2. The function prove iterates the multiplicity μ, computes all possible connections in F^μ and checks provability according to Theorem 5. It is initialized with multiplicity 1.

The path-checking algorithm is parameterized with two functions, which express the specific properties of the logic under consideration. The function initialize determines the initial value for the substitution σ and the multiplicity μ while unify-check$(A,\bar{A},F^\mu,\sigma)$ tries compute a substitution that unifies A and $\bar{A}$, extends σ, and leads to an acyclic reduction ordering in F^μ.

For classical logic initialize(F,n) computes a pair (σ, μ) with $\sigma = \emptyset$ and $\mu(u)=n$ for all $u \in \Gamma$. unify-check($(A, \bar{A}, F^\mu, \sigma)$ computes a most general (term) unifier σ_Q of $\sigma(label(A))$ and $\sigma(label(\bar{A}))$, as well as the induced reduction ordering $\lhd := (< \cup \sqsubseteq_Q)^+$. It returns σ_Q if $\lhd$ is irreflexive and fails otherwise or if the two atoms cannot be unified.

Because of the stepwise increase of the multiplicity the path checking mechanism described in Figure 3 is obviously not very efficient and also not able to decide that a given first-order formula is invalid. In an efficient implementation the multiplicity for each suitable position is determined dynamically *during* the path-checking process. Other techniques that were used in theorem provers based on the usual connection method can be applied as well.

3. PROVING THEOREMS IN CONSTRUCTIVE LOGIC

As program synthesis and verification often relies on constructive arguments, systems for automated program development must be supported by proof search procedures for intuitionistic logic. Independently from the philosophical differences between classical and intuitionistic logic the main distinction between these two logics can be expressed by a different treatment of $\forall$, $\Rightarrow$, and $\neg$. Whereas in the classical sequent calculus only the quantifier rules affected by the eigenvariable condition are not permutable, in the intuitionistic sequent calculus in addition the rules dealing with $\forall$, $\Rightarrow$, and $\neg$ in the succedent are not permutable.

A matrix method for intuitionistic logic must therefore not only check if two connected atomic formulae can be unified but also if they can both be reached by applying the same sequence of sequent rules. Only then they form a leaf in a sequent proof. In the matrix characterization this is reflected by an additional *intuitionistic substitution* σ_J, which has to make the *prefixes* of the connected positions identical, where a prefix of a position u is a string consisting of variables and constants which essentially describes the location of u in the formula tree.

For this purpose the positions labelled with atoms, $\forall$, $\Rightarrow$, or $\neg$ receive an additional *intuitionistic type* according to the following table.

intuitionistic type ϕ successor polarity	$(\neg A)^1$ A^0	$(A \Rightarrow B)^1$ A^0, B^1	$(\forall x A)^1$ A^1	P^1 A^0	(*P* atomic) —
intuitionistic type ψ successor polarity	$(\neg A)^0$ A^1	$(A \Rightarrow B)^0$ A^1, B^0	$(\forall x A)^0$ A^0	P^0	(*P* atomic) —

Positions of type ψ correspond to the application of non-permutable sequent rules and are constants in a prefix string whereas ϕ-positions are variables. This makes it possible to use unification to determine the ψ-positions that must be reduced before a ϕ position in a valid sequent proof[1] and to develop a matrix-characterization for intuitionistic validity whose formulation is almost identical to the one for classical logic.

The *prefix* $pre(u)$ of an atomic position u is a string $u_1 u_2 \ldots u_n$ where $u_1 < u_2 < \ldots < u_n = u$ are the elements of $\Psi \cup \Phi$ (the sets of ψ- and ϕ-positions) that dominate u in the formula tree. An *intuitionistic substitution* σ_J is a mapping from positions of type ϕ to (possibly empty) strings over $\Psi \cup \Phi$. It induces a relation $\sqsubset_J \subseteq \Psi \times \Phi$ in the following way: if $\sigma_J(u)=p$, then $v \sqsubset_J u$ for all characters $v \in \Psi$ occurring in p.

Definition 7. (Complementarity in Intuitionistic Logic)
Let $\sigma := (\sigma_Q, \sigma_J)$ be a *combined substitution* consisting of a first-order substitution σ_Q and an intuitionistic substitution σ_J.

1. σ is *J-admissible* iff the induced *reduction ordering* $\lhd:=(<\cup\sqsubset_Q\cup\sqsubset_J)^+$ is irreflexive and $|\sigma_J(\mathrm{pre}(v))|\leq|\sigma_J(\mathrm{pre}(u))|$ holds for all $u \in \Gamma$ and all $v \in \Delta$ occuring in $\sigma_Q(u)$.

2. A connection $\{u,v\}$ is *σ-complementary* iff $\sigma_Q(label(u))=\sigma_Q(label(v))$ and $\sigma_J(\mathrm{pre}(u))=\sigma_J(\mathrm{pre}(v))$.

In the intuitionistic sequent calculus formulas of type ϕ can be copied. An *intuitionistic multiplicity* $\mu_J:\Phi\to\mathbb{N}$ encodes the number of distinct instances of ϕ-subformulas that need to be considered during the proof search. It can be combined with a quantifier multiplicity μ_Q and leads to an indexed formula F^μ.

Theorem 8. (Matrix Characterization for Intuitionistic Logic (Wallen, 1990))
A formula F is intuitionistically valid iff there is a multiplicity $\mu := (\mu_Q, \mu_J)$, a J-admissible combined substitution $\sigma = (\sigma_Q, \sigma_J)$, and a set of σ-complementary connections such that every path through F^μ contains a connection from this set.

Example 9. *Consider the formula F_1^μ from Figure 1 with $\mu:=(\mu_Q,\mu_J)$ where $\mu_Q(a_2) = 2$, $\mu_Q(u) = 1$ otherwise and $\mu_J \equiv 1$. The set of ψ-positions in F_1^μ is $\{a_0, a_6, a_8, a_{11}, a_{15}, a_{17}, a_{18}, a_{20}, a_{22}, a_{24}, a_{26}, a_{27}\}$, and the set of ϕ-positions is $\{a_2, a_{2a}, a_3, a_{3a}, a_4, a_5, a_7, a_9, a_{10}, a_{12}, a_{16}, a_{19}, a_{23}\}$. In the following, ϕ-positions will be indicated by capital letters. ε denotes the empty string.*

For the six connections which are used to show the classical validity of F_1 in Example 3 we have $\mathrm{pre}(A_3)=a_0A_2A_3$, $\mathrm{pre}(a_{27})=a_0a_{11}a_{27}$, $\mathrm{pre}(A_{3a})=a_0A_{2a}A_{3a}$, $\mathrm{pre}(a_{26})=a_0a_{11}a_{26}$, $\mathrm{pre}(a_8)=a_0A_4A_5a_6A_7a_8$, $\mathrm{pre}(A_{19})=a_0a_{11}A_{12}a_{18}A_{19}$, $\mathrm{pre}(A_9)=a_0A_4A_5a_6A_7A_9$, $\mathrm{pre}(a_{20})=a_0a_{11}A_{12}a_{18}a_{20}$, $\mathrm{pre}(A_{10})=a_0A_4A_5A_{10}$, $\mathrm{pre}(a_{24})=a_0a_{11}a_{22}A_{23}a_{24}$, and $\mathrm{pre}(A_{16})=a_0a_{11}A_{12}a_{15}A_{16}$.

The prefixes of the six connections can be unified by $\sigma_J = \{A_2\backslash\varepsilon, A_{2a}\backslash\varepsilon, A_3\backslash a_{11}a_{27}, A_{3a}\backslash a_{11}a_{26}, A_4\backslash\varepsilon, A_5\backslash a_{11}a_{22}, A_7\backslash a_{18}a_{20}, A_9\backslash\varepsilon, A_{10}\backslash a_6a_{15}a_{24}, A_{12}\backslash a_{22}a_6, A_{16}\backslash a_{24}, A_{19}\backslash a_{20}a_8, A_{23}\backslash a_6a_{15}\}$, while the terms can be unified by $\sigma_Q = \{a_2\backslash b, a_{2a}\backslash a, a_4\backslash a, a_{13}\backslash a\}$ as before.

The combined substitution $\sigma=(\sigma_Q,\sigma_J)$ is J-admissible, because the induced reduction ordering $\lhd:=(<\cup\sqsubset_Q\cup\sqsubset_J)^+$ is irreflexive. Thus F_1 is intuitionistically valid.

Theorems 5 and 6 hold accordingly with the intuitionistic definitions of complementarity and multiplicity. Therefore our path checking algorithm presented in Figure 3 can be used for intuitionistic logic as well. We only have to provide the logic-specific functions `initialize` and `unify-check`.

For intuitionistic logic the function $\texttt{initialize}(F,n)$ computes a pair (σ, μ) where $\sigma=(\emptyset, \emptyset)$ is a combined substitution and $\mu(u)=n$ for all $u \in \Gamma \cup \Phi$. The function $\texttt{unify-check}((A, \bar{A}, F^{\mu}, \sigma)$ with $\sigma = (\sigma_Q, \sigma_J)$ computes a most general term unifier σ_{Q_1} of $\sigma_Q(label(A))$ and $\sigma_Q(label(\bar{A}))$ as well as a most general prefix-unifier σ_{J_1} of $\sigma_J(\text{pre}(A))$ and $\sigma_J(\text{pre}(\bar{A}))$. It returns $\sigma_1 := (\sigma_{Q_1}, \sigma_{J_1})$ if σ_1 is *J-admissible* and fails otherwise or if either of the two unifications fails.

To compute the intuitionistic substitution we apply a specialized string unification algorithm (Otten and Kreitz, 1996). String unification in general is quite complicated but prefixes are a very restricted class of strings. Prefixes are strings without duplicates. In two prefixes p and q, corresponding to atoms of the same formula, equal symbols can only occur within a common substring at the beginning of p and q. These restrictions enable us to use a much more efficient algorithm for computing a minimal set of most general unifiers.

The unification algorithm is based on a series of transformation rules that are repeatedly applied to a singleton set of prefix equations $\mathcal{E}Q = \{p=q\}$ and an empty substitution $\sigma_J = \emptyset$. The procedure stops if $\mathcal{E}Q$ is empty and returns the resulting substitution σ_J as most general unifier. As the transformation rules can be applied nondeterministically, the set of most general unifiers consists of the results of all successfully finished transformations.

Our unification algorithm is parameterized by a set of transformation rules in order to be adaptable to a variety of logics. For intuitionistic prefix unification the peculiarities of the logic are expressed by a set of 10 transformation rules (see (Otten and Kreitz, 1996)). These rules enable us to compute a single most general unifier in linear time. Furthermore, a parallel application of the rules to a set of prefix equations allows us to decide in quadratic time if there is *no* general unifier.

4. RECONSTRUCTING SEQUENT PROOFS FROM MATRIX PROOFS

While matrix methods are very efficient for proving the validity of a given formula they cannot directly be used within sequent or natural-deduction based proof assistants. Although in principle it would be possible to embed the connection method as *trusted external refiner*, a technique supported by the upcoming release 5 of the NuPRL proof development system (Constable et al., 1986), a matrix proof can only be used to establish the *truth* of a given formula. If, however, the formula is a part of a program derivation, one must be able to extract a piece of code from the proof, which according to the *proofs-as-program paradigm* (Bates and Constable, 1985), is essentially the same as providing a constructive sequent proof. In order to integrate matrix methods into proof assistants it is therefore necessary to *reconstruct* a sequent proof from a given matrix proof.

As matrix-proofs are compact representations of sequent proofs, converting matrix methods into sequent proofs means re-introducing the redundancies that had been avoided during proof search. Obviously, the conversion should be performed without additional search since otherwise reconstructing the sequent proof would be as difficult as finding the proof in the first place.

The conversion algorithm that we will describe in this section complements the matrix-based proof procedures presented above. It is equally uniform in its design and consults tables whose data represent the peculiarities of various classical and non-classical logics with respect to matrix and sequent calculi. Basically, it traverses the formula tree of the formula F^μ in an order that respects the induced reduction ordering $\lhd = (<\cup\sqsubseteq_Q\cup\sqsubseteq_J)^+$ generated during proof search. It selects the appropriate sequent rule for each visited node and instantiates quantifiers according to the substitution σ_Q.

As $\lhd$ does not completely encode all the non-permutabilities of sequent rules, we have to add *wait*-labels dynamically during the conversion process. These labels prevent non-invertible sequent rules from being applied too early, which means that no proof relevant formulae are deleted prematurely. At β-nodes, which cause a sequent proof to branch, the reduction ordering has to be divided appropriately and certain redundancies (e.g. *wait*-labels) need to be eliminated in order to ensure completeness. We explain our method by a small example.

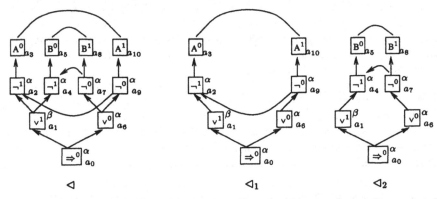

Consider the formula $F_2 \equiv \neg A \vee \neg B \Rightarrow \neg B \vee \neg A$ and its matrix proof represented by the reduction ordering $\lhd$, which consists of the formula tree of F_2 (straight arrows), the induced relation $\sqsubseteq_J$ (curved arrows), and the connections between atoms (curved lines). After reducing the β-position a_1 the reduction ordering is split into two suborderings $\lhd_1$, $\lhd_2$ and the conversion continues separately on each of the suborderings. To guarantee completeness, the operation *split* not only splits the reduction ordering $\lhd$ but also removes positions and arrows from each $\lhd_i$ (i.e. $\{a_7, a_8\}$ from $\lhd_1$ and $\{a_9.a_{10}\}$ from $\lhd_2$) which are no longer relevant for the corresponding branch of the sequent proof. The result of the splitting process is shown on the right hand of the above diagram.

The proof reconstruction process traverses the formula tree of F as follows

1. Select a position u from the set P_o of *open positions* that is not "blocked" by some arrow in $\lhd$.
2. Select a sequent rule according to the polarity and the label of u. If necessary, instantiate a variable according to σ_Q.
3. Mark u as visited, remove it from P_o and add instead its immediate successor position(s) to P_o.

$$\frac{\overline{A \vdash A}\;\; ax.}{\neg A, A \vdash}\;\neg l \qquad \frac{\overline{B \vdash B}\;\; ax.}{\neg B, B \vdash}\;\neg l$$

$$\frac{\dfrac{}{\neg A \vdash \neg B, \neg A}\;\neg r \quad \dfrac{}{\neg B \vdash \neg B, \neg A}\;\neg r}{\dfrac{\neg A \vee \neg B \vdash \neg B, \neg A}{\dfrac{\neg A \vee \neg B \vdash \neg B \vee \neg A}{\vdash \neg A \vee \neg B \Rightarrow \neg B \vee \neg A}\;\Rightarrow r}\;\vee r}\;\vee l$$

	P_o	u	rule	applied to
◁	$\{a_0\}$	a_0	$\Rightarrow r$	$(\neg A \vee \neg B \Rightarrow \neg B \vee \neg A)^0$
	$\{a_1, a_6\}$	a_6	$\vee r$	$(\neg B \vee \neg A)^0$
	$\{a_1, a_7, a_9\}$	a_1	$\vee l$	$(\neg A \vee \neg B)^1$
◁₁	$\{a_2, a_9\}$	a_9	$\neg r$	$\neg A^0$
	$\{a_2, a_{10}\}$	a_{10}	—	A^1
	$\{a_2\}$	a_2	$\neg l$	$\neg A^1$
	$\{a_3\}$	a_3	$ax.$	A^0, A^1
◁₂	$\{a_4, a_7\}$	a_7	$\neg r$	$\neg B^0$
	$\{a_4, a_8\}$	a_8	—	B^1
	$\{a_4\}$	a_4	$\neg l$	$\neg B^1$
	$\{a_5\}$	a_5	$ax.$	B^0, B^1

Figure 4   Sequent proof for F_2 and corresponding traversal steps of ◁

The traversal process and the resulting sequent proof for F_2 are depicted in Figure 4. Note that starting the traversal with a_0, a_6, a_7 instead of a_0, a_6, a_1 is not prevented by "blocking" arrows in ◁. This choice, however, would lead to a partial sequent proof that cannot be completed. Reducing a_7, i.e. applying $\neg r$ on $\neg B^0$, deletes the relevant formula $\neg A^0$ (position a_9). For this reason, our conversion algorithm adds two *wait*-labels dynamically to a_9 and a_7 and avoids a deadlock during traversal.

The technical details of our conversion procedure and the efficient elimination of redundancies after β-splits are quite subtle. An extensive discussion and algorithmic description can be found in (Schmitt and Kreitz, 1996; Schmitt and Kreitz, 1998).

5. INTEGRATING INDUCTION TECHNIQUES

The procedure for converting matrix proofs into sequent proofs suggests viewing the connection method as a proof planner for first-order logic that can be used to extend the reasoning capabilities of proof assistants by fully automated proof procedures. As formal reasoning about programs often requires inductive arguments the same methodology should be applied to integrate techniques from inductive theorem proving as well. Here, an annotated rewrite technique, called rippling (Bundy et al., 1993), has been used successfully to plan the reasoning steps from the induction hypothesis to the induction conclusion. This technique, however, shows certain weaknesses when dealing with program synthesis through inductive proofs, since in this case existentially quantified variables need to be instantiated. In fact, many program derivations require both first-order and inductive proof methods to be applied simultaneously, since both techniques are not strong enough to solve the problem independently.

Example 10. *The formula* $F_3 \equiv \forall x\, \exists y\; y^2 \leq x \wedge x < (y+1)^2$ *specifies an algorithm for computing the integer square root of a natural number x. A (top-down) proof of this formula will proceed by induction and lead to the following two subgoals*

(1) $\vdash \exists y\; y^2 \leq 0 \wedge 0 < (y+1)^2$, *and*

(2) $\exists y\; y^2 \leq x \wedge x < (y+1)^2 \vdash \exists y\; y^2 \leq x+1 \wedge x+1 < (y+1)^2$

While the base case of the induction (1) can be solved by standard arithmetical reasoning about zero, no single rippling sequence will be able to rewrite the conclusion of the step case (2) into the induction hypothesis, as the choice of y in the conclusion (y_c) strongly depends on the properties of the y in the hypothesis (y_h). If $(y_h+1)^2 \leq x+1$ then y_c must be y_h+1 in order to make the first conjunct valid. Otherwise y_c must be y_h in order to satisfy the second conjunct. Rippling would be able to rewrite the conclusion into the hypothesis in each of these two cases but it requires logical inferences to create the case analysis and to instantiate the existentially quantified variable.

On the other hand, logical proof methods alone would not be able to detect the case distinction either, as they would have to prove the non-trivial lemmata $x<(y+1)^2 \Rightarrow x+1<(y_h+1+1)^2$ for the first case and $y_h^2 \leq x \Rightarrow y_h^2 \leq x+1$ for the second. Of course, it is easy to prove the step case of the induction, if one already provides the crucial lemmata $\forall z \forall t\ z \leq t \Rightarrow z \leq t+1$ and $\forall s \forall r\ s<r^2 \Rightarrow s+1<(r+1)^2$ as well as the case analysis $\forall u \forall v\ u \leq v \lor v<u$ (using $a \leq b$ as abbreviation for $\neg(b<a)$), as the following matrix proof with multiplicity 2 for the conclusion shows.

$$
\begin{bmatrix}
y_h^2 \leq^1 x &
\overbrace{\begin{matrix} Z \leq^1 T+1 \\ {}\\ {-}Z \leq^0 T \end{matrix}} &
\begin{matrix} Y_{c1}^2 \leq^0 x+1 \\ {}\\ x+1 <^0 (Y_{c1}+1)^2 \end{matrix} &
\overbrace{\begin{matrix} U \leq^1 V \\ {}\\ V <^1 U \end{matrix}} &
\begin{matrix} Y_{c2}^2 \leq^0 x+1 \\ {}\\ x+1 <^0 (Y_{c2}+1)^2 \end{matrix} &
\begin{matrix} S <^0 R^2 \\ {}\\ S+1 <^1 (R+1)^2 \end{matrix} &
x <^1 (y_h+1)^2
\end{bmatrix}
$$

$$\sigma_Q = \{Z \backslash y_h^2,\ T \backslash x,\ Y_{c1} \backslash y_h,\ V \backslash x+1,\ U \backslash (y_h+1)^2,\ Y_{c2} \backslash y_h+1,\ S \backslash x,\ R \backslash y_h\}$$

But without the guidance of techniques that try to rewrite subformulae in the conclusion into the corresponding subformulae of the hypothesis one would have to search thousands of lemmata about arithmetics to find the ones that complete the proof, which would make the proof procedure far from being efficient.

It is therefore necessary to combine logical proof search techniques with controlled rewrite techniques such as rippling in order to improve the degree of automation when reasoning inductively about program specifications.

A first step in this direction (Pientka and Kreitz, 1998) has shown that a combination of rippling, *reverse rippling*, and simple first-order techniques can be used to generate the case analysis and to solve synthesis problems like the above automatically. The approach first decomposes the induction hypothesis by logical rules; uses sinks and wave-fronts to identify the corresponding subformulae in the conclusion; applies (forward) rippling rules to rewrite the components of the hypothesis; uses reverse rippling and matching to find a substitution and a rippling sequence that connects the conclusion with the result of rippling; and finally performs a consistency check to merge the individual substitutions into a conditional substitution for the conclusion as a whole. The search for a rippling sequence is based on the *rippling-distance* strategy introduced in (Kurucz, 1997; Bibel et al., 1998). The resulting rippling proof together with the case analysis is translated back into a sequent proof that can be executed by the NuPRL proof development system (Constable et al., 1986).

Since the only weakness of the above approach lies in the sequent-based logical proof search, it suggests an integration of the above techniques into a matrix based theorem prover. Essentially this will lead to an even more compact matrix characterization of validity and thus to further reductions of the search space in inductive theorem proving. In the following we will outline the fundamental steps towards a combination of rippling and matrix-based theorem proving.

The techniques described in (Pientka and Kreitz, 1998) enable us to generate *conditional substitutions* as a solution for a given synthesis problem. The conditions generated in the process will lead to a case analysis in the first step of a top-down sequent proof while each of the resulting subgoals can be proven by "conventional" proof techniques. A justification of this approach comes from the observation that a formula F is valid if and only if there is a set $\{c_1,..,c_n\}$ of logical constraints such that $C = c_1 \vee .. \vee c_n$ and each of the formulae $F_i = c_i \Rightarrow F$ are logically valid. This observation, which can be proven by the cut rule, is the basis of the following modified characterization theorem.

Theorem 11. *A formula F is (intuitionistically) valid iff there is a set $\{c_1,..,c_n\}$ of constraints such that $C = c_1 \vee .. \vee c_n$ is valid and for all i there is*

- *a multiplicity $\mu_i := (\mu_{Q_i}, \mu_{J_i})$,*
- *an admissible combined substitution $\sigma_i := (\sigma_{Q_i}, \sigma_{J_i})$, and*
- *a set C_i of σ_i-complementary connections*

such that every path through $F_i^\mu = c_i \Rightarrow F^{\mu_i}$ contains a connection from C_i.

Another compactification comes from the observation that a pair $\{A^1, \bar{A}^0\}$ of connected atomic formulae does not necessarily have to be equal under a given substitution σ. As complementary connections correspond to leaves in a sequent proof we only have to require that the negative atom A, which would occur on the left side of the sequent, *implies* $\bar{A}$ under σ. The implication, however, is not a general logical implication, but one that can be proven by standard decision procedures or by rewriting $\bar{A}$ into A. Thus a reasonable extension of the notion of complementarity is to consider *directed connections* $(A^1, \bar{A}^0)$ and to require A to imply $\bar{A}$ with respect to a given theory[2] $\mathcal{T}$, denoted by $A \Rightarrow_{\mathcal{T}} \bar{A}$.

Definition 12.
A directed connection (u^1, v^0) is *complementary* with respect to a theory $\mathcal{T}$ under a given combined substitution $\sigma := (\sigma_Q, \sigma_J)$ if and only if $\sigma_J(\text{pre}(u)) = \sigma_J(\text{pre}(v))$ and either $\sigma_Q(label(u)) = \sigma_Q(label(v))$ or $\sigma_Q(label(u)) \Rightarrow_{\mathcal{T}} \sigma_Q(label(v))$.

Basing a proof procedure on the above definition and the characterization given in Theorem 11 enables us to prove inductive specification theorems with existential quantifiers without having to provide domain lemmata and case-splits beforehand. Instead we extend the usual term-unification process by rippling and other theory-based reasoning techniques, which guarantee that the complementarity conditions are satisfied whenever the extended unification succeeds.

Another efficiency improvement during proof search comes from the observation that sinks and wave-fronts establish a strong relation between individual subformulae of the induction hypothesis and the conclusion. They help to identify connections that will be relevant for the proof and should be investigated first by the path-checking algorithm. By this we can reduce the search space, which is particularly helpful when searching for connections involving rippling. We conclude this section with a small example that shows the advantages of the extensions discussed above.

Example 13. *Consider F_3 from example 10, which – after unfolding the abbreviation for $\leq$ – reads as $\exists y \ \neg(x<y^2) \wedge x<(y+1)^2 \vdash \exists y \ \neg(x+1<y^2) \wedge x+1<(y+1)^2$, and its matrix below, where variables of γ-quantifiers are denoted by capital letters.*

$$\left[\begin{array}{c} \overset{\boxed{2}}{\overbrace{\qquad\qquad}} \\ x<^1(y_h+1)^2 \quad x<^0 y_h^2 \qquad \begin{array}{c} x+1<^1 Y_c^2 \\[4pt] \underset{\boxed{1}}{\underbrace{\qquad\qquad\qquad}} \quad x+1<^0(Y_c+1)^2 \end{array} \end{array} \right]$$

As connections should only run between atoms of the induction hypothesis and the corresponding axioms of the conclusion, the matrix contains only two useful connections $(x<^1(y_h+1)^2, \ x+1<^0(Y_c+1)^2)$ and $(Y_c^2<^1 x+1, \ y_h^2<^0 x)$. Since x and y_h are constants neither of the two connections can be unified and we have to use the rippling techniques described in (Pientka and Kreitz, 1998) to show their complementarity. In the first case $\boxed{1}$ this eventually leads to the substitution $\sigma_{Q_1}=\{Y_c\backslash y_h+1\}$. As the instantiated second connection does not describe an arithmetically valid implication, which can easily be checked by arithmetical decision procedures, we add the open goal $x+1<(y_h+1)^2$ as prerequisite c_1 (i.e. with opposite polarity 0) to the matrix and have thus established the validity of the sequent under this condition.

To complete the proof we now try to establish the validity of the sequent under the negated condition $c_2 = x+1<^1(y_h+1)^2$. By connecting this condition to $x+1<^0(y_c+1)^2$ we get $\sigma_{Q_2}=\{Y_c\backslash y_h\}$ which also makes the connection $\boxed{2}$ an arithmetically valid implication. According to theorem 11 we have thus shown the intuitionistic validity of the given sequent.

From a technical point of view, the above proof has synthesized a case distinction, which is added to the matrix, and has increased the multiplicity of the the conclusion to 2, as illustrated in the indexed matrix below.

$$\left[\begin{array}{c} \overset{\boxed{2}}{\overbrace{\qquad}} \quad \overset{\boxed{1}}{\overbrace{\qquad}} \\ x<^1(y_h+1)^2 \quad x<^0 y_h^2 \qquad \begin{array}{c} x+1<^1 Y_c^2 \quad \boxed{x+1<^0(y_h+1)^2} \\[4pt] \underset{\boxed{1}}{\underbrace{\qquad\qquad}} x+1<^0(Y_c+1)^2 \quad \boxed{x+1<^1(y_h+1)^2} \end{array} \\ \underset{\boxed{2}}{\underbrace{\qquad\qquad\qquad}} \end{array} \right]$$

Under the substitution $\sigma_Q = \{Y_{c1}\backslash y_h+1, Y_{c2}\backslash y_h\}$ the indicated four connections are complementary w.r.t the theory of arithmetic and span the indexed matrix in the conventional way.

6. CONCLUSION

We have presented a coherent account of matrix-based constructive theorem proving that combines proof search procedures for first-order intuitionistic logic with induction techniques. Besides proving the validity of a given formulae our combined method can also guide the development of proofs and programs in interactively controlled proof assistants. It enables us to greatly increase the degree of automation in these systems without having to sacrifice their elegance, the expressiveness of their underlying logics, or their interactive capabilities. Matrix methods can thus be used as the central inference engine during the verification, synthesis, or optimization of programs.

Our key concept is to view matrix-based proof methods as proof planners that do not underlie the typical limitations of sequent or natural deduction calculi when searching for a solution to a given problem. During a derivation they can be called either as *trusted refiner* or as mechanism which generates a proof plan that will later be executed by the proof assistant.

Obviously, this concept is not restricted to first-order or inductive theorem proving. In a similar way we can also integrate proof procedures for other important logics, such as modal logics (Kreitz and Otten, 1999) or linear logic (Kreitz et al., 1997), or higher-level strategies for program synthesis (Kreitz, 1996; Kreitz, 1998). In many of these cases we can rely on already known successful techniques that were originally implemented independently and view their results as plans for the actual derivation. By executing this plan within a proof assistant like NuPRL, Coq, or Alf we will eventually gain the amount of trust that is needed for the development of reliable applications.

In the future we will strengthen the integration of proof planning techniques into matrix-based theorem proving and investigate to what extent general planning and search techniques can be used to generate proof plans explicitly. We also intend to embed known synthesis, verification, and optimization techniques into proof assistants by using the same methodology. Our ultimate goal is to combine our experience with reasoning about group communication systems (Kreitz et al., 1998) and the above techniques into a highly automated proof environment for the development of safety-critical systems.

Christoph Kreitz
Department of Computer Science, Cornell-University,
Ithaca, NY, U.S.A.

Jens Otten, Stephan Schmitt
FB Informatik, Darmstadt University of Technology,
Darmstadt, Germany

Brigitte Pientka
Department of Computer Science, Carnegie Mellon University,
Pittsburgh, PA, U.S.A.

C. KREITZ, J. OTTEN, S. SCHMITT, AND B. PIENTKA

NOTES

1. This methodology is inspired by the admissibility condition for first-order substitutions in Definition 1, where $\sqsubset_Q$ determines which δ-positions must be reduced before certain γ-positions in order to satisfy the eigenvariable-condition.

2. This concept, which resembles the theory connections discussed in (Bibel, 1992), could also be extended to unary or n-ary connections w.r.t some theory $\mathcal{T}$.

REFERENCES

Altenkirch, T., Gaspes, V., Nordström, B., and von Sydow, B. (1994). *A user's guide to ALF*. University of Göteborg.

Bates, J. L. and Constable, R. L. (1985). Proofs as programs. *ACM Transactions on Programming Languages and Systems*, 7(1):113–136.

Bibel, W. (1981). On matrices with connections. *Journal of the ACM*, 28:633–645.

Bibel, W. (1987). *Automated Theorem Proving*. Vieweg Verlag, second edition.

Bibel, W. (1992). *Deduktion – Automatisierung der Logik*. Oldenbourg.

Bibel, W., Korn, D., Kreitz, C., and Schmitt, S. (1996). Problem-oriented applications of automated theorem proving. In Calmet, J. and Limongelli, C., editors, *Design and Implementation of Symbolic Computation Systems*, LNCS 1126, pages 1–21.

Bibel, W., Korn, D., Kreitz, C., Kurucz, F., Otten, J., Schmitt, S., and Stolpmann, G. (1998). A multi-level approach to program synthesis. In Fuchs, N., editor, *Seventh International Workshop on Logic Program Synthesis and Transformation (LOPSTR'97)*, LNAI 1463, pages 1–25.

Bundy, A., Stevens, A., van Harmelen, F., Ireland, A., and Smaill, A. (1993). Rippling: a heuristic for guiding inductive proofs. *Artificial Intelligence*, 62(2):185–253.

Constable, R. L., Allen, S. F., Bromley, H. M., Cleaveland, W. R., Cremer, J. F., Harper, R. W., Howe, D. J., Knoblock, T. B., Mendler, N. P., Panangaden, P., Sasaki, J. T., and Smith, S. F. (1986). *Implementing Mathematics with the NuPRL proof development system*. Prentice Hall.

Dowek, G. and et. al (1991). *The Coq proof assistant user's guide*. Institut National de Recherche en Informatique et en Automatique. Report RR 134.

Kreitz, C. (1996). Formal mathematics for verifiably correct program synthesis. *Journal of the IGPL*, 4(1):75–94.

Kreitz, C., Otten, J., and Schmitt, S. (1996). Guiding Program Development Systems by a Connection Based Proof Strategy. In Proietti, M., editor, *Proceedings of the Fifth International Workshop on Logic Program Synthesis and Transformation*, LNCS 1048, pages 137–151. Springer Verlag.

Kreitz, C., Mantel, H., Otten, J., and Schmitt, S. (1997). Connection-Based Proof Construction in Linear Logic. In McCune, W., editor, *Proceedings of the 14th Conference on Automated Deduction*, LNAI 1249, pages 207–221. Springer Verlag.

Kreitz, C. (1998). Program synthesis. In Bibel, W. and Schmitt, P., editors, *Automated Deduction – A Basis for Applications*, chapter III.2.5, pages 105–134. Kluwer.

Kreitz, C., Hayden, M., and Hickey, J. (1998). A proof environment for the development of group communication systems. In Kirchner, C. and Kirchner. H., editors, 15th *International Conference on Automated Deduction*, LNAI 1421, pages 317–332. Springer Verlag.

Kreitz, C. and Otten, J. (1999). Connection-based Theorem Proving in Classical and Non-classical Logics. *Journal for Universal Computer Science*, 5(3):88–112.

Kurucz, F. (1997). Realisierung verschiedender Induktionsstrategien basierend auf dem Rippling-Kalkül. Diplomarbeit, Darmstadt University of Technology.

Mantel, H. and Kreitz, C. (1998). A matrix characterization for MELL. 6th *European Workshop on Logics in Artificial Intelligence, European Workshop, JELIA '98*, LNAI 1489, pages 169–183, Springer Verlag.

Otten, J. and Kreitz, C. (1995). A connection based proof method for intuitionistic logic. In Baumgartner, P., Hähnle, R., and Posegga, J., editors, *Proceedings of the 4th Workshop on Theorem Proving with Analytic Tableaux and Related Methods*, LNAI 918, pages 122–137. Springer Verlag.

Otten, J. and Kreitz, C. (1996). T-String-Unification: Unifying Prefixes in Non-Classical Proof Methods. In Moscato, U., editor, *Proceedings of the 5th Workshop on Theorem Proving with Analytic Tableaux and Related Methods*, LNAI 1071, pages 244–260. Springer Verlag.

Pientka, B. and Kreitz, C. (1998). Instantiation of existentially quantified variables in inductive specification proofs. In 4th *International Conference on Artificial Intelligence and Symbolic Computation*, LNAI 1476, pages 247–258. Springer Verlag.

Schmitt, S. and Kreitz, C. (1995). On transforming intuitionistic matrix proofs into standard-sequent proofs. In Baumgartner, P., Hähnle, R., and Posegga, J., editors, *Proceedings of the 4th Workshop on Theorem Proving with Analytic Tableaux and Related Methods*, LNAI 918, Springer Verlag.

Schmitt, S. and Kreitz, C. (1996). Converting non-classical matrix proofs into sequent-style systems. In McRobbie, M. and Slaney, J., editors, *Proceedings of the 13th Conference on Automated Deduction*, LNAI 1104, pages 418–432. Springer Verlag.

Schmitt, S. and Kreitz, C. (1998). Deleting redundancy in proof reconstruction. In de Swaart, H., editor, *International Conference TABLEAUX-98*, LNAI 1397, pages 262–276. Springer Verlag.

Wallen, L. (1990). *Automated deduction in nonclassical logic*. MIT Press.

STEFFEN HÖLLDOBLER AND HANS–PETER STÖRR

COMPLEX PLANS IN THE FLUENT CALCULUS

1. INTRODUCTION

Imagine an autonomous agent performing a task in the real world. Its performance is based on an internal plan. From a low level point of view, the world is its own representation and the actions of the aforementioned plan are simple commands controlling the effectors of the agent. At a higher level of abstraction, the world is internally represented by states and (primitive) actions are transformations on the space of states. In this article we do not want to discuss how actions on the higher level lead to commands on the lower level or whether the abstract level is needed or not, although these are very interesting and active open research problems. We also do not want to deal with another burning question of how the agent got hold of its plan. The plan may be given to it by a programmer, it may have (semi-)automatically generated the plan from the initial state, the goal state and the descriptions of the primitive actions it is able to perform or it may have learned it from examples. For the purpose of this article we just assume that a plan at the abstract level is given.

But how should such a plan look like? In most studies performed so far, such a plan is simply a sequence of so–called primitive actions, which transform one state into another. For example, in the blocks world a simple plan may be used to stack all blocks into a tower. In such a plan the sequence in which the blocks are stacked is often fixed. E.g., if block a, b and c are on the table, then the plan "stack block b on top of a and stack block c on top of b" leads to the desired tower. This plan, however, cannot be used if there is a different number of blocks on the table. Moreover, the plan is unnecessarily precise, because the sequence of blocks is not important if we are just interested in building a tower of all blocks. Intuitively, we would like to add another layer of abstraction. We would like to abstract from the sequence of blocks used and from the number of available blocks. However, this involves more complex actions, viz. non–deterministic choice operators and recursive actions.

More formally, the question addressed in this article is whether the execution of a given plan p in a given initial situation s yields a given goal g. Thereby the fact that the execution of p in s leads to the fulfillment of g should be a logical consequence of an appropriate axiomatization of situations, actions and causality (see (McCarthy,

S. Hölldobler (ed.), Intellectics and Computational Logic, 207–223.
© 2000 *Kluwer Academic Publishers.*

1963; McCarthy and Hayes, 1969)). This problem was extensively studied for *simple* plans consisting of sequences or partial orderings of primitive actions (e.g. (Bibel, 1986; Reiter, 1991; Große et al., 1996)). However less attention was given to *complex* plans including conditional and recursive actions as well as non–deterministic choice operators (see Section 7).

This article is organized as follows. First, we demonstrate the need for complex plans by a simple example, the omelette baking problem, in Section 2. Then, we present the planning language used in this article as well as its semantics in Section 3. Thereafter, we discuss and formally define the notions of executability, correctness and termination of plans in Section 4. A formalization of complex plans by a completed equational logic program with an unification complete equational theory is given in Section 5. Up to this point the whole approach is developed independently of a concrete representation of states. We instantiate our approach by specifying states as multisets of fluents in Section 6. This leads to a formalization of reasoning about complex plans in the fluent calculus (Hölldobler and Schneeberger, 1990). Finally, we relate our solution to other approaches known from the literature in Section 7 and discuss some open problems and outline future research in Section 8.

2. THE OMELETTE BAKING PROBLEM

A cook has a finite supply of eggs, at least one of which is good, and a saucer. He can break an egg into the saucer, can smell at the saucer to determine whether the egg is good and can empty the saucer into the sink. His goal is to have a good egg in the saucer and nothing else.

This is a simplified version of a problem presented in (Levesque, 1996). For several reasons a simple plan cannot solve this problem:

- The action of breaking the egg is non–deterministic in that the cook does not know in advance whether the egg is good, and consequently has to react on the outcome of the action.

- The cook does not know in advance how may eggs he has to break before the first good one is in the saucer. In other words, he does not know in advance how many break and throw away actions he has to perform.

However, a complex plan can give an apparently straightforward solution:

Egg2Saucer

    where   (1)

Egg2Saucer $\Leftarrow$ *Break*; *if*(*Badegg*, *Emptysc*; *Egg2Saucer*, ε).

Intuitively, the action *Egg2Saucer* is a recursive procedure, whose body consists of the simple action *Break*, representing the breaking of an egg, followed by a conditional action. Within the condition *Badegg* the egg is tested to determine if it is bad, and depending on the outcome either the saucer is emptied (*Emptysc*) followed by a recursive call to *Egg2Saucer* or the procedure terminates with the empty plan ε.

3. A COMPLEX PLANNING LANGUAGE

We now give a formal description of the syntax and semantics of a language for complex plans which allows for conditional execution of plans, recursion and the choice of objects as parameters for actions, while at the same time minimizing complexity.

We intend to formalize reasoning about complex plans in a model, where *states* are snapshots of the universe at a given moment and *actions* are the only means to change from one state to another (see (McCarthy, 1963; McCarthy and Hayes, 1969)). For the moment we abstract from a specific representation of states. For example, states could be sets of propositional fluents as in the situation calculus or multisets of resources as in the fluent calculus.

Let $\mathcal{Z}$ be the set of states, $\mathcal{A}$ be a set of parameterized action names denoting *primitive actions*, $\mathcal{C}$ a set of parameterized condition names denoting *Conditions* and $\mathcal{H}$ be a set of parameterized procedure heads. Now we are ready to introduce the set $\mathcal{P}$ of *complex plans*, whose elements p are defined by the following expression in BNF:

$p = \varepsilon \mid a; p \mid if(c, p, p); p \mid h; p$
where
;   is the concatenation operator
ε is the empty plan,
a is a primitive action,
if   is a conditional,
c is a condition and
h is the head of a procedure definition.

A complex plan may be augmented by *procedures*, which are described by expressions of the form

$h / c \Leftarrow p$
where
h is the head of a procedure definition,
c is a condition and
p is a complex plan.

Let $\mathcal{D}$ denote the set of procedure definitions an agent uses for the description of his plan.

One should observe that the last action in each plan is ε. For notational convenience we often omit this occurrence of ε. We also omit the condition c and / in a procedure definition if c denotes a tautology.

The meaning of a primitive action $a \in \mathcal{A}$ is given by a set of triples of the form $\langle z, a, z' \rangle$, where $\{z, z'\} \subseteq \mathcal{Z}$. The set of such triples is denoted by $\mathcal{E}$. Intuitively, $\langle z, a, z' \rangle$ denotes that action a transforms state z into state z'.

Similarly, the meaning of the conditions is given by a set $\mathcal{V}$ of pairs $\langle c, z \rangle$, where $z \in \mathcal{Z}$, $c \in \mathcal{C}$. $\langle c, z \rangle$ denotes that condition c holds in state z.

The stepwise execution of a plan p in a state z is defined by the following transformation $\rightsquigarrow: \mathcal{Z} \times \mathcal{P} \to \mathcal{Z} \times \mathcal{P}$:

$$(z, a; p) \rightsquigarrow (z', p) \qquad \text{if } \langle z, a, z' \rangle \in \mathcal{E},$$
$$(z, if(c, p_1, p_2); p) \rightsquigarrow (z, App\,(p_1, p)) \qquad \text{if } \langle c, z \rangle \in \mathcal{V},$$
$$(z, if(c, p_1, p_2); p) \rightsquigarrow (z, App\,(p_2, p)) \qquad \text{if } \langle c, z \rangle \notin \mathcal{V},$$
$$(z, h; p) \rightsquigarrow (z, App\,(p'\sigma, p))$$
$$\text{if } \exists h', \sigma \,:\, (h'/c \Leftarrow p') \in \mathcal{D} \wedge h = h'\sigma \,\wedge\, \langle c\sigma, z \rangle \in \mathcal{V}$$

where App appends complex plans and σ denotes a substitution.

One should observe that the definition of $\rightsquigarrow$ allows several forms of non–determinism.

- $\mathcal{E}$ may contain triples of the form $\langle z, a, z_1 \rangle$ and $\langle z, a, z_2 \rangle$, where $z_1 \neq z_2$. E.g., this allows the specification of a break action which requires an egg as a condition and yields non–deterministically either a good or a bad egg in the saucer.

- In the execution of a procedure the condition may be used as a non–deterministic choice operator, which chooses one object out of all objects satisfying this condition.[1] For example, consider the procedure

$$Fillbox\,(x) \,/\, Ontable(y) \,\Leftarrow\, Putin\,(y, x); \; if(Full\,(x), \varepsilon, Fillbox\,(x))$$

used to fill a box x with blocks y standing on a table. The primitive action $Putin\,(y, x)$ puts block y in box x, and the condition $Full\,(x)$ determines whether box x is full. While executing the plan $Fillbox\,(a)$ in a state where the blocks $b_1, \ldots, b_n$ are on the table, the sequence in which the blocks are selected is not determined, since the substitution σ used in the definition of $\rightsquigarrow$ may be any substitution which binds x to a and y to some block b_i, $i \in \{1, \ldots, n\}$, on the table, thus satisfying the choice operator $Ontable(y)$.

Because of these non–determinisms the execution of a complex plan can sometimes take one of several execution paths. Formally, these paths are represented by *derivations* wrt $\rightsquigarrow$. Derivations and their length are defined as usual. A derivation $((z_i, p_i))_{i=0}^{n}$ wrt $\rightsquigarrow$ *terminates* if $p_n = \varepsilon$, i.e. the there is nothing left to execute. It *fails* if $p_n \neq \varepsilon$ and there is no (z_{n+1}, p_{n+1}) such that $(z_n, p_n) \rightsquigarrow (z_{n+1}, p_{n+1})$. In other words, it fails if there is no way for the agent to execute the next step of the plan.

4. EXECUTABILITY, CORRECTNESS AND TERMINATION OF COMPLEX PLANS

Returning to the initial question posed in the introduction we consider an initial state z_0 and a complex plan p_0. Furthermore, let g be a predicate over states which represents the conditions that should be satisfied in a goal state. Several questions arise immediately:

- When is p_0 executable in z_0 ?

- Does p_0 terminate if it is executed in z_0 ?

- Is p_0 correct?

A short reflection reveals that the questions are ill–posed without further considerations. What precisely is meant by executability, termination and correctness of plans? Since complex plans may contain non–deterministic actions and choice operators, the precise definition of these notions depends on the risks an agent is willing to take.

From the viewpoint of a sceptical agent who takes no risks, all possible derivations $((z_i, p_i))_{i=0}^n$ are to be considered. If the agent wants to succeed in every case the following conditions should be met:

- It doesn't want to get stuck – the next action of the plan should always be executable. We express this condition formally by defining the requirement of executability of a plan such that a plan p_0 is *executable* in state z_0 iff no derivation $((z_i, p_i))_{i=0}^n$ wrt $\rightsquigarrow$ fails.

- The agent wants to know beforehand that he will finish the execution at some time. This is expressed by defining termination as follows: the plan p_0 *terminates* when executed from a state z_0 iff there is an upper bound for the length of possible derivations.

- The agent wants to be sure to meet its goal. Thus, the plan p_0 is *correct* for state z_0 wrt the condition g iff for all terminating derivations $((z_i, p_i))_{i=0}^n$ the condition g holds in state z_n.

For the purpose of this article we stick to these rather strong notions. One may consider to weaken these as discussed in section 8.

To express these properties we introduce a four–placed relation $\rightarrow$ on $\mathcal{Z} \times \mathcal{P} \times \mathbf{N} \times (\mathcal{Z} \cup \{\bot\})$ which describes the complete execution of the program under a limited number of steps. It expresses successful execution:

$$z_0 \xrightarrow[m]{p_0} z_n$$

with $z_n \in \mathcal{Z}$ holds iff there is a terminating derivation $((z_i, p_i))_{i=0}^n$ of length $n \leq m$, . It expresses failure as well:

$$z_0 \xrightarrow[m]{p_0} \bot$$

holds iff there exists a derivation $((z_i, p_i))_{i=0}^n$ which either fails or is of length $n > m$. Using this relation, we establish the following proposition, whose proof is straightforward by case analysis.

Proposition 1. *A complex plan $p_0 \in \mathcal{P}$ is executable in a state $z_0 \in \mathcal{Z}$, terminates and is correct wrt. the condition g iff*

$$\exists m \in \mathbf{N} \; \forall z_g \in (\mathcal{Z} \cup \{\bot\}) : \left[z_0 \xrightarrow[m]{p_0} z_g \;\;\; \rightarrow \;\;\; z_g \neq \bot \wedge g(z_g) \right].$$

5. A LOGICAL FORMALIZATION OF COMPLEX PLANS

We are now going to express the properties of a complex plan with the help of an equational logic program (ELP). To achieve a degree of modularity we abstract from the actual description of the specific planning domain. We only require it to be expressed as an ELP whose semantics is defined by the set of first order formulas Δ_D which complies to the interface specified in the following paragraphs. An example for such an ELP is given in section 6.

A basic requirement for our formalization is that the states are reified, i.e. represented as terms. Thus, there is a injective mapping $\cdot^\tau$ from the set of states $\mathcal{Z}$ to a set of terms $\mathcal{T}$ assigning to each state its term representation.[2] Furthermore, conditions are represented as terms as well. The predicate $Valid(c, z^\tau)$ denote the fact that the condition c holds in the state z and the predicate $Goalstate(z^\tau)$ represents the goal g of the planning problem. Δ_D represents the planning domain described by $\mathcal{E}$ and $\mathcal{V}$ if the following holds:

$$
\begin{aligned}
\Delta_D &\models z_1^\tau = z_2^\tau & \text{iff} \quad & z_1 = z_2 \\
\Delta_D &\models Causes(z_1^\tau, a, z_2^\tau) & \text{iff} \quad & \langle z_1, a, z_2 \rangle \in \mathcal{E} \\
\Delta_D &\models Valid(c, z^\tau) & \text{iff} \quad & \langle c, z \rangle \in \mathcal{V} \\
\Delta_D &\models Goalstate(z^\tau) & \text{iff} \quad & g(z) \text{ holds.}
\end{aligned}
$$

In addition, Δ_D is assumed to be consistent and complete, i.e.,

$$
\begin{aligned}
\Delta_D &\not\models Causes(z_1^\tau, a, z_2^\tau) & \text{iff} \quad & \Delta_D \models \neg Causes(z_1^\tau, a, z_2^\tau) \\
\Delta_D &\not\models Valid(c, z^\tau) & \text{iff} \quad & \Delta_D \models \neg Valid(c, z^\tau) \\
\Delta_D &\not\models Goalstate(z^\tau) & \text{iff} \quad & \Delta_D \models \neg Goalstate(z^\tau).
\end{aligned}
$$

Δ_D should also contain an unification complete equational theory,[3] thus

$$\Delta_D \not\models z_1^\tau = z_2^\tau \qquad\qquad \text{iff} \quad \Delta_D \models z_1^\tau \neq z_2^\tau \;.$$

Furthermore, Δ_D should not contain any of the predicate symbols *App*, *Proc*, *World*, *Continuable*, *Doplan*, *Planfails*, and *Natnum*, which will be used in the following to model the execution of plans.

Δ_D can be specified in detail as soon as we have committed ourselves to the representation of states. Since our planning language and its semantics is indifferent to this commitment, we have just given conditions for Δ_D. As an example we instantiate our approach in the following section within the fluent calculus by using multisets of fluents to represent states; the mapping $\cdot^\tau$ and the concrete Δ_D are given there. For the moment we concentrate on the formalization of complex plans.

In the following we assume that all formulas are universally closed. Plans are concatenated with the help of a ternary predicate *App* denoting the append relation on lists as usual.

$$App\,(\varepsilon, p, p).$$
$$App\,(\,h; t\,, p,\ h; t'\,) \leftarrow App\,(t, p, t').$$
(2)

The set $\mathcal{D}$ of procedure definitions is represented by a ternary predicate *Proc* such that for each $h\,/\,c \Leftarrow b \in \mathcal{D}$ we have a fact of the form

$$Proc\,(h, c, b).$$
(3)

Now we can go on to represent our transformation $\rightsquigarrow$ by a four–placed predicate *World* :

$$
\begin{aligned}
&World\,(z_1,\ h; t\,, z_2, t) && \leftarrow Causes\,(z_1, h, z_2).\\
&World\,(z,\ if(h, p, p'); t\,, z, t') && \leftarrow Valid\,(h, z),\ App\,(p, t, t').\\
&World\,(z,\ if(h, p, p'); t\,, z, t') && \leftarrow \neg Valid\,(h, z),\ App\,(p', t, t').\\
&World\,(z,\ h; t\,, z, t') && \leftarrow Proc\,(h, c, b),\ Valid\,(c, z),\ App\,(b, t, t').
\end{aligned}
$$
(4)

To aid checking for failing derivations the predicate *Continuable* holds if there is a way to continue the execution of a plan p in a state z, i.e. if it does not hold, a derivation ending in (z, p) fails.

$$Continuable\,(z, p) \leftarrow World\,(z, p, s', p').$$
(5)

The four–placed relation $\rightarrow$ describing the possible executions of a program is represented with the help of the predicate *Doplan* . $\bot$ is a constant denoting that a plan has failed, 0 is a constant denoting the number zero and s is a unary function representing the successor function on natural numbers. The predicate

$$Doplan\,(z_0^\tau, p_0^\tau, s^m(0), z_n^\tau) \quad \text{is true}$$

iff

$$z_0 \xrightarrow[m]{p_0} z_n \ ,$$

i.e. there exists either a terminating derivation $\big((z_i, p_i)\big)_{i=0}^{n}$ of length $n \leq m$, or $z_n = \bot$ and there exists a failing derivation or a derivation of a length greater n (see previous section). Expressed in a recursive way one gets:

$$
\begin{aligned}
&Doplan\,(z_0, \varepsilon, n, z_0).\\
&Doplan\,(z_0, p, 0, \bot) && \leftarrow\ p \neq \varepsilon.\\
&Doplan\,(z_0, p_0, s(n), z_n) && \leftarrow\ p_0 \neq \varepsilon,\ World\,(z_0, p_0, z_1, p_1),\\
&&& \quad\ Doplan\,(z_1, p_1, n, z_n).\\
&Doplan\,(z_0, p_0, s(n), \bot) && \leftarrow\ p_0 \neq \varepsilon,\ \neg Continuable\,(z_0, p_0).
\end{aligned}
$$
(6)

A plan fails, iff it may lead to a state that is not a goal state:

$$Planfails\,(z_0, p_0, n) \leftarrow Doplan\,(z_0, p_0, n, z_n),\ \neg Goalstate\,(z_n).$$
(7)

Finally, the natural numbers are represented by the predicate *Natnum* supported by the unification complete equational theory contained in Δ_D: [4]

$$Natnum\,(0).$$
$$Natnum\,(s(n)) \leftarrow Natnum\,(n). \tag{8}$$

Now let

$$\Delta = \Delta_D \cup Comp(\{(2), (3), (4), (6), (7), (8)\})$$

be our axiomatization of complex plans, where *Comp* denotes the Clark completion (see e.g.Clark, 1978). The following proposition states that Δ is correct and complete. Recall that g is a predicate over states denoting the condition to be satisfied in the final state.

Proposition 2. p_0 *is executable in* z_0, *terminates and is correct wrt* g *iff*

$$\exists n \in \mathbf{N}: \Delta \models \forall z_g : [Doplan\,(z_0^\tau, t_0^\tau, s^n(0), z_g) \to z_g \neq \bot \wedge g(z_g)].$$

Sketch of proof: [5] First, one can prove by induction on the structure of plans that the predicate *App* models the concatenation of plans. Second, *Proc* (h, c, b) is implied by Δ iff it represents ground instantiations of procedures $h\,/\,c \Leftarrow b$ in $\mathcal{D}$. Based on these lemmata one can prove by case analysis that *World* represents the execution relation $\rightsquigarrow$:

$$\forall z_1, z_2 \in \mathcal{Z}, \ p_1, p_2 \in \mathcal{P}:$$
$$(z_1, p_1) \rightsquigarrow (z_2, p_2) \text{ iff } \Delta \models World\,(z_1^\tau, p_1, z_2^\tau, p_2).$$

Induction on n shows that *Doplan* represents the execution relation $\rightarrow$:

$$\forall z_0 \in \mathcal{Z}, \ p_0 \in \mathcal{P}, \ z_g \in (\mathcal{Z} \cup \{\bot\}):$$
$$z_0 \xrightarrow[n]{p_0} z_g \text{ iff } \Delta \models Doplan\,(z_0^\tau, p, s^n(0), z_g^\tau).$$

An application of Proposition 1 yields the desired result.   □

In order to reason about plans we use the predicate *Planfails* as applied in the following theorem:

Theorem 3. p_0 *is executable in* z_0, *terminates and is correct wrt* Goalstate *iff*

$$\Delta \models \exists n : Natnum\,(n) \wedge \neg Planfails\,(z_0^\tau, p_0^\tau, n) \ .$$

The proof is straightforward by case analysis.

6. A FLUENT CALCULUS FORMALIZATION OF THE OMELETTE BAKING PROBLEM

The formalization presented in the previous section is independent of the representation of states and actions. In order to completely solve the omelette baking problem, we have to choose an appropriate representation. We opt for the fluent calculus (Hölldobler and Schneeberger, 1990), a purely first order formalization, in which the frame problem is solved without the need to state any frame axioms or laws of inertia.

Within the fluent calculus, a state is a multiset of fluents. Fluents are represented by first order terms $f_1, \ldots, f_n$, which contain no occurrence of the symbols $\circ$ and $\emptyset$. Hence, a state is a multiset of the form $\dot{\{} f_1, \ldots, f_n \dot{\}}$.[6] Multisets of fluents are represented with the help of a binary function symbol $\circ$ which is written infix and satisfies the equational theory AC1, which consists of the equations

$$
\begin{array}{ll}
x \circ (y \circ z) = (x \circ y) \circ z & \text{(associativity)} \\
x \circ y = y \circ x & \text{(commutativity)} \\
x \circ \emptyset = x & \text{(unit element)}
\end{array}
$$

together with the axioms of equality. In order to reason about negated equalities, this theory is turned into a so-called unification complete theory AC1*. AC1* is then built into the unification computation and SLDENF–resolution can be used to determine whether a query follows from a normal logic program (see (Hölldobler and Thielscher, 1995)). There is a straightforward mapping $\cdot^\tau$ from multisets of fluents to their corresponding term representations. Let $\mathcal{M}$ be a multiset of terms, then

$$
\mathcal{M}^\tau = \left\{
\begin{array}{ll}
\emptyset & \text{if } \mathcal{M} = \dot{\emptyset}, \\
f \circ \mathcal{M}_1^\tau & \text{if } \mathcal{M} = \dot{\{}f\dot{\}} \,\dot{\cup}\, \mathcal{M}_1.
\end{array}
\right.
$$

Actions are represented in the fluent calculus with the help of a frame assumption. Consequently, each triple in $\mathcal{E}$ is represented by a ternary predicate *Action* , whose arguments encode the condition, the name and the effect of the action. Condition and effect are multisets of those fluents, which are affected by the action. For example, in the omelette baking problem the actions are represented by

$$
\begin{array}{l}
Action\,(\ominus, Break, \Longleftrightarrow). \\
Action\,(\ominus, Break, \overset{\text{\tiny $))$}}{\Longleftrightarrow}). \\
Action\,(\overset{\text{\tiny $))$}}{\Longleftrightarrow}, Emptysc, \emptyset). \\
Action\,(\Longleftrightarrow, Emptysc, \emptyset).
\end{array}
\tag{9}
$$

where $\ominus$ and $\ominus$ represent a good and a bad, smelly egg in the supply, and $\Longleftrightarrow$ and $\overset{\text{\tiny $))$}}{\Longleftrightarrow}$ represent a good and a bad egg in the saucer respectively.

The predicates *Causes* and *Valid* can now be represented by the clauses

$$
Causes\,(c \circ r, a, e \circ r) \leftarrow Action\,(c, a, e).
\tag{10}
$$

and

$$Valid\,(\mathsf{T}, z).$$ (11)
$$Valid\,(Badegg, \ominus \circ z).$$

respectively, where the constant T represents the truth value "true". The procedure *Egg2Saucer* , as defined in (1), is represented by the following clause:

$$Proc\,(Egg2Saucer, \mathsf{T}, Break\,; if\,(Badegg,\ Emptysc\,; Egg2Saucer,\ \varepsilon)).$$ (12)

To represent the goal we use the auxiliary predicate $In\,(m, z)$, which is true iff z contains m:

$$In\,(m, z) \leftarrow z = m \circ r.$$ (13)

The actual goal is that there is a good egg in the saucer, and no bad one:

$$Goalstate\,(z) \leftarrow In\,(\Longleftrightarrow, z),\ \neg In\,(\overset{\text{\tiny{\textit{}}}}{\smile}, z).$$ (14)

Now let

$$\Gamma = AC1^* \cup Comp(\{(2), (3), (4), (6), (7), (8), (9), (10), (11), (12), (13), (14)\})$$

be our fluent calculus formalization of the omelette baking problem. It is straightforward to verify that

$$\forall z :\ [Doplan\,(\ominus \circ \ominus \circ \ominus \circ \ominus, Egg2Saucer, s^{16}(0), z)$$
$$\rightarrow z \neq \mathsf{T} \wedge \exists s' : [z = \Longleftrightarrow \circ s'] \wedge \neg \exists s'' : [z = \overset{\text{\tiny{\textit{}}}}{\smile} \circ s'']]$$

is a logical consequence of Γ, and thus

$$\exists n :\ [Natnum\,(n) \wedge \neg Planfails\,(\ominus \circ \ominus \circ \ominus \circ \ominus, Egg2Saucer, n)].$$

as well. (An upper bound for the number of steps in the derivation can easily be given as the number of available eggs times the number of steps required for one execution of *Egg2Saucer*).

There is a straightforward implementation of Γ in Prolog by computing with the clause form of the definitions and using SLDENF–resolution. In fact, by checking carefully the cases, where equational reasoning is really needed, and giving a Prolog predicate for computing AC1–unifiers, SLDNF–resolution can be used. The Prolog program is given in the Appendix.

7. RELATION TO OTHER APPROACHES

There is a number of other approaches to the problem of reasoning about complex plans.

The work of Manna and Waldinger (Manna and Waldinger, 1987) is in a sense quite uncompromising. They establish a very complex plan theory whose main purpose is the ability to represent complex plans as terms, thus enabling generation of plans from the constructive proof of a logical formula stating the existence of a plan.[7] To be able to prove termination, this approach uses first order logic augmented by well–founded induction. Manna and Waldinger draw their ideas from their work on program synthesis. One may regard actions as computer instructions and the world as a huge data structure. Thus, the plan and the agents environment are both determinisic. Unfortunately, their formalism seems to be much too complex to be of practical use.

Stephan and Biundo (Biundo and Stephan, 1993; Stephan and Biundo, 1995) use variants of a modal logic DL for the interactive generation of recursive plans. They focus on the generation of recursive plans by refinement of domain specific plan schemata with the help of the interactive theorem prover KIV.

A close relation exists to the situation calculus based GOLOG language defined in (Levesque et al., 1997). The core idea of GOLOG is to give the user a means for specifying high level programs, which are translated into a second order logic formula. A proof of this formula in conjunction with a specification of the environment yields an action sequence, which can be executed by the agent.

The focus of the GOLOG development is different from the approach in this paper. A GOLOG plan is just a template which yields many action sequences which may be not executable, have dead ends etc. The task of the GOLOG interpreter is to find an action sequence which is executable and terminates. This may be done online or offline (Giacomo et al., 1998). Our approach instead focuses on the verification of a plan in a possibly non–deterministic environment which may contain non–deterministic elements only in a way that every possible choice of the agent leads it to its goal, i.e. every action sequence the program yields should be executable and terminate. This removes the load of runtime planning from the agent.

In contrast to the mentioned situation calculus based work our approach avoids the use of second order constructs for two reasons:

- The procedure definitions are translated into clauses of the logical formulas instead of being terms as in (Manna and Waldinger, 1987). With this translation one loses the possibility of quantification over procedure definitions and thus it is impossible to generate plans by proving a formula stating the existence of a plan. On the other hand, this approach is much less complex than the work of Manna and Waldinger (Manna and Waldinger, 1987) and avoids the use of second order formulas introduced in (Levesque et al., 1997) for this purpose.

- For the sceptical agent, who wants to know in advance that the plan execution terminates after n steps, it is sufficient to use the n-th approximation of the transitive closure of the $\leadsto$ relation describing the stepwise execution of the plan. With the use of a unification complete equational theory this is first order definable in contrast to the use of the full transitive closure. One should note however that it is not possible in our approach to prove that the plan does *not* terminate if it contains a loop. This would require proving that the plan fails for all limits $n \in \mathbf{N}$ of the execution length and thus requires induction.

In contrast to the above–mentioned formalisms, our approach can cope with the issues which arise out of non–determinism.

Recently, White translated GOLOG into an extended linear logic (White, 1998). While the transformation seems to be quite straightforward, the variant of linear logic used by White is non–standard. On the other hand, there is a close relation between the fluent calculus and linear logic as formally shown in (Große et al., 1996). Since the fluent calculus admits a standard and well understood semantics it seems to be preferable to the corresponding fragments of linear logic.

8. OPEN PROBLEMS AND FUTURE RESEARCH

We intend to use the planning language presented in this article to program autonomous robots. In order to do so we have to solve a variety of open problems. Actions like *Break* or *Emptysc* have to be translated into control commands for the effectors of the robot. On the other hand, the effectors of such an autonomous agent should not just receive commands from a high level planning language. Many tasks such as moving along a line should be performed within a low level circuit connecting the robots sensors to its effectors. But where precisely is the borderline between a so–called reflexive and a so–called deliberative behavior and how precisely do the two levels interact? Here we expect that we can learn from discrete control theory if we discover connections between this theory and reasoning about situations, actions and causality.

In a real environment the execution of an action may not lead to the expected effect. Constant monitoring based on an agent's sensors is required to determine states in which the plan must be modified or where replanning is needed. What precisely should a robot do if it observes an unexpected state change in the middle of a plan execution? First solutions to this problem were presented in (Giacomo et al., 1998). The problem itself is not trivial and good solutions depend very likely on specific domains since from a theoretical point of view replanning is as complex as planning in the worst case. Moreover, what should the robot do if the unexpected change of the state involves some sort of concept the robot is unaware of. For example, the robot may be trained to behave in the blocks world. While moving around a block, the block slips out of the robot's arm, hits the ground and breaks into three parts. What should the robot do if it has never learned anything about broken blocks?

An approach to this problem can be found in (Kennedy, 1998) which proposes an architecture for detecting the "unusualness" of an event on the basis of distinctions between model-based anticipations and actual reality. Although this work only touches on the problem of concept creation, it does provide a mechanism which enables a robot to detect that none of its current concepts are sufficient and it therefore needs to discover new ones.

Related to the problem of unexpected changes ("miracles") is the problem of conceivable but improbable outcomes ("surprises"). The concept of a sceptical agent used in this article seems too strong in a real world setting. If it was not known in the omelette baking problem that there is at least a good egg, there would be no plan which satisfies the cook as a sceptical agent. He would have to consider in advance going to a store to buy eggs, and because it is possible that there are no eggs in the store he would have to consider going to a farm ... ad infinitum. A cook as a brave agent would just break the eggs, and if they are no good, he would start planning again.

The complex plans considered in this article are given by the user. In future we would like to see an automated reasoning system generating or synthesizing these plans either from examples or from a given specification. The synthesis of recursive plans is still a wide open field to be addressed in the future.

The use of SLDENF poses some problems as well. The SLDENF derivation tree may contain massive redundancy in some cases. For instance if a box is to be filled with blocks on the table the derivation tree would contain branches for every sequence of blocks put into the box. But the actual sequence of blocks is unimportant for the box to be full after the execution of the plan. The use of lemmata or reduction rules in such a case might help.

9. ACKNOWLEDGEMENTS

The authors would like to thank Michael Thielscher and some anonymous referees for their valuable comments on earlier versions of this article.

Dresden University of Technology,
Dresden, Germany

APPENDIX: A PROLOG PROGRAM

We give below a Prolog program for the simplified version of the omelette baking
problem. In the Prolog program terms with o as well as plans are represented by lists.
The predicate acl_split(X, Y, Rest) solves the AC1–equation $X \circ Rest = Y$.

Domain independent part

```
acl_split([], T, T).
acl_split([E|R], T, R1) :-
    multi_minus(T,E,T1),
    acl_split(R,T1,R1).

multi_minus([E|R],E,R) :- !.
multi_minus([E1|R1],E,[E1|R2]) :-
    multi_minus(R1, E, R2).

world(Z1,[A|P],Z2,P) :- causes(Z1,A,Z2).
world(Z1,[if(H,PA,PB)|P],Z1,PN) :-
    holds(H,Z1), append(PA,P,PN).
world(Z1,[if(H,PA,PB)|P],Z1,PN) :-
    \+ holds(H,Z1), append(PB,P,PN).
world(Z1,[H|P],Z1,PN) :-
    proc(H,C,B), holds(C,Z1),
    append(B,P,PN).

continuable(Z1,P1) :- world(Z1,P1,_Z2,_P2).

doplan(S0,[],_M,S0).
doplan(_S0,_P0,0,fail).
doplan(S0,P0,M,SN) :-
    P0\=[],  M > 0, M1 is M-1,
    world(S0,P0,Z1,P1), doplan(Z1,P1,M1,SN).
doplan(S0,P0,M,fail) :-
    P0\=[], M > 0, \+ continuable(S0,P0).

planfails(S0,P0,N) :- doplan(S0,P0,N,SN),
    \+ goalstate(SN).

nat(0).
nat(X1) :- nat(X), X1 is X+1.
```

Domain dependent part

```
action([eg],break,[sg]).
action([eb],break,[sb]).
action([sg],emptysc,[]).
action([sb],emptysc,[]).

causes(Z1,A,Z2) :- action(C,A,E),
    ac1_split(C,Z1,R), append(E,R,Z2).

holds(true,Z).
holds(badegg,Z) :- ac1_split([sb],Z,_).

proc(egg2saucer,true,
    [break,
        if(badegg,[emptysc,egg2saucer],[])
    ]).

goalstate(Z) :- SN \= fail,
    ac1_split([sg],Z,_),
    \+ ac1_split([sb],Z,_).
```

Query

To check that the plan *Egg2Saucer* solves the problem for the case of three bad eggs and one good egg the Prolog interpreter has to prove

```
:- nat(N), \+ planfails([eb,eb,eg,eb],
                        [egg2saucer],N).
```

This yields the answer $N = 16$, i.e. the plan succeeds in at most 16 steps. The query

```
:- doplan([eb,eb,eg,eb],[egg2saucer],16,Z).
```

yields the possibly reached final states within the limit of 16 steps:

```
Z = [sg, eb, eb, eb] ;
Z = [sg, eb, eb] ;
Z = [sg, eb] ;
Z = [sg] ;
```

NOTES

1. This is similar to the $\pi(x)\sigma$ construct of GOLOG (Levesque et al., 1997).

2. The term representation of a state may be either a term describing the history of the present state, as in the situation calculus, or a direct representation of the state, as in the fluent calculus (see next section).

3. This can be the Clark theory of equality or, in the case of the fluent calculus (see below), an unification complete equational theory.

4. Induction axioms are not necessary for our purpose; more comments on that are given in the discussion.

5. The full proof can be obtained along the lines presented in (Störr, 1997).

6. The symbols used to denote sets and the usual operations on sets are also used here to denote multisets and the operations defined on multisets, but we stack a · on top of them.

7. A further reason for the high complexity seems to be the use of the situation calculus: a large part of the plan theory is used to bind plan terms to specific situations during the execution of a plan by introducing the extra situation argument.

REFERENCES

Bibel, W. (1986). A deductive solution for plan generation. *New Generation Computing*, 4:115–132.

Biundo, S. and Stephan, W. (1993). A new logical framwork for deductive planning. In *Proceedings of the International Joint Conference on Artificial Intelligence*, pages 32–38.

Clark, K. L. (1978). Negation as Failure. In Gallaire, H. and Minker, J., editors, *Workshop Logic and Data Bases*, pages 293–322. Plenum Press.

Giacomo, G. D., Reiter, R., and Soutchanski, M. (1998). Execution monitoring of high-level robot programs. In Cohn, A. G., Schubert, L., and Shapiro, S. C., editors, *Principles of Knowledge Representation and Reasoning: Proceedings of the Sixth International Conference (KR'98).*, pages 453–464. Morgan Kaufmann Publishers, Inc., San Francisco.

Große, G., Hölldobler, S., and Schneeberger, J. (1996). Linear deductive planning. *Journal of Logic and Computation*, 6(2):233–262.

Hölldobler, S. and Schneeberger, J. (1990). A new deductive approach to planning. *New Generation Computing*, 8:225–244. A short version appeared in the Proceedings of the German Workshop on Artificial Intelligence, Informatik Fachberichte *216*, pages 63-73, 1989.

Hölldobler, S. and Thielscher, M. (1995). Computing change and specificity with equational logic programs. *Annals of Mathematics and Artificial Intelligence*, 14:99–133.

Kennedy, C. M. (1998). A conceptual foundation for autonomous learning in unforeseen situations. In *IEEE International Symposium on Intelligent Control (ISIC/CIRA/ISAS'98)*, Gaithersburg, Maryland.

Levesque, H., Reiter, R., Lespérance, Y., Lin, F., and Scherl, R. (1997). Golog: A logic programming language for dynamic domains. *Journal of Logic Programming*, Special Issue 'Action and Change'.

Levesque, H. J. (1996). What is planning in the presence of sensing? Technical report, Department of Computer Science, University of Toronto, Canada.

Manna, Z. and Waldinger, R. (1987). How to clear a block: A theory of plans. *Journal of Automated Reasoning*, 4(3):343–377.

McCarthy, J. (1963). Situations and actions and causal laws. Stanford Artificial Intelligence Project: Memo 2.

McCarthy, J. and Hayes, P. J. (1969). Some philosophical problems from the standpoint of Artificial Intelligence. In Meltzer, B. and Michie, D., editors, *Machine Intelligence 4*, pages 463 – 502. Edinburgh University Press.

Reiter, R. (1991). The frame problem in the situation calculus: A simple solution (sometimes) and a completeness result vor goal regression. In Lifschitz, V., editor, *Artificial Intelligence and Mathematical*

Theory of Computation: Papers in Honor of John McCarthy, pages 359–380. Academic Press, San Diego, CA.

Stephan, W. and Biundo, S. (1995). Deduction-based refinement planning. Technical Report RR-95-13, Germen Research Center for Artificial Intelligence (DFKI).

Störr, H.-P. (1997). Bedingte und Rekursive Aktionen im Fluent–Kalkül. Master's thesis, Dresden University of Technology. (in German).

White, G. (1998). Golog and linear logic programming. Technical report, Dept. Computer Science, Queen Mary and Westfield College, University of London.

GERHARD LAKEMEYER AND HECTOR J. LEVESQUE

QUERYING AOL KNOWLEDGE BASES

— *Preliminary Report* —

1. INTRODUCTION

For agents to behave successfully, they often need to reason about what they know and do not know about the world. For example, an agent may choose a particular sensing action only after it realizes that it is missing an important piece of information. From a knowledge representation point of view, the idea would be to supply the agent with a suitable knowledge base (KB) and provide it with an appropriate mechanism to query the KB. In order to get a glimpse of the complexity of the kinds of queries that might arise when actions are involved, let us consider the following example.

Suppose we have a robot that knows nothing about the initial state of the environment except that it is less than 20 units away from a wall. The robot is also able to read its sonar, which tells it when it is getting close to a wall, where close means, say, less than 10 units between the wall and the robot. The sonar does not tell the robot the exact distance, though. Assume we have somehow suitably encoded the robot's information about the world and its actions. The robot, being in the initial state and concerned about its distance to the wall, may then want to pose questions like these to its knowledge base:

1. Am I currently close? Answer: unknown.

2. Do I know exactly how many units I am away from the wall? Answer: no.

3. Will the distance to the wall be more than 20 units after I move 1 unit away from the wall? Answer: no.

4. Will I know whether I am close to the wall after reading the sonar? Answer: yes.

Observe that queries (2) and (4) involve explicit reference to the agent's own knowledge, which calls for a sufficiently expressive (epistemic) query language. If we want to formalize examples like the above, two main questions need to be answered:

225

S. Hölldobler (ed.), Intellectics and Computational Logic, 225–244.

how do we represent the agent's knowledge about actions and the initial state and how do we specify a query mechanism which gives the robot the intended answers? For the representation part we will essentially lean on the standard answer given in the framework of the situation calculus. To specify the result of a query, we use the logic $\mathcal{AOL}$, which was recently proposed by Lakemeyer and Levesque (Lakemeyer and Levesque, 1998) and which amalgamates both the situation calculus and Levesque's logic of only knowing. $\mathcal{AOL}$ gives an account of reasoning about ordinary actions, sensing actions, knowledge about knowledge and actions, and only knowing. The latter is particularly useful when it comes to specifying what a KB knows, since it allows us to draw conclusions not only about what is known but also about what is *not* known given the sentences in the KB. In this paper, we show how to specify a query mechanism within $\mathcal{AOL}$ and investigate some of its properties. In particular, we show that queries can sometimes be reduced to ordinary first-order reasoning, even though $\mathcal{AOL}$ itself is second-order and queries may contain epistemic modalities.

The rest of the paper is organized as follows. In Sections 2 and 3, we briefly review the situation calculus and the logic $\mathcal{OL}$, respectively. In Section 4, we introduce the logic $\mathcal{AOL}$ semantically and discuss how knowledge and action are modelled within this framework. In Section 5, we define how to query an agent's knowledge at an abstract level. In Section 6, we consider concrete knowledge bases and discuss the issue of query evaluation there. Section 7 presents a brief summary and suggests areas of future work.

2. THE SITUATION CALCULUS

One increasingly popular language for representing and reasoning about the preconditions and effects of actions is the situation calculus (McCarthy, 1963). We will only go over the language briefly here noting the following features: all terms in the language are one of three sorts, ordinary objects, actions or situations; there is a special constant S_0 used to denote the *initial situation*, namely that situation in which no actions have yet occurred; there is a distinguished binary function symbol *do* where $do(a, s)$ denotes the successor situation to s resulting from performing the action a; relations whose truth values vary from situation to situation, are called relational *fluents*, and are denoted by predicate symbols taking a situation term as their last argument; similarly, functions varying across situations are called functional fluents and are denoted analogously; finally, there is a special predicate $Poss(a, s)$ used to state that action a is executable in situation s.

Within this language, we can formulate theories which describe how the world changes as the result of the available actions. One possibility is a *basic action theory* of the following form (Reiter, 1991):

- Axioms describing the initial situation, S_0.

- Action precondition axioms, one for each primitive action a, characterizing $Poss(a, s)$.

- Successor state axioms, one for each fluent F, stating under what conditions $F(\vec{x}, do(a, s))$ holds as a function of what holds in situation s. These take the place of the so-called effect axioms, but also provide a solution to the frame problem (Reiter, 1991).

- Domain closure and unique names axioms for the primitive actions.

- A collection of foundational, domain independent axioms.

In (Lin and Reiter, 1994) the following foundational axioms are considered:[1]

1. $\forall s \forall a. S_0 \neq do(a, s)$.

2. $\forall a_1, a_2, s_1, s_2. do(a_1, s_1) = do(a_2, s_2) \supset (a_1 = a_2 \wedge s_1 = s_2)$.

3. $\forall P. P(S_0) \wedge [\forall s \forall a.(P(s) \supset P(do(a, s)))] \supset \forall s P(s)$.

4. $\forall s. \neg(s < S_0)$.

5. $\forall s, s', a. (s < do(a, s') \equiv (Poss(a, s') \wedge s \leq s'))$,
   where $s \leq s'$ is an abbreviation for $s < s' \vee s = s'$.

The first three axioms serve to characterize the space of all situations, making it isomorphic to the set of ground terms of the form $do(a_1, \cdots, do(a_n, S_0) \cdots)$. The third of these is a second-order induction axiom that ensures that there are no situations other than those accessible using do from S_0. The final two axioms serve to characterize a $<$ relation between situations.

3. THE LOGIC $\mathcal{OL}$

The language of $\mathcal{OL}$ is a modal first-order dialect with equality and function symbols plus a countably infinite set of standard names $\mathcal{N} = \{{}^\#0, {}^\#1, {}^\#2, \ldots\}$ which will serve as our universe of discourse. As discussed in more detail in (Levesque, 1984; Levesque and Lakemeyer, 2000), standard names allow interesting distinctions between *de dicto* and *de re* beliefs (see below for an example). Terms and atomic formulas are defined as usual. A term is called *primitive* if it consists of a function symbol followed by standard names as arguments. Similarly a formula is called primitive if it consists of a predicate symbol followed by standard names. Arbitrary formulas of $\mathcal{OL}$ are constructed in the usual way from the atomic formulas, equality, the connectives $\neg$ and $\vee$, the quantifier $\forall$,[2] and the modal operators K and O, where $K\alpha$ should be read as "the agent knows α" and $O\alpha$ as "the agent only knows α." *Sentences* are formulas without free variables. A formula is called *objective* if it does not contain any modal operators. Vector notation will be used freely for sequences, for example, $\forall \vec{x}$ for $\forall x_1 \cdots \forall x_k$.

The semantics of $\mathcal{OL}$ is based on the familiar notion of a world, which assigns meaning to the nonlogical symbols of the language. $\mathcal{OL}$ makes the assumption that all worlds have as their universe of discourse the same set which is isomorphic to the standard names, that is, an individual is identified with a unique name. A world is then completely specified by providing the meaning of every primitive term and formula:

Definition 1. *A world w is a function from primitive expressions into $\{0, 1\} \cup \mathcal{N}$, where $w[p] \in \{0, 1\}$ for primitive formulas p, and $w[t] \in \mathcal{N}$ for primitive terms t.*

Given a world w, the denotation of an arbitrary ground term t is defined recursively as

$|n|_w = n$, where n is a standard name.

$|f(t_1, \ldots, t_k)|_w = w[f(n_1, \ldots, n_k)]$, where $n_i = |t_i|_w$.

We often write $|\vec{t}|_w$ instead of $\langle |t_1|_w, \ldots, |t_k|_w \rangle$.

While the truth of objective sentences is determined by a single world w, the meaning of sentences of the form $K\alpha$ and $O\alpha$ is defined relative to a *set* of worlds e. $K\alpha$ holds if α is true in all worlds of e. $O\alpha$ holds if $K\alpha$ holds and, in addition, every world that satisfies α is also a member of e. This way e minimizes what is known besides α. e is also called an *epistemic state*

The semantic rules which determine the truth of a sentence α at a given world w and epistemic state e (denoted as $e, w \models \alpha$) are defined as follows:

$$
\begin{array}{lll}
e, w \models F(\vec{t}) & \text{iff} & w[F(\vec{n})] = 1 \text{ and } \vec{n} = |\vec{t}|_w, \text{ where } F(\vec{t}) \text{ is atomic.} \\
e, w \models t_1 = t_2 & \text{iff} & |t_1|_w = |t_2|_w \\
e, w \models \neg\alpha & \text{iff} & e, w \not\models \alpha \\
e, w \models \alpha \vee \beta & \text{iff} & e, w \models \alpha \text{ or } e, w \models \beta \\
e, w \models \forall x\alpha & \text{iff} & e, w \models \alpha_n^x \text{ for all } n \in \mathcal{N} \\
e, w \models K\alpha & \text{iff} & \text{for all } w' \in e, e, w' \models \alpha \\
e, w \models O\alpha & \text{iff} & \text{for all } w', w' \in e \text{ iff } e, w' \models \alpha
\end{array}
$$

A formula α is valid ($\models_{OL} \alpha$) iff $e, w \models \alpha$ for all worlds w and all sets of worlds e.[3] We sometimes write $w \models \alpha$ if α is an objective sentence.

Here we only briefly discuss the operators K and O. For a detailed discussion of $\mathcal{OL}$, we refer the reader to (Levesque, 1990) and (Levesque and Lakemeyer, 2000). K has the usual properties of the logic $K45$ or *weak S5* (Hughes and Cresswell, 1968) whose characteristic axioms are:

K: $K(\alpha \supset \beta) \supset (K\alpha \supset K\beta)$

4: $K\alpha \supset KK\alpha$

5: $\neg K\alpha \supset K\neg K\alpha$

The Barcan formula ($\forall x K\alpha \supset K\forall x\alpha$) is also valid since we are assuming a fixed universe of discourse (Hughes and Cresswell, 1968). While K is very well understood, this is less the case for O except perhaps when O is applied to an objective sentence. Consider an atomic sentence p. It is easy to see that the only epistemic state e where Op is satisfied is $e = \{w \mid w \models p\}$, that is, the set of all worlds where p is true. It is the "iff" in the semantic rule of O which has the effect of maximizing e. As a result, the objective sentences known at e are exactly the logical consequences of p, which captures the idea that p is all that is known. Note that the meaning of O crucially depends on e as well as on the complement of e. In particular, for $O\alpha$ to be true, α has to be known and all worlds not in e have to falsify α. The story becomes much more complicated with arbitrary formulas in the scope of O. For example, as shown in (Levesque, 1990), using O it is possible to fully reconstruct and extend Moore's Autoepistemic Logic (Moore, 1985b). However, in this paper we will not be concerned with such issues, and all the examples used here consider only knowing applied to objective sentences.

3.1. Querying a Knowledge Base in $\mathcal{OL}$

One important application of $\mathcal{OL}$ is that it allows us to succinctly specify what it means to query a knowledge base KB, where KB consists of a set of objective sentences and the query can be any sentence in $\mathcal{OL}$.[4]

At the most abstract or *knowledge level*,[5] the knowledge of an agent is simply a collection of worlds e. Querying e can be defined as:

$$\text{ASK}[\alpha, e] = \begin{cases} yes & \text{if } e \models K\alpha \\ no & \text{if } e \models K\neg\alpha \\ unknown & \text{otherwise.} \end{cases}$$

In the case where knowledge is represented by a finite set of objective sentences KB, the corresponding set of worlds is $\Re[\text{KB}] = \{w \mid w \models \text{KB}\}$. It is not hard to show that

Theorem 2. (Levesque) *Let* KB *be objective and* α *a sentence. Then* $\text{ASK}[\alpha, \Re[\text{KB}]] = yes$ *iff* $\models_{\mathit{OL}}$ OKB $\supset$ $K\alpha$.

To see the utility of O, consider an agent who knows the standard name for the current temperature, say $20°C$. If this is all she knows then it should follow that she knows what the temperature is and yet has no idea what the barometric pressure is. In $\mathcal{OL}$ this can be expressed using KB = $\{temperature = 20°C\}$.[6] Then we obtain:

$\text{ASK}[\exists x K(temperature = x), \Re[\text{KB}]] = yes.$
$\text{ASK}[\exists x K(pressure = x), \Re[\text{KB}]] = no.$

Note that in order to return the answer *no* in the second example it is essential that we make the assumption that KB is *all* the agent knows. Note, in particular, that while OKB $\supset$ $\neg\exists x K(pressure = x)$ is valid in $\mathcal{OL}$, KKB $\supset$ $\neg\exists x K(pressure = x)$ is *not* simply because knowing the sentences in the KB does not rule out knowing more such as the barometric pressure. In fact, a more accurate reading of $K\alpha$ would be knowing *at least* α.

While a query may contain any number of modal operators, Levesque was able to show that computing the answer does not require any modal reasoning at all, but can be reduced to classical first-order reasoning alone (Levesque, 1984; Levesque, 1990). The key idea is that any subformula $K\phi(\vec{x})$ within a query α, where $\vec{x}$ are the free variables in ϕ, is replaced by an objective sentence which characterizes the known instances of ϕ for the given KB. We will not go through the technical details here, but instead illustrate the method using the above example. Since the temperature is known to be 20°, $K(temperature = x)$ is replaced by $x = 20°$, and evaluating whether $O\text{KB} \supset K\exists x K(temperature = x)$ is valid reduces to evaluating $O\text{KB} \supset K\exists x(x = 20°)$, which in turn reduces to evaluating whether the nonmodal sentence $\text{KB} \supset \exists x(x = 20°)$ is valid, which indeed it is. Similarly, since the denotation of *pressure* is not known, $K(pressure = x)$ is replaced by FALSE,[7] and $O\text{KB} \supset K(\neg \exists x K(pressure = x))$ is valid because $\text{KB} \supset \neg \exists x \text{FALSE}$ is valid.

4. THE LOGIC $\mathcal{AOL}$

In (Lakemeyer and Levesque, 1998), $\mathcal{AOL}$ was introduced both by providing a non-standard semantics and a set of foundational axioms together with soundness and completeness results. Here we only deal with the semantics, since it is sufficient for our purposes and also a natural extension of the semantics of $\mathcal{OL}$.

The language of $\mathcal{AOL}$ is a dialect of the second-order predicate calculus, like the situation calculus introduced in Section 2. Again we have three sorts: ordinary objects, actions and situations. (Among the situation variables we reserve the variable *now* for special use.) The constant S_0, the function *do*, and special predicate $Poss(a, s)$ are exactly as before. We will however require two new special predicates, $SF(a, s)$ and $K_0(s)$. The set of (relational and functional) fluents as well as the set of action function symbols is assumed to be finite.

For simplicity, we also make the following restrictions: there are no constants or functions of the situation sort other than S_0 and *do*; action functions do not take situations as arguments; all ordinary object functions are fluents; and all predicates other than those mentioned above are fluents. Finally, we assume that fluents only have situation terms as arguments in the final position.

As in $\mathcal{OL}$ we assume a fixed countably infinite domain of ordinary objects, isomorphic to the set of standard names $\mathcal{N}$.[8]

To deal with knowledge in $\mathcal{AOL}$, the biggest change is that we imagine that in addition to S_0 and its successors, there are an uncountable number of other initial and non-initial situations considered as possible epistemic alternatives. To state what is known in S_0, we use K_0. Informally, taking S_0 to be the situation counterpart to the given world w in $\mathcal{OL}$, K_0 is the counterpart to the given epistemic state e in $\mathcal{OL}$. In other words, $K_0(s)$ is intended to hold if s is a situation considered by the agent in S_0 to be possible. How knowledge changes when performing an action a in situation s is governed by $SF(a, s)$ and $Poss(a, s)$. Roughly, SF returns the value sensed by the action a at situation s.[9] For example, the truth of $SF(sonar, s)$ may indicate that the robot's sonar has registered in situation s that it is close to the wall. For more details about SF the reader is referred to Section 4.2.

4.1. Semantics

Recall that in $\mathcal{OL}$, there are worlds corresponding to all possible interpretations of the predicate and function symbols (over the domain of standard names). Different applications, of course, will use different subsets as part of the given e, but the complement of e is still relevant because of only knowing. We need the same in $\mathcal{AOL}$ with respect to K_0, but more: we need to allow for all possible interpretations of the predicate and function symbols *after all possible sequences of actions*. That is, to ensure that it is possible to know the initial value of a term or formula without also necessarily knowing its value in successor situations, it is necessary that there be initial situations that agree on the values of all terms and formulas but that have successors that disagree on these values. Thus instead of defining a world as a function from primitive expressions to suitable values as we did in $\mathcal{OL}$, we define a world in $\mathcal{AOL}$ as a function from primitive expressions and sequences of actions to these values. We then define a situation as a pair consisting of a world and a sequence of actions.

Worlds and situations

More precisely, besides the standard names for objects, the standard names for actions are terms of the form $A(t_1, \ldots, t_n)$ where A is an action function and each t_i is a standard name; there are no standard names for situations, since there will be more situations than expressions in the language. The primitive terms $\mathcal{T}$ are object terms of the form $f(t_1, \ldots, t_n)$ where each t_i is a standard name, and $f(x_1, \ldots, x_n, s)$ is a functional fluent. The primitive formulas $\mathcal{P}$ are atoms of the form $F(t_1, \ldots, t_n)$ where each t_i is a standard name, and $F(x_1, \ldots, x_n, s)$ is a relational fluent, or F is one of *Poss* or *SF*. Note that except for *Poss* and *SF*, primitive expressions are all fluents with the situation argument suppressed.

Let Act^* be the set of all sequences of standard names for actions including the empty sequence ϵ.

Definition 3. An $\mathcal{AOL}$ world w is a function:

$$w : (\mathcal{P} \times Act^*) \cup (\mathcal{T} \times Act^*) \longrightarrow \{0, 1\} \cup \mathcal{N}$$

such that

$w[p, \vec{a}] \in \{0, 1\}$ *for all* $p \in \mathcal{P}$.

$w[t, \vec{a}] \in \mathcal{N}$ *for all* $t \in \mathcal{T}$.

Let $\mathcal{W}$ *denote the set of all* $\mathcal{AOL}$ *worlds.*

Definition 4. An $\mathcal{AOL}$ situation *is a pair* $(w, \vec{a})$, *where* $w \in \mathcal{W}$ *and* $\vec{a} \in Act^*$. *An* initial *situation is one where* $\vec{a} = \epsilon$.

Definition 5. An action model M *is a pair* $\langle e, w \rangle$, *where* $w \in \mathcal{W}$ *and* $e \subseteq \mathcal{W}$.

As in $\mathcal{OL}$, w is taken to specify the actual world, and e specifies the epistemic state as those worlds an agent has not yet ruled out as being the actual one. As we will see below, a situation term s will be interpreted semantically as an $\mathcal{AOL}$ situation $(w, \vec{a})$, consisting of a world and a sequence of actions that have happened so far. A fluent $p(s)$ will be considered true if $w[p, \vec{a}] = 1$.

Because situations cannot have standard names, to interpret formulas with variables, we need to use variable maps. A variable map ν maps object, action, and situation variables into standard names for objects and actions, and into $\mathcal{AOL}$ situations, respectively. In addition, ν assigns relations of the appropriate type[10] to relational variables. For a given ν, ν_o^x denotes the variable map which is like ν except that x is mapped into o.

The meaning of terms

We write $| \cdot |_{M,\nu}$ for the denotation of terms with respect to an action model $M = \langle e, w \rangle$ and a variable map ν. Then

$|n|_{M,\nu} = n$, where n is a standard name;

$|f(\vec{t}, t_s)|_{M,\nu} = w'[f(|\vec{t}|_{M,\nu}), \vec{a}]$, where $f(\vec{t}, t_s)$ is a
functional fluent, and $|t_s|_{M,\nu} = (w', \vec{a})$;

$|A(\vec{t})|_{M,\nu} = A(|\vec{t}|_{M,\nu})$, where $A(\vec{t})$ is an action term;

$|S_0|_{M,\nu} = (w, \epsilon)$;

$|do(t_a, t_s)|_{M,\nu} = (w', \vec{a} \cdot a)$, where $|t_s|_{M,\nu} = (w', \vec{a})$, and $|t_a|_{M,\nu} = a$;

$|x|_{M,\nu} = \nu(x)$, where x is any variable, including predicate variables.

Observe that in a model $M = \langle e, w \rangle$, the only way to refer to a situation that does not use the given world w is to use a situation variable.

The meaning of formulas

We write $M, \nu \models \alpha$ to mean formula α comes out true in action model M and variable map ν:

$M, \nu \models F(\vec{t}, t_s)$ iff $w'[F(|\vec{t}|_{M,\nu}), \vec{a}] = 1$, where
$F(\vec{t}, t_s)$ is a relational fluent, and $|t_s|_{M,\nu} = (w', \vec{a})$;

$M, \nu \models X(\vec{t})$ iff $|\vec{t}|_{M,\nu} \in \nu(X)$, where X is a relational variable;

$M, \nu \models Poss(t_a, t_s)$ iff $w'[Poss(|t_a|_{M,\nu}), \vec{a}] = 1$, where $|t_s|_{M,\nu} = (w', \vec{a})$;

$M, \nu \models SF(t_a, t_s)$ iff $w'[SF(|t_a|_{M,\nu}), \vec{a}] = 1$, where $|t_s|_{M,\nu} = (w', \vec{a})$;

$M, \nu \models K_0(t_s)$ iff $|t_s|_{M,\nu} = (w', \epsilon)$ and $w' \in e$;

$M, \nu \models t_1 = t_2$ iff $|t_1|_{M,\nu} = |t_2|_{M,\nu}$;

$M, \nu \models \neg\alpha$ iff $M, \nu \not\models \alpha$;

$M, \nu \models \alpha \vee \beta$ iff $M, \nu \models \alpha$ or $M, \nu \models \beta$;

$M, \nu \models \forall x. \alpha$ iff $M, \nu_o^x \models \alpha$ for all o of the appropriate sort (object, action, situation, relation).

Let Γ be a set of formulas and α a formula. Then Γ logically implies α if for all action models $M = \langle e, w \rangle$ and variable maps ν, if $M, \nu \models \gamma$ for all $\gamma \in \Gamma$, then $M, \nu \models \alpha$. α is valid if α is logically implied by the empty set.

If α does not mention K_0, that is, the truth of α does not depend on e, we also write $w, \nu \models \alpha$ instead of $M, \nu \models \alpha$. Also, if α is a sentence, we simply write $M \models \alpha$.

4.2. Knowledge and Action

To determine what is known initially (that is, in situation S_0), we only need to consider K_0. More precisely, a sentence is known initially just in case it holds in all situations s for which $K_0(s)$ holds. To find out what holds in successor situations, we use the predicates SF and $Poss$. First note that the logic itself imposes no constraints on either SF or $Poss$; it is up to the user in an application to write appropriate axioms. For $Poss$, these are the precondition axioms, which specify necessary and sufficient conditions under which an action is executable. So we might have, for example,

$$Poss(\text{adv}, s) \equiv (wdist(s) > 0)$$

as a way of saying that the robot is able to advance 1 unit if its current distance from the wall is at least 1 unit. For SF, the user must write *sensed fluent axioms*, one for each action type, as discussed in (Levesque, 1996). The idea is that $SF(a, s)$ gives the condition sensed by action a in situation s. So we might have, for example,

$$SF(\text{sonar}, s) \equiv (wdist(s) < 10)$$

as a way of saying that the sonar sensing action in situation s tells the robot whether or not the distance to the wall in s is less than 10 units. In case the action a has no sensing component (as in simple physical actions, like moving), the axiom should state that $SF(a, s)$ is identically TRUE. Having defined SF as a predicate, we essentially confine ourselves to sensing truth values. If we want the result of a sense action to be the value of a term such as a sonar measuring the actual distance to the wall, we can do so by simply redefining SF as a function and treating TRUE and FALSE as special values returned by SF. To keep the presentation simple, however, we ignore this issue here.

With these terms, we can now define $K(s', s)$ as an abbreviation for a formula that characterizes when a situation s' is accessible from an arbitrary situation s: [11]

$$K(s', s) \doteq \forall R[\ldots \supset R(s', s)]$$

where the ellipsis stands for the conjunction of

$\forall s_1, s_2. \ Init(s_1) \wedge Init(s_2) \wedge K_0(s_2) \supset R(s_2, s_1)$
$\forall a, s_1, s_2. \ R(s_2, s_1) \wedge (SF(a, s_2) \equiv SF(a, s_1)) \wedge$

$$(Poss(a, s_2) \equiv Poss(a, s_1)) \supset$$
$$R(do(a, s_2), do(a, s_1)).$$

To get some intuitions about this definition let us consider the K-relation at an initial situation and after one action A has happened. Let s be an initial situation. The situations which are K-related to s are precisely those initial situations s' for which $K_0(s')$ holds. Now consider $do(A, s)$ and assume $Poss(A, s)$ holds, that is, A was indeed possible in s. The situations which are K-related to $do(A, s)$ are precisely those situations $do(A, s')$ such that $K_0(s')$ holds, that is, s' was accessible initially, and both s and s' agree on their respective values for $Poss$ and SF. In particular, in case A is a sensing action, we discard all those situations from our epistemic state (the situations reachable via K) which differ in the actual value being sensed in s. The general picture is best reflected by the fact that the above definition satisfies the successor state axiom for a predicate K proposed in (Scherl and Levesque, 1993) as a solution to the frame problem for knowledge and later reformulated in (Levesque, 1996), whose notation we follow here:

Theorem 6. *(Lakemeyer and Levesque, 1998). The following is a theorem of $\mathcal{AOL}$:*
$$\forall a, s, s'. \, Poss(a, s) \supset K(s', do(a, s)) \equiv$$
$$\exists s''. \, s' = do(a, s'') \wedge K(s'', s) \wedge Poss(a, s'')$$
$$\wedge \, [SF(a, s) \equiv SF(a, s'')].$$

Given K, knowledge can then be defined in a way similar to possible-world semantics (Kripke, 1963; Hintikka, 1962; Moore, 1985a) as truth in all accessible situations. Similarly, only knowing a sentence α at a situation s means that all and only those situations with the same action history as s are accessible. To denote that two situations s and s' involve the same sequence of actions from perhaps different initial situations we write $C(s', s)$, which is an abbreviation for a second-order sentence. More precisely,

$C(s, s') \doteq \forall R[\ldots \supset R(s, s')],$
    where the ellipsis stands for
$\forall s_1, s_2[Init(s_1) \wedge Init(s_2) \supset R(s_1, s_2)] \wedge$
$\forall a, s_1, s_2[R(s_1, s_2) \supset R(do(a, s_1), do(a, s_2))]$

Knowing and only knowing are then denoted using the following macros, where α may contain the special situation variable *now*. Let α_s^{now} refer to α with all occurrences of *now* replaced by s. Then

    $\textbf{Knows}(\alpha, s) \doteq \forall s' K(s', s) \supset \alpha_{s'}^{now}$
    $\textbf{OKnows}(\alpha, s) \doteq \forall s' C(s', s) \supset (K(s', s) \equiv \alpha_{s'}^{now}),$
    where s' is a new variable occurring nowhere else in α.

While the first argument of **Knows** and **OKnows** is understood to be a formula of $\mathcal{AOL}$, we also write macro expressions **Knows**(α, s), where α itself contains **Knows**.

To make this well-defined, we assume that macro expansion works from the innermost occurrence of Knows to the outside.

For example, Knows($\neg$Knows($Broken(x, now), now), S_0$) stands for

$$\forall s K(s, S_0) \supset (\neg \forall s' K(s', s) \supset Broken(x, s))$$

and should be read as "the agent knows in S_0 that it does not know that x is broken." (Note that it is important to evaluate the sentence starting from the innermost occurrence of Knows in order to handle *now* properly.)

5. ASK

In this section we want to define a version of ASK at the knowledge level which is appropriate in the context of $\mathcal{AOL}$. Later we will also be concerned with knowledge represented by $\mathcal{AOL}$-knowledge bases.

Recall that in $\mathcal{OL}$ ASK came with two arguments, a query α and an epistemic state e. In $\mathcal{AOL}$, it seems clear that we need at least a sequence of actions $\vec{a}$ as another argument because we may want to ask questions about what is known *after* a number of actions $\vec{a}$ have been performed. Note that, in $\mathcal{OL}$, the real world plays no role when answering a query since everything that is known follows from the epistemic state e alone. It is not so clear whether this is also true in $\mathcal{AOL}$. In fact, there are at least two interpretations of ASK, one where the real world is needed as an extra argument, at least sometimes, and one where it is not.

To start with the latter, the idea is that we are given a pair $(e, \vec{a})$ with the understanding that e contains those worlds which are considered possible *after* the agent has already performed the actions $\vec{a}$. In particular, the result of any sensing that occurred as part of $\vec{a}$ is reflected in e in that those worlds which previously belonged to e but did not agree with what was being sensed were removed. Under that view we can ask a query about what holds after doing $\vec{a}$ by simply looking at what is true in all worlds in e indexed by $\vec{a}$. The reader is referred to (Lakemeyer and Levesque, 1999) for a formalization of this idea.

Another view, and the one we consider here in more detail, is to always take e to be the set of worlds which the agent considers possible *initially*. In this case we are interested in asking queries about what the agent knows about the future, that is, after performing any number of actions $\vec{a}$. Here the real world plays an essential role, sometimes. For example, if we ask what the robot knows about the distance to the wall after reading its sonar, then the answer depends on the actual wall distance in the real world. While access to the real world is needed in this case, there are queries of a more hypothetical nature where the real world can still be ignored. The idea is to ask what is known initially about what the world would be like after doing some actions.[12] For example, even though the robot knows nothing about the wall distance initially, it nevertheless knows that it will know *whether* it is close to the wall after reading its sonar. To find this out, the actual world itself is not needed. Instead, all possible ways the actual world might be like need to be considered.

With these preliminaries we now turn to formally defining ASK where e is the set of worlds considered possible initially. Let α be a query, $M = \langle e, w \rangle$ an action model, and $\vec{a}$ a sequence of actions. Roughly, $\text{ASK}[\alpha, M, \vec{a}]$ returns *yes* just in case the agent knows α after executing $\vec{a}$ starting in the initial situation. Formally:

$$\text{ASK}[\alpha, M, \vec{a}] \;=\; \left\{ \begin{array}{ll} \textit{yes} & \text{if } M \models \text{Knows}(\alpha, do(\vec{a}, S_0)) \\ \textit{no} & \text{if } M \models \text{Knows}(\neg\alpha, do(\vec{a}, S_0)) \\ \textit{unknown} & \text{otherwise.} \end{array} \right.$$

A few words about the kinds of formulas which should be considered legal queries are in order at this point. First of all, given the way we have defined Knows, we should allow α to contain *now* as a free variable. For example, if we ask the robot if the wall distance is initially less than 20, then the answer should be *yes* just in case in all initial situations the robot considers possible, the wall distance is less than 20. Hence our query should be $\alpha = wdist(now) < 20$, and we obtain

$\text{ASK}[\alpha, M, S_0] = yes$ iff $M \models \text{Knows}(\alpha, S_0)$ iff $\forall s K(s, S_0) \supset wdist(s) < 20$.

We assume that *now* is the only free variable allowed in a query so that we can safely ignore variable maps in the definition of ASK. These are the only formal restrictions we impose. In the following, *query* always refers to an $\mathcal{AOL}$-formula which contains at most *now* as a free variable.

Note, however, that there are queries which give us peculiar results. For assume the robot knows nothing (for example, if e is the set of all worlds) and its initial wall distance in S_0 is 7. Then $M \models (wdist(S_0) = 7)$ and $M \models \forall x \neg\text{Knows}(wdist(now) = x, S_0)$. However, we still get $\text{ASK}[(wdist(S_0) = 7), M, \vec{a}] = yes$ for any sequence of actions $\vec{a}$. This is because $M \models \forall s K(s, do(\vec{a}, S_0)) \supset (wdist(S_0) = 7)$ follows immediately from the assumption $M \models (wdist(S_0) = 7)$ and, hence, $M \models \text{Knows}(wdist(S_0) = 7, \vec{a})$. The problem has to do with how knowledge is defined using Knows, which is the standard approach in the situation calculus. In particular, any sentence (no free variables) is invariably known to be true or known to be false. There are ways to avoid anomalies like the above by imposing certain syntactic restrictions. For example, one could rule out the use of S_0 within a query.[13] For simplicity, however, we will not concern ourselves with this issue here except to claim that all the example queries to follow will be of a reasonably restricted but still useful kind.

As we have argued above, if e is interpreted as the set of worlds considered possible initially, then ASK in general needs the real world (as part of M) as one of its arguments. On the other hand, if we are only interested in what the agent knows initially about possible future courses of events, then the real world should play no role after all. The following theorem establishes that this is indeed the case.

Theorem 7. *Let α be a query, $M = \langle e, w \rangle$ an action model, w' an arbitrary world, and $M' = \langle e, w' \rangle$. Then $\text{ASK}[\alpha, M, \epsilon] = \text{ASK}[\alpha, M', \epsilon]$.*

For this reason we will also write $\text{ASK}[\alpha, e]$ instead of $\text{ASK}[\alpha, M, \epsilon]$.

6. $\mathcal{AOL}$ KNOWLEDGE BASES

So far, we have only talked about the agent's knowledge in the abstract, namely as a set of worlds, which include all possible ways they could evolve in the future. Let us now turn to representing the agent's knowledge symbolically and see how this connects with the abstract (knowledge level) view taken so far.

Recall that an application domain in the situation calculus is typically characterized by the following types of axioms: action precondition axioms, successor state axioms, and axioms describing the initial situation (Reiter, 1991). When there are sensing actions, there is also a fourth type called *sensed fluent axioms* specifying what the outcome of sensing is.

$\mathcal{AOL}$-knowledge bases, as we envisage them, consist of formulas of these types and they have a special syntactic form.

An $\mathcal{AOL}$-formula ϕ is called *simple* in s, where s is a situation variable, if ϕ is first-order, ϕ does not mention K_0, s occurs only free in ϕ, and s is the only situation term occurring in ϕ.

In the following, let A be an action and F a fluent. Let $\phi(\vec{u})$ denote a formula whose free variables are among the variables in $\vec{u}$.

Let $s \preceq s'$ denote that situation s' is a successor of s, which is defined as:

$$s \preceq s' \doteq \forall R[\ldots \supset R(s, s')]$$

with the ellipsis standing for the conjunction of

$\forall s_1. R(s_1, s_1)$
$\forall a, s_1. R(s_1, do(a, s_1))$
$\forall s_1, s_2, s_3. R(s_1, s_2) \wedge R(s_2, s_3) \supset R(s_1, s_3)$

Action Precondition Axioms:
$\quad \forall s \forall \vec{x}. now \preceq s \supset [Poss(A(\vec{x}), s) \equiv \phi(\vec{x}, s)],$[14]
$\quad$ where $\phi(\vec{x}, s)$ is simple in s.

Sensed Fluent Axioms:
$\quad \forall s \forall \vec{x}. now \preceq s \supset [SF(A(\vec{x}), s) \equiv \phi(\vec{x}, s)]$
$\quad$ where $\phi(\vec{x}, s)$ is simple in s.

Successor State Axioms:
$\quad \forall s \forall a \forall \vec{x}. now \preceq s \supset [Poss(a, s) \supset [F(\vec{x}, do(a, s)) \equiv \phi(\vec{x}, a, s)]],$
$\quad$ where $\phi(\vec{x}, a, s)$ is simple in s.

Initial State Axioms:
$\quad \phi(now)$, where ϕ is simple in now.

A knowledge base is then a collection of formulas

$$KB = KB_0 \cup KB_{Poss} \cup KB_{SF} \cup KB_{ss},$$

where KB_0, KB_{Poss}, KB_{SF}, and KB_{ss} contain the initial state axioms, action preconditions, sensed fluent axioms, and successor state axioms, respectively.

Similar to $\mathcal{OL}$, we define the epistemic state corresponding to a KB as the set of all worlds satisfying the formulas in KB, where *now* is interpreted by initial situations. Formally,

$$\Re[KB] = \{w \mid w, \nu_{(w,\epsilon)}^{now} \models KB\}.$$

6.1. An Example

Here we consider the robot example (see also (Lakemeyer and Levesque, 1998)) in more detail. Imagine the robot lives in a 1-dimensional world, where it can move towards or away from a fixed wall. The robot also has a sonar sensor that tells it when it gets too close to the wall, say, less than 10 units away. The sonar does not, however, tell the robot the exact distance to the wall. So we might imagine three actions, adv and rev which move the robot one unit towards and away from the wall, and a sonar sensing action. We have a single fluent, $wdist(s)$, which gives the actual distance from the robot to the wall in situation s.

We begin by defining precondition axioms, sensed fluent axioms and successor state axioms, all parameterized by *now*. Let $Close(s)$ be the following abbreviation:

$$Close(s) \doteq wdist(s) < 10.$$

Let $ALL(now)$ stand for the set of these formulas:

$\forall s.now \preceq s \supset Poss(\text{adv}, s) \equiv wdist(s) > 0$

$\forall s.now \preceq s \supset Poss(\text{rev}, s) \equiv \text{TRUE}$

$\forall s.now \preceq s \supset Poss(\text{sonar}, s) \equiv \text{TRUE}$

$\forall s.now \preceq s \supset SF(\text{adv}, s) \equiv \text{TRUE}$

$\forall s.now \preceq s \supset SF(\text{rev}, s) \equiv \text{TRUE}$

$\forall s.now \preceq s \supset SF(\text{sonar}, s) \equiv Close(s)$

$\forall s.now \preceq s \supset$
    $\forall a, z. wdist(do(a, s)) = z \equiv$
        $a = \text{adv} \wedge z = wdist(s) - 1$
        $\vee\ a = \text{rev} \wedge z = wdist(s) + 1$
        $\vee\ z = wdist(s) \wedge a \neq \text{adv} \wedge a \neq \text{rev}$

Let $KB = ALL(now) \cup \{(wdist(now) < 20)\}$, that is the robot knows how its actions work and that it is initially less than 20 units away from the wall.

Let the real world w be any world such that $w \models ALL(now)_{S_0}^{now} \wedge (wdist(S_0) = 6)$, that is, the actions indeed behave as the robots expects them to and the actual wall distance is 6, that is, the robot is close to the wall. Finally, let $M = \langle \Re[\text{KB}], w \rangle$ be our action model.[15]

Here is a list of queries we can ask the robot and their respective answers.[16]

1. ASK[$Close(now), M, \epsilon$] = *unknown*.
   Initially, the robot does not know if it is close, since all it knows is that the distance is below 20.

2. ASK[$Close(now), M, \text{sonar}$] = *yes*.
   The sonar-action will tell the robot that it is close.

3. ASK[$Close(now), M, \text{sonar} \cdot \text{adv}$] = *yes*.
   Advancing can only take the robot closer, not further away from the wall.

4. ASK[$Close(now), M, \text{sonar} \cdot \text{rev}$] = *unknown*.
   After moving one unit away from the wall, though, the robot is left in doubt about whether it is close. For example, for all the robot knows, it could have been 9 units away from the wall before doing rev.

5. ASK[$\exists x(x = wdist(now)) \wedge (x < 20) \wedge$
   $\text{Knows}((x = wdist(now)), now), M, \epsilon$] = *no*.
   While the robot knows that the wall distance is less than 20, it does not know its exact value.

6. ASK[$\text{Knows}(Close(now), do(\text{sonar}, now)) \vee$
   $\text{Knows}(\neg Close(now), do(\text{sonar}, now)), M, \epsilon$] = *yes*.
   The robot knows that reading the sonar will tell it whether it is close or not.

7. ASK[$\text{Knows}(Close(now), do(\text{rev}, do(\text{sonar}, now))) \vee$
   $\text{Knows}(\neg Close(now), do(\text{rev}, do(\text{sonar}, now))), M, \epsilon$] = *unknown*.
   Similar to query (4), the robot knows that doing rev leads to losing the information about closeness.

6.2. Asking Queries in the Initial Situation

We already saw that answering queries at S_0 does not depend on what the real world is like. Now we can go even further and show that for a given knowledge base, the result of ASK can be completely specified using OKnows in a way similar to Theorem 2.

Theorem 8. *Let* KB *be a knowledge base as defined above,* α *a query. Then* ASK[$\alpha, \Re[\text{KB}]$] = *yes iff* $\models$ OKnows(KB, S_0) $\supset$ Knows(α, S_0).

While this theorem gives us a symbol level account of ASK when applied to the initial situation, we should be concerned about the fact that it requires fairly heavy machinery, that is, a full-fledged second-order logic to obtain this result. Does this mean that we need a second-order theorem prover to answer queries? While this may be the case in general, there are interesting special cases where we can get away with ordinary first-order logic, an issue we now turn to.

Suppose we are given the KB of the robot example and we want to evaluate query (5), which is strictly about what is known about the initial situation:

$$\alpha = \exists x (x = wdist(now)) \wedge (x < 20) \wedge \text{Knows}((x = wdist(now)), now).$$

It seems that the answer to this query depends only on the contents of KB_0, which is $\{(wdist(now) < 20)\}$. Moreover, since we are only concerned with a static snapshot of the world, we might as well drop all mention of situations and ask the query in terms of $\mathcal{OL}$ with $KB_0' = \{(wdist < 20)\}$ and $\alpha' = \exists x (x = wdist) \wedge (x < 20) \wedge K(wdist = x)$. With Theorem 2, finding the value of $\text{ASK}[\alpha', \Re[KB_0']]$ means determining whether $OKB_0' \supset K\alpha'$ or $OKB_0' \supset K\neg\alpha'$ is valid. Given Levesque's reduction to first-order reasoning, the latter is valid because the $KB_0' \supset \neg[\exists x (x = wdist) \wedge (x < 20) \wedge \forall x.\text{FALSE}]$ is. Hence, the answer to our original query (5) is *no*.

Indeed, we can show that this idea of reducing queries about the initial situation to corresponding queries in $\mathcal{OL}$ works in general, as long as we confine ourselves to queries which result from translating formulas of $\mathcal{OL}$ into $\mathcal{AOL}$. Such a translation was first proposed in (Lakemeyer, 1996) and works as follows:

Definition 9. *Given any term or formula ϕ in $\mathcal{OL}$, the corresponding term or formula $\phi[s]$ in $\mathcal{AOL}$, where s is any situation term, is defined as follows.*

$x[s] = x$ *if x is a variable*
$n[s] = n$ *if n is a standard name*
$f(t_1, \ldots, t_n)[s] = f(t_1[s], \ldots, t_n[s], s)$ *if $f(\vec{t})$ is a term in $\mathcal{OL}$*
$F(t_1, \ldots, t_n)[s] = F(t_1[s], \ldots, t_n[s], s)$ *if $P(\vec{t})$ is an atomic formula in $\mathcal{OL}$*
$(t_1 = t_2)[s] = (t_1[s] = t_2[s])$
$(\neg\alpha)[s] = \neg\alpha[s]$
$(\alpha \vee \beta)[s] = \alpha[s] \vee \beta[s]$
$(\forall x\alpha)[s] = \forall x\alpha[s]$
$(K\alpha)[s] = \text{Knows}(\alpha[now], s)$
$(O\alpha)[s] = \text{OKnows}(\alpha[now], s)$

For example, let $\alpha = OP(a) \supset \neg\exists x KP(x)$. Then
$\alpha[S_0] = [\forall s C(s, S_0) \supset (K(s, S_0) \equiv P(a(s), s))] \supset \neg\exists x (\forall s K(s, S_0) \supset P(x, s))$.
Note that we tacitly assume that for each predicate and function symbol in α there is a corresponding fluent of the same name in $\mathcal{AOL}$.

Theorem 10. *Let KB be a knowledge base such that* $\text{OKnows}(KB, S_0)$ *is satisfiable. Let* KB_0 *be the part of* KB *which specifies what is known about the initial situation and let* $KB_0\downarrow$ *be* KB_0 *with all occurrences of now removed. (Hence $KB_0\downarrow$ is a set of objective sentences in $\mathcal{OL}$.) Let α be a sentence in $\mathcal{OL}$. Then*

$$\text{ASK}[\alpha[now], \Re[KB]] = yes \text{ iff } \models_{ol} OKB_0\downarrow \supset K\alpha.$$

What about queries about situations other than the initial one? Here we have only obtained preliminary results so far. To illustrate the basic idea, let us consider a single action A, which is not a sensing action, and let us assume that

$$M \models \text{Knows}(Poss(A, now) \land SF(A, now) \equiv \text{TRUE}, S_0),$$

that is, the agent knows both that the action is possible and that SF is true under all circumstances because A is not used for sensing. In this case, the situations accessible after doing A are precisely the A-successors of all initial situations in $\Re[\text{KB}]$.

Let KB_A consist of a finite set of formulas $\phi^{now}_{do(A, now)}$, where ϕ is simple in now. Furthermore assume that

$$\text{KB}_A \models \phi^{now}_{do(A, now)} \text{ iff } M \models \text{Knows}(\phi^{now}_{do(A, now)}, S_0) \text{ for all } \phi \text{ simple in } now.$$

Intuitively, KB_A represents in a finite way what the agent believes the world is like after doing A. Then we obtain the following:

Theorem 11. *Let* $\text{OKnows}(\text{KB}, S_0)$ *be satisfiable,* ϕ *a formula simple in* now, *and* α *any sentence in* $\mathcal{OL}$. *Then*

1. $\text{ASK}[\phi^{now}_{do(A, now)}, \Re[\text{KB}]] = \text{ASK}[\text{Knows}(\phi, do(A, now)), \Re[\text{KB}]]$

2. $\text{ASK}[\alpha[do(A, now)], \Re[\text{KB}]] = yes \text{ iff } \models_{ol} \text{OKB}_A \downarrow \supset K\alpha.$

The first part of the theorem tells us that there is no difference between knowing that ϕ holds after doing A and knowing that after doing A it is known that A holds. The second part tells us essentially that, as long as we can finitely characterize what is known after doing an action,[17] queries about the resulting state can be rephrased in terms of queries in $\mathcal{OL}$ and hence can be reduced to first-order reasoning. The question then, of course, is whether KB_A can be easily obtained. In general, the answer is probably no. This is because Lin and Reiter (LR) (Lin and Reiter, 1997) have shown that knowledge about the world after doing an action may not be first-order representable even if the initial knowledge base is first-order. However, LR were also able to characterize special cases of successor state axioms for which KB_A is first-order and can be obtained by *progressing* the contents of the initial KB. In a sequel to this paper (Lakemeyer and Levesque, 1999) we have shown that LR's ideas can indeed be adapted to $\mathcal{AOL}$. In particular, we develop a version of progression for what LR call *context-free* knowledge bases. Our definition is actually somewhat more general than theirs since we consider sensing actions which they do not.

7. CONCLUSIONS

In this paper, we used the logic $\mathcal{AOL}$ to define suitable knowledge bases for agents who need to reason about their actions and what they know about the world. In analogy to earlier results by Levesque, we defined a function ASK to query such knowledge bases and showed that ASK can be defined in terms of only knowing in $\mathcal{AOL}$ if we ask queries about what is known initially, which includes knowledge about future actions. If we limit ourselves further to queries about the initial situation only, then query evaluation in $\mathcal{AOL}$ can be transformed into query evaluation in $\mathcal{OL}$, which has the advantage of being purely first-order, whereas $\mathcal{AOL}$ is second-order. Finally, in a sequel to this paper (Lakemeyer and Levesque, 1999), we have extended these ideas to queries about non-initial situations by suitably progressing an initial knowledge base according to what actions have been performed.

ACKNOWLEDGMENTS

We would like to thank Alexander Hägele. Early versions of some of the ideas presented in this paper first appeared in his M.Sc. thesis (Haegele, 1998).

Gerhard Lakemeyer
Aachen University of Technology
Aachen, Germany

Hector J. Levesque
University of Toronto
Toronto, Canada

NOTES

1. In addition to the standard axioms of equality.

2. Other logical connectives like $\wedge$, $\supset$, and $\equiv$ and the quantifier $\exists$ are used freely and are defined in the usual way.

3. Levesque used so-called *maximal sets* to define validity, a complication we ignore here for simplicity.

4. Levesque (Levesque, 1984; Levesque, 1990) argues why a modal epistemic language like $\mathcal{OL}$ is strictly more expressive than a classical first-order language.

5. The terms *knowledge level* and *symbol level* are due to Newell (Newell, 1981).

6. $20°C$ is used only as mnemonic for a standard name.

7. FALSE can be thought of as an abbreviation of $\forall x(x \neq x)$.

8. In (Lakemeyer and Levesque, 1998), standard names were encoded using a special constant 0 together with a unary function *succ*. This was done in order to facilitate the axiomatization. Since in this paper we are only dealing with $\mathcal{AOL}$ semantically, we stick to the same representation of standard names as in $\mathcal{OL}$.

9. For simplicity, we assume that only truth values are sensed.

10. The type determines the arity and the sort of each argument of the relations the variable ranges over. Since, in our examples, the type will always be obvious from the context, we leave this information implicit.

11. We could have defined K as a predicate in the language as is usually done, but we have chosen not to in order to keep the formal apparatus as small as possible.

12. Such hypothetical reasoning about possible courses of actions is needed in planning, for example.

13. One would also want to restrict quantification to range only over the successors or predecessors of a given situation. For instance, in $\mathcal{AOL}$ the sentence $\forall s Poss(\textsf{sonar}, s)$ makes little sense since is unsatisfiable. This is because the semantics includes *all* conceivable situations and there are some where $Poss(\textsf{sonar}, s)$ is false.

14. See the previous footnote for why quantification over situations needs to be relative to a given situation (*now*).

15. Strictly speaking, we also need to specify the natural numbers and at least the $<$-relation over them. For simplicity, we ignore this issue here and assume that simple arithmetic is built-in.

16. For proofs of some of the answers see (Lakemeyer and Levesque, 1998).

17. It is not hard to generalize the theorem to more than one action.

REFERENCES

Burgard, W., Cremers, A. B., Fox, D., Hähnel, D., Lakemeyer, G., Schulz, D., Steiner, W., Thrun, S., The Interactive Museum Tour-Guide Robot, in: *Proceedings of the 15th National Conference on Artificial Intelligence (AAAI-98)*, pp. 11–18, 1998.

del Val, A. and Shoham, Y., A Unified View of Belief Revision and Update. *Journal of Logic and Computation* Special Issue on Actions and Processes, 4, 1994, pp. 797–810. Haegele, A., On the interaction with knowledge bases in dynamic worlds (in German), M.Sc. thesis, University of Bonn, 1998.

Halpern, J. Y. and Lakemeyer, G., Levesque's Axiomatization of Only Knowing is Incomplete. *Artificial Intelligence* 74(2), 1995, pp. 381–387.

Halpern, J. Y. and Moses, Y. O., A Guide to Completeness and Complexity for Modal Logics of Knowledge and Belief. *Artificial Intelligence*, 54, 1992, pp. 319–379.

Hintikka, J., *Knowledge and Belief: An Introduction to the Logic of the Two Notions*. Cornell University Press, 1962.

Hughes, G. E. and Cresswell, M. J., *An Introduction to Modal Logic*, Methuen and Company Ltd., London, England, 1968.

Kaplan, D., Quantifying In, in L. Linsky (ed.), *Reference and Modality*, Oxford University Press, Oxford, 1971.

Kripke, S. A., Semantical considerations on modal logic. *Acta Philosophica Fennica* 16, 1963, pp. 83–94.

Lakemeyer, G., A Logical Account of Relevance, *Proc. of the 14th International Joint Conference on Artificial Intelligence (IJCAI-95)*, Morgan Kaufmann, 1995, pp. 853–859.

Lakemeyer, G., Only Knowing in the Situation Calculus, *Proc. of the Fifth International Conference on Principles of Knowledge Representation and Reasoning*, Morgan Kaufmann, San Francisco, 1996, pp. 14–25.

Lakemeyer, G. and Levesque, H. J., AOL: a logic of acting, sensing, knowing, and only knowing. *Proc. of the Sixth International Conference on Principles of Knowledge Representation and Reasoning*, Morgan Kaufmann, San Francisco, 1998.

Lakemeyer, G. and Levesque, H. J., Query Evaluation and Progression in AOL Knowledge Bases, to appear in: *Proceedings of the 16th International Joint Conference on Artificial Intelligence*, Morgan Kaufmann, San Francisco, 1999.

Levesque, H. J., Foundations of a Functional Approach to Knowledge Representation, *Artificial Intelligence*, 23, 1984, pp. 155-212.

Levesque, H. J., All I Know: A Study in Autoepistemic Logic. *Artificial Intelligence*, North Holland, 42, 1990, pp. 263–309.

Levesque, H. J., What is Planning in the Presence of Sensing. AAAI-96, AAAI Press, 1996.

Levesque, H. J. and Lakemeyer, G., *The Logic of Knowledge Bases*, Monograph, MIT Press, forthcoming.

H. J. Levesque, R. Reiter, Y. Lespérance, F. Lin, and R. B. Scherl. GOLOG: A logic programming language for dynamic domains. *Journal of Logic Programming*, 31, 59-84, 1997.

Lin, F. and Reiter, R., State constraints revisited. *J. of Logic and Computation, special issue on actions and processes*, 4, 1994, pp. 665–678. Lin, F. and Reiter, R., How to Progress a Database. *Artificial Intelligence*, 92, 1997, pp.131-167.

McCarthy, J., *Situations, Actions and Causal Laws*. Technical Report, Stanford University, 1963. Also in M. Minsky (ed.), *Semantic Information Processing*, MIT Press, Cambridge, MA, 1968, pp. 410–417.

Moore, R. C., A Formal Theory of Knowledge and Action. In J. R. Hobbs and R. C. Moore (eds.), *Formal Theories of the Commonsense World*, Ablex, Norwood, NJ, 1985, pp. 319–358.

Moore, R. C., Semantical Considerations on Nonmonotonic Logic. *Artificial Intelligence* 25, 1985, pp. 75–94.

Newell, A., The Knowledge Level, *AI Magazine* 2(2), pp. 1–20.

Reiter, R., The Frame Problem in the Situation Calculus: A simple Solution (sometimes) and a Completeness Result for Goal Regression. In V. Lifshitz (ed.), *Artificial Intelligence and Mathematical Theory of Computation*, Academic Press, 1991, pp. 359–380.

Reiter, R., Proving Properties of States in the Situation Calculus. *Artificial Intelligence*, 64, 1993, pp. 337-351.

Scherl, R. and Levesque, H. J., The Frame Problem and Knowledge Producing Actions. in *Proc. of the National Conference on Artificial Intelligence (AAAI-93)*, AAAI Press, 1993, 689–695.

REINHOLD LETZ

PROPERTIES AND RELATIONS OF TABLEAU AND CONNECTION CALCULI

1. INTRODUCTION

The connection or matings method (Andrews, 1981; Bibel, 1981; Bibel, 1987) and tableau calculi with connections like model elimination (Loveland, 1968) are related paradigms in automated deduction. While this is intuitively evident, the precise relations and differences have not been sufficiently investigated so far. In this paper, we give a thorough exposition of the two frameworks and illustrate that a careful analysis of the relations may lead to advances in automated deduction in general. We begin with a brief comparison of the inherent principles of both paradigms.

First, the tableau method in general (Smullyan, 1968; Fitting, 1996) is a *tree-oriented* deductive paradigm based on the *subformula principle*, which permits a well-founded decomposition of a formula into certain subformulae. Further typical proof-theoretic virtues of the framework are the *confluence* of the calculus and the possibility of *saturation* of a branch (possibly up to a Hintikka set). Traditionally, tableau calculi have no reference to connections. When integrating connections as a control structure into tableaux (Letz et al., 1992; Letz et al., 1994), the confluence and hence the possibility of branch saturation is lost, but the gain is *goal-orientedness*, which renders tableaux successful in automated deduction for classical logic (Moser et al., 1997).

In the connection or matings method (Andrews, 1981; Bibel, 1981; Bibel, 1987), on the other hand, the notion of a connection is of central importance. The kernel of this framework is to call a set of connections M—called *mating*—*spanning* for a formula if every appropriately defined *path through* the formula contains a connection from M. First and foremost, the concept of a spanning mating has no deductive content, it provides just a declarative (graph-theoretic) characterization of logical validity or inconsistency. The fact that both frameworks are considered as closely related has the following simple reason. The most natural method for finding and identifying a spanning mating as such is to use a tree-oriented path checking procedure which decomposes the formula, like in the tableau framework, but guided by connections. The majority of those connection *calculi* in (Bibel, 1987) can therefore be viewed as

S. Hölldobler (ed.), Intellectics and Computational Logic, 245–261.

connection *tableau* calculi. This accounts for the fact that connection tableaux and the connection method are generally considered as similar methods.

In this paper, refinements of matings will be developed and related with properties of tableaux. Depending on whether one starts off from the matings framework or uses connection tableau calculi like model elimination, the generation of clause copies is handled differently. The matings paradigm suggests to generate clause copies once and for all at the beginning of the path search whereas model elimination performs a dynamic clause copying during the tableau construction. We compare both methodologies concerning the possibility of integrating redundancy elimination techniques like failure caching and calculi extensions like factorization. Since with every tableau one can naturally associate a mating, it is interesting to transfer refinements of matings to tableaux and vice versa. In the matings framework, we emphasize the importance of the properties of *fully connectedness* and *minimality* of a mating for redundancy elimination in automated deduction. The essential notions considered in the tableau paradigm are *connectedness*, *path connectedness*, *strictness*, and *regularity*. We investigate whether the notions in one framework can be naturally identified in the other one. The paper proves the following two new results. It is demonstrated that, for each minimal spanning mating, there exists a closed strict connection tableau with this mating. This assures that the minimality on matings can be used for search pruning in connection tableaux. But we also show that the existence of a regular such tableau is not guaranteed. There are minimal spanning matings for which there exist no closed regular connection tableaux. This means that the matings paradigm has no natural correlate of the notion of regularity in tableaux. This has the interesting consequence that the static framework of matings contains a source of redundancy that can only be identified and eliminated by using the dynamic paradigm of tableaux. This does not mean that tableaux are superior to matings. In (Letz, 1998b), it is shown that, for one and the same mating, there may be (superexponentially) many different regular connection tableaux. In other terms, the mapping from regular connection tableaux to matings is not injective. Together these results prove that each of the paradigms alone is not sufficient when one attempts to achieve optimal redundancy elimination, and that there is a large potential of cross-fertilization between the frameworks.

The paper is organized as follows. In the next section, we shortly review the main concepts and properties of clausal connection tableau calculi. In Section 3, the matings kernel of the connection method is presented including the concept of so-called multiplicities of a formula. Section 4 introduces multiplicity-based variants of connection tableau calculi and compares the respective iterative-deepening methodologies with the ones based on tableau complexity. In the fifth section, refinements of matings like fully connectedness and minimality are investigated. Section 6 applies the developed matings properties to tableaux; here it is shown that, for every minimal spanning mating, there exists a closed strict connection tableau; furthermore, we show that some minimal spanning matings have no regular connection tableau proofs. In the final section, we mention future research perspectives based on the integration of matings and tableaux.

2. CLAUSAL TABLEAUX WITH CONNECTION CONDITIONS

Before starting with the presentation of connection tableaux, the meaning of some basic concepts and notations will be determined. We use standard conventions for denoting terms and literals, variables will be denoted with the letters x, y, z (with subscripts). The proof systems we will consider are all working on *clausal formulae*, which are conjunctions $F = c_1 \wedge \cdots \wedge c_n$ of *clauses*. A *clause* is a string of the form $L_1 \vee \cdots \vee L_n$ where the L_i are literals. It is essential for our work that different occurrences of a literal in a clause and a formula can be distinguished. Therefore, occurrences of literals in a clausal formula are denoted with triples $\langle L, i, j \rangle$ where L is the literal with unique identifier i in the clause c_j in F. The *complement* $\sim L$ of a literal L is A if L is of the form $\neg A$, and $\neg L$ otherwise. For formulae in clausal form, the calculus of free-variable tableaux (Fitting, 1996; Letz, 1998) can be reformulated in a particularly simple and condensed form.

Definition 1. (Clausal tableau) *A clausal tableau is a downward-oriented tree in which all nodes except the root node are labeled with literals (and other control information). For every non-leaf node N in a clausal tableau, the sequence $N_1, \ldots, N_m$ of its immediate successor nodes is called* the node family below N; *if the nodes $N_1, \ldots, N_m$ are labeled with literals $L_1, \ldots, L_m$, respectively, then the clause $L_1 \vee \cdots \vee L_m$ is termed* the tableau clause below N; *the tableau clause below the root node is called the* start *or* top clause *of the tableau. Let F be a conjunction of clauses; a clausal tableau is said to be a clausal tableau for F if every tableau clause in T is an instance of a clause in F.*

The most successful structural refinement of clausal tableaux concerning automated deduction is to use links or *connections* to guide the proof search. The condition comes in two variants, a weaker one, which we term *path connectedness*, and a stricter one, simply called *connectedness*, which we prefer. The resulting tableau calculi can be formulated as consisting of three inference rules.

Definition 2. (Connection tableau calculus) *Let F be a conjunction of clauses $c_1 \wedge \cdots \wedge c_n$.*

(Start rule) *At the beginning, select a clause from F and take it as top clause of the tableau. All new branches are considered as open. The start rule can be used only once as the initial step of the tableau construction.*

Then select an open branch B in the current tableau with leaf node N (called subgoal*) and literal label K. Two types of inference rules may be applied.*

(Extension rule) *Select a clause c_j from F. If c_j contains variables, rename them, i.e., obtain a variant $c'_j = L_1 \vee \cdots \vee L_m$ in which all variables are different from the variables in T, otherwise let $c'_j = c_j$. If there is a most general unifier σ for $\sim K$ and a literal L_i in c'_j, attach a new node family $N_1, \ldots, N_m$ to the subgoal*

N and label the nodes with the literals $L_1, \ldots, L_m$, respectively. Then consider all new branches as open *except the one ending in N_i, which is considered as* closed. *Finally, apply the substitution σ to the formulae in the tableau. We will say that the new node family (the clause c'_j) was entered at the node N_i (the literal occurrence $\langle L_i, i, j' \rangle$).*

(Closure or reduction rule) *If N has an ancestor node N' with literal L on the branch B such that there is a most general unifier σ for $\sim K$ and L, then consider B as* closed *and apply σ to the tableau.*

Furthermore, we assume that the nodes in the clausal tableau are additionally labeled with the occurrences $\langle L_i, i, j' \rangle$ of the respective literals in the used clauses or clause copies.

The *path connection tableau calculus* is identical except that the extension rule is generalized to the *path extension rule* which permits that *any* node from the branch B may be used as a unification partner for L_i. We mention this variant because it corresponds to the connection calculi in (Bibel, 1987). The connection tableau calculus, on the other hand, is a generalization of (weak) model elimination (Loveland, 1968; Loveland, 1978). Completeness proofs can be found in (Letz, 1998a). In Figure 1, two closed clausal tableaux are displayed, on the lefthand side a path connection tableau and on the righthand side a connection tableau. Note that closed path connection tableaux may contain the occurrence of pure clauses (i.e. clauses with unconnected literals) whereas closed connection tableaux cannot, as discussed below.

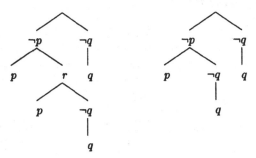

Figure 1   (Path) connection tableaux for the formula $(\neg p \lor \neg q) \land (p \lor r) \land (p \lor \neg q) \land q$.

Although with the integration of connections into the tableau framework the fundamental proof-theoretic property of *confluence*[1] is lost, the new calculus becomes competitive in automated deduction, because it permits a *goal-oriented* search. But, when searching for closed connection tableaux, a systematic branch saturation procedure like in (Smullyan, 1968) cannot be used. Instead one uses the well-known two-step methodology of iterative deepening search (Stickel, 1988). On each iteration level, only tableaux up to a certain complexity are permitted. The favoured complexity measures are the number of (closed) branches or the maximal depth of a tableau, called *inference* and *depth* bound, respectively. The bounds differ strongly in their worst-case complexities. While it is straightforward to recognize that the verification of the existence of a tableau with k inferences is an NP-complete problem, the corresponding problem for the depth bound seems much harder (it is not even clear whether it is in PSPACE). A combination of both bounds, the *weighted-depth bound*, which is integrated in the theorem prover SETHEO (Moser et al., 1997; Ibens and Letz, 1997) turned out to be very successful in practice (although the weighted-depth bound and the depth bound have the same abstract worst-case complexity).

The pure connection tableau calculus contains lots of redundancies. The following refinement implements a basic structural pruning mechanism.

Definition 3. (Regularity) *A clausal tableau is* regular *if no literal appears more than once on a branch.*

Experiments have shown that with this refinement a significant search pruning effect can be achieved. For example, the presence of clauses in a formula expressing the symmetry or the commutativity of a relation like $R(x, y) \vee \neg R(y, x)$ or $R(x, y, z) \vee \neg R(y, x, z)$ do not automatically lead to the existence of infinitely many tableaux for the formula when regularity is used.

A further reduction of the search space can be achieved with methods of *failure caching* (Astrachan and Stickel, 1992), which avoid repetitions of subgoal solutions with the same or more special substitutions. Only the *local* variant (Letz et al., 1994; Letz, 1998a) is successful in practice, which was termed *anti-lemma* mechanism in (Letz et al., 1994). Failure caching methods, however, are very expensive and difficult to implement. Finally, one should mention additional inference rules like *factorization* or *folding up* (Letz et al., 1994). Those may have a proof shortening effect and can be viewed as controlled integrations of the (atomic) cut rule. Although these additional inference rules increase the search space, they may be beneficial if a proof can be found on an earlier iterative-deepening level.

3. THE MATINGS CONCEPT IN THE CONNECTION METHOD

Based on work by Prawitz (Prawitz, 1960; Prawitz, 1969), the *connection method* was introduced by Andrews (Andrews, 1981) and Bibel (Bibel, 1981; Bibel, 1987)— we shall use Bibel's terminology as reference point. As already mentioned in the Introduction, the kernel of the connection method is not a deductive system, but a declarative syntactic characterization of logical validity or inconsistency. While, in the original papers, the connection method represents logical validity directly, we work with the dual variant representing inconsistency, which makes no difference concerning the employed notions and mechanisms. Furthermore, we work on the clausal case only.

Definition 4. (Path, connection, mating, spanning property) *Given a clausal formula* $F = c_1 \wedge \cdots \wedge c_n$, *a path through* F *is a set of* n *literal occurrences in*

F, *exactly one from each clause in* F. *A* connection *in* F *is a two-element subset* $\{\langle K, i, k\rangle, \langle L, j, l\rangle\}$ *of a path through* F *such that* K *and* L *are literals with the same predicate symbol, one negated and one not. Any set of connections* M *in* F *is called a* mating *in* F; *the pair* $\langle M, F\rangle$ *is termed a* connected formula. *A mating* M *is said to be* spanning *for* F *if every path through* F *is a superset of a connection in* M.

A conjunction of propositional clauses F is unsatisfiable if and only if there is a spanning mating for F. In the first-order case, the notions of multiplicities and unification come into play.

Definition 5. (Multiplicity, unifiable connection, mating) *First, a* multiplicity *is just a mapping* $\mu : \mathbb{N} \longrightarrow \mathbb{N}_0$ *which is then extended to clausal formulae, as follows. Given a multiplicity* μ *and two clausal formulae* $F = c_1 \wedge \cdots \wedge c_n$ *and* $F' = c_1^1 \wedge \cdots \wedge c_1^{\mu(1)} \wedge \cdots \wedge c_n^1 \wedge \cdots \wedge c_n^{\mu(n)}$ *where every* c_i^k *is a variable-renamed variant of* c_i, *we call* F' *a* (μ-)multiplicity *of* F. *A connection* $\{\langle K, i, k\rangle, \langle L, j, l\rangle\}$ *is termed* unifiable *if the atoms of* K *and* L *are. A mating is* unifiable *if there is a simultaneous unifier for all its connections.*

Theorem 6. *A clausal formula* F *is unsatisfiable if and only if there is a unifiable spanning mating for a multiplicity of* F. (Bibel, 1987)

Obviously, it is decidable whether a clausal formula has a unifiable and spanning mating. We will briefly consider the complexity of this decision problem. Interestingly, this problem is closely related with the problem of finding an unsatisfiable ground instance of a quantifier-free (clausal) formula. First, if there is a unifiable spanning mating for a clausal formula F with unifier σ, then every ground instance of $F\sigma$ is unsatisfiable, hence F has an unsatisfiable ground instance. In the other direction, when a clausal formula F has an unsatisfiable ground instance $F\sigma$, then there is a unifiable spanning mating for F with simultaneous unifier σ.

The consideration of those problems dates back to work of Prawitz ((Prawitz, 1960), and more directly to (Prawitz, 1969)). The problem naturally occurs when one considers the well-known early approaches in automated deduction like the Davis/Putnam procedures (Davis and Putnam, 1960; Davis et al., 1962). In those procedures the unsatisfiability of a first-order Skolem formula Φ is proved by systematically building increasing sets of ground instances of the quantifier-free part—the *matrix*—of Φ, which are then checked by propositional decision procedures. A crucial point which determines the efficiency of this approach concerns the manner how the respective ground instances are generated. In the original procedures, no information of the connection structure of the matrix of Φ was used, but a systematic substitution of terms from the Herbrand universe of Φ was performed, which is obviously unmanageable in practice. Just recently, in (Plaisted, 1992), Plaisted developed a linking and a hyperlinking method in which the selection of ground terms is guided by unification. In contrast, Prawitz proposed as an improvement not to build ground instances of the formula but to work directly on variable-renamed copies of the matrix of Φ and to determine an unsatisfiable set of ground instances by using unification on the connections in the set of copies. While the recognition of the unsatisfiability of a ground formula is a coNP-complete problem, the complexity of recognizing the existence of an unsatisfiable ground instance of a quantifier-free formula is complete for Σ_2^p which is presumably higher located in the polynomial hierarchy. This result is proven in (Voronkov, 1998). The latter paper contains a wealth of results on the decidability and worst-case complexities of multiplicity-based formula instantiation problems.

4. MATINGS-BASED CONNECTION PROCEDURES

The former decidability result suggests a two-step methodology of *iterative-deepening* proof search, as performed with the connection tableau procedures. The outer loop is concerned with increasing the multiplicity whereas the inner procedure explores the finite search space determined by the given multiplicity. Although there are different methods for identifying a unifiable and spanning mating for some multiplicity of a formula, one of the most natural ways is exemplified with a procedure which is similar to the connection tableau calculi, but without a renaming of the clauses in the given multiplicity.

Definition 7. ((Path) Connection tableau calculus without renaming) *The two calculi are the same as the ones given in the previous section except that*

1. *they work on a multiplicity F' of the input formula,*

2. *no renaming is permitted in a (path) extension step, and*

3. *the computed substitution σ is also applied to the clauses in F'.*

The connection procedure C_1^1 on pages 108f. in (Bibel, 1987), for example, is based on the path connection tableau calculus without renaming. For the subsequent investigations, the following weakening of the notion of regularity will play an important rôle.

Definition 8. (Strictness) *A clausal tableau in which the nodes are labeled with literal occurrences is said to be* strict *if no literal occurrence appears more than once on a branch.*

This notion is closely related with what is called *strictness* in general tableau calculi (Smullyan, 1968; Fitting, 1996). Obviously, strictness is properly weaker than regularity (Definition 3). There is the following fundamental difference between the two types of calculi, the ones with and the ones without renaming. For the calculi without renaming, it is guaranteed that there are only finitely many regular or strict (path) connection tableaux for each multiplicity of the input formula. That is, no additional limit on the tableau complexity has to be given to assure termination of the tableau search procedure for a given multiplicity.

4.1. Tableau complexity vs. formula multiplicity

Unfortunately, currently there exist no successful implementations of multiplicity-based connection (tableau) procedures. When comparing both types of tableau calculi and the corresponding iterative-deepening methodologies, it will become clear why.

The crucial difference of this type of tableau calculi from the ones of the previous section is that with multiplicity-based bounds static complexity limits are put on the input multiplicity whereas the tableau complexity is not directly bounded. As a matter of fact, when using strictness or regularity, also the depth of the tableaux is bounded, viz. by the number of clauses in the input multiplicity. But one may safely conjecture that the use of the pure multiplicity bound is much too rough in order to be successful in practice (think of a multiplicity with hundreds of clauses). Instead one may limit the *cardinality of the matings* to be considered or the *number* of clauses in a multiplicity. This should work better in practice, although it is easy to see that, for both new limits, the corresponding formula instantiation problem remains Σ_2^p-complete. But worst-case complexity results have to be taken with a grain of salt when it comes to practice, as illustrated by the success of the weighted-depth bound mentioned in Section 2.

There are also two important further differences concerning the effectiveness of the search pruning mechanisms mentioned at the end of Section 2. The first is that the beneficial effect of factorization and folding up (permitting that a proof is found on an earlier iterative-deepening level) cannot occur in the multiplicity-based case, since those rules can only reduce the tableau size, but have no influence on the unifiability and spanning properties of matings. Failure caching is even more problematic in the multiplicity-based case, for the following reason. In order to preserve completeness, not only the solution substitution of a subgoal N (and its branch) has to be considered, but also the substitutions applied to all clauses used in the subrefutation of N. This renders failure caching practically useless for the multiplicity-based calculi.

Finally, in the multiplicity-based case, there is an additional source of redundancy which has directly to do with the use of multiplicities. Fortunately, this redundancy can easily be removed. Consider the clausal formula

$$F = \neg P(a) \wedge (P(x) \vee \neg Q(y)) \wedge (Q(a) \vee Q(b)).$$

In Figure 2, two closed connection tableaux for the multiplicity $F' = c_1 \wedge c_2^1 \wedge c_2^2 \wedge c_3$ of F are displayed; also, the attached clause variants and the substitutions to be applied in the inference steps are given.

It is evident that the two tableaux are variants of each other obtainable by exchanging the positions of the clauses c_2^1 and c_2^2. This obvious redundancy can be avoided by using the proviso that any variant c_i^{k+1}, $k > 0$, of an initial clause c_i can be selected for extension only if the clause variant c_i^k in the multiplicity was already used in the tableau. This way the redundant tableau on the right cannot be constructed any more.

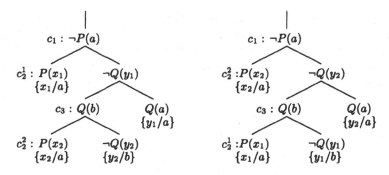

Figure 2 Multiplicity-based duplication of connection tableaux.

5. IMPORTANT REFINEMENTS OF MATINGS

It is interesting to relate properties of matings with one another and with properties of clausal tableaux. In this section, we will develop some fundamental refinements of the matings concept, clarify their relations, and discuss issues of computational complexity. In order to simplify the presentation of the subsequent definitions, we use the following abbreviated notation. A literal occurrence is said to be *in* a mating M if it is contained in some connection of M, and a clause is said to be *in* a mating M if one of its literals is in M.

Definition 9. (Fully connected mating) *A connected formula $\langle M, F \rangle$ is called* fully connected *if, whenever a literal occurrence in a clause c in F is in M, then every literal occurrence in c is in M.*

Definition 10. (Essential connection, minimal mating) *A connection C is termed* essential *in a clausal formula F if there is a path through F containing only the connection C. A connection C in a mating M in a clausal formula F is called* essential *in M if there is a path through F containing C and no other connection in M. A mating M is called* minimal *if each of its connections is essential in M.*

The general motivation for developing complete refinements of matings is to achieve redundancy elimination in the first-order case. In contrast to the proposition case, where always the full set of connections in a formula can be taken, in the first-order case, with every connection that is added to a mating, an additional unification problem has to be solved. The restriction to minimal matings keeps the simultaneous unification problem as easy as possible. The set M of essential connections of a formula, on the other hand, must be a subset of any spanning mating. Consequently, if M is not simultaneously unifiable, then the formula has no unsatisfiable ground instance.

In order to illustrate the notions, consider the propositional clausal formula

$$F = (\neg p \vee \neg q) \wedge (\neg p \vee q) \wedge (p \vee \neg q) \wedge (p \vee q).$$

The eight connections in F are spanning. The formula has two minimal spanning matings, each consisting of six connections, as depicted in Figure 3. In the figure, clauses are displayed horizontally, paths and connections vertically. Note that only four connections are essential in the formula, the connections common to both minimal spanning matings.

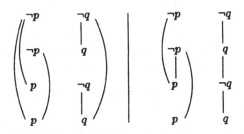

Figure 3   Two minimal spanning matings in a clausal formula.

Proposition 11. *Every minimal spanning mating is fully connected.*

Proof: Assume indirectly, the minimal spanning mating M in a formula F to have a connection C containing a literal occurrence from a clause c_k in F such that some other literal occurrence $\langle L, i, k \rangle$ in c_k were not in M. Because of the spanning property, every path through $\langle L, i, k \rangle$ must have a connection from $M \setminus \{C\}$ as a subset. Since $\langle L, i, k \rangle$ is in no connection, every path through c_k and hence any path through F must have a connection from $M \setminus \{C\}$ as a subset. This would mean that $M \setminus \{C\}$ be spanning for F, contradicting the minimality assumption of M. □

We also wish to mention the computational complexities involved in those concepts. First, it is evident that the property of being fully connected can be decided in linear time. Next, we consider the essentiality of a connection.

Proposition 12. *The verification of the essentiality of a connection in a clausal formula F is NP-complete.*

Proof: First, evidently, for any essential connection C in a clausal formula, we can guess a path through the formula containing only C in linear time. In order to recognize the NP-hardness of the problem, one can use a linear reduction of the satisfiability problem for clauses. Let F be any clausal formula. Obtain F' by simply adding the two unit clauses p and $\neg p$ to F. Then the connection containing the literal occurrences in those two clauses is essential in F' if and only if F is satisfiable. □

Finally, let us turn to the complexity of recognizing the minimality of a mating M. As a matter of fact, the problem is in NP. For any connection $C \in M$, we can guess a path through F containing only C in linear time, and there are only linearly many connections, which gives a quadratic total complexity. When considering the NP-hardness of the problem, however, the simple trick of the previous proof does not work. So we can formulate as an important open problem to decide the precise complexity of recognizing the minimality of a mating.

6. MATINGS IN TABLEAUX

How can the developed matings refinements be used on tableaux? This is obvious for the calculi without renaming, since the clause copies to be used in a tableau are determined in advance. Whenever an extension or reduction step is performed in the construction of a tableau for a multiplicity F' which involves two tableau nodes N and N' with corresponding literal occurrences $\langle K, i, k \rangle$ and $\langle L, j, l \rangle$, respectively, then we say that the connection $\{\langle K, i, k \rangle, \langle L, j, l \rangle\}$ in F' is *used* in the tableau. With *the mating* of a tableau for F' we mean the set of connections in F' used in the construction of the tableau. For connection tableau calculi with renaming, one can also define the *mating of* a tableau, the only difference being that the set of clause copies may increase during the tableau construction.

The interesting observation can be made that the mapping from tableaux to matings need not be injective. In (Letz, 1998b) it is shown that there may be (superexponentially) many regular closed connection tableaux with the same spanning mating. For this result, formulae of the type underlying the matings in Figure 3 were used. The latter paper also presents a method for removing particular cases of this form of redundancy in tableau search procedures. The results in (Letz, 1998b) demonstrate that tableaux can profit a lot from matings information. Here we wish to consider the potential of refinements of matings like fully connectedness and minimality.

Proposition 13. *The mating of any closed connection tableau (without renaming) is fully connected.*

Proof: This follows trivially from the definition of the connection tableau calculi (Definitions 2 and 7).   □

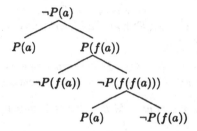

Figure 4 Closed path connection tableau with not fully connected mating.

Note that this property is not guaranteed for path connection tableaux, In Figure 4, a closed path connection tableau (without renaming) for the input (multiplicity)

$$\neg P(a) \wedge (P(x) \vee P(f(x))) \wedge (\neg P(x) \vee \neg P(f(x))) \wedge (P(x) \vee \neg P(f(x)))$$

is shown. The literal occurrence $\neg P(f(f(a)))$ in the tableau is not in the mating of the tableau. So, the connection tableau calculus can be viewed as a method for generating only fully connected spanning matings.

However, the mating of a closed connection tableau need not be minimal. An example of such a tableau is displayed in Figure 5. But we have the converse result that, for every minimal spanning mating, there is a closed connection tableau with this mating. In order to prove this fundamental relation between matings and tableaux, we need some more terminology.

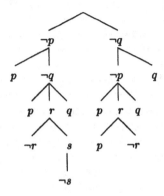

Figure 5   Closed connection tableau with nonminimal mating.

Definition 14. (Relevant literal occurrence) *A literal occurrence $\langle L, i, k \rangle$ in a clausal formula F is called* relevant *in a mating M in F if $\langle L, i, k \rangle$ is in some subset M' of M that is minimally spanning for F; A clause is called* relevant *in a mating M if every literal occurrence in the clause is relevant in M.*

Definition 15. (Strengthening) *Let $\langle M, F \rangle$ be a connected formula, c_k any clause in F, $\langle L, i, k \rangle$ any literal occurrence in c_k, and S_i^k the set of other literal occurrences in c_k. The strengthening of $\langle M, F \rangle$ by $\langle L, i, k \rangle$, written $\langle L, i, k \rangle \triangleright \langle M, F \rangle$, is the pair $\langle M', F' \rangle$ defined as follows.*

- *The formula F' is obtained from F by shortening the clause c_k to a unit clause by deleting all literal occurrences in S_i^k from the clause.*

- *M' is the set of connections in M that do not contain literals in S_i^k.*

If $S = L_1, \ldots, L_n$ is a sequence of literal occurrences from different clauses, then we abbreviate $L_n \triangleright (\cdots \triangleright (L_1 \triangleright \langle M, F \rangle))$ by writing $S \triangleright \langle M, F \rangle$.

Clearly, if $\langle M', F' \rangle$ is the strengthening of a connected formula $\langle M, F \rangle$, then M' is a mating in F'. Furthermore, if M is spanning for F, then M' must be spanning for F'. In the following, we will make use of the following lemma.

Lemma 16. (Mating Lemma) *Let M be a spanning mating for a clausal formula F, c_k any relevant clause in M, $\langle L, i, k \rangle$ any literal occurrence in c_k, and $\langle M', F' \rangle = \langle L, i, k \rangle \rhd \langle M, F \rangle$. Then, F' contains a relevant clause c_l with a literal occurrence $\langle K, j, l \rangle$ and the connection $\{ \langle L, i, k \rangle, \langle K, j, l \rangle \}$ is in M'.*

Proof: From the relevance of $\langle L, i, k \rangle$ in $\langle M, F \rangle$ it follows that $\langle L, i, k \rangle$ is relevant in $\langle M', F' \rangle$. This means that there is a subset M'' of the mating M' such that M'' is minimally spanning for F' and there is a literal occurrence $\langle K, j, l \rangle$ such that the connection $\{ \langle L, i, k \rangle, \langle K, j, l \rangle \}$ is in M''. The minimality of M'' and Proposition 11 give us that M'' is fully connected, i.e., every literal occurrence in c_l is in M''. Consequently, since M'' is minimal and spanning, every literal occurrence in c_l is relevant in M'', hence c_l is relevant in $M' \supseteq M''$. $\square$

Now, we are well-equipped to prove the intended result. The interesting part of this result is already settled on the ground case, which we consider first. Note that, in the ground case, the calculi with or without renaming coincide. We will show completeness for *strict* connection tableaux. Interestingly, this further refinement of connection tableaux will help in the completeness proof, since it guarantees termination.

Proposition 17. *For every minimal unifiable spanning mating for a ground clausal formula F, there exists a closed strict connection tableau (without renaming) for F with this mating.*

Proof: Since F is ground, the simultaneous unifier must be the empty substitution and may be ignored. In the proof, we apply a technique that is in the spirit of the method used in (Letz et al., 1994; Letz, 1998a). First, we specify a deduction procedure for connection tableaux, then we show by induction that during execution of this procedure an invariant is preserved which eventually leads to a closed tableau with the required properties.

Tableau procedure. First, attach any relevant clause c_i in F as top clause of the tableau T. As long as the tableau is not yet closed, let N with literal occurrence $\langle L, i, k \rangle$ and corresponding clause c_k in F be any subgoal, and let P be the sequence of literal occurrences on the branch from the root down to the subgoal N.

1. if N has an ancestor N' on the branch with literal occurrence $\langle \sim L, j, l \rangle$ and there is a connection in M containing both literal occurrences, perform a reduction step using N',

2. otherwise, consider $\langle M', F' \rangle = P \rhd \langle M, F \rangle$. Select a relevant clause c_l in M' containing a literal occurrence $\langle \sim L, j, l \rangle$ such that $\{ \langle L, i, k \rangle, \langle \sim L, j, l \rangle \}$ is in M'. Perform an extension step by entering the clause c_l at $\langle \sim L, j, l \rangle$.

First, evidently, the mechanism of clause selection in the procedure admits solely the construction of *strict* connection tableaux. Furthermore, just because of the strictness restriction, there can be only branches of finite length. Consequently, the procedure must terminate either because every leaf is closed or because no clause c_l exists for extension which meets the conditions stated in the procedure. We prove by induction on the branch length that the second alternative can never occur, since, for any subgoal N of an open branch that cannot be closed by a reduction step, there exists such a clause (this is the invariant). The induction base, for $n = 1$ and N being the root node, is trivial. For the induction step from branch length n to $n + 1$, $n > 1$, consider any open branch of length $n + 1$ with subgoal N labeled with $\langle L, i, k \rangle$. Let further be P the set of literal occurrences on the branch from the root down to the predecessor of N. By the induction assumption, the clause c_k is relevant in $\langle M', F' \rangle = P \triangleright \langle M, F \rangle$. Hence, by the Mating Lemma, F' contains a clause c_l with a literal occurrence $\langle \sim L, j, l \rangle$ such that the connection $\{\langle L, i, k \rangle, \langle \sim L, j, l \rangle\}$ is in M' (connectedness), and c_l is relevant in M'. Since every literal occurrence on the branch is contained in a unit clause in F' and since, by assumption, N cannot be closed by a reduction step, no literal in $P \cup \{\langle L, i, k \rangle\}$ can be contained in c_l (strictness).   □

Since the calculi considered in this paper have the ground projection property (Baaz and Leitsch, 1992), the lifting of ground completeness results to the first-order case is straightforward (Letz, 1998a; Letz, 1998b).

How can this property be exploited for redundancy elimination in automated deduction? A straightforward application would be the following. Use a proof search procedure based on strict connection tableaux and prune every tableau whose mating is not minimal. The just proved result then assures the completeness of this refined procedure.

However, we can observe that one cannot be sure whether instead of strictness the stronger notion of regularity may be demanded. At least it can be proven that not every minimal spanning mating will be captured this way.

Proposition 18. *There are minimal spanning matings for which there exist no closed regular connection tableaux.*

Proof: The proof is carried out in two parts. First, we consider the formula

$$F = (\neg p \vee \neg q) \wedge (\neg p \vee q) \wedge (p \vee \neg q) \wedge (p \vee q)$$

used in Figure 3 and the minimal spanning mating

$$M = \{\{\neg p^1, p^3\}\{\neg p^2, p^3\}\{\neg p^2, p^4\}\{\neg q^1, q^2\}\{\neg q^3, q^2\}\{\neg q^3, q^4\}\}$$

on the right of Figure 3 with the upper indices indicating the clause numbers. We demonstrate that there is no closed regular connection tableau for this mating with the top clause $c_1 = \neg p \vee \neg q$. The left subgoal $\neg p^1$ has only one connection in M, a so-called *isolated* connection, into clause c_3. From there, the $\neg q^3$-subgoal can only be connected into clause c_4, following the other connection would violate the regularity. From there, the q^4-subgoal has an isolated connection into c_3, which cannot be used, since it violates the regularity. So there is no closed regular connection tableau with top clause c_1 for the mating M.

In the second part, we construct a formula and a mating for which this holds for any start clause. This can easily be done by using the duplication technique developed in (Letz et al., 1994). We modify the given formula by adding the clauses $c_2' = \neg p' \vee q'$, $c_3' = p' \vee \neg q'$, $c_4' = p' \vee q'$ and by replacing the clause c_1 with the new clause $\neg p \vee \neg q \vee \neg p' \vee \neg q'$. As the set of matings we take the matings in the old formula plus the analogous six connections between the primed literal occurrences. It is evident that this mating is minimal and spanning. For the new formula, independent of the start clause, at some point we must enter the modified first clause for the first time. If we enter it at a primed respectively unprimed literal, then before this inference step only primed respectively unprimed literals appear in the tableau. This is because the first clause is the only one containing both primed and unprimed literals. Consequently, as a corollary of the first part of the proof, for the given mating, there will be no regular closed subtableau for the newly attached subgoal $\neg p^1$ respectively $\neg p'^1$. □

This counterexample shows that, when using regularity in connection tableaux, one does not capture all minimal spanning matings. In addition to the fact that this is proof-theoretically interesting it has a strong consequence for redundancy elimination in the matings framework. It means that the static framework of matings contains a source of redundancy that cannot be identified by looking at the matings alone. This phenomenon also explains the success of the regularity restriction for search pruning in connection tableaux.

7. FURTHER RESEARCH

We conclude with pointing to some future promising research perspectives using matings in tableaux and vice versa. First, it should be settled whether, for every unsatisfiable clausal formula F, there exists a closed regular connection tableau with a minimal mating in F. This property would be sufficient in order to assure the completeness of a connection tableau proof procedure permitting only minimal matings and using full regularity in place of strictness. Furthermore, the results developed here should be extended to connection tableau calculi with additional inference rules like factorization and folding up. Finally, a naturally arising approach would be not to compute minimal matings separately but to check the minimality property of matings dynamically during the tableau construction. This raises the important question of the computational complexity of checking the minimality of a mating in a regular or strict connection tableau. Note that these problems might be easier than verifying the minimality of a mating in general, since the tableau size and structure come into play. Regardless of these worst-case complexity results, an important future research topic will be the development of practically efficient algorithms for detecting the minimality or the nonminimality of matings.

Munich University of Technology
Munich, Germany

NOTES

1. A calculus is confluent if it cannot run into dead ends (see, e.g., (Letz, 1998a)).

REFERENCES

P. Andrews. (1981). Theorem Proving via General Matings. *Journal of the Association for Computing Machinery*, 28(2):193–214.

O. W. Astrachan and M. E. Stickel. (1992). Caching and Lemmaizing in Model Elimination Theorem Provers. *Proceedings of the 11th Conference on Automated Deduction (CADE-11)*, LNAI 607, pages 224–238, Springer.

M. Baaz and A. Leitsch. (1992). Complexity of Resolution Proofs and Function Introduction. *Annals of Pure and Applied Logic*, 57:181–215.

W. Bibel. (1981). On Matrices with Connections. *Journal of the ACM*, 28:633–645.

W. Bibel. (1987). *Automated Theorem Proving*. Vieweg, second edition.

M. Davis and H. Putnam. (1960). A Computing Procedure for Quantification Theory. *Journal of the ACM*, 7:201–215.

M. Davis, G. Logemann, and D. Loveland. (1962). A Machine Program for Theorem Proving. *Communications of the ACM*, 5(7):394–397.

M. Fitting. (1996). *First-Order Logic and Automated Theorem Proving*, Springer, seconnd edition.

O. Ibens and R. Letz. (1997). Subgoal Alternation in Model Elimination. In *Proceedings of TABLEAUX'97*, LNAI 1227, pages 201–215, Springer.

R. Letz, J. Schumann, S. Bayerl, and W. Bibel. (1992). SETHEO: A High-Performance Theorem Prover. *Journal of Automated Reasoning*, 8(2):183–212.

R. Letz, K. Mayr, and C. Goller. (1994). Controlled Integration of the Cut Rule into Connection Tableaux Calculi. *Journal of Automated Reasoning*, 13:297–337.

R. Letz. (1998). Clausal Tableaux. In W. Bibel, P. H. Schmitt, editors, *Automated Deduction. A basis for applications*, Vol. 1, pages 39–68, Kluwer.

R. Letz. (1998). Using Matings for Pruning Connection Tableaux. In *Proceedings of the 15th Conference on Automated Deduction (CADE-15)*, LNAI 1421, pages 381–396, Springer.

R. Letz. (1999). First-order Tableau Methods. In M. D'Agostino, D. Gabbay, R. Hähnle, J. Posegga, editors, *Handbook of Tableau Methods*, pages 125–196, Kluwer.

D. W. Loveland. (1968). Mechanical Theorem Proving by Model Elimination. *Journal of the ACM*, 15(2):236–251.

D. W. Loveland. (1978). *Automated Theorem Proving: a Logical Basis*. North-Holland.

M. Moser, O. Ibens, R. Letz, J. Steinbach, C. Goller, J. Schumann, K. Mayr. (1997). SETHEO and E-SETHEO. *Journal of Automated Reasoning*, 18:237–246.

S.-J. Lee and D. Plaisted. (1992). Eliminating Duplication with the Hyper-Linking Strategy. *Journal of Automated Reasoning*, 9(1):25–42.

D. Prawitz. (1960). An Improved Proof Procedure. *Theoria*, 26:102–139.

D. Prawitz. (1969). Advances and Problems in Mechanical Proof Procedures. *Machine Intelligence*, 4:59–71, Edinburgh U. Press.

R. M. Smullyan. (1968). *First-Order Logic*. Springer.

M. A. Stickel. (1988). A Prolog Technology Theorem Prover: Implementation by an Extended Prolog Compiler. *Journal of Automated Reasoning*, 4:353–380.

A. Voronkov. (1998). Herbrand's theorem, automated reasoning and semantic tableaux. In *Proceedings of LICS-98*.

ERICA MELIS AND JÖRG H. SIEKMANN

CONCEPTS IN PROOF PLANNING

1. INTRODUCTION: THE PROOF PLANNING PARADIGM

Knowledge-based proof planning is a new paradigm in automated theorem proving. Its motivation partly comes from an increasing disillusionment by many researchers in the field of automated deduction, who feel that traditional techniques have been pushed to their limit and – as important as these developments have been in the past – will not be sufficient to reach the goal of a mathematical assistant system. Human mathematicians – among other differences – have a long term plan for a complex proof which is clearly not represented at the calculus-level of individual inference steps. Moreover a mathematician in a well established field has a whole battery of proof strategies, techniques, and tricks of the trade at his disposal.

How can these abilities be simulated on a machine? The idea is as follows: As opposed to traditional automated theorem proving (see, e.g., (Loveland, 1978; Chang and Lee, 1973) for standard monographs) which searches for a proof at the *object-level* of the underlying logic calculus, proof planning constructs a plan that represents a proof at a more abstract level. Here the representation of a proof, at least while it is developed, consists of a sequence of macro-operators, such as the application of a homomorphism, the expansion of a definition, the application of a lemma, some simplification, or the differentiation of a function. Each of these operators can in principle be expanded into a sequence of inference steps, say, in natural deduction (ND), and is therefore, in accord with tactical theorem proving (Gordon et al., 1979), called a tactic. Now if an individual tactic of this kind, which may also be a call to a traditional automated theorem prover, a fast decision procedure, or a computer algebra system, is extended by pre- and postconditions, then it is called a method and one can *plan* such a sequence of methods in the classical AI-planning paradigm. This was the central idea when proof planning was introduced in (Bundy, 1988).

A plan is a sequence of such methods, where the precondition of a method *matches* the postcondition of its predecessor in that sequence. This well-known view of a plan leads naturally to a new engine for automated theorem proving: a STRIPS-like planner (Fikes and Nilsson, 1971) – or any other planner – can be used to *plan* such a

S. Hölldobler (ed.), Intellectics and Computational Logic, 263–276.
© 2000 *Kluwer Academic Publishers.*

sequence of methods that transforms the proof assumptions into the theorem. Standard heuristics and techniques from AI-planning can now be employed.

Moreover, proof planning provides means of *global search control* that correspond to mathematical intuition, as opposed to the local and syntactic search heuristics which are commonly used for search control in automated theorem proving.

The purpose of this paper is primarily a methodological discussion of *representational issues* in proof planning. This appears to be timely as in the different research groups different representations emerged from the actual practice of particular application domains. For instance, in $CIAM$ (Bundy et al., 1991) the control knowledge that consists of a single difference reduction heuristic is represented in the preconditions of methods, in ΩMEGA (Benzmueller et al., 1997) too, some control knowledge was represented in particular methods thereby precluding further attempts to easily modify or extend, to learn or to generalize the control knowledge. We shall suggest some standard notions for proof planning and their representation based on today's AI-planning methodology. In particular, we define plans, methods, control-rules, and strategies.

2. BASICS OF PLANNING

A planning problem consists of an *initial state* that describes some initial situation and of *goals* to be achieved. A planning domain is defined by *operators* that represent actions. The operators have specifications to be used in the planning process. In STRIPS notation (Fikes and Nilsson, 1971), the specifications are called preconditions and effects. Preconditions specify the conditions of the planning state that have to be satisfied for the operator to be applicable, whereas effects describe the potential changes of the planning state caused by an operator application. Effects can be represented (in STRIPS notation) by add-lists ($\oplus$) and delete-lists ($\ominus$). Note that preconditions and effects usually are literals formulated in an *object-level* language such as (on A B) or (arm-holds A). However, some planners, e.g., Prodigy (Minton et al., 1989) allow for additional preconditions formulated in a *meta-level* language that restrict the instantiations of parameters.

A partial plan is a partially ordered set of operators with additional instantiation constraints and auxiliary constraints. A partial plan can be seen as an implicit representation for sets of instantiated operator sequences (potential solutions) that are consistent with the ordering, instantiation, and auxiliary constraints. A solution of a problem, a complete plan, is a linearization of a partial plan (a sequence of actions) that transforms the initial state into a goal state, i.e., a state in which the goals hold.

The operation of a (partial order) planner repeatedly *refines* a partial plan, i.e., it adds steps and constraints and thus resticts the set of potential solutions until a complete plan can be picked from its set of potential solutions. Table 1 shows a simplified backward planning algorithm (that does not handle goal interactions). It starts with a partial plan π_0 defined by the problem to be solved. π_0 consists of steps t_0 and t_∞ that are instantiations of the dummy operators start and finish, respectively. They have the initial state as $\oplus$-effects and the goals as preconditions, respectively. π_0 also represents the order constraint $t_0 \prec t_\infty$. The introduction of a step into a partial plan removes an open goal g from the goal agenda G (it satisfies g) and may introduce new open subgoals and constraints and this is continued until no open goals are left and a solution is found or until no operator is applicable anymore. Note that while most planners plan backward, the execution of a plan works forward.

`Backwards-Refine-Plan`(π, G)

Termination: if goal agenda G empty, **then** `Solution`.
if no operator applicable, **then** `Fail`.

Goal Selection: Choose open goal $g \in G$.

Operator Selection:
- For each operator M
 for each $\oplus$-effect e of M
 let σ be the matcher $\sigma(e) = g$
 if application-conditions$(\sigma(M)) = true$
 then M is applicable.
- Choose one applicable M (backtracking point)
 insert M into π
 insert constraints into π
 update G.

Recursion: Call `Backwards-Refine-Plan` on the refined partial plan π.

Table 1 Outline for backward planning

A diversity of refinement algorithms has been developed in AI (see, e.g. (Weld, 1994; Kambhampati, 1996)), among them two kinds of hierarchical planning: precondition abstraction (Sacerdoti, 1974) and operator abstraction planning (Tate, 1977), also called hierarchical task network (HTN)-planning. Precondition abstraction first searches in an abstract space by ignoring certain object-level preconditions of operators. These ignored goals are then considered later at a lower hierarchical level. Operator abstraction employs complex (i.e. non-primitive) operators that may represent complex actions. A complex operator can be expanded into a partial (sub)plan. Note that the expansion of non-primitive operators refines a partial plan by introducing new steps and constraints. Since only primitive actions can be executed, all complex operators have to be expanded before a plan can be executed.

Search is involved in each of the planning algorithms, independent of which space they search (state-space, plan-space, abstract-space). Hence, the process of planning can be viewed as a sequence of heuristically guided decisions, i.e., as a choice from a set of candidates, such that the choice eventually leads to a complete plan. These decisions include choosing which open goal to satisfy next, which planning operator to introduce in order to satisfy this goal, and which instantiations to choose for a parameter. In any case, the decisions which goal to satisfy next and which operator to choose influence the way the search space is traversed and thus the efficiency of the search. Therefore, many search strategies that fix a particular preference have been described in the planning literature, e.g., in (Pollack et al., 1997; Koehler, 1998). For instance, one of these strategies always prefers the goal g that produces the least number of alternative applicable methods.

Some advanced planners such as Prodigy (Veloso et al., 1995) use explicit control-rules to guide the search. This employment of control-rules changes the basic planning algorithm of Table 1 into the following algorithm in Table 2.

Backwards-Refine-PlanC(π, G)

Termination: if goal agenda G empty, **then** Solution.
                if no operator applicable, **then** Fail.
Goal Selection: Evaluating control-rules (for goals) returns G' with $G' \subseteq G$.
                Choose open goal $g \in G'$.

Operator Selection:
- Evaluating control-rules (for operators) returns O'.
- For each operator $M \in O'$
  for each $\oplus$-effect e of M
    let σ be the matcher $\sigma(e) = g$
      if application-conditions$(\sigma(M)) = true$
      then M is applicable.
- Choose one applicable M (backtracking point)
    insert M into π
    insert constraints into π
    update G.

Recursion: Call Backwards-Refine-PlanC on the refined partial plan π.

Table 2 Outline for controlled backward planning

3. CONCEPTS IN PROOF PLANNING

Now we introduce the basic concepts of proof planning and briefly describe how they are realized in the ΩMEGA system. The initial state in proof planning is a collection of sequents, the proof assumptions, and the goal is the sequent to be proven. A proof planning domain consists of operators, called *methods*, of control-rules and maybe theory-specific solvers.

Definition 1. *A partial proof plan is a partially ordered set of instantiated methods and a* complete proof plan *(a solution of a problem) is a sequence of instantiated methods that transfers the initial state into a goal state.*

ΩMEGA 's Planner employs both, operator abstraction and precondition abstraction. As a generalization of the standard notion of operator abstraction planning, ΩMEGA's complex methods can be expanded *recursively* into primitive methods that correspond to inference rules of the ND-calculus. A calculus-level proof of a theorem is a complete plan consisting of *instantiated primitive* methods. Each expansion of the non-primitive methods is stored in the hierarchically structured proof plan data structure (PDS) (Benzmueller et al., 1997).

3.1. Methods

What are methods? Methods are data structures that encode mathematical proof methods. They represent inferences that are typically more complex than the single inference steps in a logical calculus. The methods should capture
  (i) common patterns in proofs, e.g. the common structure of an induction proof
      or
  (ii) common proof techniques such as simplification or the computation of a
      derivative and similar macrosteps that are called tactics in tactical theorem
      proving.
  How can we discover methods? One heuristic for knowledge acquisition not only from mathematical (text)books is the following: More often than not the importance of a method is indicated by *naming* it. Named mathematical methods are, for instance, a proof by diagonalization or by induction, the application of an important theorem such as the Hauptsatz of Linear Algebra (each n-dimensional vector space has a basis of n linearly independent vectors), the Hauptsatz of Number Theory (each natural number can be uniquely represented as the product of prime numbers), etc. The mathematical monograph *Introduction to Real Analysis* (Bartle and Sherbert, 1982) introduces mathematical methods by referring, for example, to the Supremum Property, to the Monotone Convergence Theorem, etc. It states as a didactic help or hint for the reader:"The next two results will be used later as methods of proof"(p.32), "We shall make frequent and essential use of this property (the Supremum property of $\mathcal{R}$)" (p.45), or "the method we introduce in this section (associated with the Monotone Convergence Theorem) ... applies to sequences that are monotone..." (p.88).
  How to represent methods? Starting from tactical theorem proving (Gordon et al., 1979), Alan Bundy's key idea (Bundy, 1988) was to represent methods as tactic + specification, where a tactic produces a calculus-level sequence of proof steps when it is executed and the specification part is used for proof planning. As we use a wider spectrum of methods now, our definition of methods is somewhat more general: we do not necessarily require the full expansion of a method to be generated by one tactic (Huang et al., 1994).

Definition 2. Methods *are planning operators, i.e., the building blocks of a proof plan. They consist of declarative specifications at the object- and meta-level and of an expansion function that realizes a schematic or a procedural expansion of the method to a partial proof plan.*

The object-level specifications correspond to the usual preconditions and effects in planning. That is, they specify the sequents that are open goals to be planned for by the method, the sequents that have to be in the planning state when the method is applied (i.e. the subgoals produced by the method), the sequents that have to be assumptions, and those that are produced as new assumptions when the method is applied in forward planning.

The meta-level specifications declaratively specify in a meta-language *local* conditions of the method's application, i.e., properties and relations of the sequents processed by the method.[1] This is in contrast to global properties, such as relations between methods, or how a method is used to prove a theorem in a particular theory or how the planning history including failed attempts and resources influence the choice of that method. The meta-level specifications preferably express the *legal* conditions for the method's application, in particular, the restrictions of the instantiation of the method's parameters. They can be encoded in application-conditions.

Depending on whether a method encodes a particular proof structure or a proof technique/procedure, the expansion of a non-primitive method can be realized schematically or procedurally: A schematic expansion defines a schematic proof tree that may contain meta-variables.[2]

In ΩMEGA, methods are represented as frame-like data structures with slots, slot names, and fillers. The slot names are *premises, conclusions, application conditions* (*appl.cond*), and *proof schema*. The *premises* and *conclusions* constitute a logical specification, in the sense that the conclusions are supposed to follow logically from the premises. Note that the sequents in the *premises* and *conclusions* are abbreviated by the labels of their proof lines. The ⊕- and ⊖-annotations indicate object-level specifications.

These specifications are used in planning for chaining methods together. The respective object-level specifications are matched with the current planning goal and with assumptions. Then the new planning state is computed from the previous state and the method's specifications.

In ΩMEGA the annotations are interpreted as follows: A ⊖-conclusion is deleted as an open goal, a ⊕-premise is added as a new open goal, a ⊖-premise is deleted as an assumption, and a ⊕-conclusion is added as an assumption. This representation of the object-level specifications is somewhat more involved than the usual preconditions and effects because both, forward planning (planning new assumptions from existing ones) and backward planning (reducing a goal to subgoals), are possible and, therefore, assumptions and open goals are both included into the planning state and the potential changes of the goals *and* the assumptions have to be represented.

In ΩMEGA the slot *proof schema* may provide a schema for the schematic expansion of the method and thereby capture the semantics of the method.

Examples of methods that encode a common proof structure are the `Diagonalization` method (Cheikhrouhou and Siekmann, 1998), `Induction` (Bundy et al., 1991), or the following method `ComplexEstimate` (Melis, 1998b) which is an estimation method used for planning limit theorems.

method: ComplexEstimate (a, b, e_1, ϵ)			
premises	L0, $\oplus$L1,$\oplus$ L2, $\oplus$L3		
conclusions	$\ominus L5$		
appl.cond	$\exists k, l, \sigma(Cas(a,b) = (k, l, \sigma))$		
proof schema	L0. Δ	$\vdash |a| < e_1$	(j)
	L1. Δ	$\vdash |k| \leq M$	(OPEN)
	L2.	$\vdash |a_\sigma| < \epsilon/2 * M$	(OPEN)
	L3. Δ	$\vdash |l| < \epsilon/2$	(OPEN)
	L4.	$\vdash b = k * a_\sigma + l$	(CAS)
	L5. Δ	$\vdash |b| < \epsilon$	(fix;L4,L1,L2,L3)

The task of ComplexEstimate in planning is to reduce the goal of estimating a complicated term b to simpler estimation goals. It suggests the existence of a real number M that satisfies these simpler goals. M has to be instantiated during planning. ComplexEstimate removes an open goal that matches L5 and introduces the three correspondingly instantiated new subgoals L1, L2, and L3. The *application condition* requires that a computer algebra system is called (Cas) that computes terms k and l such that b can be represented as a linear combination $(k * a_\sigma + l)$ of a_σ.[3]

The very essence of ComplexEstimate is represented in the *proof schema* whose right-most entries are justifications. They can name ND-rules, methods, or tactics (e.g., CAS for a computer algebra tactic or ATP for calling a classical theorem prover). For the purpose of a short presentation of ComplexEstimate, 'fix' abbreviates a whole subproof of $|b| < \epsilon$ from the lines L4, L1, L2, and L3. The schematic expansion of ComplexEstimate introduces a subplan into the PDS that is obtained from the *proof schema*. This subplan may contain meta-variables.

3.2. Control Knowledge

Although proof plans are abstract representations of proofs and therefore plans are usually much shorter than calculus-level proofs, the search space is still exponential and potentially infinite. Therefore, means for controlling and restricting the search space are needed. Control knowledge can be distinguished along several dimensions, for instance, legal vs. heuristic control knowledge and local vs. global control.

In the following, we shall substantiate, how the different types of control-knowledge should be represented. Essentially, our suggestion is to represent legal and local knowledge in *application conditions* of methods and – most importantly – to represent heuristic knowledge in control-rules. Implicit control knowledge is encoded in tactics and strategies.

3.2.1. Control-Rules

Informed search can advantageously replace blind local search in domains, where enough control knowledge exists. Mathematics surely is a domain, where control knowledge, i.e. ways of attacking a problem, has been accumulated even over hundreds of years. The problem is, however, to extract this knowledge and to represent it appropriately.

Since methods should ideally correspond to mathematically meaningful steps, the control knowledge in proof planning should correspond to some mathematical 'intuition' on how to proceed in a proof.

Some of this control knowledge may be represented locally within a particular method, however, not all control aspects can be represented in this local manner. In accordance with a common principle in AI, we advocate an explicit representation of control knowledge in proof planning by declarative control-rules and its separation from the factual knowledge as well as its modular implementation.

As known from AI-research (Laird et al., 1987; Minton et al., 1989), separately implemented and declaratively represented control-rules ease the modification and extension of the control knowledge considerably. When new control information comes up in new cases of problem solving, then the control-rules can be modified and new control-rules can be introduced easily, as opposed to a re-implemention of an built-in procedurally implemented control. For instance, when the control is changed or generalized or when new methods are introduced into the domain, a re-implementation of the methods is not necessary. Rather, the set of control-rules can be extended or modified.

Because of their level of abstraction, control-rules are often well-suited for producing explanations on how a proof is found, and thus they can be naturally communicated and devised. Indeed, it is an important aspect of mathematical teaching to explain and teach control knowledge. For instance, the authors of the introduction to a computer-based calculus course (Davis et al., 1994) state that:

> "Today's popular texts present most of the tools (derivatives, differential equations, definite integrals, series expansion and approximation, data fitting, linearizations, vectors, dot products, line integrals, gradients, curls, and divergences) but end up focusing too much on the tools and not enough on their *uses*. The successful calculus course produces students who recognize a calculus situation and who know what calculus tools to bring to bear on it. This is the goal of Calculus & Mathematica."

Meta-reasoning about resources, the state of the partial proof, about failed proof attempts, etc. can be captured in control-rules and last but not least, the declarative representation by rules can be a basis for automated learning of control-rules, as realized, e.g., in (Minton, 1989; Leckie and Zukerman, 1998).

For all these reasons, in ΩMEGA global (heuristic) control knowledge is represented by declarative control-rules rather than in methods as it is done in the proof planner *CIAM*. Even if the implementation format of a method allows the direct encoding of this knowledge, it might be disadvantageous. For example, the order of goals to work on next, could be encoded into a method. However, if the situation in planning becomes resource-bounded, then the control has to be changed and should prefer goals that are simple to satisfy within a given amount of time/space but the evaluation of resources is not local to methods and in any case the direct coding would be too inflexible.

In ΩMEGA, the control-rules guide the planner in its decision making. Control-rules have an antecedent and a consequent. The antecedent encodes the global context of the decision. It is used by the planner to recognize whether the rule fires at a given node in a plan search tree. The consequent of a rule encodes the advice that can be used to *select* a specified subset of the available candidates, to *reject*, or to *prefer* one candidate over another. The first two types of advice prune the search space, while prefer-rules change the default order without excluding other alternatives.

Corresponding to the choices the planner has to make, we have the following classes of control-rules in ΩMEGA:

- `operator` for choosing among several methods,

- `sequent` for choosing among goals (in backward planning) or assumptions (in forward planning),

- `binding` for choosing instantiations of method parameters, and

- `strategy` for choosing a planning strategy.

Here is a simple example for an `operator` control-rule used in planning limit theorems. This rule expresses the heuristic that, in case the goal is an inequality, `Solve`, `SOLVE*`, `UnwrapHyp` should be preferred candidate methods in the given order, where `Solve` passes an inequality goal to the constraint solver, `SOLVE*` reduces a more complicated inequality to a simpler one that can be passed to the constraint solver, in case an appropriate assumption exists in the planning state, and `UnwrapHyp` extracts a particular subformula from an assumption in order to prepare the application of `ComplexEstimate`. This control-rule is then represented as follows:

```
(control-rule prove-inequalities
       (kind operator)
       (if (goal-matches (?goal (?x < ?y))))
       (then (prefer ((Solve ?goal)
                      (SOLVE* ?goal)
                      (UnwrapHyp ?goal)))))
```

In its antecedent, the control-rule may use decidable meta-predicates to inspect the current planning state, the planning history, the current partial proof plan, the constraint state (in case a constraint solver is employed in proof planning as in ΩMEGA), resources, the theory in which to plan, typical models of the theory, etc. The meta-predicates in the following rules inspect the planning history and failed planning attempts (`failed-method`) and the current planning state (`most-similar-subterm-in`).

```
(control-rule case-analysis-critic
       (kind operator)
       (if (and (failed-method (wave))
                (failure-condition (trivial ?C))))
       (then (prefer (CaseSplit (?C or not ?C)))))
```

The `case-analysis-critic` rule expresses the heuristic that if the wave method is not applicable at some stage because a formula C is not trivially provable, then it may be useful to introduce a `CaseSplit` method into the plan. This rule represents a rational reconstruction of one of Ireland's 'critics' that we shall discuss below.

3.3. Strategies

The process of finding a plan can be seen as a repeated refinement and modification. Refinement operations take a partial plan and add steps and constraints to it, whereas modification operations take a partial plan and modify, i.e., change it. We call such operations *strategies*.

Definition 3. *A strategy is an operation on partial plans that returns a partial plan. This operation determines its search space and restricts the way to traverse it.*

Strategies can be very diverse. Examples for planning strategies are forward planning, backward planning, difference-reducing backward planning (Hutter, 1990; Bundy et al., 1990), case-based planning, precondition abstraction, instantiation of meta-variables, and expansion of abstract methods.

Conceptually, strategies differ from methods which are building blocks of a plan. Therefore we represent and implement them differently form methods. Some control knowledge is procedurally encoded into the strategies' algorithms. The representation of strategies may be parametrized, e.g., by termination conditions, a set of methods, and by a set of control-rules which make some of the control in the strategy explicit.

A multi-strategy planner (Melis, 1998c) can employ several strategies in one planning process. Now, picking an appropriate strategy requires *strategic control knowledge* which can again be declaratively represented in strategic control-rules.

An example for a strategic control-rule formalizes the heuristic that if a complex method M is rendered 'unreliable' in the partial plan and if enough time resources are available, then the expansion strategy is called with parameter M.

```
(control-rule expand-method
       (kind strategy)
       (if (and (complex-op(?M)
                and (unreliable(?M)
                     and (less (minimum time))))))
       (then (prefer expand(?M))))
```

The purpose of this multi-strategy proof planning is a flexible use of different strategies and the capability to switch between strategies. Moreover, the strategy concept is a means to structure the vast amount of mathematical knowledge that is available in real application scenarios.

4. CRITICS RECONSIDERED

Using the conceptual understanding of proof planning as outlined so far, in particular of the role of methods, control knowledge, and strategies, we shall now analyze some of the *critics* introduced by Ireland and Bundy in (Ireland and Bundy, 1996). We shall show how some of them can be reconstructed by methods, strategies, and control-knowledge.

Proof critics are a means to cope productively with failures in planning proofs based on mathematical induction. They are an *exception handling mechanism* which exploits the partial success of a proof plan, although the planning failed at some particular stage of the search for a proof. Critics are based upon the partial satisfaction of the application conditions of the wave method (Ireland and Bundy, 1996) in $C I \! A \! M$. The wave method rewrites an (annotated) subterm t of the current planning goal g using an (annotated) conditional rewrite $(Cond \rightarrow LHS \Rightarrow RHS)$. Roughly, in $C I \! A \! M$ the application conditions of wave are

1. there is an appropriate subterm t
2. LHS matches t and the matcher respects the annotation
3. $Cond$ is trivially derivable from the hypotheses of g.

Several critics analyze the reasons why the wave method was not applicable although it should have been applicable for the planning to succeed. Reasons can be that there is no appropriate term t, that there is only a *partially* matching rewrite, that no rewrite rule matches at all, or that $Cond$ is not easily derivable from the hypotheses of g. Depending on these reasons, different critics are applied in order to automatically patch the proof attempt by speculating a lemma, by goal generalization, by introducing a case-split, or by revising the induction scheme.

In the following, we briefly describe, when these critics are called and how they work. We analyze them in terms of the concepts introduced earlier and re-describe them in our conceptual framework. This way we can distinguish between different impacts of the different critics on proof plans and generalize some of them.

4.0.1. Lemma Critics

The lemma speculation and lemma calculation critics deal with a failure of the second condition of the wave method since no (annotated) rewrite matches a subterm t. As a reaction to this failure, the lemma critic constructs a rewrite and validates it in order to continue the rewriting successfully.

From our conceptual point of view, meta-level reasoning about the failure and the heuristic of constructing a rewrite can be represented by control-rules. The constructed rewrite becomes an open goal in planning and, when proved, can be used for continuing the proof planning. This allows for a generalization of the critics in the sense that meta-level reasoning with control-rules may react to failed *application conditions* of methods – even different from wave – that require the existence of a certain lemma in the planning state.

4.0.2. Case Analysis

The case analysis critic deals with a failure of the third application condition of wave. As a reaction to this failure, the case analysis critic computes a tautologous disjunction D (e.g., $Cond \lor \neg Cond$) and immediately inserts the step case-split(D) into the partial plan such that the wave method is now applicable in the $Cond$ branch of the plan. From our point of view, this case analysis critic can be replaced by a control-rule that chooses an instantiation of the case-split method as shown in the case-analysis-critic control-rule.

Furthermore, the idea of the critic can be generalized: In mathematical theorem proving the need for a case-split is often discovered only later. For instance, often $Cond$ is not tried to be proven before using the conditional rewrite but only later. In this case, CaseSplit has to be introduced by a particular refinement strategy that inserts a method while keeping the whole subproof as one of its branches of the case-split. This later introduction of a case split differs from the ordinary backward planning since the subgoal s occurring while planning for a main goal g is no longer satisfied by a method that applies $Cond \rightarrow h$ which reduced s to s'.

Moreover, this case-split strategy is no longer bound to the particular wave method anymore and the type of non-provability of $Cond$ can be generalized. The generalized conditions for calling this strategy can be expressed in the antecedent of a strategic control-rule.

So in summary, critics as introduced by Ireland and Bundy serve several very valuable purposes. While some of these purposes can be generalized by the conceptually clearer representation as strategies or control-rules, many other critics are just as valuable the way they are and should still serve as a local exception handling mechanism.

5. CONCLUSION

Automated proof planning has several advantages over classical automated theorem proving: It can employ classical automated theorem provers as methods and at the same time search for a plan at a level that is far more abstract than the level of a logical calculus. The methods represent mathematically meaningful proof steps and the control knowledge therefore corresponds to mathematical intuition. Employing this control knowledge yields an *informed search behaviour* that is superior to the search in classical automated theorem proving (see, e.g., the empirical results in (Melis, 1998a)).

In particular, the search at a more abstract level can find proofs of a length far beyond those of classical systems. For example, the OTTER prover (McCune, 1990) searches spaces of several billion clauses and the maximal proof length that can be found that way is around several hundred resolution or paramodulation steps. With proof planning we could potentially find a *plan* of several hundred steps that could then be expanded into an object-level proof of several thousand steps. Proofs of that length are not uncommon in program verification tasks. For example, the VSE verification system (Hutter et al., 1996), which is now routinely used for industrial applications in the German Centre for Artificial Intelligence (DFKI) at Saarbrücken, successfully synthesized proofs of up to 8,000 and 10,000 steps in the verification of a television and radio switching program. Often these proofs represent many weeks or even months of labor, where about 80% of the steps were successfully generated by the machine and the remaining 20% by manual interaction of the verification engineer. These proofs are, by their very length, one or two orders of magnitude beyond fully automated methods but may come into the range of possibilities, if the proof planning paradigm turns out to be successful in these settings as well.

Further advantages of knowledge-based proof planning not addressed in this paper are that a general-purpose machinery (the planning technology) is combined with domain-specific knowledge (methods and control-rules), and thus proofs in specific mathematical theories such as calculus can now be handled not only with special-purpose provers such as Bledsoe's IMPLY (Bledsoe et al., 1972) but in a general setting. The ΩMEGA system, for example, was the first to solve the open problem (open for computer based systems) of LIM* (see (Melis, 1998b)).

Finally, high-level plans can be communicated much more naturally to the user and can yield understandable explanations and proof presentations as we may find them typically in a mathematical paper or text book.

ACKNOWLEDGMENTS

We thank the ΩMEGA Group in Saarbrücken, in particular Lassaad Cheikhrouhou, Andreas Meier, Volker Sorge, Michael Kohlhase; Dieter Hutter from the VSE-team at the DFKI, and the Edinburgh Dream Group, in particular, Alan Bundy and Julian Richardson, for helpful discussions.

Erica Melis
Universität des Saarlandes
Saarbrücken, Germany

Jörg H. Siekmann
Universität des Saarlandes and DFKI Saarbrücken
Saarbrücken, Germany

NOTES

1. e.g. that a subformula of an employed asssumption equals the processed goal
2. Meta-variables are place holders for syntactic objects such as terms and formulae.
3. a_σ is the term resulting from applying σ to a. $||, *, +, /$ denote the absolute value function, multiplication, addition, and division in the real numbers, respectively.

REFERENCES

Bartle, R. and Sherbert, D. (1982). *Introduction to Real Analysis*. John Wiley& Sons.

Benzmueller, C., Cheikhrouhou, L., Fehrer, D., Fiedler, A., Huang, X., Kerber, M., Kohlhase, M., Konrad, K., Meier, A., Melis, E., Schaarschmidt, W., Siekmann, J., and Sorge, V. (1997). OMEGA: Towards a mathematical assistant. In McCune, W., editor, *CADE-14*, pages 252–255, Springer.

Bledsoe, W., Boyer, R., and Henneman, W. (1972). Computer proofs of limit theorems. *Artificial Intelligence*, 3(1):27–60.

Bundy, A. (1988). The use of explicit plans to guide inductive proofs. In Lusk, E. and Overbeek, R., editors, *CADE-9*, pages 111–120, Springer.

Bundy, A., van Harmelen, F., Hesketh, J., and Smaill, A. (1991). Experiments with proof plans for induction. *Journal of Automated Reasoning*, 7:303–324.

Bundy, A., van Harmelen, F., Ireland, A., and Smaill, A. (1990). Extensions to the rippling-out tactic for guiding inductive proofs. In Stickel, M., editor, *CADE-10*, Springer.

Chang, C.-L. and Lee, C.-T. (1973). *Symbolic Logic and Mechanical Theorem Proving*. Computer Science Classics. Academic Press.

Cheikhrouhou, L. and Siekmann, J. (1998). Planning diagonalization proofs. In *AIMSA-98*, Springer.

Davis, W., Porta, H., and Uhl, J. (1994). *Calculus & Mathematica*. Addison-Wesley.

Fikes, R. and Nilsson, N. (1971). STRIPS: A new approach to the application of theorem proving to problem solving. *Artificial Intelligence*, 2:189–208.

Gordon, M., Milner, R., and Wadsworth, C. (1979). *Edinburgh LCF: A Mechanized Logic of Computation*.

Huang, X., Kerber, M., Kohlhase, M., and Richts, J. (1994). Methods - the basic units for planning and verifying proofs. In *Jahrestagung für Künstliche Intelligenz KI-94*, Springer.

Hutter, D. (1990). Guiding inductive proofs. In Stickel, M., editor, *CADE-10*, Springer.

Hutter, D., Langenstein, B., Sengler, C., Siekmann, J., Stephan, W., and Wolpers, A. (1996). Deduction in the verification support environment (VSE). *Third International Symposium of Formal Methods Europe*, pages 268–286.

Ireland, A. and Bundy, A. (1996). Productive use of failure in inductive proof. *Journal of Automated Reasoning*, 16(1-2):79–111.

Kambhampati, S. (1996). Refinement planning: Status and prospectus. In *AAAI-96*, pages 1331–1336.

Koehler, J. (1998). Solving complex tasks through extraction of subproblems. In Simmons, R., Veloso, M., and Smith, S. (eds), *AIPS-98*, pages 62–69.

Laird, J., Newell, A., and Rosenbloom, P. (1987). SOAR:an architecture for general intelligence. *Artificial Intelligence*, 33(1):1–64.

Leckie, C. and Zukerman, I. (1998). Inductive learning of search control rules for planning. *Artificial Intelligence*, 101(1-2):63–98.

Loveland, D. (1978). *Automated Theorem Proving: A Logical Basis*. North Holland, New York.

McCune, W. (1990). Otter 2.0 users guide. Technical Report ANL-90/9, Argonne National Laboratory, Maths and CS Division, Argonne, Illinois.

Melis, E. (1998a). AI-techniques in proof planning. In *ECAI-98*, pages 494–498, Wiley.

Melis, E. (1998b). The "limit" domain. In Simmons, R., Veloso, M., and Smith, S. (eds), *AIPS-98*, pages 199–206.

Melis, E. (1998c). Proof planning with multiple strategies. In *workshop: Strategies in Automated Deduction*.

Minton, S. (1989). Explanation-based learning: A problem solving perspective. *Artificial Intelligence*, 40:63–118.

Minton, S., Knoblock, C., Koukka, D., Gil, Y., Joseph, R., and Carbonell, J. (1989). *PRODIGY 2.0: The Manual and Tutorial*. Carnegie Mellon University. CMU-CS-89-146.

Pollack, M., Joslin, D., and Paolucci, M. (1997). Flaw selection strategies for partial-order planning. *Journal of Artificial Intelligence Research*, 6:223–262.

Sacerdoti, E. (1974). Planning in a hierarchy of abstraction spaces. *Artificial Intelligence*, 5(2):115–135.

Tate, A. (1977). Generating project networks. In *IJCAI-77*, pages 888–893. Morgan Kaufmann.

Veloso, M., Carbonell, J., Pérez, M. A., Borrajo, D., Fink, E., and Blythe, J. (1995). Integrating planning and learning: The PRODIGY architecture. *JETAI Journal*, pages 81–120.

Weld, D. (1994). An introduction to least committment planning. *AI magazine*, 15(4):27–61.

J. A. ROBINSON

PROOF = GUARANTEE + EXPLANATION

1. LOGIC IS NOT THE WHOLE STORY.

Twenty years ago I wrote the following:

> Logic deals with what follows from what. ... The correctness of a piece ... does not depend
> on what the reasoning is about.
>
> (Robinson, 1979, p. 1)

I believed then that this explanation of logic is enough to account also for real proofs. I have now come to appreciate the shortcomings of this point of view. While I have no doubts that this really is the way that formal logic works, and while I still value highly the first order predicate calculus as the tangible and practical result of developing this idea in full and rigorous detail, I now see that formal logic is by no means the whole story if what we are after is an understanding of real mathematical proofs. There is so much more going on in a real mathematical proof than merely the abstract logical relations between its constituent assertions. It is only a dim and partial light that formal logic sheds on how proofs provide us (as they do) with knowledge and understanding. Considerable supplementation of the current state of our science of proofs is needed for it to serve as an adequate basis for explaining the amazing power of real mathematical proofs to affect our minds.

2. WHAT ARE REAL MATHEMATICAL PROOFS LIKE?

Saunders Mac Lane (Mac Lane, 1986) has sketched a professional's view of the nature of mathematical proof which I summarise in the equational slogan which is the title of this essay. He maintains that every real proof has two different aspects:

> Proof in mathematics is both a means to understand why some result holds and a way to achieve
> precision. As to precision, we have now ... an absolute standard of rigor.
>
> (Mac Lane, 1986, p. 337).

Amplifying the second aspect, he goes on to say that a mathematical proof is rigorous and precise [only?] when it is (or could be) written out in the notation of the first order predicate calculus as a correct formal deduction from the axioms (say, those

277

S. Hölldobler (ed.), Intellectics and Computational Logic, 277–294.

of Zermelo-Fraenkel) of set theory. He does not favour any particular formulation of the first order predicate calculus, and indeed he implies that the particular choice of formulation is not important. He does not even insist that it should be the first order predicate calculus which is to act as the definitive logical formalism. As far as he is concerned, one gathers that any of the various higher order logics, or modal logics, or intuitionistic logics, would be just as admissible as the official formalization standard for proofs. It seems that what really matters to him is simply that the inference steps of the proof be formal. What this means is that they can be seen to exemplify abstract inference patterns in ways which are not dependent on the meanings of the constituent notions:

> ... the test for the correctness of a proposed proof is by formal criteria and not by reference to the subject matter at issue.
>
> (Mac Lane, 1986, p. 378)

Valid inferences, that is, depend only on the form, and not on the content, of their constituent propositions: only on their syntactical shape, and not on their intuitive meaning. This view of valid inference patterns as merely abstract formal schemata is very much the defining fundamental doctrine for modern logic. Already implicit in the work of Aristotle, its modern version has come down to us in a direct line from Frege and Hilbert through Russell and Whitehead, Gödel, Herbrand, Gentzen, Church and Quine, to name only the leading figures in the tradition. As one of the most important principles of modern logic, it should always be central in expositions of the subject. That is why, twenty years ago, I did my best to articulate it in the introduction to my book on resolution (Robinson, 1979):

> Logic deals with what follows from what. .... The correctness of a piece of reasoning, it is found, does not depend on what the reasoning is about (we can see that the conclusion *all epiphorins are turpy* follows from the premises *all epiphorins are febrids* and *all febrids are turpy*, without understanding any of the nonlogical words) so much as on how that reasoning is done; on the pattern of relationships between the various constituent ideas rather than on the actual ideas themselves.
>
> To get at the relevant aspects of such reasoning, logic must abstract its form from its content. We must disregard the epihorins and the febrids and the turpiness and see the general truth that *all A are C* follows from *all A are B* and *all B are C* quite independently of the particular nature of the *A, B* and *C* that happen to occupy those places in the reasoning pattern.

3. MATHEMATICIANS DON'T TAKE THIS ABSTRACT LOGICAL APPROACH VERY SERIOUSLY.

They pay at most lip service to this doctrine. Witness Professor Mac Lane's rueful acknowledgement (Mac Lane, 1986, p. 377):

> To be sure, practically no one actually bothers to write out such formal proofs. In practice, a proof is a sketch, in sufficient detail to make possible a routine translation of this sketch into a formal proof. When a proof is in doubt, its repair is usually just a partial approximation of the

fully formalized version. What is at hand is not the practice of absolute rigor, but a standard of absolute rigor.

This obvious gap between the ideal and the practical has in fact (as far as I know) received little or no attention neither from mathematicians nor, surprisingly, from logicians. Since real proofs as found in the mathematical literature and in the live lectures of everyday mathematical practice are so different from the ideal proofs of logically formalized mathematics, one would think that there would have been more curiosity shown towards the discrepancy, and some serious attempts to explain it.

In the introduction to his *Begriffschrifft* in 1879 Frege (Frege, 1967) used a vivid analogy to illustrate the dual aspect of mathematical argumentation. He likened his proposed formal system to a microscope. A microscope is a device which reveals the minute details of the visible surface structure of whatever is being observed through its lenses. These details are not normally visible, or even known, to the observer because of their small size. The scale of a microscopic image typically differs by several orders of magnitude from the macroscopic image obtained by the naked eye. Frege likens what the naked eye sees to what the mathematician sees when contemplating and performing a mathematical proof. At this level, it is the overall structure and the architectural organization of a proof which are paramount: the finer details are left unelaborated. The implication of Frege's analogy is that these details would even get in the way of the understanding and would obscure and diminish the force of the proof. Too much detail causes difficulty in viewing the big picture: one cannot discern the forest for the trees.

It is the explanation component of a proof that the mathematicians's natural unaided vision is seeing when he or she is assimilating or appreciating it. This large-scale, high-level view of the situation is emergent. It simply disappears under the microscope. One should not expect to find it by increasing the magnification.

The guarantee component of a proof is simply another way of viewing the verification of the syntactic correctness of the fine structure of the formalized proof (assuming it has been formalized). If the formalization is complete, such a verification can be accomplished by a purely mechanical procedure and is of little or no cognitive interest. One does not usually expect such a mechanical verification to be done by the unaided mind. Whether done with mechanical help or not, the formal verification of the proof of a theorem sheds little or no explanatory light on why the theorem is true.

The dual view captured in Mac Lane's equation surely fits the facts. For the most part (although sometimes a proof may establish its result without affording an explanation why it holds) a proof does indeed seem to have two different roles: to be a proof-as-guarantee and to be a proof-as-explanation. Formal logic and so-called proof theory unfortunately concentrate on the former. The reason for this may be as simple as that the latter is in some sense a psychological process, having to do with the way the mind (or if you insist, the brain) is designed and how it responds to the flow of information delivered by the proof. And that is far more difficult to deal with.

4. PROOFS-AS-GUARANTEES ARE RELATIVELY WELL-UNDERSTOOD AND COMPARATIVELY UNINTERESTING.

I have come to think that the role of proof-as-guarantee is the least interesting of the two. At least, it is no longer as interesting as it once was. Indeed, it is because of the development, since Frege, of the technical machinery of formal logic, and, since Gödel and Herbrand, of its mechanization in the form of proof-checking and proof-finding algorithms and semi-algorithms, that a proof-as-guarantee is today a relatively routine and even a theoretically trivial thing. The main outcome of this entire (brilliant) formal development seems to have been to create tools for exposing and isolating logical relationships at the cost of hiding the peculiarly magical explanatory power and psychological effectiveness of the elegant and convincing proofs-as-explanations which are the glory of mathematics. All we can do with our formal tools is to translate, or recast, a proof-as-explanation into a large static network of primitive formal inference patterns each of which is too small, and too commonplace, to recapture the dynamics of the intellectual moves, and the power of the cognitive force, of the unformalized natural intuitive proof. Formalization extracts the content of the proof, sets it aside, and displays only the hollow logical shell, the syntactic skeleton, which is no more than a kind of parsing diagram of the proof.

The explanatory process caused by the cognitive internalization of a proof, on the other hand, seems to me to be both (far) more important, (far) more interesting, and (far) more challenging. Now that the twentieth-century mission of formal logic has been essentially completed, it is time to undertake a deeper and more systematic study of this cognitive process. There is an enormous literature of real proofs to serve as data, and there is a plethora of unanswered questions about how these real proofs accomplish their task.

5. WE COULD START WITH QUESTIONS CONCERNING THE NATURE OF FORMALIZATION ITSELF

Consider the question: when we formalize a proposition or a proof, how do we know that, and indeed what is meant by saying that, the formalization is correct? The well-known discussion by Imre Lakatos (Lakatos, 1976) of the proof of Euler's famous equation

$$\text{vertices} + \text{faces} - \text{edges} = 2$$

for simple 3-dimensional polyhedra is much concerned with this question. Lakatos' thesis is that in real mathematical thinking and research the act of formalization is one of the most mysterious and most difficult to get right. Obviously there has to be an appropriate degree of similarity between the formalized version and the original informal version (of a concept, or a proposition). But how can we assert formally what this correspondence is? And how do we decide whether what we assert is true or not? It is futile – simply the start of an infinite regression – to formalize a meta-assertion about a formalized assertion. The informal meta-assertion cannot be guaranteed true by formalized argumentation. If we can satisfy ourselves of its correctness (and there are many examples where we are able to do just that) we must be doing so in some essentially informal way.

Once the formalization of a proposition has been accomplished and verified, the rest of the proof is often relatively easy. Computational logic has in fact progressed far enough in this century for us to be able to understand why this is so. It is because it is now possible, in principle, to submit a fully formalized statement to a mechanized proof-finding procedure for verification. The difficulty of the mechanical verification is of a different sort from the difficulty of the formalization itself: it is only a matter of its computational complexity. We are prevented from finding a formal proof (of a provable formal statement) only by the practical intractability of the search. Otherwise the process is under complete intellectual control and its nature is well understood.

6. HOW CAN WE BEGIN TO BUILD A SCIENCE OF PROOFS-AS-EXPLANATIONS?

How can we adequately capture the idea that a real explanatory proof is a process that works on any normal human mind, producing new knowledge and understanding in that mind? The short answer is: we must begin empirically, by making observations and finding out what actually happens when proving something is going on.

What is there to observe? Well, proofs are essentially performances. We must watch how proofs are performed, and try to fathom what happens as a result. The traditional logical approach has accustomed us to think of proofs only as structured static texts. Nothing happens in such proofs. They just exist, like geometrical figures. If we confine our attention to proofs in this sense it is as though we only ever experience music in the form of the structured, silent, static scores written down by the composers in the traditional music notation. Studying these scores is of course important, but there is much more to music than descriptive diagrams. There is the entirely different, dynamic, active reality which is the living music. The musical score is just an abstraction from, or a description of, or even an algorithm for generating, the living music – one might almost say, it is a formalization of the music. The music itself is what happens when it is performed, either in the open and in public in the usual way, or in the private mental performances which some people can conjure up in their musical imaginations.

To observe how real proofs work, then, we must attend performances of them, or perform them ourselves, if we can. Proofs are like stories: we must listen to them as they are told and follow the plot. They are dramas: they must be acted. A formal proof is only the score, only the script, only the instructions for producing the real proof. The real proof is the series of cognitive events called for in the script. As the proof proceeds so do the stages of the evolution of the (subjective) mental state of seeing that, and knowing why, the theorem is true. The proof can makes this happen even if the mind has previously harbored doubt about the truth of its conclusion, even if there was previously a conviction that the conclusion could not possibly be true.

7. PROOF PERFORMANCE EXPERIMENTS.

For some years now I have been trying to observe the effects of proof performances by setting up introspective cognitive experiments and conducting them on myself. In each of these experiments I look for a theorem in the mathematical literature which (a) I can understand but which (b) I find incredible, and which (c) has a proof which initially seems to be within my capability of understanding by means of a reasonable effort on my part.

As to (a), the theorem should ideally be a proposition whose meaning I can immediately grasp. This means that the statement of the theorem should if possible contain no concepts that I do not already understand. I try to avoid choosing a proposition in which there are one or more notions I do not already know and I would have to look up and become familiar with. Finding out what the meaning of a statement is can be a very interesting process in itself, but to include it in the proof performance experiment would complicate the experiment unduly.

As to (b), it is best if I initially doubt the truth of the proposition to the extent of supposing that there may well be a counterexample to it. A performance of the proof will have to overcome this doubt, and replace it with an insightful rational conviction that the proposition is true. It must make it clear that there can be no counterexample.

As to (c), I do not always know in advance that the available proof will be within my power to understand it. Even if it involves the introduction of no notions which are unknown to me it may still demand that I already know facts which I do not already know. Sometimes it is obvious in advance that the effort to perform the proof will be enormous, and so I do not even try. For example, Professor Wiles' recent proof of Fermat's Last Theorem would be a wonderful candidate for such an experiment, but his proof is certainly too advanced and difficult to be performed properly by me, or indeed by any person not a specialist in the various areas of mathematics that Professor Wiles uses in his proof.

Once the selection is made, the experiment consists simply of learning to perform the given proof and monitoring the process. If all goes well, I can then routinely experience, explicitly, the crucial moments in the proof when my collection of rational beliefs is revised (or, on subsequent performances, once more reinforced) by the incorporation of the appropriate new beliefs involved in the proof. It is not like reading a story once and then forgetting it. It is more like learning to play a piece of music on the piano and retaining the knowledge more or less permanently. The modification of beliefs is a matter of mental changes which take time, like the slow acquisition, by repetitive practice, of the many small modules of motor skill which permit the playing of difficult passages in the piece.

Anyone can do these experiments. This is the way to observe the phenomena for which a theory of real proofs must account. Let us take an example. In one such experiment, I chose a theorem which states that for all positive integers n there is always a prime bigger than n *and moreover that the next prime after n is no bigger than $2n$.*

This proposition is known in the literature as Bertrand's Conjecture although it actually remained a conjecture for only five years before it was first proved (by Chebychev in 1850). The proposition is easy to understand. All one needs is to know what prime numbers are. When I first came across it I was quite taken aback by the strong upper bound $2n$. My surprise was due to my knowledge of the much weaker upper bound established in the well-known theorem by Euclid which states that for all positive integers n there is always a prime bigger than *and moreover that the next prime after n is never bigger than $n! + 1$.*

> Euclid's proof is designed to dispel one's fear that there may be a counterexample, namely, a positive integer, call it P, such that there is no prime bigger than P. But any of the prime divisors of the number $P! + 1$ is a prime bigger than P – primes no bigger than P divide $P!$ and therefore do not divide $P! + 1$.

Euclid's elegant proof had always given me the impression that the next prime number after n might, in some cases, be nearly as large as $n! + 1$ itself. I was very struck therefore, by the proposition that the next prime after n is never bigger than $2n$. In fact, since $2n$ is even, the next prime after n is actually as big as $2n$ only in the single case that $n = 1$. For all other n the next prime after n is always less than $2n$.

The proof I learned to perform is by Erdös. It was his first big proof, published in 1932 when he was only 18. It took me quite a long time to learn to perform it (it was like learning to play a difficult piece on the piano). It is an example of how sometimes a proof draws on facts and ideas which seem wholly extraneous to the proposition being proved. (Gentzen's Hauptsatz states essentially that if a proposition is [formally] provable at all, then it is formally provable using only notions which are present in the statement of the proposition itself. It is hard to believe, is it not, that this assertion holds for informal "real" proofs?).

I have discussed my experiment with Erdös' proof in detail elsewhere (Robinson, 1990) and here I will consider only its main ideas, but in some detail. It turns out that the proof depends on surprisingly few new and interesting facts. Most of these are lesser known (at least they were to me) properties of the binomial coefficients. Recall that the binomial coefficients are all the positive integers of the form $n!/m!(n - m)!$, where n is any nonnegative integer and m is any nonnegative integer no larger than n. I will denote the number $n!/m!(n - m)!$ by $C(n, m)$ for short.

Arranging these numbers in the pattern known as Pascal's Triangle:

$$C(0, 0)$$
$$C(1, 0) \qquad C(1, 1)$$
$$C(2, 0) \qquad C(2, 1) \qquad C(2, 2)$$
$$C(3, 0) \qquad C(3, 1) \qquad C(3, 2) \qquad C(3, 3)$$
$$C(4, 0) \qquad C(4, 1) \qquad C(4, 2) \qquad C(4, 3) \qquad C(4, 4)$$

etc.,

illustrates three interesting numerical facts:

1. the numbers at the apex and down each side are all equal to 1;

2. every other number is the sum of its two nearest neighbors above;

3. the sum of the numbers in the nth row is 2^n.

Erdös' proof uses some less observable but even more interesting properties. They particularly concern the central binomial coefficients, both the even ones $C(2n, n) = (2n)!/(n!)(n!)$ and the odd ones $C(2n + 1, n)$.

We consider the prime-power representations of the even central binomial coefficients. If p^k is any term in the representation of $C(2n, n)$ as a product of powers of prime numbers, then

$$p^k \text{ is less than } 2n, \tag{1}$$

$$\text{if } p \text{ is between } n \text{ and } 2n, k \text{ is } 1, \tag{2}$$

$$\text{if } p \text{ is between } 2n/3 \text{ and } n, k \text{ is } 0, \tag{3}$$

$$\text{if } p \text{ is greater than } 2n, k \text{ is } 0. \tag{4}$$

The content of these bare assertions is much more vividly brought home with the help of a graphical display revealing the striking patterns involved. The following table displays, in the nth row, the exponents of all the primes in the prime power representation of $C(2n, n)$. The value of n runs from 201 to 231. The ith column corresponds to the ith prime. Thus row 201 shows that $C(402, 201)$ is the product of the terms 2^4, 3^1,.etc.

Property (1) is revealed by the small size of the exponents even in the leftmost columns corresponding to the smallest primes. Properties (2) and (3) stand out because of the way each row ends in the run of 0s corresponding to the primes between $2n/3$ and n, followed by the run of 1s corresponding to the primes between n and $2n$. Property (4) is reflected in the fact that the entries in each row all correspond to primes less than $2n$. One notices that in each row there are runs of consecutive 0s of shorter length than that corresponding to Property (3). In fact, property (3) is just a special case of a more general property:

$$\text{if each power of } p \text{ less than } 2n \text{ lies between } 2n/(2r + 1) \text{ and } n/r, \\ \text{for some integer r, then } k = 0. \tag{3.1}$$

E.g., if n is 201, the sixth prime 13 lies between $2n/31 = 12 \ 30/31$ and $n/15 = 13 \ 2/5$, while its square 169 lies between $2n/3 = 402/3 = 134$ and $n = 201$; so we have a 0 in column 6 of row 201. Property (3.1) thus underlies the pattern displayed by the bands of 0s and 1s which dominate the appearance of this array. I computed the display for all n up to 1000 and thus obtained a sort of "spectrum" analyzing the prime-power decomposition of the numbers $C(2n, n)$. This [Table 0, anm. ed.] is just an extract of 30 consecutive rows from the 1000 rows of that larger display. The patterns visible in such displays of relevant facts seem to have a very strong positive effect on the understanding. In this case the characteristically "flat" prime power decomposition of the numbers $C(2n, n)$ on which Erdös' argument depends leaps to the eye, and thereafter lingers in the mind.

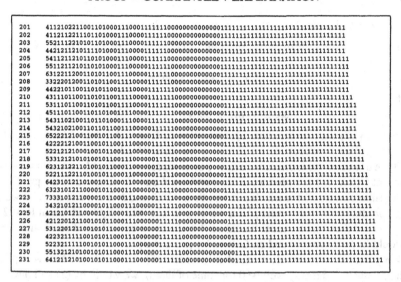

```
201   411210221100110100011100011111110000000000000001111111111111111111111111111111
202   411211221110110100011100011111110000000000000001111111111111111111111111111111
203   552111221010110100011100011111100000000000000011111111111111111111111111111111
204   442121121011110100011100011111100000000000000011111111111111111111111111111111
205   541121121011010100011100011111100000000000000011111111111111111111111111111111
206   551121121011010100010001110000011111000000000001111111111111111111111111111111
207   631221120011010110011100011111100000000000000011111111111111111111111111111111
208   332220120011010110011100011111100000000000000011111111111111111111111111111111
209   442201100110110110011100011111100000000000000011111111111111111111111111111111
210   431110110011010110011110000111111000000000000011111111111111111111111111111111
211   531110110011010110011110000111111000000000000011111111111111111111111111111111111
212   451110110011011010011110000111111000000000000011111111111111111111111111111111111
213   543110210011011010001110000111111000000000000011111111111111111111111111111111111
214   543210210011011011001110000011111000000000000111111111111111111111111111111111111
215   652221210011001011001110000011111000000000000111111111111111111111111111111111111
216   422221210011001011001110000011111000000000000011111111111111111111111111111111111
217   522121210001001011001110000011111000000000000011111111111111111111111111111111111
218   533121210101001011001110000001111000000000000011111111111111111111111111111111111
219   623121221101001011000011000000011110000000000001111111111111111111111111111111111
220   522111221101001011000011000000011110000000000001111111111111111111111111111111111
221   642310121101001011000011000000111110000000000001111111111111111111111111111111111
222   632310121100001011000011000000111110000000000011111111111111111111111111111111111
223   733310121100001011000011000000111110000000000011111111111111111111111111111111111
224   343210121100001011000011000000111110000000000011111111111111111111111111111111111
225   421210121100001011000011000000111110000000000011111111111111111111111111111111111
226   421220121100101011000011000000111110000000000011111111111111111111111111111111111
227   531220121100101011000011000000111110000000000011111111111111111111111111111111111
228   422321111100101011000011000000111110000000000011111111111111111111111111111111111
229   522321111100101011000011000000111110000000000001111111111111111111111111111111111111
230   551321210100101011000011000000111110000000000011111111111111111111111111111111111111
231   641211210100101011000011000000111110000000000011111111111111111111111111111111111111
```

Erdös makes use of one more fact of which I was not previously aware:

the product of all primes less than x is less than 4^x.   (5)

In establishing (5), Erdös uses the odd central binomial coefficients in a clever, but intelligible and brief, subproof, which I will not discuss further here.

The main part of his proof is a clever combination of these five facts. Of course, for a complete understanding of the result, these facts themselves also need to be made evident. However, we will defer that issue until we have understood the main line of reasoning.

First, then, we are asked to assure ourselves that Bertrand's Conjecture holds for all n less than 4000: that for all n between 2 and 4000 inclusive, there is a prime bigger than n and less than $2n$. We can check this, somewhat laboriously, by consulting a table of primes for each n.

However, Erdös makes this obvious more quickly and neatly by considering the sequence of primes:

$$2, 3, 5, 7, 13, 23, 43, 83, 163, 317, 631, 1259, 2503, 5003.$$

Each consecutive pair $\langle p_i, p_{i+1} \rangle$ in the series satisfies the condition

$$p_{i+1} < 2p_i .$$ (*)

Since any number n between 2 and 4000 inclusive satisfies $p_i \leq n < p_{i+1}$ for some i, and therefore

$$2p_i \leq 2n < 2p_i + 1$$ (**)

we have, by applying (*) to (**), $p_{i+1} < 2p_i \leq 2n < 2p_{i+1}$ i.e., $p_{i+1} < 2n$.

This means that if Bertrand's Conjecture were false, there would be an N with the properties

$$N \text{ is not less than } 4000 \qquad (6)$$

and

$$\text{there is no prime between } N \text{ and } 2N. \qquad (7)$$

Because of (7) the prime power representation of $C(2N, N)$ would (in view of (2), (3) and (4)) be a product of terms p^k with p less than $2N/3$.

By rearranging the terms in the prime-power representation of $C(2N, N)$ we could represent $C(2N, N)$ as a product of two numbers A and B. A would be the product of those prime powers p^k for which p is less than $2N/3$ and k is either 1 or 0. B would be the product of prime powers p^k for which p is less than $2N/3$ and k is at least 2.

We could then find an upper bound on A and also an upper bound on B, and hence we could find an upper bound on $C(2N, N)$ [alias $A\dot{B}$].

For an upper bound on A, we need only refer to (5). Even if $k = 1$ for every prime in the product (and it may well be 0 for some of them), we would by (5) still have

$$A \text{ is less than } 4^{2N/3}. \qquad (8)$$

For an upper bound on the product B, we need only reflect that since, because of (1), every term p^k in the product B is less than $2N$, and since k is at least 2, the prime p in each of these terms must be less than $\sqrt{2N}$. That means that there can be no more than $\sqrt{2N}$ of such primes, and thus no more than $\sqrt{2N}$ of such terms. So B would not be as big as the $\sqrt{2N}$ th power of $2N$:

$$B \text{ is less than } (2N)^{\sqrt{2N}}. \qquad (9)$$

Combining the upper bounds for A and B given by (8) and (9) we infer an upper bound on $C(2N, N)$.

$$C(2N, N) \text{ [alias } A \cdot B] \text{ is less than } 4^{2N/3}(2N)^{\sqrt{2N}} \qquad (10)$$

Next we find a lower bound on $C(2N, N)$. $C(2N, N)$ is the largest of the combinatorial coefficients

$$C(2N, 0), C(2N, 1), \ldots, C(2N, N-1), C(2N, 2N)$$

comprising the $2N$th row of Pascal's Triangle. The sum of these $2N + 1$ numbers is $2^{2N} = 4^N$. This sum can be rearranged as a sum of $2N$ numbers, by adding together $C(2N, 0)$ and $C(2N, 2N)$, so that we then have only $2N$ summands of which $C(2N, N)$ is the largest :

$$4^N = C(2N, 0) + C(2N, 2N) + C(2N, 1) + \ldots + C(2N, 2N-1).$$

If we then replace each of the $2N$ summands by the number $C(2N, N)$, the sum on the right will only be increased. In fact it will become equal to $2N \cdot C(2N, N)$. So then we will have:

$$4^N \text{ is less than } 2N \cdot C(2N, N).$$

Hence (dividing both sides of this inequality by $2N$) it must be that

$$4^N/2N \text{ is less than } C(2N, N) \tag{11}$$

and this give us a lower bound for $C(2N, N)$.

The lower bound given by (11) for $C(2N, N)$ is of course less than the upper bound given by (10) for $C(2N, N)$, so we can write

$$4^N/2N \text{ is less than } 4^{2N/3}(2N)^{\sqrt{2N}}, \tag{12}$$

multiply both sides of this inequality by $2N$, getting:

$$4^N \text{ is less than } 4^{2N/3}(2N)^{(1+\sqrt{2N})}, \tag{12.1}$$

divide both sides by $4^{2N/3}$, getting:

$$4^{N/3} \text{ is less than } (2N)^{(1+\sqrt{2N})}, \tag{12.2}$$

rewrite the left hand side as a power of 2, getting:

$$2^{2N/3} \text{ is less than } (2N)^{(1+\sqrt{2N})}. \tag{12.3}$$

Erdös now completes the proof by showing that (12.3) and (6) together entail;

$$N \text{ is less than 4000} \tag{13}$$

which directly contradicts

$$N \text{ is not less than 4000.} \tag{6}$$

This contradiction shows that there can be no counterexample N to Bertrand's Conjecture.

To see why (12.3) and (6) entail (13), we perform the following ingenious symbolic computation. First: write $2N$ as the sixth power of its sixth root:

$$2N = (\sqrt[6]{2N})^6 \tag{i}$$

and note that since $\sqrt[6]{2N}$ is less than $\lfloor \sqrt[6]{2N} \rfloor + 1$ we have

$$2N \text{ is less than } (\lfloor \sqrt[6]{2N} \rfloor + 1)^6. \tag{ii}$$

Here $\lfloor x \rfloor$ is the *floor* of x, i.e., the largest integer not greater than x.

Now, $x + 1$ is less than 2^x for all x greater than 2. Since $\lfloor \sqrt[6]{2N} \rfloor$ is greater than 2 in view of (6), we can put it for x in this inequality and get:

$$\lfloor \sqrt[6]{2N} \rfloor + 1 \text{ is less than } 2^{\lfloor \sqrt[6]{2N} \rfloor} \tag{iii}$$

and therefore, substituting into (ii) the right hand side of (iii) for the left hand side of (iii):

$$2N \text{ is less than } (2^{\lfloor \sqrt[6]{2N} \rfloor})^6. \tag{iv}$$

Since $\lfloor x \rfloor$ is less than or equal to x, for all x, can remove the floor from the right hand side of (iv), giving:

$$2N \text{ is less than } (2^{\sqrt[6]{2N}})^6. \tag{v}$$

Cubing both sides of (12.3) gives

$$2^{2N} \text{ is less than } (2N)^{3+3\sqrt{2N}} \tag{vi}$$

We put the right hand side of (v) for the left hand side of (v) in (vi):

$$2^{2N} \text{ is less than } (2^{\sqrt[6]{2N}})^{6(3+3\sqrt{2N})} \tag{vii}$$

and multiply out the exponent expression:

$$2^{2N} \text{ is less than } (2^{\sqrt[6]{2N}})^{18+18\sqrt{2N}}. \tag{viii}$$

Now, since 18 is less than $2\sqrt{2N}$ when N is greater than 50, which we know it is in view of (6), we can replace the first 18 in (viii) by $2\sqrt{2N}$:

$$2^{2N} \text{ is less than } (2^{\sqrt[6]{2N}})^{2\sqrt{2N}+18\sqrt{2N}}. \tag{ix}$$

We then perform the addition in the exponent expression:

$$(x)\,2^{2N} \text{ is less than } (2^{\sqrt[6]{2N}})^{20\sqrt{2N}}$$

and use the identity $(a^b)^c = a^{bc}$ to simplify the right hand side:

$$2^{2N} \text{ is less than } 2^{\sqrt[6]{2N}\cdot 20\sqrt{2N}},$$

rearrange the order of the factors in the exponent:

$$2^{2N} \text{ is less than } 2^{20\sqrt{2N}\sqrt[6]{2N}},$$

re-express the square root and the sixth root as fractional exponents:

$$2^{2N} \text{ is less than } 2^{20(2N)^{1/2}(2N)^{1/6}},$$

use the identity $a^b a^c = a^{b+c}$:

$$2^{2N} \text{ is less than } 2^{20(2N)^{1/2+1/6}},$$

and add the fractional exponents:

$$2^{2N} \text{ is less than } 2^{20(2N)^{2/3}}. \tag{xi}$$

Now, since (xi) is an inequality between two powers of 2 we also have a corresponding inequality between the two exponents:

$$2N \text{ is less than } 20(2N)^{2/3} \tag{xii}$$

whence, dividing both sides of (xii) by $(2N)^{2/3}$, we get:

$$(2N)^{1/3} \text{ is less than } 20.$$

Cubing both sides then gives

$$2N \text{ is less than } 8000$$

whence, finally, dividing both sides by 2, we have the inequality

$$N \text{ is less than } 4000 \tag{13}$$

which contradicts (6) and thus completes the main argument.

8. WHAT IS THE EXPLANATION FOR THE CRUCIAL PROPERTIES (1) TO (4)?

The basic fact on which they rest is a beautiful algorithmic formula (due to Legendre) for computing the exponents of the primes in the prime power decomposition of the factorial function. His formula gives the exponent of the prime p in the prime-power representation of $n!$ as the infinite sum:

$$\lfloor n/p \rfloor + \lfloor n/p^2 \rfloor + \lfloor n/p^3 \rfloor + \lfloor n/p^4 \rfloor + \lfloor n/p^5 \rfloor + \lfloor n/p^6 \rfloor + \ldots$$

in which the floor terms eventually become and remain 0 because the fractions become and remain less than 1.

For example, suppose we want to compute the exponent of 3 in the prime power decomposition of 100! This exponent is the sum of the series

$$\lfloor 100/3 \rfloor + \lfloor 100/3^2 \rfloor + \lfloor 100/3^3 \rfloor + \lfloor 100/3^4 \rfloor + \lfloor 100/3^5 \rfloor + \lfloor 100/3^6 \rfloor + \ldots$$
$$= 33 + 11 + 3 + 1 + 0 + 0 + \ldots$$
$$= 48.$$

The terms of the series represent the fact that among the integers from 1 to 100 there are 33 multiples of 3, 11 of which, in turn, are also multiples of $3^2 = 9$, 3 of which, in turn, are also multiples of $3^3 = 27$, one of which, finally, is also a multiple of $3^4 = 81$. None of the higher powers of 3 divide 100!. To count how many occurrences of 3 there are in the product 100!, we observe that the 33 multiples of 3 contribute 33 occurrences of 3, the 11 multiples of 9 contribute another 11 occurrences of 3, the 3 multiples of 27 contribute another 3 occurrences of 3, and finally the single multiple of 81 contributes one more occurrence of 3. The total number of occurrences of 3 is thus 48.

This counting method applies in general: to count the number of times the prime p occurs in $n!$ we sum the series:

$$\lfloor n/p \rfloor + \lfloor n/p^2 \rfloor + \lfloor n/p^3 \rfloor + \lfloor n/p^4 \rfloor + \lfloor n/p^5 \rfloor + \lfloor n/p^6 \rfloor + \cdots$$

which we can do because the terms become and stay zero when the powers of p exceed n.

It is then easy to see how, by combining the series for $(2N)!$ and $n!$, and rearranging the terms, we can count the number of times the prime p occurs in the number $C(2n, n) = (2N)!/(n!)^2$. The formula then turns out to be:

$$(\lfloor (2N)/p \rfloor - 2\lfloor n/p \rfloor) + (\lfloor (2N)/p^2 \rfloor - 2\lfloor n/p^2 \rfloor) + \cdots . \qquad (***)$$

In many ways it is this formula which is the key to the entire argument.

Let us first define the function $F(x) = \lfloor 2/x \rfloor - 2\lfloor 1/x \rfloor$ so that we can then write this formula compactly as:

$$F(p/n) + F(p^2)/n) + \cdots$$

and focus our attention on the surprising, and crucial, properties of the function $F(x)$.

9. THE FUNCTION $F(X) = \lfloor 2/X \rfloor - 2\lfloor 1/X \rfloor$

First, observe that, for any a, $\lfloor 2a \rfloor$ never exceeds $2\lfloor a \rfloor$ by more than 1. To see this, write

$$a = \lfloor a \rfloor + f(a), \text{ where } 0 \leq f(a) < 1.$$

so that

$$2a = 2\lfloor a \rfloor + 2f(a), \text{ where } 0 \leq 2f(a) < 2.$$

and

$$\lfloor 2a \rfloor = 2\lfloor a \rfloor + \lfloor 2f(a) \rfloor \text{ where } 0 \leq \lfloor 2f(a) \rfloor < 2.$$

This means that the function F takes on only the values 0 and 1, for all $x > 0$. We will need the following three properties of F:

$$F(x) = 0 \text{ for all } x \geq 2 \qquad (A)$$

since both $\lfloor 2/x \rfloor$ and $2\lfloor 1/x \rfloor$ are 0 for all $x \geq 2$.

$$F(x) = 0 \text{ for } 2/(2m + 1) < x \leq (1/m), m = 1, 2, \ldots, \qquad (B)$$

since $\lfloor 2/x \rfloor$ and $2\lfloor 1/x \rfloor$ agree only in these intervals (this value being 2m).

$$F(x) = 1 \text{ for } (1/m) < x \leq 2/(2m-1), m = 1, 2, \ldots, \qquad \text{(C)}$$

since in these intervals, $\lfloor 2/x \rfloor$ is $2m - 1$, but $2\lfloor 1/x \rfloor$ is $2m - 2$.

The crucial assertions:

$$p^k \text{ is less than } 2n, \qquad (1)$$

$$\text{if } p \text{ is between } n \text{ and } 2n, \text{ k is 1}, \qquad (2)$$

$$\text{if } p \text{ is between } 2n/3 \text{ and } n, \text{ k is 0}, \qquad (3)$$

$$\text{if } p \text{ is greater than } 2n, \text{ k is 0}. \qquad (4)$$

can now be clearly seen to be consequences of the series (***), by virtue of the properties (A), (B) and (C) of the function F.

As to (1), each term of (***) is either 0 or 1, since all its terms vanish after the rth, where r is the largest exponent for which p^r is less than $2n$. So the sum k of the series is at most r; hence p^k is at most p^r.

As to (2), if $n < p \leq 2n$, then $1 < p/n \leq 2$, then $F(p/n) = 1$ (by (C), with $m = 1$).

As to (3), if p is between $2n/3$ and n, then $F(p/n) = 0$ (by (B), with m = 1).

As to (4), if p is greater than $2n$, then $p/n > 2$ and therefore $F(p/n) = 0$ by (A).

Assertion (5), is that the product of primes no larger than x is itself no larger than 4^x. Its explanation is rather tedious and unenlightening, and we omit it here. The interested reader can find the details in (Aigner et. al., 1998, p. 8).

I find that Erdös' overall proof now stays in my mind as a collection of relatively few leading ideas dealing with interesting combinatorial phenomena. Over the period I have been learning the proof, I have tried to make myself as familiar as possible with these phenomena by means of extensive empirical observations, consisting of numerical and symbolic computations. The familiarity of these ideas has caused them by now to take on an aura of certainty, and has served to install them in my mind as established resources which can be triggered at will and as necessary when reviewing the proof.

10. SUMMARY OF THE IDEAS IN PROOF

The major phenomena dealt with in Erdos' proof are the peculiarly flat manner in which the numbers $C(2n, n)$ are constructed from the primes smaller than $2n$, and the surprising gap between $2n/3$ and n, within which no primes are available as its factors. It is also noteworthy that *all* of the primes between n and $2n$ enter into the prime-power decomposition of $C(2n, n)$ with an exponent of only 1. Even the relatively few primes less than n which have exponents larger than 1 are restricted from contributing more than $2n$ to the overall product. So, for example, when n is 201, $C(2N, n)$ is

41078559755523569773296843789533529044419483659514564121566639691487817195
45615462480893015234783450107182436577113596240

and this number has to be a product of prime-power factors *all of which are less than* 402. This means that there must be at least $46 = log_{401} C(402, 201)$ (roughly) such factors. There are in fact only 32 primes less than $402/3$. So if there were no primes between 201 and 402 then there would be only 32 primes available, and, so to speak, there could be no $C(402, 201)$.

If we repeat this little scenario for $C(4002, 2001)$ we get a similar result. There are only 217 primes less than $4002/3$. But we need at least $log_{4001} C(4002, 2001) = 333$. And so it goes. This is the intuition behind Erdös' approach.

The mind seems to be hungry for headlines or key ideas which capture the gist of a proof. In this case the headline seems to be something like: if the number $C(2n, n)$ were deprived of primes between n and $2n$ it could not exist.

When we survey a real proof in this high-level, outline way, and fix our attention on its main idea or ideas, we can better intuitively appreciate its overall plan. We understand the proof as an explanation, in a sense, even though our view of it is neither rigorous nor complete. With only the overall plan before it, the mind is not concerned with the details. For the purpose of obtaining a (higher-level) understanding, it even seems essential that the (lower-level) details should be ignored. If too many details enter into the primary sketch, we simply lose sight of the main architecture of the proof – we are unable to see the big picture.

We are surely dealing here with the same intellectual and psychological issue as is encountered, for example, in structured programming – the need to cope with conceptual complexity. A well-designed program – in fact a well-designed anything – must be organized in a hierarchical manner so that, at all levels of detail, including the topmost level, there is no more complexity for the mind to handle in a single mental scene than it can comfortably manage. There is evidently some sort of mental buffer, of limited capacity, in which we enact the scenes of the proof.

In my experience with these proof performance experiments, few written mathematical expositions are carefully designed to assist the mind in this respect. Written expositions of a proof are too often merely dumps of the details, in all their complexity, with little or no guidance as to the conceptual organization underlying them, let alone the informal intuitions from which they may have sprung.

Oral presentations seem to be a quite different matter. It is quite notable how much better the style of exposition in a spoken lecture or seminar tends to be than the usual written proofs found in journals and books. Oral exposition at its best is very much less rigid and less formal. The good expositor can and does employ all manner of helpful devices to help the mind of the listener to grasp what is going on. Not the least important, the expositor can monitor the proof recipient's body language and facial expressions for signs of comprehension or lack of it, and can try to modify the flow of explanatory ideas accordingly. *Feedback* is vital in expounding a proof. The entire point of what one is doing is to try to bring about a state of understanding in the mind of the recipient – the only reason that one is performing the proof is to try to get across to the recipient why the result is true – so it pays to monitor, as best one can, his or her mental states. One therefore stays alert for any sort of signal indicating something about these mental states, and one checks on them frequently by asking "Is that clear so far" , "Do you see that?", "OK?" and so on.

The thrust of these and similar observations arising from experience with real proofs is to underline the need for a model of the mind of the proof recipient, as well as a model of proof performance and assimilation (and proof effectiveness), to add to the familiar model of reasoning supplied by formal logic. Formal logic is limited, deliberately and indeed fruitfully, to being the mathematical theory of written proof texts and diagrams. This has grown into a successful, important, powerful and beautiful theory which can today boast of deep and lasting results. What is needed now, in addition, is an equally successful scientific theory of proof performance and proof internalization, based on a suitable model of the thinking subject and its dynamics.

Performing a proof for a person (the recipient) other than oneself surely requires the performer to maintain a representation of the state of understanding, or state of knowledge, in the mind of the recipient. The proof performance consists of stages of awakening, focusing, guiding and in general trying to control and manipulate, the two innate mental mechanisms, *entailment perception* and *assent diffusion*, which seem to be built-in primitive capabilities of every human mind and must be prominent features of any useful model of it.

Entailment perception is the (partial) psychological (subjective) correlate of the (objective) logical relationship exhibited in *valid* inference patterns. Entailment perception is however capable of error. It is possible that it could respond positively to an instance of an objectively invalid inference pattern by mistakenly perceiving it as valid. It is also possible that it could be unable to respond positively to what is objectively a valid inference. In the perception of an entailment, the conclusion is not necessarily seen as true (indeed, it may not even be true). What is perceived is the implicative relationship between the premises and conclusion: what the mind perceives is that the conclusion must be true *if* the premises are. The question of the truth or falsehood of the propositions themselves is not at issue.

The mechanism of assent diffusion causes the conclusion to be seen to be true, *if* the premises are seen be true. Assent diffusion can propagate the perception of truth through an entire internalized inferential network, provided that the mind perceives the initial premises of the proof as true.

Formal logic has tended to fix its interest on *primitive* perceived entailments – inference patterns (such as modus ponens, or universal instantiation) of minimal complexity which almost everyone perceives as valid because of an unlearned, built-in, entailment perception mechanism which has evolved with our species. These primitive relationships seem to be incapable of being dissolved into networks of simpler or smaller inferences. But they are, in general, too small to be interesting or useful in describing real proofs, which in practice are composed of larger inferences.

We will need to develop a suitable set of ideas for explaining how an objective syntactical inference pattern causes the entailment perception. This will not be easy. The task is reminiscent of the classical A.I. problem of understanding how our brains accomplish *vision*. It will require much careful empirical study of the assimilation of real proofs by real recipients. The methodology and instrumentation of such studies must become more sophisticated. Introspective experiments must be matched by observation of proof recipients who are assimilating proofs as they are being performed. Such studies need improved instruments for observing the brain in detail.

There is much to be done. What are we waiting for? Let us begin!

Syracuse University
Syracuse, U.S.A.

REFERENCES

Robinson, J. A. *Logic: Form and Function*. North Holland, 1979.

Mac Lane, S. *Mathematics: Form and Function*. Springer, 1986.

Robinson, J. A. Natural and Artificial Reasoning. In *Natural and Artificial Parallel Computation*, MIT Press, 1990.

Frege, G. Begriffschrifft, a formula language, modeled upon that of arithmetic, for pure thought. In *From Frege to Gödel*, Harvard, 1967.

Lakatos, I. *Proofs and Refutations*. Cambridge University Press, 1976

Aigner, M. and Ziegler, G.M. *Proofs from THE BOOK*. Springer, 1998.

JOHANN SCHUMANN

AUTOMATED THEOREM PROVING
IN HIGH-QUALITY SOFTWARE DESIGN

1. INTRODUCTION

The amount and complexity of software developed during the last few years has
increased tremendously. In particular, programs are being used more and more in
embedded systems (from car-brakes to plant-control). Many of these applications are
safety-relevant, i.e. a malfunction of hardware or software can cause severe damage
or loss. Tremendous risks are typically present in the area of aviation, (nuclear) power
plants or (chemical) plant control (Neumann, 1995). Here, even small problems can
lead to thousands of casualties and huge financial losses. Large financial risks also
exist when computer systems are used in the area of telecommunication (telephone,
electronic commerce) or space exploration. Computer applications in this area are not
only subject to safety considerations, but also security issues are important.

All these systems must be designed and developed to guarantee *high quality* with
respect to safety and security. Even in an industrial setting which is (or at least should
be) aware of the high requirements in Software Engineering, many incidents occur.
For example, the Warshaw Airbus crash (Neumann, 1995), pg. 46, was caused by an
incomplete requirements specification. Uncontrolled reuse of an Ariane 4 software
module was the reason for the Ariane 5 disaster (Lions et al., 1996). Some recent
incidents in the telecommunication area, like illegal "cloning" of smart-cards of D2-
GSM handies (Spiegel, 1998), or the extraction of (secret) passwords from German
T-online users (c't, 1998) show that also in this area serious flaws can happen.

Due to the inherent complexity of computer systems, most authors claim that only
a *rigorous* application of *formal methods* in all stages of the software life cycle can
ensure high quality of the software and lead to real safe and secure systems. In this
paper, we will have a look, in how far automated theorem proving can contribute to a
more widespread application of formal methods and their tools, and what automated
theorem provers (ATPs) must provide in order to be useful. We will justify our
observations with results of case studies, most of which have been carried out with the
theorem prover SETHEO (Letz et al., 1992; Goller et al., 1994).

S. Hölldobler (ed.), Intellectics and Computational Logic, 295–312.
© 2000 *Kluwer Academic Publishers.*

2. FORMAL METHODS AND DEDUCTION

Formal methods in general refer to the use of techniques from logic and discrete mathematics in specification, design and construction of computer systems and software (Kelly, 1997). Formal methods are based on logic and require the explicit and concise notation of all assumptions. Reasoning is performed by a series of inference steps of the underlying logic (formal proof).

Formal methods can be applied during various stages of the software life cycle and on different levels of "formality". (Kelly, 1997), pg. 7 distinguishes between three levels of formalization: on the lowest level, mathematical concepts and notations are used to express the requirements and assumptions. However, the analysis (if there is any) is only performed in an informal way. On the second level, formal specification languages are located. Also based on mathematical concepts, the underlying (denotational or operational) semantics of the specification language allows to perform formal reasoning. On this level, we find the classical specification languages like Z, VDM, and others, some with computer support (like syntax-controlled editors, type-checkers, or simulators). Finally, the third level concerns formal specification languages with a comprehensive environment including (automated) theorem provers and proof checkers.

Of course, the effort spent on formal methods substantially increases as the level of formalization rises. However, for the design of High-Quality Software, a considerable level of formal reasoning (with computer support) is necessary. Only then, even intricate errors can be detected, and safety and security properties can be guaranteed. Such a level usually requires proving lots of theorems on a very formal, detailed level. Doing this by hand is not only a very time-consuming, but also error prone task. Hence, computer support for (or, ideally automatic processing of) the proof obligations is necessary. Practical application of formal methods in industry (see e.g. (Weber-Wulff, 1993)), however, poses additional requirements on methods and tools: they must be *usable* and *user friendly*. This implies that a tool should

- support the entire software life cycle,

- fit smoothly into existing software development procedures,

- exhibit a fast learning curve,

- hide non-problem-specific details (e.g., existence of a prover), and

- be suited for real applications.

The last issue means that, for example, a tool must rather be able to handle trivial, but lengthy code (e.g., legacy code, macro code) than dealing with complex recursive algorithms (just think at the famous "quick-sort" example). Today's tools supporting formal methods are using *interactive theorem provers*, *model checkers*, and to a less extend, *automated theorem provers*.

2.1. Interactive Theorem Provers

Traditionally, interactive theorem provers like ACL2 (Kaufmann and Moore, 1996), EVES (Craigen and Saaltink, 1996), HOL (Gordon, 1987), Isabelle (Paulson, 1994), KIV (Reif, 1992), NqThm (Boyer and Moore, 1988), and PVS (Crow et al., 1995) — just to name a few — are being used to tackle proof tasks arising in many applications. These systems have a highly expressive input language. A higher order logic or customized logic can be defined formally and used within this framework. Formal definitions of theories can be used for the semi-automatic generation of induction schemes and simplifiers. Interactively activated *tactics* process the goals of the current theorem to be proven. Most systems furthermore contain an interactive (mostly emacs-based) user interface which allows to work on the open goals and to control the data base of theorems already proven.

Interactive theorem provers can be customized for specific applications and domains. To this end, the prover is augmented with definitions of specific logics and libraries of domain-specific tactics. Nevertheless, the proof of a theorem in general requires many interactions. Proof times of several months (e.g., (Schellhorn and Ahrendt, 1998; Havelund and Shankar, 1996)) are not an exception. Furthermore, the user must have a detailed know-how of the custom logic and the prover itself. For example, many proofs in (Paulson, 1997b) "[. . .] require deep knowledge of Isabelle". Despite their power, interactive theorem provers are only of limited usability in an industrial environment, because of their long learning curve and their relatively little degree of automatic processing.

2.2. Model Checking

On the other hand, Model Checkers for propositional (temporal) logic are more and more used in important applications. Originating from the area of hardware design and verification, these automatic tools provide an efficient means to tackle (large) proof tasks which have a finite state space (e.g., finite automata). Prominent systems are e.g., SMV (Burch et al., 1992), SPIN (Holzmann, 1991), Step, murphi (Dill, 1996), or μcke. Logics, specifically suited for the description of finite automata and their properties (e.g., CTL (Burch et al., 1990)) and convenient input languages facilitate the use of Model Checkers. Their ability to generate *counter-examples* when a conjecture cannot be proven provides valuable feed-back for the user.

Recently, Model Checkers have been extended (see e.g. (Burkart, 1997) or Mona (Klarlund and Møller, 1998)) to handle infinite domains which have a finite model property (i.e., if a model exists it has a finite size). Nevertheless, Model checkers usually cannot be applied in applications where recursive functions and data structures are used. Furthermore, most systems are not able to produce a formal proof (as a sequence of inference steps) which can be checked (or proof-read) externally (but see e.g., the Concurrency Workbench (Moller, 1992; Cleaveland et al., 1993)). Rather, the user has to rely on the correctness of the implementation[1]. The most severe reduction for the practical applicability of Model Checkers is the limit of the size of the state space they can handle. Despite numerous approaches (e.g., (Clarke et al., 1994)), proof tasks must be broken down or abstracted carefully in order to avoid state space explosion.

2.3. Automated Theorem Provers

Automated theorem provers (ATPs) for first order predicate logic (e.g. OTTER (Mc-Cune, 1994a), Gandalf (Tammet, 1997), METEOR (Astrachan and Loveland, 1991), SETHEO (Letz et al., 1992; Letz et al., 1994; Moser et al., 1997), SNARK (Stickel et al., 1994), SPASS (Weidenbach et al., 1996) . . . [2]) can handle full first order logic. Nevertheless, they are only used very rarely in applications in the area of Software Engineering. Although, due to intensive research (e.g., the German "Schwerpunkt Deduktion" (Bibel and Schmitt, 1998)), these systems have gained tremendously in power, one is tended to ask: "Why are they not used?" and "Is there really a gap between Higher-Order logic interactive theorem proving[3] and decision procedures?"

Currently, most Automated Theorem Provers (ATPs) are like racing cars: although very fast and powerful, they cannot be used for everyday traffic, because essential things (like head-lights) are missing. The classical architecture of an ATP (i.e., a highly efficient and tuned search algorithm) will and must be extended into several directions in order to be useful for real applications.

For the rest of this paper, we are concerned with the topic how, and in which way automated provers are to be extended in order to be applicable in the area of High Quality Software Design. We can identify *direct application* (i.e., proof obligations are already suited for direct processing by an ATP), *integration* of ATPs into interactive theorem provers, and the *adaptation* of automated provers towards practical applicability.

3. DIRECT APPLICATIONS

Racing tracks are specifically suited for racing cars. In our application area, domains can be identified which are suited for direct processing with an ATP. Obviously, the formal method should be close to First Order Logic (FOL), or a logic which can be translated effectively into FOL. Furthermore, the proof obligations must be of a complexity (size of the formula and size of the induced search space) which can be handled within current-technology theorem provers and the proof tasks must be provable without application of induction[4]. If these requirements are not met, it might be better not to use a general purpose ATP, but some special purpose algorithm. E.g., in PLANWARE (Burstein and Smith, 1996) the designers had enough information about how to find a solution that they "were able to throw out the theorem prover" (Smith, 1998). In this paper, we will have a look at three specific systems which directly apply automated theorem provers: PIL/SETHEO, NORA/HAMMR, and AMPHION.

3.1. PIL/SETHEO

PIL/SETHEO is a prototypical tool for the automatic verification of authentication protocols (Schumann, 1997; Dahn and Schumann, 1998; Schumann, 1999b). Authentication protocols are used in most distributed applications (e.g., internet, electronic commerce, wireless telephone networks) to identify the communication partners and to establish a secure communication, e.g., by exchanging encryption keys. Due to the importance of these protocols, their verification is vital. Several formal approaches to guarantee security properties (c.f. (Meadows, 1994; Geiger, 1995) for an overview) have been developed in the past: using modal logics of belief (e.g., (Burrows et al., 1989; Burrows et al., 1990; Gong et al., 1990; Syverson and van Oorschot, 1994; Abadi and Tuttle, 1991; Kessler and Wedel, 1994; Kindred and Wing, 1996)), Model Checking (Kindred and Wing, 1996), and approaches based on communicating sequential processes (Paulson, 1997a; Paulson, 1997b; Lowe, 1996).

PIL/SETHEO can analyze authentication protocols using the modal BAN-logic (Burrows et al., 1989) or the AUTLOG-logic (Kessler and Wedel, 1994). These logics are often employed in early stages of protocol development, because they are able to handle freshness properties (an important class of security properties) and produce short and informative proofs. Given the specification of a protocol and additional assumptions, PIL/SETHEO transforms the formulas into first order logic and starts the prover SETHEO. Proofs found by SETHEO are then automatically translated into a problem-oriented, human-readable form. An example for input and output for a simple protocol (a slight modification of the RPC-handshake (Satyanarayanan, 1987)) is shown in Figure 1. Proofs are in general found within a few seconds of run-time. Rather than going into details (which can be found in (Schumann, 1997; Dahn and Schumann, 1998)), Figure 1 illustrates an extremely important feature of PIL/SETHEO (as of any successful application): it hides any evidence of the automated theorem prover and first order logic. Both, input and output are in problem-oriented form (here, a modal belief logic), and the user does not need to have any knowledge about the prover's details.

3.2. NORA/HAMMR

Reuse of approved software components is an important method for ensuring high quality in software systems. NORA/HAMMR (Schumann and Fischer, 1997; Fischer et al., 1998) is a tool for the deduction-based retrieval of components from a library of reusable components. Using a contract-based approach, the library modules are identified by a VDM/SL specification of their pre- and post-conditions. In order to retrieve components, a query specification (also in VDM/SL) is given. Then, the library is automatically searched for matching modules. Matching components usually have a weaker pre-condition than the query, and a stronger post-condition (for details on different ways of retrieval see (Fischer, 1999)).

The tool NORA/HAMMR is designed for optimal usability. A graphical user interface (see Figure 2) allows to enter the query, browse selected components from

```
Objects:
  principal A,B;
  sharedkey K_a_b, Kp_a_b;
  statement N_a, N_b;
Assumptions:
  A believes sharedkey K_a_b;
  B believes sharedkey K_a_b;
  A believes B controls
        sharedkey K_a_b;
  B believes sharedkey Kp_a_b;
  A believes fresh N_a;
  B believes fresh N_b;
Idealized Protocol:
  message 1: A -> B
        {N_a}(K_a_b);
  message 2: A <- B
        {f(N_a),N_b}(K_a_b);
  message 3: A -> B
        {N_b}(K_a_b);
  message 4: A <- B
        {sharedkey Kp_a_b}
          (K_a_b);
Conjectures: after message 4:
  B believes A believes N_b;
```

Theorem 1. *conjecture.*

Proof. We show directly that

$$conjecture. \tag{1}$$

Because of *Message-Meaning*, *Assumption2*, and by *Message3*

$$\vdash B \models A \mid\sim N_B. \tag{2}$$

Because of *Theorem*

$$conjecture \Leftarrow \; \vdash B \models A \models N_B. \tag{3}$$

Because of *Nonce-Verification*: $A \models B \models C \Leftarrow A \models B \mid\sim C \wedge A \models \#C$. Hence by (2) and by *Assumption6* $\neg$ *conjecture*. Hence by (3) *conjecture*. Thus we have completed the proof of (1).   q.e.d.

Figure 1 Example input and output of PIL/SETHEO

the library, and control the search process which is structured as a *pipeline* of filters of increasing deductive power. The filters are capable of efficiently discarding non-matching components. Starting with signature matchers and simplification filters, most of the interesting components can be preselected. A subsequent model checking filter tries to identify non-matching components. Finally, a first-order theorem prover processes the matching relation. If a proof can be found, the library component can be safely reused. Hence, only a tiny fraction of proof tasks is processed by the automated prover. This ensures *short answer-times*, one of the most important requirements for this kind of applications.

The filter pipeline can be configured by the user, but the control of the provers is kept invisible from the user. Therefore, the tool only requires knowledge about the (problem-oriented) specification language VDM/SL. NORA/HAMMR (see Figure 2 for a screen-shot) has been evaluated extensively on a large library on functions about lists (Fischer et al., 1998). The automated provers Protein (Baumgartner and Furbach, 1994), SETHEO and SPASS (Weidenbach et al., 1996) have been used for the experiments. With a run-time limit of 60 seconds, a recall (percentage of retrieved matching components) of more than 71% (SPASS) could be obtained. If all provers are

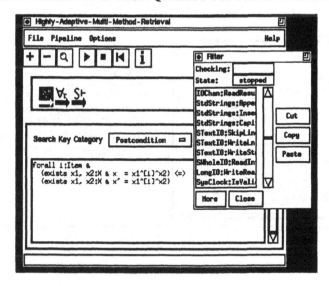

Figure 2   Graphical User Interface of NORA/HAMMR

running in a parallel competitive mode (see Section 5.2), the recall could be increased
to 80% which is acceptable for practical purposes.

3.3. Amphion

The main application area of AMPHION (Lowry et al., 1994) is the automatic synthesis
of astrodynamic (FORTRAN-) programs out of a given subroutine library (NAIF).
Specifications are entered in a graphical way as shown in Figure 3 (taken from (Lowry
et al., 1998)). All bodies (here Jupiter, Sun, space-craft) and their relationship as well
as the desired function (here to calculate the boresight angle between the Space-craft
Galileo and the Sun) are entered using graphical elements. From this, an internal
formal specification of the problem is automatically generated and processed by the
automated prover SNARK (Stickel et al., 1994). Its result corresponds to the sequence
of library calls necessary to calculate the desired function. Finally, a post-processor
converts this data structure into the desired FORTRAN program (Figure 3).

This tool is widely used within NASA and has been extended to handle several other
domains. Here again, hiding the prover and its logic is important. Only then, this tool
can be used by non-specialists in the area of theorem proving. Further features of this
kind of application come immediately into mind: proofs as a result are important, the
domain is rather restricted (only a linear sequence of subroutine calls) but nevertheless
important. However, more complex application domains probably would require at
least some kind of user interactions and/or specific adaptations and extensions to bare-

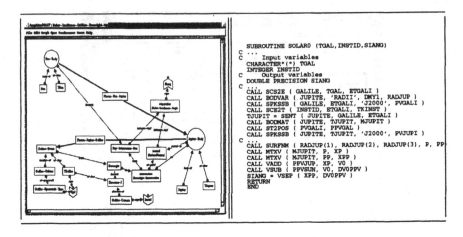

Figure 3   Example input and output of AMPHION

bone automated theorem provers (e.g., inclusion of decision procedures (Lowry and van Baalen, 1995)). Both directions will be discussed in the following.

4. INTEGRATION INTO INTERACTIVE PROVERS

The goal of integrating automated theorem provers into interactive provers is to relieve the user from tedious, error-prone and low-level work. Only major decisions — the "central proof ideas" — will have to be provided by the human user, whereas trivial tasks are performed automatically. Such a system architecture can profit much from the reasoning power of automated theorem provers. For typical applications, e.g., in verification, more than about 90% of the Higher-Order logic constructs[5] can easily be transformed into one or more first order proof tasks. According to (Reif, 1998), ideally about 25–30% of these tasks can be handled automatically. The others must be further broken down by the user. We will have a look at two prominent systems which combine interactive theorem provers with high-performance automated theorem proving: ILF and KIV.

4.1. ILF

ILF (Dahn et al., 1994) is an interactive proof environment ("Proof-Pad") which allows the interactive construction of complex proofs by using tactics. The system has been successfully applied to problems from mathematics (Mizar (Dahn and Wernhard, 1997)), hardware verification (verification of a microprocessor (Wolf and Kmoch, 1997)) and the verification of communication protocols (Dahn and Schumann, 1998).

This work showed its usability in the area of High-Quality software and hardware design.

For the verification of software protocols, an interface to the specification language Z has been defined and implemented (Dahn and Schumann, 1998). Z specifications are directly translated into ILF's sorted first order predicate logic. With the help of a graphical user interface and a tactics-based language, the proof tasks can be broken down into individual subgoals. Each subgoal is first tried by one of the connected automated provers (OTTER (McCune, 1994a), SETHEO (Letz et al., 1992; Goller et al., 1994), and Discount (Denzinger, 1995; Denzinger and Pitz, 1992)[6]). The time-limit for the automatic tries — which are performed in parallel (see Section 5.2) — is set to several seconds. If during this time no proof could be found, the user has to further break down the proof obligation.

A unique feature of ILF is its capability to present the user a problem-oriented, human readable proof. Such a proof consists of a "patchwork" of small proofs, found by the automated provers and by the interactive application of tactics. By using a common (natural deduction-style) calculus, the Block calculus (Dahn and Wolf, 1994), all proofs can be represented in a uniform style. This proof is then automatically post-processed and typeset to obtain a LaTeX-document (see also Figure 1, right-hand side for an example).

4.2. KIV and Automated Theorem Provers

KIV (Reif et al., 1997) is an interactive verifier, specifically suited for the verification of High-Quality software. Many industrial applications of KIV, e.g., the verification of an Airbag controller (Reif, 1998) demonstrates the practical usability of this system. Based on dynamic logic, reasoning can be performed manually and by tactics. As with any interactive system, the time to find a proof can be considerably. For example, for the verification of certain refinement steps for a PROLOG Abstract Machine implementation (Börger and Rosenzweig, 1995), proof times of up to two months have been reported in (Schellhorn and Ahrendt, 1998)[7].

Hence, one aim of KIV's developers is to use automated theorem provers to process simple proof tasks without user interaction. To this end, the prover $_3\mathcal{T}^{A}\!P$ (Hähnle et al., 1992; Hähnle, 1993; Beckert and Hähnle, 1992) was integrated into KIV, and experiments on the expected performance of SETHEO, SPASS, Otter, and Protein (Baumgartner and Furbach, 1994) have been performed for selected domains (Schellhorn and Reif, 1998). One key-problem which was identified is the preprocessing of axioms: when working with the interactive system, one usually loads all theories (e.g., theory of natural numbers and arithmetic, lists, trees) which might be needed for the ongoing verification. When interactive steps are performed, the human user usually knows which of the axioms is to be applied. Most automated theorem provers, however, are overwhelmed by the sheer number of axioms (often several hundreds) which are included in the formula. Therefore, a powerful mechanism for the preselection of axioms is vital. A straight-forward method has been integrated into KIV (see Section 5.1.1) which performs very well.

5. ADAPTATION OF AUTOMATED PROVERS

Although automated theorem provers for first order logic have become very powerful, they need to be adapted in order to be useful for the intended application. This is due to the fact that most ATPs have been designed and evaluated with the aim to solve small, but hard problems as they typically occur in mathematics. The large collection of problems in the TPTP benchmark library (Sutcliffe et al., 1994) reflects this fact: most problems are specifically formalized and prepared for automated deduction. Proof tasks from applications in the area of high quality software design usually poses quite different requirements for the automated theorem prover (cf. (Schumann, 1999a)). Extensions needed to meet these requirements include handling of non-first order logics (e.g., inductive problems, modal logics), efficient equality and theory treatment, handling of non-theorems (i.e., giving useful feed-back if a conjecture cannot be proven), post-processing of proofs, etc. Due to space restrictions we will focus on only two topics: preprocessing of the formulas and parallel execution in order to reduce the prover's answer time. Although all extensions mentioned above are important, experience with many case studies (cf. (Schumann, 1999a)) revealed that these issues are central for a successful application.

5.1. Preprocessing

In most applications, proof obligations are generated automatically by the application system. Because this usually involves a transformation between different logics, the generated formulas can contain many redundancies and lots of axioms which will not be needed for finding a proof. Automated theorem provers, however, are extremely sensitive with respect to the number of (unnecessary) clauses added to the formula. Therefore, it is important to perform a powerful *preprocessing* of the formula with the goal of optimizing it without affecting its provability.

5.1.1. Preselection of Axioms

In general, the task of selecting the appropriate axioms which contribute to the proof is as hard and undecidable as the proof task itself. Therefore, approximations are necessary. For domains with a rich signature and a hierarchical structured theory, a straight-forward and powerful method has been developed in (Schellhorn and Reif, 1998): given a formula, one selects only such (sub-)theories which are on the branch from the theory, required by the theorem to the root of the hierarchy. For example, to prove a theorem about the length of a list using the append operator, only the axioms belonging to the sub-theories of lists and natural numbers with addition have to be added. So, axioms, defining multiplication (which usually also belong to the theory of natural numbers) can be omitted. This mechanism is a part of the interactive system KIV (Section 4.2) and has been evaluated in (Schellhorn and Reif, 1998) with theorems, coming from the domain of graphs. With the full set of axioms (more than 500 axioms), SETHEO could show 18 example theorems ((Schellhorn and Reif, 1998), pg. 238). The axiom reduction yields less than 100 axioms which enabled SETHEO to solve 29 problems[8]. Similar methods have been integrated into ILF and NORA/HAMMR.

5.1.2. Simplification

Proof tasks which are being generated automatically, typically contain parts which are not useful for the current proof obligation. Examples are parts which are obviously not usable ("pure" parts or tautologies, e.g., $\mathcal{F} \wedge \text{TRUE}$). Such sub-formulas can be removed without affecting the logical properties of the formula, thus reducing the theorem prover's search space considerably.

Very old versions of SETHEO (Letz et al., 1988) contained such preprocessing modules. However, due to the general focus on problems which are already simplified and minimized, this aspect had been totally neglected by most ATP designers. Simplification should be performed as soon as possible (i.e., already on the level of the application) and on all subsequent levels (application logic, first order logic, clausal normal form). Typical ways of simplifying a formula which directly come into mind are:

- removal of obviously tautological parts (e.g., TRUE, FALSE, $p \vee \neg p$).

- optimization of the quantifies with the aim of producing Skolem functions with minimal length and small sets of clauses (cf. e.g. (Eder, 1985; Nonnengart et al., 1998)).

- simplification of the formula with respect to underlying theories. This means that e.g., $\text{cons}(X, Y) = []$ can be simplified to FALSE.

- formulas of the form $\forall X : (X = a \rightarrow \mathcal{F}[X])$ and some arbitrary $\mathcal{F}$ can be replaced by: $\mathcal{F}[X \backslash a]$. This means that all unconditional equations are applied to the whole formula and then removed. This kind of simplification is particular helpful when processing induction cases like $\forall L : L = [] \rightarrow \mathcal{F}$.

However, much more sophisticated ways of simplification are possible and desirable. Some methods, using semantic information have been implemented in the system NORA/HAMMR (Fischer et al., 1998). Here, simplification is also used to decide (where possible) if the theorem can be valid or not. In particular in applications, where most of the proof obligations are non-theorems, this turns out to be extremely helpful. But this is by far not the end. Experience with interactive theorem provers and symbolic algebra systems (e.g., Mathematica (Wolfram, 1991)) reveals that simplifiers are *the* central and most intricate parts of such a system. Therefore, elaborate simplification of a proof task should not only be performed during the preprocessing phase, but also during the search for the proof.

5.2. Parallel Execution

Most applications of automated theorem provers share a common and important requirement: short answer time. In particular for systems like NORA/HAMMR, KIV, or AMPHION where the user is *waiting* for the answer ("results while-u-wait"), short response times are vital for the acceptance of such a tool. Furthermore, the automated prover hooked to the system should be able to handle reasonably complex proof obligations, and the behavior of the prover should be "smooth". This means that proof tasks which are somewhat similar to each other should also exhibit a similar behavior w.r.t. response times.

A paradigm which is able to support the above requirements is the exploitation of *parallelism*. As has been demonstrated in (Kurfeß, 1990), automated theorem proving exhibits an enormous potential of parallelism. With the widespread availability of modern architectures like coupled multi-processor systems and large (often idle) networks of powerful workstations, parallel processing of proof tasks has gained practical importance.

Of the many approaches of parallel theorem proving which have been explored (see e.g. (Suttner and Schumann, 1993; Schumann et al., 1998) for an overview), the models of *competition* and (static) *partitioning* seem to be the most appropriate ones for applications. In a competitive model, all processes must solve the same (entire) proof task, but can use different parameters (p-SETHEO (Wolf, 1998)) or parameter ranges (SiCoTHEO (Schumann, 1995)). The first process which finds a solution, wins and aborts the other processes. If the search parameters for each process exhibit a behavior which is sufficiently different from the others, good speed up values can be obtained while reducing the answer times. As an additional advantage, the model does not rely on high communication bandwidth and low latency, because interprocess communication is limited to start-up and shut-down of the system.

On the contrary, a static partitioning approach (e.g., SPTHEO (Suttner, 1995)) splits up the formula into many independent parts which are searched individually and in parallel. This model also produces good scalability and efficiency. In contrast to dynamic partitioning (like PARTHEO (Schumann and Letz, 1990)), static partitioning is easier to implement on arbitrary architectures and has substantially lower requirements on the communication means.

6. CONCLUSIONS

In this paper, we have investigated how first-order automated theorem provers can be applied to the development of High Quality Software. Formal methods which facilitate the design, development and verification need support by powerful, yet user-friendly tools. Here, automated theorem provers can be used to relieve the user from tedious, error-prone work on details of the proof obligations. We have identified two ways of applying ATP, namely direct applications and their integration into interactive provers and verifiers. However, automated provers without modifications can be applied only in very few cases, because they lack several important features. In this paper, we presented work on the following central issues: preprocessing of proof obligations and efficient control by exploitation of parallelism.

The enormous potential of automated provers can be used in practical applications only if important core requirements, identified in successful case studies are met:

- evidence of the automated prover must be hidden.

- automated provers must support handling of finite domains in an efficient way (e.g., by exploiting model generation techniques or by integrating decision procedures).

- ATPs must be able to handle *obvious* non-theorems appropriately, and must give feed-back in such cases (e.g., a counter-example).

- pragmatic issues must be obeyed more carefully, e.g., precisely defined input language, implementation restrictions (like reserved identifiers, length of symbols). In research-oriented environments, these issues are often overlooked and neglected. However, they are important prerequisites for real successful applications of automated theorem provers.

With carefully chosen application domains and theorem provers which meet the above requirements and are adapted accordingly, automated theorem provers are powerful enough to help to really bring forward industrial-applicable formal methods tools for the development of High-Quality Software.

ACKNOWLEDGMENTS

This work is supported by the Deutsche Forschungsgemeinschaft (DFG) within the Habilitation-grant Schu908/5-1,Schu908/5-2,and SFB 342/A5. Partial funding for this paper was provided by NASA RTOP 519-50-22.

NASA Ames / Caelum Research Corp.
Moffett Field, Ca., USA

NOTES

1. This was also a point of critique when Model generators (Finder (Slaney, 1994) and Mace (McCune, 1994b)) were used in the area of finite quasi-groups.

2. See (Sutcliffe and Suttner (editors), 1997) for a broader overview.

3. Note, that some ITP's (e.g., PVS (Rajan et al., 1995)) already combine interactive theorem proving with decision procedures (e.g., model checking with μ-calculus and linear arithmetic solver).

4. Otherwise, special purpose inductive provers (e.g., Oyster/Clam (Bundy et al., 1990)) or interactive provers must be used to handle the proof task itself, or to generate first order subproblems ("base case, step case") out of the given proof task.

5. This figure results from estimates, given by several researchers to the author.

6. Whereas the first two provers can handle arbitrary formulas in first order logic with equality, Discount is restricted to problems which consist of equations only. In this domain, however, Discount is extremely powerful.

7. Although the topic of this case study might seem a little academic, its complexity and size resembles a typical demanding industrial application.

8. OTTER exhibits a similar behavior: it could solve 24 with all axioms and 31 with the reduced set of axioms ((Schellhorn and Reif, 1998), pg. 238).

REFERENCES

Abadi, M. and Tuttle, M. R. (1991). A Semantics for a Logic of Authentication. In *Proc. of the Tenth Annual ACM Symp. on Principles of Distributed Computing*, pages 201–216. ACM press.

Astrachan, O. and Loveland, D. (1991). METEORs: High Performance Theorem Provers using Model Elimination. In Boyer, R., editor, *Automated Reasoning: Essays in Honor of Woody Bledsoe*. Kluwer Academic Publishers.

Baumgartner, P. and Furbach, U. (1994). PROTEIN: A *PROver* with a Theory Extension *Interface*. In *Proc. 12th International Conference on Automated Deduction (CADE 12)*, volume 814 of LNAI, pages 769–773. Springer.

Beckert, B. and Hähnle, R. (1992). An Improved Method for Adding Equality to Free Variable Semantic Tableau. In Kapur, D., editor, *Proc. 11th International Conference on Automated Deduction (CADE 11)*, volume 607 of *LNAI*, pages 507 – 521. Springer.

Bibel, W. and Schmitt, P., editors (1998). *Automated Deduction: a Basis for Applications*, volume 8-10. Kluwer.

Börger, E. and Rosenzweig, D. (1995). The WAM — definition and compiler correctness. In *Logic Programming: Formal Methods and Practical Applications*, volume 11 of *Studies in Computer Science and Artificial Intelligence*. North-Holland.

Boyer, R. S. and Moore, J. S. (1988). *A Computational Logic Handbook*. Academic Press.

Bundy, A., van Harmelen, F., Horn, C., and Smaill, A. (1990). The Oyster-Clam System. In Stickel, M. E., editor, *Proc. 10th International Conference Automated Deduction (CADE 10)*, volume 449 of *Lecture Notes in Computer Science*, pages 647–648. Springer.

Burch, J. R., Clarke, E. M., McMillan, K. L., Dill, D., and Hwang, L. J. (1992). Symbolic Model Checking: 10^{20} States and Beyond. *Information and Computing*, 98(2):142–170.

Burch, J. R., Clarke, E. M., McMillan, K. L., and Dill, D. L. (1990). Sequential Circuit Verification Using Symbolic Model Checking. In *Proc. 27th ACM/IEEE Design Autom. Conf.* IEEE Comp. Soc. Press.

Burkart, O. (1997). *Automatic Verification of Sequential Infinite-state Processes*, volume 1354 of *Lecture Notes in Computer Science*. Springer.

Burrows, M., Abadi, M., and Needham, R. (1989). A Logic of Authentication. In *ACM Operating Systems Review 23(5) / Proceedings of the Twelfth ACM Symposium on Operating Systems Principles*. ACM Press.

Burrows, M., Abadi, M., and Needham, R. (1990). A Logic of Authentication. *ACM Transactions on Computer Systems*, 8(1):18–36.

Burstein, M. B. and Smith, D. (1996). ITAS: A Portable Interactive Transportation Scheduling Tool Using a Search Engine Generated from Formal Specifications. In *Proceedings of the 3rd International Conference on AI Planning Systems (AIPS-96)*, pages 35–44. AAAI Press.

Clarke, E. M., Grumberg, O., and Long, D. E. (1994). Model checking and abstraction. *ACM Transactions on Programming Languages and Systems*, 16(5):1512–1542.

Cleaveland, R., Parrow, J., and Steffen, B. (1993). The Concurrency Workbench: A semantics-based tool for the verification of concurrent systems. *ACM Transactions on Programming Languages and Systems*, 15(1):36–72.

Craigen, D. and Saaltink, M. (1996). Using EVES to Analyze Authentication Protocols. Technical Report TR-96-5508-05, ORA Canada.

Crow, J., Owre, S., Rushby, J., Shankar, N., and Srivas, M. (1995). A Tutorial Introduction to PVS. In *WIFT'95 Workshop on Industrial strength formal specification techniques, Boca Raton, Fl, USA*.

c't (1998). T-online: Hacker knacken Zugangsdaten. *c't Computermagazin*, (7/98):62ff.

Dahn, B. I., Gehne, J., Honigmann, T., Walther, L., and Wolf, A. (1994). Integrating Logical Functions with ILF. Technical Report Preprint 94-10, Humboldt University Berlin, Department of Mathematics.

Dahn, B. I. and Wernhard, C. (1997). First Order Proof Problems Extracted from an Article in the MIZAR Mathematical Library. In *Proceedings of the 1st International Workshop on First-Order Theorem Proving (FTP)*, pages 58–62. RISC Linz, Austria.

Dahn, B. I. and Wolf, A. (1994). A Calculus Supporting Structured Proofs. *Journal for Information Processing and Cybernetics (EIK)*, (5–6).

Dahn, I. and Schumann, J. (1998). Using Automated Theorem Provers in Verification of Protocols. In Bibel, W. and Schmitt, P., editors, *Automated Deduction. A basis for applications*, chapter III.8, pages 195–224. Kluwer.

Denzinger, J. (1995). Knowledge-Based Distributed Search Using Teamwork. In *Proceedings ICMAS-95*, pages 81–88. AAAI-Press.

Denzinger, J. and Pitz, W. (1992). The DISCOUNT System. User Manual. SEKI Working Paper SWP-92-16, Universität Kaiserslautern.

Dill, D. L. (1996). The Murphi Verification System. In Rajeev Alur and Thomas A. Henzinger, editors, *Proceedings of the Eighth International Conference on Computer Aided Verification CAV*, volume 1102 of *Lecture Notes in Computer Science*, pages 390–393. Springer.

Eder, E. (1985). An Implementation of a Theorem Prover based on the Connection Method. In Bibel, W. and Petkoff, B., editors, *AIMSA: Artificial Intelligence Methodology Systems Applications*, pages 121–128. North–Holland.

Fischer, B. (1999). *Deduction Based Software Component Retrieval*. PhD thesis, TU Braunschweig. (forthcoming).

Fischer, B., Schumann, J., and Snelting, G. (1998). Deduction based component retrieval. In Bibel, W. and Schmitt, P., editors, *Automated Deduction. A basis for applications*, chapter III.11, pages 265–292. Kluwer.

Geiger, J. (1995). Formale Methoden zur Verifikation kryptographischer Protokolle. Fortgeschrittenenpraktikum, Institut für Informatik, Technische Universität München. (in German).

Goller, C., Letz, R., Mayr, K., and Schumann, J. (1994). SETHEO V3.2: Recent Developments (System Abstract). In *Proc. 12th International Conference on Automated Deduction (CADE 12)*, volume 814 of LNAI, pages 778–782. Springer.

Gong, L., Needham, R., and Yahalom, R. (1990). Reasoning about Belief in Cryptographic Protocols. In *Proc. of IEEE Symposium on Security and Privacy, Oakland, Ca., USA*, pages 234–248. IEEE.

Gordon, M. (1987). A proof generating system for higher-order logic. Technical Report 103, Univ. of Cambridge, Computer Laboratory.

Hähnle, R. (1993). *Automated Theorem Proving in Multiple–Valued Logics.* Oxford University Press.

Hähnle, R., Beckert, B., Gerberding, S., and Kernig, W. (1992). The Many–Valued Tableau–Based Theorem Prover $_3T^A P$. Technical report, IBM Germany Scientific Center Institute of Knowledge Based Systems.

Havelund, K. and Shankar, N. (1996). Experiments in Theorem Proving and Model Checking for Protocol Verification. In *FME '96, Oxford, UK.*

Holzmann, G. J. (1991). *Design and Validation of Computer Protocols.* Prentice Hall.

Kaufmann, M. and Moore, J. S. (1996). ACL2: An industrial strength version of NqThm. In *Compass'96: Eleventh Annual Conference on Computer Assurance.* National Institute of Standards and Technology.

Kelly, J. (1997). *Formal Methods Specification and Analysis Guidebook for the Verification of Software and Computer Systems. Volume II: A Practitioner's Guide.* NASA.

Kessler, V. and Wedel, G. (1994). AUTLOG — An Advanced Logic of Authentication. In *Proc. IEEE Computer Security Foundations Workshop IV*, pages 90–99. IEEE.

Kindred, D. and Wing, J. (1996). Fast, automatic checking of security protocols. In *2nd USENIX Workshop on Electronic Commerce*, pages 41–52.

Klarlund, N. and Møller, A. (1998). Mona version 1.2. User Manual. Brics technical report, BRICS, University of Aarhus, Denmark.

Kurfeß, F. (1990). *Parallelism in Logic — Its Potential for Performance and Program Development.* PhD thesis, Technische Universität München.

Letz, R., Mayr, K., and Goller, C. (1994). Controlled Integration of the Cut Rule into Connection Tableau Calculi. *Journal Automated Reasoning (JAR)*, (13):297–337.

Letz, R., Schumann, J., and Bayerl, S. (1988). SETHEO – A SEquential THEOremprover for first order logic. Technical report, ATP–Report, Technische Universität München.

Letz, R., Schumann, J., Bayerl, S., and Bibel, W. (1992). SETHEO: A High-Performance Theorem Prover. *Journal of Automated Reasoning*, 8(2):183–212.

Lions, J. L. et al. (1996). Ariane 5 flight 501 failure report.

Lowe, G. (1996). SPLICE-AS: A case study in using CSP to detect errors in security protocols. Technical report, Programming Research Group, Oxford.

Lowry, M. et al. (1998). The Amphion system. URL: http://ic-www.arc.nasa.gov/ic/projects/amphion.

Lowry, M., Philpot, A., Pressburger, T., and Underwood, I. (1994). Amphion: Automatic Programming for Scientific Subroutine Libraries. In *Proc. 8th Intl. Symp. on Methodology for Intelligent Systems, Charlotte, NC, USA*, pages 326–335.

Lowry, M. and van Baalen, J. (1995). META-AMPHION: Synthesis of efficient domain-specific program synthesis systems. In *Proceedings of the 10th Knowledge-Based Software Engineering Conference*, pages 2–10.

McCune, W. (1994a). OTTER 3.0 Reference Manual and Guide. Technical Report ANL-94/6, Argonne National Laboratory, Argonne, Il, USA.

McCune, W. (1994b). A Davis-Putnam program and its application to finite first-order model search: Quasigroup existence problems. Technical report, Argonne National Laboratory, Argonne, IL, USA.

Meadows, C. A. (1994). Formal verification of Cryptographic Protocols: A Survey. In *Proc. AsiaCrypt.*

Moller, F. (1992). *The Edinburgh Concurrency Workbench (Version 6.1).* Department of Computer Science, University of Edinburgh.

Moser, M., Ibens, O., Letz, R., Steinbach, J., Goller, C., Schumann, J., and Mayr, K. (1997). The Model Elimination Provers SETHEO and E-SETHEO. *Journal of Automated Reasoning*, 18:237–246.

Neumann, P. G. (1995). *Computer Related Risks*. ACM Press.

Nonnengart, A., Rock, G., and Weidenbach, C. (1998). On Generating Small Clause Normal Forms. In *Proc. CADE-15*, number 1421 in LNAI, pages 397–411. Springer.

Paulson, L. (1997a). Proving properties of security protocols by induction. In *PCSFW: Proceedings of The 10th Computer Security Foundations Workshop*. IEEE Computer Society Press.

Paulson, L. C. (1994). *Isabelle: A Generic Theorem Prover*, volume 828 of LNCS. Springer.

Paulson, L. C. (1997b). Mechanized proofs of security protocols: Needham-Schroeder with public keys. Technical Report 413, University of Cambridge, Computer Laboratory.

Rajan, S., Shankar, N., and Srivas, M. (1995). An Integration of Model-Checking with Automated Proof Checking. In *Proc. CAV '95*, volume 939 of *LNCS*, pages 84–97. Springer.

Reif, W. (1992). The KIV System: Systematic Construction of Verified Software. In Kapur, D., editor, *Proc. 11th International Conference on Automated Deduction (CADE 11)*, volume 607 of LNAI, pages 753–757. Springer.

Reif, W. (1998). Correct Software for Safety-Critical Systems. invited talk, SPPD meeting during CADE-15.

Reif, W., Schellhorn, G., and Stenzel, K. (1997). Proving system correctness with KIV 3.0. In McCune, W., editor, *Proceedings of the 14th International Conference on Automated deduction (CADE 14)*, volume 1249 of *LNAI*, pages 69–72. Springer.

Satyanarayanan, M. (1987). Integrating Security in a Large Distributed System. Technical Report CMU-CS-87-179, CMU.

Schellhorn, G. and Ahrendt, W. (1998). *The WAM Case Study: Verifying Compiler Correctness for PROLOG with KIV*, chapter III.7, pages 165–194. In (Bibel and Schmitt, 1998). Kluwer.

Schellhorn, G. and Reif, W. (1998). Theorem proving in large theories, chapter III.11. In (Bibel and Schmitt, 1998). Kluwer.

Schumann, J. (1995). SiCoTHEO — Simple Competitive parallel Theorem Provers based on SETHEO. In *Proc. of PPAI'95, Montreal, Ca.*

Schumann, J. (1997). Automatic Verification of Cryptographic Protocols with SETHEO. In *Conference on Automated Deduction (CADE) 14*, LNAI, pages 87–100. Springer.

Schumann, J. (1999a). *Automated Theorem Proving in Software Engineering*. Habilitation, Technische Universität München, Institut für Informatik. in preparation.

Schumann, J. (1999b). Automatische Verifikation von Authentifikationsprotokollen. *KI*. Springer.

Schumann, J. and Fischer, B. (1997). NORA/HAMMR: Making Deduction Based Component retrieval Practical. In *Proc. 12th Conf. on Automated Software Engineering (ASE)*, pages 246–254. IEEE Press.

Schumann, J. and Letz, R. (1990). PARTHEO: a High Performance Parallel Theorem Prover. In Stickel, M. E., editor, *Proc. 10th International Conference on Automated Deduction (CADE 10)*, volume 449 of *Lecture Notes in Computer Science*, pages 40 – 56. Springer.

Schumann, J., Suttner, C., and Wolf, A. (1998). Parallel theorem provers based on SETHEO, chapter II.7, pages 261–290. In (Bibel and Schmitt, 1998). Kluwer.

Slaney, J. (1994). FINDER: Finite domain enumerator. In Bundy, A., editor, *Proc. 12th International Conference Automated Deduction*, volume 814 of *Lecture Notes in Artifical Intelligence*, pages 798–801. Springer.

Smith, D. (1998). Deductive support for software development. invited talk, SPPD meeting during CADE-15.

Spiegel (1998). Aussichten eines Klons. *Der Spiegel*, 18.

Stickel, M., Waldinger, R., Lowry, M., Pressburger, T., and Underwood, I. (1994). Deductive Composition of Astronomical Software from Subroutine Libraries. In *Proc. 12th International Conference on Automated Deduction (CADE 12)*, volume 814 of LNAI, pages 341–355. Springer.

Sutcliffe, G. and Suttner, C., editors. (1997). *Journal Automated Reasoning*, volume 18.

Sutcliffe, G., Suttner, C., and Yemenis, T. (1994). The TPTP Problem Library. In *Proc. 12th International Conference on Automated Deduction (CADE 12)*, volume 814 of LNAI, pages 252–266. Springer.

Suttner, C. and Schumann, J. (1993). Parallel Automated Theorem Proving. In Kanal, L., Kumar, V., Kitano, H., and Suttner, C., editors, *Parallel Processing for Artificial Intelligence I*, pages 209–257. Elsevier.

Suttner, C. B. (1995). *Static Partitioning with Slackness*. DISKI. infix-Verlag.

Syverson, P. F. and van Oorschot, P. (1994). On Unifying Some Cryptographic Protocol Logics. In *Proc. of the IEEE Comp. Soc. Sympos. on Research in Security and Privacy*, pages 14–28.

Tammet, T. (1997). Gandalf. *Journal of Automated Reasoning*, 18(2):199–204.

Weber-Wulff, D. (1993). Selling formal methods to industry. In *FME '93: Industrial-Strength Formal Methods*, volume 670 of *LNAI*, pages 671–678. Springer.

Weidenbach, C., Gaede, B., and Rock, G. (1996). Spass and Flotter version 0.42. In McRobbie, M. A. and Slaney, J. K., editors, *Proc. 13th International Conference Automated Deduction*, volume 1104 of *Lecture Notes in Artifical Intelligence*, pages 141–145. Springer.

Wolf, A. (1998). p-SETHEO: Strategy Parallelism in Automated Theorem Proving. In *Proceedings of 7th International Conference on Analytic Tableaux and Related Methods*, LNAI. Springer.

Wolf, A. and Kmoch, A. (1997). Einsatz eines automatischen Theorembeweisers in einer taktikgesteuerten Beweisumgebung an einem Beispiel aus der Hardware-Verifikation. SFB Bericht SFB342/20/97A, Technische Universität München.

Wolfram, S. (1991). *Mathematica–A System for Doing Mathematics by Computer*. Addison-Wesley, Reading, MA, USA, second edition.

ANTJE STROHMAIER

A COMPLETE NEURAL NETWORK ALGORITHM FOR HORN-SAT

1. PRELIMINARIES

Neural Networks are mainly used for classification and similar tasks, involving subsymbolic information. Nevertheless, they are also suited to deal with symbolic problems such as logic problem solving and optimization, where it can be made use of the possibility to process several tasks in parallel. Another aspect in parallel problem solving is the existence of a wide range of results given in parallel complexity theory, where parallel algorithms based on parallel random access machines (PRAMs) are designed to reduce time complexity of problem solving. As neural networks consist of units that are much simpler than PRAMs, these results cannot be directly transferred to the design of neural network algorithms. In this paper we therefore show how to combine the fields of symbolic problem solving by means of Neural Networks and parallel complexity theory to develop a neural network algorithm that solves propositional SAT-problems within the time bounds given by the results of complexity theory.

As this paper deals with a subject combining several very different fields of computer science, this first section consists of a very brief introduction to the relevant notions and results of propositional logic, parallel complexity theory and neural networks. After describing the kind of problems to be solved, we will briefly review some relevant complexity classes and classify some problems of propositional logic within them. We then describe shortly the kind of neural network used to solve the problems.

1.1. Propositional Logic

In this paper, we deal with problems of propositional logic. Propositional variables will be described by single lower case letters $p, q, r, \ldots$, possibly extended by indices. We only deal with propositional formulas in *conjunctive normal form*, i.e. each formula consists of a conjunction of disjuncts (so-called clauses), where the number of literals (i.e. propositional variables possibly preceded by a negation sign) may be restricted. A propositional formula ϕ is said to be in n-CNF ("n-conjunctive normal form") if it

S. Hölldobler (ed.), Intellectics and Computational Logic, 313–325.
© 2000 *Kluwer Academic Publishers.*

is written as

$$\phi = \bigwedge_{i=1}^{m} \bigvee_{j=1}^{n} l_{ij}$$

A propositional formula is *Horn*, if each clause contains at most one positive literal. A propositional formula is *satisfiable* if there exists a model for it, i.e. a truth assignment for the propositional variables such that the formula evaluates to *true* with this assignment. A propositional formula is *unsatisfiable* if there exists no model for it.

The problem class HORN-SAT consists of all Horn formulas that are satisfiable. The problem of deciding if a formula belongs to this class is known to be Ptime-complete (Jones and Laaser, 1977), whereas the same problem for any formula in 2-CNF (not necessary Horn) is in the closure of $\mathcal{NL}^*$, a subclass of $\mathcal{NC}$ i.e. solvable in polylogarithmic time (Cook and Luby, 1988).

1.2. Relevant Results from Complexity Theory

Parallel complexity theory deals with methods to parallelize sequential algorithms or to find new parallel algorithms. An important subject is the question, if a problem is optimally or at least efficiently parallelizable, i.e. if the work needed to solve a problem (computed by the product of time and parallel hardware needed) equals the time needed for a single processor or is at most multiplied by a power of the logarithm of the problem size, respectively. On the other hand, there exist problems that are called "non-parallelizable". These are problems where in the worst case, no speed-up can be expected by using more than one processor as the known algorithms to solve the problem are inherently sequential.[1]

A central role in parallel complexity theory is played by the problem class hierarchy $\mathcal{NC}$.[2] $\mathcal{NC}$ consists of the infinite union of the classes $\mathcal{NC}^i$ where each $\mathcal{NC}^i$ is defined through

$$\mathcal{NC}^i = \text{ATM}(\log n, \log^k n)$$

This means each problem that belongs to $\mathcal{NC}^i$ can be solved by an Alternating Touring Machine (ATM) with $\log n$ space in $\log^k n$ time. The union $\mathcal{NC}$ of these subclasses can then be characterized through

$$\mathcal{NC} = \text{ATM}(\log n, polylog(n)) = \text{PRAM}(poly(n), polylog(n)).$$

This means that problems in $\mathcal{NC}$ can also be solved by means of a polynomial amount of hardware (i.e. RAM processors) in polylogarithmic time. We give an overview over the class hierarchy in $\mathcal{NC}$ in Figure 1.

Very similar to the problem $\mathcal{P} \stackrel{?}{=} \mathcal{NP}$ it is assumed that $\mathcal{NC} \neq \mathcal{P}$, without a proof existing up to now. So it is assumed that all problems that are complete for $\mathcal{P}$ are not parallelizable in the sense explained above. For this paper we are mainly interested in parallelizing subsets of propositional logic. It is known that the problem class HORN-SAT is complete for $\mathcal{P}$, so we cannot expect any speedup by parallelizing any algorithm for the whole problem class. Nevertheless, there exist subclasses that are known to

Figure 1 The class hierarchy of $\mathcal{NC}$. The classes $\mathcal{L}$ and $\mathcal{NL}$ consist of problems solvable with logarithmic space by a deterministic or nondeterministic Touring machine, respectively. $\mathcal{NL}^*$ is the closure of $\mathcal{NL}$.

be parallelizable. But the classical problem of parallel complexity theory is to find algorithms that are as fast as possible, whereas the polynomial amount of hardware allowed to speed up the algorithms is less than realistic. It cannot be assumed that we can use that much hardware if, for example, we look at very large scale databases, whose contents has to be searched in parallel by e.g. a cubic number (in the number of items of the database) of processors. Therefore, it is especially interesting to look for the speed up that can be achieved with at most a linear amount of hardware. This is what we want to restrict ourselves to in this paper.

Below, we give a summary of some known complexities for subsets of propositional logic. n-SAT then is the problem of deciding the satisfability of a formula in n-CNF.

1. 3-SAT, where each variable occurs maximally 3 times, is in $\mathcal{P}$ ((Papadimitriou, 1991)).

This is an interesting result, as the general 3-SAT problem is $\mathcal{NP}$-complete.

2. HORN-SAT is complete for $\mathcal{P}$ and can be decided in linear time (Jones and Laaser, 1977; Dowling and Gallier, 1984).

Under the assumption that $\mathcal{P} \neq \mathcal{NC}$ we therefore cannot expect to find a parallelization for the whole problem class. But there exist subsets, that are known to be parallelizable:

3. 2-SAT is in $\mathcal{NL}^*$ (Cook and Luby, 1988).

4. 2-UNIT is $\mathcal{NL}$-complete (Jones et al., 1976).

where $\mathcal{NL}^*$ is the completion of $\mathcal{NL}$, i.e. contains all problems that are $\mathcal{NC}^1$-reducible to a problem in $\mathcal{NL}$ (Cook, 1985)—a subclass of $\mathcal{NC}^2$. 2-UNIT contains all formulas in 2-CNF, that can be proved to be satisfiable by only using unit resolution.

1.3. Neural Networks

Definition 1. *A* unit *of a neural network is a computational element, that is defined by the following parameters:*

- *an activation function g, which computes the* potential *of the unit,*

- *an output function f, which computes the unit's output*

- *a threshold θ, which influences the output function*

The state of a unit U_i at time t is defined by a pair $\langle p_i(t), o_i(t) \rangle$ where

- $p_i(t) := g(U_i, t)$ *the potential of the unit and*

- $o_i(t) := f(U_i, t)$ *the output of he unit*

The state of a neural network with n units at time t is described by a tuple $\vec{O}(t) = \langle o_1(t), \ldots, o_n(t) \rangle$ of the outputs of all units. The state $\vec{O}(t)$ of a neural network is *called* stable, *if* $\vec{O}(t) = \vec{O}(t+1)$. *The recomputation of a units output at time* $t+1$ *from the state of the network at time* t *is called an* update. *The update of all units of the network can be done synchronously, i.e. for all units at the same time, or asynchronously.*

The connection structure of the network is characterised by the type of connection between the units and their strength, the so-called weight. Connection can bear the following features, where we consider only directed connections[3]:

Bilateral connections: Information is sent from unit U_i *to unit* U_j. *The connection is written* (U_i, U_j), *its weight is designated by* w_{ji}.

Higher-order connections: Information is sent from units $U_{i1}, \ldots U_{ik}$ *together to unit* U_j. *The connection is written* $((U_{i1}, \ldots, U_{ik}), U_j)$, *its weight is designated by* $w_{ji1\ldots ik}$.

The activation function used in this paper computes the sum of weighted inputs to a unit. In the case of bilateral connections this is

$$g(U_i, t+1) = \sum_{j=1}^{n} w_{ij} o_j(t) \qquad (1)$$

If higher-order connections are used, the weighted outputs of all input units of such a connection have to be multiplied. The activation function then has the form

$$g(U_i, t+1) = \sum_{j=1}^{m} w_{ij1\ldots jn_j} \prod_{k=1}^{n_j} o_{jk}(t)$$

Units that receive input via higher-order connections are therefore called *Sigma-Pi-units*.

The output function used here is the following threshold function

$$f(U_i, t+1) = \begin{cases} 1 & \text{if } g(U_i, t+1) > \theta_i \\ 0 & \text{if } g(U_i, t+1) < \theta_i \\ f(U_i, t) & \text{if } g(U_i, t+1) = \theta_i \end{cases}$$

Units with this kind of output function are called binary threshold units, as they only have two possible outputs that are controlled by the threshold.

A unit is called *active*, if its output is greater than zero. Units can be *selfactivating* which means that a unit that once receives external activation stays active. A unit may also be *clamped*, which mans its output is fixed externally to a preset value.

A neural network is called *directed*, if it contains only directed connections.

2. A COMPLETE NEURAL ALGORITHM FOR HORN-SAT

This section describes the construction of the neural network for a given formula and the algorithm performed by this network.

2.1. Principle of the algorithm

The following algorithm is constructed for propositional Horn formulas in 3-CNF.[4] Furthermore, every non-Horn 2-SAT problem can be described by a 3-HORN-SAT problem by means of equivalence elimination and variable renaming. This follows from the fact that the problem classes 2-UNIT and 2-UNSAT are both complete for the complexity class $\mathcal{NL}$ (Jones et al., 1976). Therefore, also arbitrary 2-SAT problems can be treated with the given algorithm.

The neural network used here is a directed network with synchronous updating. We use a binary threshold Sigma-Pi-unit for each distinct variable occurring in the formula. The units are named with the respective variable names. Furthermore, two special units representing *true* and *false* are used. The *true*-unit is selfactivating. All other units have a threshold of 0.5, the weights are all set to 1. A directed and possibly higher-order connection from unit(s) $p_1(,\ldots,p_k)$ to unit q is described by (p_1,q) or $((p_1,\ldots,p_k),q)$ respectively. For a given 3-CNF Horn formula the corresponding network is construced in the following way:

- For every positive unit clause p a connection (*true*,p) is introduced.

- For every negative unit clause $\neg p$ a connection (p,*false*) is introduced.

- For each clause of the form $\neg p \lor q$ we introduce a connection (p,q).

- For each clause of the form $\neg p \lor \neg q$ we introduce a higher-order connection from p and q to *false*, written $((p,q),false)$.

- For each clause of the form $\neg p \lor \neg q \lor r$ we introduce a higher order connection from p and q to r, written $((p,q),r)$.

The resulting neural network has $n+2$ units where n is the number of distinct variables in the formula. The next step is to compute the transitive closure of the subgraph, which results from only considering bilateral connections in the network and regarding the resulting structure as a graph. For this purpose we construct the adjacency matrix A of this subgraph. The adjacency matrix A of a graph (V,E) with $|V| = n$ is an n-dimensional matrix whose elements are defined in the following way: a_{ij} is the element in the i-th row and j-th column. For the algorithm the diagonal of the matrix is additionally filled with 1. We define

$$a_{ij} = \begin{cases} 1 & \text{if } (i,j) \in E \text{ or } i = j \\ 0 & \text{else} \end{cases}$$

Then rising the matrix to the power of $2n$ with boolean matrix multiplication gives the transitive closure of the subgraph of bilateral connections. This corresponds to the transitive closure of the 2-CNF part of the formula and can be computed in logarithmic time when using $O(n^{2.376})$ processors and multiplying the matrix with itself, then multiplying the resulting matrix with itself and so forth (Coppersmith and Winograd,

1987). The resulting matrix describes the connections that can be added to the neural network.

With the network now obtained, the satisfiability of a whole family of formulas can be decided without further need to modify the network significantly: If a new set of facts (i.e. unit clauses) is used, new connection from *true* and to *false*, respectively, must be added, but the rest of the network remains the same. Furthermore, it is possible to pose queries and compute the answer with the network.

Example 2. *We consider the following propositional Horn formula ϕ:*

$$(\neg u \lor \neg t \lor v) \land (\neg s \lor t) \land (\neg r \lor s) \land (\neg p \lor \neg q \lor r)$$

At first, the neural network in Figure 2 (a) is constructed. The subgraph of bilateral connections has the adjacency matrix given in Figure 4 (a), where the diagonal is already filled with 1. After one multiplication of the matrix with itself, we already obtain the transitive closure (see Figure 4 (b)). The network now can be extended as shown in Figure 2 (b). The units true *and* false *are unconnected, because the formula does not contain any unit clauses (i.e. facts).*

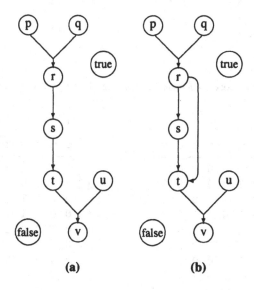

(a)   (b)

Figure 2   The neural Network for the formulas before (a) and after (b) computation of the transitive closure.

After construction of the network, it can be used for several different tasks by simply adding the respective connections. If the given formula is considered as a logic program, we can first construct a network only representing the rules of the program.

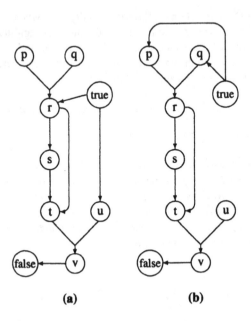

(a)   **(b)**

Figure 3   The neural network of the formula. (a) Answering the query ¬r ∨ ¬u ∨ v. (b) Answering the
query ¬p ∨ ¬q ∨ v.

	p	q	r	s	t	u	v
p	1	0	0	0	0	0	0
q	0	1	0	0	0	0	0
r	0	0	1	1	0	0	0
s	0	0	0	1	1	0	0
t	0	0	0	0	1	0	0
u	0	0	0	0	0	1	0
v	0	0	0	0	0	0	1

	p	q	r	s	t	u	v
p	1	0	0	0	0	0	0
q	0	1	0	0	0	0	0
r	0	0	1	1	1	0	0
s	0	0	0	1	1	0	0
t	0	0	0	0	1	0	0
u	0	0	0	0	0	1	0
v	0	0	0	0	0	0	1

(a)   (b)

Figure 4   The adjacency matrix of the subgraph (a) und (b) from Figure 2

The resulting network can then be used to represent different logic programs with different sets of facts by adding the connections from *true* to the units representing the respective variables. The main task for such a network then should be query answering as described in the following section.

2.2. *Query Answering and Satisfiability*

The computation of answers to queries to a propositional logic programm can be supported by the construction described above in the following manner:

1. Construct the network only for the rules of the logic program. Later-on add the connections defining the facts (i.e. unit clauses).

2. For a given query $\bigvee_i \neg p_i \vee \bigvee_j q_j$ for each i add a connection $(true, p_i)$ and for each j add a connection $(q_j, false)$.

After construction of this network, all units are initialized with output 0, i.e. are inactive. The *true*-unit is clamped with output 1 and all other units are repeatedly synchronously updated until the network reaches a stable state. If in the stable state the *false*-unit is active, this represents a positive answer to the query: Answering the query $\bigvee_i \neg p_i \vee \bigvee_j q_j$ to a logic program P corresponds to deciding the unsatisfiability of the formula $P \wedge \bigwedge_i p_i \wedge \bigwedge_j \neg q_j$. Activation of the *false*-unit at the end of the computation then shows the unsatisfiability of this formula. If we have the task to decide the satisfiability of a formulas, so we can use the same procedure with one difference: The *false*-unit must not be activated in the stable state of the network. The number of time steps needed until the network has reached a stable state then corresponds to the length of the longest directed path between two units, if the network is considered as a graph.

As we only consider propositional problems, loops need not be considered in a special way: Units belonging to a loop can only be activated, if at least one of the units in the loop is activated by input from "outside" the loop. As activation of units does not decay with time, after maximally one propagation of activation through the loop this part of computation is complete.[5] If after such a computation the *false*-unit really remains inactive, then the states of the other units give a model for the formula in question. In order to construct further models of the formula, arbitrary units can be clamped with an output of 1. Updating of the remaining units then gives models, if the *false*-unit still remains inactive.

Furthermore, in this way the logical consequences of a given set of facts can be computed. This is done by adding the respective connections from *true* to the units representing the facts. All units that will become active during the updating process represent logical consequences of the logic programm represented by the rules and facts encoded in the network structure.

Example 3. *We again consider the example formulas 2. We want to know if*

1. $\phi \vdash (\neg r \vee \neg u \vee v)$ *and*

2. $\phi \vdash (\neg p \vee \neg q \vee v)$.

For the first query we add the connections (true, r), (true, u) *and* (v, false). *The true-unit is clamped with output 1. The network needs 5 steps to reach a stable state, where the false-unit is active. This means a positive answer to the first query. The resulting network is given in Figure 3 (a).*

For the second query we add the connections (true, p), (true, q) *and* (v, false). *After clamping the true-unit with output 1 an 5 steps the false-unit remains still inactive, as unit u is not activated and consequently also v remains inactive. As a consequence the second query is answered negatively. The resulting network is given in Figure 3 (b). The result can also be interepreted in the following way: A counter example, i.e. a model for the formula* $\phi \wedge p \wedge q \wedge \neg v$ *has been found. It is represented by the state of the network, i.e. a truth assignment where the following set of variabels is assigned* true: $\{p, q, r, s, t\}$.

The effect of computing the transitive closure of the 2-CNF network part is not be seen very well here, as it results only in a reduction of the computation by one step (by the direct connection from r to t).

2.3. Complexity of the Algorithm

In this section the time and space complexity of the algorithm is described. Space here means the amount of parallel hardware needed (i.e. in general the number of PRAM processors or neural units). If n is the number of distinct propositional variables in the given formula, then the following ressources are necessary:

1. Construction of the preliminary network needs at worst $O(n)$ time for each of the n units. This is the case if each variable shares a common clause with each other variable.[6]

2. Computation of the transitive closure of the 2-SAT subgraph needs $O(\log^2 m)$ time and $O(m^{2.376})$ PRAM processors (Coppersmith and Winograd, 1987), where $m \leq n$ is the number of distinct variables occurring in a clause with 2 literals.

3. Extension of the preliminary network by the connections computed in step 2 needs $O(n)$ time for each of the $O(n)$ units.

In total we need linear time and a less than cubic number of processors, where only in the computation of transitive closure the power of PRAM processors is needed. Construction of the network up to this point is only necessary once. Afterwards the network can be used for a whole class of problems, that differ in the given facts and the task (query answering or satisifability testing).

Once the network is constructed, answering a given query or deciding the satisfiability of a given formula needs the following ressources:

1. Posing a query to the network consists of adding some connections. This needs constant time for each of the $O(n)$ units.

2. Computing the answer or deciding the satisfiability of the formulas needs constant time in case of a pure 2-CNF formula (because of the transitive closure then computed over the whole graph). For a 3-CNF formula the maximal time needed is linear in the number of clauses of length 3.

3. RELATED WORK

In (Ullman and van Gelder, 1986) a parallel algorithm for logic program query answering is presented. In contrast to the idea presented in this paper, they always compute the complete transitive closure of the whole (slightly differently represented) graph (including the higher order parts). But this has to be done in *every* query answering process again. Therefore in *every* answer computation nearly a cubic amount of PRAM processors is needed. They have a need for $O(n^{2.376})$ processors and $\log^k n$ time for every query in contrast to a single need for $O(n^{2.376})$ processors and $\log^k n$ time and later-on only $O(n)$ processors and $O(n)$ time. This means we trade a factor of n^2 processors for a factor of $n/\log^k n$ time.

The system as a whole resembles the one developed in (Shastri and Ajjanagadde, 1993) with the difference, that they do not compute the transitive closure. But this computation exactly assures that the time needed to compute an answer to a given query corresponds to the results known from complexity theory.

In (Kanellakis, 1988) a class of so-called DATALOG programs, i.e. logic programs solvable in $\mathcal{NC}$ is defined:

Definition 4. *A DATALOG-program consists of a set of rules $\mathcal{R}$ (i.e. Horn formulas) of the form*

$$A_0 \leftarrow A_1, \ldots, A_m \qquad m \geq 1$$

where each atom A_i has the form $r_j(X_1, \ldots, X_{k_j})$ without constants or other function symbols (i.e. we use predicate logic here).

For DATALOG programs several characterisations of their complexity are given. As every DATALOG program can be written as a propositional Horn formula, the algorithm given in this paper guarantees, that for a given DATALOG program a neural network is generated, that really solves the given problem in the time given by the characterisation of parallel complexity.

The recurrent networks used in (Kalinke and Störr, 1996) work with a similar principle to compute logical consequences from a given logic program. But they again do not compute a transitive closure. As the clause structure there is represented by an internal layer of hidden units with different thresholds and weights, computing the transitive closure could not be done by simply multiplying the adjacency matrix of a graph. Even if the connections needed for a transitive closure were known, it would be difficult to integrate them into the neural network, as the clause structure there is represented so different. It would become necessary to add new units, not only new connections, where also the thresholds and weights would have to be determined – an obviously much more difficult task. Otherwise the layered structure of the networks had to be violated.

The algorithm presented here corresponds to the second algorithm described in (Dowling and Gallier, 1984). Their algorithm perform a breadth-first-pebbling on the graph of the formula. But this exactly corresponds to successive propagation of activation in the network from *true* to *false*. Because of this correspondence, the algorithm described here behaves in exactly the same way as the second one in (Dowling and Gallier, 1984). Therefore, their proof of completeness and soundness also applies here. The problems discussed in (Scutella, 1990) occurring when the graph contains loops can only occur when the third "call-by-need" algorithm in (Dowling and Gallier, 1984) is used, as this one relies on depth-first search. The algorithm presented here performs parallel search on all units of the network. Furthermore we use a bottom-up strategy by means of starting with *true* and propagating activation to *false*. In contrast, the call-by-need algorithm in (Dowling and Gallier, 1984) uses top-down search.

4. CONCLUSION

The system presented here reflects the results known from parallel complexity theory. But exactly because of this, in the general case it is not adequate in the sense of (Bibel, 1991), where adequacy means that the difficulty of a problem is reflected by a mechanism's time and amount of hardware needed to solve it: The computation of the transitive closure needs a nearly cubic number of processors, whereas it is known that HORN-SAT can be solved in linear time by a sequential algorithm. Although this linearity itself can rely on a cubic number of clauses (and therefore may not be a real linear complexity compared to number of distinct variables in a formula), this shows that acceleration of the computation has to be paid for with much more hardware.[7]

TLC GmbH
Frankfurt, Germany

NOTES

1. An example for a nonparallelizable problem is the unification problem for variable term bindings in predicate logic (Dwork et al., 1984).

2. which stands for "Nicks's class" named after Nicholas Pippenger.

3. Undirected connections where information can be send in both directions can be modelled by two directed connections with identical weight.

4. This is no restriction, as every HORN-SAT problem can be represented by means of a 3-CNF formula.

5. Here we suppose that all units outside the loop sending input to units inside the loop have already reached their final state of activation.

6. One should note that the linear time complexity of the sequential algorithm given in (Dowling and Gallier, 1984) refers to the *length* of the given formula, which itself can be cubic in the number of distinct variables.

7. One should note that because of the assumed distinctness of $\mathcal{P}$ and $\mathcal{NC}$ an optimal parallelization cannot be obtained.

REFERENCES

Arbib, M. (1995). *The Handbook of Brain Theory and Neural Networks*. MIT press.

Bibel, W. (1991). Perspectives on automated deduction. In Boyer, R. S., editor, *Automated Reasoning: Essays in Honor of Woody Bledsoe*, pages 77-104. Kluwer Academic, Utrecht.

Cook, S. and Luby, M. (1988). A simple parallel algorithm for finding a satisfying truth assignment to a 2-CNF formula. *Information Processing Letters*, 27:141-145.

Cook, S. A. (1985). A taxanomy of problems with fast parallel algorithms. *Information and Control*, 64:2-22.

Coppersmith, D. and Winograd, S. (1987). Matrix multiplication via arithmetic progression. In *Proc. 28th Ann. ACM Symp. on Theory of Computing*, pages 1-6.

Dowling, W. F. and Gallier, J. H. (1984). Linear time algorithms for testing the satisfiability of propositional horn formulae. In (Scutella, 1990), pages 267-284.

Dwork, C., Kanellakis, P. C., and Mitchell, J. C. (1984). On the sequential nature of unification. *Journal of Logic Programming*, 1:35-50.

Jones, N., Lien, Y., and Laaser, W. (1976). New problems complete for nondeterministic log space. *Mathematical Systems Theory*, 10:1-17.

Jones, N. D. and Laaser, W. T. (1977). Complete problems for deterministic polynomial time. *Journal of Theoretical Computer Science*, 3:105-117.

Kalinke, Y. and Störr, H.-P. (1996). Rekurrente neuronale Netze zur Approximation der Semantik akzeptabler logischer Programme. In Bornscheuer, S.-E. and Thielscher, M., editors, *Fortschritte in der Künstlichen Intelligenz*, volume 27, page 27. Dresden University Press.

Kanellakis, P. (1988). Logic programming and parallel complexity. In Minker, J., editor, *Foundations of Deductive Databases and Logic Programming*, chapter 14, pages 547-585. Morgan Kaufman.

Papadimitriou, C. (1991). On selecting a satisfying truth assignment. In *Symposium on Foundations of Computer Science*, pages 163-169.

Scutella, M. G. (1990). A note on Dowling and Gallier's top-down algorithm for propositional horn satisfiability. *Journal of Logic Programming*, 8:265-273.

Shastri, L. and Ajjanagadde, V. (1993). From associations to systematic reasoning: A connectionist representation of rules, variables and dynamic bindings using temporal synchrony. *Behavioural and Brain Sciences*, 16(3):417-494.

Ullman, J. D. and van Gelder, A. (1986). Parallel complexity of logical query programs. In *Symposium on Foundations of Computer Science*, pages 438-454.

MICHAEL THIELSCHER

NONDETERMINISTIC ACTIONS IN THE FLUENT CALCULUS: DISJUNCTIVE STATE UPDATE AXIOMS

1. INTRODUCTION

Research in Artificial Intelligence aims at explaining and modeling intelligent behavior in terms of computational processes (Schalkoff, 1990). The classical approach towards this goal assumes intelligent behavior to be a result of correct reasoning on correct representations. In turn, this reasoning is understood by means of formal logic (McCarthy, 1958). The research area of Cognitive Robotics (Lespérance et al., 1994; Shanahan, 1996) is concerned with the application of this AI approach to a crucial aspect of intelligent behavior, namely, performing actions in a dynamic world. The famous Frame Problem (McCarthy and Hayes, 1969) inevitably arises in this context. Straightforward solutions exist only if it is possible for an intelligent agent to acquire complete information about world states. The early STRIPS approach (Fikes and Nilsson, 1971) and modern efficient planning techniques such as (Kautz and Selman, 1996), for instance, are restricted to problems in which this assumption of complete state information holds. Yet most of intelligent behavior concerns acting under partial information, and this is where the Frame Problem becomes a fundamental challenge which, thirty years after its discovery, is still in the focus of attention (Shanahan, 1997).

Within the setting of classical logic, the Fluent Calculus constitutes a successful attempt to address the Frame Problem as regards both the representational aspect (since no effect axiom or any other axiom needs to mention non-effects) and, at the same time, the inferential aspect (since carrying over persistent fluents from one situation to the next does not require separate deduction steps for each). Moreover, all this is achieved without relying on complete knowledge of the initial or any other situation. In (Thielscher, 1999) we have demonstrated the expressive power of the Fluent Calculus via a new approach to this axiomatization paradigm, where we started off from the Situation Calculus in the version that uses successor state axioms as a solution to the representational aspect of the Frame Problem (Reiter, 1991). We have illustrated how the Fluent Calculus, or a novel version thereof, can be viewed

327

S. Hölldobler (ed.), Intellectics and Computational Logic, 327–345.

as the result of gradually improving the concept of successor state axioms in view of the inferential aspect and without losing the representational merits. The key is to gradually apply the principle of reification, which means to use terms instead of atoms as the formal denotation of statements. Along the path leading from successor state axioms to what we call *state update axioms* lies an intermediate approach, namely, the alternative formulation of successor state axioms described by (Khalil, 1996), in which atomic fluent formulas are reified. This alternative design inherits the representational advantages and additionally addresses the inferential Frame Problem. Yet it does so only under the restriction that complete knowledge is available of the values of the relevant fluents in the initial situation. The Fluent Calculus, and in particular the notion of state update axioms, can then be viewed as a further improvement in that it overcomes this restriction by carrying farther the principle of reification to conjunctions of fluents. As the main result we have proved that, much like in (Reiter, 1991), a suitable collection of what these state update axioms can be automatically derived from a complete (wrt. the relevant fluents and actions) set of single effect axioms, provided actions do not have potentially infinitely many effects (Thielscher, 1999).

The purpose of the present paper is to extend this primary result for the Fluent Calculus to actions with indeterminate effects. The importance of this extension when it comes to modeling other than artificially simplified action domains, is common knowledge in the field by now; see, e.g., (Sandewall, 1994; Shanahan, 1997; Born-scheuer and Thielscher, 1997). In particular in (Lin, 1996) it has been illustrated how the formulation of *disjunctions* of successor state axioms can be used to solve the representational Frame Problem for nondeterministic actions. In the following section we illustrate by means of examples how these disjunctions can be reified to *disjunctive* state update axioms, by which both the representational and the inferential Frame Problem are solved. Much like in the special case of deterministic actions, along the path to this solution by means of the Fluent Calculus lies the dual form of successor state axioms of (Khalil, 1996) extended to nondeterministic actions. As before, however, this approach solves inferential aspect only in case of complete knowledge of the initial situation. In Section 3 we then present a fully mechanic method to derive disjunctive state update axioms from an arbitrary collection of Situation Calculus style effect axioms for both deterministic and nondeterministic actions, provided the actions do not have potentially infinitely many effects. The axiomatization thus obtained correctly reflects the initial effect axioms plus the assumption of these providing a complete account of possible changes.

2. FROM SITUATION CALCULUS TO FLUENT CALCULUS

2.1. Successor State Axioms (I)

Reasoning about actions is inherently concerned with change: Properties expire, objects come into being and cease to exist, true statements about the state of affairs at some time may be entirely wrong at another time. The first and fundamental challenge of formalizing reasoning about actions is therefore to account for the fact that most properties in the real world possess just a limited period of validity. This unstable nature of properties which vary in the course of time has led to calling them "fluents." In order to account for fluents changing their truth values in the course of time as consequences of actions, the Situation Calculus paradigm (McCarthy and Hayes, 1969) is to use so-called situation arguments to limit the range of validity of a fluent to a specific situation. The performance of an action then brings about a new situation in which certain fluents may no longer hold.

As an example which will be used throughout the paper, we consider the nondeterministic action of dropping a pin onto a checkerboard: The pin may land inside a white square, inside a black square, or touch both.[1] To axiomatize this action and its effects by means of the Situation Calculus, let $White(x)$ and $Black(x)$ be two fluents meaning that (parts of) pin x are on a white and a black square, respectively, and let $Have(x)$ be a fluent representing that pin x is currently held. By the term $Drop(x)$ we denote our action. We use the general binary predicate $Holds(f, s)$ to indicate that fluent f holds in situation s, and the predicate $Poss(a, s)$ to indicate that it is possible in situation s to perform action a. The latter is used to specify the preconditions of our action as follows:[2]

$$
\begin{aligned}
Poss(Drop(x), s) &\equiv \\
Holds(Have(x), s) &\wedge \neg Holds(White(x), s) \wedge \neg Holds(Black(x), s)
\end{aligned}
\tag{1}
$$

In order to specify indeterminate effects, in (Lin, 1996) a further foundational predicate $Caused(f, v, s)$ is introduced to indicate that fluent f is caused to have truth value v in situation s, where v can be either of the constants $true$ and $false$. The following two foundational axioms state that if a fluent is caused to have truth value $true$ or $false$ in a situation, then it holds or holds not, respectively, in that situation:

$$
\begin{aligned}
Caused(f, true, s) &\supset Holds(f, s) \\
Caused(f, false, s) &\supset \neg Holds(f, s)
\end{aligned}
\tag{2}
$$

With the aid of this additional predicate, the following axiom expresses the fact that our example action always has the effect that the pin being dropped is no longer held:

$$
Poss(Drop(x), s) \supset Caused(Have(x), false, Do(Drop(x), s))
\tag{3}
$$

This is a deterministic effect axiom. The additional, indeterminate effect of dropping the pin is formalized by the following axiom (Lin, 1996):

$$
\begin{aligned}
Poss(Drop(x), s) \supset \; &[\, Caused(White(x), true, Do(Drop(x), s)) \\
&\wedge Caused(Black(x), false, Do(Drop(x), s))\,] \vee \\
&[\, Caused(White(x), false, Do(Drop(x), s)) \\
&\wedge Caused(Black(x), true, Do(Drop(x), s))\,] \vee \\
&[\, Caused(White(x), true, Do(Drop(x), s)) \\
&\wedge Caused(Black(x), true, Do(Drop(x), s))\,]
\end{aligned}
\tag{4}
$$

This formula describes a nondeterministic effect as can be seen by the consequent of the implication being a disjunction of possible combinations of effects. The two effect axioms (3) and (4), along with (1) and (2), suffice to draw the right conclusions about the effects of dropping a pin. Suppose, for instance, of two pins, a hair pin and a safety pin, it is known that the former is currently held and not lying on a white nor a black square while the latter touches a white one. More formally, consider the assertion,

$$Holds(Have(HairPin), S_0) \wedge \neg Holds(White(HairPin), S_0)$$
$$\wedge \neg Holds(Black(HairPin), S_0) \wedge Holds(White(SafetyPin), S_0) \qquad (5)$$

where S_0 denotes the current situation. Let $S_1 = Do(Drop(HairPin), S_0)$, then our axiomatization supports the conclusion that $\neg Holds(Have(HairPin), S_1)$, and also that $Holds(White(HairPin), S_1) \vee Holds(Black(HairPin), S_1)$.

However, our effect axioms do not suffice to conclude, for instance, that the safety pin still touches a white square. This deficiency is due to the Frame Problem, which has been uncovered as early as in (McCarthy and Hayes, 1969). In order to obtain this and other intuitively expected conclusions, a number of non-effect axioms (or "frame axioms") need to be supplied, like the following, which says that a pin lying on a white square is not affected by dropping another pin:

$$White(x, s) \supset White(x, Do(Drop(y), s)) \qquad (6)$$

Now, the Frame Problem is concerned with the problems that arise from the apparent need for non-effect axioms like (6). Actually there are two challenging aspects: The *representational* Frame Problem is concerned with the proliferation of axioms which allow to conclude that a non-affected fluent does not change its value. The *inferential* Frame Problem describes the computational difficulties raised by the presence of many non-effect axioms when it comes to making inferences on the basis of an axiomatization: Suppose that for a proof some properties were needed in situations other than the ones where they are given or obtained as effects of an action. Then one-by-one each of these properties has to be carried from the latter to the former through each intermediate situation by means of separate non-effect axioms.

With regard to the representational aspect, successor state axioms as defined in (Reiter, 1991) provide a solution which is optimal in the sense that it requires no extra frame axioms at all. The key idea is to combine, in a determined fashion, several effect axioms into a single one. The result, more complex than simple effect axioms like (3) but still mentioning solely effects, is designed in such a clever way that it implicitly contains sufficient information also about non-changes of fluents.

The procedure by which these axioms are set up is the following. Suppose $F(\vec{x})$ is among the fluents one is interested in. On the assumption that a fixed, finite set of actions is considered relevant, it should be possible to specify with a single formula $\gamma_F^+(\vec{x}, a, s)$ all circumstances by which $F(\vec{x})$ would be caused to become true. That is to say, $\gamma_F^+(\vec{x}, a, s)$ describes all actions a and conditions relative to situation s so that $F(\vec{x})$ is a positive effect of performing a in s. A dual formula, $\gamma_F^-(\vec{x}, a, s)$, defines the circumstances by which fluent $F(\vec{x})$ is caused to become false. Consider, for example, our fluent $Have(x)$. The one action we are interested in, $Drop(x)$, causes the corresponding instance of $Have$ to become false according to (3). Hence an adequate definition of $\gamma_{Have}^{-}(x, a, s)$ is the formula $[a = Drop(x)]$, while $\gamma_{Have}^{+}(x, a, s)$ should be equated with a logical contradiction.

On the basis of suitable definitions for both γ_F^{+} and γ_F^{-}, a complete account can be given of how the truth value of fluent F in a new situation depends on the old one, namely,

$$Poss(a, s) \supset$$
$$Holds(F(\vec{x}), Do(a, s)) \equiv \gamma_F^{+}(\vec{x}, a, s) \vee [Holds(F(\vec{x}), s) \wedge \neg \gamma_F^{-}(\vec{x}, a, s)]] \quad (7)$$

This is the general form of *successor state axioms*. It says that the fluent F holds in a new situation if, and only if, it is either a positive effect of the action being performed, or it was already true and the circumstances were not such that the fluent had to become false. Notice that both γ^{+} and γ^{-} talk exclusively about effects (positive and negative), not at all about non-effects. Nonetheless, by virtue of being bi-conditional, a successor state axiom implicitly contains all the information needed to entail any non-change of the fluent in question. For whenever neither $\gamma_F^{+}(\vec{x}, a, s)$ nor $\gamma_F^{-}(\vec{x}, a, s)$ is true, then (7) rewrites to the simple equivalence $F(\vec{x}, Do(a, s)) \equiv F(\vec{x}, s)$.

Given the formulas γ_{Have}^{+} and γ_{Have}^{-} from above, the successor state axiom for $Have(x)$ is

$$Poss(a, s) \supset$$
$$Holds(Have(x), Do(a, s)) \equiv Holds(Have(x), s) \wedge a \neq Drop(x) \quad (8)$$

In (Lin, 1996) it has been argued that the generalization to *disjunctions* of successor state axioms can be used to solve the representational Frame Problem in case of actions with indeterminate effects. To this end, each single alternative outcome of a nondeterministic action is represented by a conjunction of successor state axioms for the relevant fluents. In turn, these conjunctions are conjoined disjunctively. The following, for instance, is an axiomatization of our example action wrt. the two fluents $White(x)$ and $Black(x)$:

$$Poss(a, s) \supset$$
$$[Holds(White(x), Do(a, s)) \equiv a = Drop(x) \vee Holds(White(x), s)$$
$$\wedge Holds(Black(x), Do(a, s)) \equiv Holds(Black(x), s)] \vee$$
$$[Holds(White(x), Do(a, s)) \equiv Holds(White(x), s) \quad (9)$$
$$\wedge Holds(Black(x), Do(a, s)) \equiv a = Drop(x) \vee Holds(Black(x), s)] \vee$$
$$[Holds(White(x), Do(a, s)) \equiv a = Drop(x) \vee Holds(White(x), s)$$
$$\wedge Holds(Black(x), Do(a, s)) \equiv a = Drop(x) \vee Holds(Black(x), s)]$$

Here the first two successor state axioms model the alternative where the pin being dropped lands on a white square only, the next two model its landing exclusively on a black square, and the bottommost two successor state axioms model its landing on both squares simultaneously. Formula (9) suffices to conclude that $Holds(White(SafetyPin), S_0)$ is not affected by action $Drop(HairPin, S_0)$: The axiom entails $Holds(White(x), Do(a, s)) \subset Holds(White(x), s)$. This is why we can spare frame axiom (6). By specifying the effects of actions in form of successor state axioms it is thus possible to avoid frame axioms altogether. This axiomatization technique therefore provides us with an in a certain sense optimal solution to the Frame Problem—as far as the representational aspect is concerned.

2.2. Successor State Axioms (II)

While successor state axioms are a good way to overcome the representational Frame Problem since no frame axioms at all are required, the inferential aspect is still present. If for a proof some properties are needed in situations other than the ones where they are given or obtained, then they have to be carried through each intermediate situation by separate instances of successor state axioms.

However, it has been shown in (Khalil, 1996) that by formulating successor state axioms in a way that is somehow dual to the scheme (7), the inferential aspect can be addressed at least to a certain extent. The key to the alternative form of successor state axioms is to devise one for each action, and not for each fluent, which gives a complete account of the positive and negative effects of that action. Suppose $A(\vec{x})$ is an action, then it should be possible to specify with a single formula $\delta_A^+(\vec{x}, f, s)$ the necessary and sufficient conditions on f and s so that f is a positive effect of performing $A(\vec{x})$ in s. In case of indeterminate effects, several of these formulas are needed, one for each alternative outcome α. This shall be indicated by an additional subscript, as in $\delta_{A,\alpha}^+(\vec{x}, f, s)$. Our example action $Drop(x)$ has three positive effects, and so we have these three formulas:

$$\delta_{Drop(x),\alpha_1}^+(x, f, s) \text{ is } f = White(x)$$
$$\delta_{Drop(x),\alpha_2}^+(x, f, s) \text{ is } f = Black(x)$$
$$\delta_{Drop(x),\alpha_3}^+(x, f, s) \text{ is } f = White(x) \vee f = Black(x)$$

For each action and each alternative outcome, a dual formula, $\delta_{A,\alpha}^-(\vec{x}, f, s)$, defines the necessary and sufficient conditions on f and s so that, as far as alternative α is concerned, f is a negative effect of performing $A(\vec{x})$ in s. In our running example, the appropriate formulas are

$$\delta_{Drop(x),\alpha_1}^-(x, f, s) \text{ is } f = Black(x) \vee f = Have(x)$$
$$\delta_{Drop(x),\alpha_2}^-(x, f, s) \text{ is } f = White(x) \vee f = Have(x)$$
$$\delta_{Drop(x),\alpha_3}^-(x, f, s) \text{ is } f = Have(x)$$

On the basis of $\delta_{A,\alpha}^+$ and $\delta_{A,\alpha}^-$, a complete account can be given of which fluents hold in situations if $A(\vec{x})$ is performed and if alternative α materializes. The actual result is then one out of the various possible alternatives. The general scheme for such a disjunction of successor state axioms of the alternative type is,

$$Poss(A(\vec{x}), s) \supset$$
$$\bigvee_\alpha \left\{ Holds(f, Do(A(\vec{x}), s)) \equiv \delta^+_{A,\alpha}(\vec{x}, f, s) \vee [Holds(f, s) \wedge \neg \delta^-_{A,\alpha}(\vec{x}, f, s)] \right\}$$

That is to say, the fluents which hold after performing the action $A(\vec{x})$ and if alternative α materializes, are exactly those which are among the positive effects or which held before and are not among the negative effects.

Given the formulas $\delta^+_{Drop,\alpha}(f, s)$ and $\delta^-_{Drop,\alpha}(f, s)$ from above, we thus obtain this disjunction of successor state axioms:

$$Poss(Drop(x), s) \supset$$
$$Holds(f, Do(Drop(x), s)) \equiv$$
$$f = White(x) \vee [Holds(f, s) \wedge f \neq Black(x) \wedge f \neq Have(x)]$$
$$\vee \; Holds(f, Do(Drop(x), s)) \equiv \tag{10}$$
$$f = Black(x) \vee [Holds(f, s) \wedge f \neq White(x) \wedge f \neq Have(x)]$$
$$\vee \; Holds(f, Do(Drop(x), s)) \equiv$$
$$f = White(x) \vee f = Black(x) \vee [Holds(f, s) \wedge f \neq Have(x)]$$

Notice that non-effects are not explicitly mentioned and no additional frame axioms are required, so the representational aspect of the Frame Problem is addressed with the alternative notion of successor state axioms just as with the original version of (Reiter, 1991) or its extension to nondeterministic actions of (Lin, 1996). The inferential advantage of the alternative design shows if we represent the collection of fluents that are true in a situation s by equating the atomic formula $Holds(f, s)$ with the conditions on f to hold in s. The following formula, for instance, constitutes a suitable description of the initial situation in our example (c.f. formula (5)):

$$Holds(f, S_0) \equiv f = Have(HairPin) \vee f = White(SafetyPin) \tag{11}$$

The crucial feature of this formula is that the situation argument, S_0, occurs only once. With this representational trick it becomes possible to obtain a complete description of a successor situation in one go, that is, by singular application of one disjunction of successor state axioms. To see why, suppose we substitute, in (10), variable x by $HairPin$ and variable s by S_0, then we can replace the three occurrences of sub-formula $Holds(f, S_0)$ of the resulting instance by the equivalent disjunction as given in axiom (11). So doing yields the formula,

$Poss(Drop(HairPin), S_0) \supset$

    $Holds(f, Do(Drop(HairPin), S_0)) \equiv$

        $f = White(HairPin) \lor [(f = Have(HairPin) \lor f = White(SafetyPin))$

                        $\land f \neq Black(HairPin) \land f \neq Have(HairPin)]$

  $\lor\ Holds(f, Do(Drop(HairPin), S_0)) \equiv$

        $f = Black(HairPin) \lor [(f = Have(HairPin) \lor f = White(SafetyPin))$

                        $\land f \neq White(HairPin) \land f \neq Have(HairPin)]$

  $\lor\ Holds(f, Do(Drop(HairPin), S_0)) \equiv$

        $f = White(HairPin) \lor f = Black(HairPin) \lor$

                $[(f = Have(HairPin) \lor f = White(SafetyPin))$

                    $\land f \neq Have(HairPin)]$

which all at once provides all derivable information of the successor situation. With the aid of (1) and given suitable axioms both for equality and for the assumption of uniqueness of names, the above can be simplified to

    $Holds(f, Do(Drop(HairPin), S_0)) \equiv$

        $f = White(HairPin) \lor f = White(SafetyPin)$

  $\lor\ Holds(f, Do(Drop(HairPin), S_0)) \equiv$

        $f = Black(HairPin) \lor f = White(SafetyPin)$

  $\lor\ Holds(f, Do(Drop(HairPin), S_0)) \equiv$

        $f = White(HairPin) \lor f = Black(HairPin) \lor f = White(SafetyPin)$

At first glance it seems that the alternative design of successor state axioms provides an overall satisfactory solution to both aspects of the Frame Problem. No frame axioms at all are needed, and one instance of a single disjunction of successor state axioms suffices to carry over to the next situation all unchanged fluents. However, the proposed method of inference relies on the very strong assumption that we can supply a complete account of what does and what does not hold in the initial situation. Axiom (11), for instance, provides such a complete specification, because it says that any fluent is necessarily false in S_0 which does not occur to the right of the equivalence symbol. Unfortunately it is impossible to formulate partial knowledge of the initial state of affairs in a similarly advantageous fashion. Of course one can start with an incomplete specification like, e.g.,

$$Holds(f, S_0) \subset [f = Have(HairPin) \lor f = White(SafetyPin)] \qquad (12)$$
$$\land f \neq White(HairPin) \land f \neq Black(HairPin)$$

which mirrors the incomplete description we used earlier (c.f. formula (5)). But then the elegant inference step from above, where we have simply replaced a sub-formula by an equivalent, is no longer feasible. In this case one is in no way better off with the alternative notion of successor state axioms; again separate instances need to be applied, one for each fluent, in order to deduce what holds in a successor situation.

2.3. Disjunctive State Update Axioms

So far we have used the concept of *reification* to denote single properties by terms. The 'meta'-predicate $Holds(f, s)$ has been introduced which relates a reified fluent f, i.e., a term meaning a proposition, to a situation term, thus indicating whether the corresponding property is true in the associated situation. When formalizing collected information about a particular situation S as to which fluents are known to hold in it, the various corresponding atoms $Holds(f_i, S)$ are conjuncted using the standard logical connectives. We have seen how the inferential aspect of the Frame Problem is addressed if this is carried out in a certain way, namely, by equating $Holds(f, s)$ with some suitable formula Ψ. The effects of an action a can then be specified in terms of how Ψ modifies to some formula Ψ' such that $Holds(f, Do(a, s)) \equiv \Psi'$. We have also seen, however, that this representation technique is still not sufficiently flexible in that it is impossible to construct a first-order formula Ψ so that $Holds(f, S_0) \equiv \Psi$ provides a correct incomplete specification of S_0. Yet it is possible to circumvent this drawback by carrying farther the principle of reification, to the extent that not only single fluents but also their conjunctions are formally treated as terms. Required to this end is a binary function which to a certain extent reifies the logical conjunction. This function shall be denoted by the symbol " ∘ " and written in infix notation. The use of this function is the characteristic feature of axiomatizations which follow the paradigm of the Fluent Calculus.

The union of all relevant fluents that hold in a situation is called the *state* (of the world) in that situation. A situation is characterized by the sequence of actions that led to it. While the world possibly exhibits the very same state in different situations, the world is in a unique state in each situation. A function denoted by $State(s)$ shall relate situations s to the corresponding states, which are reified collections of fluents.

Modeling entire states as terms allows the use of variables to express mere partial information about a situation. The following, for instance, is an incomplete account of the situation S_0 in our example (c.f. (5) and (12)):

$$\exists z\, [\ State(S_0) = Have(HairPin) \circ White(SafetyPin) \circ z$$
$$\wedge\ \forall z'.\ z \neq White(HairPin) \circ z' \wedge z \neq Black(HairPin) \circ z'\ ] \tag{13}$$

That is, of the initial state it is known that both $Have(HairPin)$ and $White(SafetyPin)$ are true and that possibly some other facts z hold, too—with the restriction that z must not include $White(HairPin)$ nor $Black(HairPin)$, of which we know they are false.

The binary function " ∘ " needs to inherit from the logical conjunction an important property. Namely, the order is irrelevant in which the conjuncts are given. Formally, order ignorance is ensured by stipulating associativity and commutativity, that is,

$\forall x, y, z. (x \circ y) \circ z = x \circ (y \circ z)$ and $\forall x, y. x \circ y = y \circ x$. It is convenient to also reify the empty conjunction, a logical tautology, by a constant, which is usually denoted by $\emptyset$ and which satisfies $\forall x. x \circ \emptyset = x$. The three equational axioms, jointly abbreviated AC1, in conjunction with the standard axioms of equality entail the equivalence of two state terms whenever they are built up from an identical collection of reified fluents.[3] In addition, denials of equalities, such as in the second part of formula (13), need to be derivable. This requires an extension of the standard assumption of "unique names" for fluents to uniqueness of states, denoted by *EUNA* (see, e.g., (Hölldobler and Thielscher, 1995; Thielscher, 1997)).

The assertion that some fluent f holds (resp. does not hold) in some situation s can now be formalized by $\exists z. State(s) = f \circ z$ (resp. $\forall z. State(s) \neq f \circ z$). This allows to reintroduce the *Holds* predicate, now, however, not as a primitive notion but as a derived concept:

$$Holds(f, s) \equiv \exists z. State(s) = f \circ z \tag{14}$$

In this way, any Situation Calculus assertion about situations constitutes an identical assertion in the Fluent Calculus.

Knowledge of effects of actions is formalized in terms of specifying how a current state modifies when moving on to a next situation. To serve this purpose, the concept of *state update axioms* has been introduced in (Thielscher, 1999). Their universal form is

$$\Delta(s) \supset \Gamma[State(Do(A, s)), State(s)] \tag{15}$$

where $\Delta(s)$ states conditions on s, or rather on the corresponding state, under which the successor state is obtained by modifying the current state according to Γ. Typically, condition $\Delta(s)$ is a compound formula consisting of $Holds(f, s)$ atoms, as defined with the foundational axiom (14). The component Γ defines the way the state in situation s modifies according to the effects of the action under consideration. Generally, actions may initiate and terminate properties. If an action has a positive effect, then the fluent f which becomes true simply needs to be coupled onto the state term via $State(Do(A, s)) = State(s) \circ f$. If an action has a negative effect, then the fluent f which becomes false needs to be withdrawn from the current state $State(s)$. The scheme $State(Do(A, s)) \circ f = State(s)$ serves this purpose. Incidentally, this scheme is the sole reason for not stipulating that " $\circ$ " be idempotent. For if it were, then the equation $State(Do(A, s)) \circ f = State(s)$ would be satisfied if $State(Do(A, s))$ contained f. Hence this equation would not guarantee that f becomes false. Vital for the scheme is also to ensure that state terms do not contain any fluent twice or more, i.e.,

$$\forall s, x, z. State(s) = x \circ x \circ z \supset x = \emptyset \tag{16}$$

On this basis, the following instance of (15) is the general form of state update axioms for deterministic actions with only direct effects:

$$\Delta(s) \supset State(Do(A, s)) \circ \vartheta^- = State(s) \circ \vartheta^+$$

where ϑ^- are the negative effects and ϑ^+ the positive effects, respectively, of action a under condition $\Delta(s)$. [4] Nondeterministic actions require a more general form of state update axioms (15), namely, where Γ is a disjunction of equations, each of which describes a possible outcome, i.e., update. The following *disjunctive* state update axiom, for example, provides a suitable specification of the (indeterminate) effect of dropping a pin:

$$Poss(Drop(x), s) \supset$$
$$State(Do(Drop(x), s)) \circ Have(x) = State(s) \circ White(x)$$
$$\lor\ State(Do(Drop(x), s)) \circ Have(x) = State(s) \circ Black(x) \qquad (17)$$
$$\lor\ State(Do(Drop(x), s)) \circ Have(x) = State(s) \circ White(x) \circ Black(x)$$

Put in words, $Have(x)$ becomes false in any case while at least one of $White(x)$ and $Black(x)$ becomes true, maybe both of them.

If in this state update axiom we substitute x by $HairPin$ and s by S_0, then we can replace the three occurrences of term $State(S_0)$ in the resulting instance by the equal term as given in axiom (13). So doing, and given that we know $Poss(Drop(HairPin), S_0)$ and setting $S_1 = Do(Drop(HairPin), S_0)$, yields,

$$\exists z\,[\ State(S_1) \circ Have(HairPin) =$$
$$Have(HairPin) \circ White(SafetyPin) \circ z \circ White(HairPin)$$
$$\lor\ State(S_1) \circ Have(HairPin) =$$
$$Have(HairPin) \circ White(SafetyPin) \circ z \circ Black(HairPin)$$
$$\lor\ State(S_1) \circ Have(HairPin) =$$
$$Have(HairPin) \circ White(SafetyPin) \circ z \circ White(HairPin)$$
$$\circ Black(HairPin)\,]$$

which implies, e.g., $Holds(White(HairPin), S_1) \lor Holds(Black(HairPin), S_1)$ and also $Holds(White(SafetyPin), S_1)$. In this way we have obtained from an incomplete initial specification a still partial description of the possible successor states, each of which includes the unaffected fluent $White(SafetyPin)$. This property thus survived the application of the state update axiom without the need to be carried over by separate application of axioms. In this way the concept of state update axioms provides a solution to both the representational and the inferential aspect of the Frame Problem which is capable of dealing with incomplete knowledge about states.

3. THE GENERAL METHOD

Having illustrated the design and use of state update axioms by example, in this section we will present a general, fully mechanic procedure by which is generated a suitable set of state update axioms from a given collection of Situation Calculus effect axioms, like the deterministic (3) and the indeterminate (4). As in the deterministic case, for our method to be feasible it is necessary that actions do not potentially have infinitely many effects, or so-called *open* effects. An example of a violation of this assumption is the following axiom, which specifies an (indeterminate) open effect:

$$Bomb(x) \wedge Holds(Nearby(x,y), s) \wedge \neg Holds(Destroyed(y), s) \supset$$
$$Caused(Destroyed(y), true, Do(Explodes(x), s)) \qquad (18)$$
$$\vee\, Caused(Destroyed(y), false, Do(Explodes(x), s))$$

That is to say, if a bomb x explodes then any intact, nearby object y may or may not be destroyed thereafter. Notice that even after instantiating the action expression *Explodes(x)* and the situation term s, the effect literals still carries a variable, y, so that the action may have infinitely many effects. State update axioms for actions with open effects are discussed in Section 4.

In what follows, we consider effect specifications of the following form, where A denotes an action and $\mathcal{F} = \{F_1, \ldots, F_m\}$ a finite, non-empty set of fluents:

$$Poss(A(\vec{x}), s) \supset$$
$$\varepsilon_{A,\mathcal{F}}(\vec{x}, s) \supset$$
$$Caused(F_1(\vec{y}_1), v_{11}, Do(A(\vec{x}), s)) \wedge \ldots \wedge Caused(F_m(\vec{y}_m), v_{1m}, Do(A(\vec{x}), s))$$
$$\vee \ldots \vee$$
$$Caused(F_1(\vec{y}_1), v_{n1}, Do(A(\vec{x}), s)) \wedge \ldots \wedge Caused(F_m(\vec{y}_m), v_{nm}, Do(A(\vec{x}), s))$$

Here, ε is a first-order formula with free variables are among $\vec{x}, s$; $v_{ij} \in \{true, false\}$; and each $\vec{y}_i$ contains only variables from $\vec{x}$. Notice that it is the very last restriction which ensures that the effect specification does not describe an open effect: Except for the situation term, all arguments of an effect F_i are bound by the action term $A(\vec{x})$. The reader may verify that the deterministic effect axiom at the beginning of Section 2.1, formula (3), fits this scheme by equating $\varepsilon_{Drop,\{Have\}}$ with a tautology and letting $v_{11} = false$, while the indeterminate effect axiom (4) fits this scheme by equating $\varepsilon_{Drop,\{White,Black\}}$ with a tautology again and setting the truth values v_{ij} ($i = 1, 2, 3$; $j = 1, 2$) accordingly. We assume that a given set $\mathcal{E}$ of effect axioms is *sound* in that a fluent F may not occur in two or more effect axioms for one and the same action unless the conditions are mutually exclusive; that is, for all actions A and sets of fluents $\mathcal{F}_1, \mathcal{F}_2$ such that $\mathcal{F}_1 \cap \mathcal{F}_2 \neq \{\}$, the unique names assumption must entail

$$\neg \exists \vec{x}, s\, [\varepsilon_{A,\mathcal{F}_1}(\vec{x}, s) \wedge \varepsilon_{A,\mathcal{F}_2}(\vec{x}, s)] \qquad (19)$$

Fundamental for any attempt to solve the Frame Problem is the assumption that a given set of effect axioms is *complete* in the sense that it specifies all relevant effects of all involved actions. Our concern, therefore, is to design state update axioms for a given set of effect specifications which suitably reflect the completeness assumption. The following instance of scheme (15) is the general form of state update axioms for actions with only direct but possibly indeterminate effects:

$$\Delta(s) \supset \quad State(Do(A, s)) \circ \vartheta_{\alpha_1}^- = State(s) \circ \vartheta_{\alpha_1}^+$$
$$\vee \ldots \vee$$
$$State(Do(A, s)) \circ \vartheta_{\alpha_n}^- = State(s) \circ \vartheta_{\alpha_n}^+$$

where, under alternative α_i, $\vartheta_{\alpha_i}^-$ are the negative effects and $\vartheta_{\alpha_i}^+$ the positive effects, respectively, of action a under condition $\Delta(s)$. The main challenge for the design of these state update axioms is to make sure that condition Δ is strong enough for the equations in the consequent to be sound. Neither must any $\vartheta_{\alpha_i}^+$ include a fluent that already holds in situation s (for this would contradict the foundational axiom about multiple occurrences, (16)), nor should any $\vartheta_{\alpha_i}^-$ specify a negative effect that is already false in s (for then *EUNA* implies that the equation be false). This is the motivation for the case distinction in item 2 of our procedure, which is shown in Fig. 1 (depticted at the end of the paper).

Our method blindly considers all combinations of conditions $\Delta_1(s) \wedge \Delta_2(s)$. Some of the state update axioms thus obtained may have inconsistent antecedent, in which case they can be removed. For the purpose of illustration, we apply our procedure to the two example effect axioms from the beginning, which we repeat here for convenience:

$$Poss(Drop(x), s) \supset Caused(Have(x), false, Do(Drop(x), s))$$

$$
\begin{aligned}
Poss(Drop(x), s) \supset \ &[\,Caused(White(x), true, Do(Drop(x), s)) \\
&\wedge Caused(Black(x), false, Do(Drop(x), s))\,] \vee \\
&[\,Caused(White(x), false, Do(Drop(x), s)) \\
&\wedge Caused(Black(x), true, Do(Drop(x), s))\,] \vee \\
&[\,Caused(White(x), true, Do(Drop(x), s)) \\
&\wedge Caused(Black(x), true, Do(Drop(x), s))\,]
\end{aligned}
$$

To begin with, any strict subset $\kappa \subseteq \{1, 2\}$ will produce an inconsistent $\Delta_1(s)$, because neither of the two effect axioms is conditioned further than by the action precondition, $Poss(Drop(x), s)$. In case $\kappa = \{1, 2\}$ we obtain $\Delta_1(s)$ as $Poss(Drop(x), s)$. Three selections α_1, α_2, and α_3 are possible, one for each of the alternatives in the second one of the two axioms. Each of these selections must include the effect described by the first axiom. Thus we obtain,

$$
\begin{array}{llll}
\vartheta_{\alpha_1}^+ \ \text{is} \ White(x) & \qquad & \vartheta_{\alpha_1}^- \ \text{is} \ Have(x) \circ Black(x) \\
\vartheta_{\alpha_2}^+ \ \text{is} \ Black(x) & \qquad & \vartheta_{\alpha_2}^- \ \text{is} \ Have(x) \circ White(x) \\
\vartheta_{\alpha_3}^+ \ \text{is} \ White(x) \circ Black(x) & \qquad & \vartheta_{\alpha_3}^- \ \text{is} \ Have(x)
\end{array}
$$

Now, since $Poss(Drop(x), s)$ requires that $Have(x)$ be true and both $White(x)$ and $Black(x)$ be false, the only $\Delta_2(s)$ which is consistent with $\Delta_1(s)$ equals $Poss(Drop(x), s)$. Then,

$$
\begin{array}{llll}
\vartheta_{\alpha_1}^+ |_{\Delta_2} \ \text{is} \ White(x) & \qquad & \vartheta_{\alpha_1}^- |_{\Delta_2} \ \text{is} \ Have(x) \\
\vartheta_{\alpha_2}^+ |_{\Delta_2} \ \text{is} \ Black(x) & \qquad & \vartheta_{\alpha_2}^- |_{\Delta_2} \ \text{is} \ Have(x) \\
\vartheta_{\alpha_3}^+ |_{\Delta_2} \ \text{is} \ White(x) \circ Black(x) & \qquad & \vartheta_{\alpha_3}^- |_{\Delta_2} \ \text{is} \ Have(x)
\end{array}
$$

because $\Delta_2(s) \models \neg Holds(Black(x), s) \wedge \neg Holds(White(x), s)$. We therefore obtain a single disjunctive state update axiom which coincides with the one we already used in Section 2.3, viz. axiom (17).

For each action A, let the following $k \geq 0$ axioms be all given effect axioms concerning A:

$$Poss(A(\vec{x}), s) \supset [\varepsilon^1_{A,\mathcal{F}_1} \supset D_1]$$

$$\vdots$$

$$Poss(A(\vec{x}), s) \supset [\varepsilon^k_{A,\mathcal{F}_k}(\vec{x}, s) \supset D_k]$$

For each subset $\kappa \subseteq \{1, \ldots, k\}$ (including the empty one) do the following.[5]

1. Let $Poss(A(\vec{x}), s) \wedge \bigwedge_{i \in \kappa} HOLDS(\varepsilon^i_{A,\mathcal{F}_i}(\vec{x}, s)) \wedge \bigwedge_{j \notin \kappa} HOLDS(\neg\varepsilon^j_{A,\mathcal{F}_i}(\vec{x}, s))$ be denoted by $\Delta_1(s)$. Select in every disjunction D_i with $i \in \kappa$ one disjunct C_i. For each such combined selection α do the following.

   1a. For each selected (via α) conjunction C_i, which is

   $$Caused(F_1(\vec{y}_1), v_1, Do(A(\vec{x}), s)) \wedge \ldots \wedge Caused(F_m(\vec{y}_m), v_m, Do(A(\vec{x}), s))$$

   let $\vartheta^+_{\alpha,i}$ be the o-term consisting of all $F_l(\vec{y}_l)$ such that v_l is *true*, and let $\vartheta^-_{\alpha,i}$ be the o-term consisting of all $F_l(\vec{y}_l)$ such that v_l is *false*.[6]

   1b. Let ϑ^+_α be the o-term consisting of all $\vartheta^+_{\alpha,i}$, and let ϑ^-_α be the o-term consisting of all $\vartheta^-_{\alpha,i}$ (where $i \in \kappa$).

2. Let $\mathcal{F}^+$ be the set of all fluents $F(\vec{y})$ that occur in ϑ^+_α for some α, and let $\mathcal{F}^-$ be the set of all fluents $F(\vec{y})$ that occur in ϑ^-_α for some α. For any pair of subsets $\widehat{\mathcal{F}}^+ \subseteq \mathcal{F}^+$ and $\widehat{\mathcal{F}}^- \subseteq \mathcal{F}^-$ (including the empty ones) let $\Delta_2(s)$ be the conjunction $\bigwedge_{f \in \widehat{\mathcal{F}}^+} Holds(f, s) \wedge \bigwedge_{f \in \widehat{\mathcal{F}}^-} \neg Holds(f, s)$ and construct the following disjunctive state update axiom:

$$\Delta_1(s) \wedge \Delta_2(s) \supset \bigvee_\alpha State(Do(A(\vec{x}), s)) \circ \vartheta^-_\alpha|_{\Delta_2} = State(s) \circ \vartheta^+_\alpha|_{\Delta_2}$$

where $\vartheta^-_\alpha|_{\Delta_2}$ is just like ϑ^-_α but without all terms $F(\vec{y})$ such that $\Delta_2(s) \models \neg Holds(F(\vec{y}), s)$, and $\vartheta^+_\alpha|_{\Delta_2}$ is ϑ^+_α without all terms $F(\vec{y})$ such that $\Delta_2(s) \models Holds(F(\vec{y}), s)$.[7]

Figure 1   Generating disjunctive state update axioms from indeterminate effect specifications.

4. CONCLUSION

Starting off from the concept of disjunctions of successor state axioms as a solution to the representational aspect of the Frame Problem in case of both deterministic and nondeterministic actions, we have gradually applied the principle of reification and thus have solved the inferential Frame Problem by means of the Fluent Calculus and in particular with the notion of disjunctive state update axioms. We have demonstrated the expressive power of this solution by showing how a suitable collection of these axioms can be automatically derived from a complete (wrt. the relevant fluents and actions) set of single effect axioms, provided actions have no open effects. A state update axiom formalizes an equational relation between the state at one situation and the state at the successor situation. These equations being symmetric, a state update axiom can be used equally for reasoning forward and backward in time. The versatility of the Fluent Calculus promises it to be applicable to more complex problems of reasoning about actions. For instance, the solution to the Ramification Problem of (Thielscher, 1997), and in particular its axiomatization in the Fluent Calculus, furnishes a ready approach for elaborating the ideas developed in the present paper so as to deal with additional, indirect effects of actions.

The version of the Fluent Calculus we used in this paper differs considerably from its roots (Hölldobler and Schneeberger, 1990) and existing extensions of the latter to actions with indeterminate effects (Brüning et al., 1993; Thielscher, 1994), e.g. in that now the full expressive power of first-order logic is exploited. For a long time, the Fluent Calculus has been viewed exclusively as a close relative of approaches to the Frame Problem which appeal to non-classical logics, namely, linearized versions of, respectively, the connection method (Bibel, 1986; Bibel, 1998) and Gentzen's sequent calculus (Masseron et al., 1993). In (Große et al., 1996), for example, the three approaches have been proved to deliver equivalent solutions to a resource-sensitive variant of STRIPS planning (Fikes and Nilsson, 1971). On the other hand, the expressiveness of the Fluent Calculus in relation to the classical Situation Calculus (McCarthy, 1963) has first been convincingly elaborated in (Thielscher, 1999). The earlier comparison of (Bibel et al., 1989), which links the aforementioned linear connection method to the Situation Calculus, covers only a restricted form of STRIPS domains and thus concerns a mere fraction of the calculi.

Moving from Situation Calculus to Fluent Calculus involves the introduction of the equational theory AC1. While the simple addition of equality axioms may constitute a considerable handicap for theorem proving (Hölldobler, 1989), a variety of efficient constraint solving algorithms have been developed for our particular equational theory (Pacholski and Podelski, 1997). Solving the inferential Frame Problem by means of state update axioms furthermore relies on the fact that the latter cover the entire change an action causes. The price of this is that the number of update axioms is, in the worst case, exponentially larger than the number of single effect axioms. However, this is perfectly acceptable as long as actions have very few effects compared to the overall number of fluents.

The essential motivation for using the Fluent Calculus is that state update axioms provide a solution not only to the representational Frame Problem, since they talk exclusively about effects, but also to the inferential Frame Problem, since one such axiom always specifies the entire relation between two consecutive situations. The inferential aspect of the Frame Problem concerns each single fluent needed by a proof in a situation other than the one where it is given or arises. This holds regardless of whether successor state axioms are used for reasoning forward in time or as a basis for regression (Reiter, 1991). If all fluents are needed in exactly the situations they are given or obtained, then the inferential Frame Problem causes no computational burden at all. The more fluents need to be carried unchanged through many intermediate situation, however, the more valuable is a solution to the inferential Frame Problem.

The restriction to actions without open effects, on the other hand, is inevitable if one aims at an explicit description of the direct effects (Thielscher, 1999). Open effects can only be implicitly specified in state update axioms, as is done in this example axiom (recall effect specification (18)):

$$Bomb(x) \supset \left[\begin{array}{l} State(Do(Explodes(x), s)) = State(s) \circ w \supset \\ \forall f, y \left[\begin{array}{c} \exists z. w = f \circ z \supset \\ f = Destroyed(y) \land Holds(Nearby(x, y), s) \land \neg Holds(f, s) \end{array} \right] \end{array} \right]$$

in which the positive effects of the action, w, is defined rather than explicitly given. It lies in the nature of open effects that a suitable state update axiom provides just an implicit definition of the required update and so does no longer solve the inferential Frame Problem at the point where such an action is performed—but of course it still covers the representational aspect.

AFTERWORD

In 1986, Wolfgang Bibel developed a linearized variant of his classical connection method (Bibel, 1981) in order to tackle both the representational and the inferential aspect of the Frame Problem within logic (Bibel, 1986). Not only must this work be viewed as a precursor of Linear Logic (Girard, 1987; Masseron et al., 1993), also the Fluent Calculus, first introduced in (Hölldobler and Schneeberger, 1990) and so christened in (Bornscheuer and Thielscher, 1997), is closely related to this linear connection method. The affinity of the three formalisms has been emphasized by several formal comparison results proving their essential equivalence for certain classes of planning problems (Große et al., 1996).

Despite, or maybe due to this close relationship, Wolfgang Bibel and I always had, and still have, strong but opposing preferences as regards the linear connection method on the one hand and the Fluent Calculus on the other. The latter stands out against the former, or so my standard argument goes, because it stays entirely within classical logic and thus admits a clear standard semantics and is readily applicable to a variety of important ontological extensions of classical planning. The former allows a most natural and intuitive specification of actions and their effects, or so Wolfgang Bibel usually counters. While this debate is far from being settled, [8] our competition always had fruitful impact on both approaches. It gave rise to the development of Transaction Logic (Bibel, 1998), which roots in the linear connection method but allows to model many further aspects of commonsense reasoning about actions. And the novel version of the Fluent Calculus developed in (Thielscher, 1999) and extended in the present paper is a result of me not being able for years to stop thinking about a more intuitive motivation and appealing syntax for this axiomatization paradigm.

The most remarkable fact is that Wolfgang Bibel was never tempted to exploit his authority nor superior position in our scientific arguments. Despite my restless spirit of opposition I could always count on his support. I owe much to him, and I want to thank him for all of it.

Dresden University of Technology
Germany

NOTES

1. According to (Lin, 1996) and (Shanahan, 1997), this example is due to Ray Reiter.

2. A word on the notation: Predicate and function symbols, including constants, start with a capital letter whereas variables are in lower case, sometimes with sub- or superscripts. Free variables in formulas are assumed universally quantified.

3. The reader may wonder why function " $\circ$ " is not expected to be idempotent, i.e., $\forall x.\, x \circ x = x$, which is yet another property of logical conjunction. The (subtle) reason for this is given below.

4. If actions have additional, indirect effects, then this gives rise to the so-called Ramification Problem; see Section 4.

5. Set κ determines which ones of the effect axioms apply in the state update axiom to be constructed.

6. If either set of fluents is empty, then the respective ϑ_i is the unit element, $\emptyset$.

7. Hence, all fluents of ϑ_α^- are ignored which are already false in s according to condition Δ_2; likewise, all fluents of ϑ_α^+ are ignored which are already true in s.

8. As Wolfgang Bibel says, "Future practice has to determine which of the two will eventually prevail." ((Bibel, 1998), p. 1555)

REFERENCES

Bibel, W. (1981). On Matrices with Connections. *Journal of the ACM*, 28:633+.

Bibel, W. (1986). A deductive solution for plan generation. *New Generation Computing*, 4:115+.

Bibel, W. (1998). Let's plan it deductively! *Artificial Intelligence*, 103(1–2):183+.

Bibel, W., del Cerro, L. F., Fronhöfer, B., and Herzig, A. (1989). Plan generation by linear proofs: on semantics. In *Proc. of the German Workshop on Artificial Intelligence*, pages 49–62. Springer, Informatik Fachberichte 216.

Bornscheuer, S.-E., Thielscher, M. (1997). Explicit and implicit indeterminism: Reasoning about uncertain and contradictory specifications of dynamic systems. *Journal of Logic Programming*, 31(1–3):119+.

Brüning, S., Hölldobler, S., Schneeberger, J., Sigmund, U., and Thielscher, M. (1993). Disjunction in resource-oriented deductive planning. In D. Miller, editor, *Proc. of the International Logic Programming Symposium*, page 670, Vancouver, Canada. MIT Press. (Poster).

Fikes, R. E. and Nilsson, N. J. (1971). STRIPS: A new approach to the application of theorem proving to problem solving. *Artificial Intelligence*, 2:189+.

Girard, J.-Y. (1987). Linear Logic. *Journal of Theoretical Computer Science*, 50(1):1+.

Große, G., Hölldobler, S., and Schneeberger, J. (1996). Linear Deductive Planning. *Journal of Logic and Computation*, 6(2):233+.

Hölldobler, S. (1989). *Foundations of Equational Logic Programming*, volume 353 of *LNAI*. Springer.

Hölldobler, S. and Schneeberger, J. (1990). A new deductive approach to planning. *New Generation Computing*, 8:225+.

Hölldobler, S. and Thielscher, M. (1995). Computing change and specificity with equational logic programs. *Annals of Mathematics and Artificial Intelligence*, 14(1):99+.

Kautz, H. and Selman, B. (1996). Pushing the envelope: Planning, propositional logic, and stochastic search. In Clancey, B. and Weld, D., editors, *Proc. of the AAAI National Conference on Artificial Intelligence*, pages 1194–1201, Portland. MIT Press.

Khalil, H. (1996). *Formalizing the Effects of Actions in First Order Logic*. Diplomarbeit, Intellectics, Dept. of Computer Science, Darmstadt University of Technology.

Lespérance, Y., Levesque, H. J., Lin, F., Marcu, D., Reiter, R., and Scherl, R. B. (1994). A logical approach to high-level robot programming—a progress report. In Kuipers, B., editor, *Control of the Physical World by Intelligent Agents, Papers from the AAAI Fall Symposium*, pages 109–119, New Orleans.

Lin, F. (1996). Embracing causality in specifying the indeterminate effects of actions. In Clancey, B. and Weld, D., editors, *Proc. of the AAAI National Conference on Artificial Intelligence*, pages 670–676, Portland. MIT Press.

Masseron, M., Tollu, C., Vauzielles, J. (1993). Generating plans in linear logic I. Actions as proofs. *Journal of Theoretical Computer Science*, 113:349+.

McCarthy, J. (1958). Programs with Common Sense. In *Proc. of the Symposium on the Mechanization of Thought Processes*, volume 1, pages 77–84, London. (Reprinted in: (McCarthy, 1990)).

McCarthy, J. (1963). *Situations and Actions and Causal Laws*. Stanford Artificial Intelligence Project, Memo 2.

McCarthy, J. (1990). *Formalizing Common Sense*. Ablex. (Edited by V. Lifschitz).

McCarthy, J. and Hayes, P. J. (1969). Some philosophical problems from the standpoint of artificial intelligence. *Machine Intelligence*, 4:463+.

Pacholski, L. and Podelski, A. (1997). Set constraints: a pearl in research on constraints. In G. Smolka, editor, *Proc. of the International Conference on Constraint Programming*, volume 1330 of *LNCS*, pages 549–561. Springer.

Reiter, R. (1991). The frame problem in the situation calculus: A simple solution (sometimes) and a completeness result for goal regression. In Lifschitz, V., editor, *Artificial Intelligence and Mathematical Theory of Computation*, pages 359–380. Academic Press.

Sandewall, E. (1994). *Features and Fluents. The Representation of Knowledge about Dynamical Systems*. Oxford University Press.

Schalkoff, R. (1990). *Artificial Intelligence: An Engineering Approach*. McGraw-Hill.

Shanahan, M. (1996). Robotics and the common sense informatic situation. In Wahlster, W., editor, *Proc. of the European Conference on Artificial Intelligence*, pages 684–688, Budapest, Hungary. John Wiley.

Shanahan, M. (1997). *Solving the Frame Problem: A Mathematical Investigation of the Common Sense Law of Inertia.* MIT Press.

Thielscher, M. (1994). Representing actions in equational logic programming. In Van Hentenryck, P., editor, *Proc. of the International Conference on Logic Programming*, pages 207–224, Santa Margherita Ligure, Italy. MIT Press.

Thielscher, M. (1997). Ramification and causality. *Artificial Intelligence*, 89(1–2):317+.

Thielscher, M. (1999). From situation calculus to fluent calculus: state update axioms as a solution to the inferential frame problem. *Artificial Intelligence*.

CHRISTIAN WAGNER

THE ILLUSION OF KNOWLEDGE

(or Why Data Is More Important than Knowledge)

1. INTRODUCTION

Reports of human expertise instil admiration and awe in us. A skilled expert might be able to play numerous games of chess in parallel (de Groot, 1965) and beat most opponents, or might pinpoint the problem in a machine within seconds or minutes where others have wasted hours without benefit.

Intriguing in these stories is not only the complexity of the problems the experts are able to tackle, but also the speed with which they operate, essentially outperforming their less expert counterparts by a factor of 10 to maybe 100 (Laird et al., 1986, Snoddy, 1926). Of course, differences in the handling of complexity might be explained with differences in knowledge. How can the differences in speed be explained, however? For machines, to achieve 100 times speed improvement, we need either a better architecture, or very different algorithms. As architecture is fixed by human physiology, seemingly, algorithms are responsible for most if not all of the differences. Algorithms, however, are part of a person's knowledge. So again, knowledge seems to be the crucial element. Or is it?

The article attempts to address this question. It will be argued that "routine" expert performance is more closely related to data than to knowledge possessed by the expert, hence creating an "illusion of knowledge". It will further argued that what often is described as "tacit" knowledge might better be categorized as data than as knowledge.

2. TYPES OF TASKS

Expert problem solving and task performance has been studied extensively, and both in terms of process and outcome, distinctive differences between experts and "novices" have been identified. For the purpose of this discussion, we focus on three "task types", where unique expert characteristics have been recognized, and which appear to require very different reasoning capabilities from the expert.

347

S. Hölldobler (ed.), Intellectics and Computational Logic, 347–359.
© 2000 Kluwer Academic Publishers.

2.1. "Routine" Expert Tasks

Widely written about (e.g., Bouwman, 1982, Marchant, 1989, Su and Govindaraj, 1986), and most focused on in this article is the "routine" task performance of experts. Independent of task domain, experts are *fast*, *effective*, and *efficient* in completing tasks they are familiar with. For example, expert programmers (e.g., Vessey 1985) are much faster in finding software bugs than novices, make fewer mistakes (i.e., make the correct diagnosis), and perform the task thoroughly, yet efficiently (i.e., do not get lost in fruitless depth-first search for problem causes).

Routine, repeated performance of the same or very similar task, is important for this level of task performance. This is well illustrated by the "power law of practice" (Snoddy, 1926) which demonstrates the relationship between time taken, accuracy, and number of trials. According to this empirically found law, performance improvements are not linear, but exponential, resulting in possible 10 or even 100 times differences between novices and experts.

It should be noted that experts, while performing a task routinely, may not be able to explain their processing. This has been documented in accounts of the study of experts (Polanyi, 1966), as well as in reports of the knowledge acquisition phase of expert system development (Waterman, 1986). The inability of experts to describe their reasoning has led to protocol studies in which experts are supposed to "think aloud", in essence verbalizing the contents of their short term memory (Ericsson and Simon, 1980). These accounts, however, reveal data, not process information and cannot be seen as evidence that routine task performance is heavily knowledge based.

2.2. Reasoning from First Principles

Reasoning from first principles as an expert skill has been identified both in human information processing, and has been used as a technique in AI (Davis, 1983). In human information processing, reasoning from first (better: general) principles is found when the expert's routine mechanisms fail, or possibly, when the expert is asked to explain his or her reasoning.

Reasoning from first principles is not required in many routine tasks, but it plays nevertheless an important rule in expert reasoning. For example, reports show that when experts cannot find a solution using routine methods, they will then rely on general principles to search for a novel solution. It is also used in scenario creation, for instance, when an expert has to design an "experiment" to help in diagnosing. Using general principles, the expert deduces how the system should perform, to then measure the difference between actual and expected performance. First principles reasoning is also used in the design of "new" machines, as well as to formalize and communicate knowledge (e.g., Polya, 1946).

2.3. Rule Induction and Knowledge Explication

Induction, generalizing from n to the $n+1^{st}$ case, is a fundamental reasoning capability of all humans (as well as other intelligent beings). However, from experts we require not only the ability to generalize, thus using the learning gathered from previous experiences. We also demand their ability to explain the performance, so that their knowledge can be transferred to others, and so that we can have confidence in their judgment. Hence we expect from experts the ability to recognize patterns that exist in the tasks they are performing, and to be able to express ("explicate") them in a way that their performance can be understood and possibly even be replicated by others. By all means, this expert capability seems to be more heavily dependent on knowledge than on data.

3. DATA AND KNOWLEDGE

In order to provide the necessary background to further discuss the contributions of knowledge and data for human expert performance, we now need to clarify the terminology of this article.

Definition 1. (Fact) *A fact is an association between a thing (an entity) and a value which describes a property of that entity, or in other words, a predicate with constants for its arguments (compare Ullman, 1988, p. 99). Facts have truth values (they are either believed to be true or false).*

Example: *My_bank_account contains $4,137.20. My_bank_account is an entity (the name suggests it is a bank account, but it does not have to be). $4137.20 is the value. The property is one of containing.*

The identifying characteristic of facts is that all their information is explicity contained. I.e., bank_account(my, $4137.20), contains all its information explicitly. In contrast, bank_account(X, $4137.20) is not a fact, but an association which states that everyone's bank account contains the said amount (one argument of the predicate is a variable).

Definition 2. (Rule) *A rule is an association (relation, relationship) between entities or between facts. Rules also have truth values. The associations can be of several different types, including implication (IF ... THEN), whole-part relationship (Is-part-of), or categorization (Is-a).*

Example 1 (implication, fact-to-fact): *IF a bank account (entity) has a positive balance (value) THEN that bank account is not overdrawn.*

Example 2 (Is-a): *A savings account is an account.*

Example 3 (Is-part-of): *Transfer of ownership is part of a purchase contract.*

Definition 3. (Data) *Data is a collection of facts.*

The definition of data as a collection of facts is widely used in computer science and information systems. Compare Gallagher (1988, pp. 51-52), Elmasri and Navathe (1989, p. 651), or Missikoff and Wiederhold (1986). It is often differentiated from information, a term frequently used in decision theory to describe whether the data changes decision maker beliefs or actions, i.e., according to Bayes' rule.

Definition 4. (Knowledge) *Knowledge is a collection of associations (rules of some form) and facts.*

Elmasri and Navathe (1989, pp. 650-651) point out that knowledge representation mechanisms "include some mechanisms for inferencing or deducing information from stored data ..." and that they use both "extensional knowledge" (facts) and "intensional knowledge" (i.e., rules), thus echoing the definition. The definition is also in agreement with Date (1990, p. 672). Wiederhold (1984) defines knowledge essentially as associations (constraint rules, procedural rules, application specific rules, but also enterprise directing *facts* and rules).

4. DATA VS. KNOWLEDGE AS THE SOURCE OF EXPERT PERFORMANCE

4.1. Impact of Data vs. Knowledge for Routine Expert Performance

As previously mentioned, the key assumptions of this article is that "routine" expert performance is primarily data driven instead of inference or knowledge driven. A data driven activity would be one that requires only one or a few data retrieval operations, such as pattern matching and result reporting. According to the findings of Card et al. (1983), such an activity should require processing times in the sub-second range, i.e., about .2s for a single "chunk" related operation. In other words, the reasoning activity required to generate the result, regardless of its complexity, would be reflected in the database through extensional, rather than intensional representation. Thus, independent of complexity, results could be generated in short and fairly constant time.

4.1.1. Experiment

To test the assumption, a small experiment was carried out in which subjects had to perform an arithmetic task (addition and multiplication) whose difficulty was varied from routine to higher levels, while performance in terms of time taken and accuracy was monitored. At the simplest level, subjects had to add two numbers of less than 10 ("A2 < 10"). Difficulty was then increased by requiring more numbers to be added (e.g., three or five), by asking subjects to multiply, instead of add, and by increasing the range of numbers. Conceptually, all these tasks are of similar difficulty, and would, completed on a computer, require the same time (for range variation, or add vs. multiply), or linear time increases (for more operands). Not so for our human subjects.

Ten subjects participated in the experiment, all of them highly educated (post-graduate level education). They had to complete 50 calculations for each activity. Table 1 summarizes the results for processing times, Table 2 for accuracy rates. Table 1 lists calculation times (in seconds) for each subject by activity, together with mean and standard deviation. For example, subject S1 spent .39 seconds on average (based on 50 calculations) to add two numbers between 1 and 9, and .85s per calculation to multiply two numbers from 1 to 9.

	S1	S2	S3	S4	S5	S6	S7	S8	S9	S10	Mean	S. Dev.
A2 < 10	0.39	0.29		0.11	0.06	0.19	0.20				0.21	0.11
A3 < 10	1.15	1.14	1.19	0.79	0.91	0.92	0.83	0.70	1.50	0.49	0.96	0.27
A5 < 10									6.26		6.26	
M2 < 10	0.85	0.36			0.37				0.56		0.53	0.20
M2 < 20			3.55	2.70	2.46		4.72	4.42		5.69	3.92	1.14

Table 1 Processing Times for Calculation Exercise.

Table 2 lists accuracy rates. An accuracy rate of 1.00 indicates that 50 out of 50 calculations were completed correctly. Table 2 contains two additional rows, showing accuracy rates and frequency for time consuming calculations (exceeding 5 seconds). For example, subject S3 has an accuracy rate of .79 for all calculations which took more than 5 seconds. S3 needed more than 5 seconds to complete a calculation in 15 out of 50 situations.

S1	S2	S3	S4	S5	S6	S7	S8	S9	S10	Mean	S. Dev.
A2 < 10	0.98	0.96		1.00	1.00	0.96	1.00				0.98	0.02
A3 < 10	0.94	0.88	0.98	0.94	1.00	0.88	1.00	0.98	0.96	1.00	0.96	0.04
A5 < 10									0.96		0.96	0.00
M2 < 10	0.94	0.97			0.96				0.96		0.96	0.01
M2 < 20			0.84	0.86	1.00		0.96	0.90		0.94	0.92	0.06
> 5s			0.79	0.86	1.00		0.90	0.80		0.80	0.86	0.07
Qty >5s			15	12	12		18	12		12	13.50	2.29

Table 2 Accuracy Rates for Calculation Exercise.

4.1.2. Interpretation

The results indicate that more complex tasks require more time and reduce accuracy. That is not surprising. Surprising is that task times rise disproportionally when compared to the "absolute" difficulty of the tasks. Adding three numbers instead of two resulted in a four-fold calculation time increase (from .21s to .96s, statistically significant, $p < .00005$, t-test). Multiplying two numbers in the range from 1 to 19 resulted in an eight-fold time increase in calculation times (from .53s to 3.92s, statistically significant, p<.0006, t-test).

Can the calculation time increase be explained through subjects' use of different algorithms, or different knowledge for different calculation tasks? Table 3 helps answering this question. Table 3 shows times taken by subjects for select calculation tasks. For example, subject S5 needed 0.8s to multiply 10 times 19.

S3		S4		S5		S7		S8		S10	
Ops	T	Ops	T	Ops	T	Ops	T	Ops	T	Ops	T
7 11	1.04	10 20	1.19	10 19	0.80	*11 11*	*0.94*	6 5	0.69	8 5	0.41
11 11	*1.04*	*11 11*	*1.19*	13 11	3.00	4 6	0.94	*11 11*	*0.69*	*11 11*	*0.41*
11 12	4.14	11 17	5.99	*11 11*	*3.40*	11 17	3.44	11 12	2.99	20 11	2.81
16 16	5.84			11 17	8.40	19 11	7.94	17 11	2.99	11 15	3.11
18 18	6.24	19 11	5.90	17 18	18.70			16 16	6.29	18 18	11.5

Table 3   Calculation Times for Select Problems.

Note that each subject had to compute 11x11. For all but one subject (S5), this was an easy task, requiring comparatively very little time. E.g., S7 needed the same time to calculate 11x11 as for 4x6. The only plausible explanation for this result is that subjects were able to recall the result, and that they did not have to compute. If a subject had to compute via normal decomposition, then 11x11 should have been about as time consuming as 11x12 (see S3 or S8 for the difference). If subjects had used a binomial to generate the result, then 16x16 should have been about as time consuming as 11x11 (see S3 and S8 for differences). Subject 4 provides further insight into time required for computation by decomposition. A more detailed analysis of protocol data reveals that S4 calculated 19x11 obtaining a wrong result, namely 201 (10x19 + 1x11) instead of 209 (10x19+1x19), suggesting calculation through decomposition. That computation required 5.90s.

We conclude that the highest levels of performance, reflected by fastest computation times and best accuracy, are achieved through data retrieval, not inference. In other words, data based processes, not knowledge based processes resulted in best performance. This does not imply, however, that experts don't use algorithms or heuristics, nor that use of these heuristics is inefficient or ineffective. On the contrary, even in the arithmetic exercise, without the ability to recall a result, subjects had to use algorithms to compute. And, more efficient algorithms, i.e., powerful decomposition heuristics, could lead to better calculation results. Use of heuristics is well documented in the research on expert vs. novice problem solving behavior (e.g., Albert et al., 1986), as is the ability of experts to reason from first (general) principles in unfamiliar problem situations. However, the use of data based techniques is also well documented. For example, given a diagnosis task, experts will invoke a "checklist" of typical problem causes and then focus in their diagnosis on eliminating causes that do not fit with observations (e.g., Su and Govindaraj, 1986, Bouwman, 1982). Here again, a data based technique is used for problem solving efficiency and reliability. However, if that technique fails, i.e., because all potential problem causes are eliminated during analysis, then the expert again has to rely on reasoning from first principles to solve the problem (in a much more slowly manner).

More specifically, there is great value in the ability of experts to generate solutions through inferences from general principles. Yet the real value of experts lies in their ability to quickly recall the result for a large number of scenarios, many of which appear as complex problems to novice problem solvers. This ability allows master chess players to make very quick decisions on a chess board that looks highly complex to the novice, or to quickly determine a company's financial strength from a look at its balance sheet.

An interesting additional observation can be made. There appear to be three performance levels, identified by different time requirements. First, there are tasks whose completion takes a short and almost constant amount of time (e.g., about .1 ... .2s), thus indicating a single (retrieval type performance). Second, there are tasks which take longer, but whose performance reflect a few multiples of the "retrieval task" times. Performance at this level might be best compared to "reflexive thinking" (Shastri and Ajjanagadde, 1993). Finally, there are tasks which require much longer time, require "reflective thinking", and possibly result in "thrashing" behavior or no solution. Differentiation between these task types will, however, require much more detailed analysis and goes beyond the scope of this article.

4.2. Solution Finding vs. Explanation

Waterman (1986) provides a beautiful example of knowledge acquisition, where an insurance claims expert is interviewed by a knowledge engineer to elicit and formalize the expert's knowledge. Waterman's expert, after reading the case detail, quickly gives an estimate of financial liability. In the then following discussion between expert and knowledge engineer, the expert explains his "reasoning", describing algorithms and heuristics used, as well as assumptions made. In the end, the lengthy computation instruction results in a financial liability figure almost identical to the value determined by the expert prior to explaining it (difference of about 1%).

The example illustrates two of the expert abilities discussed previously. First, the ability to quickly generate a solution to a "routine' problem. Second, the ability to generate the result in "non-routine" mode, through inference from general principles and heuristics. (Of course, the ability to explain the solution based on general principles implies that the expert has previously embarked on a process of rule induction and explication, thus demonstrating also the ability to explicate knowledge).

Another intriguing point of Waterman's example is that the expert's initial estimate and the result obtained from inference are almost, but not entirely, identical. This strongly suggests that the expert used two different methods to find the solution. In other words, the expert was not rapidly and quietly completing all the calculations he later explained to the knowledge engineer. Instead, he first used a very efficient (and likely heavily data based) process, that, because of the expert's experience, in its result closely matched the later reasoning process.

4.3. Data Based Reasoning Associated with Human Heuristics and Biases

An interesting piece of evidence for the importance of data based reasoning comes from the study of decision making heuristics and biases. This research looks at decision maker deviations from rational behavior and their explanation. Numerous such heuristics and corresponding biases have been found and repeatedly validated through empirical study.

One type of behavior (Tversky and Kahneman, 1983) was an incorrect assessment of the likelihood of probabilistic events. To determine a likelihood, subjects would not use analytic (rule based) forms of probability assessment, but would go by the number of occurrences they were able to recall from memory (a data based approach, called *availability heuristic*).

Illustration: *Subjects were asked to estimate the occurrence, within four pages of a novel, of words of the form ____ing. Another group of subjects was asked to estimate the occurrence of words of the form ____n_ Estimates for _ing words were higher than for _n_ words, although the former are a subset of the latter. However, since it is easier for subjects to recall words ending in _ing (see Tversky and Kahneman for empirical proof), their estimates were reversed.*

Another empirically verified type of behavior was the use of the simple heuristic "anchoring and adjustment" (Tversky and Kahneman, 1982, p. 14). Using this heuristic, a decision maker would find a solution not by deriving it from first principles, but by selecting a known, closest case to fit the problem (anchor), and then adjusting for differences between the present problem and the one retrieved from memory.

Example: *Suppose a person knows the distance between earth and moon (about 384,000km), but not the distance between earth and sun. Asked about the distance to the sun, the person will use the known distance as an anchor, and will adjust (i.e., add some distance), and adjust for differences between the two objects relationship to the earth. A typical estimate then might be 1 million, or maybe 10 million km.*

Decision maker biases of this kind were found among decision makers, regardless of their expertise, as a "natural" behavior. Both demonstrate reasoning that is heavily data based, with little additional knowledge based processing.

4.4. Reasoning with Tacit (Implicit) Knowledge

In recent years, tacit knowledge has received increased attention as a source of highest level expertise. Nonaka and Takeuchi (1995) for instance discusses the role of tacit knowledge in organizational knowledge creation and considers it a source of competitive advantage. The concept of tacit knowledge, however, was first proposed by Polanyi (1966). Polanyi's views about tacit knowledge can be stated as follows.

Definition 5. (Tacit Knowledge) *A set of facts and rules, of which only the resulting (i.e., implied) facts are observable by the knowledge owner. The resulting component, called Term 2, is considered "specifyably known." The unobservable component (Term 1) is considered "tacitly known".*

Example 1: *A loan officer reviews the facts of a loan application and rejects the application. Asked "why did you reject it?" she cannot give a meaningful explanation ("it did not warrant acceptance"), because she is not aware why he rejected it. Term 2 (specifyably known) - loan rejection, (fact).*

Term 1 (tacitly known) - facts, such as monthly income, monthly debt service, rule stating "reject an application if monthly debt service exceeds 20% of monthly income."

Example 2: *After completing a job interview, the interviewing manager concludes that the job applicant was lying to her, but is unaware how she came to that conclusion ("it's just a hunch").*

Term 2 (specifyably known) - the applicant was lying (fact).

Term 1 (tacitly known/observed) - the applicant rubbed her ear-lobes repeatedly during the interview (fact), increased face-touching is a sign of deception (rule).

4.5. Interpreting Tacit Knowledge and Knowledge Explication

For the purpose of our argument, two questions are particularly relevant. First, is there tacit knowledge, and second, is it best described as knowledge or as data?

The first question can be positively answered. For example, in several experiments, Lewicky et al. (1987, 1988) found that subjects were able to improve their performance in cognitive tasks over thousands of trials, but were unable to explain the rule that governed their performance, even when offered US$100 rewards. In another study, Reber and Lewis (1977) found that through task performance subjects become better at the task as well as better in explaining their performance (explication), however that their performance increase surpasses their improvement in explaining the performance. In yet another study, Mathews at al. (1989) demonstrated empirically that when a subject group, while learning a task, explained its knowledge to a control group, the control group performed at about half the level of accuracy of the first group. This suggests the existence of some hidden, not expressed knowledge among the experimental group.

The question of knowledge versus data has been empirically addressed in a study by Reber et al. (1980). This study found that "knowing the rule" hindered subjects' task performance compared to simple pattern matching performance. Perruchet et al. (1990) further add to the evidence for data driven performance.

In summary, then, tacit "knowledge" exhibits characteristics related closely to those discussed concerning other aspects of expert performance. Experts possess tacit knowledge, likely learnt in the course of many trials of task performance. This knowledge appears to be represented in data patterns that can be efficiently (fast) and effectively (goal achieving) invoked by the expert. When asked to explicate their "knowledge" experts may or may not be able to do, but even if they can, their ability to describe their "knowledge" will lack behind their actual task performance.

4.6. Machine versus Human Reasoning

The above discussion has focused largely on human expert reasoning, and has drawn conclusions based on the behavioural and functional characteristics of human reasoning. Bibel (1988), however, made similar observations for automated deduction. He points out that despite significant advances in logical inference speed, no significant gains were made in finding new proofs to old problems, in fact that simple problems can pose significant difficulty to these automated reasoners. Bibel identifies three causes: too simple control regimes, poor expressive power, and badly understood human reasoning (resulting in inadequate problem representation).

One of Bibel's proposed solutions to the problem is "reduction", that is, finding an alternate representation, where simple algorithms (i.e., a simple do-loop) apply, which possibly can be carried out in parallel. That argument relates to the one made earlier for human reasoning. Where in machine reasoning the solution path might be "find alternate representation, then use simple algorithm for that representation", for humans we may suggest "find alternate representation, then use table lookup (or pre-compiled solution)". In that context, Hölldobler (1990) points out that the reduction technique, combined with parallel processing of isolated connections, can lead to a very significant decrease in processing time, comparable with the time differential that exists between reflective and reflexive reasoning (Shastri and Ajjanagadde, 1993).

5. CONCLUSIONS

The discussion has provided several arguments indicating that for humans (and possibly machines), data based performance is significantly more important than knowledge based performance. This is true for "routine" expert task performance (where the processing can be explained), and for tasks where we rely on experts' tacit "knowledge" (where the processing cannot be explained). It appears that expert performance for both task types relies on learning "patterns of co-occurrence and covariation" (Reber, 1993) some of which can be explained in rule form by the expert and some of which cannot be explained. The expert will know more rules and may be able to furnish them "after the fact" to explain prior task performance (compare de Groot, 1965), but will know exceedingly more data patterns which are the true source of his or her expertise. In that sense again, understanding one's own knowledge and reasoning in terms of supposedly applied rules, is an illusion.

One might conclude then that if (human) expertise stems from data instead of knowledge, building intelligent machines that rely heavily on knowledge based processes is fruitless. Not so. After all, the reasoning characteristics of people and computers are different. People are very slow in processing, but extremely efficient in pattern matching and data recall. Computers have almost the opposite performance characteristics, and — with every new generation — are gaining particularly in their processing performance. Hence, processing mechanisms such as deductive reasoning, which are not very appropriate for people to carry out, can be very appropriate for computers. This appears to be relevant especially when an approach is chosen that combines problem reformulation with use of relatively simple algorithms.

Furthermore, the inability of human experts to explain their reasoning through rules, does not mean that rules cannot explain it. Hence, application areas for machine reasoning exist both in infering rules from data (data mining), and in then using those rules to generate higher levels of machine based expertise. Thus, one of the key application areas for machine intelligence will be the area of data mining techniques, in order to better explain expertise that otherwise cannot be explained. Similarly, self-training artificial neural networks, even though they do not "understand" the patterns they are representing, seem an appropriate area to better approximate expert performance.

And yet, in absence of a more formal, knowledge based, understanding of human expert performance, the most beneficial information systems support may come from better data management, data representation, and data retrieval methods. Therefore, the best way to create higher levels of performance in machines may come from databases, combined with case based reasoning tools and truth maintenance systems.

City University of Hong Kong,
Kowloon, Hong Kong

REFERENCES

Albert, D.S., Munson, R., and Resnik, M.D. Reasoning in Medicine, *Johns Hopkins University Press*, 1988.

Andreasen, M.M. "The Use of Systematic Design in Practice". In Yoshikawa, H., *Design and Synthesis*, Elsevier, 1985.

Bibel, W. "Advanced Methods in Automated Deduction". In Siekmann, J. *Advanced Topics in Artificial Intelligence*, Springer, 1988, 41-59.

Bouwman, M.J. "The Use of Accounting Information: Expert versus Novice Behavior". In Ungson, G.R. and Braunstein, D.N. *Decision Making: An Interdisciplinary Inquiry*, Kent, 1982.

Card, S.K., Moran, T.P., and Newell, A. *The Psychology of Human-Computer Interaction*, Lawrence Erlbaum Associates, 1983.

Date, C.J. *An Introduction to Database Systems*, Addison Wesley, 1990.

de Groot, A.D. *Thought and Choice in Chess*, Mouton, 1965.

Davis, R. "Reasoning from First Principles in Electronic Troubleshooting". *International Journal of Man-Machine Studies*, 19, 1983, 403-423.

Ericsson, K.A. and Simon, H.A. "Verbal Reports as Data". *Psychological Review*, 87, 3, May 1980, 215-251.

Gallagher, J.P. *Knowledge Systems for Business: Integrating Expert Systems and MIS*, Prentice Hall, 1988.

Elmasri, R. and Navathe, S. *Fundamentals of Database Systems*, Benjamin/Cummings, 1989.

Hölldobler, S. "On the Artificial Intelligence Paradox". *Behavioral and Brain Sciences*, 1993, 463-464.

Hölldobler, S. "A Structured Connectionist Unification Algorithm". *Proceedings of the AAAI National Conference on Artificial Intelligence*, 1990, 587-593.

Lewicky, P., Czyzewska, M., and Hoffman, H. "Unconscious Acquisition of Complex Procedural Knowledge". Journal of Experimental Psychology: Learning, Memory, and Cognition, 13, 1987, 523-530.

Lewicky, P., Hill, T., and Bizot, E. "Acquisition of Procedural Knowledge about a Pattern of Stimuli that Cannot Be Articulated". *Cognitive Psychology*, 20, 1988, 24-37.

Laird, J., Rosenbloom, P., and Newell, A. Universal Subgoaling and Chunking, *Kluwer Academic Publishers*, 1986.

Marchant, G. "Analogical Reasoning and Hypothesis Generation in Auditing". *The Accounting Review*, 64, 3, 1989, 500-513.

Mathews, R.C., Buss, R.R., Chinn, R., Stanley, W.B., Blanchard-Fields, F., Cho, R.-J., and Druhan, B. "The Role of Implicit and Explicit Processes in Learning from Examples: A Synergistic Effect". *Journal of Experimental Psychology: Learning, Memory, and Cognition*, 15, 1989, 1083-1100.

Missikoff, M. and Wiederhold, G. "Toward a Unified Approach for Expert and Database Systems", in Kerschberg, L. (ed.), *Expert Database Systems* (*Proceedings of the First International Workshop on Expert Database Systems 1984*), Benjamin/Cummings, 1986.

Newell, A. and Simon, H.A. *Human Problem Solving*, Prentice Hall, 1972.

Nonaka, I. and Takeuchi, H. *The Knowledge Creating Company: How Japanese Companies Create the Dynamics of Innovation*, Oxford University Press, 1995.

Perruchet, P., Gallego, J., and Savy, I. "A Critical Reappraisal of the Evidence for Unconscious Abstraction of Deterministic Rules in Complex Experimental Situation". *Cognitive Psychology*, 22, 1990, 493-516.

Polanyi, M. *The Tacit Dimension*, Doubleday, 1966.

Polya, G. *How to Solve It*, Princeton University Press, 1946.

Reber, A.S. *Implicit Learning and Tacit Knowledge*, Oxford University Press, 1993.

Reber, A.S., Kassin, S.M., Lewis, S., and Cantor, G.W. "On the Relationship between Implicit and Explicit Modes in the Learning of a Complex Rule Structure". *Journal of Experimental Psychology: Human Learning and Memory*, 6, 1980, 492-502.

Reber, A.S. and Lewis, S. "Toward a Theory of Implicit Learning: The Analysis of the Form and Structure of a Body of Tacit Knowledge". *Cognition*, 5, 1977, 333-361.

Shastri, L. and Ajjanagadde, V. "From Simple Associations to Systematic Reasoning: A Connectionist Representation of Rules, Variables and Dynamic Bindings Using Temporal Synchrony". *Behavioral and Brain Sciences*, 1993, 417-451.

Snoddy, G. S. "Learning and Stability". *Journal of Applied Psychology*, 10, 1926, 1-36.

Su, Y.D. and Govindaraj, T. "Fault Diagnosis in Large Dynamic System Experiments on a Training Simulator". *IEEE Transaction on Systems, Man, and Cybernetics*, 16, 1, 129-141.

Tversky, A. and Kahneman, D. "Extensional vs. Intuitive Reasoning: The Conjunction Fallacy in Probability Judgment". *Psychological Review*, 1983, 293-315.

Tversky, A., Kahneman, D. "Judgment under Uncertainty: Heuristics and Biases". In Kahneman, D., Slovic, P., and Tversky, A. *Judgment under Uncertainty: Heuristics and Biases*, Cambridge University Press, 1982.

Ullman, J.D. *Principles of Database and Knowledge-Base Systems*, Vol. 1, Computer Science Press, 1988.

Vessey, I. "Expertise in Debugging Computer Programs: A Process Analysis". *International Journal of Man-Machine Studies*, 23, 1985, 459-494.

Waterman, D.A. *A Guide to Expert Systems*, Addison-Wesley, 1986.

Wiederhold, G. "Knowledge and Database Management", *IEEE Software*, January 1984.

CHRISTOPH WALTHER

CRITERIA FOR TERMINATION

1. INTRODUCTION

Proving the termination of algorithms is one of the challenges in program verification. Termination proofs can be quite complicated, e.g. proving the termination of McCarthy's 91-function

function $f91(x\!:\!\mathsf{nat})\!:\!\mathsf{nat} \Leftarrow$
    if $\ x > 100$
        then $x - 10$
        else $\ f91(f91(x+11))$
    fi

or Takeuchi's function

function $tak(x,y,z\!:\!\mathsf{nat})\!:\!\mathsf{nat} \Leftarrow$
    if $\ x \leq y$
        then y
        else $\ tak(tak(x-1,y,z), tak(y-1,z,x), tak(z-1,x,y))$
    fi

require a sophisticated argumentation, cf. (Manna, 1974; Moore, 1979; Feferman, 1991; Knuth, 1991), and for other algorithms as e.g.

function $col(x\!:\!\mathsf{nat})\!:\!\mathsf{nat} \Leftarrow$
    if $\ x \leq 1$
        then x
        else if $\ even(x)$
                then $col(x/2)$
                else $\ col(3x+1)$
        fi
    fi

(attributed to Collatz) termination is an open problem for more than 50 years (Gardner, 1983). On the other hand, proof procedures exist which verify the termination of "standard" procedures for arithmetic functions, as e.g.

S. Hölldobler (ed.), *Intellectics and Computational Logic*, 361–386.
© 2000 *Kluwer Academic Publishers.*

function $gcd(x, y : \text{nat}) : \text{nat} \Leftarrow$
    if $y = 0$
      then x
      else if $x \geq y$
           then $gcd(x - y, y)$
           else if $x = 0$
               then y
               else $gcd(x, y - x)$
              fi
        fi
  fi,

for sorting, or for operations on trees and graphs etc. without any human advice (Walther, 1994b; Giesl, 1995; Giesl et al., 1998). Hence termination can be proved in a uniform way in some cases at least.[1]

In this paper we illustrate which problems must be solved for proving the termination of an algorithm. We formulate some sufficient criteria and demonstrate their success and failure by examples. We also define classes of algorithms by simple syntactic requirements, whose termination usually is easier to verify compared to the general case.

Informally, the termination of an algorithm means that each computation involving the algorithm halts after finitely many steps. A computation of a machine M is modelled by a function eval which maps *expressions* of a program into *values* of the machine. The function eval is called the *interpreter* of M and is formally given as a partial function eval : EXPR $\mapsto$ VAL, where VAL is the set of all values of M and EXPR denotes the set of expressions of a program P, consisting of calls of procedures defined by P as well as calls of *base operations* provided by the machine M.

We need some *syntax* to represent *values*, *expressions* and *programs*, and we use standard notions of predicate logic, cf. e.g. (Gallier, 1986), and term rewriting, cf. e.g. (Avenhaus, 1995; Baader and Nipkow, 1998), for that purpose. In particular, we write $\mathcal{T}(\Sigma, \mathcal{V})_s$ for the set of *many-sorted terms* of sort s over some S-sorted signature Σ for function symbols, a set $\mathcal{V}$ of variable symbols and a set S of sort symbols, where $S = \{\text{nat}, \text{bool}\}$ throughout the paper. $\mathcal{T}(\Sigma)_s$ abbreviates the set of all *ground terms* of sort s. We sometimes write terms as strings, i.e. $f s_1 \ldots s_n$ is written instead of $f(s_1, \ldots, s_n)$, and we use $\mathcal{T}(\Sigma, \mathcal{V})_w$ etc. as a shorthand notation for the cartesian product $\mathcal{T}(\Sigma, \mathcal{V})_{s_1} \times \ldots \times \mathcal{T}(\Sigma, \mathcal{V})_{s_k}$, where $w = s_1 \ldots s_k \in S^+$.

For sake of simplicity, we assume a machine M which operates on *natural numbers* and *boolean values* only.[2] Natural numbers are represented by the nullary base operation 0 (for zero) and the unary base operation $succ$ denoting the successor function. So natural numbers are formally given by the set $\mathcal{T}(\{0, succ\})_{nat} = \{0, succ(0), succ(succ(0)), \ldots \}$ of ground terms over 0 and $succ$ and we use $\{true, false\}$ as the set of boolean values. Subsequently, we write $\mathcal{C}_{nat}$ as an abbreviation for $\mathcal{T}(\{0, succ\})_{nat}$, $\mathcal{C}_{bool}$ as an abbreviation for $\{true, false\}$, and we use $\mathcal{C} := \mathcal{C}_{nat} \cup \mathcal{C}_{bool}$ instead of VAL to denote the set of all values on which M operates.

The machine M offers 4 additional base operations, viz. the predecessor operation $pred$: nat $\to$ nat, a test operation $zero$: nat $\to$ bool, and two conditionals if_s : bool $\times s \times s \to s$, where $s \in S$. $\Sigma(M) := \{0, succ, true, false, pred, zero, if_{nat}, if_{bool}\}$ is the set of all names of base operations known to the machine M.

We now extend our development by a concept for *functional programs* to be executed by M: A *functional procedure* F is an expression of the form **function** $f(x_1: s_1, \ldots, x_n: s_n):s \Leftarrow R_f$ such that the *formal parameters* $x_1, \ldots, x_n$ of F are distinct variables of sort $s_1, \ldots, s_n$ respectively and the *body* R_f of F is a term of sort s containing only variable symbols from $\{x_1, \ldots, x_n\}$.

A sequence $P = \langle F_1, \ldots, F_k \rangle$ of functional procedures **function** f_j ... is a *functional program* iff for each $j \in \{1, \ldots, k\}$ the body of F_j contains only function symbols from $\Sigma(M) \cup \{f_1, \ldots, f_j\}$. Due to this requirement, each functional procedure F_j is defined only by using base operations, by previously defined procedures $F_1, \ldots, F_{j-1}$, and by *recursion*, as f_j may occur in the body of F_j. Note that our requirement for functional programs excludes *mutual recursion*. We let $\Sigma(P)$ denote the set of all names of base operations plus all names of operations defined by a functional program P, i.e. $\Sigma(P) := \Sigma(M) \cup \{f_1, \ldots, f_k\}$. Hence the set $\mathcal{T}(\Sigma(P))$ of ground terms represents the set of expressions EXPR$(P) := \mathcal{T}(\Sigma(P))$ of the functional program P, to be evaluated by the interpreter eval to the values of M.[3]

For instance, $P = \langle F_{plus} \rangle$ is a functional program, where the functional procedure F_{plus} is defined as

function $plus(x:\text{nat}, y:\text{nat}):\text{nat} \Leftarrow$
$\quad if_{nat}(zero(x), y, succ(plus(pred(x), y)))$.

To ease readability, we use abbreviations like "$x = 0$" for "$zero(x)$", "n" for "$succ^{(n)}(0)$", "**if** b **then** t_1 **else** t_2 **fi**" for "$if_s(b, t_1, t_2)$", "$1 + x$" for "$succ(x)$" and "$x - 1$" for "$pred(x)$". We also use the standard mathematical notation for function symbols if appropriate. E.g.

function $times(x, y:\text{nat}):\text{nat} \Leftarrow$
$\quad$ **if** $x = 0$
$\qquad$ **then** 0
$\qquad$ **else** $times(x - 1, y) + y$
$\quad$ **fi**

defines a functional procedure F_{times} and

function $ge(x, y:\text{nat}):\text{bool} \Leftarrow$
$\quad$ **if** $y = 0$
$\qquad$ **then** $true$
$\qquad$ **else** **if** $x = 0$
$\qquad\qquad$ **then** $false$
$\qquad\qquad$ **else** $ge(x - 1, y - 1)$
$\qquad$ **fi**
$\quad$ **fi**

defines a procedure F_{ge} in a more readable notation, and $\langle F_{plus}, F_{times}, F_{ge} \rangle$ is a functional program.

2. OPERATIONAL SEMANTICS AND TERMINATION

Having defined the syntax of the kind of functional programs we are concerned with, we now provide a semantics for these programs. This is achieved by defining a so-called *evaluation calculus*, i.e. a calculus whose inference rules stipulate how an *expression* from $T(\Sigma(P))$ is transformed step by step, such that eventually a *value* from C is obtained (sometimes):

Definition 1. (Evaluation Calculus for M)
Let $s \in S$, $t, r \in T(\Sigma(P))_{nat}$, $p_1, p_2 \in T(\Sigma(P))_s$, $b, b' \in T(\Sigma(P))_{bool}$, $P = \langle \ldots, \mathbf{function}\, f(x_1:s_1,..,x_n:s_n):s \Leftarrow R_f, \ldots \rangle$ *and* $f(u_1,\ldots,u_n) \in T(\Sigma(P))$. *Then the evaluation calculus for the machine* M *is given by the following inference rules:*

(1) $\dfrac{succ(t)}{succ(r)}$, if $t \to r$; (2) $\dfrac{pred(0)}{0}$

(3) $\dfrac{pred(succ(t))}{t}$, if $t \in C_{nat}$; (4) $\dfrac{pred(t)}{pred(r)}$, if $t \to r$;

(5) $\dfrac{zero(0)}{true}$ (6) $\dfrac{zero(succ(t))}{false}$, if $t \in C_{nat}$;

(7) $\dfrac{zero(t)}{zero(r)}$, if $t \to r$; (8) $\dfrac{if_s(true, p_1, p_2)}{p_1}$

(9) $\dfrac{if_s(false, p_1, p_2)}{p_2}$ (10) $\dfrac{if_s(b, p_1, p_2)}{if_s(b', p_1, p_2)}$, if $b \to b'$;

(11) $\dfrac{f(u_1,\ldots,u_n)}{\sigma(R_f)}$, *where* σ *is a substitution defined as* $\sigma = \{x_1/u_1,\ldots,x_n/u_n\}$.

We call $\to$ *the evaluation relation of* M, *where* $t \to r$ *holds iff some inference rule*

$$\dfrac{t}{r}$$, *if* $B(t,r)$;

exists, such that the application requirement $B(t,r)$ *is satisfied.*

The terms $u_1, \ldots, u_n$ in rule (11) are the *actual parameters* of the *procedure call* $f(u_1, \ldots, u_n)$. Here procedure calls are implemented by the parameter passing discipline *call-by-name* (sometimes also called *call-by-need*), and the corresponding evaluation strategy is called *lazy evaluation*. This is because an actual parameter only is evaluated if its value really is required for the evaluation of a procedure call, cf. Section 4[4].

We use the evaluation calculus to compute values from expressions of a functional program, and e.g. 2 is obtained by an evaluation of the procedure call $plus(1,1)$, because $plus(1,1) \to^* 2$.[5]

The evaluation relation is *deterministic* and all values are *minimal* w.r.t. $\to$. In addition, $\to$ is *well founded* (or *noetherian*), if restricted to expressions from $\mathcal{T}(\Sigma(\mathsf{M}))$:[6]

Theorem 2. *For all* $t, r_2, r_2 \in \mathcal{T}(\Sigma(P))$:

(i) $r_1 = r_2$, *if* $r_1 \leftarrow t \to r_2$,

(ii) $t \notin C$ *iff* $t \to r$ *for some* $r \in \mathcal{T}(\Sigma(P))$, *and*

(iii) $(\mathcal{T}(\Sigma(\mathsf{M})), \to)$ *is a well-founded set.*

Proof: (i), (ii) By structural induction upon t. (iii) If $t \to r$ and $t \in \mathcal{T}(\Sigma(\mathsf{M}))$, then r has strictly less symbols than t, as proved by structural induction upon t. $\square$

As a consequence of Theorem 2, for each expression $t \in \mathcal{T}(\Sigma(P))$ at most one value $q \in C$ exists, such that $t \to^* q$. Hence we define the interpreter eval of M as the *partial* function eval : $\mathcal{T}(\Sigma(P)) \mapsto C$ satisfying $\mathrm{eval}(t) = q$ iff $t \to^* q$.[7] This means that the machine M comes up with the result $\mathrm{eval}(t)$, as e.g. 2, if called with an expression $t \in \mathcal{T}(\Sigma(P))$, as e.g. $plus(1,1)$, provided the evaluation of t succeeds.

The interpreter eval only is a *partial* function, since by the rule for procedure calls, $(\mathcal{T}(\Sigma(P)), \to)$ generally is not a well-founded set. For instance, $P = \langle \ldots,$ function $inner(x:\mathrm{nat}):\mathrm{nat} \Leftarrow inner(1+x), \ldots \rangle$ may rise an *infinite* evaluation $inner(0) \to inner(1) \to inner(2) \to \ldots$ of $inner(0)$. This means that the evaluation of $inner(0)$ does not succeed, and we write $\mathrm{eval}(inner(0)) = \propto$ in such a case.

However, the interpreter is a *total* function if restricted to expressions from the *empty* program. So a non-value expression t always can be evaluated, if t consists of calls to base operations only, cf. Theorem 2(iii). For certain functional programs, as e.g. $\langle F_{plus}, F_{times}, F_{ge} \rangle$, this property may also hold, and we call a functional program *terminating*, if infinite evaluations are impossible:

Definition 3. (Termination of Functional Programs) *A functional program* P *terminates iff* $(\mathcal{T}(\Sigma(P)), \to)$ *is a well-founded set.*

Since our development excludes mutual recursion, the termination of a functional program can be expressed by a notion of termination for *functional procedures*:

Definition 4. (Termination of Functional Procedures) *Let* $P = P' \oplus \langle F \rangle$ *be a functional program, such that* P' *terminates. Then the* functional procedure F terminates *iff* P *terminates*.

By this definition, the termination of a functional program $P = \langle F_1, \ldots, F_k \rangle$ can be proved by considering the functional procedures of P step by step, starting from the empty program. All we need is a requirement for the termination of a functional procedure F, where we may already assume the termination of the other functional procedures called in the body of F.

Subsequently we aim to develop some criteria for the termination of functional procedures in order to gain some insights into the difficulty of proving the termination of functional programs.

3. DENOTATIONAL SEMANTICS OF FUNCTIONAL PROGRAMS

Denotational semantics provide an alternative approach to the *operational* semantics of functional programs defined by the interpreter eval. Since denotational semantics uses semantical notions of first-order predicate logic, it is in particular useful for our purpose: For each functional program P, we consider a $\Sigma(P)$-algebra $D_P = (\mathcal{D}, \delta_P)$, where the carrier $\mathcal{D}$ of D_P is separated into the sets $\mathcal{D}_{nat} := \mathcal{C}_{nat} \cup \{\perp_{nat}\}$ and $\mathcal{D}_{bool} := \mathcal{C}_{bool} \cup \{\perp_{bool}\}$. This means that the carrier of D_P consists of the values of the machine M plus two symbols denoting *undefinedness* for each sort. The interpretation function δ_P associates each function symbol $f : s_1 \times \ldots \times s_n \to s$ from $\Sigma(P)$ with a (total) *monotonic* function $\delta_{P,f} : \mathcal{D}_{s_1} \times \ldots \times \mathcal{D}_{s_n} \to \mathcal{D}_s$.[8]

In case of base operations g, $\delta_{P,g}$ is explicitly given, as e.g. the interpretation of $pred$ is defined by $\delta_{P,pred}(0) := 0$, $\delta_{P,pred}(succ(q)) := q$ and $\delta_{P,pred}(\perp_{nat}) := \perp_{nat}$. D_P "respects" the values of M, i.e. $\delta_{P,0} := 0$, $\delta_{P,succ}(q) := succ(q)$ if $q \in \mathcal{C}_{nat}$, and $\delta_{P,succ}(\perp_{nat}) := \perp_{nat}$. For function symbols f which are introduced by a functional procedure F, $\delta_{P,f}$ is defined as the *least fixpoint* of the *functional* obtained from F, see e.g. (Manna, 1974).

As usual, we write $D_P(t)$ for the interpretation of an expression $t \in \mathcal{T}(\Sigma(P))$ by D_P. In denotational semantics, non-termination of functional procedures is modelled by the symbols for undefinedness, as e.g. $\delta_{P,inner}(d) := \perp_{nat}$ for all $d \in \mathcal{D}_{nat}$. More generally, the relation between operational and denotational semantics is expressed by the following theorem:

Theorem 5. (Equivalence of Operational and Denotational Semantics)
Either eval$(t) = D_P(t)$ *or* eval$(t) = \infty$ *and* $D_P(t) = \perp_s$ *for each functional program* P *and each* $t \in \mathcal{T}(\Sigma(P))_s$.

By Theorem 5, the denotational semantics of functional programs can be defined in such a way, that the interpretation $D_P(t)$ of t corresponds to the result of evaluating t by eval iff such an evaluation succeeds, and t is interpreted as "undefined" otherwise.

4. CALL-BY-NAME TERMINATION

Let $F = \textbf{function } f(x^*:w):s \Leftarrow R_f$ and let $P = P' \oplus \langle F \rangle$ be a functional program, such that P' terminates.[9] Then F does not terminate, if there is an *infinite* sequence S of expressions $f(s_0^*)$, $f(s_1^*)$, $f(s_2^*)$, ... such that the evaluation of $f(s_i^*)$ leads to the evaluation of $f(s_{i+1}^*)$ for all $i \in \mathbb{N}$. On the contrary, if each call $f(s^*)$ of f necessitates only *finitely* many recursive calls, say $f(s_1^*), \ldots, f(s_h^*)$, then F terminates, because the evaluation of the last recursive call $f(s_h^*)$ necessitates calls $g(r^*)$ of procedures from the *terminating* functional program P' at most. Consequently, proving termination of F requires proving the absence of an infinite sequence of recursive calls like S above.

The key point in the definition of S is the requirement "*the evaluation of $f(s_i^*)$ leads to the evaluation of $f(s_{i+1}^*)$*". This requirement is formally captured by the notion of a *necessary subevaluation*: Let $Occ(t)$ denote the set of all *occurrences* (or *positions*) of a term t (including the "trivial" occurrence ε) and let $t|_\pi$ denote the subterm of t at occurrence $\pi \in Occ(t)$. Then we write $t \mathrel{\lrcorner} \pi$ for a non-value expression t of a functional program P and some $\pi \in Occ(t)$ iff the evaluation of t by eval necessitates the evaluation of the subterm $t|_\pi$:

Definition 6. (Necessary Subevaluation $t \mathrel{\lrcorner} \pi$) *Let P be a functional program, $t \in \mathcal{T}(\Sigma(P))\backslash\mathcal{C}$ and $\pi \in Occ(t)$. Then the evaluation of t necessitates the evaluation of $t|_\pi$, in symbols $t \mathrel{\lrcorner} \pi$, iff $\pi = \varepsilon$ or $t = f(t_1, \ldots, t_n)$, $\pi = i\pi'$, $t_i \mathrel{\lrcorner} \pi'$ and*

(i) $f \in \{succ, pred, zero, if_s\}$ *and* $i = 1$, *or*

(ii) $f = if_s$, $i = 2$ *and* $t_1 \to^* true$, *or*

(iii) $f = if_s$, $i = 3$ *and* $t_1 \to^* false$, *or*

(iv) $P = \langle \ldots, \textbf{function } f(x_1:s_1, \ldots, x_n:s_n):s \Leftarrow R_f, \ldots \rangle$ *and* $\sigma(R_f) \mathrel{\lrcorner} \xi$ *for some* $\xi \in Occ(R_f)$ *such that* $R_f|_\xi = x_i$ *and* $\sigma = \{x_1/t_1, \ldots, x_n/t_n\}$.

By (i), the first argument t_1 of an application $f(t_1, \ldots)$ of a base operation f must always be evaluated if $f(t_1, \ldots)$ is to be evaluated. The only exception from this rule are terms of form $succ(succ(\ldots(0)\ldots))$, as those terms already represent values, and consequently no further evaluation is needed (and possible). The evaluation of the *then*-part t_2 of a conditional $if(t_1, t_2, t_3)$ is only necessary, if the condition t_1 evaluates to *true*, cf. (ii), and the evaluation of the *else*-part t_3 is required, if t_1 evaluates to *false*, cf. (iii). This entails in particular, that no branch of the conditional is considered, if the evaluation of t_1 fails by non-termination. Finally, an actual parameter t_i must be evaluated on the evaluation of a procedure call $f(t_1, \ldots, t_n)$, if the *instantiated* procedure body $\sigma(R_f)$ is evaluated at some occurrence ξ, where ξ selects the formal parameter x_i in the (non-instantiated) procedure body R_f, cf. (iv) and Figure 1.

The notion of a necessary subevaluation mirrors the lazy evaluation strategy implemented by the interpreter eval, because for the evaluation of an expression t, only

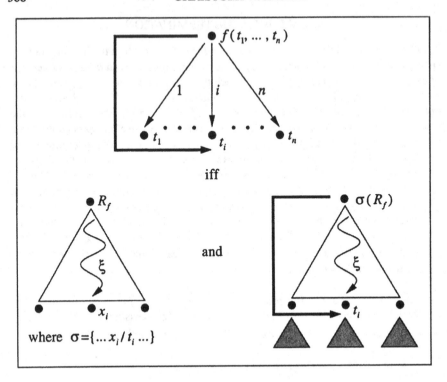

Figure 1   Necessary subevaluations of actual parameters

subterms $t|_\pi$ with $t \dashv \pi$ are considered. Lemma 7 illustrates the relation between necessary subevaluations and the interpreter eval:

Lemma 7. *For all $t \in \mathcal{T}(\Sigma(P))$:*
eval$(t) = \propto$ *iff* $t \dashv \pi$ *and* eval$(t|_\pi) = \propto$ *for some* $\pi \in Occ(t)$, *cf. Figure 2.*

Proof: The *only-if* case is obvious, and the *if*-case is proved by Noetherian induction upon the length of the evaluation sequence of t.   □

To investigate the termination of a functional procedure $F =$ **function** $f(x^* : w) : s \Leftarrow R_f$ which is added to a terminating functional program P' yielding $P = P' \oplus \langle F \rangle$, we consider a certain $\Sigma(P)$-algebra $D(\gamma) = (\mathcal{D}, \delta(\gamma))$: The interpretation function $\delta(\gamma)$ of $D(\gamma)$ coincides with the interpretation function $\delta_{P'}$ of the $\Sigma(P')$-algebra $D_{P'}$ for the function symbols from $\Sigma(P')$, i.e. $\delta(\gamma)_g = \delta_{P',g}$ for all $g \in \Sigma(P')$, and $\delta(\gamma)_f := \gamma$ for some function $\gamma \in [\mathcal{D}_w \rightarrow \mathcal{D}_s]$. In other words, $D(\gamma)$ gives a meaning to all function symbols from $\Sigma(P)$ such that the function symbols from $\Sigma(P')$ are associated with the (total) function computed by eval, cf.

Theorem 5, and f is associated with some arbitrary monotonic function γ. Using the notion of necessary subevaluations and the $\Sigma(P)$-algebra $D(\gamma)$, now a criterion for the termination of a functional procedure F can be formulated:

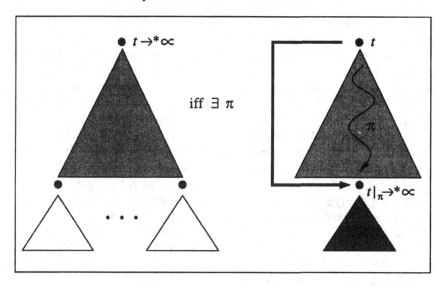

Figure 2 Evaluation of expressions and necessary subevaluations

Definition 8. (call-by-name Termination) *A functional procedure F terminates "call-by-name" iff some well-founded relation $\gg \subset \mathcal{D}_w \times \mathcal{D}_w$ and some function $\phi \in [\mathcal{D}_w \to \mathcal{D}_s]$ exists, such that*

(i) $D(\phi)(s^*) \gg D(\phi)(\sigma(t^*))$ *for all* $\sigma = \{x^*/s^*\}$ *with* $s^* \in \mathcal{T}(\Sigma(P))_w$ *and for all* $\pi \in Occ(R_f)$ *with* $R_f|_\pi = ft^*$ *and* $\sigma(R_f) \downharpoonleft \pi$, *and*

(ii) ϕ *satisfies* F, *i.e.* $D(\phi) \models \forall x^* : w\ f(x^*) \equiv R_f$.[10]

For each procedure call fs^*, *call-by-name* termination demands that the interpretation $D(\phi)(\sigma(t^*))$ of the parameter list $\sigma(t^*)$ which belongs to an *executed* recursive call $f\sigma(t^*)$ has to be *smaller* w.r.t. some well-founded relation $\gg$ than the interpretation $D(\phi)(s^*)$ of the argument list s^* belonging to the initial procedure call fs^*. The interpretation of the arguments is fixed by the semantics of P', except for the function symbol f of the functional procedure whose termination is under investigation. However, by requirement (ii) one may assume that the interpretation ϕ of f is "compatible" with the definition of f, when proving (i). In other words, $\downharpoonleft$ determines the sequences S of procedure calls $fs_0^*, fs_1^*, fs_2^*, \ldots$ to be considered and $\gg$ guarantees that these sequences are finite, where ϕ is used to verify that the arguments $s_0^*, s_1^*, s_2^*, \ldots$ of the procedure calls in S are ordered w.r.t. $\gg$.

Theorem 9. *A functional procedure F terminates iff F terminates* call-by-name.

Proof: "$\Rightarrow$" Let $\gg \subset \mathcal{D}_w \times \mathcal{D}_w$ such that $q^* \gg r^*$ iff some $p^*, u^* \in \mathcal{T}(\Sigma(P))_w$ exist such that $q^* = D_P(p^*)$, $r^* = D_P(u^*)$ and the evaluation of fp^* leads to the evaluation of fu^*. Then $\gg$ is well founded, because by the termination of $P = P' \oplus \langle F \rangle$, each sequence of recursive calls necessitated by a procedure call $f...$ is finite. We choose $\phi := \delta_{P, f}$, i.e. ϕ is the function computed by eval, therefore $D(\phi) = D_P$, and ϕ satisfies F. Now if $R_f|_\pi = ft^*$ and $\sigma(R_f) \dashv \pi$, then the evaluation of fs^* leads to the evaluation of $f\sigma(t^*)$, hence $D_P(s^*) \gg D_P(\sigma(t^*))$, and F terminates *call-by-name*.

"$\Leftarrow$" Let $M := \{r^* \in \mathcal{T}(\Sigma(P))_w \mid \text{eval}(fr^*) = \propto$ and $\text{eval}(r_i) \neq \propto$ for each $i \in \{1, \ldots, |w|\}$ with $fr^* \dashv i\}$, and let $s^* \in M$, such that $D(\phi)(s^*)$ is $\gg$-minimal among all elements of M. Then $\text{eval}(\sigma(R_f)) = \propto$, because $fs^* \to \sigma(R_f)$, where $\sigma = \{x^*/s^*\}$. Since P' terminates, $\sigma(R_f)$ has a subterm $\sigma(R_f)|_\pi = fu^*$ such that $\sigma(R_f) \dashv \pi$ and $\text{eval}(fu^*) = \propto$ for some $\pi \in Occ(\sigma(R_f))$.

Let $> \subset \mathcal{T}(\Sigma(P))_w \times \mathcal{T}(\Sigma(P))_w$ such that $a^* > b^*$ iff $fa^*|_\rho = fb^*$ and $fa^* \dashv \rho$ for some $\rho \in Occ(fa^*)\backslash\{\varepsilon\}$. Then fb^* is a proper subterm of fa^* if $a^* > b^*$, hence $>$ is well founded and we prove $u^* \in M$ by Noetherian induction upon $>$.

Since $\text{eval}(fu^*) = \propto$, fu^* cannot be a proper subterm of fs^*, hence $\sigma(R_f)|_\pi = fu^*$ implies $R_f|_\pi = ft^*$, where $\sigma(t^*) = u^*$ for some $t^* \in \mathcal{T}(\Sigma(P), \mathcal{V})_w$. Consequently $D(\phi)(s^*) \gg D(\phi)(\sigma(t^*)) = D(\phi)(u^*)$, because F terminates *call-by-name*, contradicting the $\gg$-minimality of $D(\phi)(s^*)$, and therefore $M = \emptyset$.

Now if $\text{eval}(fs^*) = \propto$ for some $s^* \in \mathcal{T}(\Sigma(P))_w$, then there must be a *smallest* procedure call fr^* with $\text{eval}(fr^*) = \propto$, i.e. $\text{eval}(r_i) \neq \propto$ for each $i \in \{1, \ldots, |w|\}$. But then $M \neq \emptyset$, hence $\text{eval}(fs^*) \neq \propto$ for any $s^* \in \mathcal{T}(\Sigma(P))_w$ and F terminates. $\square$

Example 10.

(i) *The functional procedure* F_{null} *defined as*

function $null(x, y : \text{nat}) : \text{nat} \Leftarrow$
    if $x = 0$
        then 0
        else $null(null(x - 1, null(x, y)), y)$
    fi

terminates call-by-name: *Let* $\phi \in [\mathcal{D}_{nat, nat} \to \mathcal{D}_{nat}]$ *such that* ϕ *satisfies* F_{null}. *Then* (*) "$\phi(q, e) \neq \perp$ *implies* $\phi(q, e) = 0$ *for all* $q \in \mathcal{C}_{nat}$ *and for all* $e \in \mathcal{D}_{nat}$", *as it is easily verified by Peano induction upon* q.

A procedure call $null(s, r)$ *necessitates the evaluation of the recursive calls* $null(null(s - 1, null(s, r)), r)$ *and* $null(s - 1, null(s, r))$. *Let* $\langle d, e \rangle \gg \langle d', e' \rangle$ *iff* $d \in \mathcal{C}_{nat}$ *and either* $d' = \perp$ *or* $d >_{nat} d'.$[11] *We find* $D_P(s) = 1 + c$ *for some* $c \in \mathcal{C}_{nat}$ *whenever the evaluation of* s *leads to a recursive call. Hence* $D(\phi)(s) = 1 + c$, *because* ϕ *satisfies* F_{null}, *and therefore* $\delta_{P, null} \sqsubseteq \phi.$[12] *So we obtain* $D(\phi)(\langle s, r \rangle) = \langle 1 + c, D(\phi)(r) \rangle$.

If $\phi(c, \phi(1 + c, D(\phi)(r))) = \perp$, *then* $\langle 1 + c, D(\phi)(r) \rangle \gg \langle \perp, D(\phi)(r) \rangle = D(\phi)(\langle null(s - 1, null(s, r)), r \rangle)$. *Otherwise* $\phi(c, \phi(1 + c, D(\phi)(r))) = 0$, *cf.* (*), *hence*

$\langle 1 + c, D(\phi)(r) \rangle \gg \langle 0, D(\phi)(r) \rangle = D(\phi)((null(s-1, null(s,r)), r))$, *and require-ment 8(i) is satisfied for the first recursive call. Since* $\langle 1 + c, D(\phi)(r) \rangle \gg \langle c, \phi(1+c, D(\phi)(r)) \rangle = D(\phi)(\langle s - 1, null(s, r) \rangle)$, *requirement 8(i) is satisfied also for the other recursive call. Since no other recursive calls are necessitated by the evaluation of* $null(s, r)$, F_{null} *terminates call-by-name.*

(ii) The functional procedure F_{outer} = **function** $outer(x : \text{nat}) : \text{nat} \Leftarrow 1 + outer(x)$ *does not terminate call-by-name: Each procedure call* $outer(s)$ *necessitates the evaluation of the recursive call* $outer(s)$ *and there is no well-founded relation* $\gg$ *satisfying* $D(\phi)(s) \gg D(\phi)(s)$.

Example 10(i) illustrates the problems to be solved if *call-by-name* termination of a functional procedure has to be verified: First, one has to "guess" a well-founded relation $\gg$ which is useful for the termination proof. Then, one has to determine the recursive calls in the body of the procedure, which are *not executed* (for a given input). Finally, one has to invent a useful *partial correctness statement* about the functional procedure, like (*) above, in order to verify requirement 8(i) for the remaining recursive calls.

Since $D_P = D(\delta_{P, f})$, we may alternatively demand $D_P(s^*) \gg D_P(\sigma(t^*))$ instead of $D(\phi)(s^*) \gg D(\phi)(\sigma(t^*))$ and "ϕ *satisfies* F" in Definition 8, such that Theorem 9 still holds. However, this would demand to guess the semantics of a functional procedure for proving its termination in any case, which is generally not required. E.g. in Example 10 we have guessed the semantics of F_{null} by the partial correctness statement (*), since (*) stipulates that $null(s, r)$ always evaluates to 0, provided the evaluation succeeds at all. However, we may alternatively use the weaker statement "$\phi(q, e) \neq \perp$ implies $1 + q >_{nat} \phi(q, e)$ for all $q \in C_{nat}$ and all $e \in \mathcal{D}_{nat}$" for proving the termination of F_{null}, which also holds for each ϕ satisfying F_{null}. And for other functional procedures, no reasoning about the semantics of F is required at all for proving F's termination, cf. Section 7. But generally some reasoning about the semantics of a functional procedure is inevitable for proving its termination.[13]

The well-founded relation $\gg$ of Definition 8 is defined on $\mathcal{D}_w$, so values can be compared with the undefinedness symbol $\perp$ in particular. This looks odd at a first glance, since termination entails the absence of undefinedness, cf. Theorem 5. By Theorem 9, we can always find a well-founded relation $\gg$ defined on C_w, such that the requirements of *call-by-name* termination are satisfied and Theorem 9 still holds. However, this stronger demand would yield harder proof obligations in some cases as generally one has to verify $\phi : C_w \to C_s$ in addition.

In Example 10(i), for instance, we would have to prove in addition, that the interpretation of $null(s - 1, null(s, r))$ is never $\perp$ in the recursive case, because otherwise $D(\phi)(\langle s, r \rangle)$ cannot be compared with $D(\phi)((null(s - 1, null(s, r)), r))$, as $\gg$ is now defined on C_w. So we had to verify (**) "$\phi(q, e) \neq \perp$ for all $q \in C_{nat}$ and all $e \in \mathcal{D}_{nat}$" too.

Hence using a well-founded relation $\gg$ defined on $\mathcal{D}_w$ may ease a termination proof considerably, as e.g. a direct proof of a statement like (**) is not required (but *implicitly* obtained), however for the price of a more difficult proof of Theorem 9.

5. CALL-BY-VALUE TERMINATION

The criterion of Definition 8 is not a very practical tool for proving the termination of a functional procedure, and it seems worthwhile to relax the requirements a bit in order to obtain a more handy recipe. Besides the problem to "guess" a useful well-founded relation $\gg$ and a partial correctness statement about F carrying the proof of 8(i), the main obstacle in applying *call-by-name* termination is the problem to determine whether some recursive call $f\sigma(t^*)$ in the body of F in fact is executed on the evaluation of a procedure call fs^*. A remedy to this problem is to replace $\sigma(R_f) \dashv \pi$ in Definition 8 by a weaker requirement, which however is easier to decide.

To this effect, we associate with each subterm $t|_\pi$ of a term t a quantifier-free formula $COND(t,\pi)$, which must be satisfied whenever $t|_\pi$ is evaluated on the evaluation of t, i.e. whenever $t \dashv \pi$ holds: Let $B(t)$ be a *subterm-tree* for t, i.e. a tree whose nodes are labelled with terms such that the root is labelled with t and each node with label $g(t_1, \ldots, t_n)$ has n sons labelled with $t_1, \ldots, t_n$ respectively. To compute $COND(t,\pi)$, we also provide some of the vertices in $B(t)$ with labels: For a node labelled with $if(b, t_1, t_2)$, the vertex to the son with label t_1 is labelled with $b \equiv true$ and the vertex to the son with label t_2 receives the label $b \equiv false$. All other vertices in $B(t)$ carry no label. Now we obtain $COND(t,\pi)$ by forming a conjunction from the set of all vertex labels on the path in $B(t)$ from the root to the node labelled with $t|_\pi$ (where $COND(t, \pi) := TRUE$ if this set is empty), cf. Figure 3.

E.g. $COND(t, 32) = zero(y) \equiv false \wedge ge(x, y) \equiv true$ and $COND(t, 333) = zero(y) \equiv false \wedge ge(x, y) \equiv false \wedge zero(x) \equiv false$ for t like in Figure 3. Subsequently, we write $COND(t, \pi) \rightarrow^* TRUE$ iff $COND(t, \pi) = TRUE$ or $COND(t, \pi) = b_1 \equiv c_1 \wedge \ldots \wedge b_h \equiv c_h$ and $b_i \rightarrow^* c_i$ for each $i \in \{1, ..., h\}$. $COND(t,\pi)$ provides requirements in form of equations which must be satisfied, if $t|_\pi$ is to be evaluated for the evaluation of t:

Lemma 11. *For all* $t \in \mathcal{T}(\Sigma(P))$ *and all* $\pi \in Occ(t)$:
If $t \dashv \pi$, *then* $COND(t, \pi) \rightarrow^* TRUE$.

Proof: By structural induction upon t. □

By Lemma 11 and Theorem 5, $D_P \models COND(t, \pi)$ is *necessary* for $t \dashv \pi$, and now we consider all recursive calls $\sigma(R_f)|_\pi = f\sigma(t^*)$ such that $D(\phi) \models COND(\sigma(R_f), \pi)$, instead of $\sigma(R_f) \dashv \pi$, for proving the termination of a functional procedure F:

Definition 12. (call-by-value Termination)
A *functional procedure* F terminates "call-by-value" *iff some well-founded relation* $\gg \subset \mathcal{D}_w \times \mathcal{D}_w$ *and some function* $\phi \in [\mathcal{D}_w \rightarrow \mathcal{D}_s]$ *exists, such that*

(i) $q^* \gg D(\phi)(\theta(t^*))$ *for all* $\theta = \{x^*/q^*\}$ *with* $q^* \in \mathcal{C}_w$ *and for all* $\pi \in Occ(R_f)$ *with* $R_f|_\pi = ft^*$ *and* $D(\phi) \models COND(\theta(R_f), \pi)$, *and*

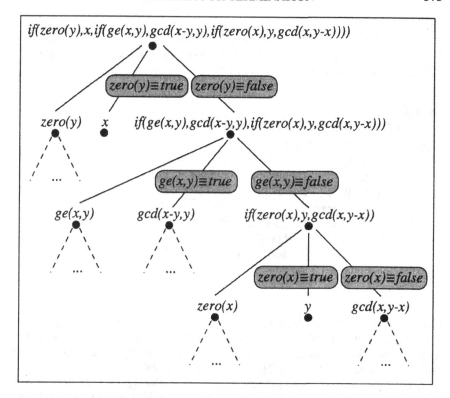

Figure 3 Labelled subterm tree $B(t)$ for the computation of $COND(t,\pi)$

(ii) ϕ satisfies F, *i.e.* $D(\phi) \models \forall x^* : w\ f(x^*) \equiv R_f$.

For each procedure call fq^*, *call-by-value* termination demands that the interpretation $D(\phi)(\theta(t^*))$ of the parameter list $\theta(t^*)$ which belongs to an *executable* recursive call $f\theta(t^*)$ has to be *smaller* w.r.t. some well-founded relation $\gg$ than the argument list q^* belonging to the initial procedure call fq^*.

Since $\sigma(R_f) \rightharpoondown \pi$ entails $D(\phi) \models COND(\theta(R_f), \pi)$, *call-by-value* termination entails *(call-by-name)* termination:

Theorem 13. *If F terminates* call-by-value, *then F terminates* (call-by-name).

Proof: Assume that $D(\phi)(s^*) \gg D(\phi)(\sigma(t^*))$ does not hold for some $s^* \in \mathcal{T}(\Sigma(P))_w$ and some $\pi \in Occ(R_f)$ such that $R_f|_\pi = ft^*$ and $\sigma(R_f) \rightharpoondown \pi$, where $\sigma = \{x^*/s^*\}$.

Let $> \subset \mathcal{T}(\Sigma(P))_w \times \mathcal{T}(\Sigma(P))_w$ such that $u^* > v^*$ iff fv^* is a proper subterm of fu^*. Then $>$ is well founded, and we may assume that s^* is $>$-minimal. Hence $s^* \in \mathcal{T}(\Sigma(P'))_w$ and $D(\phi)(s^*) \in \mathcal{C}_w$, because P' terminates. If $\sigma(R_f) \rightharpoondown \pi$, then

$D_P \models COND(\sigma(R_f), \pi)$ by Lemma 11, hence $D(\phi) \models COND(\sigma(R_f), \pi)$ because $\delta_{P,f} \sqsubseteq \phi$. But then $D(\phi) \models COND(\theta(R_f), \pi)$ where $\theta = \{x^*/D(\phi)(s^*)\}$, hence $D(\phi)(s^*) \gg D(\phi)(\theta(t^*))$, because F terminates *call-by-value*, and with $D(\phi)(\theta(t^*)) = D(\phi)(\sigma(t^*))$ a contradiction is obtained.   □

Example 14.

(i) *The functional procedure* F_{mod2} *defined as*

function $mod2(x:\text{nat}):\text{nat} \Leftarrow$
    if $x = 0$
       then 0
       else if $x - 1 = 0$
           then 1
           else if $mod2(x - 2) = 0$
                then 0
                else $1 + mod2(2 \times \lfloor x/2 \rfloor)$
              fi
          fi
       fi

terminates call-by-value:[14] *Let* $\phi \in [\mathcal{D}_{nat} \to \mathcal{D}_{nat}]$ *such that* ϕ *satisfies* F_{mod2}*. Then* (*) "$\phi(r) \neq \bot$ *implies* $\phi(r) = 0$ *or* $odd(r)$ *for all* $r \in C_{nat}$", *as it is easily verified by a two-step Peano induction. For a procedure call* $mod2(q)$*, the recursive calls* $mod2(q - 2)$ *and* $mod2(2 \times \lfloor q/2 \rfloor)$ *have to be considered:*

If $D(\phi) \models q \neq 0 \land q \neq 1$, *then* $q >_{nat} q - 2 = D(\phi)(q - 2)$. *If* $D(\phi) \models q \neq 0 \land q \neq 1 \land mod2(q - 2) \neq 0$, *then* $\phi(q - 2) \notin \{\bot, 0\}^{15}$, *hence* $odd(q - 2)$ *by* (*)*. Consequently also* $odd(q)$ *is true, and we obtain* $q >_{nat} q - 1 = D(\phi)(2 \times \lfloor q/2 \rfloor)$*. Hence requirement 12(i) is satisfied for both recursive calls,* F_{mod2} *terminates call-by-value.*

(ii) *The functional procedure* F_{louie} *defined as*

function $louie(x:\text{nat}):\text{nat} \Leftarrow$
    if $x = 0$
       then 0
       else $louie(louie(x - 1))$
    fi

terminates call-by-value: *Let* $\phi \in [\mathcal{D}_{nat} \to \mathcal{D}_{nat}]$ *such that* ϕ *satisfies* F_{louie}*. Then* (*) "$\phi(r) \neq \bot$ *implies* $\phi(r) = 0$ *for all* $r \in C_{nat}$", *as it is easily verified by Peano induction upon* r*. For a procedure call* $louie(q)$*, the recursive calls* $louie(louie(q - 1))$ *and* $louie(q - 1)$ *have to be considered:*

Let $\gg$ *be the well-founded relation defined by* $d \gg d'$ *iff* $d \in C_{nat}$ *and either* $d' = \bot$ *or* $d >_{nat} d'$*. If* $D(\phi) \models q \neq 0$, *then* $q \gg q - 1 = D(\phi)(q - 1)$*. If* $\phi(q - 1) = \bot$, *then* $q \gg \bot = D(\phi)(louie(q - 1))$*, and if* $\phi(q - 1) \neq \bot$, *then* $\phi(q - 1) = 0$ *by* (*)*, hence* $q \gg 0 = D(\phi)(louie(q - 1))$ *also in this case. Since requirement 12(i) is satisfied for both recursive calls,* F_{louie} *terminates call-by-value.*

Call-by-value termination is easier to verify than *call-by-name* termination, simply because it has not to be determined whether an *executable* recursive call will be *executed* in fact. As a consequence, however, *call-by-value* termination only provides a sufficient termination requirement, as there are terminating functional procedures, which do not terminate *call-by-value*:

Example 15. *The (terminating) functional procedure F_{null} from Example 10 does not terminate* call-by-value, *since there is no well-founded relation $\gg$ such that $\langle q, r \rangle \gg \langle q, r \rangle$ for some $q, r \in C_{nat}$. In other words, F_{null} does not terminate* call-by-value, *because the body of F_{null} contains a recursive call $null(x, y)$, which results in non-termination, if executed. However, since $null(x, y)$ is never executed, this recursive call does not spoil the* (call-by-name) *termination of F_{null}.*

However, *call-by-value* termination *equivalently* characterizes the successful evaluation of each term, if procedure calls in a functional program P are implemented by the parameter passing discipline *call-by-value* (instead of the *call-by-name* discipline). The corresponding evaluation strategy is called *eager evaluation* and is obtained by restricting all actual parameters in rule (11) of the evaluation calculus (cf. Definition 1) to be *values* only, yielding

$$(11') \quad \frac{f(u_1, \ldots, u_n)}{\sigma(R_f)} \text{ , if } \sigma = \{x_1/u_1, \ldots, x_n/u_n\} \text{ and } u_1, \ldots, u_n \in C.$$

For procedure calls with non-value arguments, a further evaluation rule is provided, viz.

$$(12) \quad \frac{f(u_1, \ldots, u_j, \ldots, u_n)}{f(u_1, \ldots, u_j', \ldots, u_n)} \text{ , if } u_j \Rightarrow u_j' \text{ ,}$$

where we write $\Rightarrow$ instead of $\rightarrow$, to distinguish *eager* evaluation from *lazy* evaluation. For instance, the procedure call $plus(1, 1)$ is evaluated to 2 also by *eager* evaluation, i.e. $plus(1, 1) \Rightarrow^* 2$.[16]

By presence of rule (12), the eager evaluation relation $\Rightarrow$ cannot be *deterministic*. However a weaker *confluence* requirement is guaranteed (and also all values are minimal w.r.t. $\Rightarrow$):

Theorem 16. *For all $t, r_1, r_2 \in \mathcal{T}(\Sigma(P))$:*

(i) *$t \notin C$ iff $t \Rightarrow r$ for some $r \in \mathcal{T}(\Sigma(P))$, and*

(ii) *$r_1 = r_2$ or $r_1 \Rightarrow t' \Leftarrow r_2$ for some $t' \in \mathcal{T}(\Sigma(P))$, if $r_1 \Leftarrow t \Rightarrow r_2$.*

Proof: By structural induction upon t.   □

As a consequence of Theorem 16, for each expression $t \in \mathcal{T}(\Sigma(P))$ at most one value $q \in C$ exists, such that $t \Rightarrow^* q$.[17] Hence eager evaluation of expressions can be modelled by a *partial* function e-eval : $\mathcal{T}(\Sigma(P)) \mapsto \mathcal{C}$, called the *eager interpreter* of P, such that e-eval$(t) = q$ iff $t \Rightarrow^* q$. Now since eager evaluation demands the evaluation of the actual parameters *before* the procedure definition is applied, actual parameters are evaluated also if their values do not contribute to the result, and this may cause non-termination in cases where lazy evaluation succeeds.

Theorem 17. e-eval$(t) \neq \propto$ *for all* $t \in \mathcal{T}(\Sigma(P))$ *iff F terminates* call-by-value *and* e-eval$(t') \neq \propto$ *for all* $t' \in \mathcal{T}(\Sigma(P'))$.

Proof: "$\Rightarrow$" If $t \in \mathcal{T}(\Sigma(P))$ is to be evaluated by the eager interpreter e-eval and $D_P \models COND(t, \pi)$ for some $\pi \in Occ(t)$, then $t|_\pi$ must be evaluated by e-eval. Hence the proof is similar to the proof of Theorem 9, where $\sigma(R_f) \lrcorner \pi$ is replaced by $D_P \models COND(\sigma(R_f), \pi)$.

"$\Leftarrow$" Let $M := \{r^* \in \mathcal{C}_w \mid \text{e-eval}(fr^*) = \propto\}$, and let q^* a $\gg$-minimal element of M. Then e-eval$(\theta(R_f)) = \propto$, because $fq^* \Rightarrow \theta(R_f)$, where $\theta = \{x^*/q^*\}$. Since e-eval$(t') \neq \propto$ for all $t' \in \mathcal{T}(\Sigma(P'))$, R_f has a subterm $R_f|_\pi = ft^*$ such that $COND(\theta(R_f), \pi) \Rightarrow^*_P$ TRUE and e-eval$(\theta(t^*)) = \propto$ for some $\pi \in Occ(\theta(R_f))$.

We may assume, that $f\theta(t^*)$ is the smallest of those terms, i.e. all proper subterms $f \ldots$ of $f\theta(t^*)$ can be evaluated by e-eval, provided e-eval evaluates the $COND$-formula for $f \ldots$ to TRUE. Then e-eval$(\theta(t^*)) = r^*$ for some $r^* \in M$, since e-eval$(t') \neq \propto$ for all $t' \in \mathcal{T}(\Sigma(P'))$. Consequently $D(\phi)(\theta(t^*)) = r^*$ and $D(\phi) \models COND(\theta(R_f), \pi)$, hence $q^* \gg D(\phi)(\theta(t^*))$, because F terminates *by-value*, contradicting the $\gg$-minimality of q^*.

Hence e-eval$(fr^*) \neq \propto$ for all $r^* \in \mathcal{C}_w$ and since e-eval$_P(t') \neq \propto$ for all $t' \in \mathcal{T}(\Sigma(P'))$, e-eval$_P(t) \neq \propto$ for all $t \in \mathcal{T}(\Sigma(P))$. $\qquad\square$

Like in the definition of *call-by-name* termination, the well-founded relation $\gg$ used for *call-by-value* termination also is defined on $\mathcal{D}_w$, yielding the same benefits as for *call-by-name* termination: If $\gg \subset \mathcal{C}_w \times \mathcal{C}_w$ had been demanded instead, then e.g. for proving the *call-by-value* termination of F_{louie} from Example 14(ii), we had to verify in addition, that the interpretation of $louie(q)$ is different from $\bot$ for each $q \in \mathcal{C}_{nat}$.[18]

Note that *call-by-name* termination requires to consider procedure calls of form $f(s_1, \ldots, s_n)$ where the actual parameters s_i are *any* expressions, whereas *call-by-value* termination considers only *values* q_i as actual parameters. This is because a successful eager evaluation of a procedure call $f(s_1, \ldots, s_n)$ entails a successful eager evaluation of each actual parameter s_i, hence it is enough to consider only values as actual parameters. However, since a successful lazy evaluation of a procedure call does not entail a successful lazy evaluation of each actual parameter in the call, the restriction to value parameters would render the *call-by-name* termination criterion unsound:

Example 18. *The functional procedure $F_{strange}$ defined as*

function $strange(x, y : \text{nat}) : \text{nat} \Leftarrow$
    if $x = 0$
        then 1
        else $strange(strange(x - 1, 0), strange(x, 0))$
    fi

does not terminate call-by-name, *because e.g.* $\text{eval}(strange(1, 0)) = \propto$. *Let* $\phi \in [\mathcal{D}_{nat,nat} \to \mathcal{D}_{nat}]$ *defined by*

$$\phi(d, e) := \left\{ \begin{array}{ll} 1 & \text{, if } d = 0, \\ \perp & \text{, else .} \end{array} \right.$$

Then ϕ satisfies $F_{strange}$ and we consider procedure calls $strange(q, r)$ with $q, r \in C_{nat}$. We find $D(\phi)(q) = 1 + c$ for some $c \in C_{nat}$ whenever the evaluation of $strange(q, r)$ leads to a recursive call, where $strange(strange(q - 1, 0), strange(q, 0))$ and $strange(q - 1, 0)$ are the only recursive calls necessitated by the evaluation of $strange(q, r)$. Hence $D(\phi)(\langle strange(q - 1, 0), strange(q, 0)\rangle) = \langle \phi(c, 0), \phi(1 + c, 0) \rangle$ and $D(\phi)(\langle q, r \rangle) = \langle 1 + c, r \rangle$.

Let $\langle d, e \rangle \gg \langle d', e' \rangle$ iff $d, e \in C_{nat}$ and either $d' = \perp$, $d >_{nat} d'$ or $d = d'$ and $e' = \perp$. If $c = 0$, then $\phi(c, 0) = 1$ and $\phi(1 + c, 0) = \perp$, hence $\langle 1 + c, r \rangle = \langle 1, r \rangle \gg \langle 1, \perp \rangle = \langle \phi(c, 0), \phi(1 + c, 0) \rangle$. If $c \neq 0$, then $\phi(c, 0) = \phi(1 + c, 0) = \perp$, hence $\langle 1 + c, r \rangle \gg \langle \perp, \perp \rangle = \langle \phi(c, 0), \phi(1 + c, 0) \rangle$. Finally $\langle 1 + c, r \rangle \gg \langle c, 0 \rangle = D(\phi)(\langle q - 1, 0 \rangle)$. Hence requirement 8(i) of call-by-name termination is satisfied for each recursive call which is necessitated by a procedure call having only value *arguments, although $F_{strange}$ does not terminate.*

6. STRONG TERMINATION

Proving the termination of a functional procedure F generally requires the *invention* of an appropriate partial correctness statement about F and a *proof* of this statement for the verification of the *call-by-value* requirement 12(i), cf. Example 14. So generally some *knowledge about the semantics* of a functional procedure is inevitable for proving its termination, and this complicates the termination proof. However, for some functional procedures termination can be proved without reasoning about a procedure's semantics. We say that such functional procedures terminate *strongly*:

Definition 19. (Strong Termination) *A functional procedure F terminates "strongly" iff some well-founded relation $\gg \subset \mathcal{D}_w \times \mathcal{D}_w$ exists, such that*

(i) $q^* \gg D(\phi)(\theta(t^*))$ *for all* $\theta = \{x^*/q^*\}$ *with* $q^* \in C_w$ *and for all* $\pi \in Occ(R_f)$ *with* $R_f|_\pi = ft^*$ *and* $D(\phi) \models COND(\theta(R_f), \pi)$

holds for all functions $\phi \in [\mathcal{D}_w \to \mathcal{D}_s]$.

If requirement 19(i) holds for *all* functions, then it holds in particular for *some* function *satisfying F,*[19] and since requirements 12(i) and 19(i) coincide, *strong* termination entails *call-by-value* termination:

Corollary 20. *If F terminates* strongly, *then F terminates* call-by-value.

Example 21.
   (*i*) *The functional procedure* F_{smod2} *defined as*

      function $smod2(x:\text{nat}):\text{nat} \Leftarrow$
          if $\ x = 0$
             then 0
             else **if** $\ x - 1 = 0$
                    then 1
                    else **if** $\ smod2(x - 2) = 0$
                           then 0
                           else $\ 1 + smod2(x - 1)$
                        fi
                  fi
             fi

terminates strongly: *For a procedure call* $smod2(q)$, *the recursive calls* $smod2(q - 2)$ *and* $smod2(q - 1)$ *have to be considered. If* $D(\phi) \models q \neq 0 \wedge q \neq 1$, *then* $q >_{nat} q - 2$ *as well as* $q >_{nat} q - 1$. *Hence requirement 19(i) is satisfied for both recursive calls, and* F_{smod2} *terminates* strongly.

   (*ii*) *The functional procedure* F_{ack} *for Ackermann's function, defined as*

      function $ack(x, y:\text{nat}):\text{nat} \Leftarrow$
          if $\ x = 0$
             then $1 + y$
             else **if** $\ y = 0$
                    then $ack(x - 1, 1)$
                    else $ack(x - 1, ack(x, y - 1))$
                fi
          fi,

terminates strongly: *Let* $\gg$ *the lexicographic order imposed by* $>_{nat}$ *on* $\mathcal{D}_{nat} \times \mathcal{D}_{nat}$. *We have to consider three recursive calls, viz.* $ack(q - 1, 1)$, $ack(q, r - 1)$ *and* $ack(q - 1, ack(q, r - 1))$, *for a procedure call* $ack(q, r)$:
   If $D(\phi) \models q \neq 0 \wedge r = 0$, *then* $\langle q, r \rangle \gg \langle q - 1, 1 \rangle$ *and if* $D(\phi) \models q \neq 0 \wedge r \neq 0$, *then*, $\langle q, r \rangle \gg \langle q, r - 1 \rangle$ *as well as* $\langle q, r \rangle \gg \langle q - 1, \phi(q, r - 1) \rangle$. *Hence requirement 19(i) is satisfied for each recursive call, and* F_{ack} *terminates* strongly.

    Since *strong* termination requires no reasoning about the semantics of the functional procedure under consideration, the *results* in *non-recursive* cases and the *contexts*, in which *recursive calls* are *embedded*, do not influence the termination behaviour of the procedure. Hence any functional procedure F' *strongly* terminates *"by construction"*, if F' is obtained from a *strongly* terminating functional procedure F only by a modification of the contexts of recursive calls and a replacement of result terms, which do not introduce new recursive calls. Consequently, *strong* termination for an infinite class of functional procedures is proved, if *strong* termination is verified for only one member of this class.

Example 22. *The functional procedure F_{gcd} from Section 1 terminates* strongly, *as it is easily verified using $\langle q, r \rangle \gg \langle q', r' \rangle$ iff $q + r >_{nat} q' + r'$. Hence the functional procedures F_{quot} defined as*

> **function** $quot(x, y : \text{nat}) : \text{nat} \Leftarrow$
>> **if** $y = 0$
>>> **then** 0
>>> **else if** $x \geq y$
>>>> **then** $1 + quot(x - y, y)$
>>>> **else** 0
>>> **fi**
>> **fi**

and F_{mod} defined as

> **function** $mod(x, y : \text{nat}) : \text{nat} \Leftarrow$
>> **if** $y = 0$
>>> **then** 0
>>> **else if** $x \geq y$
>>>> **then** $mod(x - y, y)$
>>>> **else** x
>>> **fi**
>> **fi**

must terminate *strongly, as both procedures are obtained from F_{gcd} only by modification of the contexts of recursive calls and replacements of result terms, without introduction of new recursive calls.*

However, *non-strongly* terminating functional procedures are sensitive for such modifications, since this changes the semantics and consequently a non terminating procedure may result.

Example 23. *Let F_{dewey} and F_{huey} functional procedures defined by*

> **function** $dewey(x : \text{nat}) : \text{nat} \Leftarrow$
>> **if** $x = 0$
>>> **then** 1
>>> **else** $dewey(dewey(x - 1))$
>> **fi**

and

> **function** $huey(x : \text{nat}) : \text{nat} \Leftarrow$
>> **if** $x = 0$
>>> **then** 0
>>> **else** $2 + huey(huey(x - 1))$
>> **fi**.

Both procedures do not terminate call-by-value, *as e.g.* e-eval$(dewey(1)) =$ e-eval$(huey(2)) = \infty$. *However, the functional procedure F_{louie} from Example 14(ii) terminates* call-by-value. *F_{dewey} results from F_{louie} by replacing 0 in the non-recursive case of F_{louie} by 1, and F_{huey} results from F_{louie} by embedding the recursive call of F_{louie} in the context $2 + \ldots$.*

7. NORMAL-RECURSIVE AND TAIL-RECURSIVE PROCEDURES

Since *strong* termination demands requirement 19(i) to hold for *each* function, it must hold in particular also for functions *not* satisfying F. Consequently *strong* termination may fail for some *call-by-value* terminating procedures:

Example 24.
(i) The functional procedure F_{mod2} from Example 14(i) does not terminate strongly: Let $\phi \in [\mathcal{D}_{nat} \to \mathcal{D}_{nat}]$ such that $\phi(d) = 1$ for all $d \in \mathcal{D}_{nat}$. Then $q \gg D(\phi)(2 \times \lfloor q/2 \rfloor)$ must hold, if $D(\phi) \models q \neq 0 \wedge q \neq 1 \wedge mod2(q-2) \neq 0$, hence $2 \gg D(\phi)(2 \times \lfloor 2/2 \rfloor) = 2$ must hold in particular. Since this is impossible for any well-founded relation $\gg$, F_{mod2} does not terminate strongly.

(ii) The functional procedure F_{louie} from Example 14(ii) does not terminate strongly: Let $\phi \in [\mathcal{D}_{nat} \to \mathcal{D}_{nat}]$ such that $\phi(d) = 1$ for all $d \in \mathcal{D}_{nat}$. Then $q \gg D(\phi)(louie(q-1))$ must hold, if $D(\phi) \models q \neq 0$, hence $1 \gg D(\phi)(louie(1-1)) = 1$ must hold in particular. Since this is impossible for any well-founded relation $\gg$, F_{louie} does not terminate strongly.

Note that the function ϕ in Example 24 does not satisfy the functional procedures under consideration, hence *call-by-value* termination is not spoiled upon the existence of these functions, cf. Example 14.

Since *strong* termination is not necessary for *call-by-value* termination but obviously is easier to verify, it seems worthwhile to recognize functional procedures for which *strong* termination coincides with *call-by-value* termination. We therefore define the class of so-called *normal-recursive* functional procedures, i.e. procedures which neither possess *nested* recursions $f(\ldots f(\ldots)\ldots)$ nor have recursive calls in the conditions of an *if*-statement:

Definition 25. (Normal-Recursive Functional Procedures) *A functional procedure $F = \text{function } f(x^*:w):s \Leftarrow R_f$ is normal-recursive iff f does not occur in t for all subterms $f(\ldots, t, \ldots)$ and $if(t, \ldots, \ldots)$ of R_f.*

For instance, the functional procedures for *col, plus, times, ge, gcd, quot* and *mod* are normal-recursive, whereas the functional procedures for *f91, tak, null, mod2, louie, smod2* and *ack* are not. Now *strong* termination also is *necessary* for *call-by-value* termination, if only normal-recursive functional procedures are considered:

Theorem 26. *F terminates* strongly *iff F terminates* call-by-value, *if F is* normal-recursive.

Proof: "⇒" By Corollary 20.
"⇐" Since *F* is normal-recursive, neither $COND(\theta(R_f), \pi)$ nor $\theta(t^*)$ contain an *f*-term, hence the *call-by-value* requirement 12(i) must hold for *any* function ϕ, and therefore *F* terminates *strongly*. □

As a consequence of Theorem 26, we must fail in proving *strong* termination for a *call-by-value* terminating procedure *F*, only if *F* is not normal-recursive. In other words, the notion of "normal-recursion" provides a trivial syntactic requirement to decide whether a test for strong termination is enough, cf. Figure 4.

Note that "normal-recursion" is not a *necessary* requirement for *strong* termination. E.g. the functional procedures for *smod2* and *ack* terminate strongly, cf. Example 21, although both procedure are not normal-recursive.

Theorem 26 does not generalize to *call-by-name* termination, i.e. there are normal-recursive *call-by-name* terminating functional procedures, which do not terminate *strongly*.

Example 27. *The functional procedure F_{nought} defined as*

function $nought(x:\text{nat}):\text{nat} \Leftarrow x \times nought(x-1)$

terminates call-by-name *and obviously is normal-recursive. However,* $nought(0) \Rightarrow^+ 0 \times nought(0) \Rightarrow^+ 0 \times (0 \times nought(0)) \Rightarrow \ldots$, *i.e.* e-eval($nought(0)$) = $\propto$, *hence F_{nought} does not terminate* call-by-value. *But then by Corollary 20, F_{nought} does not terminate* strongly *either.*

However, *strong* termination coincides with *call-by-name* termination for a proper subclass of the normal-recursive functional procedures: A normal-recursive procedure *F* is *tail-recursive* iff each recursive call $f(\ldots)$ is neither embedded in another procedure call nor in a call of a base operation different from if. I.e., if the body of *F* contains a term *t* of form $g(\ldots f(\ldots)\ldots)$, then $t = if(b, \ldots f(\ldots)\ldots)$.

Definition 28. (Tail-Recursive Functional Procedures)
A normal-recursive *procedure $F =$* **function** $f(x^*:w):s \Leftarrow R_f$ *is tail-recursive iff $t = f(\ldots)$, $t = if(\ldots)$ or f does not occur in t for all subterms t of R_f.*

E.g. the functional procedures for *col*, *ge*, *gcd* and *mod* are tail-recursive, whereas the procedures for *plus*, *times*, *quot* and *nought* are not. The functional procedures for *null*, *mod2*, *smod2*, *ack* and *louie* are not tail-recursive, because these procedures are not normal-recursive.

The class of tail-recursive procedures is well-known, in particular because PROLOG procedures and loops of imperative programs straightforwardly can be translated to tail-recursive functional procedures and vice versa. For tail-recursive procedures, *strong* termination also is necessary for (*call-by-name*) termination:

Theorem 29. F *terminates* strongly *iff* F *terminates* (call-by-name), *if* F *is* tail-recursive.

Proof: "$\Rightarrow$" By Corollary 20 and Theorem 13.
"$\Leftarrow$" Let $\theta = \{x^*/q^*\}$ such that $q^* \in \mathcal{C}_w$. Then "$r \downarrow \rho$ for all subterms r of $\theta(R_f)$ and for all $\rho \in Occ(r)$ such that $r|_\rho = f(\dots)$ and $COND(r, \rho) \to^* \text{TRUE}$ " can be proved by induction upon ρ. Hence *call-by-name* termination of F entails *call-by-value* termination of F. But then F terminates *strongly* by Theorem 26, because F is normal-recursive. $\qquad\square$

As a consequence of Theorem 29, for proving the termination of a *loop* in an imperative program, no partial correctness statement about the semantics of the loop is required.

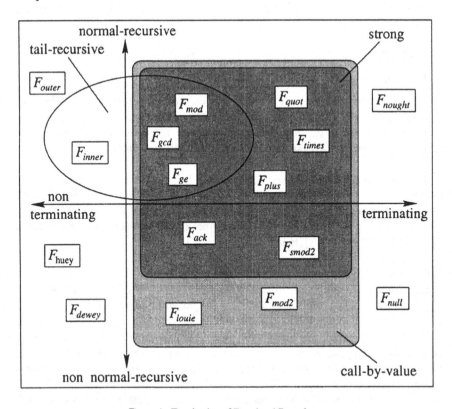

Figure 4   Termination of Functional Procedures

Figure 4 summarizes the results by relating *call-by-name, call-by-value* and *strong* termination w.r.t. *normal-recursive* and *tail-recursive* functional procedures.

8. CONCLUSION

Challenge problems for termination analysis, like the 91-function, Ashcroft's procedure for list reversal (Manna, 1974), Takeuchi's and Collatz' functions etc. provide a valuable source for theoretical investigations (not only w.r.t. termination), but are by no means typical examples of useful software. As procedures designed for practical purposes usually are *normal-recursive*, a test for *strong* termination is enough in practice. The only relevant exception from this argumentation are terminating non-normal recursive procedures with recursive calls in conditions (like *smod2*), which e.g. "naturally" occur for operations on tree-like structures. The functional procedure

```
function sub_sexpr(x, y : sexpr) : bool ⟸
    if  x = y
        then true
        else if  atom(y)
                then false
                else if  sub_sexpr(x, car(y))
                        then true
                        else  sub_sexpr(x, cdr(y))
                     fi
             fi
    fi
```

is an example and the procedure *value* from (Boyer and Moore, 1979) is another one. However, although not normal-recursive, these procedures also terminate *strongly*.

Therefore *strong* termination provides a solid formal base for an *automated* termination analysis of procedures with *eager* semantics. The main challenge is to *invent* a well-founded relation ≫ such that the strong termination requirement 19(i) can be *proved*, where an *induction theorem prover*, e.g. (Boyer and Moore, 1979; Walther, 1994a) can be used for this verification.

For computing the "right" relation ≫, an a-priori fixed relation does the job in almost all realistic cases for procedures computing arithmetic functions or operating on linear lists, viz. $>_{nat}$ and comparing lists by their length respectively (Walther, 1994b; Giesl et al., 1998).[20] However, sometimes this is not enough for procedures working on more elaborate data structures, as e.g. graphs or tree-like structures, and (machine generated) polynomial orders have been proved successful for termination analysis in this domain (Giesl, 1995; Giesl et al., 1998).

These proposals are developed further for the termination analysis of procedures also operating on *non-free* data structures, as e.g. sets (Sengler, 1996; Sengler, 1997).[21] Another interesting development, which is in particular useful for *loop-programs*, is the termination analysis for functional programs in which not all procedures terminate: Often the procedures of a program can be separated into *interface* procedures and *auxiliary* procedures, where the latter cannot be called from outside. In such a scenario it is enough that only the interface procedures terminate, whereas termination for the auxiliary procedures must be guaranteed for certain inputs only, viz. the inputs provided by the calls of the auxiliary procedures in the program, cf. (Brauburger, 1997; Giesl et al., 1998; Brauburger, 1999).

One key to success for *automated* termination proofs in languages with *eager* semantics is the fact that requirement 19(i) of strong *termination* can be encoded by a predicate logic formula, thus getting rid of the operational nature of termination. However, for *lazy* languages the trivial computation of *COND* must be replaced by some deductive concept modelling the necessary subevaluations given by ↵ . Hence proofs for *call-by-name* termination must mirror the evaluation of expression to some extent, and this constitutes an increased difficulty of automated termination analysis for lazy languages as compared to the eager case, cf. (Panitz and Schmidt-Schauß, 1997; Panitz, 1997).

ACKNOWLEDGMENTS

I am grateful to M. Bormann, J. Brauburger, J. Giesl and D. McAllester for valuable comments on a draft of this paper.

Darmstadt University of Technology
Darmstadt, Germany

NOTES

1. Of course, these proof procedures must be *incomplete* as the set of all total recursive functions is not semi-decidable.

2. All results presented subsequently straightforwardly carry over to more elaborate data structures, as *lists* or *trees*.

3. Note that *values* are *expressions* too, since $C \subset \mathcal{T}(\Sigma(P))$.

4. Since we are interested in the termination of algorithms only, we restrict lazy evaluation to procedure calls and do not consider infinite data structures, which would be obtained by e.g. dropping the side conditions of rules 3 and 6.

5. $\to^+$ is the transitive closure of $\to$ and $\to^*$ is the reflexive closure of $\to^+$.

6. A relation $> \subset A \times A$ is *well-founded* and $(A, >)$ is a *well-founded set* iff there is no infinite sequence $a_1 > a_2 > a_3 > \ldots$ of elements from A.

7. By Theorem 2(ii) no value can be evaluated further, hence $\mathsf{eval}(q) = q$ for all values $q \in C$.

8. Monotonicity of a function $\phi : \mathcal{D}_{s_1} \times \ldots \times \mathcal{D}_{s_n} \to \mathcal{D}_s$ is defined w.r.t. the "more-defined-or-equal"-relation $\sqsubseteq$ on the cartesian product $\mathcal{D}_{s_1} \times \ldots \times \mathcal{D}_{s_n}$, where $(d_1, \ldots, d_n) \sqsubseteq (e_1, \ldots, e_n)$ iff either $d_i = \bot$ or $d_i = e_i$ for all $i \in \{1, \ldots, n\}$. ϕ is *monotonic* iff $(d_1, \ldots, d_n) \sqsubseteq (e_1, \ldots, e_n)$ entails $\phi(d_1, \ldots, d_n) \sqsubseteq \phi(e_1, \ldots, e_n)$. We let $[\mathcal{D}_{s_1} \times \ldots \times \mathcal{D}_{s_n} \to \mathcal{D}_s]$ denote the set of all monotonic functions $\phi : \mathcal{D}_{s_1} \times \ldots \times \mathcal{D}_{s_n} \to \mathcal{D}_s$, see e.g. (Manna, 1974) for more details.

9. "$f(x^* : w)$" is an abbreviation for "$f(x_1 : s_1, \ldots, x_n : s_n)$", where $x^* = x_1 \ldots x_n$ and $w = s_1 \ldots s_n$.

10. The symbol $\equiv$ denotes equality of first-order predicate logic.

11. $>_{nat} \subset C_{nat} \times C_{nat}$ denotes the "usual" greater-relation on natural numbers, e.g. $succ(succ(0))$ $>_{nat} succ(0) >_{nat} 0$.

12. ϕ satisfies F iff ϕ is a fixpoint of the functional associated with F and since $\delta_{P,f}$ is the *least* fixpoint of this functional, $\delta_{P,f} \sqsubseteq \phi$ must hold.

13. Guessing the semantics of a procedure seems to be the only way for proving termination in "hard" cases, as e.g. for Takeuchi's function, cf. (Moore, 1979; Knuth, 1991) and for Ashcroft's function (Manna, 1974). Also the termination proofs for the 91-function were performed in this way (Manna, 1974; Dershowitz and Manna, 1979; Knuth, 1991), except a solution presented in (Feferman, 1991). Recently (Giesl, 1997) presented a proof based on a weaker (machine generated) partial correctness statement.

14. $\lfloor x/2 \rfloor$ is the truncated division by 2, e.g. $\lfloor 3/2 \rfloor = 1$ and $\lfloor 4/2 \rfloor = 2$.

15. $D(\phi) \models t \neq 0$ abbreviates $D(\phi) \models zero(t) \equiv false$, which entails $D(\phi)(t) \neq \perp$ and $D(\phi)(t) \neq 0$.

16. Generally, $t \Rightarrow^* q$ entails $t \to^* q$ for all $t \in \mathcal{T}(\Sigma(P))$ and all $q \in C$, but the evaluations may differ in the intermediate steps as $t \Rightarrow r$ does not entail $t \to r$ for certain $t, r \in \mathcal{T}(\Sigma(P))$.

17. By Theorem 16(ii), $\Rightarrow$ is *strongly confluent*, hence $\Rightarrow$ is *confluent* (Newman, 1942), and the statement follows by 16(i).

18. The benefits of using a relation $\gg \subset \mathcal{D}_w \times \mathcal{D}_w$ for *call-by-value* termination, i.e. the use of *partial* instead of *total* correctness statements, were observed by J. Giesl, who proved a theorem corresponding to the "if"-part of Theorem 17 (Giesl, 1997). Our notion of *call-by-name* termination was inspired by this observation. However, due to the nature of lazy evaluation, the proof of Theorem 9 requires a more complicated argumentation, cf. (Walther, 1998).

19. Since each functional associated with a functional procedure F has *one* fixpoint at least, cf. (Manna, 1974), at least *one* function satisfying F exists.

20. By a moderate restriction of this approach, (McAllester and Arkoudas, 1996) even propose a programming discipline (comparable to a more "liberal" form of primitive recursion), in which only *terminating* procedures can be defined.

21. *Freely* and *non-freely* generated data structures differ in the notion of equality, which is the equality on values in the former and a *congruence relation* on values in the latter case.

REFERENCES

Avenhaus, J. (1995). *Reduktionssysteme*. Springer.

Baader, F. and Nipkow, T. (1998). *Term Rewriting and All That*. Cambridge University Press.

Boyer, R. and Moore, J. S. (1979). *A Computational Logic*. Academic Press, Boston.

Brauburger, J. (1997). Automatic Termination Analysis for Partial Functions using Polynomial Orderings. In *Proceedings of the 4th International Static Analysis Symposium (SAS '97), Paris, France*, LNCS 1302, pages 330–344. Springer.

Brauburger, J. (1999). *Automatic Termination Analysis for Functional and Imperative Programs*. Doctoral Dissertation TU Darmstadt, Infix, St. Augustin, Germany.

Dershowitz, N. and Manna, Z. (1979). Proving termination with multiset orderings. *CACM*, 22(8):465–476.

Feferman, S. (1991). Proofs of termination and the "91" function. In Lifschitz, V., editor, *Artificial Intelligence and Mathematical Theory of Computation*, pages 47–63. Academic Press, Boston.

Gallier, J. H. (1986). *Logic for Computer Science: Foundations of Automatic Theorem Proving*. Harper and Row, New York.

Gardner, M. (1983). *Wheels, Lifes and other Mathematical Amusements*. W. H. Freeman and Company, New York.

Giesl, J. (1995). *Automatisierung von Terminierungsbeweisen für rekursiv definierte Algorithmen*, volume 96 of *DISKI*. Doctoral Dissertation TU Darmstadt, Infix, St. Augustin, Germany.

Giesl, J. (1997). Termination of Nested and Mutually Recursive Algorithms. *Journal of Automated Reasoning*, 19:1–29.

Giesl, J., Walther, C., and Brauburger, J. (1998). Termination Analysis for Functional Programs. In Bibel, W. and Schmitt, P., editors, *Automated Deduction — A Basis for Applications*, volume 3, pages 135–164. Kluwer Academic Publishers.

Knuth, D. (1991). Textbook examples of recursion. In Lifschitz, V., editor, *Artificial Intelligence and Mathematical Theory of Computation*, pages 207–229. Academic Press, Boston.

Manna, Z. (1974). *Mathematical Theory of Computation*. McGraw-Hill.

McAllester and Arkoudas (1996). Walther Recursion. In *Proceedings of the 13th International Conference on Automated Deduction (CADE-13), New Brunswick, USA*, LNAI 1104, pages 643–657. Springer.

Moore, J. S. (1979). A Mechanical Proof of the Termination of Takeuchi's Function. *Information Processing Letters*, pages 176–181.

Newman, M. A. H. (1942). On theories with a combinatorical definition of 'equivalence'. *Annals of Mathematics*, 43(2):223–243.

Panitz, S. (1997). *Generierung statischer Programminformation zur Kompilierung verzögert ausgewerteter funktionaler Programmiersprachen*. Doctoral Dissertation, Johann Wolfgang Goethe-Universität, Frankfurt am Main, Germany.

Panitz, S. and Schmidt-Schauß, M. (1997). TEA: Automatically Proving Termination of Programs in a Non-Strict Higher-Order Functional Language. In *Proceedings of the 4th International Static Analysis Symposium (SAS '97), Paris, France*, LNCS 1302, pages 345–360. Springer.

Sengler, C. (1996). Termination of Algorithms over Non-freely Generated Data Types. In *Proceedings of the 13th International Conference on Automated Deduction (CADE-13), New Brunswick, USA*, LNAI 1104, pages 121–136. Springer.

Sengler, C. (1997). *Induction on Non-Freely Generated Data Types*, volume 160 of *DISKI*. Doctoral Dissertation, Infix, St. Augustin, Germany.

Walther, C. (1994a). Mathematical Induction. In Gabbay, D., Hogger, C., and Robinson, J., editors, *Handbook of Logic in Artificial Intelligence and Logic Programming*, volume 2. Oxford University Press.

Walther, C. (1994b). On proving the Termination of Algorithms by Machine. *Artificial Intelligence*, 71(1):101–157.

Walther, C. (1998). *Recursion, Induction, Verfication*. Course Notes, TU Darmstadt.

Epilogue

In the beginning was the Connection Method, and the Connection Method was with The Scientist, and the Connection Method was The Scientist. The same was in the beginning with The Scientist.

Through it all valid formulae were proven; and without it was not any thing proven that was provable. In it was the spanning mating and the spanning mating was the characterization of validity. And the characterization was presented to the scientific community, but the community comprehended it not.

There was a man sent from The Scientist, whose name was Elmar. The same came as a witness, to bear witness of the Connection Method that all researchers through him might believe. He himself had not invented the Connection Method, but came only to bear witness of its superiority. The true inference method, which gives light to every researcher was coming into the field of automated deduction.

It was in the field, and though the field was changed by it, the scientific community did not recognize it. It came unto its own, but its own did not receive it. But as many as received it, to those who believed in its superiority, He gave the right to become the children of Intellectics — children born not of natural descent, nor of human decision, but selected by The Scientist.

And the Connection Method became a theorem prover, and dwelt among us. And we beheld its efficiency, the efficiency of the One and Only, which came from the The Scientist, full of elegance and efficiency.

Elmar bare witness of it. He spoke up at conferences, saying, „This was it of which I wrote, 'The method that is a special case of mine, surpasses it because it was before my method.' " And because of its superiority we have all published one paper after another. For the calculus was given by Gentzen, but elegance and efficiency came through the Connection Method. No researcher has ever fully recognized the The Scientist, but the One and Only Method, which comes from the The Scientist's heart, has made him known.

And this is the testimony of Elmar, when the scientific community sent researchers and scholars to ask him, „What is your method?" And he confessed, and denied not; but confessed, „It is not the One and Only." And they asked him, „What then? Is it the tableaux method?" And he said, „It is not." „Is it model elimination?" And he answered, „No." Then said they unto him, „What is it? We must give an answer to them that sent us. What do you say about yourself?" He replied, „I am the voice of one calling in the desert, 'Make straight the way for The Scientist' ", as spoken by Frege, the prophet.

And they which were sent were of the Resolution. And they asked him, and said unto him, „Why then do you teach, if your method is not the One and Only, nor the tableaux method, nor model elimination?" „I teach the consolution," Elmar replied, „but among you stands a method, which you do not know. It is the one which surpasses mine and whose efficiency I am not worthy to compare."

This happened at Kaiserslautern, beyond the Rhine, where Elmar was teaching.

S. Hölldobler (ed.), *Intellectics and Computational Logic*, 387.

APPLIED LOGIC SERIES

1. D. Walton: *Fallacies Arising from Ambiguity*. 1996   ISBN 0-7923-4100-7
2. H. Wansing (ed.): *Proof Theory of Modal Logic*. 1996   ISBN 0-7923-4120-1
3. F. Baader and K.U. Schulz (eds.): *Frontiers of Combining Systems*. First International Workshop, Munich, March 1996. 1996   ISBN 0-7923-4271-2
4. M. Marx and Y. Venema: *Multi-Dimensional Modal Logic*. 1996
        ISBN 0-7923-4345-X
5. S. Akama (ed.): *Logic, Language and Computation*. 1997   ISBN 0-7923-4376-X
6. J. Goubault-Larrecq and I. Mackie: *Proof Theory and Automated Deduction*. 1997
        ISBN 0-7923-4593-2
7. M. de Rijke (ed.): *Advances in Intensional Logic*. 1997   ISBN 0-7923-4711-0
8. W. Bibel and P.H. Schmitt (eds.): *Automated Deduction - A Basis for Applications*. Volume I. Foundations - Calculi and Methods. 1998   ISBN 0-7923-5129-0
9. W. Bibel and P.H. Schmitt (eds.): *Automated Deduction - A Basis for Applications*. Volume II. Systems and Implementation Techniques. 1998   ISBN 0-7923-5130-4
10. W. Bibel and P.H. Schmitt (eds.): *Automated Deduction - A Basis for Applications*. Volume III. Applications. 1998   ISBN 0-7923-5131-2
        (Set vols. I-III: ISBN 0-7923-5132-0)
11. S.O. Hansson: *A Textbook of Belief Dynamics*. Theory Change and Database Updating. 1999   Hb: ISBN 0-7923-5324-2; Pb: ISBN 0-7923-5327-7
    Solutions to exercises. 1999.   Pb: ISBN 0-7923-5328-5
        Set: (Hb): ISBN 0-7923-5326-9
        Set: (Pb): ISBN 0-7923-5329-3
12. R. Pareschi and B. Fronhöfer (eds.): *Dynamic Worlds from the Frame Problem to Knowledge Management*. 1999   ISBN 0-7923-5535-0
13. D.M. Gabbay and H. Wansing (eds.): *What is Negation?* 1999 ISBN 0-7923-5569-5
14. M. Wooldridge and A. Rao (eds.): *Foundations of Rational Agency*. 1999
        ISBN 0-7923-5601-2
15. D. Dubois, H. Prade and E.P. Klement (eds.): *Fuzzy Sets, Logics and Reasoning about Knowledge*. 1999   ISBN 0-7923-5911-1
16. H. Barringer, M. Fisher, D. Gabbay and G. Gough (eds.): *Advances in Temporal Logic*. 2000   ISBN 0-7923-6149-0
17. D. Basin, M.D. Agostino, D.M. Gabbay, S. Matthews and L. Viganò (eds.): *Labelled Deduction*. 2000   ISBN 0-7923-6237-3
18. P.A. Flach and A.C. Kakas (eds.): *Abduction and Induction*. Essays on their Relation and Integration. 2000   ISBN 0-7923-6250-0
19. S. Hölldobler (ed.): *Intellectics and Computational Logic*. Papers in Honor of Wolfgang Bibel. 2000   ISBN 0-7923-6261-6

KLUWER ACADEMIC PUBLISHERS – DORDRECHT / BOSTON / LONDON